Dictionary of Literary Biography • Volume Seventy-seven

British Mystery Writers,
1920-1939

Dictionary of Literary Biography • Volume Seventy-seven

British Mystery Writers, 1920-1939

Edited by
Bernard Benstock
University of Miami

and

Thomas F. Staley
University of Texas, Austin

A Bruccoli Clark Layman Book
Gale Research Inc. • Book Tower • Detroit, Michigan 48226

Matthew J. Bruccoli and Richard Layman, *Editorial Directors*
C. E. Frazer Clark, Jr., *Managing Editor*

Manufactured by Edward Brothers, Inc.
Ann Arbor, Michigan
Printed in the United States of America

**Library of Congress Cataloging-in-
Publication Data**

British mystery writers, 1920-1939/edited by Bernard
 Benstock and Thomas F. Staley.
  p. cm.–(Dictionary of literary biography; v. 77)
 "A Bruccoli Clark Layman book."
 Includes index.
 ISBN 0-8103-4555-2
  1. Detective and mystery stories. English–History and
 criticism. 2. Detective and mystery stories, English–
 Bio-bibliography. 3. Authors, English–20th century–Bio-
 graphy–Dictionaries. I. Benstock, Bernard. II. Staley,
 Thomas F. III. Series.
 PR888.D4B7 1988
 823'.0872'09–dc19
                                          88-30048
                                          CIP

Contents

Contents

Plan of the Series

The advisory board, the editors, and the publisher of the *Dictionary of Literary Biography* are joined in endorsing Mark Twain's declaration. The literature of a nation provides an inexhaustible resource of permanent worth. We intend to make literature and its creators better understood and more accessible to students and the reading public, while satisfying the standards of teachers and scholars.

To meet these requirements, *literary biography* has been construed in terms of the author's achievement. The most important thing about a writer is his writing. Accordingly, the entries in *DLB* are career biographies, tracing the development of the author's canon and the evolution of his reputation.

The purpose of *DLB* is not only to provide reliable information in a convenient format but also to place the figures in the larger perspective of literary history and to offer appraisals of their accomplishments by qualified scholars.

The publication plan for *DLB* resulted from two years of preparation. The project was proposed to Bruccoli Clark by Frederick G. Ruffner, president of the Gale Research Company, in November 1975. After specimen entries were prepared and typeset, an advisory board was formed to refine the entry format and develop the series rationale. In meetings held during 1976, the publisher, series editors, and advisory board approved the scheme for a comprehensive biographical dictionary of persons who contributed to North American literature. Editorial work on the first volume began in January 1977, and it was published in 1978. In order to make *DLB* more than a reference tool and to compile volumes that individually have claim to status as lit-

erary history, it was decided to organize volumes by topic, period, or genre. Each of these freestanding volumes provides a biographical-bibliographical guide and overview for a particular area of literature. We are convinced that this organization—as opposed to a single alphabet method—constitutes a valuable innovation in the presentation of reference material. The volume plan necessarily requires many decisions for the placement and treatment of authors who might properly be included in two or three volumes. In some instances a major figure will be included in separate volumes, but with different entries emphasizing the aspect of his career appropriate to each volume. Ernest Hemingway, for example, is represented in *American Writers in Paris, 1920-1939* by an entry focusing on his expatriate apprenticeship; he is also in *American Novelists, 1910-1945* with an entry surveying his entire career. Each volume includes a cumulative index of subject authors and articles. Comprehensive indexes to the entire series are planned.

With volume ten in 1982 it was decided to enlarge the scope of *DLB*. By the end of 1986 twenty-one volumes treating British literature had been published, and volumes for Commonwealth and Modern European literature were in progress. The series has been further augmented by the *DLB Yearbooks* (since 1981) which update published entries and add new entries to keep the *DLB* current with contemporary activity. There have also been *DLB Documentary Series* volumes which provide biographical and critical source materials for figures whose work is judged to have particular interest for students. One of these companion volumes is entirely devoted to Tennessee Williams.

We define literature as the *intellectual commerce of a nation*: not merely as belles lettres but as that ample and complex process by which ideas are generated, shaped, and transmitted. *DLB* entries are not limited to "creative writers" but extend to other figures who in their time and in their way influenced the mind of a people. Thus the series encompasses historians, journalists, publishers, and screenwriters. By this means readers of *DLB* may be aided to perceive literature not as cult scripture in the keeping of intellectual high priests but firmly positioned at the center of a nation's life.

DLB includes the major writers appropriate to each volume and those standing in the ranks immediately behind them. Scholarly and critical counsel has been sought in deciding which minor figures to include and how full their entries should be. Wherever possible, useful references are made to figures who do not warrant separate entries.

Each *DLB* volume has a volume editor responsible for planning the volume, selecting the figures for inclusion, and assigning the entries. Volume editors are also responsible for preparing, where appropriate, appendices surveying the major periodicals and literary and intellectual movements for their volumes, as well as lists of further readings. Work on the series as a whole is coordinated at the Bruccoli Clark Layman editorial center in Columbia, South Carolina, where the editorial staff is responsible for accuracy of the published volumes.

One feature that distinguishes *DLB* is the illustration policy–its concern with the iconography of literature. Just as an author is influenced by his surroundings, so is the reader's understanding of the author enhanced by a knowledge of his environment. Therefore *DLB* volumes include not only drawings, paintings, and photographs of authors, often depicting them at various stages in their careers, but also illustrations of their families and places where they lived. Title pages are regularly reproduced in facsimile along with dust jackets for modern authors. The dust jackets are a special feature of *DLB* because they often document better than anything else the way in which an author's work was perceived in its own time. Specimens of the writers' manuscripts are included when feasible.

Samuel Johnson rightly decreed that "The chief glory of every people arises from its authors." The purpose of the *Dictionary of Literary Biography* is to compile literary history in the surest way available to us—by accurate and comprehensive treatment of the lives and work of those who contributed to it.

The *DLB* Advisory Board

Foreword

As noted in *DLB 70: British Mystery Writers, 1860-1919* the writing of mysteries, generally in the form of novels and short stories but also at times as dramatic presentations, has provided an increasingly significant contribution to literature in Britain (as well as in America and on the European continent) since the advent of the Gothic novel at the end of the eighteenth century. Scholars have enjoyed tracing the roots of the mystery form back to much earlier cultures, particularly to Greek tragedy, inadvertently acknowledging that as long as criminal acts and behavior are an aspect of human activity crime will provide subject matter for works of literature. Yet nineteenth-century writers laid the foundation for modern mystery fiction, which in its various forms and manifestations has held sway in the twentieth century as a highly popular component of both mass culture and serious literary expression.

Despite the attempts of writers to define the mystery form during the so-called Golden Age of the mystery in England (the period from about 1913 to 1930 when the puzzle mystery reached a degree of heightened preciosity) the genre is remarkable for its varying guises and classifications. The relationship between the Gothic novel, which flourished in Victorian England, and the mystery is clear, for example, in the works that Sheridan Le Fanu began writing in the early 1860s and in precursors of the mystery such as Angus Reach's romance *Clement Lorimer* (1848-1849). Although the fiction of the supernatural has continued to influence the mystery, Edgar Allan Poe's four detective stories published in the 1840s established an emphasis on ratiocination over atmosphere that has been far more influential in determining the overall direction of detective fiction. The success of Wilkie Collins's *The Woman in White* (1860) and *The Moonstone* (1868), along with Sir Arthur Conan Doyle's Sherlock Holmes (created in 1887), popularized the basic detective narrative, focusing on the investigative detective, frequently a "serial" figure like Holmes himself, appearing throughout a succession of novels and stories.

Detective fiction has its analogue in the crime story and in its unusual variant, the inverse crime narrative, where the emphasis shifts from the reader's assembling the pieces of the puzzle into a revelatory pattern along with the detective to the observation of the investigator arriving at (or in some cases failing to arrive at) the completed puzzle already known to the reader. In both types of crime narrative the crime and the criminal are featured at the expense of the detective, and detection is limited to an ancillary function. Many of these crime narratives are essentially psychological thrillers, with focuses ranging from the elements of aberrant human behavior to the workings of the thoroughly pathological criminal mind, and a fine line, if any at all, separates mainstream psychological fiction from the psychological crime thriller.

Crime/detection fiction also shares roots with the pure adventure story, and elements of the adventure tale have often been retained in the less genteel variants of the crime/detective story, often resurfacing in fictions that feature or culminate in "the chase" or "the hunt," depicted either from the perspective of the hunter or the hunted—or both. In turn, the adventure/chase phenomenon of exciting crime narratives evolves naturally into the espionage novel. This variant of the mystery has increased in popularity since World War II, but the espionage novel came to prominence at the time of World War I in the works of Edgar Wallace, John Buchan, William Le Queux, and E. Phillips Oppenheim. Spy fiction more often than not retains its affinities with crime and detection in methods of operation, while frequently containing strong political implications and propagandistic intentions.

What is frequently termed the thriller or the suspense novel covers a wide area, subsuming the detective story, which in itself has often been divided between the genteel puzzle narrative that looks to be almost exclusively English (with American imitators) and that reached its zenith (or nadir) in the Golden Age of the 1920s and 1930s, and the fiction of hard-boiled "realism" that was its contemporary American cousin and alternative (but has been adopted by occasional British practitioners as well). Scholars have viewed that violent American phenomenon as either a reaction against the effete English variety of detective novel or a native by-product of nineteenth-century Western fiction urbanized and brought up to date. Yet bloody crime fiction already existed during the formative period of detective fiction in Victorian Britain, and violence, with its own didactic purposes, was characteristic of serious fiction of the age as well.

The nineteenth-century phenomenon of "middle-culture" literary art blurred the distinction between serious literature and popular fiction, a balanced attitude that only a handful of authors in the twentieth century have sought to establish for themselves. Most mystery fiction since the cultic prominence of Conan Doyle's detective has been written by authors who specialize almost exclusively in it, although an author of prestige has on occasion been known to indulge in the writing of thrillers, usually under an assumed name. From the nineteenth century on, writers best known for their work in other genres have tried their hand at the popular form, at times creating literature that satisfies both worlds. In the period between the world wars, such novelists as Graham Greene, W. Somerset Maugham, C. P. Snow, and J. B. Priestley practiced the mystery form. In fact, all of Greene's early fiction depended upon the conventions of mystery fiction, and throughout his career his "entertainments" bear witness to their influence upon him. With prose fiction, and particularly the novel, fixed as the primary literary vehicle of the bourgeois era of the nineteenth and twentieth centuries, the mystery novel in its various guises has claimed a prominent position, with a pedigree of its own, in mainstream literary art. That pedigree was legitimized in the period just after World War I when the mystery solidified as a form and attracted a large and enthusiastic audience. *DLB 77: British Mystery Writers, 1920-1939* discusses many of the writers responsible for the flourish of the modern mystery, such as Margery Allingham, Agatha Christie, Ngaio Marsh, Dorothy L. Sayers, and Josephine Tey; also included are authors who extended the genre, such as Eric Ambler, the master of the spy novel, who replaced the false glamour and improbabilities of earlier thrillers with realism and subtle plotting.

This is the second *DLB* volume of British mystery writers; subsequent volumes will cover the period from World War II to the present. Because there has been little scholarship devoted to individual mystery writers except for the most prominent, this volume is particularly useful as a stimulus to further study. Writers are best defined by what they wrote, and so the primary bibliography for each entry contains as many published books as could be verified in reliable sources. Since mystery writing of the period covered here is often formulaic, it has frequently been adequate to discuss works representative of an author's career or to describe in general terms the fiction a writer produced.

The history of mystery fiction, in Great Britain as in America, recounts the evolution of a literary form from a means of popular entertainment to a mode of expression through which the exigencies of everyday life are examined. There is no more compelling subject than crime, particularly murder; the century-and-a-half-long tradition of mystery fiction, which is the systematic literary attempt to come to terms with violent crime, deserves our closest attention.

—Thomas F. Staley and Bernard Benstock

Acknowledgments

This book was produced by Bruccoli Clark Layman, Inc. Karen L. Rood is senior editor for the *Dictionary of Literary Biography* series. Jean W. Ross and Charles Lee Egleston were the in-house editors.

Production coordinator is Kimberly Casey. Art supervisor is Cheryl Crombie. Copyediting supervisor is Joan M. Prince. Typesetting supervisor is Kathleen M. Flanagan. Laura Ingram and Michael D. Senecal are editorial associates. The production staff includes Rowena Betts, Charles D. Brower, Amanda Caulley, Patricia Coate, Mary Colborn, Holly Deal, Sarah A. Estes, Eric Folley, Cynthia Hallman, Judith K. Ingle, Warren McInnis, Kathy S. Merlette, Sheri Beckett Neal, Virginia Smith, and Mark Van Gunten. Jean W. Ross is permissions editor. Joseph Caldwell and Susan Todd, photography editors, and Joseph Matthew Bruccoli and Penney L. Haughton did photographic copy work for the volume.

The editors also wish to acknowledge the admirable research and organizational support of Joan Seay.

Walter W. Ross and Rhonda Marshall did the library research with the assistance of the reference staff at the Thomas Cooper Library of the University of South Carolina: Daniel Boice, Cathy Eckman, Gary Geer, Cathie Gottlieb, David L. Haggard, Jens Holley, Dennis Isbell, Jackie Kinder, Marcia Martin, Jean Rhyne, Beverly Steele, Ellen Tillett, Carol Tobin, and Virginia Weathers. Peter Howard of Serendipity Books, Berkeley, California, helped locate elusive books.

The editors are particularly grateful to Otto Penzler and the Mysterious Bookshop for their generous assistance in providing illustrations and archival material for use in this volume.

Dictionary of Literary Biography • Volume Seventy-seven

British Mystery Writers, 1920-1939

Dictionary of Literary Biography

Margery Allingham

(20 May 1904-30 June 1966)

B. A. Pike

BOOKS: *Blackkerchief Dick* (London: Hodder & Stoughton, 1923; Garden City, N.Y.: Doubleday, Page, 1923);

Water in a Sieve (London: French, 1925);

The White Cottage Mystery (London: Jarrolds, 1928);

The Crime at Black Dudley (London: Jarrolds, 1929); republished as *The Black Dudley Murder* (Garden City, N.Y.: Doubleday, Doran, 1929);

Mystery Mile (London: Jarrolds, 1930; Garden City, N.Y.: Doubleday, Doran, 1930);

Look to the Lady (London: Jarrolds, 1931); republished as *The Gyrth Chalice Mystery* (Garden City, N.Y.: Doubleday, Doran, 1931);

Police at the Funeral (London: Heinemann, 1931; Garden City, N.Y.: Doubleday, Doran, 1932);

Other Man's Danger, as Maxwell March (London: Collins, 1933); republished as *The Man of Dangerous Secrets* (Garden City, N.Y.: Doubleday, Doran, 1933);

Sweet Danger (London: Heinemann, 1933); republished as *Kingdom of Death* (Garden City, N.Y.: Doubleday, Doran, 1933);

Death of a Ghost (London: Heinemann, 1934; Garden City, N.Y.: Doubleday, Doran, 1934);

Rogues' Holiday, as Maxwell March (London: Collins, 1935; Garden City, N.Y.: Doubleday, Doran, 1935);

Flowers for the Judge (London: Heinemann, 1936; Garden City, N.Y.: Doubleday, Doran, 1936);

The Shadow in the House, as Maxwell March (Lon-

Margery Allingham

don: Collins, 1936; Garden City, N.Y.: Doubleday, Doran, 1936);

Mr. Campion: Criminologist (Garden City, N.Y.: Doubleday, Doran, 1937);

Dancers in Mourning (London: Heinemann, 1937; Garden City, N.Y.: Doubleday, Doran, 1937); republished as *Who Killed Chloe?* (New York: Avon, 1943);

The Case of the Late Pig (London: Hodder & Stoughton, 1937);

The Fashion in Shrouds (London: Heinemann, 1938; Garden City, N.Y.: Doubleday, Doran, 1938);

Mr. Campion and Others (London: Heinemann, 1939);

Black Plumes (London: Heinemann, 1940; Garden City, N.Y.: Doubleday, Doran, 1940);

Traitor's Purse (London: Heinemann, 1941; Garden City, N.Y.: Doubleday, Doran, 1941); republished as *The Sabotage Murder Mystery* (New York: Avon, 1943);

The Oaken Heart (London: Michael Joseph, 1941; Garden City, N.Y.: Doubleday, Doran, 1941);

Dance of the Years (London: Michael Joseph, 1943); republished as *The Gallantrys* (Boston: Little, Brown, 1943);

Coroner's Pidgin (London: Heinemann, 1945); republished as *Pearls Before Swine* (Garden City, N.Y.: Doubleday, Doran, 1945);

Wanted: Someone Innocent (New York: Stamford House, 1946);

The Case Book of Mr. Campion (New York: American Mercury, 1947);

More Work for the Undertaker (London: Heinemann, 1948; Garden City, N.Y.: Doubleday, 1949);

Deadly Duo (Garden City, N.Y.: Doubleday, 1949)—comprises *Wanted: Someone Innocent* and *Last Act;* republished as *Take Two at Bedtime* (Kingswood, Surrey: World's Work, 1950);

The Tiger in the Smoke (London: Chatto & Windus, 1952; Garden City, N.Y.: Doubleday, 1952);

No Love Lost (Kingswood, Surrey: World's Work, 1954; Garden City, N.Y.: Doubleday, 1954)—comprises *The Patient at Peacocks Hall* and *Safer Than Love;*

The Beckoning Lady (London: Chatto & Windus, 1955); republished as *The Estate of the Beckoning Lady* (Garden City, N.Y.: Doubleday, 1955);

Hide My Eyes (London: Chatto & Windus, 1958); republished as *Tether's End* (Garden City, N.Y.: Doubleday, 1958); republished as *Ten Were Missing* (New York: Dell, 1961);

Crime and Mr. Campion (Garden City, N.Y.: Doubleday, 1959);

Three Cases for Mr. Campion (Garden City, N.Y.: Doubleday, 1961);

The China Governess (Garden City, N.Y.: Doubleday, 1962; London: Chatto & Windus, 1963);

The Mysterious Mr. Campion (London: Chatto & Windus, 1963);

The Mind Readers (New York: Morrow, 1965; London: Chatto & Windus, 1965);

Mr. Campion's Lady (London: Chatto & Windus, 1965);

Mr. Campion's Clowns (London: Chatto & Windus, 1967);

Cargo of Eagles, by Allingham and Youngman Carter (London: Chatto & Windus, 1968; New York: Morrow, 1968);

The Allingham Casebook (London: Chatto & Windus, 1969; New York: Morrow, 1969);

The Allingham Minibus (London: Chatto & Windus, 1973; New York: Morrow, 1973);

The Margery Allingham Omnibus (London: Penguin, 1982).

OTHER: *Six Against the Yard,* by Allingham and others (London: Selwyn & Blount, 1936); republished as *Six Against Scotland Yard* (Garden City, N.Y.: Doubleday, 1936).

Margery Allingham is preeminent among the writers who brought the detective story to maturity in the decades between the two world wars. She created an aristocratic, unassuming detective called Albert Campion, who matured from "just a silly ass" of the 1920s to an eminent intelligence veteran forty years later. He ranks high among the great detectives of fiction but does so unobtrusively, disdaining self-advertisement. Other recurrent characters contribute richly to the Campion series: Campion's wife, Amanda; his manservant, Lugg; and his police associates, Stanislaus Oates and Charlie Luke. The novels and stories in which they appear are among the most distinguished in the genre—vivacious, stylish, observant, shapely, intricate, and witty. They are unfailingly intelligent and imaginative, even when they do not wholly succeed.

Allingham regarded the mystery novel as a box with four sides—"a Killing, a Mystery, an Enquiry and a Conclusion with an Element of Satisfaction in it." Once inside the box, she felt secure: the genre gave her the discipline she felt she needed, while allowing her imagination full

Allingham leaving the Quai des Orfevres, Paris headquarters of the French police force

play to provide the "Element of Satisfaction." This she abundantly did, from her first crime novel in 1928 to her last in 1968.

Margery Louise Allingham was born in Ealing, a western suburb of London, and not, as one of her dust jackets claims, in the "old house in the wilds of Norman Essex" in which she was raised. She was the first child of two cousins, Herbert John Allingham and his wife, Emily Jane (Hughes) Allingham, whom she later described as "second generation London Irish," pink in their political sympathies. Both parents were writers, carrying on a strong tradition that flourished in their family for four generations. Herbert Allingham edited the *Christian Globe*, a nonconformist weekly owned by his father, and also ran the *London Journal* before he abandoned journalism to become a prolific free-lance pulp writer for both children and adults. His wife sold stories to women's magazines, and her sister Maud Hughes founded and edited *Picture Show*, a successful film magazine. Margery Allingham's

cousin, Emily Jane Hughes, also wrote for women's magazines.

Herbert John Allingham's decision to give up journalism came soon after his daughter's birth, and she was only a few months old when the family moved from Ealing to Layer Breton, a remote village southwest of Colchester, on the edge of the Essex marshes. Here they lived in a Georgian rectory that became open house to a circle of writers and journalists; and here Margery Allingham began writing, earning her first fee at the age of eight for a story published in one of her aunt's journals.

Allingham wrote steadily through her school days, at first in Colchester and later as a boarder at the Perse School for Girls in Cambridge, where she wrote, produced, and performed in a costume play. After her return to London in 1920 she enrolled at the Regent Street Polytechnic, where she studied drama and speech training in a successful attempt to overcome a childhood stammer. Here she wrote the verse play *Dido and Aeneas*, which was performed at St. George's Hall and the Cripplegate Theatre; Allingham played a leading role, and the scenery was designed by Philip Youngman Carter, whom she would marry in 1927.

The Allinghams retained a house on Mersea Island, a few miles from Layer Breton, and here Margery Allingham found the material for her first novel, the adventure story *Blackkerchief Dick* (1923), which was published when she was nineteen. Two years earlier she had participated in a series of séances, during which messages ostensibly from seventeenth-century pirates and smugglers were received. Long afterwards her husband maintained that these occult communications were "entirely the product of Margery's dynamic imagination," so that *Blackkerchief Dick* is wholly a work of fiction and not, as was originally claimed, a fictional rendering of a true story transmitted from beyond the grave. Whatever its origins, it was warmly received: the *Bookman* for October 1923 welcomed a "thoroughly entertaining" story, written "with an ease and finish given to few young writers."

Besides *Dido and Aeneas*, Allingham wrote other plays: *Water in a Sieve*, a one-act comedy published by French in 1925, and "Without Being Naturally Qualified" (unpublished). The title of the latter was based on a quotation from George Bernard Shaw, who responded with detailed criticism when she sent him a copy. She was also persuaded by her father to write a serious novel

5

about the Bright Young People of the 1920s, but she found herself frustrated by the tension between her natural gaiety and the earnest intensity of her theme, and the book was never published.

As a result of this failure, Allingham decided to "escape into the Mystery," which she felt was "at once a prison and a refuge" to a writer unsure of her aims but confident of her powers. *The White Cottage Mystery* was her first essay in detection, written as a serial for the *Daily Express* in 1927 and published as a book by Jarrolds a year later. It was an auspicious debut, confident in narrative, effective as a mystery, and with a remarkably bold conclusion. The victim is a sadistic brute whose death is investigated by an elderly Scotland Yard inspector called W. T. Challoner. His son is at hand when the corpse is discovered, and when the trail leads to France, they follow it together. At the end W. T. throws up the case, revealing the truth and the clue that led to it only after seven years have passed.

In 1929 Albert Campion made his debut as a minor character and, for a time, a suspect in *The Crime at Black Dudley* (1929; published in the United States as *The Black Dudley Murder*, 1930), a melodramatic novel that is effective in atmosphere but less secure in its handling of the detective element. Campion's noble lineage, vacant look, and, most significantly, his characteristic modesty, the unassuming stance that he never abandons in all his eventful career, are quickly established.

Throughout the 1920s and 1930s Allingham found it necessary to write in other fields to make a living. Since her books were "not then all that profitable," she worked hard to earn time for the writing she really wished to do. In her preface to *The Mysterious Mr. Campion* (1963) she distinguishes between her "right hand writing," which she did for pleasure and creative satisfaction, and her "left hand writing," which was commissioned and subject to editorial supervision. In the early years of her marriage she was producing ten thousand words a week, shaping the plot of a film into a story for the *Girl's Cinema*, another of her aunt's papers. Later the left-hand work became more congenial and less of a chore. She wrote magazine fiction for Lord Northcliffe's *Answers*, in the tradition of her father. At a more sophisticated level, she produced a series of Campion stories for the *Strand Magazine*, nine of which were later collected with other stories in *Mr. Campion and Others* (1939). They are elegant little puzzles with a high degree of fin-

ish, and it is perhaps significant that Lugg, who is not known for his polish, is replaced in these stories by an anonymous manservant. From 1937 to 1944 Allingham also wrote for *Time and Tide* in a conscious attempt to widen her range. Though most of her contributions are reviews of current novels, she also wrote an occasional light essay.

The right-hand books were written in the country: *Mystery Mile* (1930) at Letherington in Suffolk; *Sweet Danger* (1933) at a rented house in Chappel, in Essex, the model for Pontisbright, the novel's setting. London was for left-hand work only, and though the Carters maintained their London base at 91 Great Russell Street, they lived in the country by preference. Allingham regarded herself essentially as a countrywoman, exiled in the city; from 1934 she and her husband made their permanent home at D'Arcy House in Tolleshunt d'Arcy, five miles from Layer Breton.

After the three apprentice novels, Allingham's work found a stylish assurance that never left her. Her powers were steadily developing throughout the 1930s, which she began with *Mystery Mile*, an engaging light adventure novel, and crowned with *The Fashion in Shrouds* (1938), at once an incisive comedy of manners and a complex crime puzzle. Seven other novels and two collections of stories also appeared during the ten years leading up to the outbreak of World War II.

The Crime at Black Dudley established a pattern for *Mystery Mile*, *Look to the Lady* (1931; published in the United States as *The Gyrth Chalice Mystery*), and *Sweet Danger* (published in the United States as *Kingdom of Death*). In all four of these novels the corpses are incidental. Though violent deaths occur, they do so only on the periphery of the action, while the main concern of those involved is to retain or gain possession of something precious. These early novels were assembled on what the author called the Plumpudding principle, whereby inventive action takes precedence over reasoned restraint. They are high-spirited larks, crammed with improbable incidents and eccentric characters, all set against the traditional idyllic landscape of a timeless England. *Look to the Lady* is especially rich in fantastic detail: the Gyrth Chalice has a legendary guardian that proves to be truly awe-inspiring; and gypsies, a bald witch, and a maddened mare add to the excitement. Despite the author's contention that the Plumpudding procedure is "no con-

Dust jacket for the first edition of Allingham's personal favorite among her novels (courtesy of Otto Penzler)

struction at all," these early books in fact benefit from the long apprenticeship. *Sweet Danger* is especially well made, with two distinct lines of action that converge in a vivid total denouement.

Campion is promoted in *Mystery Mile* from minor zany to principal knight-errant, a status he retains for the rest of his career, which comprises seventeen more novels and some thirty stories. This book is also notable for the introduction of two of his chief henchmen, the old lag Magersfontein Lugg, and the dependable policeman Stanislaus Oates. Lugg is a marvelous "character" in the sense of an exaggerated personality that operates on a level of engaging fantasy rather than stern reality. Allingham felt the need to comment on his role and to justify his failure to age over the years, as most of her characters do. She saw him as the personification of Campion's sense of humor, an essential extension of his employer's more seemly persona, with a force beyond his

basic humanity that frees him from the need to age. In fact, cerebral justification of Lugg is unnecessary, since the books would be immeasurably the poorer without him.

Lugg is a former cat burglar who has lost his figure ("a hillock of a man, with a big pallid face which reminded one irresistibly of a bull terrier") and now functions improbably as Campion's manservant and self-appointed censor, mournfully enlivening his employer's routines with caustic observations on current circumstances and bodeful predictions for the future. His relationship with Campion is a dazzling variation on the traditional interdependence of master and man, established largely through entertaining dialogue that allows their deep mutual affection to emerge through the veil of derision thrown over it. As a result, Lugg can function as a genuine aide when the need arises (in *Traitor's Purse*, 1941, for instance). Much of his charm derives from his speech, an offhand basic Cockney with baroque flourishes that lift it clear of any actual utterance known to man. His later career is documented as the series progresses: his night in the wood in *Look to the Lady*, his increasing social pretensions in *Flowers for the Judge* (1936), his narrow escape from death in *The Case of the Late Pig* (1937), his stint as a butler in *Dancers in Mourning* (1937), his book of quotations in *The Fashion in Shrouds*, his war effort in *Coroner's Pidgin* (1945), and his reprieve from dismissal in *More Work for the Undertaker* (1948).

Oates is less flamboyant, particularly in the earlier years, where he makes the mistakes and Campion corrects them. Only in the later books does he come fully into his own: in *More Work for the Undertaker*, where his tour around his old manor develops into a star turn; and in *Cargo of Eagles* (1968), where he holds court in the basement of the ultimate in reactionary London clubs.

Sweet Danger also introduces the Lady Amanda Fitton. She, too, is an essential element in Campion's armory, quite apart from the fact that she finally resolves his sexual tensions by marrying him. As Lugg is his humor, so Amanda is his yardstick, his judgment and sense of proportion: she helps to define his insights, direct his thoughts, and decide his courses of action. She is eighteen, a redhead with honey-brown eyes and a triangular smile, radiating youth, intelligence, health, and beauty. She has mechanical skills rare in one of her age and sex, an expertise in electricity that makes her a God-given ally in the

Pontisbright treasure hunt. Her spirit is indomitable, her gaiety infectious, her loyalty unquestionable, her resource unfailing: "eager generosity" is "her mainspring." *Sweet Danger* ends with an unconventional love scene in which Campion agrees to wait until Amanda is ready to come to him. On her next appearance, in *The Fashion in Shrouds*, the agreed years have passed, and she is twenty-four, a valuable member of the Alandel aeronautics team, with the look of "a Botticelli angel" and a boundless enthusiasm for her work that makes Campion, at thirty-eight, "aware of a chill" at his distance from her world of young ideals and endeavors. The sequel here to their odd, yet tender, love scene in *Sweet Danger* is a mock engagement that is broken spectacularly for reasons that do not become clear until later; when we next meet them, in *Traitor's Purse*, they are genuinely engaged, but Campion is suffering from amnesia and uncertain what their relationship is. Only in the later novels are we given any indication that they are capable of a deep emotional commitment to each other, and then only obliquely in the pain that Campion involuntarily causes Amanda. However, the end of *Traitor's Purse* does resolve their emotional difficulties, after a complex sequence of doubts and misunderstandings. Though Campion's civilized inhibitions still bedevil his emergence from his amnesia, the sight of Amanda is sufficient to shock him into full awareness of how great his loss would be were he to let her go. Finally, he simply claims her, feeling for "the first time in his life . . . completely adult. His hesitancy, his qualms, his intellectual doubts seemed suddenly the stuff of childhood." Later books focus on widely differing stages in the development of their marriage, notably Campion's comic first encounter with his infant son Rupert and the panic that engulfs him when Amanda comes dreadfully close to being stabbed to death (again, perhaps, he values her most when he thinks he might lose her).

In a brief preface to *Death of a Ghost* (1934) Allingham draws a distinction between the early adventures of "frankly picaresque" character and the "less highly coloured but even more grave difficulties" which were to engage Campion in his more mature years. The herald of the new era is *Police at the Funeral*, which was published in 1931, two years before *Sweet Danger* brought the first phase to a close. It is a model detective story, elegantly written, cunningly wrought, and rich in character and atmosphere. Here Campion is properly subdued to a daunting new environment, a somber Cambridge household under the thumb of an implacable old widow. Nothing in the earlier books suggests the range and intensity of characterization which the author now reveals. Uncle William Faraday is a comic humbug in the tradition of Falstaff, forever disclaiming his actual frailties while protesting virtue where none exists. Simultaneously Allingham exposes the sly sadism of her dead cousin through a series of eerie retrospective insights into a truly ugly nature.

Three years later *Death of a Ghost* confirmed the promise of its predecessor and again showed Allingham extending her range, this time among a colony of artists in London's Little Venice. The novel is only in part a whodunit, since the killer's identity is established well before the end. The closing chapters constitute a coda to the main action, with Campion risking his life to coax the killer into the open, successfully, but with a shocking outcome. He is challenged here as never before and feels his way to the killer's identity by an intuitive process culminating in "what he could only regard as a species of revelation."

Flowers for the Judge continued the line of cultural mysteries. It is a more uneven performance, occasionally uncertain in tone and with a dispiriting wash of sentiment laid over certain scenes and characters. Two lines of action converge on the publishing firm of Barnabas in Holborn, where a disappearance develops into a death. Campion's dual investigation seems curiously detached from the central development, whereby the law moves ponderously against the wrong man. A contrasting lightness distinguishes *The Case of the Late Pig*, in which Allingham's "attempt to combine Mr. Campion's newly acquired responsible mood with his earlier light-hearted adventures" resulted in one of her perfect books. Campion tells the story himself, in a blithe, easy style reminiscent of P. G. Wodehouse's. The action, too, has convolutions worthy of the comic master, but the sinister gaiety Allingham achieves is all her own.

As further evidence of her expanding powers, she produced in the same year her most ambitious novel to that date, *Dancers in Mourning*. The action centers on Jimmy Sutane, the star of a revue based on the alleged memoirs of William Faraday, known as Uncle William. A campaign of persecution is in full swing against Sutane, and an addition to the cast of his show seems ill-judged and therefore inexplicable. Campion is present when the first death occurs, and he and Uncle William remain on hand to observe Sutane

*Allingham at tea with two of her dogs, circa
1960 (Popperfoto)*

and his entourage. But Campion is no longer a
neutral observer: a sudden passion for Sutane's
wife overwhelms him, eroding his detachment
and clouding his judgment so that he fails to dis-
cern the killer's identity until very late in the day.
Every development in the case is scrupulously rendered in terms of human personality, and the narrative is deeply satisfying as an illumination of
character and as a complex murder story.

The Fashion in Shrouds, which followed a year
later, is even more impressive as a demonstration
of Allingham's contention that a sophisticated
crime story may coexist in the same narrative
with an incisive novel of manners. Her special concern here is to reinforce the traditional view that
the sexes are interdependent and the only
proper "human entity" is "a man and a woman."
Two eminent career women demonstrate the
point: Campion's sister Val, a dress designer, and
Georgia Wells, an actress. For all their success,
they cannot overcome "the dreadful primitive
weakness of the female of any species." They discover this truth while deeply involved in an intricate murder mystery set against an elegant background of haute couture and high living.

Georgia is the pivot on which the double action
turns: the emotional tensions arise from her decision to annex Val's lover, and the murders occur
because the victims loved her enough to marry
her. Val and Georgia dictate the style of the
novel, which faithfully reflects their self-
conscious cleverness and occasional tendency to
go too far. Allingham later acknowledged that
the book was overwritten and trimmed it for inclusion in a 1965 omnibus.

When war came in 1939, Allingham was
well on with *Black Plumes* (1940), her only mature
novel to exclude Campion. Though she finished
the book more quickly than she had intended, it
shows no sign of haste: the action moves with
stately menace toward a vivid climax, in which
both killer and murder weapon are spectacularly
revealed. Instead of Campion, the investigator is
Bridie, a soft-spoken man from the Orkneys,
over whose "small steady eyes" wool is not easily
pulled. In ambience and tone the novel recalls
Flowers for the Judge; in both books the mystery
threatens a close-knit family firm beset by suspicion and fear when a partner is murdered.

Allingham's next books were written while
Britain waited to be invaded. Essex, facing the
Low Countries across the North Sea, must have
seemed especially vulnerable, and Allingham
flew the flag at home with exemplary courage
and determination while her husband was serving abroad. She became involved in Air Raid Pre-
cautions work, served as First Aid Commandant
for her district, and organized the billeting and
care of evacuees from London. She was also set
to function as the local agent of a British Resistance, should such a movement have become a reality. D'Arcy House became a temporary military
base for eight officers and two hundred men of
the Cameronians. Weapons and explosives were
stored in the grounds and emergency food supplies in the garage.

As the range of her activities indicates, the
war stirred deep feelings in Allingham, and they
were expressed in her writing. A letter from
Allingham's publisher in *Time and Tide,* July
1940, reads like a rallying cry, confirming her
faith in the individual's passion for all that he
holds dear as the essential feature of the nation's
strength. In 1941 she published *The Oaken Heart,*
based on letters written to American friends and
shaped into a book at the suggestion of Doubleday, her American publisher. Under a light disguise of fiction, it records the life of D'Arcy
House and its neighborhood as they adapted to

war and the threat of invasion. The book was intended to stir America into joining the Allies in the fight against Germany. In *Traitor's Purse*, published the same year, Campion finds himself driven by "a deep and lovely passion for his home, his soil, his blessed England." As a novel, *Traitor's Purse* is taut and feverish, with insistent tensions all converging on Campion. He is in an appalling situation: he alone holds the key to Britain's salvation, but a blow on the head has routed his memory. Much of the novel's fascination lies in Campion's gradual discovery of himself, professionally as a detective and personally as Amanda's lover.

The next novel, *Dance of the Years* (1943; published in the United States as *The Gallantrys*), was the author's only attempt at mainstream fiction. Though she was ambitious for its success and had intended it as a full-scale dynastic saga based on her family's history, it tailed off after a promising start into "a precis of a larger scheme." The need to earn enough to maintain her home, coupled with the demands made on her by her many responsibilities, caused her to finish the book too quickly.

Her next Campion novel, *Coroner's Pidgin* (published in the United States as *Pearls Before Swine*), showed no decline of powers or diminution of spirits. Uniquely, it was written without the close collaboration of her husband, whose active service kept him abroad during its completion. The earlier action in the book defines the domestic tensions among another self-contained smart set, but later developments achieve a larger excitement, grander altogether than what has gone before. The richness and range of the characterization are remarkable, and there are many intense and memorable moments, not least the macabre opening sequence, in which Lugg and the Dowager Lady Carados maneuver a dead woman up the stairs to Campion's flat.

When *More Work for the Undertaker* appeared in 1948, Allingham apologized in the dedication to "all old and valued clients . . . for unavoidable delay in delivery of goods." In fact, the absence of any books since the publication of *Coroner's Pidgin* three years earlier marked the beginning of a reduced rate of production that the author maintained for the rest of her life. There were thirteen novels in the fourteen years from 1928 to 1941, but only eight in the twenty-four years from 1945 to 1968.

Of the seven postwar novels, none is richer than *More Work for the Undertaker*, a consummate entertainment flawed only by a certain lack of definition in the character of the villain. It is an Allingham treasure house, sinister yet festive in atmosphere and alive with wit and fancy. Campion completely outclasses Charlie Luke, the author's new young policeman, whose "pile-driver personality" nonetheless takes the reader by storm. Equally fine are the undertaker, Bowels, and the Palinodes, the family of bizarre intellectuals around whom the case revolves.

Allingham's greatest success came in 1952 with *The Tiger in the Smoke*, the novel most often named as her best. It is a somber book, much the darkest in the canon, and though the whodunit element is absent, the level of tension is high. The Tiger is Jack Havoc, a vicious killer on the run in a fog-bound London, seeking the key to a treasure that obsesses him. For the author he is a new departure, "the first genuinely evil person" she had created. Against such an adversary Campion is out of his depth, content to leave the hunt to Luke. At a high point of the action, Havoc is confronted by Campion's uncle, Canon Avril, in a classic encounter of good and evil. The old priest's power affects the younger man so profoundly that he finds it, for the first time, less than easy to kill. Canon Avril is the greatest of the novel's many triumphs, a man for whom God alone can judge the actions of men; others are the Tiger himself, a dangerous animal, vicious from the cradle, and a freakish band of street musicians led by a neurotic albino.

Allingham's personal favorite among her novels, *The Beckoning Lady* (published in the United States as *The Estate of the Beckoning Lady*), was published in 1955. There are strong autobiographical elements in the narrative: Minnie Cassands is something of a self-portrait, and her husband Tonker is derived from Youngman Carter. The celebration at the Beckoning Lady "mirrors something of what a summer party could be like at Tolleshunt d'Arcy," and the absurd routines imposed on Minnie by her income tax adviser clearly had their origin in a real-life frustration. The setting is Pontisbright, and Uncle William is, sadly, one of the victims. Campion determines to avenge his old friend, but otherwise this is one of his lightest undertakings. Because it is shaped with a veteran's craft and concern, the mystery is continually absorbing, but there are many self-indulgent digressions. Charlie Luke suffers a virtual betrayal at his author's hands: his integrity and force are sacrificed to the prevalent languor, and diffident love reduces him to an abject travesty of his true self.

Hide My Eyes (1958; published in the United States as *Tether's End*) restores him to prominence and to his customary command. Though Campion contributes crucially, and Luke himself shuts his eyes to an essential truth, it is very much his case, built up from isolated details that coalesce in his mind to form a pattern. The action covers a single day in which disparate events interlock in a grim and complex design. Because the pressure does not yield, the excitement is concentrated and continuous. At the beginning of the day Luke broods over the tenuous scraps that might be evidence, but that night he arrests his man. His quarry is "a well-trained animal without imagination or moral sense," different from Havoc because he is cooler and more calculating. The day through which we follow him finally destroys his image of himself, forcing him to acknowledge his common humanity with the rest of mankind. The action moves with a kind of elemental certainty to a final confrontation between good and evil.

Four years passed before the appearance of *The China Governess* (1962). One of the author's most studied and serious works, it combines a characteristic coziness with a harsher awareness of contemporary doubts and tensions. Most of the characters involved are either deceived or deceiving, on a scale that governs their lives. An identity crisis is the core of the action, the need of Timothy Kinnit to learn his true parentage. In the course of his quest, the novel explores heredity, asserting continually that no amount of social conditioning can eliminate inherited traits: Timothy's heredity declares itself in his looks, his voice, his gestures, and his temperament. The theme of illusion and reality is subtly extended: to a garrulous nanny, whose romantic view of life deliberately excludes unpleasant truths; and to Timothy's adoptive family, around whom a far-reaching pattern of guilt takes shape.

The Mind Readers (1965) is the last of Allingham's completed novels; before *Cargo of Eagles* was finished, she had died of cancer, at Colchester, six weeks after her sixty-second birthday. Though *The Mind Reader* was comparatively ill-received, it has many saving graces: acute intelligence, contagious zest, lavish invention, and intense commitment to its unusual theme. The narrative looks confidently to the future, while also harking back to the high exuberance of the early adventure novels. Essentially, this is an esca-

pade, in which sinister powers plot to possess a treasure, while Campion and his henchmen strive to make it secure. The title indicates the nature of the treasure: a device for reading people's minds, discovered by two of Amanda's great-nephews. Campion, for once, can only watch and wonder–at his own deliverance from imminent death, and finally at the spectacular denouement engineered by the boys. After a tangled action, the novel ends on a clear note of hope. The death of a traitor inspires a patriotic outburst reminiscent of that in *Traitor's Purse,* and the spies and schemers who seek to control the device are wholly confounded.

The publisher's brief preface to the posthumously published *Cargo of Eagles* confirms the care and craftsmanship that went into Allingham's work: the "whole fabric" of the story "had been mapped out long before her death," so that her husband was able to finish it, as she herself would have done, according to plan. The book has the force and coherence of a unified whole, in no way diminished by the enforced collaboration. The action is set in a dour estuary village called Saltey, in East Anglia, where the locals obstruct authority as a matter of course and wild gangs of teenage "tearaways" roar up and down on motorcycles. For the last time, Allingham absorbs a raw modern phenomenon into the traditional fabric of one of her novels, accurately presenting the "ton-up types" as joyless and destructive, while ensuring that they do not jeopardize the essentially civilized tone of a characteristic Allingham entertainment. For all its surliness, Saltey is Allingham territory, with a picturesque history, a local legend, treasure to be found, and Campion on hand to find it before the enemy. Like everyone else, he follows the signs to the wrong conclusion but recovers to control the final sequence with an assurance matching anything in his long career, literally unmasking the villain and stage-managing the subsequent revelations with a shrewd showmanship calculated to achieve exactly the effects he wants. For Campion, there were to be two more adventures, written by Youngman Carter, but for Allingham this was the end.

Besides her novels, Allingham wrote four novellas and sixty-four stories, published in a wide variety of journals and anthologies. The novellas are more overtly romantic in tone than the novels and exclude Campion. They were collected in two volumes, *Deadly Duo* (1949; published in the United Kingdom as *Take Two at Bedtime,* 1950) and *No Love Lost* (1954). Five collections of Allingham stories appeared in the author's lifetime, and two more have been assembled since her death.

Youngman Carter's touching account of his wife in his preface to *Mr. Campion's Clowns* (1967) gives a warm picture of a gay and generous woman, with kindness and courage and a rare gift for friendship. Though not an orthodox Christian, she was "deeply religious," with her own tenets of belief. She was greatly attached to her house and garden and loved to share them with her many friends. Her marriage brought her enduring happiness; and for over forty years her husband was also her collaborator, helping to plan each book and designing the wrappers for most of them. After her death he achieved in *Cargo of Eagles* and his own two sequels a lively pastiche of her characteristic mode.

In that mode she had "precious few peers and no superiors," as the *Sunday Times* once claimed. She remains one of the most diverting and alluring of mystery novelists, zestful in narrative and dialogue, and supremely devious in her designs. She showed acute insight into character, and her books abound in witty and accurate observations of people, with an especially keen eye for an eccentric. Her sense of place carried her with ease from the chic resorts of the beau monde to a desolate island and a reeking dump. She had a vivid vein of fantasy, and very few of her jokes misfire. If the tone falters at times, there are no flat pages: her early training made her incapable of dullness. As a stylist she reached a high level of conscious elegance, from which she moved on to the graceful, pointed precision of her later manner.

Despite family resemblances between one novel and another, Allingham never repeated herself or wrote to a formula. Aware of the need to adapt her work to a changing world, she devised new forms, often taking risks and continually testing her range. She experimented freely, not always with success, but invariably with conviction and intelligence. Always an expert storyteller, she became a true novelist as she matured, refining and deepening her fictions to encompass significant themes, exploring the great abstractions: love and justice, good and evil, illusion and truth. Her work attains classic status and will not be forgotten; not for nothing was she compared to Charles Dickens and Robert Louis Stevenson.

Eric Ambler

(28 June 1909-   )

Joan DelFattore
University of Delaware

BOOKS: *The Dark Frontier* (London: Hodder & Stoughton, 1936);

Uncommon Danger (London: Hodder & Stoughton, 1937); republished as *Background to Danger* (New York: Knopf, 1937);

Epitaph for a Spy (London: Hodder & Stoughton, 1938; New York: Knopf, 1952);

Cause for Alarm (London: Hodder & Stoughton, 1938; New York: Knopf, 1939);

The Mask of Dimitrios (London: Hodder & Stoughton, 1939); republished as *A Coffin for Dimitrios* (New York: Knopf, 1939);

Journey into Fear (London: Hodder & Stoughton, 1940; New York: Knopf, 1940);

Skytip, with Charles Rodda, as Eliot Reed (New York: Doubleday, 1950; London: Hodder & Stoughton, 1951);

Judgment on Deltchev (London: Hodder & Stoughton, 1951; New York: Knopf, 1951);

Tender to Danger, with Rodda, as Eliot Reed (New York: Doubleday, 1951); republished as *Tender To Moonlight* (London: Hodder & Stoughton, 1952);

The Schirmer Inheritance (London: Heinemann, 1953; New York: Knopf, 1953);

The Manas Affair, with Rodda, as Eliot Reed (London: Collins, 1953; New York: Doubleday, 1953);

Charter to Danger, with Rodda, as Eliot Reed (London: Collins, 1954);

The Night-Comers (London: Heinemann, 1956); republished as *State of Siege* (New York: Knopf, 1956);

Passport to Panic, with Rodda, as Eliot Reed (London: Collins, 1958);

Passage of Arms (London: Heinemann, 1959; New York: Knopf, 1960);

The Light of Day (London: Heinemann, 1962; New York: Knopf, 1963); republished as *Topkapi* (New York: Bantam, 1964);

The Ability to Kill, and Other Pieces (London: Bodley Head, 1963);

A Kind of Anger (London: Bodley Head, 1964; New York: Atheneum, 1964);

Eric Ambler

Dirty Story (London: Bodley Head, 1967; New York: Atheneum, 1967);

The Intercom Conspiracy (New York: Atheneum, 1969; London: Weidenfeld & Nicolson, 1970);

The Levanter (London: Weidenfeld & Nicolson, 1972; New York: Atheneum, 1972);

Doctor Frigo (London: Weidenfeld & Nicolson, 1974; New York: Atheneum, 1974);

Send No More Roses (London: Weidenfeld & Nicolson, 1977); republished as *The Siege of the Villa Lipp* (New York: Random House, 1977);

The Care of Time (London: Weidenfeld & Nicolson, 1981; New York: Farrar, Straus & Giroux, 1981);

Here Lies: An Autobiography (London: Weidenfeld & Nicolson, 1985; New York: Farrar, Straus & Giroux, 1986).

SHORT STORIES: "The Army of the Shadows," in *The Queen's Book of the Red Cross* (London: Hodder & Stoughton, 1939);
"The Intrusions of Dr. Czissar" ("A Bird in the Tree," "The Case of the Emerald Sky," "Case of the Gentleman Poet," "Case of the Landlady's Brother," "Case of the Overheated Flat," "The Case of the Pinchbeck Locket"), in *Sketch* (London, 1940);
"The Blood Bargain," in *Winter's Crimes 2,* edited by George Hardinge (London: Macmillan, 1970).

MOTION PICTURES: *The Way Ahead,* screenplay by Ambler and Peter Ustinov, Fox, 1944;
The October Man, screenplay by Ambler, Eagle Lion, 1947;
One Woman's Story, screenplay by Ambler, Stanley Haynes, and David Lean, Universal, 1949;
Highly Dangerous, screenplay by Ambler, Lippert, 1950;
The Clouded Yellow, screenplay by Ambler, General Film Distributors, 1950;
The Magic Box, screenplay by Ambler, British Lion Film Corporation, 1951;
Encore, screenplay by Ambler and others, Paramount, 1951;
The Promoter, screenplay by Ambler, Universal, 1952;
Rough Shoot, screenplay by Ambler, United Artists, 1953;
The Cruel Sea, screenplay by Ambler, Universal 1953;
Lease of Life, screenplay by Ambler, General Film Distributors, 1954;
The Purple Plain, screenplay by Ambler, United Artists, 1954;
Battle Hell, screenplay by Ambler, Distributors Corporation of America, 1957;
A Night to Remember, screenplay by Ambler, British Lion Film Corporation, 1958;
The Wreck of the Mary Deare, screenplay by Ambler, M-G-M, 1960.

OTHER: "The Army of the Shadows," in *The Queen's Book of the Red Cross* (London: Hodder & Stoughton, 1939);
To Catch a Spy: An Anthology of Favorite Spy Stories, edited by Ambler (London: Bodley Head, 1964; New York: Atheneum, 1965);
Arthur Conan Doyle, *The Adventures of Sherlock Holmes,* introduction by Ambler (London: Murray-Cape, 1974).

Eric Clifford Ambler was born in southeast London. His father, Alfred Percy Ambler, and his mother, Amy Madeleine Andrews, were music hall entertainers. Under their professional names, Amy and Reg Ambrose, they gave puppet shows and performed as living marionettes. As a boy Eric Ambler was attracted to the life of a music hall performer, but his parents insisted on educating him for a more conventional career. Ambler therefore attended Colfe's Grammar School in London, where he was extremely unhappy. His conflicts with academic authority in general, and with certain schoolmasters in particular, later provided the background for the bitter memories of one of his best-known characters, Arthur Abdel Simpson (*The Light of Day,* 1962, and *Dirty Story,* 1967). However, despite his rebelliousness (he later described himself as "a kind of juvenile delinquent"), Ambler was a competent student. At the age of fifteen he won an engineering scholarship to Northampton Polytechnic, a branch of London University. He left before graduation in order to begin an apprenticeship in electrical engineering, but after a year of that he returned to his original career goal: the music halls.

In 1929, disillusioned with show business after a year of touring England as a vaudeville comedian and songwriter, Ambler took a job writing advertising copy. By this time he had written two novels, four plays, and a number of songs, but he had not succeeded in publishing anything. Ignoring the advice of a literary agent who, having read one of his novels, advised him to go into some other line of work, Ambler continued to write. He finally succeeded in having two of his plays produced by amateur performers. He was much more successful in his work as a copywriter, and by 1937 he had become the director of a large London advertising agency.

Despite his success in business and his apparent failure as a creative writer, Ambler was not willing to settle down to the life of a London advertising executive. His political views and his personal convictions were very far to the left, and although he never joined the Communist party, he had no sympathy for the capitalist system. He also had an intense desire to do creative work in an area in which he could make significant improvements. As he later explained, "What happened was simply *having failed* at playwriting, *having failed* as a songwriter, *failed* as an engineer, I looked around for something I could change and decided it was the thriller-spy story. The detective story genre has been worked over and worked over, but no one had looked at the thriller. It was still a dirty word. So I decided to intellectualize it, insofar as I was able."

Ambler's first thriller was accepted for publication in 1936 by Hodder and Stoughton, and their advance of thirty pounds more than doubled his lifetime earnings as a creative writer. As Ambler cheerfully admits, *The Dark Frontier* is an unwieldy and amateurish book. Its protagonist, Prof. Henry Barstow, suffers a blow on the head and wakes up believing that he is Conway Carruthers, an experienced secret agent. He then takes it upon himself to defeat the conspiracy of big business, in the shape of international cartels and armament firms, to exploit the individual for corporate profit. The character of Carruthers was intended to parody the right-wing, superman image of the thriller hero exemplified by Bulldog Drummond, but Ambler lost control of his material, and the book turned into a kind of fantasy. It does, however, contain an interesting bit of foresight. Barstow/Carruthers invades the Balkan stronghold of an evil scientist in order to prevent him from perfecting his new invention: an atom bomb. The political and scientific sophistication which led Ambler to anticipate the importance of the atom bomb nearly a decade before the real bomb was finally developed became a characteristic of his best work.

The Dark Frontier was successful enough to induce Hodder and Stoughton to offer Ambler a contract for three books at one hundred pounds a book. He promptly produced a second thriller, *Uncommon Danger* (1937; published in the United States as *Background to Danger*). In this book a freelance journalist, Kenton, recklessly agrees to carry some papers through a border checkpoint for a man he has just met. He finds himself involved in an international conspiracy created by such conglomerates as Pan-Eurasian Petroleum and Imperial Armour Plating Trust. In placing the blame for world tension on international corporations, cartels, and consortia rather than on governments, Ambler was influenced by the work of John Buchan and of Francis Beeding (pseudonyms of John Leslie Palmer and Hilary Aidan St. George Saunders). They had written thrillers in which individual heroes defeat conspiracies hatched by groups of rich, powerful, and respected men. Ambler also followed, and eventually surpassed, Buchan and Beeding in the use of innocent and/or politically naive protagonists

who are drawn into adventures by circumstances outside their control. Buchan and Beeding, however, were essentially right-wing writers; and their thrillers, unlike Ambler's, usually end with a restoration of order and an affirmation of the honor of the Establishment.

After the publication of *Uncommon Danger* Ambler decided to leave the security of his agency directorship in order to devote all of his time to creative work. In 1938 he moved to Paris, where he lived on fifteen dollars a week, associated with writers like Cyril Connolly and Brian Howard, and became, as he later expressed it, "quite the little intellectual snob." Ambler had always had an intense interest in history, and now he read widely in that area. His increasingly sophisticated insight into political movements and sociological phenomena became an important factor in his writing. He also used specific incidents from continental history as background for his stories, such as the Battle of Preussisch-Eylau, which he summarized in the prologue to *The Schirmer Inheritance* (1953). In addition to history, he read a good deal of philosophy and psychology, notably the works of Nietzsche and Jung. He went into psychoanalysis because he was frightened by the latent violence which he perceived in his own fantasies, and he emerged with a greater understanding of the sources of human aggression and an increased ability to verbalize that understanding.

The first novel Ambler wrote in Paris, *Epitaph for a Spy* (1938), resembles Maugham's Ashenden stories in its emphasis on the pragmatic aspects of espionage. The epitaph mentioned in the title is spoken over the crushed body of the dead spy at the end of the story: " 'He needed the money.' " The spy, however, is not the central figure of the novel. Its protagonist-narrator, Josef Vadassy, is coerced into acting as a counterspy for French intelligence by the threat of deportation from France. In the motivations of these two characters Ambler expresses the carrot-and-stick philosophy which runs through all his novels. In Ambler's world people do things to gain something or to avoid something. There are very few real idealists or patriots in these stories, and their survival rate is close to zero.

The Hungarian-born Vadassy is a typical Ambler protagonist: naive, inoffensive, and unassertive to the point of timidity. Through no fault of his own he is stateless; no consul will speak on his behalf, and no country will welcome him if

Ambler, standing, with his parents, Amy Madeleine Andrews and Alfred Percy Ambler, and his brother Maurice in 1920 (courtesy of Eric Ambler)

he is expelled from France. Vadassy's political isolation and his consequent vulnerability externalize Ambler's view of the essential personal isolation of the ordinary man trying to survive in a hostile or, at best, an indifferent world.

Epitaph for a Spy was followed closely by *Cause for Alarm* (1938), whose protagonist resembles Vadassy in his innocence and naiveté. Far from being a struggling refugee, however, Marlow is a mildly complacent member of the British middle class who travels to Milan as the representative of an armaments firm. Nevertheless, his bowler hat and furled umbrella–and even the security of his British passport–are no protection against the determination of foreign agents to use him for their own purposes. With the help of a Russian, Zaleshoff, Marlow finally succeeds in escaping across the mountains into Yugoslavia and from there to England. Marlow's own experi-

ences and Zaleshoff's lectures and example change Marlow's view of life, and the English society that he had once accepted unquestioningly now strikes him as trivial, unreal, and probably doomed.

Unlike earlier thriller writers, Ambler was aggressively left-wing. In his prewar novels he often portrayed Communists, usually Russians or Germans, as "wise old men" figures who clarify for the naive protagonist the true nature of international politics in general and of the capitalist conspiracy in particular. The character of Zaleshoff in *Cause for Alarm* is that kind of tutelary figure. Although Ambler later modified his views when he realized that totalitarian socialism, like capitalism, exploits the individual and interferes with his rights and liberties, his rejection of the jingoistic xenophobia of writers like Sapper (Herman Cyril McNeile) contributed a great deal to the intellectualization and liberalization of the thriller genre.

Up to this point Ambler's novels had been received reasonably well by critics and by the public, but in 1939 he published his first outstanding book, *The Mask of Dimitrios*. It was the Book-of-the-Month Club selection for September 1939, and it has never been out of print. Its protagonist, Charles Latimer, is a British scholar and writer of detective stories who is permitted to view a corpse in a police morgue. He is told that it is the body of a criminal named Dimitrios. Probing into the history of this dead criminal and listening to the narratives of the people who had known him, Latimer peels away layer after layer of the illusion with which Dimitrios has surrounded himself. He finds greater and greater evil: theft, pimping, white slave traffic, drug dealing, treason, and murder. At last Latimer strips away the final illusion: Dimitrios is not dead but alive as a citizen of an accommodating South American country. Moreover, Dimitrios has become a respected member of the board of directors of an international banking firm.

Ambler's interest in the work of Carl Jung is evident in his portrayal of Dimitrios as a representative of the collective or communal evil which pervaded prewar Europe. Decadent himself, Dimitrios externalizes and personifies the decadence of the world around him. Conversely, the quality of evil embodied in Dimitrios reflects the dark side of the soul of each individual whom he confronts. Thus the figure of Dimitrios embodies both the collective evil of a society and the private evil of each individual in it. Like Milton's Satan, he repels and attracts because he personifies that which the spectator longs to deny but fears that he must, after all, acknowledge as his own.

In 1939 Ambler married Louise Smith Crombie, an artist from New Jersey whom he had met in Paris. When war broke out in Europe they returned to England, where Ambler wrote *Journey into Fear* (1940). Its protagonist is a senior engineer sent by a British munitions company to supply the Turkish navy with new armaments in preparation for the war which is now inevitable. German agents attempt to delay the project by hiring an assassin to kill the engineer, Graham. As he attempts to escape, Graham finds himself trapped on board a small cargo boat with Banat, the assassin. *Journey into Fear* provides a brilliant analysis of the range of responses that Graham experiences in his role as percipient prey. After seek-

ing to avoid Banat or to defend himself from him, Graham succumbs to a morbid fascination with the person and presence of the man who plans to kill him.

Banat intends, quite passionlessly, to murder Graham for five thousand French francs plus expenses. (The explanation offered by a Turkish policeman, "He is very fond of gambling, and is always short of money," recalls Ambler's epitaph for a spy.) Yet, although Graham is horrified by the evil that Banat represents, he is an arms merchant, a salaried dealer in death on a much larger scale than Banat could ever achieve. His only advantage over Banat is the sanction of society, but it is a society in which good and evil have lost their meaning.

Journey into Fear was to be Ambler's last novel for eleven years. Shortly after its publication he enlisted in the British army as a private in the artillery. He was assigned to the antiaircraft battery stationed at Chequers, Winston Churchill's country home, for the purpose of protecting Churchill when he was in residence there. In 1943 Ambler served in Italy, and the first-hand experience he gained of battles and their aftermath served as background for scenes in several of his postwar novels, notably *Send No More Roses* (1977). In 1944 Ambler, by then an officer, was transferred to Army Kinematography, where he remained for the rest of the war. He became assistant director with the rank of lieutenant colonel. On 15 October 1945 he was awarded the American Bronze Star for his contribution to Anglo-American relations in preparing the documentary film *United States* (1945). Ambler worked with combat film units and helped to make ninety-six educational and training films. He also collaborated with Peter Ustinov on the script of *The Way Ahead* (1944), a feature film depicting the transition of a group of raw recruits into an effective fighting unit. Carol Reed directed the film, which starred Ustinov and David Niven.

During the war four of Ambler's novels were made into films, but he did not participate actively in the filming because of his military responsibilities. Joseph Cotten wrote the screenplay for *Journey into Fear* (1942), which starred Cotten, Orson Welles, Dolores Del Rio, and Agnes Moorehead. In 1943 *Background to Danger* was released, based on Ambler's novel *Uncommon Danger*. It starred George Raft, Sydney Greenstreet, and Peter Lorre. *The Mask of Dimitrios*, starring Zachary Scott, Sydney Greenstreet, and Peter Lorre, was released in 1944. *Hotel Reserve* (1946),

Ambler in 1927 (courtesy of Eric Ambler)

based on *Epitaph for a Spy*, starred James Mason and Herbert Lom.

After he had been discharged from the army in 1946, Ambler went to work as a writer of screenplays. He was attracted to a career in screenwriting because he believed that there were going to be major innovations in the British film industry. As he had done when he began writing thrillers, Ambler welcomed the opportunity to make substantial changes in the medium in which he worked. Much of his writing was done for J. Arthur Rank's Cineguild, where the "front office" seldom interfered with the creative filmmakers. However, in their attempts to transform the British cinema, the new filmmakers produced material which cost too much and lacked popular appeal. Although Ambler's own films were reasonably well received, they were neither brilliant nor strikingly innovative.

After writing four consecutive screenplays, Ambler began to alternate his work in films with the writing of novels. He collaborated with another screenwriter, Charles Rodda, on five novels which were published in the 1950s under the pseudonym Eliot Reed. He also began to publish again under his own name. The novels of his "second period" are darker and more cynical than his earlier work. "When you had cleared the Nazis away," he observed, "all these other shits were still there." Ambler now numbered among these the Communists he had once admired. The repressive policies of the totalitarian Communist states had finally convinced Ambler that communism offers no more hope for individual liberty or for the recognition of the importance of the ordinary man than capitalism does.

Judgment on Deltchev (1951) was written in response to the show trial of Nikola Petkov, accused of having plotted to overthrow the Bulgarian government. A French diplomat who had attended the trial gave Ambler an account of the injustices committed there, including an attempt by the authorities to hamper Petkov's defense by withholding the insulin that he needed. Ambler's view of the situation is clear from the first paragraph of *Judgment on Deltchev:* "When treason to the state is defined simply as opposition to the government in power the political leader convicted of it will not necessarily lose credit with the people. . . . His trial, therefore, is no formality but a ceremony of preparation and precaution. He must be discredited and destroyed as a man so that he may safely be dealt with as a criminal." The story which follows outlines the steps by which this is done to Yordan Deltchev, a popular but rebellious political leader.

Reaction to *Judgment on Deltchev* was mixed. Predictably, readers with socialistic tendencies were alarmed and incensed by this evidence of Ambler's changed attitude toward left-wing political groups. He received a large number of angry and, in some cases, abusive letters. Other readers responded to the change in his style rather than to the change in his ideology, pointing out that *Judgment on Deltchev* has more authority but less adventure than Ambler's earlier novels. Roderick MacLeish of the *Washington Post* ranked *Judgment on Deltchev* as Ambler's "masterpiece," while Ambler's friend Raymond Chandler was disappointed in it. In a letter to a friend Chandler wrote, "It is not so much that Ambler has let himself get too intellectual as that he has let it become apparent that he was being intellectual." In a way, Chandler's criticism of Ambler's new style was a backhanded compliment. Ambler had set out, fifteen years earlier, to intellectualize the thriller. With *Judgment on Deltchev*, he had unquestionably done it.

Ambler's next novel, *The Schirmer Inheritance*, made it clear that he intended to adhere to his new style of writing. Although *The Schirmer Inheritance* resembles *The Mask of Dimitrios* in some respects—they are both quest novels, and both portray the tensions and aberrations of the characters as reflections of the unsettled state of society—*The Schirmer Inheritance* is more carefully structured, more thoughtful, and less exciting than Ambler's earlier work. Almost half the book is taken up with the legal complexities and the practical problems encountered by a lawyer who seeks among the thousands of displaced persons in postwar Europe the missing heir to an American fortune. Perhaps because of its comparative lack of adventure, *The Schirmer Inheritance* was not particularly popular.

During the 1950s and 1960s Ambler continued to work as a screenwriter. Three of his screenplays were original stories (*The October Man*, 1947; *Highly Dangerous*, 1950; and *Battle Hell*, 1957), but most of them were based on books by other authors, such as H. G. Wells, W. Somerset Maugham, Arnold Bennett, Geoffrey Household, and H. E. Bates. His most successful film was an adaptation of Nicholas Monsarrat's novel *The Cruel Sea* (1953). Ambler was nominated for an Academy Award for that screenplay, but the Oscar went to Daniel Taradash for *From Here to Eternity*. Ambler also worked for a year on the

screenplay of *Mutiny on the Bounty*, for which he is said to have received an advance of one hundred thousand dollars as well as a salary of three thousand dollars a week. He had been instructed to rewrite the story in order to make the role of Fletcher Christian, intended for Marlon Brando, more important than the role of Captain Bligh, which was to be played by Trevor Howard. He thought that he had solved the problem when he discovered that Christian and Bligh had met long before they sailed together on the *Bounty*, but the producers refused to let Ambler use that material because they believed that the public, accustomed to the story as it had been presented in the 1935 film with Charles Laughton and Clark Gable, would not accept a major change of that kind. Brando, who had script approval, rejected all of Ambler's screenplays because they did not give him a large enough role. After fourteen attempts, Ambler gave up. The film was finally made with a script written by Charles Lederer.

In 1956 Ambler published *The Night-Comers*, the story of a British engineer and a Eurasian girl trapped in the headquarters of a revolutionary army fighting to take over the capital city of an island off the coast of Indonesia. Although there is a great deal of violence in the story, it is outside the control of the protagonists, whose role is essentially passive. They are spectators of a drama in which they may be hurt or killed but whose outcome they cannot affect. Despite some fine scenes, *The Night-Comers* is a talky and slow-moving story, and it lacks the complexity and depth of Ambler's best work.

In 1958 Ambler and his wife Louise were divorced, and later that year he married Joan Harrison. Like Ambler, Harrison was a successful screenwriter. Her credits include *Saboteur*, *Suspicion*, and *Jamaica Inn*. In 1940 she received two Academy Award nominations: Best Original Screenplay for *Foreign Correspondent*, with Charles Bennett (the award went to Preston Sturges for *The Great McGinty*); and Best Screenplay for the adaptation of Daphne Du Maurier's novel *Rebecca*, with Robert E. Sherwood (the award went to Donald Ogden Stewart for *The Philadelphia Story*). She also produced a number of films and television programs, including *Alfred Hitchcock Presents*.

Ambler made two excursions into television in the 1950s: the CBS series *Climax!* did an adaptation of *Epitaph for a Spy*, and Ambler created the popular television show *Checkmate*. That series, which ran for four years (1959-1962), was made up of seventy one-hour episodes starring Sebas-

tian Cabot as a retired teacher and Doug Mc-
Clure and Anthony George as his former students. Most of the episodes were set in San Francisco, where the series characters had an investigative agency.

Ambler's next novel, *Passage of Arms* (1959),
won the Crime Writers Association's Critics
Award (the Golden Dagger). Like several of Ambler's earlier novels, such as *Uncommon Danger*
and *Cause for Alarm*, *Passage of Arms* recounts the
story of a traveling businessman who finds himself involved in the machinations of organized
groups of international profiteers. However, the
villains in *Passage of Arms* are not so wicked, nor
is the protagonist so virtuous, as the corresponding characters in the earlier novels. Greg Nilsen
is shrewd and sophisticated enough to realize
that he is skirting the law when he agrees to play
the part of the nominal owner of a cargo of armaments, but he succumbs to the temptations of
money and adventure. Unlike many of Ambler's
other protagonists, Nilsen is not pressured into becoming involved in the conspiracy; he makes his
decisions freely, and those decisions bring him
closer to the moral state of the villains. Some of
the villains, on the other hand, demonstrate a degree of moderation and even of honor which
brings them closer to the moral state of the protagonist. Ambler extends this perception of moral rel-
ativity to the political realm, and Nilsen learns
that the labels "Communist" and "Fascist" are
only different ways of spelling "Power." Moderation or despotism in the use of that power are simply human acts, unaffected by the political colora-
tion of the men in whose hands the power rests.

In 1960 the editors of *Life* magazine asked
Ambler to cover the Los Angeles trial of Dr.
Raymond Bernard Finch and Carole Tregoff, accused of having murdered Finch's wife, Barbara.
Ambler did so. A year later he attended another
murder trial, this time in London. The defen-
dant was James Hanratty, accused of having murdered Michael John Gregsten and of having
raped and seriously injured Valerie Storie. In
both cases the juries brought in verdicts of
guilty; Finch and Tregoff went to prison, and
Hanratty was hanged.

Ambler had, over the years, collected a few
other essays on real-life murder: "The Ability to
Kill," a study of murderers who are "morally de-
fective" in that they feel no compunction for
what they have done; "The Reporter," an account of Ambler's experiences in covering a murder trial at the Old Bailey for an American news

*Dust jacket for the first edition of Ambler's novel about au-
thor Charles Latimer's discovery of the true identity of master
criminal Dimitrios*

agency; and "The Lizzie Borden Memorial Lectures," written for the American magazine *Holiday*, in which Ambler imitates the style of
Thomas De Quincey's essay "On Murder Considered as One of the Fine Arts" in order to plead
for the restoration and preservation of the buildings in which famous crimes have been committed. Ambler gathered these together with an expanded version of the *Life* magazine article on
Finch and Tregoff, the essay he had written on
the Hanratty case, and assorted other essays and
published them as *The Ability to Kill, and Other
Pieces* (1963).

Ambler lost the notes for the novel which
should have followed *Passage of Arms* when his
Bel Air home was destroyed by a brush fire in
1961, and he then wrote an entirely different
story. *The Light of Day*, for which he received his
second Golden Dagger Award, introduces one of

his most popular protagonists, Arthur Abdel Simpson. The illegitimate son of an Egyptian mother and an English father, Simpson adds new dimensions to the word *bastard*. As a boy he retaliates against a schoolmaster who has caned him by pouring concentrated sulphuric acid on the saddle of the schoolmaster's bicycle. As an adult he is weak, vain, ineffectual, dishonest, and spiteful. He also has a potbelly, thinning hair, indigestion, and bad breath. His chief virtues are cunning, resilience, and a well-developed talent for finding the main chance. Yet, to the reader who has enough of a sense of humor to see it, Simpson has the charm and the sting of familiarity. Like any picaresque hero, Simpson exaggerates the vices and follies which plague the human race, but he does not falsify them.

Simpson has lost his British citizenship and is not particularly welcome anywhere, so he wanders among the Balkan countries as a tourist guide and driver (officially), and as a pimp, con man, and petty thief (unofficially). When he becomes involved with criminals who have smuggled guns into Turkey and are planning to rob the Topkapi museum in Istanbul, he does not waste time considering ways and means of foiling the villains; he proceeds directly to considering ways and means of saving his own skin. The brisk, racy, sometimes mildly scatological style in which Simpson narrates the tale of his tribulations adds the final touch of humor to the novel.

The Light of Day was made into a film, *Topkapi* (1964), starring Peter Ustinov, Melina Mercouri, Maximilian Schell, Robert Morley, and Akim Tamiroff. Monja Danischewsky, who wrote the screenplay, was nominated for the Writers Guild Award. The film enjoyed both critical and popular success.

Arthur Abdel Simpson makes a second appearance in *Dirty Story*, for which Ambler won his third Golden Dagger Award. Simpson becomes involved in a larger and more dangerous conspiracy: an attempt on the part of SMMAC (Société Minière et Métallurgique de l'Afrique Centrale) to take over a piece of mineral-rich land controlled by UMAM (Ugazi Mining and Development Corporation). As often happens in Ambler's novels, the governments which nominally control the disputed area of land are, in fact, unimportant. The real power is in the hands of big business. In order to gain control of an area rich in rare earths, SMMAC sends in a military force complete with mortars and submachine guns. Simpson stumbles into becoming a mercenary

serving as an officer in this force, answering to the code name Spearhead. Although some humor arises from the disparity between Simpson's position and his disposition, *Dirty Story* is distinctly heavier than *The Light of Day*. Its conclusion, however, is pure irony. Simpson, the quintessential stateless man, manages to set himself up as an emerging nation and looks forward to making a steady income from the sale of passports.

Between the two Simpson stories, Ambler wrote *A Kind of Anger* (1964), in which Piet Maas, a Dutch journalist working in Paris, is assigned to search for a young woman who has witnessed an assassination. The murdered man, Col. Ahmed Arbil, is a former Iraqi diplomat who was granted political asylum in Switzerland when his sympathy with the Kurdish nationalist movement brought him into disfavor with the Iraqi government. Maas succeeds in locating the young woman, Lucia Bernardi, and they plan to sell Arbil's papers to the highest bidder. The story contains an account of an attempted suicide which was, as Ambler later confirmed, based on Raymond Chandler's unsuccessful attempt to shoot himself. *A Kind of Anger* won the Mystery Writers of America's Edgar Allan Poe Award.

In 1968 Ambler and his wife, who had been dividing their time between Los Angeles and London with frequent trips to the Middle East, the south of France, and Switzerland, settled into a permanent home in Clarens, Switzerland, on the eastern end of Lake Leman (the setting of Rousseau's *Nouvelle Heloise*). They continue to travel, often in connection with Ambler's books, but most of his work since 1968 has been done there.

Immediately following the successful return of Arthur Simpson in *Dirty Story*, Ambler brought back another character, Charles Latimer of *The Mask of Dimitrios*, for a second appearance. As he does in the earlier novel, Latimer steps out of his relatively secure and innocent milieu to do research into the history of a criminal who has been brought, by coincidence, to Latimer's attention. The criminal in *The Intercom Conspiracy* (1969), however, is much more sophisticated than Dimitrios. He and his partner are not pimps or white slavers but respected men in responsible positions who organize a paper crime in which the only blood that is shed is that of the overly inquisitive Latimer. Colonels Jost and Brand, each the head of his country's secret service, purchase a small subscription newsletter to publish in bulletin form some of the secret information to which they have access. They publish five such bulletins, each compromising a different country. The colonels' intent is to induce the secret services of the countries involved to bid against one another for the purchase of the newsletter and the assurance that the publication of this information will cease. Their plan works, and they retire on the proceeds. However, Jost's neighbor Latimer learns enough to link him, and through him Brand, with the conspiracy. Brand believes, mistakenly, that Jost has betrayed him and takes steps to see that Latimer never publishes what he knows. Jost later suggests that, Brand's mentality being what it is, Latimer is probably embedded in a construction project somewhere between Ferney-Voltaire and Strasbourg.

Like *The Mask of Dimitrios, The Intercom Conspiracy* is told by several voices, each recounting part of the story and each contradicting the attitudes and conclusions of the other voices. The central figure is Theodore Carter, the victimized editor of the newsletter. Since the colonels have arranged matters so that they remain well in the background, Carter finds himself alone in facing the serious displeasure of five secret service organizations, including the CIA and the KGB. Understandably upset, he behaves much as Arthur Abdel Simpson would have done: he worries about saving himself and builds up a wall of rationalizations between himself and the recognition of his own failures. By the end of the story, however, he has demonstrated enough initiative and endurance to justify the beginnings of a new sense of self-respect.

By the time he wrote *The Intercom Conspiracy* Ambler was firmly established as a leading thriller author. The man who had received thirty pounds for *The Dark Frontier* demanded—and, it is rumored, got—an advance of twenty thousand pounds for *The Intercom Conspiracy*. His next book, *The Levanter* (1972), was even more successful, probably because Ambler had managed once again to anticipate the trend of world events. This book, which centers around the activities of Palestinian guerrillas, was published on 21 June 1972. On 5 September 1972 the Olympic Games at Munich were disrupted by the murder of eleven Israeli athletes by Arab terrorists. Early sales of *The Levanter* included thirty-five thousand hardback copies in New York City alone.

The Levanter takes the form of an account by the harassed protagonist of what he maintains is the true story of the events in which he has been involved. (A similar narrative technique is used in

Dust jacket for the first American edition of Ambler's 1940 novel about an English armaments engineer pursued by a Turkish assassin hired by German agents during the early days of World War II (courtesy of Otto Penzler)

The Light of Day and *Send No More Roses,* among other books by Ambler.) Michael Howell, a "Levantine mongrel" of mixed parentage, heads the prestigious Agence Howell, an import-export firm operating primarily in the Middle East. He becomes involved with Salah Ghaled, a Palestinian guerrilla leader who has abandoned the Palestinian Liberation Organization because he feels that it is too moderate. Members of Ghaled's organization have planted in Tel Aviv a number of bombs which can be set off by remote control from a ship, and he forces Howell to provide the ship. Howell, who has until now been conservative to the point of timidity, reacts with exceptional courage and initiative. Tel Aviv is saved, but some of the bombs are found disguised as batteries manufactured by the Agence Howell. The authorities produce a false confession which Ghaled had extorted from Howell at gunpoint as a form of insurance, and Howell becomes the prey of an hysterical press. For once, an Ambler character is telling the truth when he says that it was not his fault.

Ambler had for some time been moving in the direction of the "straight" political novel as opposed to the thriller, and with *The Levanter* he seems to have taken the final step. Although Ambler won the Crime Writers Association's Golden Dagger Award (his fourth) for *The Levanter*, some critics were disappointed in the book because of its talkiness and its relative lack of action. Those critics were even more disappointed in Ambler's next book, *Doctor Frigo* (1974). Peter Prescott summarized this point of view in his *Newsweek* review: "When his most recent novel, *The Levanter*, appeared, I grumbled that nothing *happened* until page 80, a poor showing for a suspense story. It seems I missed Ambler's drift: in this new novel [*Doctor Frigo*] nothing happens until page 240." (The novel contains 247 pages.)

Doctor Frigo is the least exciting of Ambler's novels because its protagonist, an intelligent man with a reasonable understanding of his own character, does what no other Ambler protagonist has done: he keeps his involvement in the crisis to a minimum. Dr. Ernesto Castillo, whose father was the victim of a political assassination in an unnamed coffee republic and is now regarded as a martyr to the liberal cause, has spent most of his life in exile in the French Antilles. He works in a French government hospital, where his taciturnity has earned him the nickname of "Dr. Frigo" ("frozen meat"). He is ordered by the French secret service to examine Manuel Villegas, the liberal party leader who will almost certainly be the next president of the coffee republic. Villegas, who was a friend and colleague of Castillo's father, wants to use Castillo for the propaganda value that his name carries in his birthplace. Pressured by the French authorities, Castillo accepts Villegas's invitation to become his personal physician. When Villegas's forces have succeeded in taking over the country and he returns to assume the presidency, Castillo is forced to go with him. However, he manages to stay clear of the political upheaval which follows and is at last allowed to return home.

One reason for Castillo's success in avoiding unnecessary political involvement is the advice of Robert L. Rosier, an American agent. Rosier's function in the novel is similar to that of the Communist agents who advised the protagonists of Ambler's prewar novels, but the "wise old man" figure is now preaching the gospel of self-preservation rather than of socialism: keep your

head, watch your back, and make your deals in advance. The atmosphere of sadness and cynicism which pervades *Doctor Frigo* is particularly strong because of the lack of excitement in the story.

Send No More Roses is a psychological novel in which the narrative perspective is entirely subjective and exquisitely unreliable. Paul Firman, a.k.a. Reinhardt Oberholzer, a.k.a. Perrivale Smythson, sets out to convince Prof. Frits Buhler Krom and two of his associates that he, Firman, is not a master criminal. Professor Krom is trying to find support for his theory that there is a type of criminal who is never caught because his knowledge of international law and his amoral cunning render him virtually uncatchable. Krom describes this type as *Der kompetente Kriminelle*, the able criminal. He believes that he has uncovered evidence to show that Firman is the head of an international organization which engages in various types of extortion, a *kompetente Kriminelle* who has been identified through sheer bad luck. Firman claims that he is not the head of the organization but the hired, if upper-level, help. Krom forces Firman to invite him and his two associates to a weekend meeting at one of his safe houses, the Villa Lipp. The meeting ends when the villa is attacked. Krom later publishes his book, based on his own observations and on the information he had obtained from Firman before the attack began. In response, Firman writes the refutation which makes up most of *Send No More Roses*. Because of the conflicting and contradictory points of view in the novel, and above all because of the admitted unreliability of the principal narrator, it is impossible to be certain which of the other incidents narrated in the book actually took place. *Send No More Roses* resembles, in this respect, William Faulkner's *Absalom, Absalom!* (1936) and *The Sound and the Fury* (1929). The story is not about events; it is about perspectives.

In his most recent novel, *The Care of Time* (1981), Ambler returned to a more conventional thriller style. Unlike most of his later books, *The Care of Time* begins with a burst of action: "The warning message arrived on Monday, the bomb itself on Wednesday. It became a busy week." The narrator, Robert Halliday, is a successful American writer; the sender of the bomb, Karlis Zander, is an agent for a Persian Gulf sheik known only as "the Ruler." Zander pressures Halliday into coming to Austria with a television crew to pretend to interview the Ruler. The real purpose of the encounter, however, is to provide an opportunity for a meeting between the Ruler and

NATO representatives regarding a NATO military base on the Ruler's territory. During the filmed interview the Ruler not only makes politically damaging statements but also displays a degree of sadism and paranoia which he has previously succeeded in concealing from the world at large. Halliday and Zander, pursued by terrorists hired by the Ruler, attempt to preserve the film so that it can be shown in Europe and America to discourage members of NATO from giving the Ruler the biological weapons he seeks. This chase scene and the bomb sequence at the beginning of the novel add excitement and suspense to the story; but the journey to the Ruler's Austrian hideaway, which makes up more than a third of the book, occasionally lapses into distracting and tedious travelogue.

Eric Ambler has received two awards for lifetime achievement: the Srenska Deckarakademins Grand Master Award (1975) and the Mystery Writers of America's Grand Master Award (1975). These awards commemorate the fact that Ambler, described by the Mystery Writers of America as "the father of the modern spy novel," replaced the false glamor, jingoistic patriotism, and simplistic plots of many earlier thriller writers with realism, subtlety, and Byzantine complexity. His characters, their motivations, and the situations into which these motivations lead them are consistently plausible. If Dashiell Hammett revolutionized the detective novel when he "gave murder back to the kind of people who commit it for reasons, not just to provide a corpse," Eric Ambler did the same for the thriller.

Bibliography:
Gerd Haffmans, ed., *Uber Eric Ambler* (Zurich: Diogenes, 1979).

References:
Ronald Ambrosetti, "The World of Eric Ambler, From Detective to Spy," in *Dimensions of Detective Fiction*, edited by Larry N. Landrum, Pat Browne, and Ray B. Browne (Bowling Green, Ohio: Popular Press, 1976), pp. 102-109;
Paxton Davis, "The World We Live In: The Novels of Eric Ambler," *Hollins Critic* (February 1971): 3-11;
Hugh Eames, *Sleuths Inc.* (New York: Lippincott, 1978);
Joel Hopkins, "An Interview with Eric Ambler," *Journal of Popular Culture*, 9 (Fall 1975): 285-293;
Clive James, "Eric Ambler," *New Review*, 1 (September 1974): 63-69;
Gavin Lambert, *The Dangerous Edge* (New York: Grossman, 1976).

Papers:
Ambler's manuscripts, correspondence, and reviews are in the Department of Special Collections, Mugar Memorial Library, Boston University.

Michael Arlen

(16 November 1895-23 June 1956)

Dorothy Goldman
University of Kent

See also the Arlen entry in *DLB 36: British Novelists, 1890-1929: Modernists.*

BOOKS: *The London Venture* (London: Heinemann, 1920; New York: Doran, 1920);

The Romantic Lady (London: Collins, 1921; New York: Dodd, Mead, 1921);

"Piracy" (London: Collins, 1922; New York: Doran, 1923);

These Charming People (London: Collins, 1923; New York: Doran, 1924);

The Green Hat (London: Collins, 1924; New York: Doran, 1924);

May Fair (London: Collins, 1925; New York: Doran, 1925);

The Acting Version of the Green Hat (New York: Doran, 1925);

Young Men in Love (London: Hutchinson, 1927; New York: Doran, 1927);

The Zoo: A Comedy in Three Acts, by Arlen and Winchell Smith (New York & London: French, 1927);

Lily Christine (Garden City, N.Y.: Doubleday, Doran, 1928; London: Hutchinson, 1929);

Babes in the Wood (London: Hutchinson, 1929; Garden City, N.Y.: Doubleday, Doran, 1929);

Men Dislike Women (London: Heinemann, 1931; Garden City, N.Y.: Doubleday, Doran, 1931);

Man's Mortality (London: Heinemann, 1933; Garden City, N.Y.: Doubleday, Doran, 1933);

Good Losers, by Arlen and Walter Hackett (London: French, 1934);

Hell! Said the Duchess (London: Heinemann, 1934; Garden City, N.Y.: Doubleday, Doran, 1934);

The Crooked Coronet (London & Toronto: Heinemann, 1937; Garden City, N.Y.: Doubleday, Doran, 1937);

The Flying Dutchman (London & Toronto: Heinemann, 1939; Garden City, N.Y.: Doubleday, Doran, 1939).

Michael Arlen

PLAY PRODUCTIONS: *Dear Father*, London, New Scala Theatre, 30 November 1924; revised as *These Charming People*, New York, Gaiety Theatre, 6 October 1925;

The Green Hat, London, Adelphi Theatre, 2 September 1925; New York, Broadhurst Theatre, 15 September 1925;

Why She Was Late for Dinner, London, Everyman Theatre, 27 November 1926;

The Zoo, by Arlen and Winchell Smith, London, King's Theatre, 23 May 1927;

Good Losers, by Arlen and Walter Hackett, London, Whitehall Theatre, 16 February 1931.

MOTION PICTURE: *The Heavenly Body*, screenplay by Arlen and Walter Reisch, M-G-M, 1944.

25

OTHER: "Gay Falcon," in *To the Queen's Taste*, edited by Ellery Queen (Boston: Little, Brown, 1946).

Michael Arlen began his writing career in journalism but quickly abandoned that field to write short stories, novels, plays, and a screenplay. He enjoyed enormous popularity at times–*The Green Hat* (1924) in particular was hugely successful–and was compared favorably with such writers as Aldous Huxley and F. Scott Fitzgerald. He was essentially a creator of nonrealistic romances written in an overtly artificial style reminiscent of Saki (Hector Hugh Munro), well outside the regular canon of detective fiction, but some of his output can be advantageously considered in its light.

Michael Arlen was born Dikran Kouyoumdjian in Bulgaria to Armenian parents. He was the youngest of a family of four sons and one daughter. In 1901 his family immigrated to England, where he attended Malvern College. When his schooling was complete, his parents expected him to enter the family business and his teachers thought that he should go up to Oxford; however, he showed an early rebellious streak by studying medicine briefly at Edinburgh University. In 1913 he moved to London and joined the fringes of the literary set. By 1916 his work was being published, mainly in Armenian papers; his first book, *The London Venture* (a collection of his journalism), was published in 1920. Subsequently he began to write under the name Michael Arlen, which he adopted legally in 1922, becoming a British citizen. Though several of his works contain criminal elements, murder, and attempted murder, such stories as "The Ancient Sin," "The Smell in the Library" (both collected in *These Charming People*, 1923), and "Farewell, These Charming People" (collected in *May Fair*, 1925), and the novels *Young Men in Love* (1927) and *Men Dislike Women* (1931) can no more be said to constitute detective fiction than can *Macbeth*.

It is in his short stories concerning Michael Wagstaffe that Arlen first uses the conventions of detective fiction. Wagstaffe appears in "The Man with the Broken Nose," "The Cavalier of the Streets," "Salute the Cavalier" (*These Charming People*), "The Crooked Coronet," and "The Gorilla of Mayfair" (*The Crooked Coronet*, 1937). Wagstaffe is outside the law, but lives by his own moral code. He persuades George Tarlyon and Ralph Wyndham Trevor (characters who reappear in other works by Arlen) that he is an Armenian ("no one would say he was an Armenian if he wasn't, would he?") and that he is about to kill Achmed Jzzit Pasha, who has kidnapped his sister to add her to his harem. Dissuading him from murder by the promise of their assistance in rescuing her, the two Englishmen go with Wagstaffe and hold down the furious Turk while Wagstaffe searches the house. Only when he does not come back is the Turk revealed as his father; Wagstaffe has stolen his valuable coin collection and Tarlyon's Rolls Royce. "He's a clever boy, Michael. . . . He is always on the lookout for what he calls the Mugs. . . . He calls himself the cavalier of the streets, but when he is up to any of his tricks he disguises himself as an Armenian. . . . [The mugs] believe him at once, on the grounds that no one would say that he was an Armenian if he wasn't." In "Salute the Cavalier" Wagstaffe takes the blame for a theft he did not commit, as some sort of payment for his seduction of Betty, the real thief, when he was at Oxford. In "The Crooked Coronet" Wagstaffe attempts to blackmail the beautiful Lady Quorn out of her wicked ways: "For each and every time that I suspect you on good grounds of having given way to your lower nature with a married or engaged man, I shall charge you the sum of one hundred pounds." But here at last he has met his match. Bluff and double bluff, blackmail, and theft succeed each other until the two principals are left having tea together–previously a euphemism for Lady Quorn's sexual peccadilloes.

Explanatory details and the presence of crime are not allowed to confuse Arlen's witty and romantic stories. Rather, he uses a criminal milieu to allow Wagstaffe to express his alienation from society, its glamorous attractions for him, and his romantic commitment to entering it on his own terms. Though these are uses to which detective fiction has been put in the past, it is hard not to see these stories as what Arlen hoped might be his assimilation on his own terms into English society.

From Arlen's second book of short stories (*May Fair*), "The Prince of the Jews" gives a more developed picture of the alienated outsider who inhabits both the criminal and the fashionable world. Julian Raphael is wanted for murder, drug smuggling, and more; but his most significant crimes are his socialism and the fact that he insults Charles Fasset-Smith, an upper-class friend of George Tarlyon. Fasset-Smith and Tarlyon fit nicely into their roles as gentlemen detectives, tracking Raphael down. The dreadfully sentimen-

Arlen with his wife, the Countess Atalanta Mercati, whom he married in 1928

tal ending to the story, in which Raphael, his mistress Manana Cohen (who has been attracted to and protected Fasset-Smith), and Fasset-Smith himself find friendship in the afterlife, surrenders any serious achievement but does reveal how important the idea of reconciliation was to Arlen—in this instance achieved by Raphael only by giving up Cohen to Fasset-Smith. When Arlen was ill in 1927, he went to recuperate in Florence, renewing there his friendship with D. H. Lawrence, who was revising *Lady Chatterley's Lover*. Lawrence used Arlen as the model for Michaelis, the Irish playwright in the book

who "pined to be where he didn't belong . . . among the English upper classes. And how they enjoyed the various kicks they got at him! And how he hated them!"

As late as 1940 Arlen wrote for *Ellery Queen's Mystery Magazine* a story whose eponymous hero Gay Falcon is, in critic Harry Keyishian's description, a "desperate character . . . rather like a more mature, sardonic Michael Wagstaffe." He eventually appeared in a series of films (fifteen in all), radio plays, and a television series, for which he became a softer, more debonair character. In the original story, the

Brigit Patmore and Arlen, circa 1920s

only one which Arlen himself wrote, the reason for Falcon's confidence that Diana Temple will not report his theft of the jewels from her safe only becomes apparent when he returns them to an insurance company.

Arlen's fortunes changed dramatically in 1924 with the publication of *The Green Hat,* which had an enormous popular success, bringing him fame and a reputed half-a-million dollars. He turned for a time to writing for the stage and screen, moving first to New York and then in 1925 to Hollywood, where he spent two years writing screenplays. In 1928 Arlen married Countess Atalanta Mercati. The couple lived in Cannes and had two children: Michael John, born in 1930, and Venetia, born in 1933.

Arlen regarded *Man's Mortality* (1933), his fourth novel, as a serious political work. Its Jules Verne-like picture of a future dominated by International Aircraft and Airways combines a rattling good yarn with serious social comment. Similar political elements can also be found in his next novel, *Hell! Said the Duchess* (1934), which supposes, four years in the future (1938), a Conservative-Fascist coalition led by Winston Churchill with Oswald Ernald Mosley (leader of

the British Union of Fascists) as minister of war. The book develops into an "allegorical fantasy," in Harry Keyishian's view, but its roots are firmly in detective fiction. Mary, Duchess of Dove, a beautiful, shy, and virtuous widow, is suddenly accused not only of living a sexually promiscuous life in London's low dives but also of committing a series of "Jane-the-Ripper" murders. When a private detective, Henry James Fancy, sees her leave her house on the night of the third murder and she later claims she was safe at home in bed, everything appears to be set for a conventional plot of suspicion, accusation, and final proof. To the private detective is added the commonly used combination of amateur detective (her cousin Col. Victor Wingless) and Scotland Yard. Even the representatives of the Yard display the proper credentials for detective fiction by ranging from the humble–Supt. G. I. Crust–to the fictionally common but actually rare combination of professional policeman and English gentleman–Sir Giles Prest-Olive and the Honorable Basil Icelin.

Though the detectives rapidly become convinced of the duchess's innocence, the discovery of the real culprit (the duchess is being impersonated by a bisexual, evil, supernatural creature called Xanthis Axaloe) takes longer. Arlen is again using the conventions of detective fiction to give an initial format to his work, one that arouses expectations of rational explanation that are rapidly abandoned for a bizarrely supernatural conclusion which usurps rationality while briefly partaking of its conviction. The brave Colonel Wingless must destroy Axaloe: "His great hands encircling Axaloe's throat, Wingless pressed down for what seemed to him an eternity. Axaloe, opening his mouth wide in his dying agony, spoke a sentence in a language that sounded like a rushing wind. Wingless, at last unloosening his hands, turned blindly away and lurched to the door.... 'There wasn't a body. There was that white dress floating in something greyish that slopped over to the floor....'" The horror of the encounter is enough to destroy Wingless too. He becomes convinced that his hands smell of Axaloe ("The monkey-house of the Zoo ... multiplied ten thousand times") and kills himself. The supernatural and political elements fuse when it is revealed that the duchess was chosen as the victim so that the defense of her innocence by the police would be interpreted by the populace as a corrupt gesture of class solidarity, and riots and anarchy would follow.

Arlen's last book of short stories, *The Crooked Coronet*, shows a greater reliance on detective conventions than any previous work, especially in "The Bearded Golfer" and "The Agreeable Widower." The former, which contains a delightful moment when a murderer's guilt is revealed by a white cat crawling out of a golf bag on the luggage rack of a train, is, however, spoiled by Arlen's again tagging on an intentionally mysterious, actually muddled, ending. The ending has always been of paramount importance in detective fiction; if a satisfactory solution is not provided, a central trust between author and reader has been violated. Arlen only fully respects this trust once, in "The Agreeable Widower." In this story both Scotland Yard and the French police, preening themselves on frustrating a confidence trickster, are startled to find themselves outwitted in the capture of a murderer by the very private detective who has been their main suspect. The ending is firmly traditional, even down to having the police take the credit from the private detective: "Ada Livermore was tried and condemned for murder at the Old Bailey in June last in what was known for many days as the 'Riviera Murder Case.' Chief-Inspector Parbold was warmly congratulated, both by his colleagues and the Press, on the solution of so difficult a case."

In 1939 Arlen returned to London, intending to stay for the duration of the war. He began writing a column for the *Tatler*, and in 1940 accepted a post as public relations officer for the western midlands region. After xenophobic questions in the House of Commons as to his suitability for the post, he resigned and rejoined his family in America. There was another trip to Hollywood, where he later claimed he did nothing and was "perfectly content." In 1946 he settled in New York, where he died ten years later of lung cancer.

Reference:
Harry Keyishian, *Michael Arlen* (Boston: Twayne, 1975).

H. C. Bailey
(1 February 1878-24 March 1961)

Nancy Ellen Talburt
University of Arkansas

BOOKS: *My Lady of Orange* (London & New York: Longmans, Green, 1901);

Karl of Erbach (New York: Longmans, Green, 1902; London: Longmans, Green, 1903);

The Master of Gray (London & New York: Longmans, Green, 1903);

Rimingtons (London: Chapman & Hall, 1904);

Beaujeu (London: Murray, 1905);

Under Castle Walls (New York: Appleton, 1906); republished as *Springtime* (London: Murray, 1907);

Raoul, Gentleman of Fortune (London: Hutchinson, 1907); republished as *A Gentleman of Fortune* (New York: Appleton, 1907);

The God of Clay (London: Hutchinson, 1908; New York: Brentano's, 1908);

Colonel Stow (London: Hutchinson, 1908); republished as *Colonel Greatheart* (Indianapolis: Bobbs-Merrill, 1908);

Storm and Treasure (London: Methuen, 1910; New York: Brentano's, 1910);

The Lonely Queen (London: Methuen, 1911; New York: Doran, 1911);

The Suburban (London: Methuen, 1912);

The Sea Captain (New York: Doran, 1913; London: Methuen, 1914);

The Gentleman Adventurer (London: Methuen, 1914; New York: Doran, 1915);

Forty Years After: The Story of the Franco-German War, 1870 (London & New York: Hodder & Stoughton, 1914);

The Highwayman (London: Methuen, 1915; New York: Dutton, 1918);

The Gamesters (London: Methuen, 1916; New York: Dutton, 1919);

The Young Lovers (London: Methuen, 1917; New York: Dutton, 1929);

The Pillar of Fire (London: Methuen, 1918);

Barry Leroy (London: Methuen, 1919; New York: Dutton, 1920);

Call Mr. Fortune (London: Methuen, 1920; New York: Dutton, 1921);

His Serene Highness (London: Methuen, 1920; New York: Dutton, 1922);

H. C. Bailey

The Fool (London: Methuen, 1921; New York: Dutton, 1927);

The Plot (London: Methuen, 1922);

Mr. Fortune's Practice (London: Methuen, 1923; New York: Dutton, 1924);

The Rebel (London: Methuen, 1923);

Knight at Arms (London: Methuen, 1924; New York: Dutton, 1925);

Mr. Fortune's Trials (London: Methuen, 1925; New York: Dutton, 1926);

The Golden Fleece (London: Methuen, 1925);

The Merchant Prince (London: Methuen, 1926; New York: Dutton, 1929);

Bonaventure (London: Methuen, 1927);

Mr. Fortune, Please (London: Methuen, 1927; New York: Dutton, 1928);

Judy Bovenden (London: Methuen, 1928);

The Roman Eagles (London: Gill, 1929);

Mr. Fortune Speaking (London & Melbourne: Ward, Lock, 1929; New York: Dutton, 1931);

Garstons (London: Methuen, 1930); republished as *The Garston Murder Case* (Garden City, N.Y.: Doubleday, Doran, 1930);

Mr. Fortune Explains (London & Melbourne: Ward, Lock, 1930; New York: Dutton, 1931);

Mr. Cardonnel (London & Melbourne: Ward, Lock, 1931);

Case for Mr. Fortune (London: Ward, Lock, 1932; Garden City, N.Y.: Doubleday, Doran, 1932);

The Red Castle (London & Melbourne: Ward, Lock, 1932); republished as *The Red Castle Mystery* (Garden City, N.Y.: Doubleday, Doran, 1932);

The Man in the Cape (London: Benn, 1933);

Mr. Fortune Wonders (London & Melbourne: Ward, Lock, 1933; Garden City, N.Y.: Doubleday, Doran, 1933);

Shadow on the Wall (London: Gollancz, 1934; Garden City, N.Y.: Doubleday, Doran, 1934);

Mr. Fortune Objects (London: Gollancz, 1935; Garden City, N.Y.: Doubleday, Doran, 1935);

The Sullen Sky Mystery (London: Gollancz, 1935; Garden City, N.Y.: Doubleday, Doran, 1935);

A Clue for Mr. Fortune (London: Gollancz, 1936; Garden City, N.Y.: Doubleday, Doran, 1936);

Mr. Fortune's Case Book (London: Methuen, 1936)—comprises *Call Mr. Fortune, Mr. Fortune's Practice, Mr. Fortune's Trials*, and *Mr. Fortune, Please*;

Clunk's Claimant (London: Gollancz, 1937); republished as *The Twittering Bird Mystery* (Garden City, N.Y.: Doubleday, Doran, 1937);

Black Land, White Land (London: Gollancz, 1937; Garden City, N.Y.: Doubleday, Doran, 1937);

This is Mr. Fortune (London: Gollancz, 1938; New York: Doubleday, Doran, 1938);

The Great Game (London: Gollancz, 1939; New York: Doubleday, Doran, 1939);

The Veron Mystery (London: Gollancz, 1939); republished as *Mr. Clunk's Text* (New York: Doubleday, Doran, 1939);

The Bottle Party (New York: Doubleday, Doran, 1940);

The Bishop's Crime (London: Gollancz, 1940; New York: Doubleday, Doran, 1941);

Mr. Fortune Here (London: Gollancz, 1940; New York: Doubleday, Doran, 1940);

The Little Captain (London: Gollancz, 1941); republished as *Orphan Ann* (Garden City, N.Y.: Doubleday, Doran, 1941);

Dead Man's Shoes (London: Gollancz, 1942); republished as *Nobody's Vineyard* (Garden City, N.Y.: Doubleday, Doran, 1942);

Meet Mr. Fortune (Garden City, N.Y.: Doubleday, Doran, 1942);

No Murder (London: Gollancz, 1942); republished as *The Apprehensive Dog* (Garden City, N.Y.: Doubleday, Doran, 1942);

The Best of Mr. Fortune (New York: Pocket Books, 1943);

Mr. Fortune Finds a Pig (London: Gollancz, 1943; Garden City, N.Y.: Doubleday, Doran, 1943);

Slippery Ann (London: Gollancz, 1944); republished as *The Queen of Spades* (Garden City, N.Y.: Doubleday, Doran, 1944);

The Cat's Whisker (Garden City, N.Y.: Doubleday, Doran, 1944); republished as *Dead Man's Effects* (London: Macdonald, 1945);

The Wrong Man (Garden City, N.Y.: Doubleday, Doran, 1945; London: Macdonald, 1946);

The Life Sentence (London: Macdonald, 1946; Garden City, N.Y.: Doubleday, 1946);

Honour among Thieves (London: Macdonald, 1947; Garden City, N.Y.: Doubleday, 1947);

Saving a Rope (London: Macdonald, 1948); republished as *Save a Rope* (Garden City, N.Y.: Doubleday, 1948);

Shrouded Death (London: Macdonald, 1950).

PLAY PRODUCTION: *The White Hawk*, by Bailey and David Kimball, London, Aldwych Theatre, 30 May 1909.

OTHER: "The Thistle Down" in *The Queen's Book of the Red Cross* (London: Hodder & Stoughton, 1939);

"A Matter of Speculation," in *Anthology 1968 Mid-Year*, edited by Ellery Queen (Frederic Dannay and Manfred B. Lee) (New York: Davis, 1968).

Round Reggie Fortune, doctor and detective, debuted in 1920–as did Hercule Poirot–and the good-living and straight-talking agent of Providence remains the chief claim to fame of his prolific author, H. C. Bailey. Fortune is a stylish character whose stories and novels bear an unmistakable stamp. In them, Bailey creates a voice almost as individual, though not so compelling, as Raymond Chandler's Philip Marlowe. When Fortune observes that "Providence expects a lot for its money" (in *Shadow on the Wall*, 1934), the statement is in his characteristic idiom. His creed, expressed in an early story, is similarly vivid: "I don't let anybody but me kill my patients." Bailey was acknowledged by his contemporary Howard Haycraft, writing in *Murder for Pleasure* (1968), as one of the five most important writers of Golden Age detective fiction of his time, and Julian Symons suggests in *Mortal Consequences* (1973) that Fortune was possibly the most popular sleuth in England between the world wars. Even Colin Watson, in *Snobbery with Violence* (1971), does not include Bailey's works with the detective stories he dissects to display the prejudices of their readers, and he pays offhand tribute to the "good-natured satirical sideswipes at English class-consciousness, cosiness and love of security [which] are characteristic of Bailey's detective fiction." Despite this general regard, few of the author's works remain or reappear in print, and the primary significance of Bailey's detective fiction appears today to be historical. Still, the Reggie Fortune works, especially the short stories, have the power to charm a contemporary reader by means of their clever and satiric detective and an ability to please with language and surprise with twists of plot.

Henry Christopher Bailey was the only son of Henry Bailey of London. He was educated at City of London School and received First Class Honours in Greats at Corpus Christi College, Oxford, in 1901. He distinguished himself by serving as coxswain of his boat crew and writing a novel, *My Lady of Orange*, which was published in the same year that he received his degree. Returning to London, he took up a position with the *Daily Telegraph* in which he continued until retirement, serving variously as dramatic correspondent, war correspondent, and leader writer. A fellow writer of detective fiction, E. C. Bentley, was also on the staff of the *Telegraph* for twenty-five of those years. In 1908 Bailey married Lydia Hayden Janet Guest, daughter of Dr. A. Hayden Guest, a Manchester physician. They had two daughters, Mary and Betty. Neighbors in Llanfairfechan, Wales, to which Bailey retired in 1946, recall him as a small, shy man, who continued to dress formally in retirement and collected postal cards. He died in 1961, leaving an estate of some fifteen thousand pounds sterling.

While a full-time journalist, H. C. Bailey also wrote an average of one novel per year, producing fifty novels and twelve volumes of short sto-

ries between 1901 and 1950. During the first twenty years of his writing career, Bailey wrote only nonmystery novels, producing twenty-nine historical romances in about as many years. It was not until 1920 that he published his first work of detective fiction, *Call Mr. Fortune*, a volume of six short stories. As a war correspondent between 1914 and 1918, he is said to have begun writing detective stories as a relief from the strain of his work. Reginald Fortune is introduced in "The Archduke's Tea," the first of eighty-five Fortune stories. According to Ellery Queen (in *101 Years' Entertainment*, 1941), Bailey had written more detective short stories about a single detective than any other author. Reggie changes little with the years, although he does marry Joan Amber, an actress, and he is variously served by a chauffeur, Sam (an individual somewhere between Lord Peter Wimsey's Bunter and Nero Wolfe's Archie Goodwin), and the most nearly equal confidant in classic detective fiction, the Honourable Sidney Lomas, C.I.D. As a physician, Reggie is neither amateur nor professional detective, but the mainspring of his being is a passion for justice, a moral indignation at the inhumanity which lies behind the acts he investigates. He does not detect for the love of the game but for love of the victim. Consequently, he is among the most ruthless of detectives.

The six short stories in *Call Mr. Fortune* are typical in length of all his stories, about half as long as the usual Rex Stout story featuring Nero Wolfe but up to twice as long as the usual Sherlock Holmes story. Favored elements which reappear in later stories are the revenge motive (often extreme and bizarre and reaching to the children of the intended victim in an almost biblical way) in "The Business Minister," the machinations of an impecunious and cold-blooded heir in "The Archduke's Tea," and professional criminals in "The Sleeping Companion." Plots typically make use of violent as well as cerebral action and conclusions which incorporate poetic and immediate–rather than legal–justice. Reggie is like Holmes in making extensive use of the physical clue found at the scene of the crime, and during the course of the Fortune works it is revealed that he knows Dutch tobacco from German, recognizes the sort of slime characteristic of a neglected pool, and knows how butterflies are captured and the environment of the gypsy moth, as well as knowing his way around a dissection table and doctor's surgery. The first stories establish some typical Bailey character types, including no-

Dust jacket for the first American edition of Bailey's 1940 collection of nine short stories featuring Reggie Fortune

bles (an archduke and a prince), professional thieves, a kidnapped girl, and a revenge-crazed business tycoon.

Five further volumes of Reggie Fortune stories appeared between 1923 and 1930, interspersed with nonmystery novels, and the last seven collections appeared between 1932 and 1940, following the publication of Bailey's first detective novel. Fortune novels appeared beginning in 1934 with *Shadow on the Wall*. Stories in each collection after the first range from those which are about practical jokes and contain more humor than crime, to works about disturbing domestic violence aimed by the obsessed at those they wish to possess or control. Stories of the lighter type include "The Sported Oak" (in *Case for Mr. Fortune*,

1932), "The Love Bird" (in *Mr. Fortune Wonders*, 1933), and "The Fight for the Crown" (in *Mr. Fortune Here*, 1940).

One of Bailey's best early stories of the darker kind, "The Unknown Murderer," appears in the second collection, *Mr. Fortune's Practice* (1923), and centers upon a wealthy woman whose motive for murder is her enjoyment of the grief of those who loved her victims with special intensity. This case has a conclusion of a type particularly favored by Bailey, both of whose serial detectives regularly bring about climaxes involving action, rescue, and prevention of further crimes instead of the reconstruction and explanation which are the hallmarks of the exploits of more sedentary detectives. The female villain is like Sir

Arthur Conan Doyle's famous character, Irene Adler, donning a male chauffeur's uniform and driving Fortune to a remote spot, luring him outside the car by a pretended breakdown, and attempting to bash his head in. Among the best of the Fortune stories are those which are similar in menace, including "The Furnished Cottage" (1925), "The Little Finger" and "The Long Dinner" (1935), and "The Dead Leaves" (1936). Children taught by their mother to revenge their father contrive the plot in the first; a benevolent thief who takes care of one of his own with Old Testament justice is the chief interest of the second; a plot to offer health and hope to poor children by murdering rich ones for pay is the chilling plan in the third; and Reggie's analysis of sparse natural clues is the high point of the fourth. The collections of stories maintain a consistent quality, and Ellery Queen's favorite, according to *Queen's Quorum*, is *Mr. Fortune Objects*, which was not published until 1935.

Bailey's first detective novel, *Garstons*, appeared in 1930, one year before the last nonmystery work, *Mr. Cardonnel*, and it featured the second of his two series detectives, the peculiar Joshua Clunk. Clunk appears in no short stories, and the Clunk novels are a noteworthy attempt by Bailey to write a mystery about a detective who is the opposite of Fortune in tastes, class, method, and milieu and about those who see justice from the receiving end. However, he is unable to make this second detective sufficiently attractive to carry the works as Reggie carries his. Clunk is a lawyer who works for his own extensive interests more than for his clients, the downtrodden victims of professional criminals or society. His world is a different social stratum from Reggie's, but each detective makes cameo appearances, in court or laboratory, in some novels of the other. Clunk's clerks are his intelligence-gathering forces, since he is seldom privy to the findings of the police; and minions Hopley, Lewis, and Fay Delicia "Madge" John display many talents and are more active than Clunk by the time the last Bailey novel, *Shrouded Death*, appeared in 1950. Despite Clunk's reputation as a shyster, he and Fortune are alike in approaching the solutions of crimes by looking directly at the evidence, championing the victims and the wrongly accused, and being eager to secure an immediate justice by means of a counterplot rather than an arrest. In fact both cooperate with the same policemen, Superintendent Bell and Inspector Underwood. They are also alike in being plump as a

result of their tastes for what each differently defines as good food: partridge and Montrachet for Fortune, sweets and more homely cooking for Clunk. Each is a man with his head full of things remembered, but Fortune's allusions are more to a wider literature and lore (everything from Gilbert and Sullivan to Johann von Schiller), Clunk's more often to chapel hymns. Fortune spends his ease with his cat, wife, or flower garden while Clunk spends his in a gospel hall built with his own money, and, as we are told in *Garstons*, "there, three times on Sundays and once in the week, Mrs. Clunk played the harmonium and Mr. Clunk preached the Larger Hope, when business allowed."

In the first three detective novels, *Garstons*, *The Red Castle* (1932), and *The Sullen Sky Mystery* (1935), featuring Clunk, the additional length provides more time than did the short-story form for assorted lovers, a greater detail concerning past crimes, and more attention to place. Each is also, broadly speaking, a maiden- or child-in-distress novel. In most of Bailey's novels, plot complications increase (mystery stories generally have one crime and one criminal), rising to a height in the Clunk novel *Dead Man's Shoes* (1942), which has three villains, three motives, and three lines of criminal activity. Similarly problematic is *No Murder* (1942), a Fortune novel in which three attempted murders fail and none of the three actual deaths is murder. Villainy in the early novels usually arises in connection with questionable business schemes, the plans of common criminals, and twisted family relationships and feuds. *The Bishop's Crime* (1940) is different. A Fortune novel, it depicts the search for a perhaps illusory church treasure and has a unified plot. The impressive female villain has an Oxford degree. Spirited children, the life of a cathedral close, clues from Dante, and an abundance of learning also add interest to this well-focused tale.

During the war years, spies, fifth columnists, black marketeers, and returning warriors make their appearance in the novels. An example is *Mr. Fortune Finds a Pig* (1943); set in Wales, it includes a plot to infect schoolchildren with typhus. The grandiose plans of a local man and would-be ruler (with a foreign wife whose native tongue is English) may suggest the Duke and Duchess of Windsor to the imaginative reader. Another war story is *The Cat's Whisker* (1944), in which Reggie works with the military and the American agent Rosen to catch German agents and the murderer.

Two very late novels, *The Life Sentence* (1946) and *Honour among Thieves* (1947), show Bailey attempting still to do new things. In the first, the interest of the novel is fixed on Rosalind Ward, a girl of sixteen, and her love affair is one of Bailey's better ones. The Cinderella motif of the plot is strained, but Reggie's rescue is timely. Alf Buck, a reformed criminal, and his younger brother, Tommy, are the main subjects of the second of these novels, in which it is Alf, not Clunk, whose counterplot achieves the real justice in the story. In *Shrouded Death* he uses many familiar devices, and he is successful in presenting a postwar society's problems, not the least of which is the unattractiveness to many citizens of the "stiff upper lip" which could be taken for granted in prewar fiction.

Bailey published *The Man in the Cape* in 1933, and it is the only detective novel which contains neither Fortune nor Clunk. In other ways, however, it has much in common with those series. There is a menaced child, a rescue, a hidden heir who murders for wealth, and an American protagonist who does not trouble himself over how the guilty die so long as no additional victims do.

In an uncollected short story, "A Master of Speculation," which was first published in *Ellery Queen's Mystery Magazine* (February 1961), a female sleuth is introduced. Brought up to better things ("The Pumphreys came over with the Conqueror and did very well out of it"), the Honourable Victoria Pumphrey finds her talents rewarded during the investigation she undertakes, and she is referred to as having a "profitable career of crime" as though she were a series figure. The character has much in common with Reggie, and it is a pity Bailey did not continue to use Miss Pumphrey, as she displays the potential to provide a vehicle for his undeniable talents that could been less fixed in his own time than the majority of his mysteries.

Bailey published 107 known works of detective fiction as well as 29 other novels. It is an impressive total, especially considering his full-time career as a journalist. Admired by professional peers and consistently read by the public of his day, he earned recognition for his achievement of a highly individual voice, character, and story

in the Reggie Fortune works, for the creation of well-structured plots, and for a notable consistency in the quality of his detective fiction. Milward Kennedy, a detective fiction writer, in a 1936 review in the *Telegraph*, describes the personality of Reggie Fortune as being as strong as any detective since Sherlock Holmes. Erik Routley, in his *The Puritan Pleasures of the Detective Story* (1972), fixes the quality of Reggie's persona by labeling him a "rebel disciple" of Holmes, pointing out that he is plump, "comfort-loving," married, and a particular champion of children.

The decline in Bailey's popularity, especially in comparison with that of Agatha Christie and her less outspoken detective, Hercule Poirot, appears attributable to several characteristics of his works. One is a parable or tale quality which contrasts sharply with the surface realism more characteristic of detective fiction today. This quality is seen in the tendency toward allegory and an emphasis on sin and poetic justice, rather than crime and the justice of the courts; and by such names as Fortune, Nosy Parker, Lady Sancreed (a church leader), and Totsbury (a town where a child's body is found buried). A second possible reason for the decline in his popularity is the fact that what are arguably Bailey's best works are in the long short story, a form much less popular today than in his time. Moreover, the stilted dialogue of often stereotypical secondary characters, outdated social comment, Golden Age stylistic affectations, and melodramatic situations are recurring elements in his work. The detective fiction of H. C. Bailey belongs too much to its day to deserve resurrection as a complete corpus, but there are gems to be found among the short stories and the novels, which will repay with wit and unexpected plot turns the attention of the discerning reader.

References:

Howard Haycraft, *Murder for Pleasure,* enlarged edition (New York: Biblio & Tannen, 1968);

Erik Routley, *The Puritan Pleasures of the Detective Story* (London: Gollancz, 1972);

Julian Symons, *Mortal Consequences* (New York: Schocken, 1973);

Colin Watson, *Snobbery with Violence* (New York: St. Martin's, 1971).

Anthony Berkeley
(A. B. Cox, Francis Iles)
(5 July 1893-9 March 1971)

Charles Shibuk

BOOKS: *Jugged Journalism,* as A. B. Cox (London: Jenkins, 1925);

The Family Witch; An Essay in Absurdity, as Cox (London: Jenkins, 1925);

Brenda Entertains, as Cox (London: Jenkins, 1925);

The Layton Court Mystery, anonymous (London: Jenkins, 1925); as Anthony Berkeley (Garden City, N.Y.: Doubleday, Doran, 1929);

The Wychford Poisoning Case, as Berkeley (London: Collins, 1926; New York: Doubleday, Doran, 1930);

The Professor on Paws, as Cox (London: Collins, 1926; New York: Dial, 1927);

Mr. Priestley's Problem, as Cox (London: Collins, 1927); republished as *The Amateur Crime* (Garden City, N.Y.: Doubleday, Doran, 1928);

Roger Sheringham and the Vane Mystery, as Berkeley (London: Collins, 1927); republished as *The Mystery at Lovers' Cave* (New York: Simon & Schuster, 1927);

The Silk Stocking Murders, as Berkeley (London: Collins, 1928; Garden City, N.Y.: Doubleday, Doran, 1928);

Cecil Disappears, as A. Monmouth Platts (London: John Long, 1928);

The Poisoned Chocolates Case, as Berkeley (London: Collins, 1929; Garden City, N.Y.: Doubleday, Doran, 1929);

The Piccadilly Murder, as Berkeley (London: Collins, 1929; Garden City, N.Y.: Doubleday, Doran, 1930);

The Second Shot, as Berkeley (London: Hodder & Stoughton, 1930; Garden City, N.Y.: Doubleday, Doran, 1931);

Top Storey Murder, as Berkeley (London: Hodder & Stoughton, 1931); republished as *Top Story Murder* (Garden City, N.Y.: Doubleday, Doran, 1931);

Malice Aforethought, as Francis Iles (London: Gollancz, 1931; New York: Harper, 1931);

A. B. Cox (photograph by Peter Davies)

The Floating Admiral, by Berkeley and others (London: Hodder & Stoughton, 1931; Garden City, N.Y.: Doubleday, Doran, 1932);

Before the Fact, as Iles (London: Gollancz, 1932; Garden City, N.Y.: Doubleday, 1932; revised edition, London: Pan, 1958);

Murder in the Basement, as Berkeley (London: Hodder & Stoughton, 1932; Garden City, N.Y.: Doubleday, Doran, 1932);

Ask a Policeman, by Berkeley and others (London: Barker, 1933; New York: Morrow, 1933);

Jumping Jenny, as Berkeley (London: Hodder & Stoughton, 1933); republished as *Dead Mrs.*

Stratton (Garden City, N.Y.: Doubleday, Doran, 1933);

Panic Party, as Berkeley (London: Hodder & Stoughton, 1934); republished as *Mr. Pidgeon's Island* (Garden City, N.Y.: Doubleday, Doran, 1934);

O England!, as Cox (London: Hamish Hamilton, 1934);

Six Against the Yard, by Berkeley and others (London: Selwyn & Blount, 1936); republished as *Six Against Scotland Yard* (Garden City, N.Y.: Doubleday, Doran, 1937);

Trial and Error, as Berkeley (London: Hodder & Stoughton, 1937; Garden City, N.Y.: Doubleday, Doran, 1937);

Not to Be Taken, as Berkeley (London: Hodder & Stoughton, 1938); republished as *A Puzzle in Poison* (New York: Doubleday, Doran, 1938);

Death in the House, as Berkeley (London: Hodder & Stoughton, 1939; New York: Doubleday, Doran, 1939);

As for the Woman, as Iles (London: Jarrolds, 1939; New York: Doubleday, Doran, 1939);

A Pocketful of One Hundred New Limericks, as Cox (London: Privately printed, 1960).

PLAY PRODUCTIONS: *Mr. Priestley's Adventure,* Brighton, Palace Theatre, 19 March 1928; as *Mr. Priestley's Night Out,* London, Royalty Theatre, 27 March 1928.

OTHER: "The Avenging Chance," as Berkeley, in *The Best Detective Stories of the Year 1929* (London: Faber, 1930); republished as *The Best English Detective Stories of the Year,* edited by Ronald Knox and H. Harrington (New York: Liveright, 1930);

"White Butterfly," as Berkeley, in *Fifty Famous Detectives of Fiction* (London: Oldhams, 1938);

"The Wrong Jar," as Berkeley, in *Detective Stories of Today,* edited by Raymond Postgate (London: Faber, 1940);

"The Lost Diary of Th*m*s A. Ed*s*n, as Iles, in *The Saturday Book 6,* edited by Leonard Russell (London: Hutchinson, 1946): 268-271;

"Dark Journey," as Iles, in *To the Queen's Taste,* edited by Ellery Queen (Frederic Dannay and Monfred B. Lee) (Boston: Little, Brown, 1946);

"Mr. Bearstowe Says," as Berkeley, in *Anthology 1965 Mid-Year,* edited by Queen (New York: Davis, 1965).

PERIODICAL PUBLICATIONS: "It Takes Two to Make a Hero," as Iles, *Collier's,* 112 (4 September 1943): 13, 60-65;

"Mr. Simpson Goes to the Dogs," as Berkeley, *Ellery Queen's Mystery Magazine* (February 1946);

"Outside the Law," as Iles, *Ellery Queen's Mystery Magazine* (June 1949);

"The Coward," as Iles, *Ellery Queen's Mystery Magazine* (January 1953).

Anthony Berkeley Cox (Anthony Berkeley, Francis Iles) was a journalist with a satiric bent, a mystery critic, and a major detective story writer and innovator whose career and wit gave new life and appeal to the detective story form at the start of its Golden Age. He was also the founder of the first and most important mystery writers' organization, London's famous Detection Club, which is still in existence. His best and most famous works–*The Poisoned Chocolates Case* (1929), *Malice Aforethought* (1931), *Before the Fact* (1932), and *Trial and Error* (1937)–are reprinted at frequent intervals.

Cox was born in Watford, Hertfordshire, England. Unlike many authors, especially today, Cox disliked personal publicity and made strenuous efforts to protect his privacy. It is known that he attended University College, London, and served in the British army in France during World War I, and he is reported by several sources to have studied for the bar. One of his novels, *Trial and Error,* does reveal extensive legal knowledge. He married Helen Macgregor in 1932; the couple had no children. Cox was one of two directors of A. B. Cox, Ltd., a firm near London's Strand, whose exact business has never been discovered. He was noted for being a genial host, an impressive letter writer, and an expert in the American idiom. He was also deeply interested in true crime cases and knowledgeable about poisons.

Cox started his literary career in the early 1920s by writing humorous sketches for *Punch.* Many were collected in *Jugged Journalism* (1925), which included a Sherlockian parody, "Holmes and the Dasher," as it might have been written by P. G. Wodehouse. The narrator is Bertie Watson, a name that spoofs Sherlock Holmes's friend and chronicler Dr. John H. Watson. A volume of short stories (*Brenda Entertains,* 1925) and two satiric novels (*The Family Witch,* 1925, and *The Professor on Paws,* 1926) quickly followed.

Cox's first attempt at a detective novel, *The Layton Court Mystery* (1925), was published anonymously. Later editions, including the American one, were signed by the author as Anthony Berkeley. In this novel Cox's series detective Roger Sheringham is easily able to deduce that an apparent case of suicide is murder and to solve a locked-room problem. He does have difficulty, however, in finding the identity of the murderer. Cox dedicated the book to his father, to whom he wrote, "I know of nobody who likes a detective story more than you do, with the possible exception of myself. So if I write one and you read it, we ought to be able to amuse ourselves at any rate." *The Layton Court Mystery* novel is light, bright, and amusing; it reflects its author's satiric bent in its reaction to the more serious work in this genre. In critic Howard Haycraft's assessment, this work "brought to the detective novel an urbane and naturalistic quality that was a welcome and needed relief."

Series detective Roger Sheringham was born two years before his creator. He studied classics and history at Oxford and excelled at rugby and golf. He served in World War I after graduation, sustaining two slight wounds in combat. A business career held no allure for Sheringham, nor did teaching or farming, but an attempt to write a novel as a lark proved to be the turning point in his career: the manuscript was accepted for publication, and the book became an immediate success. He continued to write novels and took frequent forays into crime journalism. Sheringham knows that his literary talent is slim; he does not think very highly of his fans. He is round-faced, stocky, and slightly below average height. He usually smokes a pipe, is very fond of beer, and talks too much in a purposeless manner.

His creator has stated, "Roger Sheringham is an offensive person, founded on an offensive person I once knew, because in my original innocence I thought it would be amusing to have an offensive detective. Since he has been taken in all seriousness, I have had to tone his offensiveness down and pretend he never was." In the introduction to *Jumping Jenny* (1933), which reveals further details of Sheringham's life, Cox says, "In matters of detection (he) knows his own limitations. He recognizes that although argument and logical deduction from fact are not beyond him, his faculty for deduction from character is a bigger asset to him; and he knows quite well that he is not infallible. He has, in point of fact, very often

been quite wrong. But that never deters him from trying again." At this early period, Sheringham seems to be a completely undisciplined and unconventional version of E. C. Bentley's Philip Trent. By the time of his last investigation, in *Panic Party* (1934), all the rough edges have been smoothed out in an effort to fit him into the conventional mold of "The Great Detective."

As far as mystery writing was concerned, Cox stated, "[I] found that detective stories paid better [than writing sketches for *Punch*]. When I find something that pays better than detective stories, I shall write that. . . ."

Cox's second detective novel, *The Wychford Poisoning Case* (1926), concerns the beautiful but indiscreet Mrs. Bentley, who is charged with the arsenic poisoning of her husband. It is Sheringham's job to save her. The author claimed that he had tried to write a psychological detective story, but the reviews were only average. Dashiell Hammett said, "His book runs at a brisk entertaining rate to a flabby and unsporting end." This novel, based on the famous Florence Maybrick case, represents Cox's weakest effort in the detective fiction field. Years later, upon maturer reflection, he felt it was overly facetious and fit only for incineration.

Roger Sheringham and the Vane Mystery (1927) was an improvement. Its plot centers on the case of a Mrs. Vane, who has fallen over a cliff under highly suspicious circumstances. Sheringham is aided by his cousin Anthony Walton (who emulates Philip Trent and falls in love with the chief suspect) and matches wits for the first time with Inspector Moresby of Scotland Yard, who is ordinary in looks and behavior and unlike anyone's conception of a professional detective. At this time Sheringham has turned to crime journalism. Intoxicated by his investigative successes, he writes articles on crime and acts as special correspondent for the *Courier*.

Mr. Priestley's Problem (1927) is the only mystery novel Cox published under his own name. It is about several crime enthusiasts who stage a murder hoax at the expense of the staid Mr. Priestley, who believes he has killed a blackmailer. He determines to evade the consequences of the crime he thinks he has committed by escaping with a beautiful girl to whom he is handcuffed. The reviewers enjoyed Cox's humor in *Mr. Priestley's Problem,* and this novel may have influenced Alfred Hitchcock's 1935 film version of John Buchan's *The Thirty-Nine Steps;* neither the heroine nor the handcuff business can be found

Caricature of Cox drawn by George Morrow to illustrate Cox's first book, Jugged Journalism, *a 1925 collection of humorous sketches written for* Punch

in Buchan's novel. *Mr. Priestley's Problem* is a charming and delightful novel, and one of its author's best efforts of the 1920s; but it is completely forgotten today.

The Silk Stocking Murders (1928), a bit more sensational than most of Cox's books, finds Sheringham and Moresby pursuing a serial murderer who uses silk stockings as nooses to strangle his victims and leaves their bodies hanging on doors. Although the reviewers thought the novel below average, it is more serious than the earlier books and in that sense represents an advance over them. The author humorously dedicated *The Silk Stocking Murders* "To A. B. Cox who very kindly wrote this book for me in his spare time."

In 1928 Cox founded the Detection Club and became its first honorary secretary. In the beginning, only authors who wrote pure detective stories could qualify for membership; thriller writers were not invited to apply. Later years saw a relaxation of the strict standards for membership.

One of Berkeley's finest works is the short story "The Avenging Chance," which many mystery critics consider to be one of the ten best short stories in the genre. It was immediately expanded to *The Poisoned Chocolates Case.* The plot revolves around finding out who sent the lethal box of candy that eventually found its way to Joan Bendix. The mystery is investigated by an organization called the Crimes Circle, which was founded by Sheringham. Although Sheringham stars in this novel, he does not shine brightly, especially when his solution is found to be incorrect.

The ineffectual but astute Ambrose Chitterwick, who debuts here and is the complete antithesis of the extroverted Sheringham, is able to propose the correct solution. *The Poisoned Chocolates Case* is also a satire on mystery readers, writers, fans, and the Detection Club. Though some critics preferred the short story, the novel was highly praised and is usually cited as the best of the books Cox wrote under the Berkeley pseudonym. It is also notable for its six possible solutions to the crime. In a recent edition of the book, mystery writer Christianna Brand has suggested a seventh possible solution.

In *The Piccadilly Murder* (1929), which was also praised by the reviewers, Mr. Chitterwick is having his tea in a posh London hotel while a murder is committed before his very eyes. This is the first Berkeley novel to dispense with Sheringham's services, but Inspector Moresby is available to lend a hand. In *The Second Shot* (1930) Sheringham investigates a fatal accident that occurs at a detective story writer's house party. There is an attempt in this book at greater depth of characterization, and also a good deal of discussion within the body of the novel about the detective story form. In addition, in his frequently quoted preface, the author proclaims that the detective novel is changing from a puzzle of time, place, motive, and opportunity to a puzzle of character. Cox tried to demonstrate this theory by using the relatively unfamiliar device of having the chief suspect narrate this tale. The result was more than competent but not outstanding. It did serve to mark Cox's development as a writer, but this first attempt to use an "inverted" viewpoint would soon be eclipsed by the "Francis Iles" novels.

A robbery is interrupted by the murder of an elderly lady in *Top Storey Murder* (1931), and Inspector Moresby is obliged to enlist the aid of Roger Sheringham, who immediately spots a vital clue. Reviews of the book were disappointing, though critic James Sandoe disagreed, calling it a first-rate detective story and the best of the Berkeley novels.

Certain members of the Detection Club, including Dorothy L. Sayers, Agatha Christie, Henry Wade, Freeman Wills Crofts, John Rhode, and others, tried their hand at writing a serial detective novel in what became *The Floating Admiral* (1931). It was Berkeley's task to write the final chapter and tie all the loose ends together. The results were better than expected, and Christianna Brand has called Berkeley's contribution masterly.

The first Francis Iles novel, *Malice Aforethought*, is the study of a caddish and cowardly doctor who murders his equally detestable wife and tries to evade the legal consequences of his crime. This novel, based on the real-life Armstrong case, represents the first major step in the advancement of Cox's theory that the detective story must expand in new directions in order to prevent self-strangulation. In *Murder for Pleasure* (1941; enlarged edition, 1968) critic Howard Haycraft characterizes the Iles novels as "penetrating psychological studies of murder and horror told from the inside out–[they] are not detective stories; for the element of detection has been subordinated to the fascinating examination of 'the events leading up to the crime' as seen and felt by the participants." R. Austin Freeman, Isabel Ostrander, Arthur Gask, C. S. Forester, and Marie Belloc Lowndes had previously worked in this inverted form, but the Iles novel was a sensation. The reviews were unanimous raves, and a group of disciples including Richard Hull and C. E. Vulliamy quickly followed in the master's footsteps in using the inverted form. Other mystery writers such as Crofts, Wade, Roy Vickers, Daphne du Maurier, and Andrew Garve bear witness to the Iles influence.

Malice Aforethought, a comedy of manners imbued with cynicism and irony, is summed up thus in *The Hundred Best Crime Stories* by Julian Symons: "If there is one book more than another that may be regarded as a begetter of the postwar realistic crime novel, it is this one." However,

though the first half of *Malice Aforethought* gives us Cox at the very top of his form, when the protagonist decides to commit a second crime, there is too sudden a change from high comedy to farce, and the result is a definite descent in quality. (C. E. Vulliamy manages in the derivative *The Vicar's Experiments*, [1932], writing under the pseudonym Anthony Rolls, to maintain an evenly balanced tone and style throughout while dealing with technical problems of a similar nature.)

Cox took a giant step forward with his next Iles novel and produced a contender for the all-time honors list. *Before the Fact* is the psychological study of a murderer as seen by his wife–who is his intended victim. It was an advance in many ways over its predecessor, especially in using the then almost unique device of telling the entire story from the viewpoint of the victim instead of the perpetrator of the crime. (It might be noted that Cox dedicated this novel to his own wife.) Reviews of the book were uniformly excellent, and Dorothea Brande said that "for sheer nightmarish horror it has seldom been surpassed." Haycraft best summed up *Before the Fact* in *Murder for Pleasure* by stating, "not many 'serious' novelists of the present era have produced character studies to compare with Iles' internally terrifying portrait of the murderer in *Before the Fact*, his masterpiece and a work truly deserving the appellations of unique and beyond price ... *Malice Aforethought* (was) a sparkling and original piece, but lacking the frightening overtones of the later effort."

A film version of this novel was directed by Alfred Hitchcock as *Suspicion* (1941) with a happy ending (widely criticized for being contrived), and Joan Fontaine received an Academy Award for her performance as Iles's protagonist. Hitchcock was once seriously interested in filming *Malice Aforethought* (with Alec Guinness), but it remained one of his many unrealized projects. However, a four-part television version was filmed in England in 1978 and presented as part of the *Mystery!* television series in America in early 1981.

Iles was to remain silent for the next seven years, but Berkeley continued with *Murder in the Basement* (1932), a prime example of the British fair-play school and a straightforward, solid tale that is unjustly forgotten today. It concerns Reginald Dane, who finds a murder victim under the basement floor of his new house. Moresby is called upon to investigate and once again enlists

Dust jacket for Cox's 1929 novel, an expansion of one of his finest short stories, "The Avenging Chance" (courtesy of Otto Penzler)

Sheringham's help in identifying the victim and finding the murderer.

In *Jumping Jenny* the chief suspect is Roger Sheringham, who must fight to prove his own innocence. The novel is ingenious and tricky; it contains at least one surprise for the unwary reader. *Panic Party* concerns a millionaire, living on a small desert island, whose attempt to perpetrate a practical joke turns sour because murder isn't funny. Fortunately, Sheringham is around to seek an unknown murderer while attempting to quell the rising panic of the island's inhabitants. This novel was very well received by the critics and is unusual in that it introduces a note of wild

farce to the proceedings. It is also Sheringham's last recorded adventure.

Cox took another giant step in 1937 with the publication of *Trial and Error*. Its central character, the inoffensive Lawrence Todhunter, finds that he is to die in six months and decides that he will try to commit what he hopes will be the perfect murder; his victim will be the most detestable human being he can discover. Todhunter's attempt is so successful that an innocent man is about to be convicted for the crime–unless Todhunter can prove that the accused is innocent. Although the reviews of *Trial and Error* were not unanimously favorable, it is easily the

41

best book Cox wrote under the Berkeley pseudonym and superior to anything else he wrote except *Before the Fact*. It is an often moving novel, written with great sympathy and compassion for its central character. If any proof were needed, *Trial and Error* provides the link (suspected, but not confirmed at this time by Cox) between Berkeley and Iles–whose name it should have carried if not for the presence of series character Ambrose Chitterwick who had appeared in two Berkeley novels. Both "The Haycraft-Queen Definitive Library of Detective-Crime-Mystery Fiction" list and James Sandoe's "Readers' Guide to Crime" place *Trial and Error*, along with *The Poisoned Chocolates Case* and *Before the Fact*, on their honor roles.

Not to Be Taken (1938) finds John Waterhouse dead from gastric ulcers, but his brother Cyril suspects foul play and demands exhumation and examination of the body. When that is accomplished, arsenic is discovered. The reviews of the book were generally good, but in spite of the author's scrupulous fair play with the reader, critics found the solution to rest on a tenuous motive that seemed to be out of keeping with the character of the guilty party.

Death in the House (1939) mixes murder with politics when a British parliamentarian dies from curare. The novel was criticized for its episodic structure by critics who failed to realize that it had originally been published as a newspaper serial. It is the final novel signed by Berkeley, and while it is not a major work, it was suspenseful, and its elements of political satire contributed to its entertainment values.

Cox's last published novel, *As for the Woman* (1939), signed by Iles, concerns a triangular situation involving a callow youth, a vain and neurotic wife who is no longer young, and her sadistic husband. It was a very adult novel for its time, and another example of its author's psychological delving into character. The reviews (but not the financial rewards) were fairly good, but *As for the Woman* was a disappointment in the light of previous Iles (and Berkeley) work. Its crime fiction element was meager, as the novel was basically concerned with adultery and revenge. Iles announced that *As for the Woman* was the first in a trilogy "about murder as the natural outgrowth of character," but he never wrote a successor, and the book was quickly forgotten.

Iles's ending for *As for the Woman* could have made it one of the most ironic and devastating mystery novels ever written if he had not chosen to add material that softened his truly crushing fi-

nale. Although it was far from being a total success, *As for the Woman* is one of Cox's most powerful and unjustly forgotten works. If it had been published a decade or two later under any other writer's name, it likely would have received much greater critical acclaim and financial reward.

The reason Cox stopped writing mystery novels has never been satisfactorily explained. Perhaps he had "found something that pays better" in reviewing, which he had begun to do for the *Daily Telegraph* in the mid 1930s. Rumor states that he had inherited a great deal of money by the time *As for the Woman* was published. John Dickson Carr, who considered Cox one of the greatest mystery writers of all time, has mentioned that Cox told him that he had written *As for the Woman* during a period of severe emotional strain. It was published right at the start of World War II and fell flat. Its failure affected Cox deeply, causing him to lose interest in writing, and no one could persuade him to continue. Cox's obituary in the *London Times* cited his extreme antipathy to paying what he considered exorbitant taxes on his literary earnings as the reason for the halt in his production.

A few short stories did appear in the early 1940s, most of which were published or reprinted in *Ellery Queen's Mystery Magazine*. Curiously, Cox is one of the few major writers who has never had a collection of short crime fiction published in book form.

During this period Cox and his wife were living quietly in an old house in St. John's Wood in London. The end of the war saw Cox (as Francis Iles) installed as crime fiction reviewer for the *Sunday Times* (London), a position he was to hold for about two decades, until he moved over to the *Guardian* in his last years. In the first supplement to *Twentieth-Century Authors*, published in 1955, Cox admitted that "there is now no secret about my being 'Francis Iles'. To regain a decent anonymity, I shall have to think about a new pseudonym."

Cox believed that his masterpiece *Before the Fact* was a failure, because he felt that he been unable to render the character and motivation of his protagonist with sufficient clarity to satisfy his own high standards. He was able to revise the novel, and the result was published in a 1958 paperback edition in England.

A disquieting glimpse of Cox in his last years is offered by Christianna Brand, who wrote that "by the time I knew him, and I knew him well, he was in bad health, a bit run to seed and degenerating into sick miserliness–hoarding his considerable wealth for heaven knows what disposal, for he often assured me that there was not a soul in the world whom he did not cordially dislike . . . but he was an excellent companion, clever, erudite, and very well read; sometimes I have thought he was really the cleverest of us all." A more optimistic view is recalled by James Sandoe, who met Cox while the latter was touring the United States by bus around 1960: "His heart was weak, but his spirit gallant . . . and he thoroughly charmed all of us who were fortunate enough to lunch with him. . . ."

A. B. Cox started his mystery writing career in a lighthearted, rather trivial manner, but became one of the best and most important crime writers of his generation. His influence (and some of his work) is still very much with readers today.

References:
Christianna Brand, Introduction to *The Floating Admiral*, by Anthony Berkeley and others (Boston: Gregg Press, 1979);

John Dickson Carr, "The Jury Box," *Ellery Queen's Mystery Magazine*, 60 (July 1972): 87-88;

Howard Haycraft, "Anthony Berkeley Cox," *Wilson Library Bulletin*, 14 (December 1939): 268;

Haycraft, *Murder for Pleasure: The Life and Times of the Detective Story* (New York: Appleton Century, 1941; enlarged edition, New York: Biblio & Tannen, 1968);

H. R. F. Keating, Introduction to *Before the Fact*, by Francis Iles (Boston: Gregg Press, 1979);

Paul R. Moy, "A Bibliography of the Works of Anthony Berkeley Cox (Francis Iles)," *Armchair Detective*, 14 (Summer 1981): 236-238;

James Sandoe, Foreword and Annotated Checklist, in *The Poisoned Chocolate Case*, by Berkeley (San Diego: Mystery Library, 1979);

Charles Shibuk, "The Literary Career of Mr. Anthony Berkeley Cox," *Armchair Detective*, 2 (April 1969): 164-168, 170.

Nicholas Blake
(C. Day Lewis)
(27 April 1904-22 May 1972)

Earl F. Bargainnier
Wesleyan College

See also the Day Lewis entries in *DLB 15: British Novelists, 1930-1959;* and *DLB 20: British Poets, 1914-1945.*

SELECTED BOOKS: *Beechen Vigil and Other Poems,* as C. Day Lewis (London: Fortune Press, 1925);

Country Comets, as Day Lewis (London: Hopkinson, 1928);

Transitional Poem, as Day Lewis (London: Hogarth Press, 1929);

From Feathers to Iron, as Day Lewis (London: Hogarth Press, 1931);

The Magnetic Mountain, as Day Lewis (London: Hogarth Press, 1933);

Dick Willoughby, as Day Lewis (Oxford: Blackwell, 1933);

A Hope for Poetry, as Day Lewis (Oxford: Blackwell, 1934);

A Question of Proof, as Nicholas Blake (London: Collins/Crime Club, 1935; New York: Harper, 1935);

Collected Poems 1929-1933, as Day Lewis (London: Hogarth Press, 1935);

Collected Poems 1929-1933 and A Hope for Poetry, as Day Lewis (New York: Random House, 1935);

A Time to Dance and Other Poems, as Day Lewis (London: Hogarth Press, 1935);

Revolution in Writing, as Day Lewis (London: Hogarth Press, 1935);

Noah and the Waters, as Day Lewis (London: Hogarth Press, 1936; New York: Transatlantic Arts, 1947);

A Time to Dance: Noah and the Waters and Other Poems; With an Essay, Revolution in Writing, as Day Lewis (New York: Random House, 1936);

Thou Shell of Death, as Blake (London: Collins/Crime Club, 1936); republished as *Shell of Death* (New York: Harper, 1936);

The Friendly Tree, as Day Lewis (London: Cape, 1936; New York: Harper, 1937);

There's Trouble Brewing, as Blake (London: Collins/Crime Club, 1937; New York: Harper, 1937);

Starting Point, as Day Lewis (London: Cape, 1937; New York: Harper, 1938);

Overtures to Death and Other Poems, as Day Lewis (London: Cape, 1938);

The Beast Must Die, as Blake (London: Collins/Crime Club, 1938; New York: Harper, 1938);

The Smiler with the Knife, as Blake (London: Collins/Crime Club, 1939; New York: Harper, 1939);

Child of Misfortune, as Day Lewis (London: Cape, 1939);

Poems in Wartime, as Day Lewis (London: Cape, 1940);

Selected Poems, as Day Lewis (London: New Hogarth Library, 1940);

Malice in Wonderland, as Blake (London: Collins/Crime Club, 1940); republished as *The Summer Camp Mystery* (New York: Harper, 1940);

The Case of the Abominable Snowman, as Blake (London: Collins/Crime Club, 1941); republished as *The Corpse in the Snowman* (New York: Harper, 1941);

Word Over All, as Day Lewis (London: Cape, 1943);

Short is the Time, Poems 1936-1943, as Day Lewis (New York: Oxford University Press, 1945);

The Poetic Image, as Day Lewis (London: Cape, 1947; New York: Oxford University Press, 1947);

Minute for Murder, as Blake (London: Collins/Crime Club, 1947; New York: Harper, 1948);

The Otterby Incident, as Day Lewis (London: Putnam's, 1948; New York: Viking, 1949);

C. Day Lewis (photograph by Christopher Smedley)

Poems 1943-1947, as Day Lewis (London: Cape, 1948; New York: Oxford University Press, 1948);

Head of a Traveler, as Blake (London: Collins/Crime Club, 1949; New York: Harper, 1949);

The Poet's Task, as Day Lewis (Oxford: Clarendon Press, 1951);

Selected Poems, as Day Lewis (Harmondsworth, U.K.: Penguin, 1951);

An Italian Visit, as Day Lewis (London: Cape, 1953; New York: Harper, 1953);

The Dreadful Hollow, as Blake (London: Collins/Crime Club, 1953; New York: Harper, 1953);

The Whisper in the Gloom, as Blake (London: Collins/Crime Club, 1954; New York: Harper, 1954);

Notable Images of Virtue, as Day Lewis (Toronto: Ryerson Press, 1954);

Collected Poems, as Day Lewis (London: Cape/Hogarth Press, 1954);

A Tangled Web, as Blake (London: Collins/Crime Club, 1956; New York: Harper, 1956);

End of Chapter, as Blake (London: Collins/Crime Club, 1957; New York: Harper, 1957);

The Poet's Way of Knowledge, as Day Lewis (Cambridge: Cambridge University Press, 1957);

Pegasus and Other Poems, as Day Lewis (London: Cape, 1957; New York: Harper, 1958);

A Penknife in My Heart, as Blake (London: Collins/Crime Club, 1958; New York: Harper, 1959);

The Widow's Cruise, as Blake (London: Collins/Crime Club, 1959; New York: Harper, 1959);

The Buried Day, as Day Lewis (London: Chatto & Windus, 1960; New York: Harper & Row, 1960);

The Worm of Death, as Blake (London: Collins/Crime Club, 1961; New York: Harper & Row, 1961);

The Gate and Other Poems, as Day Lewis (London: Cape, 1962);

The Deadly Joker, as Blake (London: Collins/Crime Club, 1963);

Requiem for Living, as Day Lewis (New York: Harper & Row, 1964);

The Sad Variety, as Blake (London: Collins/Crime Club, 1964; New York: Harper & Row, 1964);

The Room and Other Poems, as Day Lewis (London: Cape, 1965);

The Lyric Impulse, as Day Lewis (Cambridge: Harvard University Press, 1965; London: Chatto & Windus, 1965);

The Morning After Death, as Blake (London: Collins/Crime Club, 1966; New York: Harper & Row, 1966);

Selected Poems, as Day Lewis (New York: Harper & Row, 1967);

The Abbey That Refused To Die, as Day Lewis (Claremorris, County Mayo, Ire.: Ballintubber Abbey, 1967);

The Private Wound, as Blake (London: Collins/Crime Club, 1968; New York: Harper & Row, 1968);

The Whispering Roots, as Day Lewis (London: Cape, 1970);

The Whispering Roots and Other Poems, as Day Lewis (New York: Harper & Row, 1970);

Poems of C. Day-Lewis, 1925-1972, edited by Ian Parsons (London: Cape/Hogarth Press, 1977).

OTHER: *Oxford Poetry, 1927,* edited, with an introduction, by C. Day Lewis and W. H. Auden (New York: Appleton, 1928);

Selected Poems by Robert Frost, introduction by Day Lewis (London: Cape, 1936);

The Mind in Chains, Socialism and Cultural Revolution, edited, with an introduction, by Day Lewis (London: F. Muller, 1937);

"A Slice of Bad Luck," as Nicholas Blake, in *Detection Medley,* edited by John Rhode (London: Hutchinson, 1939);

A New Anthology of Modern Verse 1920-1940, edited, with an introduction, by Day Lewis and L. A. G. Strong (London: Methuen, 1941);

Howard Haycraft, *Murder for Pleasure: The Life and Times of the Detective Story,* English edition, introduction by Blake (London: Davies, 1942);

"The Assassin's Club," as Blake, in *Murder for the Millions,* edited by Frank Owen (New York: Fell, 1946);

"It Fell to Earth," as Blake, in *Armchair Detective Reader,* edited by Ernest Dudley (London: Boardman, 1948);

"A Study in White," as Blake, in *Queen's Awards,* fourth series, edited by Ellery Queen (Frederic Dannay and Manfred B. Lee (Boston: Little, Brown/London: Gollancz, 1949);

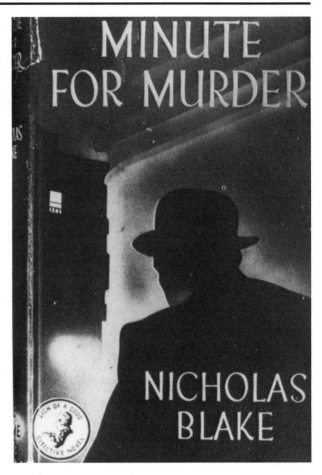

Dust jacket for the first American edition of Day Lewis's postwar masterpiece, a murder mystery involving a poisoning, set during the last days of World War II

The Chatto Book of Modern Poetry, 1915-1955, edited by Day Lewis and John Lehmann (London: Chatto & Windus, 1956);

"Mr. Prendergast and the Orange," as Blake, in *Great Stories of Detection,* edited by R. C. Bull (London: Barker, 1960);

English Lyric Poems, 1500-1900, edited by Day Lewis (New York: Appleton-Century-Crofts, 1961);

The Collected Poems of Wilfred Owen, edited, with an introduction, by Day Lewis (London: Chatto & Windus, 1963);

"Long Shot," in *Twentieth Anniversary Annual,* edited by Queen (New York: Random House, 1965);

An Anthology of Modern Verse, edited by Day Lewis and Strong (London: Methuen, 1967).

Nicholas Blake was the crime-fiction pseudonym of Cecil Day Lewis, poet, translator of Virgil, critic, and editor. His twenty detective novels, sixteen featuring the cases of amateur detective

Nigel Strangeways, are the equal in their genre to his poetry in its genre. This dual success in both a popular form and the most elite of literary forms is a remarkable achievement and an indication of the breadth of his interests and talents. Although he stated that he wrote his first detective novel because he needed one hundred pounds to repair a leaking roof, he never apologized for his detective fiction. He admitted that it enabled him to give up teaching, which he did not enjoy, and he never tried to hide the identity of Nicholas Blake, though both the novels and his mystery criticism, including reviews for the *Spectator* for many years, continued to be published under that name.

Day Lewis was Anglo-Irish, born in Ballintubber, Ireland, the son of Frank Cecil Day-Lewis, a curate of the Church of Ireland, and Kathleen Blake Squires Day-Lewis. On the death of his mother when he was four, he and his father moved to England, where his father served in various parishes, and he was raised by an aunt. He attended Wilkie's School and Sherborne School and went to Wadham College, Oxford, on a grant, receiving his M.A. in 1927. He was an unwilling schoolmaster at Summer Fields, Larchfield, and Cheltenham schools until 1935, when his detective fiction enabled him to devote all of his time to writing. His 1928 marriage to Constance Mary King, daughter of one of his Sherborne teachers, ended in divorce in 1951; in the same year he married actress Jill Balcon. There were two children by each marriage.

From 1935 to 1938 Day Lewis was a member of the Communist Party Great Britain. He never actually resigned; as he states in *The Buried Day* (1960), his autobiography, "I just quietly faded out." By the end of World War II, his Marxist views had all but disappeared, and there is no evidence of them in the Blake novels after the first three; indeed, the late *The Sad Variety* (1964) is an anti-Communist thriller. Except for five years of wartime service as editor in the Ministry of Information, Day Lewis's career from 1935 to his death consisted of writing or editing eighty books, occasional lecturing, and serving as director of the publishing firm Chatto and Windus from 1954, the latter providing the background for *End of Chapter* (1957). He was elected Professor of Poetry at Oxford for 1951-1956; served as Norton Professor of Poetry at Harvard, 1964-1965 (the source for *The Morning After Death*, 1966); and held many other distinguished lectureships. He was awarded honorary degrees

from the Universities of Exeter and Hull and Trinity College, Dublin, as well as being named an Honorary Fellow of Wadham College, Oxford. Other honors included the positions Vice-President (1958) and Companion of Literature (1964) of the Royal Society of Literature, Honorary Member of the American Academy of Arts and Letters, and Member of the Irish Academy of Letters. He was named Commander, Order of the British Empire in 1950 and ended his literary life as Poet Laureate of England (1968-1972).

In his introduction to the English edition of Howard Haycraft's *Murder for Pleasure* (1942), Blake described detective fiction as "the Folk-Myth of the Twentieth Century," with the detective as fairy godmother. Since he believed that guilt is present in everyone and that the force of religion has weakened for many people, detective fiction offers a substitute for religious ritual in harmlessly releasing or absolving that sense of guilt. It is in this "fantasy-representation of guilt" that the value of detective fiction lies. However, the fantasy is equally important: "evil must, both for myth-making and entertainment, be volatised by a certain measure of fantasy." These statements on the function and method of detective fiction are important in understanding Blake's intent and accomplishment.

In his novels Blake exhibited certain characteristics that are evidence of his being a poet. He used literary allusions, leitmotivs, striking figures of speech, and parallel chapter titles. He was an expert on various English accents and dialects, from the Dorset peasant to the London businessman. The novels are often symmetrical in structure, with the final pages returning to the incidents of the first. One should never assume that the first pages of a Blake novel are simply exposition–more likely they contain some key to the novel's problem. He also enjoyed experimenting with structure–shifting points of view, juxtaposing action and explanation, disarranging time sequence–and writing mysteries which are practically outside the limits of the genre, such as *A Tangled Web* (1956) and *The Private Wound* (1968). This experimentation is a principal reason for the variety of the Blake novels. Another notable characteristic is his use of his own experience in the novels, including places lived, positions held, even a traumatic love affair; and he has many writers as characters. Except for the four thrillers, the novels present family murders, usually requiring digging into the past to reveal relationships and motives. (The three most common motives

Day Lewis at age forty-five (photograph by Irving Penn)

phors, but has few eccentricities. As a detective, he belongs to the ratiocinative school. He develops theories on the basis of evidence found by the police, but relies even more on the psychology of the people involved in a case. His enjoyment of, as he says, "setting a cat among the pigeons" and his boyish exhibitionism make him seem less formidable as a detective than he is; but he also has an "inordinate curiosity" as to people, "particularly the pathological states of mind," and an almost perfect verbal memory. He usually thinks of a number of possible solutions to a crime; then he *thinks.* As his logic plays over his "tail-chasing arguments," he comes to the correct solution but leaves the reader in a dizzy whirl. Likable, normal, but a master of reasoning: these are the qualities of Nigel Strangeways.

Five major repeated characters appear with Strangeways: three are police, and two are women. Strangeways works well with the police. His uncle Sir John Strangeways is an assistant commissioner of Scotland Yard, and in the early cases is often the source of Nigel's involvement. Detective-Inspector Blount, a bland, bald Scot, is the official detective in five cases; he is succeeded by Inspector Wright, who is saturnine and "hatchet faced," in three others. They supply facts, while Strangeways provides theories. In *Thou Shell of Death* (1936) Strangeways meets Georgia Cavendish, a famous woman explorer. In the next novel they are married. Strangeways discusses his cases with her and even uses her as an agent provocateur, and in *The Smiler with the Knife* (1939) she is the central character, infiltrating a Fascist conspiracy, while he plays a negligible role. Georgia is killed in the blitz, and for a time there is no romantic interest in Strangeways's life, but then he has an affair with sculptor Clare Massinger. They eventually live together, but it is her choice not to marry. As a result of Strangeways's relationships with these two women, the novels are divided chronologically into three groups. Seven were written between 1935 and 1941, the last six of which might be called the "Georgia" novels. As Blake was working for the Ministry of Information during World War II, no other novels appeared until 1947, and then there were nine by 1966. In the first three of these Strangeways is mourning Georgia's death. In the last six his affair with Clare Massinger is a major element, and they can be termed the "Clare" novels.

Strangeways is introduced in *A Question of Proof* (1935), which presents murder at a boys'

are revenge, madness, and greed.) Other elements often employed include a chase of some kind, comic set pieces, the frequent use of children or teenagers as characters, romance, long final explanations, and suicide or insanity rather than arrest and punishment for the murderer.

Blake is generally supposed to have modeled Nigel Strangeways on his friend and fellow poet W. H. Auden. Certainly there is a physical resemblance. Strangeways is tall, with a deceptively docile appearance, sandy-colored hair, and shortsighted pale blue eyes. He sprawls, is somewhat clumsy and untidy, and has a huge appetite. He loves puns, literary allusions, and mixed meta-

school and for which Blake used his teaching experience. Asked to help a friend suspected of murdering one of the boys, Strangeways discovers the murderer, but not before another victim dies. The understanding of schoolboys and masters is obvious, the comic scenes—particularly a car chase, a tea party, and Strangeways's initiation into the boys' secret society, the Black Spot—are hilarious, and the time problem which is the heart of the mystery is cleverly explained. *Thou Shell of Death* is a country-house mystery involving the death of a celebrated air ace, Fergus O'Brien, who has certain similarities to T. E. Lawrence. It is the first of the novels whose answer lies buried in the past, and its plot is a conscious variation on Cyril Tourneur's *The Revenger's Tragedy* (1607). The solution is complicated for Strangeways by snow, a blackmailer, the victim's secretiveness, and his own attraction to Georgia, who is the chief suspect for much of the novel. Though he is married to Georgia in *There's Trouble Brewing* (1937), Strangeways is away in Dorset solving the mystery surrounding the death of a brewer whose remains are found boiled in one of his copper vats. Though complex in plotting and effective in its minor characters, the novel suffers from Strangeways's facetiously playing up to the image of the eminent detective; his attempts at being Sherlock Holmes seem merely silly, and the more than twenty pages of final explanation are tedious.

If *There's Trouble Brewing* is relatively weak, its successor is one of Blake's four best novels. The opening line of *The Beast Must Die* (1938) is "I am going to kill a man." This technique would seem to make it an inverted story with the killer known, but Blake uses that expectation as a narrative trick. The first third of the novel consists of the diary of Felix Lane, a detective novelist who is determined to avenge the hit-and-run death of his son. The diary traces his search for and discovery of the driver of the car. Lane's attempt at murder fails, but then his intended victim is murdered. Strangeways and Georgia enter at this point. The solution is brilliantly constructed, and though Strangeways calls this "my most unhappy case," it is not for readers.

The next novel, *The Smiler with the Knife*, is the first of Blake's thrillers. In this book Georgia and Nigel fake a separation so that she can enter into a Fascist conspiracy to overthrow the British government. The pre-World War II unease in Great Britain is presented with skill, but the last half of the book degenerates into an unintention-

ally comic escape-and-chase sequence. The leader of the conspiracy is known, and the interest is on whether Georgia can escape with the plans. She burns a stately home, blinding the villain; disguises herself as Santa Claus; endures a chase in a huge truck; disguises herself again as a eurythmic dancer; and finally has to fight the blinded villain in a totally dark room. It is all quite amusing, but very improbable.

After giving Georgia such a large role, Blake omitted her completely from *Malice in Wonderland* (1940; published in the United States as *The Summer Camp Mystery*), the weakest of all the novels. Set at a vacation camp that is being ruined by practical jokes, it does not contain a murder, although a German spy is killed; and the characters are either stereotypes or inanities. Apparently intended to be satirical in the manner of Evelyn Waugh, it fails to sustain the satire or the mystery. Much better is *The Case of the Abominable Snowman* (1941; published in the United States as *The Corpse in the Snowman*). Another country-house-in-the-winter mystery, it contains as suspects, in the words of Georgia, "a trollop, an Anglo-Saxon squire, an American wife, a rolling stone, a fribble, and a quack," one of whom is a totally evil person; there are also two delightful children and Georgia's scatty cousin Clarissa, who exists in her own eighteenth-century world. Suicide and murder are joined here, as in *Thou Shell of Death*, to confound the reader, and Strangeways is in top form as psychologist-detective.

Minute for Murder (1947), Blake's first novel after World War II, is generally regarded as his masterpiece. Based upon his wartime job, it takes place in the Visual Propaganda Division of the Ministry of Morale between the defeats of Germany and Japan. The director's secretary-mistress is poisoned in the presence of eight people, including Strangeways. The tension of five years of war and the necessarily close contact of the Ministry officials, plus the possibility of treason and the certainty of blackmail, provide all sorts of red herrings, but Strangeways's major problem is to solve the inexplicable disappearance from the murder room of the poison capsule. The novel ends with his listening to a confrontation between the two principal suspects, and he describes it as "a pretty naked exhibition of mutual antipathy." It is a superbly dramatic denouement to one of the great British detective novels. It was followed by *Head of a Traveler* (1949), a novel that demonstrates the relationship between the dual careers of its author. The character Robert Seaton is a major modern poet whose family becomes involved in murder. Strangeways is a great admirer of Seaton, and thus the novel has much to say on the meaning of being a poet. The leitmotiv of Plash Meadow, Seaton's house, and the puns, allusions, and situations related to heads—the corpse is found headless—give the novel a structural unity that is evidence of Blake's craftsmanship. Most interesting is the enigmatic conclusion: Strangeways knows the murderer's identity but cannot decide whether to reveal his knowledge; the ending is left open to this unusual novel. Not on the same level is *The Dreadful Hollow* (1953). The murderer is evident so early, as are the subterfuges supposed to eliminate her as a suspect and the past family history, that there is little suspense. The red herring of poison-pen letters is not developed, and altogether the work comes close to the inadequacy of *Malice in Wonderland*.

In *The Whisper in the Gloom* (1954) Clare Massinger and Strangeways have known each other for some time, but here she learns that he is a detective, she saves his life, and their love affair commences. This thriller centers on a mysterious message given by a dying man to a twelve-year-old boy. It is filled with more coincidence than any other Blake novel; the boy and his streetwise chum are rather too clever; there is a massive shootout that includes army which takes place at a stately home; and the ending seems indebted to Alfred Hitchcock's *The Man Who Knew Too Much*. Far superior is *End of Chapter*. Another of Blake's most acclaimed works, it takes place at the publishing firm of Wenham and Geraldine. Since Blake was a director of Chatto and Windus publishers, the setting is authentic. The discussions of writing and publishing are interwoven into the plot so that they never seem extraneous dressing. Millicent Miles, an unpleasant popular writer, is murdered, and the reasons are again deep in the past. The suspects and red herrings are handled with finesse, and Strangeways's sympathy for the murderer, who commits suicide, provides an added dimension. Without question, *End of Chapter* is one of Blake's best.

Strangeways and Clare are on a cruise of the Greek Isles in *The Widow's Cruise* (1959). A middle-aged femme fatale and an obnoxiously precocious little girl are murdered. The people on the ship are the usual varied lot: an acerbic bishop's wife, a Greek "stud," a troubled teenager, a fake expert on the classics and a real one, and another blackmailer. Much fun is had at the ex-

Day Lewis with Jill Balcon, his second wife, at their Campden Hill Road home, 1953 (courtesy of Sean Day-Lewis)

pense of psychoanalysis and its practitioners, and the scenery is sketched effectively without being excessively obtrusive. However, the central plot premise is difficult to accept. After Strangeways stretches his explanation to its limit, once again the murderer commits suicide.

The superior Blake novel of the five published in the 1960s is the first, *The Worm of Death* (1961). It finds Strangeways and Clare living together in a house in Greenwich. Nearby is the house of Dr. Piers Loudron (modeled on Blake's own house). When the doctor disappears and then is found in the Thames, Strangeways is asked to investigate. He finds himself pitted against a psychopath, finally on a ruined barge in the river, where for the third time he is saved by Clare. The atmosphere of riverside London is evoked with extraordinary imagery and detail in this book; and the members of the Loudron family, the entanglements of the past, and particularly the relationships of parents and children are masterfully treated in this work, which is as much a psychological novel as it is a mystery.

The Sad Variety is another thriller and much like *The Whisper in the Gloom*. This time a child, Lucy Wragby, is kidnapped by Communists to force her scientist father to reveal a recent discovery. Lucy is incredibly calm for a ten-year-old about her ordeal; again snow is a significant factor; and there is a slam-bang finish, with Strangeways and Clare leading the charge to rescue Lucy. Effective in its way, it is still not classic Blake. Nor is *The Morning After Death*, Strangeways's last case, which carries him to Cabot University in New England. Based upon the author's period at Harvard as Norton Professor of Poetry, it contains the murder of a professor; satire of American academia; references to American literary figures, especially Emily Dickinson (the title is from one of her poems); a confrontation between the murderer and Strangeways at Walden Pond; Strangeways's infidelity to Clare with a graduate student; and a chase after a football game leading to the murderer's suicide. In spite of all these ingredients, it ends Strangeways's career on a lower standard than Blake's best: *The Beast Must Die, Minute for Murder, End of Chapter*, and *The Worm of Death*.

Between 1956 and 1968 Blake wrote four novels without Strangeways. Each is quite different from the others. *A Tangled Web* is based upon the famous John Williams case of 1912 but is presented in a 1950s setting. Though a murder occurs, there is little mystery as to the murderer; rather, the novel is concerned with love, power, and betrayal of trust. The reader feels sympathy for the murderer and disgust for the "friend" who betrays him, as is Blake's intent, for the action is presented from the viewpoint of the young woman who loves the murderer. With coincidentally the same plot premise as Patricia Highsmith's *Strangers on a Train* (1950), *A Penknife in My Heart* (1958) is an ironic story of two weak men who agree to perform murders for each other and whom nemesis overtakes in the form of the guilt and gradual self-awareness of one. Perhaps Blake's most symmetrical novel, it offers both melodramatic action and psychological characterization. *The Deadly Joker* (1963) is a classical village detective novel, with John Waterson, a Strangeways-like retired inspector of schools, as narrator and amateur detective. A series of practical jokes in Netherplash Cantorum leads to the death of the beautiful Indian wife of the new squire. The romantic relationships are complex, and though the murderer is somewhat obvious, Blake manages to offer a number of possible suspects and plot twists. (This is the only one of the novels not published in the United States.)

Blake's last mystery is his most intriguing, for *The Private Wound* is to a large, if undocumented, degree autobiographical. A comparison of it to *The Buried Day*, Day Lewis's autobiography, provides numerous parallels between Dominic Eyre, the Anglo-Irish writer in the novel, and his creator; and the novel's passionate love affair in late 1930s Ireland is surely a fictional representation of a similar experience of the author, mentioned in *The Buried Day*. A murder and its punishment are interwoven with the love affair and with Irish religion, politics, and culture to form an unconventional but penetrating work. In this valedictory to mystery fiction, Blake used the form to re-create a traumatic period of his own life, and in so doing produced his most disturbingly original novel.

Nicholas Blake's reputation is that of one of the principal detective writers to appear in the 1930s, perhaps *the* principal British *male* writer. Just as the name of Cecil Day Lewis would appear on nearly any list of the twenty major British poets of the twentieth century, so would that of Nicholas Blake appear on a similar list of the most significant writers of twentieth-century British detective fiction. If the list were limited to males, he would be in the top ten. His novels have been praised both in England and the United States by critics of all persuasions, and recently a new generation of readers has discovered him with the publication of his detective novels in the Harper Perennial paperback series. In Nigel Strangeways, Blake not only paid a compliment to his friend Auden but also created one of the most compassionate, sensible, and likable of British detectives. The variety, the literate stylishness, the clever plotting, the experimentation with form, the unusual depth of characterization, and, as Julian Symons has said, the "bubbling high spirits" of Blake's novels place them among the assured classics of detective fiction.

References:

Winslow Dix, "The Second Incarnation of C. Day Lewis," *Chronicle of Higher Education*, 19 March 1979, pp. R13-R14;

Clifford Dyment, *C. Day Lewis* (London: Longmans, Green, 1955).

Papers:
There are collections of Day Lewis manuscripts and other papers at the British Museum, University of Liverpool, New York Public Library, and State University of New York at Buffalo.

Leo Bruce
(Rupert Croft-Cooke)

(20 June 1903-10 June 1979)

Nancy Pearl

BOOKS: *Songs of a Sussex Tramp,* as Rupert Croft-Cooke (Steyning, Sussex: Vine Press, 1922);

Tonbridge School: A Poem, as Croft-Cooke (Tonbridge, U.K.: Free Press, 1923);

Songs South of the Line, as Croft-Cooke (London: Lincoln Torrey, 1925);

The Viking, as Croft-Cooke (London: Privately printed for B. Rota, 1926);

How Psychology Can Help, as Croft-Cooke (London: Daniel, 1927);

Some Poems, as Croft-Cooke (Rochester, U.K.: Galleon Press, 1929);

Banquo's Chair, as Croft-Cooke (London: Deane, 1930);

Troubadour, as Croft-Cooke (London: Chapman & Hall, 1930);

Give Him the Earth, as Croft-Cooke (London: Chapman & Hall, 1930; New York: Knopf, 1931);

Night Out, as Croft-Cooke (London: Jarrolds, 1932; New York: Dial, 1932);

Cosmopolis, as Croft-Cooke (London: Jarrolds, 1932; New York: Dial, 1933);

Release the Lions, as Croft-Cooke (London: Jarrolds, 1933; New York: Dodd, Mead, 1934);

Her Mexican Lover, as Croft-Cooke (London: Mellifont Press, 1934);

Picaro, as Croft-Cooke (London: Jarrolds, 1934; New York: Dodd, Mead, 1934);

Tap Three Times, as Croft-Cooke (London & New York: French, 1934);

Shoulder the Sky, as Croft-Cooke (London: Jarrolds, 1935);

Blind Gunner, as Croft-Cooke (London: Jarrolds, 1935);

Crusade, as Croft-Cooke (London: Jarrolds, 1936);

Kingdom Come, as Croft-Cooke (London: Jarrolds, 1936);

Darts, as Croft-Cooke (London: Bles, 1936);

God in Ruins: A Passing Commentary, as Croft-Cooke (London: Fortune Press, 1936);

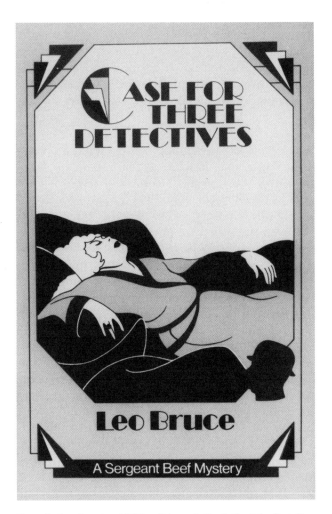

Dust jacket for the 1980 edition of Croft-Cooke's first Sergeant Beef mystery

Case for Three Detectives, as Leo Bruce (London: Bles, 1936; New York: Stokes, 1937);

Case without a Corpse, as Bruce (London: Bles, 1937; New York: Stokes, 1937);

Pharaoh with His Waggons and Other Stories, as Croft-Cooke (London: Jarrolds, 1937);

The World is Young, as Croft-Cooke (London: Hodder & Stoughton, 1937); republished as

Escape to the Andes (New York: Messner, 1938);

How to Get More Out of Life, as Croft-Cooke (London: Bles, 1938);

The Man in Europe Street, as Croft-Cooke (London: Rich & Cowan, 1938; New York: Putnam's, 1938);

Rule, Britannia, as Croft-Cooke (London: Jarrolds, 1938);

Same Way Home, as Croft-Cooke (London: Jarrolds, 1939; New York: Macmillan, 1940);

Case with Four Clowns, as Bruce (London: Davies, 1939; New York: Stokes, 1939);

Case with No Conclusion, as Bruce (London: Bles, 1939);

Case with Ropes and Rings, as Bruce (London: Nicholson & Watson, 1940);

Glorious, as Croft-Cooke (London: Jarrolds, 1940);

The Circus Has No Home, as Croft-Cooke (London: Methuen, 1941; revised and augmented edition, London: Falcon Press, 1950);

Ladies Gay, as Croft-Cooke (London: Macdonald, 1946);

Octopus, as Croft-Cooke (London & New York: Jarrolds, 1946); republished as *Miss Allick* (New York: Holt, 1947);

Case for Sergeant Beef, as Bruce (London: Nicholson & Watson, 1947);

How to Enjoy Travel Abroad, as Croft-Cooke (London: Rockliff, 1948);

The Moon in My Pocket: Life with the Romanies, as Croft-Cooke (London: Sampson Low, Marston, 1948);

Rudyard Kipling, as Croft-Cooke (London: Home & Van Thal, 1948; Denver: Swallow, 1948);

Wilkie, as Croft-Cooke (London: Macdonald, 1948); republished as *Another Sun, Another Home* (New York: Holt, 1949);

The White Mountain, as Croft-Cooke (London: Falcon Press, 1949);

Brass Farthing, as Croft-Cooke (London: Laurie, 1950);

A Football for the Brigadier and Other Stories, as Croft-Cooke (London: Laurie, 1950);

Gala Night at "The Willows," by Croft-Cooke and Gladys Bronwyn Stern (London: Deane, 1950);

Neck and Neck, as Bruce (London: Gollancz, 1951);

Cities, by Croft-Cooke and Noel Barber (London: Wingate, 1951);

Three Names for Nicholas, as Croft-Cooke (London: Macmillan, 1951);

The Sawdust Ring, by Croft-Cooke and W. S. Meadmore (London: Odhams, 1951);

Buffalo Bill: The Legend, The Man of Action, The Showman, by Croft-Cooke and Meadmore (London: Sidgwick & Jackson, 1952);

The Life for Me, as Croft-Cooke (London: Macmillan, 1952);

Nine Days with Edward, as Croft-Cooke (London: Macmillan, 1952);

Cold Blood, as Bruce (London: Gollancz, 1952);

Harvest Moon, as Croft-Cooke (London: Macmillan, 1953; New York: St. Martin's Press, 1953);

The Blood-Red Island, as Croft-Cooke (London & New York: Staples, 1953);

Fall of Man, as Croft-Cooke (London: Macmillan, 1955);

At Death's Door, as Bruce (London: Hamilton, 1955);

A Few Gypsies, as Croft-Cooke (London: Putnam's, 1955);

Seven Thunders, as Croft-Cooke (New York: St. Martin's Press, 1955; London: Macmillan, 1956);

Sherry, as Croft-Cooke (London: Putnam's, 1955; New York: Knopf, 1956);

The Verdict of You All, as Croft-Cooke (London: Secker & Warburg, 1955);

Dead for a Ducat, as Bruce (London: Davies, 1956);

Death of Cold, as Bruce (London: Davies, 1956);

The Tangerine House, as Croft-Cooke (London: Macmillan/New York: St. Martin's Press, 1956);

Port, as Croft-Cooke (London: Putnam's, 1957);

The Gardens of Camelot, as Croft-Cooke (London: Putnam's, 1958);

Dead Man's Shoes, as Bruce (London: Davies, 1958);

A Louse for the Hangman, as Bruce (London: Davies, 1958);

Barbary Night, as Croft-Cooke (London: Eyre & Spottiswoode, 1958);

Our Jubilee Is Death, as Bruce (London: Davies, 1959);

The Quest for Quixote, as Croft-Cooke (London: Secker & Warburg, 1959); republished as *Through Spain with Don Quixote* (New York: Knopf, 1960);

Smiling Damned Villain: The True Story of Paul Axel Lund, as Croft-Cooke (London: Secker & Warburg, 1959);

Dust jacket for Croft-Cooke's 1974 mystery which takes place on a holiday cruise from England

The Altar in the Loft, as Croft-Cooke (London: Putnam's, 1960);

English Cooking: A New Approach, as Croft-Cooke (London: W. H. Allen, 1960);

Furious Old Women, as Bruce (London, Davies, 1960);

Jack on the Gallows Tree, as Bruce (London: Davies, 1960);

Thief, as Croft-Cooke (London: Eyre & Spottiswoode, 1960; Garden City, N.Y.: Published for the Crime Club by Doubleday, 1961);

Die All, Die Merrily, as Bruce (London: Davies, 1961; New York: British Book Centre, 1961);

The Drums of Morning, as Croft-Cooke (London: Putnam's, 1961);

Madeira, as Croft-Cooke (London: Putnam's, 1961);

A Bone and a Hank of Hair, as Bruce (London: Davies, 1961);

Clash by Night, as Croft-Cooke (London: Eyre & Spottiswoode, 1962);

Nothing Like Blood, as Bruce (London: Davies, 1962);

The Glittering Pastures, as Croft-Cooke (London: Putnam's, 1962);

Wine and Other Drinks, as Croft-Cooke (London: Collins, 1962);

Crack of Doom, as Bruce (London: Davies, 1963); republished as *Such Is Death* (New York: British Book Centre, 1963);

Bosie: The Story of Lord Alfred Douglas, His Friends and Enemies, as Croft-Cooke (London: W. H. Allen, 1963; Indianapolis: Bobbs-Merrill, 1964);

Cooking for Pleasure, as Croft-Cooke (London & Glasgow: Collins, 1963);

The Numbers Came, as Croft-Cooke (London: Putnam's, 1963);

Tales of a Wicked Uncle, as Croft-Cooke (London: Cape, 1963);

The Last of Spring, as Croft-Cooke (London: Putnam's, 1964);

Death in Albert Park, as Bruce (London: W. H. Allen, 1964);

The Wintry Sea, as Croft-Cooke (London: W. H. Allen, 1964);

The Gorgeous East: One Man's India, as Croft-Cooke (London: W. H. Allen, 1965);

Death at Hallows End, as Bruce (London: W. H. Allen, 1965; New York: British Book Centre, 1966);

Paper Albatross, as Croft-Cooke (London: Eyre & Spottiswoode, 1965; London & New York: Abelard-Schuman, 1968);

Death on the Black Sands, as Bruce (London: W. H. Allen, 1966);

The Purple Streak, as Croft-Cooke (London: W. H. Allen, 1966);

The Wild Hills, as Croft-Cooke (London: W. H. Allen, 1966);

Feasting with Tigers: A New Consideration of Some Late Victorian Writers, as Croft-Cooke (London: W. H. Allen, 1967; New York: Holt, Rinehart & Winston, 1968);

The Happy Highways, as Croft-Cooke (London: W. H. Allen, 1967);

Death of a Commuter, as Bruce (London: W. H. Allen, 1967);

Death at St. Asprey's School, as Bruce (London: W. H. Allen, 1967);

Death on Romney Marsh, as Bruce (London: W. H. Allen, 1968);

Three in a Cell, as Croft-Cooke (London: Eyre & Spottiswoode, 1968);

The Ghost of June: A Return to England and the West, as Croft-Cooke (London: W. H. Allen, 1968);

Exotic Food: Three Hundred of the Most Unusual Dishes in Western Cookery, as Croft-Cooke (London: Allen & Unwin, 1969; New York: Herder & Herder, 1971);

The Sound of Revelry, as Croft-Cooke (London: W. H. Allen, 1969);

Wolf from the Door, as Croft-Cooke (London: W. H. Allen, 1969);

Death with Blue Ribbon, as Bruce (London: W. H. Allen, 1969; New York: London House & Maxwell, 1970);

Death on Allhallowe'en, as Bruce (London: W. H. Allen, 1970);

Exiles, as Croft-Cooke (London: W. H. Allen, 1970);

Death by the Lake, as Bruce (London: W. H. Allen, 1971);

The Licentious Soldiery, as Croft-Cooke (London: W. H. Allen, 1971);

Under the Rose Garden, as Croft-Cooke (London & New York: W. H. Allen, 1971);

While the Iron's Hot, as Croft-Cooke (London: W. H. Allen, 1971);

The Unrecorded Life of Oscar Wilde, as Croft-Cooke (London: W. H. Allen, 1972; New York: McKay, 1972);

The Dogs of Peace, as Croft-Cooke (London: W. H. Allen, 1973);

Nasty Piece of Work, as Croft-Cooke (London: Eyre Methuen, 1973);

Death in the Middle Watch, as Bruce (London: W. H. Allen, 1974);

Death of a Bovver Boy, as Bruce (London: W. H. Allen, 1974);

The Caves of Hercules, as Croft-Cooke (London: W. H. Allen, 1974);

The Long Way Home, as Croft-Cooke (London: W. H. Allen, 1974);

Conduct Unbecoming, as Croft-Cooke (London: W. H. Allen, 1975);

Circus: A World History, by Croft-Cooke and Peter Cotes (London: Elek, 1976);

The Green, Green Grass, as Croft-Cooke (London: W. H. Allen, 1977).

OTHER: John Mair, Christopher Hollis, Richard Blake Brown, and others, *Major Road Ahead: A Young Man's Ultimatum,* edited, with a prefatory letter, by Croft-Cooke (London: Methuen, 1939);

Segismundo Casado, *The Last Days of Madrid: The End of the Second Spanish Republic,* translated by Croft-Cooke (London: Davies, 1939);

The Circus Book, edited by Croft-Cooke (London: Sampson Low, Marston, 1948);

"Death in the Garden," in *The Evening Standard Detective Book* (London: Gollancz, 1950);

"Murder in Miniature," in *The Evening Standard Detective Book,* second series (London: Gollancz, 1951).

Rupert Croft-Cooke, who wrote his best-known detective novels under the pseudonym Leo Bruce, was born in Edenbridge, Kent, to Hubert Bruce Cooke and Lucy Taylor Cooke. He attended Tonbridge School in Kent and Wellington College (now Wrekin College) before studying at the University of Buenos Aires in 1923-1926. While living in Buenos Aires, Croft-Cooke founded a weekly, *La Estrella,* and edited it in 1923-1924. He worked as an antiquarian bookseller in 1929-1931 and lectured at the English Institute Montana, Zugerberg, Switzerland, in 1931. In 1940 he entered the British intelligence corps, and two years later he served with distinction in the Madagascar campaign, earning the British Empire Medal. He was given command of the Third (Queen Alexandra's Own) Gurka Rifles in 1943 and in 1944 became a captain and field security officer for the Poona District. An instructor at the British intelligence school in Karachi in 1945, he was field security officer for the Delhi District in 1945-1946. He returned to England in 1946 and became a book critic for the *Sketch* (London), leaving in 1953 to devote his full time to his writing.

Croft-Cooke's experiences abroad are not reflected in his mystery novels, which are relentlessly British in their settings and characters. The detectives in the two well-known series he wrote as Leo Bruce are a Cockney policeman, Sgt. William Beef, who, flushed with beer and a few successful cases, quits the police force to open up his own detective agency; and Carolus Deene, a widower and an independently wealthy former paratrooper, who is now history master at a minor public school. The author of the well-received *Who Killed William Rufus? And Other Mysteries of History,* Deene became a gentleman detec-

LEO BRUCE
A CAROLUS DEENE MYSTERY

Such Is Death

Dust jacket for the 1986 edition of the mystery in which school-master Carolus Deene solves the villain's "ideal" murder

tive through his research into historical mysteries.

The first Bruce novels feature Sergeant Beef and are narrated by the not entirely likable Lionel Townsend, who is ostensibly the author of accounts of Beef's cases. Townsend is a snob who looks down at Beef's supposed inferiority in class, education, and intelligence, and he presents Beef as a beer-drinking, darts-playing buffoon who merely stumbles through luck onto the solutions to his cases. The relationship between chronicler and subject remains touchy throughout the eight Sergeant Beef mysteries (1936-1952). Townsend frequently makes it clear to Beef that he is doing Beef a favor by recording his cases for posterity.

In *Case with No Conclusion* (1939), however, Beef rebels against Townsend's narrative treatment. This fourth novel in the series is the first

to follow Beef's adventures after he has retired from the police force, and in the first chapter Beef complains in detail that he is losing potential clients because of the way Townsend is writing about him. Beef mentions the favorable treatment Anthony Gethryn, Albert Campion, and Dr. Gideon Fell get from their authors. He also charges that Townsend overemphasizes his accent—which, in fact, makes the first three books of the series, especially *Case without a Corpse* (1937), difficult to read. Townsend agrees to make the changes Beef wants in the hope that both readership and cases will increase, and, indeed, in later books Beef's accent is hardly noticeable, while Townsend's snobbishness has diminished but has not disappeared.

The first Beef novel, *Case for Three Detectives* (1936), is an ingenious locked-room mystery, in which three famous detectives, Simon Plimsoll, Amer Picon, and Monsignor Smith (thinly disguised versions of Peter Wimsey, Hercule Poirot, and Father Brown), are shown up by the lowly Sergeant Beef. The three offer plausible solutions to the murder while Beef listens and then explains what really happened. Beef describes his method of detection in *Case with Ropes and Rings* (1940): "I don't do a lot of skylarking with microscopes and that, and I have no opinion at all of what they call psychology. I just use my loaf." He is contemptuous of other policemen's methods, and in fact policemen are not well regarded in any of the Beef novels. As a character in *Case for Three Detectives* puts it, "My dear chap, when you've seen as much of them as I have you'll know that they don't think at all. They just guess." In any of Bruce's mysteries, despite the fair clues given to the reader, it is difficult to outreason the detective or to identify the murderer before the end of the book. In the intricately plotted *Cold Blood* (1952), for example, Beef shows that what appeared to be murder was really suicide and what seemed to be an obvious suicide was in fact murder.

Three years after the last Beef novel appeared in 1952 Bruce introduced Carolus Deene. As a result of the response to his historical research, Deene is asked to solve many present-day crimes. Although his headmaster, Hugh Gorringer, and his housekeeper, Mrs. Stick, do not want him to pursue these extracurricular interests, Deene accepts all cases because, as he explains in *Our Jubilee Is Death* (1959), he does not "like murder anywhere by anyone for any motive at all. . . . It's monstrously presumptuous." Like

Beef, Deene is unimpressed by the police work that he witnesses. Yet–except for one member of the local police force, John Moore, who appears in several early novels–the police tell him they are better equipped than he to solve crimes. Like Beef, however, Deene sees his own methods of detection as vastly different from and far superior to those of the police. "He had never believed greatly in forensic chemistry or the use of the microscope or even, except in rare cases, finger prints" (*A Bone and a Hank of Hair*, 1961). Instead he relies heavily on intuition: "He trusted little more than his instincts, his gift of logic, and insight into motives" (*Death in the Middle Watch*, 1974). In *Furious Old Women* (1960), for example, he has "a strange superstitious feeling that ahead of him lay great evil and perhaps danger, that the death of Millicent Griggs, horrible though it was, would prove to be only a part of something more menacing and beastly." In *Crack of Doom* (1963), one of the best Deene novels, intuition plays an important role in his investigation of a so-called perfect murder: the murderer acted solely from a desire to kill for the experience itself and had no discernible motive in choosing his victim. Deene gets "a whiff of something abnormal and hellish" when he begins investigating this case.

Despite Deene's intuitions, his solutions to cases are based on more than feelings. Bruce rarely relies on trick solutions or coincidence, though in *Nothing Like Blood* (1962) one of the characters happens to be adept at tightrope walking, and she helps Deene catch the murderer through this unlikely talent.

The best of the Deene novels were written in the late 1950s and the early 1960s, beginning with *Our Jubilee Is Death* and continuing through *Death in Albert Park* (1964). Some of the early

Deene novels appear somewhat derivative. The first, *At Death's Door* (1955), for example, is reminiscent of Agatha Christie's *The ABC Murders* (1936). The best of the Deene novels include memorable minor characters, such as the victim in *Our Jubilee Is Death*, an unloved and unlovely mystery writer. Part of *A Bone and a Hank of Hair* is set in an artist colony in Cornwall, which is peopled by such obviously named writers as Oswald Auden and Sacheverell Spender. *Death in Albert Park* contains another well-drawn minor character: Goggins, who does not finish eating one meal until the next one begins.

A Bone and a Hank of Hair is typical of the best Deene novels in its intricate plot. A man appears to have murdered each of his three wives, but Deene discovers that he has murdered none of them. In *Crack of Doom* coincidence complicates the plot when the murder victim turns out to be the murderer's long-lost brother, and the murderer must kill again to cover up the original crime.

The earliest Bruce novels are somewhat dated by their reflection of the prejudices and stereotypical outlooks of their times. Thurston, in the first Beef novel, *Case for Three Detectives*, is described as having "the jolly German simplicity and sentimentality." These novels also contain undertones of the anti-Semitism of upper-class British society during the 1930s. Women get the short shrift as well. In *Case for Three Detectives* Townsend describes "awful parties in London at which women with unpleasant breath advocate free love and nudism." Bruce's few female characters tend to be unconvincing stereotypes.

Yet, despite these limitations, Leo Bruce is clearly one of the best of the mystery writers of his day, and his intricately plotted and consistently interesting novels deserve to be read.

Leslie Charteris
(12 May 1907-   )

Joan DelFattore
University of Delaware

BOOKS: *X Esquire* (London & Melbourne: Ward, Lock, 1927);

The White Rider (London: Ward, Lock, 1928; Garden City, N.Y.: Doubleday, Doran 1930);

Meet the Tiger (London: Ward, Lock, 1928); republished as *Meet—the Tiger!* (Garden City, N.Y.: Doubleday, Doran, 1929); republished as *The Saint Meets the Tiger* (New York: Sun Dial Press, 1940);

The Bandit (London & Melbourne: Ward, Lock, 1929; Garden City, N.Y.: Doubleday, Doran, 1930);

Daredevil (London & Melbourne: Ward, Lock, 1929; Garden City, N.Y.: Doubleday, Doran, 1929);

Enter the Saint (London: Hodder & Stoughton, 1930; Garden City, N.Y.: Doubleday, Doran, 1931);

Knight Templar (London: Hodder & Stoughton, 1930; republished as *The Avenging Saint* (Garden City, N.Y.: Doubleday, Doran, 1931; London: Pan Books, 1949);

The Last Hero (London: Hodder & Stoughton, 1930; Garden City, N.Y.: Doubleday, Doran, 1930); republished as *The Saint Closes the Case* (New York: Sun Dial Press, 1941; London: Pan Books, 1960); republished as *The Saint and the Last Hero* (New York: Avon Books, 1953);

Alias the Saint (London: Hodder & Stoughton, 1931); republished as *Wanted for Murder* (Garden City, N.Y.: Doubleday, Doran, 1931);

Featuring the Saint (London: Hodder & Stoughton, 1931); republished as *Wanted for Murder* (Garden City, N.Y.: Doubleday, Doran, 1931);

She Was a Lady (London: Hodder & Stoughton, 1931); republished as *Angels of Doom* (Garden City, N.Y.: Doubleday, Doran, 1932); republished as *The Saint Meets His Match* (London: Hodder & Stoughton, 1950; New York: Sun Dial, 1941);

Getaway (London: Hodder & Stoughton, 1932; Garden City, N.Y.: Doubleday, Doran,

Leslie Charteris

1933); republished as *Saint's Getaway* (Garden City, N.Y.: Sun Dial Press, 1933);

The Holy Terror (London: Hodder & Stoughton, 1932); republished as *The Saint vs. Scotland Yard* (Garden City, N.Y.: Doubleday, Doran, 1932; London: Pan Books, 1949);

The Brighter Buccaneer (London: Hodder & Stoughton, 1933; Garden City, N.Y.: Doubleday, Doran, 1933);

Once More the Saint (London: Hodder & Stoughton, 1933); republished as *The Saint and Mr. Teal* (Garden City, N.Y.: Doubleday, Doran, 1933; London: Hodder & Stoughton, 1950);

Boodle (London: Hodder & Stoughton, 1934); republished as *The Saint Intervenes* (Garden City, N.Y.: Doubleday, Doran, 1934);

The Misfortunes of Mr. Teal (London: Hodder & Stoughton, 1934; Garden City, N.Y.: Doubleday, Doran, 1934); republished as *The Saint in London* (New York: Sun Dial Press, 1941; London: Hodder & Stoughton, 1966);

The Saint Goes On (London: Hodder & Stoughton, 1934; Garden City, N.Y.: Doubleday, Doran 1935);

The Saint in New York (London: Hodder & Stoughton, 1935; Garden City, N.Y.: Doubleday, Doran, 1935);

The Saint Overboard (London: Hodder & Stoughton, 1936; Garden City, N.Y.: Doubleday, Doran, 1936);

The Ace of Knaves (London: Hodder & Stoughton, 1937; Garden City, N.Y.: Doubleday, Doran, 1937); republished as *The Saint in Action* (New York: Sun Dial Press, 1938);

Thieves' Picnic (London: Hodder & Stoughton, 1937; Garden City, N.Y.: Doubleday, Doran, 1937); republished as *The Saint Bids Diamonds* (New York: Triangle, 1942; London: Hodder and Stoughton, 1950); republished as *The Saint at a Thieves' Picnic* (New York: Avon, 1951);

Follow the Saint (Garden City, N.Y.: Doubleday, Doran, 1938; London: Hodder & Stoughton, 1939);

Prelude for War (London: Hodder & Stoughton, 1938; Garden City, N.Y.: Doubleday, Doran, 1938); republished as *The Saint Plays with Fire* (New York: Triangle, 1942; London: Hodder & Stoughton, 1951);

The First Saint Omnibus (London: Hodder & Stoughton, 1939; Garden City, N.Y.: Doubleday, Doran, 1939);

The Happy Highwayman (London: Hodder & Stoughton, 1939; Garden City, N.Y.: Doubleday, Doran, 1939);

The Saint in Miami (Garden City, N.Y.: Doubleday, Doran, 1940; London: Hodder & Stoughton, 1941);

The Saint Goes West (London: Hodder & Stoughton, 1942; Garden City, N.Y.: Doubleday, Doran, 1942);

The Saint Steps In (Garden City, N.Y.: Doubleday, Doran, 1943; London: Hodder & Stoughton, 1944);

The Saint on Guard (Garden City, N.Y.: Doubleday, 1944; London: Hodder & Stoughton, 1945); abridged as *The Sizzling Saboteur* (New York: Avon, 1956); abridged again as *The Saint on Guard* (New York: Avon, 1958);

Lady on a Train (Hollywood, Calif., 1945);

The Saint Sees It Through (Garden City, N.Y.: Doubleday, 1946; London: Hodder & Stoughton, 1947);

Call for the Saint (London: Hodder & Stoughton, 1948; Garden City, N.Y.: Doubleday, 1948);

Saint Errant (Garden City, N.Y.: Doubleday, 1948; London: Hodder & Stoughton, 1949);

The Second Saint Omnibus (Garden City, N.Y.: Doubleday, 1951; London: Hodder & Stoughton, 1952);

The Saint in Europe (Garden City, N.Y.: Doubleday, 1953; London: Hodder & Stoughton, 1954);

The Saint on the Spanish Main (Garden City, N.Y.: Doubleday, 1955; London: Hodder & Stoughton, 1956);

The Saint Around the World (Garden City, N.Y.: Doubleday, 1956; London: Hodder & Stoughton, 1957);

Thanks to the Saint (Garden City, N.Y.: Doubleday, 1957; London: Hodder & Stoughton, 1958);

Señor Saint (Garden City, N.Y.: Doubleday, 1958; London: Hodder & Stoughton, 1959);

The Saint to the Rescue (Garden City, N.Y.: Doubleday, 1959; London: Hodder & Stoughton, 1961);

Trust the Saint (Garden City, N.Y.: Doubleday, 1962; London: Hodder & Stoughton, 1962);

The Saint in the Sun (Garden City, N.Y.: Doubleday, 1963; London: Hodder & Stoughton, 1964);

Spanish for Fun (London: Hodder & Stoughton, 1964);

Vendetta for the Saint (Garden City, N.Y.: Doubleday, 1964; London: Hodder & Stoughton, 1965);

The Saint in Pursuit (Garden City, N.Y.: Doubleday, 1970; London: Hodder & Stoughton, 1971);

The Saint and the People Importers (London: Hodder Paperbacks, 1971; Garden City, N.Y.: Doubleday, 1972);

Paleneo: A Universal Sign Language (London: Hodder & Stoughton for Interlix A. G., 1972).

MOTION PICTURES: *The Saint's Double Trouble,* screenplay by Charteris and Ben Holmes, RKO, 1940;

The Saint's Vacation, screenplay by Charteris and Jeffrey Dell, RKO, 1941;

The Saint in Palm Springs, screen story by Charteris, RKO, 1941;

Lady on a Train, screen story by Charteris, Universal, 1945;

River Gang, screenplay by Charteris, Universal, 1945;

Two Smart People, screenplay by Charteris and Ethel Hill, MGM, 1946;

Tarzan and the Huntress, screenplay by Charteris, Jerry Grushkin, and Rowland Leigh, RKO, 1947.

OTHER: Juan Belmonte y Garcia and Manuel Chaves Nogales, *Juan Belmonte, Killer of Bulls: The Autobiography of a Matador,* translated by Charteris (London: Heinemann, 1937; Garden City, N.Y.: Doubleday, Doran, 1937);

The Saint Meets The Tiger, introduction by Charteris (Indianapolis: Charter, 1980).

Leslie Charteris is the creator of Simon Templar (the Saint), best known of the modern gentleman outlaws and hero of the longest-running fictional series written by a single author.

Charteris was born in Singapore on 12 May 1907 and learned to speak Chinese and Malay before he learned the English alphabet. At the age of ten he acquired his first typewriter and, as he later remarked, "promptly began to write for money." He produced several issues of an ambitious newsletter which included features, puzzles, and illustrations. The illustrations were matchstick figures of the type which Charteris later used as his famous Saint logotype.

Charteris's father, S. C. Yin, was a surgeon, businessman, and civic leader. He was also an enthusiastic traveler, and by the time Charteris reached adolescence his parents had taken him around the world three times. Until he was twelve years old Charteris was educated privately. Apart from his formal studies he was an avid reader, especially of boys' adventure fiction of the type found in the *Chums* serials. He also worked his way through an entire encyclopedia.

In 1919 Charteris left Singapore for England. He was enrolled in Falconbury School, Purley, Surrey, until 1922 and then in Rosall School, Fleetwood, Lancashire, until 1924.

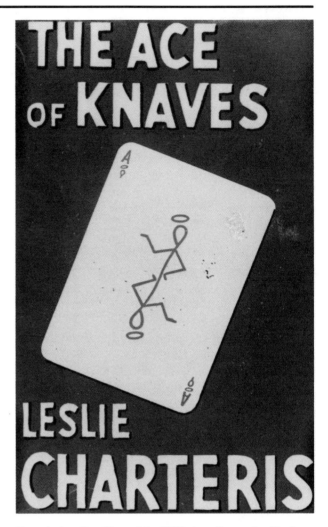

Dust jacket for Charteris's 1937 installment in his long-running series recounting the adventures of Simon Templar, alias the Saint (courtesy of Otto Penzler)

Charteris disliked school intensely, although his size, athletic ability, and unwillingness to tolerate any nonsense discouraged his schoolmates from bullying him. He particularly disliked the policy of strict regimentation which was characteristic of British public schools at that time. He could discipline himself to do whatever he had to in order to reach what he regarded as worthwhile goals, but mortification for its own sake—for example, poor food, early rising, and cold baths—struck him as pointless. He was even less impressed by the stereotyped thought patterns which he was expected to adopt as his own. When he ran the school magazine, it was frequently censored or suppressed because of his unorthodox editorial policies and opinions. This rebellious attitude toward precedent and authority became the basis of both the content and the style of some of his best stories.

Charteris entered King's College, Cambridge, after what he later described as "an interregnum of agreeable debauchery in Paris, playing at being an art student and learning fluent French by osmosis." He read law for one year and passed the first part of his tripos, but when his first novel was accepted for publication, he decided that he had had all the formal education he needed. In spite of his parents' protests, he left Cambridge and began a career as a freelance writer. He was nineteen years of age.

Charteris's first novel, *X Esquire* (1927), was his fourth publication. At the age of eleven he had had a poem accepted in a boys' magazine; at sixteen he had sold a short story; and in January 1925 Hutchinson's *Sovereign Magazine* had published the short story "One Crowded Hour." *X Esquire* is a highly improbable story about a masked hero who deals out justice to criminals who are, for one reason or another, beyond the reach of the law. The Saint would later carry out the same kind of justice, but far more convincingly. In *X Esquire* the police are incredibly cooperative, going so far as to place the archvillain under house arrest in order to allow the hero to murder him by lifting him into the air and snapping his back across a chair. Charteris later referred to *X Esquire* as "an appallingly bad book."

Although he continued to write thriller stories, Charteris found it necessary to undertake other forms of employment in order to support himself during the years before he became an established author. He drove a bus during the English general strike of 1926, served as an auxiliary policeman, blew up balloons for a game booth in a traveling fair, and worked as a bartender and as a professional bridge player. He went to Malaya to prospect for gold and to fish for pearls, but he also accepted less glamorous jobs such as working in a tin mine and on a rubber plantation.

In 1926 Charteris changed his name by deed poll from Leslie Charles Bowyer Yin to Leslie Charles Charteris Bowyer-Ian. Since he was not yet of legal age he had to accede to his father's wishes in the matter of the surname, but he referred to himself thereafter as Leslie Charteris. In 1946, when he became an American citizen, he changed his name formally to Leslie Charteris.

Charteris's second novel, *The White Rider* (1928), is overwritten and poorly constructed, but it is an improvement over *X Esquire.* Its hero, Peter Lestrange, shows traces of the lounging,

laughing, impudent buccaneer who would eventually emerge as the Saint. Although this book, like *X Esquire,* contains echoes of Sapper (Herman Cyril McNeile) and Edgar Wallace, Charteris's own style was beginning to emerge.

In *Meet The Tiger* (1928) Charteris created the character of Simon Templar, although he had at that time no idea of making him a series hero. Templar is twenty-seven years of age, over six feet tall, lean and strong, black-haired and blue-eyed, irreverent, adventuresome, and charming. Charteris would later regret having given Templar's age in this book, since it naturally raised questions when, fifty years later, the Saint was still vaulting over fences or even, it is tastefully suggested, into beds. At the time, however, Templar was only one of a series of heroes who embodied Charteris's emerging view of the ideal man.

Meet the Tiger also introduced Patricia Holm, the Saint's first and most important romantic interest. Unlike many early thriller heroines, beautiful blond Patricia is far from being helpless. Although she appeals to the Saint for assistance, she herself plays an active and courageous role not only in this adventure but also in several of the later stories.

The hero of Charteris's next book, *The Bandit* (1929; originally published as a serial entitled *The Black Cat* in the *Empire News),* is unique in the British thriller literature of that period. Ramon Francisco de Castila y Espronceda Manrique is, as his name suggests, the antithesis of the big, beefy, British hero epitomized in Sapper's Bulldog Drummond. Manrique is unashamedly Latin, with sleek black hair, an equally sleek moustache, a small build, and non-English manners. Charteris's rejection of the mindless xenophobia of writers like Sapper and Dornford Yates (Cecil William Mercer) could hardly have been expressed more strongly. Although he did not write another novel about Manrique, Charteris reminded his readers of him when, in "The Inland Revenue" (*The Holy Terror,* 1932), he credited the Saint with having written a thriller novel with a "dago" hero.

Daredevil (1929) also anticipates the Saint stories and novels. It features a hero with the unlikely name of Storm Arden, who is cast in the same mold as Charteris's character Peter Lestrange. One of the supporting characters in *Daredevil* was to become part of the Saint saga as Templar's constantly frustrated would-be nemesis, Chief Inspector Teal of Scotland Yard. Teal's characterization is reasonably complete: chubby, deceptively somnolent, competent, and cautious (" 'Fat men didn't ought to touch alcohol,' " he frequently observes). He works with Storm Arden in *Daredevil*.

Charteris's early work attracted the attention of Percy Montague Haydon, controlling editor of a group of weekly and monthly periodicals owned by the Amalgamated Press. Haydon was particularly interested in a new (in 1929) weekly periodical, the *Thriller*, which featured detective and adventure stories. He persuaded Edgar Wallace, with some difficulty and for a high fee, to write "Red Aces" for the first issue. He then persuaded Charteris, with less difficulty and for a much lower fee, to write "The Story of a Dead Man" for the fourth issue. Charteris's "The Secret of Beacon Inn" appeared in the ninth issue, and after that he became a regular contributor. Haydon, who became one of Charteris's closest friends, later provided the inspiration for the character of Monty Hayward, one of the Saint's companions in adventure.

At this point in his career Charteris began using a series hero rather than creating a new hero for each story. Since most of Charteris's heroes were of the same general type, it saved him the trouble of inventing new details for each one. It also increased the popularity of the stories by inducing readers to become interested in the continuing adventures of a familiar character. Charteris chose Simon Templar as his series hero and placed him at the head of a gang known as the Five Kings. The Saint was the joker, and his companions represented the four suits.

The stories in the *Five Kings* series were later revised and reprinted in such books as *The Last Hero* (1930), *Knight Templar* (1930), and *The Holy Terror*. Several of Charteris's other stories were also revised and reprinted in book form, with the Saint replacing the original hero. "The Story of a Dead Man," for example, appeared in *Featuring the Saint* (1931), with Simon Templar in the role originally played by a character named Jimmy Traill. In the same book, "The Secret of Beacon Inn" became "The National Debt," and the name of the original hero–Rameses Smith–became an alias for the Saint. Charteris later experimented with a different series hero, Lyn Peveril, but after writing three Peveril stories he decided that the Saint was the better character.

The Saint is a multifaceted character whose startling shifts from laughing mischief to utter deadliness account for a good deal of his popularity. Like Robin Hood, with whom he is often compared, he robs from the rich to give to the poor–less his substantial commission, which he calls his "collection fee." But the Saint's victims are always corrupt in some way, and his fleecing of them is presented as a kind of justice.

The justice that the Saint represents can, on occasion, extend beyond mere robbery. The Saint believes that while capital punishment may not deter members of the general public from committing crimes, it certainly deters its object from committing any more. Charteris eventually stopped writing stories in which the Saint deliberately and passionlessly executes someone, not because he softened toward criminals but because he began to feel that evil is too pervasive and too complex to be substantially reduced by the death of one individual. He concluded, therefore, that it is misleadng to write scenes which result in a sense of purification when a villain who has seemed to embody evil (and thereby to limit it) is destroyed. However, Charteris never apologized for the hard line that the Saint takes in the earlier books. Pestered about the real-life implications of the Saint's actions, Charteris said, "I was writing adventure stories, not sociological theses."

Even in the stories which include premeditated killings, such as *The Last Hero, Knight Templar,* "The Impossible Crime" (*Alias the Saint*, 1931), "The Million Pound Day" (*The Holy Terror*), *The Saint in New York* (1935), and "The Well-Meaning Mayor" (*The Happy Highwayman*, 1939), the Saint is never presented as a bully. He is always willing to risk his own life in order to administer justice in cases in which the law is hopelessly entangled in its own red tape. He has no license to kill, and despite the private sympathy of individual police officers, he seldom has the support of the law. He pits his wit and skill against the wit and skill of his adversaries, sharing with them the additional danger of police interference.

In 1931 Charteris married his first wife, Pauline Schishkin. They had one daughter, Patricia Ann. Their marriage ended in divorce in 1937. Charteris was married and divorced twice more before meeting his present wife, the former actress Audrey Long. They have been married since 1952.

Having heard that American magazines paid much higher rates for stories than British magazines did, Charteris left England for the United States in 1932. His stories sold well there, so he moved to Hollywood, where he wrote film stories and screenplays. He also wrote *The Saint in New York*, the story of Templar's defeat of highly placed New York racketeers. *The Saint in New York* (published first in the *American Magazine* and then in book form) sold better in both the United States and Britain than anything Charteris had written before. Further, its popularity inspired readers to look for copies of his earlier books. Charteris's decision to use a series hero proved to be a commercial as well as a literary success, and the Saint saga was firmly established.

By 1936 the popularity of the Saint was great enough to warrant the establishment of a fan club, the Saint Club, which is still in existence. In conformity with the Robin Hood ideals of the Saint himself, the club dues and the small profits derived from the sale of merchandise (e.g., ties, key chains, photographs, stationery) were used to support an eight-bed ward in the Invalid and Crippled Children's Hospital, Plaistow. When the advent of nationalized medicine made it unnecessary for the club to continue its support of the hospital, these funds were donated to the Arbour Youth Centre in the London district of Stepney. Each member of the club receives a rule book, a membership card, and an annual appeal for funds for the youth center, written by Charteris himself.

The popularity of the Saint continued to grow, and in 1938 RKO purchased the film rights to the character and began their series with *The Saint in New York* (1938). The script was reasonably faithful to the original story, but RKO's choice of a leading actor was unfortunate. Louis Hayward, a small man with a nervous manner and a rapid delivery, failed to convey the sense of authority and the drawling humor which the role required. RKO's next choice, George Sanders, played the Saint in five films: *The Saint Strikes Back* (1939; based on the 1931 Saint novel *She Was a Lady*), *The Saint in London* (1939; based on "The Million Pound Day" in *The Holy Terror*), *The Saint's Double Trouble* (1940; original story), *The Saint Takes Over* (1940; original story), and *The Saint in Palm Springs* (1941; original story, later published in *The Saint Goes West*, 1942). The best of these films is unquestionably *The Saint in London*, directed by John Paddy Carstairs, a friend of Charteris who had a good deal of sympathy with the character and with the spirit of the Saint stories. Unfortunately, although Sanders's build and features were ideal for the part, his sneering insolence and excessively slow pacing robbed the character of the air of dash and daring which is his trademark. Moreover, Sanders's

Charteris in the late 1930s

performance, particularly in the later films, gave audiences the impression that he was unbearably bored with the role–as indeed he was. Sanders's increasing boredom was understandable, since the scripts became worse and worse. Charteris is credited with having written two scripts and written the screen story for one other, but the producers paid little attention to his observations about the lack of originality and even of logic in the scripts which were finally filmed. Charteris was so appalled by the results that when he was told that a New York movie house had been criticized for showing *The Saint's Double Trouble* at a children's performance, he agreed with the protestors. "After all," he asked, "what had those wretched innocent little children done to deserve being forced to sit through such a dull stupid film as that?"

RKO tried filming two more stories, *The Saint's Vacation* (1941; based on the 1932 *Getaway*) and *The Saint Meets the Tiger* (1943; based on *Meet the Tiger*), with a British actor, Hugh Sinclair, in the title role. However, his portrayal of the Saint as a dashing and deadly desperado was seriously undermined by his inability to fire a gun without squeezing his eyes shut. In the final RKO Saint film, *The Saint's Girl Friday* (1954; also called *The Saint Returns* and *The Saint's Return*), Louis Hayward was no more impressive than he had been sixteen years earlier. Two Saint films were made in France, one with Felix Marten and one with Jean Marais, but they were of such poor quality that Charteris refused to allow them to be shown outside of France or to allow any more French Saint films to be made. In 1941 RKO cast George Sanders (followed by his brother, Tom Conway) as the Falcon, a series hero allegedly based on the hero of Michael Arlen's story "The Gay Falcon" (1940). These films were so similar to the Saint films, however, that Charteris won a lawsuit against RKO, and the company was ordered to terminate the series.

Although Charteris had no desire to appear in films as Simon Templar, he did play the role of the Saint in a photographic version of *The Saint in Palm Springs* which appeared in *Life* magazine in May 1941. This pictorial presentation was originally intended to commemorate the centennial of the publication of Edgar Allan Poe's "Murders in the Rue Morgue."

In 1944 NBC Radio began a series of *Saint* programs. The Saint was played by several actors: Edgar Barrier, Brian Aherne (in Charteris's opinion, the best), Barry Sullivan, Vincent Price, and Tom Conway. The Saint also appeared in comic strip form in several newspapers, including the *New York Herald Tribune*, the *London Evening Standard*, and the *Manchester Evening News*. Charteris, who had written the comic strip *Secret Agent X-9* in the 1930s, produced these comics himself for ten years. A second series of *Saint* comic strips was produced some years later, but they were written by other authors under Charteris's supervision.

By this time Charteris was spending most of his time in the United States; and on 27 July 1946 he became an American citizen. He lived for a time in California, then settled in Florida. During the summers he toured the country in a trailer which he had designed himself. He later purchased a home in Michigan.

During the years before World War II Charteris wrote stories in which the Saint encountered a succession of individual villains—murderers, con men, thieves, drug dealers—and dealt with them summarily and effectively. At the end of the adventure the reader was satisfied that the villain was thoroughly eliminated and that the world was a little cleaner than it had been before. With the rise of Nazism, however, the importance of individual villains began to wane. As Charteris explained in his foreword to *The Second Saint Omnibus* (1951), once World War II began,

something had to be lost from the Saint stories. If the Saint continued to fight individual villains, who were by then a relatively minor threat to world security, their defeat would seem correspondingly insignificant. If, on the other hand, the Saint tackled the Nazi menace, his contribution would have to be seen as one among thousands. "And never could there be the complete catharsis of the old formula—the villain defeated, the crime foiled or avenged, and the sun shining again, all through the cleverness and courage of one crusader with whom a reader might identify himself."

The austerity which accompanied World War II affected not only the plots of the Saint books but also the character of the Saint himself. He had begun to lose some of his flamboyance even before the war began, but even what might otherwise have remained of his boyish exuberance would have been out of place in the wartime novels. Delight in the game of danger is an admirable quality when one is risking one's own life voluntarily; but it would have been an unthinkably callous reaction to opportunities for adventure which arose from the sufferings caused by the war. Some of the Saint's self-sufficiency, too, was lost in the wartime novels. In order to do anything at all against fifth columnists, saboteurs, and spies, he needed at least some support from an organization. This was provided through the mysterious Mr. Hamilton in Washington, who gave the Saint information, transportation, and supplies, and occasionally drew his attention to a conspiracy that he could not otherwise have discovered. Therefore, although the Saint's courage and ingenuity played their part in the Allied cause, the wartime stories lacked the glamour of the earlier books; and no one understood why this was so better than Charteris himself did. "To be one of the million ants that dragged down the dragon is a noble thing, you have been taught to think, and you accept it; but it is not the same as being Saint George in your own shining armor, with your foot on the dragon's neck, and your single sword in its heart."

Even after World War II was over, the Saint could not go back to his earlier way of life. He did not age year by year, but neither did he remain fixed in a state of extended adolescence; and the ebullience that he had displayed as a younger man would have been inappropriate in the more mature Saint of the postwar books. William Vivian Butler, in his study of the Saint, divides his development into stages: the *Meet the*

Tiger Saint (not yet a major hero), the very British Saint (an impudent rakehell), the Anglo-American Saint (an older, more polished man of the world), the wartime Saint (the "next-best-thing-to-a-G-man Saint"), and the cosmopolitan Saint who emerged after World War II and flourished for fifteen years. As Butler observes, "there's something a little lost and melancholy" about the quieter, more cynical Simon Templar who wanders alone from one hotel to another, enjoying the company of numerous acquaintances but separated permanently from the close friends of the earlier books. Charteris was often asked to bring back the earlier supporting characters, especially Patricia Holm, but he was no longer interested in writing that kind of story. The Saint's lone-wolf isolation was an important part of the character as Charteris now saw him because it was the logical consequence of the choices that Charteris had allowed the Saint to make. A wandering buccaneer cannot expect domestic comfort or the continued companionship of devoted friends who have, after all, their own lives to live; and, in an increasingly complex world, he cannot expect that an attack on a villain will achieve the same results that it used to.

Although the postwar Saint stories lack some of the fun and excitement of the earlier books, they are, on the whole, more imaginative and better written. In his earlier stories Charteris had often devised clever and original methods of inverting confidence tricks so that they backfired on the would-be swindlers; now he applied the same kind of ironic inversion to a wide range of literary conventions. For example, in "The Reluctant Nudist" (which had the distinction of appearing in the *Continental Nudist* magazine as well as in *The Saint Around the World,* 1956) Charteris reverses several clichés. What appears to be the hackneyed story of a wealthy uncle supporting a dependent nephew turns out to be just the reverse; and certain generally accepted standards of behavior, such as the desirability of holding a steady job in order to keep clothes on one's back, are subjected to subtle but effective mockery. In "The Sporting Chance" (*The Saint Around the World,*) the Saint becomes, literally, a fisher of men; and in "The Perfect Sucker" (*Thanks to the Saint,* 1957) the con artist is honest and the would-be victim just misses becoming an unwilling thief.

Many of the Saint's postwar adventures display a depth of human understanding which was missing from the earlier thrillers. In "The Spanish Cow" (*The Saint in Europe,* 1953), for example, the Saint is touched by the pain of a loud and unattractive woman who would, in an earlier story, have been nothing more than the disagreeable female she first appears to be. In another story, "The Pearls of Peace" (*Sẽnor Saint,* 1958), the Saint robs a blind man of beads which the man believes to be pearls in order to allow him to keep the one thing of real value that he has. In stories like these Charteris focused on the kind of experience which is less dramatic and less exciting, but more real and more universal, than the blood-and-thunder heroics of the earlier books.

In addition to writing new Saint stories Charteris edited the *Saint Mystery Magazine* (also known as the *Saint Detective Magazine* and the *Saint Magazine*) which he started in the spring of 1953. The *Saint Magazine* usually included an editorial by Charteris, a new or reprinted Saint story (or, in later issues, an article by Charteris entitled "Instead of the Saint"), and mystery stories by other writers, including Agatha Christie, Dorothy L. Sayers, E. Phillips Oppenheim, Sax Rohmer, and Wallace. The magazine, which ran for 141 issues, was one of the better examples of this type of publication. It was interesting and literate and, for a time, commercially successful. The American edition eventually had a circulation of eight million and the British edition (sold in Great Britain and in the Commonwealth countries) reached a similar figure. The French and Dutch editions had circulations of five million copies each. However, as competition became keener and as the supply of Saint stories ran low and other stories became more difficult to acquire, the *Saint Magazine* ceased production. The last issue appeared in October 1967.

During the 1950s and early 1960s Charteris received offers for the television rights to the Saint. However, remembering what producers, directors, and scriptwriters had done to the character in the RKO films, he was not anxious to rush into a television series. Eventually, Robert Baker of Tempean Films made him an acceptable offer. Charteris did try to maintain the greatest possible control over the series, primarily by insisting upon having approval of both the synopsis and the completed script of each episode in advance of filming. However, the producer and the script supervisor, concerned with the probable reactions of British and American audiences and American sponsors, and immersed in the practical problems of filming at high speed and on widely varied locations, often disagreed with

Charteris's comments. He was particularly incensed by the tendency of the scriptwriters and the script supervisor to reverse his inverted clichés, so that instead of surprise endings the stories had conventional endings. For example, in writing the script for "The Reluctant Nudist" under the title "The Persistent Patriots," the television writers not only eliminated the nudists, which, of course, they had to do, but also made the nephew dependent upon the uncle, spoiling the whole point of the story. Another source of annoyance was the scriptwriters' policy of softening the Saint's reactions to criminals. In the original script of "Recoil," for example, a criminal falls off a fire escape and the Saint looks "shaken." Although Charteris realized that television taboos made it impossible for the Saint to throw the man over the railing himself, he did feel that "At least this is a chance to get over some of the Saint's real toughness. Let him just look grim, tight-lipped, and cold." In the end, the shot of the Saint after the villain's fall was eliminated altogether. Often, however, Charteris was simply told that the changes he had suggested could not be implemented for various reasons, and the television Saint was a much milder figure than the Saint of the books ever was.

The choice of an actor to play the Saint on television was, of course, a serious matter. At first it seemed almost certain that Patrick McGoohan, who had played the lead in *Danger Man* and would later write and star in *The Prisoner*, would play the role of the Saint. However, he lacked the humor and the touch of devilment which were important to the role. He also objected, at that time, to playing any part which required him to use a gun. Roger Moore, who had played the leads in *Ivanhoe*, *The Alaskans*, and *Maverick* (after playing second lead to James Garner), actively sought the role of the Saint. At first it was thought that he was too young and too good-looking to play the Saint, but in time most of those who had had reservations—including Charteris—came to regard Moore as quite a good Saint. As Butler observes, "Moore may not have been everyone's idea of the Saint (I doubt if any actor could be), but he caught the rather difficult note of mischievous authority brilliantly."

The original Saint series ran for 118 one-hour episodes, the first 71 in black and white and the remaining episodes in color. Production began in March 1962 and ended in August 1968. It was an extremely popular program and was eventually dubbed into several languages and shown all over the world. Two two-part episodes, *The Saint and the Fiction-Makers* and *Vendetta for the Saint,* were made into feature films. Ten years after the end of the first series Robert Baker produced a second series, this time with Ian Ogilvy in the title role. Unfortunately, this series was allotted very poor time slots in both Britain and the United States, and it ran for only one season.

When the television writers had used up most of the original Saint stories, they began creating new plots for the television scripts. Some of the better scripts were later adapted into book form, reversing the usual process of adapting a book into a script. Although Charteris had not written these stories, he supervised the adaptations very closely, and he revised the completed stories before they were published in book form. Later, he supervised the adaption into book form of some of Donne Avenell's outlines for the *Saint* comic strips.

Charteris's corrections and revisions of the material submitted to him by these collaborators were often substantial. For example, in the original draft of "The Pastor's Problem" (*Count on the Saint,* 1980) the Saint quickly befriends a man accused of having assaulted an old woman. Charteris pointed out to the adapter, Graham Weaver, that the Saint would hardly have been sympathetic to one accused of such a crime. He also pointed out the implausibility of a sequence in which the accused man, having escaped from the police, remained in the neighborhood until they caught him again. The final story, which incorporates Charteris's suggestions, is quite different from the original draft.

Despite the demands made on his time by the Saint books, films, magazines, comic strips, and television programs, Charteris has always enjoyed a variety of activities. For years he was an enthusiastic deep-sea fisherman and was involved in many other sporting activities. He is a recognized, if sometimes unorthodox, connoisseur of food and wine and has written a number of articles on the subject. From 1966 until 1968 he wrote a regular column for *Gourmet* magazine. Although he is not an admirer of Sir Arthur Conan Doyle's work, Charteris, collaborating with Anthony Boucher (as Denis Green) on the scripts for a Sherlock Holmes radio series, wrote more Holmes stories than Conan Doyle had.

One of Charteris's most important interests apart from the Saint is the study of language. He has long held the belief that the most boring and least practical way to learn a language is to study its grammar, and he supported this point of view by writing *Spanish for Fun* (1964), an unconventional but effective explanation of functional Spanish usage. He also created Paleneo, a form of picture language which is based on concepts rather than on the words used to express those concepts in any particular language. The Paleneo sign for "fear," for example, is a pair of matchstick knees knocking together; "love" is a heart; and "nothing" is an empty circle. His book *Paleneo: A Universal Sign Language* was published in 1972.

Charteris and his wife presently divide their time between England and the south of France, with occasional visits to Ireland. He regards himself as retired and refuses all requests for interviews and personal appearances. He did, however, consent to write a new introduction for the Charter Books reprint of *The Saint Meets the Tiger* (1940), published in 1980. Looking back over his career as an author, Charteris writes, "I was always sure that there was a solid place in escape literature for a rambunctious adventurer such as I dreamed up in my own youth, who really believed in the old fashioned romantic ideals and was prepared to lay everything on the line to

bring them to life. . . . That is how and why the Saint was born, and why I hope he may eventually occupy a niche beside Robin Hood, d'Artagnan, and all the other immortal true heroes of legend. Anyway, on this date, I can say that I'll always be glad I tried."

References:
William Vivian Butler, *The Durable Desperadoes* (London: Macmillan, 1973);

William O. G. Lofts and Derek J. Adley, *The Saint and Leslie Charteris* (Bowling Green, Ohio: Popular Press, 1972);

John Nieminski, compiler, *The Saint Magazine Index: Authors and Titles Spring 1953-October 1967* (Owensboro, Ky.: Cook & McDowell, 1980);

Colin Watson, *Snobbery with Violence: Crime Stories and Their Audience* (London: Eyre & Spottiswoode, 1971), pp. 145ff.

Papers:
The Special Collections Room at Mugar Memorial Library, Boston University, houses the Leslie Charteris Collection, which includes correspondence, typescripts, screenplays, television and radio scripts, books, magazines, and memorabilia.

Agatha Christie

(15 September 1890-12 January 1976)

H. R. F. Keating

BOOKS: *The Mysterious Affair at Styles: A Detective Story* (London: Lane, 1920; New York: Dodd, Mead, 1927);

The Secret Adversary (London & New York: Lane, 1922; New York: Dodd, Mead, 1922);

The Murder on the Links (London: Lane, 1923; New York: Dodd, Mead, 1923);

Poirot Investigates (London: Lane, 1924; New York: Dodd, Mead, 1925);

The Secret of Chimneys (London: Lane, 1925; New York: Dodd, Mead, 1925);

The Road of Dreams (London: Bles, 1925); republished as *Poems* (London: Collins, 1973; New York: Dodd, Mead, 1973);

The Murder of Roger Ackroyd (London: Collins, 1926; New York: Dodd, Mead, 1926);

The Big Four (London: Collins, 1927; New York: Dodd, Mead, 1927);

The Mystery of the Blue Train (London: Collins, 1928; New York: Dodd, Mead, 1928);

Partners in Crime (London: Collins, 1929; New York: Dodd, Mead, 1929);

The Under Dog (London: Readers Library, 1929);

The Seven Dials Mystery (London: Collins, 1929; New York: Dodd, Mead, 1929);

Giant's Bread, as Mary Westmacott (London: Collins, 1930; Garden City, N.Y.: Doubleday, Doran, 1930);

The Murder at the Vicarage (New York: Dodd, Mead, 1930; London: Collins, 1935);

The Mysterious Mr. Quin (London: Collins, 1930; New York: Dodd, Mead, 1930);

The Floating Admiral, includes contributions by Christie, G. K. Chesterton, Dorothy L. Sayers, and others (London: Hodder & Stoughton, 1931; Garden City, N.Y.: Doubleday, Doran, 1932);

The Sittaford Mystery (London: Collins, 1931); republished as *The Murder at Hazelmoor* (New York: Dodd, Mead, 1931);

The Thirteen Problems (London: Collins, 1932); republished as *The Tuesday Club Murders* (New York: Dodd, Mead, 1933); republished as *Miss Marple's Final Cases* (London: Collins, 1972);

Agatha Christie (photograph by Popperfoto)

Peril at End House (London: Collins, 1932; New York: Dodd, Mead, 1932);

The Hound of Death and Other Stories (London: Odhams Press, 1933);

Lord Edgeware Dies (London: Collins, 1933); republished as *Thirteen at Dinner* (New York: Dodd, Mead, 1933);

Why Didn't They Ask Evans? (London: Collins, 1934); republished as *The Boomerang Clue* (New York: Dodd, Mead, 1935);

Murder on the Orient Express (London: Collins, 1934); republished as *Murder in the Calais Coach* (New York: Dodd, Mead, 1934);

Unfinished Portrait, as Westmacott (London: Collins, 1934; New York: Doubleday, 1934);

Parker Pyne Investigates (London: Collins, 1934); republished as *Mr. Parker Pyne, Detective* (New York: Dodd, Mead, 1934);

Black Coffee (London: Ashley, 1934; Boston: Baker, 1934);

The Listerdale Mystery and Other Stories (London: Collins, 1934);

Murder in Three Acts (New York: Dodd, Mead, 1934); republished as *Three Act Tragedy* (London: Collins, 1935);

Death in the Clouds (London: Collins, 1935); republished as *Death in the Air* (New York: Dodd, Mead, 1935);

The A.B.C. Murders: A New Poirot Mystery (London: Collins, 1936; New York: Dodd, Mead, 1936);

Cards on the Table (London: Collins, 1936; New York: Dodd, Mead, 1937);

Murder in Mesopotamia (London: Collins, 1936; New York: Dodd, Mead, 1936);

Murder in the Mews and Other Stories (London: Collins, 1937); republished as *Dead Man's Mirror and Other Stories* (New York: Dodd, Mead, 1937);

Death on the Nile (London: Collins, 1937; New York: Dodd, Mead, 1938);

Dumb Witness (London: Collins, 1937); republished as *Poirot Loses a Client* (New York: Dodd, Mead, 1937);

Appointment with Death (London: Collins, 1938; New York: Dodd, Mead, 1938);

Hercule Poirot's Christmas (London: Collins, 1938); republished as *Murder for Christmas* (New York: Dodd, Mead, 1939); republished as *A Holiday for Murder* (New York: Avon, 1947);

Murder Is Easy (London: Collins, 1939); republished as *Easy to Kill* (New York: Dodd, Mead, 1939);

Ten Little Niggers [novel] (London: Collins, 1939); republished as *And Then There Were None* (New York: Dodd, Mead, 1940);

The Regatta Mystery and Other Stories (New York: Dodd, Mead, 1939);

One, Two, Buckle My Shoe (London: Collins, 1940); republished as *The Patriotic Murders* (New York: Dodd, Mead, 1941);

Sad Cypress (London: Collins, 1940; New York: Dodd, Mead, 1940);

Evil Under the Sun (London: Collins, 1941; New York: Dodd, Mead, 1941);

N or M? (London: Collins, 1941; New York: Dodd, Mead, 1941);

The Body in the Library (London: Collins, 1942; New York: Dodd, Mead, 1942);

The Moving Finger (New York: Dodd, Mead, 1942; London: Collins, 1943);

Five Little Pigs (London: Collins, 1942); republished as *Murder in Retrospect* (New York: Dodd, Mead, 1942);

The Mystery of the Baghdad Chest (London: Bantam, 1943);

The Mystery of the Crime in Cabin 66 (London: Bantam, 1943);

Poirot and the Regatta Mystery (London: Bantam, 1943);

Poirot on Holiday (London: Todd, 1943);

Problem at Pollensa Bay, and The Christmas Adventure (London: Todd, 1943);

The Veiled Lady, and The Mystery of the Baghdad Chest (London: Todd, 1944);

Death Comes as the End (New York: Dodd, Mead, 1944; London: Collins, 1945);

Towards Zero [novel] (London: Collins, 1944; New York: Dodd, Mead, 1944);

Absent in the Spring, as Westmacott (London: Collins, 1944; New York: Farrar & Rinehart, 1944);

Ten Little Niggers [play] (London: French, 1945); republished as *Ten Little Indians* (New York & London: French, 1946);

Appointment with Death [play] (London: French, 1945);

Sparkling Cyanide (London: Collins, 1945); republished as *Remembered Death* (New York: Dodd, Mead, 1945);

The Hollow [novel] (London: Collins, 1946; New York: Dodd, Mead, 1946);

Poirot Knows the Murderer (London: Todd, 1946);

Murder on the Nile (New York: French, 1946; London: French, 1948);

Come, Tell Me How You Live, as Agatha Christie Mallowan (London: Collins, 1946; New York: Dodd, Mead, 1946);

The Labours of Hercules: Short Stories (London: Collins, 1947); republished as *Labors of Hercules: New Adventures in Crime by Hercule Poirot* (New York: Dodd, Mead, 1947);

Witness for the Prosecution and Other Stories (New York: Dodd, Mead, 1948);

The Rose and the Yew Tree, as Westmacott (London: Heinemann, 1948; New York: Rinehart, 1948);

Taken at the Flood (London: Collins, 1948); republished as *There Is a Tide* (New York: Dodd, Mead, 1948);

Crooked House (London: Collins, 1949; New York: Dodd, Mead, 1949);

The Mousetrap and Other Stories (New York: Dell, 1949); republished as *Three Blind Mice and Other Stories* (New York: Dodd, Mead, 1950);

A Murder Is Announced (London: Collins, 1950; New York: Dodd, Mead, 1950);

They Came to Baghdad (London: Collins, 1951; New York: Dodd, Mead, 1951);

The Under Dog and Other Stories (New York: Dodd, Mead, 1951);

They Do It with Mirrors (London: Collins, 1952); republished as *Murder with Mirrors* (New York: Dodd, Mead, 1952);

The Hollow [play] (London: French, 1952; New York: French, 1952);

Mrs. McGinty's Dead (London: Collins, 1952; New York: Dodd, Mead, 1952);

A Daughter's a Daughter, as Westmacott (London: Heinemann, 1952);

After the Funeral (London: Collins, 1953); republished as *Funerals Are Fatal* (New York: Dodd, Mead, 1953);

A Pocket Full of Rye (London: Collins, 1953; New York: Dodd, Mead, 1954);

The Mousetrap (New York: French, 1954; London: French, 1954);

Witness for the Prosecution [play] (London: French, 1954; New York: French, 1954);

Destination Unknown (London: Collins, 1954); republished as *So Many Steps to Death* (New York: Dodd, Mead, 1955);

Hickory, Dickory, Dock (London: Collins, 1955); republished as *Hickory, Dickory, Death* (New York: Dodd, Mead, 1955);

The Burden, as Westmacott (London: Heinemann, 1956);

Dead Man's Folly (London: Collins, 1956; New York: Dodd, Mead, 1956);

Spider's Web (London: French, 1957; New York: French, 1957);

4:50 from Paddington (London: Collins, 1957); republished as *What Mrs. McGillicuddy Saw!* (New York: Dodd, Mead, 1957);

Towards Zero [play], by Christie and Gerald Verner (New York: Dramatists Play Service, 1957; London: French, 1958);

Ordeal by Innocence (London: Collins, 1958; New York: Dodd, Mead, 1959);

Verdict (London: French, 1958);

The Unexpected Guest (London: French, 1958);

Cat among the Pigeons (London: Collins, 1959; New York: Dodd, Mead, 1960);

Go Back for Murder (London: French, 1960);

The Adventures of the Christmas Pudding, and Selection of Entrées (London: Collins, 1960);

Double Sin and Other Stories (New York: Dodd, Mead, 1961);

13 for Luck! A Selection of Mystery Stories for Young Readers (New York: Dodd, Mead, 1961; London: Collins, 1966);

The Mirror Crack'd from Side to Side (London: Collins, 1962); republished as *The Mirror Crack'd* (New York: Dodd, Mead, 1963);

Rule of Three: Afternoon at the Seaside, The Patient, The Rats, 3 volumes (London: French, 1963);

The Clocks (London: Collins, 1963; New York: Dodd, Mead, 1964);

A Caribbean Mystery (London: Collins, 1964; New York: Dodd, Mead, 1965);

Surprise! Surprise! (New York: Dodd, Mead, 1965);

At Bertram's Hotel (London: Collins, 1965; New York: Dodd, Mead, 1965);

Star Over Bethlehem and Other Stories, as Mallowan (London: Collins, 1965; New York: Dodd, Mead, 1965);

Third Girl (London: Collins, 1966; New York: Dodd, Mead, 1967);

13 Clues for Miss Marple (New York: Dodd, Mead, 1966);

Endless Night (London: Collins, 1967; New York: Dodd, Mead, 1968);

By the Pricking of My Thumbs (London: Collins, 1968; New York: Dodd, Mead, 1968);

Hallowe'en Party (London: Collins, 1969; New York: Dodd, Mead, 1969);

Passenger to Frankfurt (London: Collins, 1970; New York: Dodd, Mead, 1970);

The Golden Ball and Other Stories (New York: Dodd, Mead, 1971);

Nemesis (London: Collins, 1971; New York: Dodd, Mead, 1971);

Fiddlers Three (London: French, 1972);

Elephants Can Remember (London: Collins, 1972; New York: Dodd, Mead, 1972);

Akhnaton (London: Collins, 1973; New York: Dodd, Mead, 1973);

Postern of Fate (London: Collins, 1973; New York: Dodd, Mead, 1973);

Hercule Poirot's Early Cases (London: Collins, 1974; New York: Dodd, Mead, 1974);

Miss Marple's Final Cases (London: Collins, 1974);

Murder on Board (New York: Dodd, Mead, 1974);

Curtain: Hercule Poirot's Last Case (London: Collins, 1975; New York: Dodd, Mead, 1975);

Sleeping Murder (London: Collins, 1976; New York: Dodd, Mead, 1976);

Christie in Paris, 1906 (courtesy of the Estate of Agatha Christie)

An Autobiography (London: Collins, 1977; New York: Dodd, Mead, 1977);

The Mousetrap and Other Plays (New York: Dodd, Mead, 1978).

PLAY PRODUCTIONS: *Black Coffee*, London, Embassy Theatre, 8 December 1930;

Ten Little Niggers, adapted from Christie's novel, London, St. James's Theatre, 17 October 1943; produced again as *Ten Little Indians*, New York, Broadhurst Theatre, 27 June 1944, 425 [performances];

Appointment with Death, adapted from Christie's novel, London, Piccadilly Theatre, 31 March 1945;

Murder on the Nile, adapted from Christie's *Death on the Nile*, London, Ambassadors' Theatre, 19 March 1946; produced again as *Hidden Horizon*, New York, Plymouth Theatre, 19 September 1946, 12;

The Hollow, adapted from Christie's novel, London, Fortune Theatre, 7 June 1951;

The Mousetrap, adapted from Christie's *Three Blind Mice*, London, Ambassadors' Theatre, 25 November 1952; New York, Maidman Playhouse, 5 November 1960;

Witness for the Prosecution, adapted from Christie's story, London, Winter Garden Theatre, 28 October 1953; New York, Henry Miller's Theatre, 16 December 1954, 645;

Spider's Web, London, Savoy Theatre, 14 December 1954; New York, Lolly's Theatre Club, 15 January 1974;

Towards Zero, adapted by Christie and Gerald Verner from Christie's novel, London, St. James's Theatre, 4 September 1956;

Verdict, London, Strand Theatre, 22 May 1958;

The Unexpected Guest, London, Duchess Theatre, 12 August 1958;

Go Back for Murder, adapted from Christie's *Five Little Pigs*, London, Duchess Theatre, 23 March 1960;

Rule of Three: Afternoon at the Seaside, The Patient, and *The Rats*, London, Duchess Theatre, 20 December 1962;

Fiddlers Three, London, 1971; Southsea, 1972;

Akhnaton and Nefertiti, New York, 1979.

RADIO: *The Mousetrap*, BBC, 1952;
Personal Call, BBC, 1960.

Agatha Christie is a towering figure in the history of crime literature for two reasons. First, she consolidated the form of the pure mystery novel, achieving in five or six of her books puzzle stories that set a standard unlikely ever to be decisively bettered. Second, she sold more books than any other writer except Shakespeare. Totaling her sales was a task that defeated her agent and publishers. Her works have been translated into more than a hundred languages. She was, in short, the most successful mystery writer the world has known.

To some extent Christie's extraordinary success can be attributed to timing. Christie began writing at the start of the Golden Age of the detective story, when mysteries were attaining worldwide popularity. As she continued to turn out books, her name became in the public mind almost a shorthand expression for the genre. Her increasing popularity had little to do with the ordinary processes of publishing publicity. Christie was a particularly retiring person; she would not have subjected herself to book-promotion appearances, and she gave very few interviews during the latter part of her life. Nor was her popularity greatly aided by translation to other media. Until almost the end of her life, the films that were made from her books were by no means great successes. Her works were not seen on television until after her death. The plays she wrote gained from the popularity of the books rather than contributed to it (though one, *The Mousetrap*, has been perennially successful, running for more than twenty-five years in London). Her work gained wide popularity in part because she wrote in plain, good English with ample dialogue. She usually sketched her characters with the lightest of touches so that they could be imaginatively fleshed out by readers from any country to fit their own particular backgrounds. Above all, she told a simple story in a straightforward manner, rarely injecting any thoughts and feelings of her own.

Perhaps she owed this last virtue to her earliest upbringing. Born in the English seaside resort of Torquay to Frederick Alvah Miller, an American with private means, and Clarissa Boehmer Miller, she never attended school, nor did she have a governess. Her mother had come to believe in an educational theory that held that the female child's mind ought to be left alone to receive its own impressions. Mrs. Christie went so far as to say that Agatha Christie (unlike her older sister, who attended the well-known girls' school Roedean) should not learn to read before the age of eight. Christie, however, taught herself to read by asking her nursemaid the names of shops they passed on their walks and comparing them with the names over their doors. Once she mastered the art, she was allowed to read voraciously. Freed of most of the customary duties of the schoolchild, she had time to give her imagination free rein, and she created in her head a whole school of her own peopled by girls to whom she gave vivid and distinctive characters, remembered clearly long afterwards when she wrote her autobiography. She also began to write stories and at the age of eleven a poem that was published in the local newspaper. Yet she had no youthful ambition to become a writer and indeed well after she had achieved regular publication did not think of herself in that light.

Christie's quiet and happy days in Torquay, which may account for the fundamental state of contentment that underlies her books, came to an end when she went to France to study singing and piano. She achieved enough proficiency to raise the possibility of concert appearances, but her considerable nervousness (she remained shy

with strangers all her life) precluded a performing career. However, her musicality almost certainly accounts for the gift of timing that was to be an essential part of her success as a writer of fiction.

Back in Torquay from her studies in France, Christie rejected an army officer to whom she had been unofficially engaged and fell in love with Archibald Christie, who was about to join the hazardous Flying Corps. They were married on Christmas Eve in 1914, and Archibald Christie immediately returned to his duties while his wife resumed her nursing work at Torquay in a Voluntary Aid Detachment.

Before long she transferred from nursing to working in the dispensary of a local hospital, and it was during lulls in the activity there that she began, in response to a challenge from her sister, to piece together the plot and characters for a detective story. Inspired by a number of Belgian refugees living in the vicinity, she created the character Hercule Poirot and eventually completed the manuscript of his first case, *The Mysterious Affair at Styles* (1920). Six publishers rejected it, but it was eventually taken by John Lane in London for the sum of twenty-five pounds. It was not published in America until 1927.

It is hard to understand why the book found so little favor with publishers. It is a good example of its genre and one that bears reading or rereading more than sixty years after its publication. Set in a large country house during the war, it tells of the murder of a somewhat despotic old lady "with a fondness for opening bazaars and playing the Lady Bountiful," recently married for the second time to a mysterious bearded man, Alfred Inglethorp, who rules the roost. A Belgian policeman refugee, one of the beneficiaries of Mrs. Inglethorpe's charity, comes eventually to unravel an extremely complicated crime.

The story is told through the eyes of Captain Hastings, a wounded officer convalescing with his friend Mrs. Inglethorpe's son at Styles Court. Hastings had met Hercule Poirot in Belgium long before, and, slow-witted though he is, he has ambitions to set up as "a Sherlock Holmes" himself. Indeed, the descent of the Poirot/Hastings pair from the Holmes/Watson pair is clear, and it is deliberate on the part of the author. She said in *An Autobiography* (1977) that, in thinking about what to call her detective, she felt he ought to have "rather a grand name—one of those names that Sherlock Holmes and

Christie in 1926, at the time of her nine-day disappearance, leaving a hotel in Harrogate (courtesy of the Estate of Agatha Christie)

his family had. . . . How about calling my little man Hercules?" Then, after hitting on the last name *Poirot* for no reason that she knew of (though possibly she had read of and forgotten Mrs. Belloc Lowndes's Hercule Popeau, a bossy, self-opinionated foreign detective working in England), she altered *Hercules* to a more likely and more euphonious *Hercule*. In a later, inferior book, *The Big Four* (1927), Christie carried the parody element to the point of giving Hercule Poirot a mysterious brother, Achille, because all celebrated detectives, Poirot is made to say, have

brothers who would be even more celebrated were it not for constitutional indolence.

The Mysterious Affair at Styles showed several traits that were to mark Christie's writing. There is, first, the underlying main puzzle, which is not quite so daring and original in this book as in the later, better ones but is nevertheless a considerable achievement for a beginning author. It consists of taking advantage of the English law of *autrefois acquit,* the ruling that no one may be tried twice for the same offense. The pair of murderous plotters deliberately court an arrest knowing that the "evidence" they have contrived can be finally disproved. In thus apparently clearing the suspect at a late stage, Christie cunningly clears him in the reader's mind as well, only to have Poirot in the final, somewhat long-winded pages of explanation incriminate the pair of plotters once again. It is an ingenious and striking device, one that stamps itself on the reader's memory and recurs in later books. *The Mysterious Affair at Styles* shows an early mastery of other devices of the detective author. Part of its main plot depends on the conspiracy and close working relationship between two characters who appear to have no connection at all. Christie linked them by making them cousins, but she skillfully conceals and at the same time reveals this relationship, which is important to the solution of the mystery.

Christie's Hercule Poirot was, in the description of Captain Hastings, "an extraordinary looking little man! He was hardly more than five feet, four inches, but he carried himself with great dignity. His head was exactly the shape of an egg, and he always perched it a little on one side. His moustache was very stiff and military. The neatness of his attire was almost incredible. I believe a speck of dust would have caused him more pain than a bullet would." Poirot regularly referred to "the little grey cells" of his brain, and he almost invariably wore a black jacket, correct striped trousers, and bow tie, adding an overcoat and muffler if the weather was anything less than steamy. It has been said that he speaks French only for the easy phrases and English for anything more complicated; this may have reflected Christie's consideration for her readers.

The Mysterious Affair at Styles sold about two thousand copies, a respectable figure in Britain at the time, and was well reviewed. "The book is put together so deftly," said an anonymous reviewer in the *British Weekly,* "that I can remember no recent book of the kind that approaches it in merit." The *London Evening News* was even more enthusiastic: "A wonderful triumph . . . in this writer there is a distinguished addition to the list of writers in this genus." The *Bookman* added: "The most ingenious and absorbingly interesting tale of sensations and mystery we have read for a long time." The book was reprinted in the year of its publication and again the next year. In various editions it has been in print ever since.

Perhaps not realizing where her highest abilities lay, Christie next wrote a story of criminal adventure instead of a puzzle novel. This misreading of her talents recurred many times in her writing life. She said in *An Autobiography* that books of this sort were "more fun and quicker to write." *The Secret Adversary* (1922) concerns two young people, Thomas Beresford (Tommy) and Prudence Cowley (Tuppence), who reappear in the Christie oeuvre over the years. Jobless in the immediate post-World War I years in London, they beome involved, through a series of blatant coincidences, in thwarting a plot to take over Britain instigated by a mysterious "Mr. Brown," whose identity is not revealed until the last pages. As a thriller, the book is by no means a bad piece of work. Tommy and Tuppence are lively characters, swapping backchat in much the manner of young people in the novels of P. G. Wodehouse. (Many years later Christie dedicated *Hallowe'en Party*, 1969, to "P. G. Wodehouse whose books and stories have brightened my life.") Christie's gifts for deceiving the reader and for swift, direct narrative do much to make the book an easy read, though it is considerably dated in method. For example, it contains such inventions as "gloves fitted with the finger-prints of a notorious burglar" and rapidly contrived happy endings for both Tommy and Tuppence, for the young American millionaire Julius P. Hersheimmer, and for Jane Finn, the American girl who had been entrusted with a secret document that could have implicated important British statesmen. Though the book's old-fashioned, nonsensical tone is a strong disadvantage from a purely literary point of view, from a sociological point of view it is a considerable plus. Because Christie used details of current everyday life simply as they were necessary to move her story along and not as intentional pieces of authorial observation, such details are all the more trustworthy as descriptions of life in that time, place, and social stratum. The attitude of the young, upper-middle-class jobless in the opening pages, which is jocular but has an undertone of real anxiety, is a

Program cover for the first production of Christie's play The Mousetrap, *which set a record for the longest continuous run in the history of legitimate theater*

good example. This kind of social description occurs all through Christie's writing.

Christie's next noteworthy book was her sixth mystery, *The Murder of Roger Ackroyd* (1926), which embodied the most daring use of the detective-story conventions by any writer up to that time and became one of the landmarks of detective literature. Its innovation, in part suggested to her by Lord Mountbatten (who later became Viceroy of India), is that the narrator turns out to be the murderer. Though this device may seem to flout the conventions of the genre, in fact it merely takes advantage of their existence to create a puzzle that is a peak of the genre's art. To bring off this feat Christie had to abandon Poirot's faithful Watson, Captain Hastings. In his place she substituted Dr. Sheppard, a new acquaintance of Poirot's and his neighbor in the country. The story is told totally in his words, and Christie contrived his narration so that nothing he says is untrue. Only occasionally does she arrange his prose in such a way as to conceal from the reader the passage of a period of time.

One instance serves well as a classic example of Christie's technique of trickery. Accompanied by Parker, the butler, Sheppard has broken into the study, where they have found the body of Roger Ackroyd. Sheppard tells how he sends Parker for the police: "Parker hurried away, still wiping his perspiring brow. I did what little had to be done. I was careful not to disturb the position of the body, and not to handle the dagger at all." The phrase "what little had to be done" is taken by almost every reader to mean some small task of tidying up. In fact, Sheppard stows in his medical bag the dictaphone that has simulated Ackroyd's voice and restores a chair to its proper place. Another example the book provides of Christie's talent is her portrayal of Dr. Sheppard's spinster sister, the gossipy Caroline. Though she is a standard character of the sort that could have been treated stereotypically, she is portrayed so well that she takes on a vivid life of her own. Caroline Sheppard is the forerunner of Christie's popular second detective, Miss Marple.

The Murder of Roger Ackroyd created a sensation. Critical comments on Christie's having made the murderer her narrator ranged from "a rotten, unfair trick" to "a brilliant, psychological tour-de-force." The book was attacked by the American writer Willard Huntington Wright (who wrote under the name S. S. Van Dine) but defended by Christie's British rival Dorothy L. Sayers. The *London News Chronicle* called it a "tasteless and unforgivable let-down by a writer we had grown to admire," while the *Daily Sketch* reviewer felt it was "the best thriller ever!" The *Daily Sketch* verdict, with the substitution of the more correct term *detective puzzle* for *thriller*, has been endorsed by many subsequent writers. The British crime novelist Celia Fremlin has called *The Murder of Roger Ackroyd* "the best and most powerful" of Christie's books. Julian Symons, another British crime writer, considers it the first of her books to show her finest skills at full stretch, and the American critic G. C. Ramsey labels it "*the* classic Christie." The publisher printed a first edition of fifty-five hundred copies, more than double the number for Christie's first book, and reprints were soon called for.

Things were not going well in Christie's personal life, however. First there was the death of her mother, and with that the job of cleaning up Ashfield, the old family home in Torquay. This task required Christie to undergo a long separation from her husband and their young daughter; when she returned home, she learned that Colonel Christie wanted a divorce so that he could marry someone else. These cumulative blows brought on a nervous breakdown. Christie left home one evening after a quarrel with her husband and went to the Yorkshire spa town of Harrogate, where she checked into a hotel under the name of the woman her husband wanted to marry. Nine days later, as a result of the great blare of publicity, she was recognized at her hotel, where she had joined the resident trio in playing light music. She was brought by Colonel Christie back to their home, being greeted at the London rail terminus by a huge crowd. This embarrassment reinforced her natural reticence, and afterward she would consent to only the rarest and most local of public appearances. Even in her autobiography, written many years later, she did not mention the episode, confining herself to the events leading up to it and the later arrangements for her divorce, in 1928.

The books that immediately followed Christie's disappearance and return were potboilers, written for money and occupation. In 1929 she took the Orient Express to the Middle East, where she met the eminent archaeologist Leonard Woolley at Ur of the Chaldees. Returning to the dig the following season, Christie met Woolley's young assistant, Max Mallowan. Christie and Mallowan were married six months later, in September 1930.

That same year *The Murder at the Vicarage* was published. It was the first novel to feature Miss Marple, who had been created for a series of short stories for an evening paper (published, together with a second series, as *The Thirteen Problems*, 1932, in England and *The Tuesday Club Murders*, 1933, in the United States). Though *The Murder at the Vicarage* deserves attention as the novel in which Miss Marple makes her official debut, it is not one of Christie's best books. She said in *An Autobiography*, "I cannot remember where, when or how I wrote it, why I came to write it, or even what suggested to me that I should select a new character . . . to act as sleuth in the story. Certainly at the time I had no intention of continuing her for the rest of my life. I did not know she was to become a rival to Hercule Poirot." One of the reasons for Miss Marple's creation, however, may well have been that Christie was getting tired of Poirot, an occupational hazard for creators of detectives of marked character. Certainly she felt, even quite early, a strong if intermittent dislike for the cocky Belgian. In an interview she gave the *Daily Mail* in 1938 she said, "Why–why–why did I even invent this detestable, bombastic, tiresome little creature?" Though she could not bring herself then to end his career, he did become a good deal less bombastic in later books.

The Murder at the Vicarage concerns the death of Colonel Protheroe, warden at the Church of St. Mary in the southern English village of St. Mary Mead, which proves to have more than its fair share of burglary, impersonation, embezzlement, and adultery, and more than its fair share of potential murderers. Miss Jane Marple, one of its parishioners, is introduced as "that terrible Miss Marple," but the narrator, the unworldly vicar Len Clement (a charming and adroitly done first-person portrait), tells how in the end "Miss Marple had been right on every count."

Miss Marple is in many ways the antithesis of Hercule Poirot. Poirot is an embodiment of so many eccentricities that he seems unreal, whereas Miss Marple has a credibility derived in part from her prototype, Caroline Sheppard, and in part from being modeled to some extent on Christie's grandmother. Where Poirot works by at least the appearance of logic and reasoning, Miss Marple works largely by intuition. Their handling of essentially the same affair can be studied in *Lord Edgeware Dies* (1933), which features Poirot, and *The Mirror Crack'd from Side to Side* (1962), in which Miss Marple is the detective.

Miss Marple depends for her successes on five linked qualities: 1) an extensive knowledge of people garnered over many years and based on the premise that the inhabitants of St. Mary Mead form a microcosm of the wider world; 2) her belief that gossip–or tittle-tattle, as she calls it–is true more often than not; 3) a gift for making connections between people's minor misdemeanors and their capacity for greater ones; 4) her intuition; and 5) her consistent, pessimistic lack of trust, which prevents her from taking anyone she meets at face value. This last quality becomes by the later books a positive nose for evil.

With marriage to Max Mallowan Christie began a period of her life in which archaeology played as large a part as crime writing. She accompanied her husband on his increasingly successful expeditions, acting as his assistant, but she also wrote during these travels, demanding only a table of sufficient sturdiness. Her time in the Middle East is reflected in such books as *Murder*

in Mesopotamia (1936), *Death on the Nile* (1937), *Appointment with Death* (1938), *Death Comes as the End* (1944), and *They Came to Baghdad* (1951). Another book arising from her travels to the archaeological sites of the Middle East, recalling, in fact, the circumstances of her decision to go there for the first time, in *Murder on the Orient Express* (1934; published in the United States as *Murder in the Calais Coach*). The British title was used for the very successful film made long after the book's publication. Max Mallowan related in his memoirs how his wife nearly lost her life under the Orient Express shortly before she wrote the story, which he had suggested to her and which she dedicated to him. He wrote: "It was lucky she lived to write the book, for not long before penning it, while standing on the railway station at Calais, she slipped on the icy platform and fell under the train. Luckily a porter was at hand to fish her up before the train started moving."

Murder on the Orient Express is another example of Christie's daring fundamental overturnings of detective-story conventions while keeping within their framework. The story is set on the great, luxurious train as it steams from Istanbul toward Calais with Hercule Poirot on board; it centers on the murder of an American businessman and collector who is later revealed as the kidnapper and murderer of the child Daisy Armstrong. Poirot knows that no one could have boarded the train after the murder–it is stalled in a snowdrift–so the killer has to be one of the passengers, an apparently unrelated lot. Small discrepancies in their testimony give him the clues that lead to the mystery's resolution, which Poirot announces to the assembled travelers while the train remains immobile: they have united to commit the murder, each having had some connection, familial or otherwise, to the kidnapped and murdered child. But, Poirot says, he intends to let the Yugoslav police believe the crime was committed by an assassin who left the train immediately thereafter.

By the time she wrote *Murder on the Orient Express*, Christie had progressed considerably from the make-believe murders of her earliest books. Here she ventured to touch on real life; the kidnapping in the book bears a marked resemblance to the Lindbergh kidnapping. In *An Autobiography* she wrote, "When I began writing detective stories I was not in any mood . . . to think seriously about crime." Eventually, though, she began to get interested in the criminal mind. "One of the pleasures of writing detective sto-

Christie, age 85, being presented to Queen Elizabeth at the 1974 film premiere of Murder on the Orient Express, *which was named Best Picture of the Year by the British Film Awards in 1975 (courtesy of the Estate of Max Mallowan)*

ries," she continued, "is that there are so many types to choose from: the light-hearted thriller, which is particularly pleasant to do; the intricate detective story with an involved plot which is technically interesting and requires a great deal of work, but is always rewarding; and then what I can only describe as the detective story that has a kind of passion behind it–that passion being to help save innocence. Because it is *innocence* that matters, not *guilt*." *Murder on the Orient Express* is this last sort of book, and it, with others, rebuts the common assumption that Christie wrote detective stories that were no more than puzzles with cardboard characters going through predictable motions.

The solution to *Murder on the Orient Express* aroused the particular ire of Raymond Chandler, who cited it in *The Simple Art of Murder* (1950), his famous denunciation of the English crime puzzle. The book was well received, however, having three reprintings in the year of its publication alone. Christie's next book, *Three Act Tragedy* (1935; published in the United States as *Murder in Three Acts,* 1934), may have benefited directly from the success of *Murder on the Orient Express;* it

was the first of her books to sell ten thousand hardback copies in Britain within a year of its publication, though it has come since to be regarded as a minor Christie work.

Another important book emerged from this calm, prosperous, and prolific period of Christie's life, during which she and Mallowan purchased the lovely Greenway House in Devon, which was to be her primary home for the rest of her life. *The A.B.C. Murders* (1936) perhaps exemplifies Christie's ingenuity better than any other book she wrote. In it Hercule Poirot is faced with a series of murders apparently committed by a madman with a fixation on the alphabet: he has started with the killing of Alice Ascher in Andover, followed by the killing of Betty Barnard in Bexhill, then by that of Sir Carmichael Clarke in Churston, each murder preceded by a taunting letter to Poirot signed "A.B.C." The trick is that the alphabet device has been designed to divert attention from Franklin Clarke's motive for killing his brother, Sir Carmichael Clarke. This is a variation on the device first used by Edgar Allan Poe in "The Purloined Letter," in which a crucial letter is "hidden" among other letters, and a murder among other murders. The book's technical challenge involved linking into a fair puzzle three murders that must be made to seem the work of a madman. Christie solved the problem partly by making her murderer go one step further than usual to hide his motive. He provides a ready-made suspect, a feeble individual saddled with the name Alexander Bonaparte Cust. Franklin Clarke happens to have become acquainted with him and persuades him to answer an advertisement for a salesman's job. His unknown employer (Clarke himself) then directs him to each of the towns where a murder is about to take place. Christie dealt with the difficulty of incorporating Cust into her story by abandoning the conventional point of view and breaking up her narrative, giving some of it to Captain Hastings and other parts to other tellers. She also made especially good use in this book of red herrings, false clues to throw readers off the track to the puzzle's solution.

In his introduction to the Collins Crime Club's fiftieth anniversary edition of *The A.B.C. Murders*, Julian Symons wrote of Christie's skill that "to construct such a device is not at all simple, as anybody who has tried will know, and to repeat it, to vary it, to offer the readers a dozen clues of which eleven are misleading while a true interpretation of the twelfth will lead to the heart of the maze–and then of course to try to make sure that this twelfth clue is *not* interpreted rightly– that is the real art of the traditional detective story, and it is the art in which Agatha Christie was supreme." He considered *The A.B.C. Murders* a prime example of Christie's talent for such deception. Other judges have heaped equal praise on the book. G. C. Ramsey selected it for detailed analysis in *Agatha Christie, Mistress of Mystery* (1967) as the classic example of her art, and Robert Barnard called it "a total success" in *A Talent to Deceive* (1980).

World War II brought about a major change in Christie's life. Her husband, eager to get into the action, enrolled in the Royal Air Force Volunteer Reserve and was sent to North Africa, where his experience of the Arab way of life was considered useful in liaison work. This meant a long separation for the couple, who had rarely been apart for more than very short periods. In her husband's absence Christie returned to the work she had done in World War I, acting as a dispenser in a London hospital this time rather than in Torquay. Greenway House had been temporarily occupied by the U.S. Navy, and

the Mallowans' home in Oxford was being used for evacuees from the London air raids. Hospital work, however, did not use all her energies, and she wrote roughly two books a year during this period. Because of the shortage of paper, two of the wartime books were not published until much later. They are the last adventure of Hercule Poirot and the last Miss Marple book. Their author had them carefully kept, deciding that they should be published only after her death.

Hercule Poirot's Christmas (1938; published in the United States as *Murder for Christmas*, 1939), with its emphasis on the traditional holiday ceremony that Christie loved especially for its food, marked the peak of the peaceful days before World War II. The book is one of Christie's bows to a subgenre of the detective story, the house party murder (in this case, that of the host, millionaire Simeon Lee), and also a rare flirtation with the locked-room puzzle, a subgenre presided over by John Dickson Carr. The few incidental details Christie uses in this book to establish character reflect the time of its writing. Pilar Estravados, a half-Spanish, half-English girl going to spend Christmas at the Lees' English country home, remarks on "how funny they were, the English! They all seemed so rich, so prosperous–their clothes–their boots–Oh! undoubtedly England was a very rich country." The South African guest, Stephen Farr, reflects that the people he sees in England are "so alike, so horribly alike! Those that hadn't got faces like sheep had faces like rabbits. . . . Even the girls, slender, egg-faced, scarlet-lipped, were of a depressing uniformity." The two guests' impressions, taken together, create a vivid if superficial picture of a country absorbed in its own affairs, hardly aware of the impending war.

The opening pages of the novel seem to provide only introductions to some of the characters as they gather for the party (a traditional device of the subgenre), but at least one physical clue has been planted. Stephen Farr, catching his first sight of Pilar and succumbing to her beauty, thinks, "This girl was different. Black hair, rich creamy pallor–eyes with the depth and darkness of night in them." Though this may seem to be only a crude characterization, Christie is telling her readers (in a way she calculates they are bound to forget) that the girl had brown eyes. Later, it is revealed that both of Pilar's parents have blue eyes; in other words, she is not who she claims to be. Other clues to the real identity of various characters (an important feature of this plot) are sown for sharper readers to spot and be misled by. Christie draws attention to Stephen's physique—the arrogant jawline, the aquiline nose—in a way that makes the attentive reader think, mistakenly, that he is the missing Lee son. Another character, the police detective Superintendent Sugden, also bears a strong likeness to members of the Lee family; Christie states four times that he draws a finger along his jawline, a gesture established as a Lee characteristic. It is because of Christie's skillful manipulation of her readers in this manner that Barnard selected *Hercule Poirot's Christmas*, in *A Talent to Deceive*, as one of "three prize specimens." In a 1956 article for *Life* British critic and novelist Nigel Dennis singled the book out for its particularly cunning use of clues.

Ten Little Niggers (1939; published in the United States as *And Then There Were None*, 1940) depends on a brilliant idea rather than a series of well-concealed clues. It features neither Poirot nor Miss Marple. Eight people are summoned to a small island off the south coast of England for a mysterious holiday. Each of them, it is revealed in a series of vignettes, has something shady in his past. When they arrive, their host appears to be absent, the only boat has been taken back to the mainland by the boatman, and there are only two servants, making a total of ten people stranded on the island. One by one the guests are murdered. The suspense grows from the questions of which guest will be murdered next, which of the last two remaining guests will prove to be the killer, and how will the final death take place. Christie placed in each bedroom of her fictional island house a framed copy of the old rhyme that inspired the book, taken from the American set of verses "Ten Little Indians," written by Septimus Winner in 1864, but known to English children of Christie's time in the version used in her story. It is this version that gives the novel its strict form and dictates the manner of the murders. For example, the sixth victim is going to die after "a bumble bee stung one and then there were Five."

The combination of predictability and suspense gave this book its particular magic, and it had a very enthusiastic reception. It was the first Christie book to be made into a successful film, *And Then There Were None* (1945), directed by René Clair. There had been a few earlier films from her books and short stories, starting in 1928 with a German production of *The Secret Ad-*

Christie and her second husband, Max Mallowan, 1970 (courtesy of the Estate of Max Mallowan)

versary under the title *Die Abenteurer G.m.b.H.* (The Adventurers Ltd.). *And Then There Were None* far surpasses these. Other film versions of the book appeared in 1966 and 1974, both directed by Harry Allen Towers.

In 1941, with war raging in Europe, Christie gave her readers a cozy story of a single death in peaceful times, *Evil Under the Sun*. In this book Poirot is on holiday by the sea, a situation incongruous with his character as it has previously been portrayed: he is supposed to hate the sea. But Christie's plot demanded a setting in which the similarity of a sunbather's motionless body to that of an adroitly murdered corpse would be evident.

Poirot makes this comparison early in the book when one of his fellow guests remarks that, though the hotel is on Smugglers Island, there ought not to be any bodies for the vacationing detective to be concerned with. "Ah, but that is not strictly true," Poirot answers. "Regard them there, lying out in rows. What are they? They are not men and women. There is nothing personal about them. They are just–bodies!" This sets up the device that will provide an alibi when the sexy actress Arlena Stuart is murdered; it is a piece of visual trickery in Christie's best vein.

Another notable device in the story, and a favorite of Christie's, is the conventional triangle turned around. The situation appears to involve a glamorous star who dallies with the husband of an ex-schoolteacher and is murdered, setting up as primary suspects the deceived wife and the star's husband. It is eventually revealed, however, that the ex-teacher and her husband have conspired to commit the murder, the husband having defrauded the victim of a large sum and needing to cover this up.

One other small device used in the book, worth pointing out because it is a method of character description that Christie typically uses, is the comparison of humans with dogs. Here Miss Brewster, a tough, athletic woman with a pleasant, weather-beaten face, is likened to a sheepdog and set in contrast to the loquacious American guest Mrs. Gardener, who is called a yapping Pomeranian. In this way Christie could make her characters vivid enough without going into much detail. In real life she was very fond of dogs and almost always had one.

Another book published at the height of the war and set in a peacetime atmosphere was *Five Little Pigs* (1942; published in the United States as *Murder in Retrospect*). One of Christie's most ingenious books, it has similarities to a crucial period in her life, though it is impossible to know whether or not she consciously drew on the facts in creating her fictions. Christie's notorious disappearance had taken place sixteen years earlier; in *Five Little Pigs* Poirot is retained to investigate a murder that had taken place sixteen years in the past. The characters include a wife with a young daughter and a husband in love with a much younger woman–just the situation that had precipitated the Christies' divorce. Amyas Crale, the self-centered painter who was murdered in the story, bore the same initials as Christie's first husband, who in turn could have been the real-life model for another character, Philip Blake, a bluff, insensitive stockbroker and "best friend" of the murdered man. Perhaps because she wrote the book in wartime, cut off from her second husband's supporting presence and the social life she normally led, Christie goes deeper into character in *Five Little Pigs* than in most of her books.

Through Poirot's investigation and the testimony during the trial, Christie builds up a composite portrait of the condemned wife, Caroline Crale, managing to resolve several differing views of her character into a credible portrait that contributes to the puzzle's solution.

The British critic and crime novelist Edmund Crispin, who pointed out that Christie achieved considerable variety in her writing, felt that she rose in *Five Little Pigs* to heights she perhaps never achieved elsewhere, except occasionally in the romance novels she wrote under the name of Mary Westmacott. Barnard called *Five Little Pigs* "beautifully tailored . . . , rich and satisfying . . . the best Christie of all." It was the first Christie book to achieve an initial British hardback sale of twenty thousand copies. In 1960 Christie adapted it for the stage as *Go Back for Murder*– without Poirot, who, she realized, came off well only as a character in books. It ran for only a short time in London.

Crooked House (1949) is worthy of mention. It features neither Poirot nor Miss Marple, but it has two of Christie's favorite ingredients, a nursery rhyme ("There was a crooked man . . .") and a poisoning, and it was one of her favorites. For a late edition she wrote a preface in which she told how the story began with her idea for the Leonides family, to which some of its important characters belong, and how it evolved in her mind over a period of years. Two of the characters may have been inspired by the pattern of the rhyme: Mr. Leonides's young wife Brenda, whom Christie called the "crooked cat"; and Laurence Brown, the invalid tutor in love with Brenda, who was seen as the "crooked mouse" caught by the cat. But in this book there is none of the close parallel between story and rhyme that gave *And Then There Were None* its framework. *Crooked House* is notable not for its form but for its shocking resolution, in which a child turns out to be the murderer. (Christie later said the publishers had wanted her to change the ending, but she refused.) It also contains fine character portraits of two children, a rare accomplishment for Christie.

Curtain: Hercule Poirot's Last Case (1975) was one of the books Christie had written during World War II but tucked away for posthumous publication. Her publishers persuaded her to allow its earlier publication, however, so that there would be a 1975 book in the long-standing "Christie for Christmas" tradition. For his final appearance Christie chose to take Poirot back to where he began, Styles Court, now a slightly run-down guest house; there she made his last words "Cher ami," addressed to his old companion Captain Hastings and neatly echoing his first recorded words, "Mon ami, Hastings!" Poirot, a paying guest at Styles Court, knows that someone among the other guests is responsible for several murders and is likely to commit more. He asks Hastings to join him in finding the murderer.

Soon a murder is committed in the house, and it is revealed only in the final pages that the dead man is the person Poirot has been hunting (Christie concealed the murderer by making him a victim) and that Poirot has killed him. To accomplish the necessary deception, Christie made all the possible suspects taller than the victim so that no one could have impersonated him except Poirot, who, being shorter than the victim, could increase his height with elevator shoes.

The idea for the book perhaps went back to the time when Christie was writing *The A.B.C. Murders*. Early in that book there is a jocular passage designed primarily to reestablish the Hastings-Poirot relationship, since Hastings had been absent through several preceding books. The Scotland Yard officer they had worked with before, ferret-faced Chief Inspector Japp, said to Poirot, "Shouldn't wonder if you ended by detecting your own death. That's an idea, that is. Ought to be put in a book." The idea of *Curtain* is also sketched out in a passage in chapter 9 of *Peril at End House* (1932). In *Curtain* Poirot deliberately brings about his own death by pushing his amyl nitrate ampules out of reach just after he has written a long letter to Hastings describing the means of his suicide and detecting his own crime, clue by clue. The death of Poirot caused a sensation throughout much of the world, making the papers even in Communist China, a tribute to Christie's enormous popularity. The affair was often treated as front-page news, and many mock obituaries were printed.

Sleeping Murder (1976) was in many ways Miss Marple's most typical case as well as her last one, and another book that allowed Christie to indulge her fondness for going back into the past for material, this time events that had occurred eighteen years earlier. Because of the additional passage of time between the writing of the book and its publication, some of its occurrences were almost half a century old by the time it was out. It was thus not only a detective novel but, in a sense, a historical one, with a wealth of period detail.

At the age of three Christie's character Gwenda Reed saw a young woman (who later proved to have been her stepmother) lying strangled at the foot of the stairs and heard a triumphant voice quote from John Webster's play *The Duchess of Malfi*, "Cover her face. Mine eyes dazzle, she died young. . . ." By coincidence Gwenda has come back as a young married woman to that very house, which she does not remember. There, odd incidents stir recollections of the past, and by chance she confides her distress to the elderly spinster Miss Marple. The progress of the ensuing investigation, carried out in part by Gwenda and her husband Giles, paints a good portrait of Miss Marple. She is first described by her nephew, Raymond West, whose wife is a distant cousin of Gwenda's: "You'll adore my Aunt Jane," he says. "She's . . . a perfect Period Piece. Victorian to the core. All her dressing-tables have their legs swathed in chintz. She lives in a village where nothing ever happens." A few paragraphs later Christie introduces her: "Miss Marple was an attractive old lady, tall and thin, with pink cheeks and blue eyes, and a gentle, rather fussy manner. Her blue eyes often had a little twinkle in them."

At a performance of *The Duchess of Malfi* Miss Marple sees Gwenda shocked into hysteria by hearing Webster's lines again. Unable to account for her reaction, Gwenda is all for putting herself in the hands of a psychiatrist. Miss Marple reveals her habitual reliance on common sense when she says, "I always think myself it's better to examine the simplest and most commonplace explanations first." She is able to convince Gwenda that in all probability she heard someone say those lines from Webster and saw a real body in the house she has come to eighteen years later. "Children are odd little creatures," Miss Marple says. "If they are badly frightened, especially by something they don't understand, they don't talk about it. They bottle it up."

Miss Marple advises Gwenda not to delve back into what happened in her house eighteen years before. But she knows that Gwenda and Giles will pursue the mystery, and she decides that she ought to be in the neighborhood in case they need help. By playing the innocent elderly gossip, she extracts information about life in the little town eighteen years earlier. Finally, the three work together, and, primarily through the women's intuitive use of the clues they find, including a letter that provides the final proof, they solve the mystery.

Part of Christie's genius in *Sleeping Murder* is avoiding the repetitious interview techniques, in which the detective talks with one person after another to gather clues. She accomplishes this by using Gwenda and Giles as subsleuths, at intervals faithfully reporting to Miss Marple. This device provides the reader enough information to solve the riddle while introducing variety into the plot without recourse to an unlikely sequence of events. The book also shows Christie at her best as a mistress of misdirection and concise character portrayal.

The last Marple book had a first hardback printing in Britain of sixty thousand copies and was a popular and critical success. But the books that Christie wrote after the war, when she was reunited with her husband and again in possession of her two country homes, showed an increasing decline in her powers. Max Mallowan continued his archaeological work in the Middle East and made the important discoveries that earned him knighthood in 1968 and that he described in such books as *Prehistoric Assyria* (1935). Christie continued to travel with him and to write both in the Middle East and at home. She was made a dame in 1971. Among her few noteworthy works after the war was *The Mousetrap,* which began as a radio play written for Queen Mary's eightieth birthday and was first produced as a stage play in 1952. *The Mousetrap* set a record for the longest continuous run in the history of legitimate theater.

After the publication of *Postern of Fate* in 1973 Christie acknowledged that she could no longer go on working. She lived a country life, gradually giving up visits to London for the opera and for meetings of the Detection Club. She was finally forced to use a wheelchair. On 12 January 1976, while her husband was wheeling her away from the lunch table, Christie quietly died.

References:

Robert Barnard, *A Talent to Deceive: An Appreciation of Agatha Christie* (New York: Dodd, Mead, 1980);

H. R. F. Keating, ed., *Agatha Christie: First Lady of Crime* (London: Weidenfeld & Nicolson, 1977; New York: Holt, Rinehart & Winston, 1977);

Jessica Mann, *Deadlier Than the Male* (Newton Abbot: David & Charles, 1981);

G. C. Ramsey, *Agatha Christie, Mistress of Mystery* (New York: Dodd, Mead, 1967; London: Collins, 1968);

A. L. Rowse, *Memories of Men and Women* (London: Eyre, 1980);

Randall Toye, comp., *The Agatha Christie Who's Who* (London: Muller, 1980; New York: Holt, Rinehart & Winston, 1980);

Nancy Blue Wynne, *An Agatha Christie Chronology* (New York: Ace, 1976).

John Collier

(3 May 1901-6 April 1980)

Marvin S. Lachman

BOOKS: *His Monkey Wife; or, Married to a Chimp* (London: Davies, 1930; New York: Appleton, 1931);

Just the Other Day: An Informal History of Great Britain since the War, by Collier and Iain Lang (London: Hamilton, 1932; New York & London: Harper, 1932);

Tom's A-Cold (London: Macmillan, 1933); republished as *Full Circle* (New York: Appleton, 1933);

Defy the Foul Fiend; or, The Misadventures of a Heart (London: Macmillan, 1934; New York: Knopf, 1934);

The Devil and All (London: Nonesuch, 1934);

Presenting Moonshine: Stories (New York: Viking, 1941; London: Macmillan, 1941);

The Touch of Nutmeg, and More Unlikely Stories (New York: Readers Club, 1943); republished as *Green Thoughts and Other Strange Tales* (New York: Editions for the Armed Services, 1945);

Fancies and Goodnights (Garden City, N.Y.: Doubleday, 1951); abridged as *Of Demons and Darkness* (London: Transworld, 1965);

Pictures in the Fire (London: Hart-Davis, 1958);

Milton's Paradise Lost: Screenplay for Cinema of the Mind (New York: Knopf, 1973).

Collections: *The John Collier Reader* (New York: Knopf, 1972; London: Souvenir, 1975);

The Best of John Collier (New York: Pocket, 1975).

MOTION PICTURES: *Sylvia Scarlett,* screenplay by Collier, Gladys Unger, and Mortimer Offner, RKO, 1936;

Elephant Boy, screenplay by Collier, Akos Tolnay, and Marcia de Silva, United Artists, 1937;

Deception, screenplay by Collier and Joseph Than, Warner Brothers, 1946;

Roseanna McCoy, screenplay by Collier, RKO, 1949;

The Story of Three Loves, screenplay by Collier, Jan Lustig, and George Froeschel, MGM, 1953;

John Collier

I Am a Camera, screenplay by Collier, Distributors Corporation of America, 1955;

The War Lord, screenplay by Collier and Millard Kaufman, Universal, 1965.

OTHER: John Aubrey, *The Scandal and Credulities of John Aubrey,* edited by Collier (London: Peter Davies, 1931; New York: Appleton, 1931);

"Please Excuse Me, Comrade," in *Ten Contemporaries: Notes Toward Their Definitive Bibliography,* second series, edited by Terence I. Armstrong as John Gawsworth (London: Joiner & Steele, 1933), pp. 109-117.

PERIODICAL PUBLICATIONS: "The Dog That Came to the Funeral," *Ellery Queen's Mystery Magazine,* 30 (December 1957): 72-80;

"The Love Connoisseur," *Ellery Queen's Mystery Magazine*, 32 (December 1958): 96-104;

"Anniversary Gift," *Ellery Queen's Mystery Magazine*, 33 (April 1959): 50-61;

"A Matter of Taste," *Ellery Queen's Mystery Magazine*, 34 (November 1959): 96-103.

Though best known as a writer of fantasies, John Collier wrote enough mysteries to become almost as famous in that genre. His short-story collection, *Fancies and Goodnights* (1951), though only ten of its fifty stories are mysteries, was selected by Ellery Queen for the "Queen's Quorum," generally acknowledged to be the definitive list of outstanding mystery short-story collections. Collier was honored with a Mystery Writers of America award in 1952 for these short stories.

John Henry Noyes Collier was born in London, 3 May 1901, to John George and Emily Noyes Collier. He was educated privately and never attended school after kindergarten. He began writing poetry at the age of nineteen and first was published in 1920. His novels and short stories during the early 1930s earned him a reputation for whimsy and caustic wit which carried across the Atlantic, and in 1935 he came to the United States under contract to RKO Pictures. He wrote many screenplays during the next thirty years and also was active in television.

Two of Collier's most famous and frequently anthologized stories, included in *Fancies and Goodnights,* demonstrate the author's skill in writing about murder and marriage. They are in the Francis Iles (A. B. Cox) tradition as they tell of husbands with motives for murdering their wives. These two stories are considered to be definitive variations on the "burial of the body in the basement," a subgenre of the mystery. In "De Mortuis," a staid New York State doctor is, to the regret of his many friends, married to a woman who has often been flagrantly unfaithful to him. When she mysteriously disappears, these friends are more than willing to assume he has buried her in his basement and to provide an alibi for him. In "Back for Christmas," the protagonist is a British doctor, also unhappily married, with an extremely domineering wife. Because he has a young mistress in the United States, eliminating his wife is especially tempting to him. The doctor and his wife are about to leave on a prolonged trip, and the cellar as a burial spot beckons to him. The ironic endings of both stories have surprised and captivated several generations of readers.

Malice domestic is a theme that would recur throughout the Collier canon. "Three Bears Cottage," is an amusing story about a retired couple who do not get along. The husband brings back some poisoned mushrooms for his wife, telling her they are "rich in vitamins D, E, A, T, and H." Again the ending is surprising, but this story is deservedly less well known because Collier, uncharacteristically, failed to create his usual sophisticated plot and characters. In "Anniversary Gift" Jensen grows to hate his wife who controls the purse strings in their household and spends much of it on pets. They are living in sunny Florida, but, perversely, he sees mirages of New York sleet, skyscrapers, and apartments in which no pets are permitted. He decides to give his wife a poisonous coral snake as a present, though he tells her it is harmless. There is still another unhappy couple in "The Dog That Came to the Funeral," in which an unfaithful wife kills her husband, the General, by substituting tap water for the penicillin solution he needs. She and her lover become worried when a dog who seems to look remarkably like the General begins to follow them. "A Matter of Taste" comes closer to being a classic detective story than any other Collier work. Sir Barnard Wigmore, consulting pathologist to the Home Office, tells of one of his famous cases, the murder of Lady Jerningham, whose husband, Sir Jervase Jerningham, was suspected of having given her poisoned chocolates.

Collier could take story ideas which had become clichés and breath new life into them. An example is "The Touch of Nutmeg Makes It," in which a group of businessmen are chatting over drinks at a private club, reminiscing about the past. One claims to be an acquitted ax-murderer and implies to his companions that he may have committed murder because the victim did not know how to prepare drinks correctly.

Using the "biter bit" plot device, which Wilkie Collins originated, Collier often has perpetrators of crime punished through their own plans going awry. Yet, because this is not always true in his stories, the reader is kept in suspense by never knowing in advance whether Collier will punish his criminals or let them go free. One of his most famous stories, "Another American Tragedy," can almost be considered *literally* a "biter bit" story since it involves a greedy, debt-ridden young man who has all of his teeth removed by a dentist and replaced with dentures. He then visits his dying, wealthy uncle whom he kills. Removing the false teeth, he impersonates the old man

Dust jacket for the first edition of Collier's 1951 collection of short stories, which won an Edgar Award from the Mystery Writers of America in 1952.

so he can effect a change in the latter's will. He expects to fool his uncle's lawyer but he does not count on having to contend with the family physician, another of Collier's doctors of dubious morality. This doctor is also currently the old man's heir. Until the very end of this story, as in many of Collier's tales, the reader is left wondering whether evil will triumph over evil.

Surprisingly, considering the jaundiced view of marriage Collier often showed in his stories, many of his best mysteries deal with love. A good example is "The Love Connoisseur" in which Harvey Macreavy, in Monte Carlo, falls in love. Collier calls it "a love so sweet and so passionate as to be better imagined than described . . . this love was a cross between a very expensive Valentine and a well upholstered electric chair." Macreavy shoots a rival for the object of his affection, but

the shot is not heard among many others that night near the casino "for it happened to be a night on which the bank was doing extremely well."

In two other excellent stories, Collier improbably, and successfully, works love into fantasy-crime tales. "Night! Youth! Paris! and the Moon!" begins with a marvelous first paragraph in which the world-weary narrator says, "Annoyed with the world, I took a large studio in Hampstead. Here I resolved to live in utter aloofness, until the world should approach me on its knees, whining it apologies." When his money runs out, he leases the studio to a beautiful female artist and retires to his trunk, left in the studio, from which he spies on her. She naively brings a man to the studio so she can show him *her* etchings, thinking he is a potential customer. When he has the wrong idea as to what she wishes to sell, and she resists his unwanted advances, he hits her on the head and, thinking he has killed her, removes her clothes and places her in the trunk. As he has the trunk shipped to Paris for disposal, she awakens, and true love with her fellow artist develops–in the trunk. In "Squirrels Have Bright Eyes" the narrator has fallen in love with Brynhild, "a superb creature, an Amazon, a positive Diana" with "four magnificent limbs, sunburned several tones darker than her blonde and huntress hair." She refuses him, saying, "No, no. I live with my guns. The world cannot utter its gross libidinous sneers at a girl who lives chastely with her Lee-Enfield, her Ballard, her light Winchester." He pretends to have himself stuffed for her, and is placed in her apartment as a "motionless companion," along with her trophies. Though she now loves him for this gesture, calling him Squirrel, he is afraid to let her know he is really alive for fear her love will not survive the disclosure. The scene is set for a typically clever Collier denouement when the narrator's rival, Captain Fenshawe-Fanshawe comes to Brynhild's apartment and makes sexual advances in his presence.

Collier's stories owe much to his talent as a screenwriter, and his economical writing style and clever use of speech create small miracles of characterization. While many of his crime stories could have been written by other mystery writers, there were others that could only have been created by someone who, in the words of critic Moses Hadas, thinks with "the logic of lunacy."

In his introduction to *The John Collier Reader* (1972) Anthony Burgess said about him, "... to write tales about hell under the floor boards, the devil as a film producer, men kept in bottles, a man who marries a chimpanzee is a sure way to miss the attentions of 'serious' chroniclers of fiction. . . . He makes literature out of the intrusion of fantasy or quiet horror into a real world closely observed, not out of the creation of a parallel world." Paul Theroux has called Collier "one of the great literary unclassifiables–it is another synonym for genius."

Collier, who was twice married, died of a stroke in Pacific Palisades, California, on 6 April 1980. The best of Collier's short stories have earned him a place with Saki (H. H. Munro), Ambrose Bierce, and Roald Dahl–those writers whose work is difficult to limit to any single genre, and who appeal to those whose taste is for the macabre and the imaginative. Since it is likely that there always will be an audience for that type of literature, the best of Collier will continue to be reprinted.

References:

Anthony Burgess, introduction to *The John Collier Reader* (New York: Knopf, 1972);

Moses Hadas, foreword to *Fancies and Goodnights* (Garden City, N.Y.: Doubleday, 1951);

Tom Milne, "The Elusive John Collier," *Sight and Sound*, 45 (Spring 1976): 104-108;

Betty Richardson, *John Collier* (Boston: G. K. Hall, 1983);

Paul Theroux, *Sunrise with Seamonsters* (Boston: Houghton Mifflin, 1985), pp. 303-308.

John Creasey

(17 September 1908-9 June 1973)

Marvin S. Lachman

SELECTED BOOKS: *Seven Times Seven* (London: Melrose, 1932);

The Death Miser, (London: Melrose, 1933);

Men, Maids, and Murder (London: Melrose, 1933; revised edition, London: Long, 1973);

Fire of Death, as M. E. Cooke (London: Fiction House, 1934);

First Came a Murder (London: Melrose, 1934; revised edition, London: Long, 1969; New York: Popular Library, 1972);

Redhead (London: Hurst & Blackett, 1934);

The Black Heart, as Cooke (London: Gramol, 1935);

The Casino Mystery, as Cooke (London: Mellifont, 1935);

The Crime Gang, as Cooke (London: Mellifont, 1935);

The Death Drive, as Cooke (London: Mellifont, 1935);

Death Round the Corner (London: Melrose, 1935; revised edition, New York: Popular Library, 1970; London: Long, 1971);

The Mark of the Crescent (London: Melrose, 1935; revised edition, London: Long, 1970; New York: Popular Library, 1972);

Number One's Last Crime, as Cooke (London: Fiction House, 1935);

The Stolen Formula Mystery, as Cooke (London: Mellifont, 1935);

The Big Radium Mystery, as Cooke (London: Mellifont, 1936);

The Day of Terror, as Cooke (London: Mellifont, 1936);

The Dummy Robberies, as Cooke (London: Mellifont, 1936);

The Hypnotic Demon, as Cooke (London: Fiction House, 1936);

The Killer Squad (London: Newnes, 1936);

The Moat Farm Mystery, as Cooke (London: Fiction House, 1936);

The Secret Fortune, as Cooke (London: Fiction House, 1936);

John Creasey (photograph by Conway Studios)

The Successful Alibi, as Cooke (London: Mellifont, 1936);

The Terror Trap (London: Melrose, 1936; revised edition, London: Long, 1970; New York: Popular Library, 1972);

Thunder in Europe (London: Melrose, 1936; revised edition, London: Long, 1970; New York: Popular Library, 1972);

Meet the Baron, as Morton (London: Harrap, 1937); as Creasey (London: Transworld, 1965); republished as *The Man in the Blue Mask* (Philadelphia: Lippincott, 1937);

Carriers of Death (London: Melrose, 1937; revised edition, London: Arrow, 1968; New York: Popular Library, 1972);

The Case of the Murdered Financier (London: Amalgamated, 1937);

Days of Danger (London: Melrose, 1937; revised edition, London: Long, 1970; New York: Popular Library, 1972);

Four Find Danger, as Michael Halliday (London: Cassell, 1937);

The Greyvale School Mystery, as Peter Manton (London: Low, 1937);

The Hadfield Mystery, as Cooke (London: Mellifont, 1937);

The Baron Returns, as Anthony Morton (London: Harrap, 1937); republished as *The Return of Blue Mask* (Philadelphia: Lippincott, 1937);

The Moving Eye, as Cooke (London: Mellifont, 1937);

Murder Manor, as Manton (London: Wright & Brown, 1937);

The Mysterious Mr. Rocco (London: Mellifont, 1937);

The Raven, as Cooke (London: Fiction House, 1937);

Stand By for Danger, as Manton (London: Wright & Brown, 1937);

Three for Adventure, as Halliday (London: Cassell, 1937);

The Baron Again, as Morton (London: Low, 1938); republished as *Salute Blue Mask!* (Philadelphia: Lippincott, 1938);

The Baron at Bay, as Morton (London: Low, 1938); republished as *Blue Mask at Bay* (Philadelphia: Lippincott, 1938);

The Circle of Justice, as Manton (London: Wright & Brown, 1938);

Death Stands By (London: Long, 1938; revised edition, London: Arrow, 1966; New York: Popular Library, 1972);

For Her Sister's Sake, as Cooke (London: Fiction House, 1938);

Four Motives for Murder, as Brian Hope (London: Newnes, 1938);

Introducing the Toff (London: Long, 1938; revised, 1954);

Menace! (London: Long, 1938; revised edition, New York: Popular Library, 1971; London: Long, 1972);

The Mountain Terror, as Cooke (London: Mellifont, 1938);

Three Days Terror, as Manton (London: Wright & Brown, 1938); as Creasey (London: New English Library, 1969);

Two Meet Trouble, as Halliday (London: Cassell, 1938);

Alias the Baron, as Morton (London: Low, 1939); republished as *Alias Blue Mask* (Philadelphia: Lippincott, 1939);

The Baron at Large, as Morton (London: Low, 1939); republished as *Challenge Blue Mask!* (Philadelphia: Lippincott, 1939);

The Crime Syndicate, as Manton (London: Wright & Brown, 1939);

Dangerous Journey, as Norman Deane (London: Hurst & Blackett, 1939); as Creasey (New York: McKay, 1974);

Death Looks On, as Manton (London: Wright & Brown, 1939);

Death on Demand, as Gordon Ashe (London: Long, 1939);

Documents of Death (London: Mellifont, 1939);

The Great Air Swindle (London: Amalgamated, 1939);

The Hidden Hoard (London: Mellifont, 1939);

Murder in the Highlands, as Manton (London: Wright & Brown, 1939);

Murder Must Wait (London: Long, 1939; revised edition, London: Long, 1969; New York: Popular Library, 1972);

The Mystery of Blackmoor Prison (London: Mellifont, 1939);

Panic! (London: Long, 1939; New York: Popular Library, 1972);

Secret Errand, as Deane (London: Hurst & Blackett, 1939); revised edition, as Creasey (New York: McKay, 1974);

The Speaker, as Ashe (London: Long, 1939); republished as *The Croaker* (New York: Holt, Rinehart & Winston, 1972);

The Toff Goes On (London: Long, 1939; revised, 1955);

The Toff Steps Out (London: Long, 1939; revised, 1955);

Call for the Baron, as Morton (London: Low, 1940); republished as *Blue Mask Victorious* (Philadelphia: Lippincott, 1940);

Death by Night (London: Long, 1940; revised edition, London: Long, 1971; New York: Popular Library, 1972);

Heir to Murder, as Halliday (London: Paul, 1940);

Here Comes the Toff, as Creasey (London: Long, 1940; New York: Walker, 1967);

The Island of Peril (London: Long, 1940; revised edition, London: Long, 1970; New York: Popular Library, 1976);

The Man from Fleet Street (London: Amalgamated, 1940);

The Midget Marvel, as Manton (London: Mellifont, 1940);

Murder Comes Home, as Halliday (London: Paul, 1940);

The Poison Gas Robberies (London: Mellifont, 1940);

Secret Murder, as Ashe (London: Long, 1940);

Terror by Day, as Ashe (London: Long, 1940);

The Toff Breaks In (London: Long, 1940; revised, 1955);

Unknown Mission, as Deane (London: Hurst & Blackett, 1940); revised edition, as Creasey (London: Arrow, 1972; New York: McKay, 1972);

The Verrall Street Affair, as Cooke (London: Newnes, 1940);

Versus the Baron, as Morton (London: Low, 1940); republished as *Blue Mask Strikes Again* (Philadelphia: Lippincott, 1940);

Who Was the Jester?, as Ashe (London: Newnes, 1940);

The Withered Man, as Deane (London: Hurst & Blackett, 1940); as Creasey (New York: McKay, 1974);

By Persons Unknown, as Jeremy York (London: Bles, 1941);

Go Away Death (London: Long, 1941; New York: Popular Library, 1976);

I Am the Withered Man, as Deane (London: Hurst & Blackett, 1941); as Creasey (London: Long, 1972; New York: McKay, 1973);

Murder by the Way, as Halliday (London: Paul, 1941);

Salute the Toff (London: Long, 1941; New York: Walker, 1971);

Sabotage (London: Long, 1941; revised edition, London: Long, 1972; New York: Popular Library, 1976);

The Toff Proceeds (London: Long, 1941; New York: Walker, 1968);

'Ware Danger!, as Ashe (London: Long, 1941);

Who Saw Him Die!, as Halliday (London: Paul, 1941);

The Case of the Mad Inventor (London: Amalgamated, 1942);

The Day of Disaster (London: Long, 1942);

Death in High Places, as Ashe (London: Long, 1942);

Foul Play Suspected, as Halliday (London: Paul, 1942);

Inspector West Takes Charge (London: Paul, 1942; revised edition, London: Pan, 1963; New York: Scribners, 1972);

Murder Most Foul, as Ashe (London: Long, 1942; revised edition, London: Transworld, 1973);

Prepare for Action (London: Paul, 1942; revised edition, London: Arrow, 1966; New York: Popular Library, 1975);

There Goes Death, as Ashe (London: Long, 1942; revised edition, London: Transworld, 1973);

The Toff Goes to Market (London: Long, 1942; New York: Walker, 1967);

The Toff Is Back (London: Long, 1942; New York: Walker, 1974);

Traitors' Doom (London: Long, 1942; New York: Walker, 1970; revised and abridged edition, London: Arrow, 1965);

Where Is the Withered Man?, as Deane (London: Hurst & Blackett, 1942); revised edition, as Creasey (London: Arrow, 1972; New York: McKay, 1972);

Who Died at the Grange?, as Halliday (London: Paul, 1942);

Accuse the Toff (London: Long, 1943; New York: Walker, 1975);

The Baron Comes Back, as Morton (London: Low, 1943);

Death in Flames, as Ashe (London: Long, 1943);

Five to Kill, as Halliday (London: Paul, 1943);

Inspector West Leaves Town (London: Paul, 1943); republished as *Go Away to Murder* (New York: Lancer, 1972);

The Legion of the Lost (London: Long, 1943; New York: Daye, 1944; revised and abridged edition, New York: Walker, 1974);

Mr. Quentin Investigates, as Morton (London: Low, 1943);

Murder at King's Kitchen, as Halliday (London: Paul, 1943);

Murder Unseen, as York (London: Bles, 1943);

No Alibi, as York (London: Melrose, 1943);

No Darker Crime (London: Paul, 1943; New York: Popular Library, 1976);

Private Carter's Crime (London: Amalgamated, 1943);

Return to Adventure, as Deane (London: Hurst & Blackett, 1943); revised edition, as Creasey (London: Long, 1974);

The Toff Among the Millions (London: Long, 1943; revised edition, London: Hamilton, 1964; New York: Walker, 1976);

Two Men Missing, as Ashe (London: Long, 1943; revised edition, London: Corgi, 1971);

The Valley of Fear (London: Long, 1943); revised as *The Perilous Country* (London: Long, 1949; New York: Walker, 1973);

Dangerous Quest (London: Long, 1944; revised and abridged edition, London: Arrow, 1965; New York: Walker, 1974);

Dark Peril (London: Paul, 1944; revised edition, London: Long, 1969; New York: Popular Library, 1975);

Gateway to Escape, as Deane (London: Hurst & Blackett, 1944); revised edition, as Creasey (London: Hutchinson / Long, 1974);

Dust jacket for the 1954 first edition of a volume in Creasey's long-running series featuring wealthy amateur detective Richard Rollison as the Toff

Inspector West at Home (London: Paul, 1944; New York: Scribners, 1973);

Introducing Mr. Brandon, as Morton (London: Low, 1944);

Murder in the Family, as York (London: Melrose, 1944; revised edition, New York: McKay, 1976);

Murder on Largo Island, as Charles Hogarth (Creasey and Ivor Ian Bowen) (London: Selwyn & Blount, 1944);

No Crime More Cruel, as Halliday (London: Paul, 1944);

Rogues Rampant, as Ashe (London: Long, 1944; revised edition, London: Transworld, 1973);

Who Said Murder?, as Halliday (London: Paul, 1944);

The Toff and the Curate (London: Long, 1944; New York: Walker, 1969); republished as *The Toff and the Deadly Parson* (New York: Lancer, 1970);

The Toff and the Great Illusion (London: Long, 1944; New York: Walker, 1967);

A Case for the Baron, as Morton (London: Low, 1945; New York: Duell, Sloan & Pearce, 1949);

The Cinema Crimes (Manchester: Pemberton, 1945);

Come Home to Crime, as Deane (London: Hurst & Blackett, 1945); revised edition, as Creasey (London: Long, 1974);

Crime with Many Voices, as Halliday (London: Paul, 1945);

Death in the Rising Sun (London: Long, 1945; revised edition, London: Long, 1970; New York: Walker, 1976);

Death on the Move, as Ashe (London: Long, 1945);

Feathers for the Toff (London: Long, 1945; revised edition, London: Hodder & Stoughton, 1964; New York: Walker, 1970);

Find the Body, as York (London: Melrose, 1945; revised edition, New York: Macmillan, 1967);

The Hounds of Vengeance (London: Long, 1945; revised, 1969);

Inspector West Regrets (London: Paul, 1945; revised edition, London: Hodder & Stoughton, 1965; New York: Lancer, 1971);

Invitation to Adventure, as Ashe (London: Long, 1945);

Reward for the Baron, as Morton (London: Low, 1945);

Yesterday's Murder, as York (London: Melrose, 1945);

Career for the Baron, as Morton (London: Low, 1946; New York: Duell, Sloan & Pearce, 1950);

Here is Danger!, as Ashe (London: Long, 1946);

Holiday for Inspector West (London: Paul, 1946);

The House of the Bears (London: Long, 1946; revised edition, London: Arrow, 1962; New York: Walker, 1975);

Murder Came Late, as York (London: Melrose, 1946; revised edition, New York: Macmillan, 1969);

Murder Makes Murder, as Halliday (London: Paul, 1946);

The Peril Ahead (London: Paul, 1946; revised edition, London: Long, 1969; New York: Popular Library, 1974);

Play for Murder, as Deane (London: Hurst & Blackett, 1946); revised edition, as Creasey (London: Arrow, 1975);

Shadow of Doom (London: Long, 1946; revised, 1970);

The Toff and the Lady (London: Long, 1946; New York: Walker, 1975);

The Toff on Ice (London: Long, 1946); republished as *Poison for the Toff* (New York: Pyramid, 1965);

The Baron and the Beggar, as Morton (London: Low, Marston, 1947; New York: Duell, Sloan & Pearce, 1950);

Dark Harvest (London: Long, 1947; revised edition, London: Arrow, 1962; New York: Walker, 1977);

Give Me Murder, as Ashe (London: Long, 1947);

Hammer the Toff (London: Long, 1947);

Keys to Crime, as Richard Martin (Bournemouth: Earl, 1947); as Creasey (Bath: Lythway, 1973);

The League of Dark Men (London: Paul, 1947; revised edition, London: Arrow, 1965; New York: Popular Library, 1975);

Lend a Hand to Murder, as Halliday (London: Paul, 1947);

Let's Kill Uncle Lionel, as York (London: Melrose, 1947; revised edition, London: Transworld, 1973; New York: McKay, 1976);

Murder Too Late, as Ashe (London: Long, 1947);

Mystery Motive, as Halliday (London: Paul, 1947); as Creasey (New York: McKay, 1974);

Run Away to Murder, as York (London: Melrose, 1947; New York: Macmillan, 1970);

The Silent House, as Deane (London: Hurst & Blackett, 1947); revised edition, as Creasey (London: Arrow, 1973);

Battle for Inspector West (London: Paul, 1948; New York: Lancer, 1971);

Blame the Baron, as Morton (London: Low, Marston, 1948; New York: Duell, Sloan & Pearce, 1951);

Close the Door on Murder, as York (London: Melrose, 1948; New York: McKay, 1973);

Dark Mystery, as Ashe (London: Long, 1948);

Engagement with Death, as Ashe (London: Long, 1948);

First a Murder, as Halliday (London: Paul, 1948); as York (London: Corgi, 1970); as Creasey (New York: McKay, 1972);

Intent to Murder, as Deane (London: Hurst & Blackett, 1948); revised edition, as Creasey (London: Arrow, 1973);

No End to Danger, as Halliday (London: Paul, 1948); as Creasey (Bath: Lythway, 1972);

Policeman's Triumph, as Manton (London: Wright & Brown, 1948);

A Rope for the Baron, as Morton (London: Low,

Marston, 1948; New York: Duell, Sloan & Pearce, 1949);

Sons of Satan (London: Long, 1948);

The Toff in Town, as Creasey (London: Long, 1948; revised edition, New York: Walker, 1977);

The Toff Take Shares (London: Long, 1948; New York: Walker, 1972);

Triumph for Inspector West (London: Paul, 1948); republished as *The Case Against Paul Raeburn* (New York: Harper, 1958);

Why Murder?, as Deane (London: Hurst & Blackett, 1948); revised edition, as Creasey (London: Arrow, 1975);

The Wings of Peace (London: Long, 1948; New York: Walker, 1978);

Vote for Murder, as Martin (Bournemouth: Earl, 1948); as Creasey (Bath: Lythway, 1973);

Books for the Baron, as Morton (London: Low, 1949; New York: Duell, Sloan & Pearce, 1952);

The Dawn of Darkness (London: Long, 1949);

The Department of Death (London: Evans, 1949);

The Dying Witnesses, as Halliday (London: Evans, 1949); as Creasey (Bath: Lythway, 1973);

The Gallows Are Waiting, as York (London: Melrose, 1949; New York: McKay, 1973);

Inspector West Kicks Off (London: Paul, 1949); republished as *Sport for Inspector West* (New York: Lancer, 1971);

Kill or Be Killed, as Ashe (London: Evans, 1949);

The League of Light (London: Evans, 1949);

A Puzzle in Pearls, as Ashe (London: Long, 1949; revised edition, London: Corgi, 1971);

The Toff and Old Harry (London: Long, 1949; revised edition, London: Hodder & Stoughton, 1964; New York: Walker, 1970);

The Toff on Board (London: Evans, 1949; revised edition, New York: Walker, 1973);

Who Killed Rebecca?, as Halliday (London: Paul, 1949);

Cry for the Baron, as Morton (London: Low, 1950; New York: Walker, 1970);

The Dark Circle, as Ashe (London: Evans, 1950);

Death to My Killer, as York (London: Melrose, 1950; New York: Macmillan, 1966);

Dine with Murder, as Halliday (London: Evans, 1950);

The Enemy Within (London: Evans, 1950; New York: Popular Library, 1977);

Fool the Toff (London: Evans, 1950; New York: Walker, 1966);

Inspector West Alone (London: Evans, 1950; New York: Scribners, 1975);

Inspector West Cries Wolf (London: Evans, 1950); republished as *The Creepers* (New York: Harper, 1952);

Kill the Toff (London: Evans, 1950; New York: Walker, 1966);

The Man Who Shook the World (London: Evans, 1950);

The Man I Didn't Kill (London: Hurst & Blackett, 1950); as Halliday (London: Mayflower-Dell, 1965); revised edition, as Creasey (London: Hutchinson, 1973);

Murder Week-End, as Halliday (London: Evans, 1950);

Murder with Mushrooms, as Ashe (London: Evans, 1950; revised edition, London: Corgi, 1971; New York: Holt, Rinehart & Winston, 1974);

No Hurry to Kill, as Deane (London: Hurst & Blackett, 1950); revised edition, as Creasey (London: Arrow, 1973);

Sentence of Death, as York (London: Melrose, 1950; New York: Macmillan, 1964);

Thief in the Night, as Manton (London: Wright & Brown, 1950);

Trap the Baron, as Morton (London: Low, 1950; New York: Walker, 1971);

Attack the Baron, as Morton (London: Low, 1951);

A Case for Inspector West (London: Evans, 1951); republished as *The Figure in the Dusk* (New York: Harper, 1952);

Dead or Alive (London: Evans, 1951; New York: Popular Library, 1974);

Death in Diamonds, as Ashe (London: Evans, 1951);

Double for Murder, as Deane (London: Hurst & Blackett, 1951); revised edition, as Creasey (London: Hutchinson, 1973);

A Knife for the Toff (London: Evans, 1951; New York: Pyramid, 1964);

Missing or Dead?, as Ashe (London: Evans, 1951);

The Prophet of Fire (London: Evans, 1951; New York: Walker, 1978);

Puzzle for Inspector West (London: Evans, 1951); republished as *The Dissemblers* (New York: Scribners, 1967);

Quarrel with Murder, as Halliday (London: Evans, 1951; revised edition, London: Corgi, 1975);

Shadow the Baron, as Morton (London: Low, 1951);

Take a Body, as Halliday (London: Evans, 1951); revised edition, as Creasey (London: Hodder & Stoughton, 1964; New York: World, 1972);

The Toff Goes Gay (London: Evans, 1951); republished as *A Mask for the Toff* (New York: Walker, 1966);

The Children of Hate (London: Evans, 1952); republished as *The Children of Despair* (New York: Jay, 1958; revised edition, London: Long, 1970); republished as *The Killers of Innocence* (New York: Walker, 1971);

Death in a Hurry, as Ashe (London: Evans, 1952);

Golden Death, as Deane (London: Hurst & Blackett, 1952);

Hunt the Toff (London: Evans, 1952; New York: Walker, 1969);

Inspector West at Bay (London: Evans, 1952); republished as *The Blind Spot* (New York: Harper, 1954); republished as *The Case of the Acid Throwers* (New York: Avon, 1960);

Lame Dog Murder, as Halliday (London: Evans, 1952); as Creasey (New York: World, 1972);

Look at Murder, as Deane (London: Hurst & Blackett, 1952);

Voyage with Murder, as York (London: Melrose, 1952);

Warn the Baron, as Morton (London: Low, 1952);

The Baron Goes East, as Morton (London: Low, 1953);

The Baron in France, as Morton (London: Hodder & Stoughton, 1953; New York: Walker, 1976);

Call the Toff (London: Hodder & Stoughton, 1953; New York: Walker, 1969);

Danger for the Baron, as Morton (London: Hodder & Stoughton, 1953; New York: Walker, 1974);

A Gun for Inspector West (London: Hodder & Stoughton, 1953); republished as *Give a Man a Gun* (New York: Harper, 1954);

The Long Search, as Ashe (London: Long, 1953); republished as *Drop Dead!* (New York: Ace, 1954);

Man on the Run, as Halliday (London: Hodder & Stoughton, 1953); as Creasey (New York: World, 1972);

Murder Ahead, as Deane (London: Hurst & Blackett, 1953);

Murder in the Stars, as Halliday (London: Hodder & Stoughton, 1953); as Creasey (New York: World, 1972);

Murder Out of the Past (Leigh-on-Sea: Barrington Gray, 1953);

No Escape from Murder, as Manton (London: Wright & Brown, 1953);

Sleepy Death, as Ashe (London: Long, 1953);

Safari with Fear, as York (London: Melrose, 1953);

Send Inspector West (London: Hodder & Stoughton, 1953); revised as *Send Superintendent West* (London: Pan, 1965; New York: Scribners, 1976);

The Toff Down Under (London: Hodder & Stoughton, 1953; New York: Walker, 1969); republished as *Break the Toff* (New York: Lancer, 1970);

Adrian and Jonathan, as Martin (London: Hodder & Stoughton, 1954);

The Baron Goes Fast, as Morton (London: Hodder & Stoughton, 1954; New York: Walker, 1972);

A Beauty for Inspector West (London: Hodder & Stoughton, 1954); republished as *The Beauty Queen Killer* (New York: Harper, 1956); republished as *So Young, So Cold, So Fair* (New York: Dell, 1958);

The Charity Murders, as Manton (London: Wright & Brown, 1954);

The Crooked Killer, as Manton (London: Wright & Brown, 1954);

Death in the Spanish Sun, as Deane (London: Hurst & Blackett, 1954);

Death in the Trees, as Ashe (London: Long, 1954);

Death Out of Darkness, as Halliday (London: Hodder & Stoughton, 1954); as Creasey (New York: World, 1971);

Double for Death, as Ashe (London: Long, 1954; New York: Holt, Rinehart & Winston, 1969);

Incense of Death, as Deane (London: Hurst & Blackett, 1954); revised edition, as Creasey (London: New English Library, 1969);

A Kind of Prisoner (London: Hodder & Stoughton, 1954; New York: Popular Library, 1975);

Nest-Egg for the Baron, as Morton (London: Hodder & Stoughton, 1954); republished as *Deaf, Dumb & Blonde* (Garden City, N.Y.: Doubleday, 1961);

Out of the Shadows, as Halliday (London: Hodder & Stoughton, 1954); as Creasey (New York: World, 1971);

The Toff at Butlin's (London: Hodder & Stoughton, 1954; New York: Walker, 1976);

The Toff at the Fair (London: Hodder & Stoughton, 1954; New York: Walker, 1968);

The Touch of Death (London: Hodder & Stoughton, 1954; New York: Walker, 1969);

Cat and Mouse, as Halliday (London: Hodder & Stoughton, 1955); republished as *Hilda Take Heed*, as York (New York: Scribners, 1957); as Halliday (London: World Distributors, 1960);

Gideon's Day, as J. J. Marric (London: Hodder & Stoughton, 1955; New York: Harper, 1955); republished as *Gideon of Scotland Yard* (New York: Berkley, 1958);

Help from the Baron, as Morton (London: Hodder & Stoughton, 1955; New York: Walker, 1977);

Inspector West Makes Haste (London: Hodder & Stoughton, 1955); republished as *The Gelignite Gang* (New York: Harper, 1956); republished as *Murder Makes Haste* (New York: Lancer, 1955); republished as *Night of the Watchman* (New York: Berkley, 1966);

The Kidnapped Child, as Ashe (London: Long, 1955; New York: Holt, Rinehart & Winston, 1971); republished as *The Snatch* (London: Transworld, 1963);

The Man Who Stayed Alive, as Ashe (London: Long, 1955);

The Mists of Fear (London: Hodder & Stoughton, 1955; New York: Walker, 1977);

Murder at End House, as Halliday (London: Hodder & Stoughton, 1955);

A Six for the Toff (London: Hodder & Stoughton, 1955; New York: Walker, 1969); republished as *A Score for the Toff* (New York: Lancer, 1972);

So Soon to Die, as York (London: Paul, 1955; New York: Scribners, 1957);

The Toff and the Deep Blue Sea (London: Hodder & Stoughton, 1955; New York: Walker, 1967);

Two for Inspector West (London: Hodder & Stoughton, 1955); republished as *Murder: One, Two, Three* (New York: Scribners, 1960); republished as *Murder Tips the Scales* (New York: Berkley, 1962);

Day of Fear, as Ashe (London: Long, 1956; New York: Holt, Rinehart & Winston, 1978);

Gideon's Week, as Marric (London: Hodder & Stoughton, 1956; New York: Harper, 1956); republished as *Seven Days to Death* (New York: Pyramid, 1958);

The Flood (London: Hodder & Stoughton, 1956; New York: Walker, 1969);

Hide the Baron, as Morton (London: Hodder & Stoughton, 1956; New York: Walker, 1978);

Kill Once, Kill Twice, as Kyle Hunt (New York: Simon & Schuster, 1956; London: Barker, 1957);

Make-Up for the Toff (London: Hodder & Stoughton, 1956; New York: Walker, 1967); republished as *Kiss the Toff* (New York: Lancer, 1971);

No Need to Die, as Ashe (London: Long, 1956); republished as *You've Bet Your Life* (New York: Ace, 1957);

Parcels for Inspector West (London: Hodder & Stoughton, 1956); republished as *Death of a Postman* (New York: Harper, 1957);

A Prince for Inspector West (London: Hodder & Stoughton, 1956); republished as *Death of an Assassin* (New York: Scribners, 1960);

Seeds of Murder, as York (London: Paul, 1956; New York: Scribners, 1958);

Sight of Death, as York (London & New York: Paul, 1956; New York: Scribners, 1958);

The Toff in New York (London: Hodder & Stoughton, 1956; New York: Pyramid, 1964);

Accident for Inspector West (London: Hodder & Stoughton, 1957); republished as *Hit and Run* (New York: Scribners, 1959);

The Black Spiders (London: Hodder & Stoughton, 1957; New York: Popular Library, 1975);

Death of a Stranger, as Halliday (London: Hodder & Stoughton, 1957; New York & London: White Lion, 1972); republished as *Come Here and Die*, as York (New York: Scribners, 1959);

Find Inspector West (London: Hodder & Stoughton, 1957); republished as *The Trouble at Saxby's* (New York: Harper, 1959); republished as *Doorway to Death* (New York: Berkley, 1961);

Frame the Baron, as Morton (London: Hodder & Stoughton, 1957); republished as *The Double Frame* (Garden City, N.Y.: Doubleday, 1961);

Gideon's Night, as Marric (London: Hodder & Stoughton, 1957; New York: Harper, 1957);

Kill a Wicked Man, as Hunt (New York: Simon & Schuster, 1957; London: Barker, 1958);

Model for the Toff (London: Hodder & Stoughton, 1957; New York: Pyramid, 1965);

Runaway, as Halliday (London: Hodder & Stoughton, 1957); as Creasey (New York: World, 1971);

The Toff on Fire (London: Hodder & Stoughton, 1957; New York: Walker, 1966);

Wait for Death, as Ashe (London: Long, 1957; New York: Holt, Rinehart & Winston, 1972);

Come Home to Death, as Ashe (London: Long, 1958); republished as *The Pack of Lies* (Garden City, N.Y.: Doubleday, 1959);

Gideon's Month, as Marric (London: Hodder & Stoughton, 1958; New York: Harper, 1958);

Kill My Love, as Hunt (New York: Simon & Schuster, 1958; London & New York: Boardman, 1959);

Murder Assured, as Halliday (London: Hodder & Stoughton, 1958);

Murder, London-New York (London: Hodder & Stoughton, 1958; New York: Scribners, 1961);

My Brother's Killer, as York (London: Long, 1958; New York: Scribners, 1959);

The Plague of Silence (London: Hodder & Stoughton, 1958; New York: Walker, 1968);

Red Eye for the Baron, as Morton (London: Hodder & Stoughton, 1958); republished as *Blood Red* (Garden City, N.Y.: Doubleday, 1960);

Strike for Death (London: Hodder & Stoughton, 1958); republished as *The Killing Strike* (New York: Scribners, 1961);

The Toff and the Stolen Tresses (London: Hodder & Stoughton, 1958; New York: Walker, 1965);

The Toff on the Farm (London: Hodder & Stoughton, 1958; New York: Walker, 1964); republished as *Terror for the Toff* (New York: Pyramid, 1965);

Black for the Baron, as Morton (London: Hodder & Stoughton, 1959); republished as *If Anything Happens to Hester* (Garden City, N.Y.: Doubleday, 1962);

Death of a Racehorse (London: Hodder & Stoughton, 1959; New York: Scribners, 1962);

Double for the Toff (London: Hodder & Stoughton, 1959; New York: Walker, 1965);

The Drought (London: Hodder & Stoughton, 1959; New York: Walker, 1967); republished as *Dry Spell* (London: Four Square, 1967);

Elope to Death, as Ashe (London: Long, 1959; New York: Holt, Rinehart & Winston, 1977);

Gideon's Staff, as Marric (London: Hodder & Stoughton, 1959; New York: Harper, 1959);

Hide and Kill, as York (London: Long, 1959; New York: Scribners, 1960);

Mark Kilby Solves a Murder, as Robert Caine Frazer (New York: Pocket, 1959); republished as *R.I.S.C.* (London: Collins, 1962); republished as *The Timid Tycoon* (London: Fontana, 1966);

Missing from Home, as Halliday (London: Hodder & Stoughton, 1959); republished as *Missing, by Jeremy York*, as York (New York: Scribners, 1960);

Thicker than Water, as Halliday (London: Hodder & Stoughton, 1959); as York (Garden City, N.Y.: Doubleday, 1962);

The Toff and the Runaway Bride (London: Hodder & Stoughton, 1959; New York: Walker, 1964);

The Crime Haters, as Ashe (Garden City, N.Y.: Doubleday, 1960; London: Long, 1961);

The Case of the Innocent Victims (London: Hodder & Stoughton, 1960; New York: Scribners, 1966);

Don't Let Him Kill, as Ashe (London: Long, 1960); republished as *The Man Who Laughed at Murder* (Garden City, N.Y.: Doubleday, 1960);

Gideon's Risk, as Marric (London: Hodder & Stoughton, 1960; New York: Harper, 1960);

Go Ahead with Murder, as Halliday (London: Hodder & Stoughton, 1960); republished as *Two for the Money*, as York (Garden City, N.Y.: Doubleday, 1962);

How Many to Kill?, as Halliday (London: Hodder & Stoughton, 1960); republished as *The Girl with the Leopard-Skin Bag*, as York (New York: Scribners, 1961);

Mark Kilby and the Miami Mob, as Frazer (New York: Pocket, 1960; London & Glasgow: Collins, 1966); republished as *The Miami Mob* in *The Miami Mob, and Mark Kilby Stands Alone* (London: Collins, 1965);

Mark Kilby and the Secret Syndicate, as Frazer (New York: Pocket, 1960); republished as *The Secret Syndicate* (London: Collins, 1963);

The Mountain of the Blind (London: Hodder & Stoughton, 1960);

Murder on the Line (London: Hodder & Stoughton, 1960; New York: Scribners, 1963);

A Rocket for the Toff (London: Hodder & Stoughton, 1960; New York: Pyramid, 1964);

Salute for the Baron, as Morton (London: Hodder & Stoughton, 1960; New York: Walker, 1973);

They Didn't Mean to Kill: The Real Story of Road Accidents (London: Hodder & Stoughton, 1960);

The Toff and the Kidnapped Child (London: Hodder & Stoughton, 1960; New York: Walker, 1965);

To Kill a Killer, as Hunt (London & New York: Boardman, 1960; New York: Random House, 1960); as Creasey (New York & London: White Lion, 1973);

To Kill or to Die, as York (London: Long, 1960; New York: Macmillan, 1965);

A Branch for the Baron, as Morton (London: Hodder & Stoughton, 1961); republished as *The Baron Branches Out* (New York: Scribners, 1967);

Death in Cold Print (London: Hodder & Stoughton, 1961; New York: Scribners, 1962);

The Edge of Terror, as Halliday (London: Hodder & Stoughton, 1961); as York (New York: Macmillan, 1963);

Follow the Toff (London: Hodder & Stoughton, 1961; New York: Walker, 1967);

The Foothills of Fear (London: Hodder & Stoughton, 1961; New York: Walker, 1966);

Gideon's Fire, as Marric (London: Hodder & Stoughton, 1961; New York: Harper, 1961);

The Hollywood Hoax, as Frazer (New York: Pocket, 1961; London: Collins, 1964);

The Man I Killed, as Halliday (London: Hodder & Stoughton, 1961); as York (New York: Macmillan, 1963);

Rogues' Ransom, as Ashe (Garden City, N.Y.: Doubleday, 1961; London: Long, 1962);

The Scene of the Crime (London: Hodder & Stoughton, 1961; New York: Scribners, 1963);

The Toff and the Teds (London: Hodder & Stoughton, 1961); republished as *The Toff and the Toughs* (New York: Walker, 1968);

Bad for the Baron, as Morton (London: Hodder & Stoughton, 1962); republished as *The Baron and the Stolen Legacy* (New York: Scribners, 1967);

Gideon's March, as Marric (London: Hodder & Stoughton, 1962; New York: Harper, 1962);

Hate to Kill, as Halliday (London: Hodder & Stoughton, 1962);

Mark Kilby Stands Alone, as Frazer (New York: Pocket, 1962); republished in *The Miami Mob, and Mark Kilby Stands Alone* (London: Collins, 1965); republished as *Mark Kilby and the Manhattan Murders* (London: Collins, 1966);

Mark Kilby Takes a Risk, as Frazer (New York: Pocket, 1962);

Policeman's Dread (London: Hodder & Stoughton, 1962; New York: Scribners, 1964);

The Terror: The Return of Dr. Palfrey (London: Hodder & Stoughton, 1962; New York: Walker, 1966);

Death from Below, as Ashe (London: Long, 1963; New York: Holt, Rinehart & Winston, 1968);

The Depths (London: Hodder & Stoughton, 1963; New York: Walker, 1967);

A Doll for the Toff (London: Hodder & Stoughton, 1963; New York: Walker, 1965);

Gideon's Ride, as Marric (London: Hodder & Stoughton, 1963; New York: Harper & Row, 1963);

Hang the Little Man (London: Hodder & Stoughton, 1963; New York: Scribners, 1963);

Leave It to the Toff (London: Hodder & Stoughton, 1963; New York: Pyramid, 1965);

The Quiet Fear, as Halliday (London: Hodder & Stoughton, 1963); as York (New York: Macmillan, 1968);

A Sword for the Baron, as Morton (London: Hodder & Stoughton, 1963); republished as *The Baron and the Mogul Swords* (New York: Scribners, 1966);

The Toff; a Comedy Thriller in Three Acts (London: Evans, 1963);

The Baron on Board, as Morton (London: Hodder & Stoughton, 1964; New York: Walker, 1968);

The Big Call, as Ashe (London: Long, 1964; New York: Holt, Rinehart & Winston, 1975);

Gideon's Lot, as Marric (New York: Harper & Row, 1964; London: Hodder & Stoughton, 1965);

Gideon's Vote, as Marric (London: Hodder & Stoughton, 1964; New York: Harper & Row, 1964);

The Guilt of Innocence (London: Hodder & Stoughton, 1964);

Look Three Ways at Murder (London: Hodder & Stoughton, 1964; New York: Scribners, 1965);

A Promise of Diamonds, as Ashe (New York: Dodd, Mead, 1964; London: Long, 1965);

The Sleep (London: Hodder & Stoughton, 1964; New York: Walker, 1968);

The Baron and the Chinese Puzzle, as Morton (London: Hodder & Stoughton, 1965; New York: Scribners, 1966);

Cunning as a Fox, as Halliday (London: Hodder & Stoughton, 1965); as Hunt (New York: Macmillan, 1965);

Gideon's Badge, as Marric (New York: Harper & Row, 1965; London: Hodder & Stoughton, 1966);

The Inferno (London: Hodder & Stoughton, 1965; New York: Walker, 1966);

Murder, London-Australia (London: Hodder & Stoughton, 1965; New York: Scribners, 1965);

The Toff and the Spider (London: Hodder & Stoughton, 1965; New York: Walker, 1966);

Danger Woman, as Abel Mann (New York: Pocket, 1966);

Murder, London-South Africa (London: Hodder & Stoughton, 1966; New York: Scribners, 1966);

Sport for the Baron, as Morton (London: Hodder & Stoughton, 1966; New York: Walker, 1969);

A Taste of Treasure, as Ashe (London: Long, 1966; New York: Holt, Rinehart & Winston, 1966);

The Toff in Wax (London: Hodder & Stoughton, 1966; New York: Walker, 1966);

Wicked as the Devil, as Halliday (London: Hodder & Stoughton, 1966); as Hunt (New York: Macmillan, 1966);

Affair for the Baron, as Morton (London: Hodder & Stoughton, 1967; New York: Walker, 1968);

A Bundle for the Toff (London: Hodder & Stoughton, 1967; New York: Walker, 1968);

A Clutch of Coppers, as Ashe (London: Long, 1967; New York: Holt, Rinehart & Winston, 1969);

The Executioners (London: Hodder & Stoughton, 1967; New York: Scribners, 1967);

The Famine (London: Hodder & Stoughton, 1967; New York: Walker, 1968);

Gideon's Wrath, as Marric (London: Hodder & Stoughton, 1967; New York: Harper & Row, 1967);

Good, God and Man: An Outline of the Philosophy of Self-ism (London: Hodder & Stoughton, 1967; New York: Walker, 1971);

Sly as a Serpent, as Halliday (London: Hodder & Stoughton, 1967); as Hunt (New York: Macmillan, 1967);

The Baron and the Missing Old Masters, as Morton (London: Hodder & Stoughton, 1968; New York: Walker, 1969);

The Blight (London: Hodder & Stoughton, 1968; New York: Walker, 1968);

Cruel as a Cat, as Halliday (London: Hodder & Stoughton, 1968); as Hunt (New York: Macmillan, 1968);

Gideon's River, as Marric (London: Hodder & Stoughton, 1968; New York: Harper & Row, 1968);

John Creasey–Fact or Fiction? A Candid Commentary in Third Person [includes *A John Creasey Bibliography* by Creasey and R. E. Briney] (White Bear Lake, Minn.: Armchair Detective, 1968; revised, 1969);

A Shadow of Death, as Ashe (London: Long, 1968; New York: Holt, Rinehart & Winston, 1976);

So Young to Burn (London: Hodder & Stoughton, 1968; New York: Scribners, 1968);

Stars for the Toff (London: Hodder & Stoughton, 1968; New York: Walker, 1968);

The Baron and the Unfinished Portrait, as Morton (London: Hodder & Stoughton, 1969; New York: Walker, 1970);

Gideon's Power, as Marric (London: Hodder & Stoughton, 1969; New York: Harper & Row, 1969);

Murder, London-Miami (London: Hodder & Stoughton, 1969; New York: Scribners, 1969);

The Toff and the Golden Boy (London: Hodder & Stoughton, 1969; New York: Walker, 1969);

The Oasis (London: Hodder & Stoughton, 1969; New York: Walker, 1970);

A Scream of Murder, as Ashe (London: Long, 1969; New York: Holt, Rinehart & Winston, 1970);

Too Good to Be True, as Halliday (London: Hodder & Stoughton, 1969); as Hunt (New York: Macmillan, 1969);

Gideon's Sport, as Marric (London: Hodder & Stoughton, 1970; New York: Harper & Row, 1970);

Last Laugh for the Baron, as Morton (London: Hodder & Stoughton, 1970; New York: Walker, 1971);

A Nest of Traitors, as Ashe (London: Long, 1970; New York: Holt, Rinehart & Winston, 1971);

A Part for a Policeman (London: Hodder & Stoughton, 1970; New York: Scribners, 1970);

A Period of Evil, as Halliday (London: Hodder & Stoughton, 1970); as Hunt (New York: World, 1971);

The Smog (London: Hodder & Stoughton, 1970; New York: Walker, 1971);

The Toff and the Fallen Angels (London: Hodder & Stoughton, 1970; New York: Walker, 1970);

As Lonely as the Damned, as Halliday (London: Hodder & Stoughton, 1971); as Hunt (New York: World, 1972);

The Baron Goes A-Buying, as Morton (London: Hodder & Stoughton, 1971; New York: Walker, 1972);

Gideon's Art, as Marric (London: Hodder & Stoughton, 1971; New York: Harper & Row, 1971);

A Rabble of Rebels, as Ashe (London: Long, 1971; New York: Holt, Rinehart & Winston, 1972);

The Unbegotten (London: Hodder & Stoughton, 1971; New York: Walker, 1972);

Vote for the Toff (London: Hodder & Stoughton, 1971; New York: Walker, 1971);

As Empty as Hate, as Halliday (London: Hodder & Stoughton, 1972); as Hunt (New York: World, 1972);

The Baron and the Arrogant Artist, as Morton (London: Hodder & Stoughton, 1972; New York: Walker, 1973);

Gideon's Men, as Marric (London: Hodder & Stoughton, 1972; New York: Harper & Row, 1972);

The Insulators (London: Hodder & Stoughton, 1972; New York: Walker, 1973);

A Splinter of Glass (London: Hodder & Stoughton, 1972; New York: Scribners, 1972);

The Toff and the Trip-Trip-Triplets (London: Hodder & Stoughton, 1972; New York: Walker, 1972);

As Merry as Hell, as Halliday (London: Hodder & Stoughton, 1973); as Hunt (New York: Stein & Day, 1974);

Burgle the Baron, as Morton (London: Hodder & Stoughton, 1973; New York: Walker, 1974);

Gideon's Press, as Marric (London: Hodder & Stoughton, 1973; New York: Harper & Row, 1973);

A Life for Death, as Ashe (London: Long, 1973; New York: Holt, Rinehart & Winston, 1973);

The Theft of Magna Carta (London: Hodder & Stoughton, 1973; New York: Scribners, 1973);

The Toff and the Terrified Taxman (London: Hodder & Stoughton, 1973; New York: Walker, 1973);

The Voiceless Ones (London: Hodder & Stoughton, 1973; New York: Walker, 1974);

The Extortioners (London: Hodder & Stoughton, 1974; New York: Scribners, 1975);

Gideon's Fog, as Marric (New York: Harper & Row, 1974; London: Hodder & Stoughton, 1975);

A Herald of Doom, as Ashe (London: Long, 1974; New York: Holt, Rinehart & Winston, 1975);

The Masters of Bow Street (London: Hodder & Stoughton, 1974; New York: Simon & Schuster, 1974);

This Man Did I Kill, as Halliday (London: Hodder & Stoughton, 1974); as Hunt (New York: Stein & Day, 1974);

The Toff and the Sleepy Cowboy (London: Hodder & Stoughton, 1974; New York: Walker, 1975);

The Baron, King-Maker, as Morton (London: Hodder & Stoughton, 1975; New York: Walker, 1975);

A Blast of Trumpets, as Ashe (London: Long, 1975; New York: Holt, Rinehart & Winston, 1976);

Gideon's Drive, as Marric (London: Hodder & Stoughton, 1976; New York: Harper & Row, 1976);

The Man Who Was Not Himself, as Halliday (London: Hodder & Stoughton, 1976); as Hunt (New York: Stein & Day, 1976);

A Plague of Demons, as Ashe (London: Long, 1976; New York: Holt, Rinehart & Winston, 1977);

The Thunder–Maker (London: Hodder & Stoughton, 1976; New York: Walker, 1976);

The Toff and the Crooked Copper (London: Hodder & Stoughton, 1977);

A Sharp Rise in Crime (London: Hodder & Stoughton, 1978; New York: Scribners, 1979);

Love for the Baron, as Morton (London: Hodder & Stoughton, 1979);

The Whirlwind (London: Hodder & Stoughton, 1979).

OTHER: *The Mystery Bedside Book*, edited by Creasey (London: Hodder & Stoughton, 1960);

Crimes Across the Sea, edited by Creasey (New York: Harper & Row, 1964; London: Harrap, 1965).

The most prolific mystery writer ever, John Creasey eventually achieved as much fame for the quality of his work as he did for its sheer quantity. Beginning in 1932 he wrote over five hundred books about heroes as diverse as Gordon Craigie, the Toff, the Baron, Roger West, Patrick Dawlish, Palfrey, and Gideon of Scotland Yard.

Creasey, the seventh of nine children, was born 17 September 1908 to Ruth and Joseph Creasey. His father was a coach maker in Surrey, England. Creasey claimed that his ambition to become a writer stemmed from the age of ten when a schoolmaster, after reading a writing exercise in which the boy had recounted an imaginary conversation between Marshal Foch and Kaiser Wilhelm, told him he could make a living out of writing. The family was poor, and Creasey was forced to leave school at the age of fourteen and support himself with a variety of clerical and factory jobs while he wrote at night. Though his family ridiculed his ambition and he received 743 rejection slips for work submitted between the ages of ten and seventeen, he persisted and finally sold a short story. His first novel, a spy story, *Seven Times Seven*, was published in 1932 when he was twenty-three. In his early days he often worked for forty-eight consecutive hours to meet a deadline on a fifty-two-hundred-word serial, for which he would receive thirteen guineas in payment. The number of books and short stories he eventually sold, well over six hundred, almost matched his early record of rejections. He proved to be so prolific that he left enough material for new works by him to be published for six years after his death.

From the beginning of his writing career Creasey's method was to write very quickly. A Walker Publishing Company publicity release (Fall 1971) cited the *Hudersfield Examiner*, which once wrote about Creasey's speed: "It is said that Mr. Creasey produces three novels at the same time, one written with his right hand and one with his left and the third dictated." Maurice Richardson, in the *London Observer*, reviewed another book by saying, "I am told that Mr. Creasey can write a book like this in three days. Having read the book, I can well believe it." In a 1971 letter to the *New York Times Book Review* Creasey, who was able to poke fun at himself, quoted Richardson and said the criticism had a "quite gentlemanly ring" compared to Newgate Callendar of the *New York Times Book Review*, whom he accused of deliberate unkindness in his reviews of books

Creasey had written more than fifteen years in the past.

Unwilling (or unable) to change his writing habits, Creasey eventually hired a series of professional readers to review his work, making note of factual and/or grammatical errors which he then corrected on revision. Many of his early novels eventually were revised and updated for republication in Great Britain and before their first publication in the United States. Of his entire output he had set aside eighty-five books which he felt were unworthy of being republished, even with revisions. From 1936 to 1961 he published no fewer than nine new books a year. Shortly before his death in 1973 he had limited his production to about eight books annually, though he seemed much more prolific because so many books were constantly being reissued throughout the world.

Creasey wrote juveniles, westerns, sports stories, romantic novels, biographies, and other nonfiction. His great fame, however, came from writing mysteries which appeared under sixteen separate names, including his own. As M. E. Cooke (his first wife's initials and name) and Peter Manton he wrote more than thirty mysteries, none about series characters; they were among those never published in the United States. Most of his successful books involved the use of series characters, many of whom proved to be extremely popular. Creasey was astonishingly versatile, creating more continuing series of other novels than any other mystery writer before or after his time.

Though he never deviated from the idea that his work must entertain, he determined early in his career that serious themes about the problems of contemporary society would be included whenever possible. In many of his books he included topics such as poverty, juvenile delinquency, political corruption, and dangers to the environment. In a 1971 publicity release by Walker Publishing Company he said, "The crime book is the only book written today dealing with the fundamental human conflict between good and evil. At its best, it is today's morality play."

Creasey's first major series character was Gordon Craigie, chief of Department Z, the counterespionage arm of British intelligence. Craigie first appeared in Creasey's sixth book, *Redhead* (1934). As World War II in Europe grew imminent, the series took on greater plausibility, and it was quite popular during the 1930s, especially books like *Thunder in Europe* (1936), *Days of Danger* (1937), and *Menace!* (1938). Trying to stay

ahead of world events, Creasey made this one of his more imaginative series. For example, as early as 1943, in *No Darker Crime*, he sends Craigie and his staff to investigate the assassinations of government representatives who are working on plans to feed the postwar world. Craigie, incidentally, unlike some of Creasey's early heroes, was a forerunner of realism in the detective story as he showed many human traits. He is often tired and impatient. Usually overworked, he feels the burden of an administrator's increasing volume of paperwork.

The Black Spiders, the last Department Z book, was published in 1957. By then the organization had merged with Department Z5, an international group operating under Harley Street physician Stanislaus Alexander Palfrey in the series which Creasey began in 1942 with *Traitors' Doom*. The Palfrey series evolved with international crime thrillers like *The Hounds of Vengeance* (1945), about the attempt to discover hidden Nazi hoards, to doomsday mysteries with many of the elements of science fiction. In *The Flood* (1956) a villain with a Messianic complex has unleashed deep-sea crustaceans with the power to cause the earth to become inundated. Needless to say, critics, while finding the book chilling, emphasized its lack of credibility. Equally unscrupulous forces release insects which can cause paralysis in *The Plague of Silence* (1958). As the Palfrey series went on, Creasey more often used real problems facing the world as plot devices. For example, *The Famine* (1967) deals with overpopulation, and *The Smog* (1970) examines massive pollution. Palfrey's foes in *The Insulators* (1972) are typical of the mad scientists Palfrey usually battles in these often allegorical novels. They are leaders of a group which, after installing its own underground nuclear arsenals throughout the world, manufactures a gas which can insulate humans against atomic radiation. They plan to use the threat of their bombs (and their control of its antidote) to blackmail and, eventually, enslave the world.

Creasey's next series, after Department Z, was one written under the pseudonym Anthony Morton regarding the Baron (John Mannering), who originally led a double life as a rich gentleman and a Raffles-type jewel thief. The first title in the series, *Meet the Baron* (1937), was written in only six days for a contest. Mannering wore a blue mask during his escapades, and when the series first appeared in the United States, the name of the hero in the titles was Blue Mask rather

Creasey posing atop a clutch of ostrich eggs in Oudtshoorn, South Africa, during a tour of the country in 1962 (photograph by Richard Creasey)

than the Baron. Eventually, after marriage to wealthy Lorna Fauntley, Mannering gives up thievery and opens a posh art and antiques store in the Mayfair section of London. He even agrees to act as a consultant to Scotland Yard on matters related to theft of objets d'art, but his former nemesis, Superintendent Bristow, remains eternally suspicious. There is little detection in the Baron series, and the books owe much to the thrillers of Edgar Wallace and Sydney Horler. Still, the series remained enormously popular with a wide variety of readers. (Jean Cocteau once called the Baron his favorite fictional character.) The Baron was less popular with some critics. Newgate Callendar, reviewing an American publication (1971) of *Trap the Baron* (1950) for the *New York Times Book Review* (13 June 1971), acknowledged Creasey's ingenious plotting but felt the author's "flat stereotyped writing" ruined the Baron books.

Richard Rollison (The Toff) was another wealthy hero who skirted the edges of the law, beginning with his 1938 series debut *Introducing the Toff*. The Toff was always one of Creasey's favorite characters, as is made clear in the enthusiastic

introduction the author wrote for the first United States publication in 1964 of *The Toff in New York* (1956). In it he gave a brief biography of Rollison, after defining a toff for American audiences as "a person who behaves handsomely." Rollison had worked his way around the world for three years to prove that, despite his wealth, he could support himself as well as find out how the rest of the world, "especially the underprivileged," live. He learned to defend himself and "won degrees (with honors) in the University of Tough Life." Back in England, Rollison puts on no airs despite his wealth and social position, and he is "impatient of featherbedding, either by royalty or by unions." A bachelor throughout the series, he has a more active love life than most Creasey series characters, and his eye for women occasionally causes him problems, as in *The Toff at the Fair* (1954), in which he is captivated by a beautiful gypsy who may be involved in the cocaine trade. When the series begins, Rollison is impatient with the police, but gradually he works well with them though he continues to maintain strong contacts with people who skirt the law in the working-class East End of London. He is aided by the characters who reappear throughout the series: for example, his loyal valet, Jolly; his broad-minded, though patrician aunt, Lady Gloria "Old Glory" Hurst; and Inspector Gryce.

Plots are minimal in the Toff series, and only many false starts and contrived complications drag them out to novel length. The books frequently start out with Rollison doing a good deed for someone only to find himself involved in a major crime. Home on leave from his army duties in *The Toff Goes to Market* (1942), Rollison uses his contacts in London's underworld to discover black marketeers who are distributing tainted food and forcing merchants to accept their illegal products. In *The Toff in New York* Rollison follows wealthy Valerie Hall from London to New York at her brother's request. When the brother is kidnapped the Toff is there to help her, showing his usual sense of honor as well as a head for heights as he walks on hotel ledges and fights a climactic battle on the 101st floor observation tower of a skyscraper. Along the way the Toff gets to imitate a Texas colonel, using what reads like an authentic drawl, and to work with a brave New York City taxi driver. In a plot right out of the pulp magazines of the 1930s, they combat "Dutch" Himmy, the gangster who has "terrorized parts of New York." In *A Bundle for the Toff* (1967) Rollison literally has a baby

*Dust jacket for the first American edition of Creasey's 1970 installment in his Inspector West series,
this case involving an attempt by outside forces to destroy the British motion
picture industry*

left on his doorstep, and a paternity suit is threatened against him. *The Toff and the Fallen Angels* (1970) sees him helping the proprietress of a home for wayward girls which someone is trying to destroy. One of the best in the entire series is *The Toff and the Kidnapped Child* (1960), in which a distraught mother, fearing her daughter has been taken away by her estranged husband, asks the Toff to investigate. The writing is a bit more subtle than usual, with the Toff's attraction for the mother well-handled.

Creasey constantly brought his Toff series up-to-date, moving into London of the infamous Teddy Boy gangs and other vicious young criminals in *The Toff and the Teds* (1961) and *The Toff and the Golden Boy* (1969). The Toff books never broke new ground in mystery fiction, but they gained great popularity because they were fast-moving thrillers about likable characters. If the Toff and the people he tried to help were very

good, the villains he confronted were extremely evil, and that, too, was part of the attraction of the series.

The Patrick Dawlish series, which Creasey wrote as Gordon Ashe, began with *Death on Demand* (1939), the year after the Toff series began. Originally the two characters were similar, with courage, physical perfection, and wealth. One difference is that Dawlish is married, and it is the kidnapping of his wife in *Wait for Death* (1957), one of the later books in the first phase of the series, which provides a crucial plot device. Dawlish and his lovely wife, Felicity, have been lured to Brighton, and while he tries to find why they are followed by a beautiful blonde in a bikini bathing suit, Felicity is stolen away. The series took a new turn after 1960 as Dawlish, a former war hero who has been fighting crime on his own, becomes a deputy assistant commissioner of the London metropolitan police, joining an international group known as the Crime Haters. He is Great Britain's delegate to the organization, and he works with representatives from every major police force in the world to thwart crimes of international significance. An early Crime Hater book in the Dawlish series, *Death from Below* (1963), proved to be one of Creasey's most suspenseful thrillers as Dawlish and his colleagues try to find out why young men and women are being systematically drowned throughout Western Europe. In this book Creasey does a good job of creating an aura of fear appropriate to horrible events taking place for unknown reasons. There were occasions when the plots in the Dawlish series were similar to those in the Palfrey books. A typical example is *A Nest of Traitors* (1970), in which investigation of a major international passport fraud scheme leads Dawlish to "The Authority," an international conspiracy to take over all the governments, banks, and industries of the world.

In 1942 Creasey, writing under his own name, introduced his series character Inspector (later Superintendent) Roger "Handsome" West of Scotland Yard, in *Inspector West Takes Charge*. The novel is a mixture of police story and thriller, with West relying heavily on his friend Mark Lessing, a wealthy London playboy. The series gradually took on more authentic qualities, and West, despite the exceptional good looks which led to his nickname, becomes a believable hero in his own right. His family is usually important to the stories, with frequent reference to the time he must spend away from his wife and two sons, Martin and Richard (the names, incidentally, of Creasey's sons by his second wife, Jean Fudge, whom he married in 1941). Even the plots grew better, rising above the formulaic level of such books as *A Beauty for Inspector West* (1954), in which a killer stalks the winners of regional beauty contests in Great Britain.

Parcels for Inspector West (1956), an example of the well-written later books in the West series, is a novel about the murder of a postal clerk just before Christmas. Although he could have delegated the unpleasant task of informing the clerk's wife and five children, West tells them himself in a poignant scene whose novelistic qualities reflected the growth in Creasey's talent. The contrast, throughout this book, of a joyous holiday season with stark murder is very effective. In *Accident for Inspector West* (1957) a nonconformist minister, known as Parson Pete, who is head of the Anti-Road Murder campaign (his own mother having been killed by a car), surprisingly

Dust jacket for the forty-fifth installment in Creasey's series featuring gentleman jewel thief Baron John Mannering

is accused of a series of hit-and-run deaths throughout London. One murder victim is a magistrate who was considered an advocate of the rights of motorists. To solve the crimes West must overcome two attempts on his life, one of which is by automobile. He also must deal with the distractions caused by the severe illness of his old friend (and superior) at Scotland Yard, Assistant Commissioner Chatsworth, who has suffered a heart attack.

Creasey wrote relatively few short stories, and those he did write were generally not up to the quality of his novels. Yet "The Greyling Crescent Tragedy" (*Ellery Queen's Mystery Magazine*, June 1966), while brief, demonstrates all that had become excellent in the West series. This is a very moving tale about a seven-year-old who awakens in the morning to find his mother murdered. What the child remembers of a quarrel he overheard before going to sleep is crucial to the discovery of the murderer.

The Inspector Folly series was written under the pseudonym Michael Halliday (they were published in the United States as by Jeremy York or Kyle Hunt). Folly is not a distinctive personality, and he is perhaps best remembered for his obesity. Another series under the Halliday pseudonym in England concerns the Fane family, a thinly disguised version of the Creaseys. Father Jonathan is a prolific mystery writer, creator of the Prince, hero of a series of over seventy books about an aristocratic private eye. Fane's sons Martin and Richard, who refer to their father as "the maestro of the twanging nerve," have read a great deal about crime and give up their respective careers in advertising and journalism to form a private detective agency.

Though he was considered highly in Great Britain, nothing John Creasey had done previously prepared mystery readers for the excellence of the Gideon series for which he used the J. J. Marric pseudonym. (The last name was a combination of those of his sons, Martin and Richard.) Procedurals, realistic novels which followed police procedures, had been written before the Gideon books, but his are considered the best of this type of detective fiction. In the United States Lawrence Treat had created a believable group of policemen as early as 1945. In 1954 Maurice Procter had published his first of many successful novels about Inspector Harry Martineau of the fictional northern British city of Granchester. Even Creasey's Roger West books had authenticity, though West usually remains the storybook hero and the individual, with his good looks and intuitive actions.

In *Gideon's Day* (1955), which begins the series, six major crimes confront Gideon during the course of a single day. While solving these crimes, Gee-Gee, as he is known to his colleagues, is undergoing strained family relations with his wife, Kate, who is incensed that her husband is so seldom at home and has left her with six children to bring up, mainly by herself. Though he has a well-deserved reputation for steeliness at work, Gideon shows humanity and flexibility in dealing with this crisis in his personal life. *Gideon's Day* was made into a film, *Gideon of Scotland Yard*, in 1959. *Gideon's Week* (1956), *Gideon's Night* (1957), and *Gideon's Month* (1958) were almost as good as the first book in blending realism and a sympathetic character, lacking only the novelty which comes with the beginning of a major series.

Going from strength to strength, Creasey produced two Gideon books in the early 1960s which stand as the peak of his career. *Gideon's Fire* (1961) was given the Edgar Allan Poe Award as the best novel of the year by the Mystery Writers of America in 1962. Anthony Boucher, in the *New York Times Book Review* (22 January 1961), maintained that this was the best of all the Gideon books, calling it "a technically dazzling handling of a large number of plots: arson, child-rape, murder domestic and financial fraud; . . each developed as fully as the average crime writer could do in a single-minded novel." London has seldom been better realized than in this book, especially the city's slums which are the target for a series of deadly fires. Gideon's humanity is continuously emphasized, especially when he is guilty of an occasional mistake during a day when he must make countless on-the-spot decisions.

Gideon's March (1962) and *Gideon's River* (1968) were also highly rated. In the *New York Times Book Review* (15 April 1962) Boucher called *Gideon's March* "the police novel at its firmest and most fascinating." London is the setting for a conference of Western leaders, with the meeting to be led off by a procession. Rumors of a possible attempt on the life of one of the leaders have been received, and Gideon is responsible for preventing an assassination. This book has been cited by historians of the mystery as prophetic, in view of the subsequent assassination of John F. Kennedy in Dallas, Texas. (The potential assassin in *Gideon's March* hates the president of the United States for being a Catholic and favoring equal rights for blacks.) The book can also be considered the precursor of an entire mystery subgenre of books involving international assassination and hijacking. However, it has proved to be far better than any of the dozens of books regarding these crimes which have followed it. Jacques Barzun and Wendell Hertig Taylor, in *A Catalogue of Crime* (1971), praised the interweaving of the personal lives of the investigators with ongoing investigations into diamond smuggling, kidnapping, and murder in *Gideon's River*, which they cite as the best of the Gideon series.

Creasey used his income to do a great deal of traveling, completing ten books while on one around-the-world trip. He made many trips to the United States, where he traveled extensively by bus and car, again writing during all of his free moments. His visits to the United States led to still another series, written under the name Robert Caine Frazer. The books are about Mark Kilby, the chief investigator for the Regal Investment Security Corporation (R.I.S.C.). Though Kilby is British and his company is based in London, R.I.S.C. has branches throughout the United States, and most of his adventures are set there. For example, *Mark Kilby and the Secret Syndicate* (1960) begins with the hijacking of a Greyhound bus in the Arizona desert. Other books are set in Miami and Hollywood, California. The Kilby series, designed for the American audience, though reprinted in England, marked a return by Creasey to a bigger-than-life hero like Palfrey or the Toff. Kilby's job is "to make sure that R.I.S.C. doesn't invest in phony schemes." He carries a switchblade in his cane; as Creasey wrote, "That and a mind that was as sharp as the blade of the knife were his only weapons." Referred to as "a Beau Brummel among detectives," Kilby is once described as "wearing a light-gray silk suit, and the fit was so flawless that it looked as if it had been built around him." A later entry in the series, *Mark Kilby Stands Alone* (1962), begins with an ocean voyage but then involves murder in New York City and its suburbs, with Kilby facing a local master criminal named Cellini.

Never one to let a usable name go to waste, with *Cunning as a Fox* Creasey inaugurated a new series in 1965 about a grandfatherly psychiatrist named Dr. Emmanuel Cellini, formerly of New York City but now practicing in London, who solves his cases as much by intuition as by detective work. There is little in the plotting in these books that is startling, but they contain better character studies of the villains than does much of Creasey's work. The Cellini series was published as by Michael Halliday in England and as by Hunt in the United States.

Creasey also wrote a historical novel tracing the early days of the British police, from 1739 to 1829, through the lives and careers of several families. He was especially proud of this book, *The Masters of Bow Street* (1974), which required more research than any of his other works but which he did not live to see published. He died of congestive heart failure on 9 June 1973, in Bodenham, Salisbury, England.

The apparently endless energy of Creasey carried over to organizational activities related to writing. With Nigel Morland he was cofounder of the British Crime Writers Association. He was also a member of the Mystery Writers of America and edited one of their annual short-story anthologies. After meeting several members on a

trip to the United States, he became an officer of the Western Writers of America. His third wife, Jeanne Williams, was a western writer, and Creasey lived for a time in Tucson, Arizona, while their marriage lasted.

Creasey was very active in British politics and ran for Parliament on four occasions, within fifteen months, as candidate of the Liberal party. His political theories were set forth during his campaigns in his proposals for an "all party alliance," a system which called for government by the best men from each party rather than one party alone. Though never coming close to winning, he steadily increased the size of the vote he received, going from 2.9 percent the first time he ran to 13.9 percent in his last election. It is likely that, if his persistence in the face of literary rejection slips is any indication, he would have eventually been elected to political office had he lived. Creasey's political thinking and philosophy were closely related and were set forth in his book *Good, God and Man: An Outline of the Philosophy of Self-ism* (1967). He also found time for social causes like Oxfam (to prevent hunger), a plan for uniting Europe, and a program of national savings, in addition to his work for road safety, including the book *They Didn't Mean to Kill: The Real Story of Road Accidents* (1960).

Once the butt of jokes among critics for the sheer quantity of his work, Creasey went on to earn the respect of most of them without ever losing his popularity with the reading public. At his best he had an apparently inexhaustible flow of ideas and the ability to generate excitement and suspense. For years unwillingness to vary the formula that had brought his early thrillers success in England had denied many of his books reprint in the United States. When he changed the direction of his Roger West series and then created George Gideon, he satisfied American publishers who said their readers wanted characters who were believable and with whom they could identify. Thus, he opened new markets for himself and obtained the critical approval he had long sought on both sides of the Atlantic. He also placed himself in the forefront of the police procedural novel, the major new trend in the mystery story of the 1950s and 1960s, for it was the enormous success of the Gideon books which solidified the popularity of the police procedural subgenre and set the stage for such important series as the Ed McBain (Evan Hunter) 87th Precinct novels, which began in 1956, and the Los Angeles police series which Elizabeth Linington began writing in 1960.

References:

Jacques Barzun and Wendell Hertig Taylor, *A Catalogue of Crime* (New York: Harper & Row, 1971);

Barzun and Taylor, Introduction to *Gideon's River* (New York: Garland, 1983);

Tom Bird, "John Creasey Remembered," *Short Stories*, 1 (July 1981): 9-12;

John Boyles, "A Word for John Creasey: J. J.

Marric's *Gideon's Risk*," *Armchair Detective*, 11 (July 1978): 282-283;

George N. Dove, *The Police Procedural* (Bowling Green, Ohio: Popular Press, 1982), pp. 177-183;

Deryk Harvey, "The Best of John Creasey," *Armchair Detective*, 7 (November 1973): 42-43;

"How to Be the Most," *Newsweek* (2 February 1959): 85-86;

Allen J. Hubin, "Meet the Author," *Armchair Detective*, 2 (October 1968): 3-5;

Francis M. Nevins, Jr., "Remembering John Creasey," *Xenophile*, 4 (June 1974): 37-38.

Freeman Wills Crofts

(1 June 1879-11 April 1957)

H. M. Klein
University of East Anglia

BOOKS: *The Cask* (London: Collins, 1920; New York: Seltzer, 1924);

The Ponson Case (London: Collins, 1921; New York: Boni, 1927);

The Pit-Prop Syndicate (London: Collins, 1922; New York: Seltzer, 1925);

The Groote Park Murder (London: Collins, 1924; New York: Seltzer, 1925);

Inspector French's Greatest Case (London: Collins, 1925; New York: Seltzer, 1925);

Inspector French and the Cheyne Mystery (London: Collins, 1926; New York: Boni, 1926);

Inspector French and the Starvel Tragedy (London: Collins, 1927); republished as *The Starvel Hollow Tragedy* (New York & London: Harper, 1927);

The Sea Mystery: An Inspector French Detective Story (London: Collins, 1928; New York & London: Harper, 1928);

The Box Office Murders: An Inspector French Case (London: Collins, 1929); republished as *The Purple Sickle Murders* (New York & London: Harper, 1929);

Bann and Lough Neagh Drainage (Belfast: His Majesty's Stationery Office, 1930);

Sir John Magill's Last Journey: An Inspector French

Case (London: Collins, 1930; New York & London: Harper, 1930);

Mystery in the Channel (London: Collins, 1931); republished as *Mystery in the English Channel* (New York & London: Harper, 1931);

Sudden Death (London: Collins, 1932; New York & London: Harper, 1932);

Death on the Way (London: Collins, 1932); republished as *Double Death* (New York & London: Harper, 1932);

The Hog's Back Mystery (London: Hodder & Stoughton, 1933); republished as *The Strange Case of Dr. Earle* (New York: Dodd, Mead, 1933);

The 12.30 from Croydon (London: Hodder & Stoughton, 1934; Melbourne & Baltimore: Penguin, 1953); republished as *Wilful and Premeditated* (New York: Dodd, Mead, 1934);

Mystery on Southampton Water (London: Hodder & Stoughton, 1934); republished as *Crime on the Solent* (New York: Dodd, Mead, 1934);

Crime at Guildford (London: Collins, 1935); republished as *The Crime at Nornes* (New York: Dodd, Mead, 1935);

The Loss of the "Jane Vosper" (London: Collins, 1936; New York: Dodd, Mead, 1936);

Freeman Wills Crofts

Man Overboard! (London: Collins, 1936; New York: Dodd, Mead, 1936); republished and abridged as *Cold-Blooded Murder* (New York: Avon, 1947);

Found Floating (London: Hodder & Stoughton, 1937; New York: Dodd, Mead, 1937);

The End of Andrew Harrison (London: Hodder & Stoughton, 1938); republished as *The Futile Alibi* (New York: Dodd, Mead, 1938);

Antidote to Venom (London: Hodder & Stoughton, 1938; New York: Dodd, Mead, 1939);

Fatal Venture (London: Hodder & Stoughton, 1939); republished as *Tragedy in the Hollow* (New York: Dodd, Mead, 1939);

Golden Ashes (London: Hodder & Stoughton, 1940; New York: Dodd, Mead, 1940);

James Tarrant, Adventurer (London: Hodder & Stoughton, 1941); republished as *Circumstan-*

tial Evidence (New York: Dodd, Mead, 1941);

The Losing Game (London: Hodder & Stoughton, 1941); republished as *A Losing Game* (New York: Dodd, Mead, 1941);

Fear Comes to Chalfont (London: Hodder & Stoughton, 1942; New York: Dodd, Mead, 1942);

The Affair at Little Wokeham (London: Hodder & Stoughton, 1943); republished as *Double Tragedy* (New York: Dodd, Mead, 1943);

The Hunt Ball Murder (London: Todd, 1943);

Mr. Sefton, Murderer (London: Vallancey, 1944);

Enemy Unseen (London: Hodder & Stoughton, 1945; New York: Dodd, Mead, 1945);

Death of a Train (London: Hodder & Stoughton, 1946; New York: Dodd, Mead, 1947);

Murderers Make Mistakes (London: Hodder & Stoughton, 1947);

Young Robin Brand, Detective (London: University of London Press, 1947; New York: Dodd, Mead, 1948);

Silence for the Murderer (New York: Dodd, Mead, 1948; London: Hodder & Stoughton, 1949);

The Four Gospels in One Story: Written as a Modern Biography (London: Longmans, Green, 1949);

Dark Journey (New York: Dodd, Mead, 1951); republished as *French Strikes Oil* (London: Hodder & Stoughton, 1952);

Many a Slip (London: Hodder & Stoughton, 1955);

The Mystery of the Sleeping Car Express (and Other Stories) (London: Hodder & Stoughton, 1956);

Anything to Declare? (London: Hodder & Stoughton, 1957).

OTHER: *The Floating Admiral*, includes contributions by Crofts, G. K. Chesterton, and others (London: Hodder & Stoughton, 1931; Garden City, N.Y.: Doubleday, Doran, 1932);

"A New Zealand Tragedy," in *The Anatomy of Murder: Famous Crimes Critically Considered by Members of The Detection Club* (London: Lane, 1936);

Six Against the Yard, includes contributions by Crofts, Margery Allingham, Anthony Berkeley, and others (London: Selwyn & Blount, 1936); republished as *Six Against Scotland Yard* (Garden City, N.Y.: Doubleday, Doran, 1936);

Double Death: A Murder Story, includes contributions by Crofts, Dorothy Sayers, Valentine Williams, and others; supervised by John Chancellor (London: Gollancz, 1939).

The son of a British army doctor from an old Cork Protestant family, Freeman Wills Crofts was born on 1 June 1879 in Dublin, Ireland. His father died while on service abroad, and later on his mother married a Church of Ireland clergyman, an archdeacon named Harding. Crofts was sent to school at the Methodist and Campbell College in Belfast. In 1896 his uncle Berkeley D. Wise, at that time chief engineer of the Belfast & Northern Counties Railway, took him on as a civil-engineering apprentice in his department. In 1899 Crofts was made a junior assistant engineer; a year later he became district engineer at Coleraine, where he also served as parish organist. In 1912 he married Mary Bellas Canning. They had no children. Their union, which was a harmonious and happy one, lasted until Croft's death. Crofts was promoted to the position of chief assistant engineer and moved to Belfast in 1923.

He became a detective-story writer relatively late in life. He described how this happened in 1939 when his first book, *The Cask* (1920), was included in Collins's "library of classics." In 1919 he was very ill, and during this period of convalescence "I became so bored that I didn't know what to do, and to try to fill the time I asked for a pencil and a few sheets of notepaper. I began to write down what seemed the most absurd and improbable things I could think of. Before I knew what was happening, a whole morning was gone." He wrote on, then read the first chapter to his wife, who was amazed (as Crofts ruefully noted) and delighted, so he continued writing until he was well enough to return to his job. Looking at the manuscript later, he found it quite promising. He began to revise, showing the results to a neighbor, Adam A. C. Mathers, whose criticism and suggestions he gratefully accepted. The book was completed, sent off to A. P. Watt, the literary agency, and accepted by Collins on the advice of John Beresford. One condition was, however, that the third part (entirely a courtroom scene) would be recast, something to which Crofts eagerly set about. His original title was a Dickens echo: "A Mystery of Two Cities"; quite understandably, Collins did not care for this, and in the end the book appeared as *The Cask. The Cask* is the story of the effort to discover who has mur-

Dust jacket for the first British edition of Crofts's 1928 novel featuring Inspector Joseph French of Scotland Yard, Crofts's best-known detective (courtesy of Otto Penzler)

dered a young woman whose body has been stuffed into a large cask and sent to England from France. After what appears to be meticulous police work a likely suspect is arrested. The novel then focuses on the efforts of detective Georges La Touche to discover how the real killer has created his alibi. *The Cask* sold one hundred thousand copies by 1939. As Crofts said, "The whole episode represented such a thrill that, as may be imagined, it was not long before I was at work on a second book, *The Ponson Case.* This also 'went,' and from then on the die was cast. I would continue writing books, even if I had to give up my railway work to do it."

In 1929 Crofts resigned from the Belfast & Northern Counties Railway. He was entrusted by the government of Northern Ireland with a compensation inquiry, the result of which was published as *Bann and Lough Neagh Drainage* (1930). Crofts and his wife then moved to the south of England. They lived first in Blackheath, then near Guildford, and finally in Worthing, where Crofts died in April 1957. By that time he had written thirty-four novels, radio plays, dozens of short stories, and contributions to several collaborative publications. Alongside writing, his second and then his main career, he cultivated as hobbies traveling, music (besides playing the organ he frequently acted as choirmaster and conducted), gardening (put to good use in his writing: e.g., the chief clue in *Fatal Venture* [1939] hinges on the blooming season of delphiniums and clarkia), and carpentry. In all, then, his was a quiet but very successful life, the external culmination point of which probably was his election to the Royal Society of Arts early in 1939.

Crofts was an unobtrusive, kindly, dependable, indeed punctilious man, sober, serious-minded, neat and correct, upright and deeply religious. The last-mentioned trait found its most prominent expression in his 1949 retelling of the four Gospels, but also informs his detective fiction, coming to the fore overtly and directly in the last phase of *Antidote to Venom* (1938). He also had a sound training in applied mathematics and engineering; extensive technical skills and experience; firsthand knowledge of workshops, warehouses, offices; and, of course, an insider's grasp of everything to do with railways. These areas of knowledge, as well as an absorbing interest in boats and shipping, furnish a solid, if rarely glamorous, backcloth to his dreams of crime and punishment.

Crofts is best known for the creation of his ingenious, but occasionally fallible detective Inspector French and the fact that his villains often have seemingly unshakable alibis. With A. C. Bentley, Agatha Christie, and Dorothy Sayers he is often credited with founding the Golden Age of English detective fiction around 1918. He was an active and distinguished member of the Detection Club and participated in such group volumes as *The Anatomy of Murder* (1936) and *Double Death* (1939), a composite murder story organized for Gollancz by John Chancellor. His popularity remained high during World War II, when around twenty of his short detection plays were produced mainly in the BBC radio series *Chief Inspector French's Cases* (plays later recast as stories in *Murderers Make Mistakes*, 1947).

Crofts is rightly called a realist writer. His obituary in the *London Times* draws attention to the fact that he used to visit the scenes of action beforehand, taking photographs and making notes

Dust jacket for the first British edition of Crofts's 1946 novel, in which Inspector French is almost killed while trying to destroy a German commando unit (courtesy of Otto Penzler)

of the locality's salient features. He often uses timetables. Crofts's moral stand never varies: crime is presented as serious, wrong, and detestable; sympathies are never guided toward the perpetrators but are reserved for the victims, the detectives, and the general public for whose protection they are at work.

In his first four novels Crofts sometimes employs gifted amateurs to solve the mystery, but in *Inspector French's Greatest Case* (1925) and after he focused on Inspector Joseph French of Scotland Yard. The last French novel was *Anything to Declare?* (1957). Like the vast majority of Crofts's characters, French himself is ordinary, yet in an extraordinary way. He is solidly and contentedly lower middle class. Of unremarkable appearance generally, he has blue eyes and is stoutly built; yet he is a fast mover when physical action is required, which is not often. Such scenes of violence are the more effective for being introduced sparingly by the author. French is kind and tolerant (except where malice and murder are concerned), in his manner smooth and affable, but he can be stern and imposing when required. He unites the qualities of a highly gifted single sleuth with those of an able organizer of collective police efforts. Some critics say he is nothing but a reasoning function, but this is simply untrue. He does reason, often until he is utterly exhausted, and that in itself makes him rather more human than some of his compeers.

French's basic assumptions are simple. The first is: "There is a reason for everything, . . . if you can only find it" (*The End of Andrew Harrison*, 1938); his second maxim is fittingly phrased as a question: "What other people [i.e., the criminals] had thought of, surely he should be able to think of too?" (*Crime at Guildford*, 1935). His third maxim is at the same time an epitome of Crofts's procedure and is best illustrated from chapter 2 of *The Sea Mystery* (1928). Here French draws a distinction between literature and reality: "there is this difference between a novel and real life. In a novel the episodes are selected and the reader is told those which are interesting and which get results. In real life we try perhaps ten or twenty lines which lead nowhere before we strike the lucky one. And in each line we make perhaps hundreds of enquiries, whereas the novel describes one. It's like any other job, you get results by pegging away." "Pegging away" or, as the same idea is worded in *Crime at Guildford*, "just sticking it" perfectly describes not only how French operates but also how Crofts represents French's adventures in crime solution. The distinctive mark of Crofts's novels is that they narrow the differential; there are always a large number of inquiries which are fruitless. The unmistakable effect of realism in Crofts's fiction arises from the application of this principle. To impatient readers it may often seem that Crofts shifts the weights too much. Others think he achieves his balance to good purpose and feel rewarded for their plodding along with French, at times lagging a bit behind, at others advancing (or thinking to advance) a little ahead of him.

Like Crofts's other investigators French is ordinary in that he does not know everything. Thus, for instance, he has no precise notion about the production of cement, something essential to solving the problems that arise in *Mystery on Southampton Water* (1934). However, he learns fast. Neither is French wholly free from personal animus. His hatred of old Mr. Gething's mur-

derer in *Inspector French's Greatest Case* is one of his greatest motivations to find the culprit. And French is keenly interested in attaining a higher income and more elevated rank.

The entire long chain of self-contained French novels gains a certain loose cohesion not only by constant references back to past cases (and even their minor characters) but also by the detective's modest ambitions. Even the pre-French Scotland Yard officers are retrospectively worked in: Burnley (of *The Cask*) retires (in *The Sea Mystery*). Tanner (of *The Ponson Case*, 1921) and Willis (of *The Pit-Prop Syndicate*, 1922) continue as French's subordinates and colleagues as he rises, in a slow process, from inspector in the first French novel (1925) to the rank of chief inspector, when the incumbent of that post, Mitchell, retires (*Mystery on Southampton Water*). French becomes superintendent (*Silence for the Murderer*, 1948) and finally chief superintendent (*Anything to Declare?*).

French is married, and his wife Emmy ("Em") sometimes takes a large part in his work. Em gives advice in various novels and even accompanies French on two steamer trips (*Found Floating*, 1937, and *Fatal Venture*). No children are mentioned, but French has a nephew (who effects the contact between Robin Brand and French in Crofts's juvenile detective novel, *Young Robin Brand, Detective* (1947). Mostly, however, his home remains a blank background to which he retires for weekend rests whenever possible.

Lastly, French is realistic in that he makes mistakes. In *The Box Office Murders* (1929) they nearly cost a young girl's life; in *Antidote to Venom* they allow the murderer to take the easy way out; in *The Hog's Back Mystery* (1933) he makes progress too slowly to prevent a follow-up murder. In *The Sea Mystery, Mystery in the Channel* (1931), and *Death of a Train* (1946) French allows himself to be fooled and is all but killed in consequence of his lapses. Very often failure stares him in the face. It never actually materializes in the stories themselves, only in further cases alluded to; but his bafflement and frustration are at times forcefully portrayed.

The endings of Crofts's novels vary little. Usually the narrator informs the reader (as in Henry Fielding's novels) about what happened after the denouement. The most dramatic example is in *Death of a Train* where French receives all the news when he regains consciousness in the hospital, having with a grenade destroyed a German commando unit, deliberately sacrificing himself in the act. Notable variations are the grand finale explanation and retrospect scenes in *The 12.30 from Croydon* (1934) and in *The Hog's Back Mystery;* in the latter book the author gives page references to help the reader look up the clues. In *Fatal Venture* the story is taken even beyond the usual winding up: French becomes a friend of a couple who had been among the suspects in the case.

Crofts is still read today. Seven of his novels are currently in print. *The Cask* exists in three editions, and Jacques Barzun and Wendell Hertig Taylor include *The Box Office Murders* among their series *Fifty Classics of Crime Fiction, 1900-1950.*

References:

Howard Haycraft, *Murder for Pleasure: The Life and Times of the Detective Story*, enlarged edition (New York: Biblio & Tannen, 1968), pp. 122-124;

Erik Routley, *The Puritan Pleasures of the Detective Story: A Personal Monograph* (London: Gollancz, 1972), pp. 124-127;

Julian Symons, *Bloody Murder: From the Detective Story to the Crime Novel: A History* (New York: Viking, 1984);

H. Douglas Thomson, "Freeman Wills Crofts," in *Masters of Mystery: A Study of the Detective Story* (London: Collins, 1931).

Lord Dunsany
(Edward John Moreton Drax Plunkett, Baron Dunsany)
(25 August 1878-25 October 1957)

Janet Egleson Dunleavy
University of Wisconsin-Milwaukee

See also the Dunsany entry in *DLB 10: Modern British Dramatists, 1900-1945.*

BOOKS: *The Gods of Pegāna* (London: Elkin Mathews, 1905; Boston: Luce, 1916);

Time and the Gods (London: Heinemann, 1906; Boston: Luce, 1917);

The Sword of Welleran, and Other Stories (London: Allen, 1908; Boston: Luce, 1916);

A Dreamer's Tales (London: Allen, 1910; Boston: Luce, 1916);

The Book of Wonder (London: Heinemann, 1912; Boston: Luce, 1913);

Five Plays (London: Richards, 1914; New York: Kennerley, 1914);

Fifty-one Tales (London: Elkin Mathews, 1915; New York: Kennerley, 1915);

A Night at an Inn: A Play in One Act (New York: Sunwise Turn, 1916; London: Putnam's, 1922);

The Queen's Enemies: A Play (New York: French, 1916; London: Putnam's, 1922);

Tales of Wonder (London: Elkin Mathews, 1916); republished as *The Last Book of Wonder* (Boston: Luce, 1916);

Plays of Gods and Men (Dublin: Talbot, 1917; London: Unwin, 1917; New York & London: Putnam's, 1917; Boston: Luce, 1917);

Tales of War (Dublin: Talbot/London: Unwin, 1918; London & New York: Putnam's, 1922);

Tales of Three Hemispheres (Boston: Luce, 1919; London: Unwin, 1920);

Unhappy Far-Off Things (London: Elkin Mathews, 1919; Boston: Little, Brown, 1919);

If: A Play in Four Acts (London: Putnam's, 1921; New York & London: Putnam's, 1922);

The Chronicles of Rodriguez (London & New York: Putnam's, 1922); republished as *Don Rodriguez: Chronicles of Shadow Valley* (New York & London: Putnam's, 1922);

The Laughter of the Gods (London: Putnam's, 1922);

Plays of Near and Far (London & New York: Putnam's, 1922);

Edward John Moreton Drax Plunkett, Baron Dunsany
(BBC Hulton)

The King of Elfland's Daughter (London & New York: Putnam's, 1924);

Alexander (London & New York: Putnam's, 1925);

Alexander, & Three Small Plays (London & New York: Putnam's, 1925; New York & London: Putnam's, 1926);

The Charwoman's Shadow (London & New York: Putnam's, 1926; New York & London: Putnam's, 1926);

The Blessing of Pan (London & New York: Putnam's, 1927; New York & London: Putnam's, 1928);

Seven Modern Comedies (London & New York: Putnam's, 1928; New York: Putnam's, 1929);

Fifty Poems (London & New York: Putnam's, 1929);

The Travel Tales of Mr. Joseph Jorkens (London & New York: Putnam's, 1931);

The Curse of the Wise Woman (New York & Toronto: Longmans, Green, 1933; London: Heinemann, 1933);

If I Were Dictator; the Pronouncements of the Grand Macaroni (London: Methuen, 1934);

Mr. Jorkens Remembers Africa (London & Toronto: Heinemann, 1934); republished as *Jorkens Remembers Africa* (New York & Toronto: Longmans, Green, 1934);

Mr. Faithful: A Comedy in Three Acts (New York & Los Angeles: French/London: French, 1935);

Up in the Hills (London & Toronto: Heinemann, 1935; New York: Putnam's, 1936);

My Talks with Dean Spanley (London: Heinemann, 1936; New York: Putnam's, 1936);

Rory and Bran (London & Toronto: Heinemann, 1936; New York: Putnam's, 1937);

Plays for Earth and Air (London & Toronto: Heinemann, 1937);

My Ireland (London: Jarrolds, 1937; New York & London: Funk & Wagnalls, 1937);

Mirage Water (London: Putnam's, 1938; Philadelphia: Dorrance, 1939);

Patches of Sunlight (London & Toronto: Heinemann/New York: Reynal & Hitchcock, 1938);

The Story of Mona Sheehy (London & Toronto: Heinemann, 1939; New York & London: Harper, 1940);

Jorkens Has A Large Whiskey (London: Putnam's, 1940);

War Poems (London & Melbourne: Hutchinson, 1941);

Wandering Songs (London & Melbourne: Hutchinson, 1943);

A Journey (London: Macdonald, 1943);

While the Sirens Slept (London & New York: Jarrolds, 1944);

The Sirens Wake (London & New York: Jarrolds, 1945);

The Donnellan Lectures, 1943 (London & Toronto: Heinemann, 1945);

A Glimpse from a Watchtower (London & New York: Jarrolds, 1946);

The Year (London & New York: Jarrolds, 1946);

The Man Who Ate the Phoenix (London & New York: Jarrolds, 1947);

The Fourth Book of Jorkens (London: Jarrolds, 1948; Sauk City, Wis.: Arkham, 1948);

To Awaken Pegasus (Oxford: Ronald, 1949);

The Strange Journeys of Colonel Polders (London & New York: Jarrolds, 1950);

The Last Revolution (London: Jarrolds, 1951);

Dunsany in his service uniform, 1914. In the Easter Rebellion of 1916 Dunsany suffered a wound which left a scar and partial paralysis on one side of his nose and mouth

His Fellow Men: A Novel (London: Jarrolds, 1952);

The Little Tales of Smethers and Other Stories (London & New York: Jarrolds, 1952);

Jorkens Borrows Another Whiskey (London: M. Joseph, 1954);

At the Edge of the World, edited by Lin Carter (New York: Ballentine, 1970);

Beyond the Fields We Know, edited by Carter (London: Pan/Ballentine, 1972);

Over the Hills and Far Away (New York: Ballentine, 1974);

The Ghosts of the Heaviside Layer (Philadelphia: Owlswick, 1980).

PLAY PRODUCTIONS: *The Glittering Gate*, Dublin, Abbey Theatre, 29 April 1909; London, Court Theatre, 6 June 1910;

King Argimenes and the Unknown Warrior, Dublin, Abbey Theatre, 26 January 1911;

The Gods of the Mountain, London, Haymarket Theatre, 1 June 1911;

The Golden Doom, London, Haymarket Theatre, 19 November 1912;

The Lost Silk Hat, Manchester, Gaiety Theatre, 4 August 1913;

A Night at an Inn, New York, Neighborhood Playhouse, 23 April 1916;

The Queen's Enemies, New York, Neighborhood Playhouse, 14 November 1916;

The Laughter of the Gods, New York, Punch and Judy Theatre, 15 January 1919;

The Murderers, Indianapolis, Shubert Murat Theatre, 14 July 1919;

If, London, Ambassadors' Theatre, 30 May 1921;

Cheezo, London, Everyman Theatre, 15 November 1921;

Lord Adrian, Birmingham, Prince of Wales's Theatre, 12 November 1923;

Fame and the Poet, Leeds, Albert Hall, 8 February 1924;

His Sainted Grandmother, London, Fortune Theatre, 8 December 1926;

The Jest of Hahalaba, London, Playroom 6, 22 March 1927;

Mr. Faithful, London, Q Theatre, 22 August 1927.

OTHER: Francis Ledwidge, *Songs of the Fields*, introduction by Dunsany (London: Jenkins, 1916);

Ledwidge, *Songs of Peace*, edited, with an introduction, by Dunsany (London: Jenkins, 1917);

Ledwidge, *Last Songs*, introduction by Dunsany (London: Jenkins, 1918);

Ledwidge, *The Complete Poems of Francis Ledwidge*, introduction by Dunsany (London: Jenkins, 1919);

Thomas Caldwell, ed., *The Golden Book of Modern English Poetry, 1870-1920*, introduction by Dunsany (London & Toronto: Dent, 1922); republished as *The Golden Book of Modern English Poetry, 1870-1930* (London: Dent, 1930);

Seumas MacCall, *Gods in Motley*, foreword by Dunsany (London: Constable, 1935);

Mary Lavin, *Tales from Bective Bridge*, introduction by Dunsany (London: M. Joseph, 1945);

George Meredith, *The Egoist,* introduction by Dunsany (London: Oxford University Press, 1947);

The Odes of Horace, translated by Dunsany (London & Toronto: Heinemann, 1947);

Mary Hamilton, *Green and Gold,* introduction by Dunsany (London: Wingate, 1948);

Annie Crone, *Bridie Steen,* introduction by Dunsany (London: Heinemann, 1949);

Judith Anne Dorothea Wentworth Blunt-Lytton, Baroness, *Drift of the Storm,* introduction by Dunsany (Oxford: Ronald, 1951);

Stanton A. Coblentz, *Time's Travellers,* introduction by Dunsany (Mill Valley, Cal.: Wings, 1952);

Arthur Machen, *A Hill of Dreams,* introduction by Dunsany (London: Richards, 1954);

The Collected Works of Horace, translated by Dunsany and Michael Oakley (London: Dent/New York: Dutton, 1961).

Extraordinarily prolific in a number of literary genres and author of translations, sketches, essays, memoirs, poems, plays, novels, tales, and short fiction that in his lifetime appealed to both popular and educated taste on both sides of the Atlantic, Edward John Moreton Drax Plunkett, eighteenth Baron Dunsany, was also a world traveler and a man of wide-ranging interests and experiences. His earliest unpublished stories were composed while he was still a schoolboy. His last stories were published three years before his death at the age of seventy-nine.

Dunsany's fantastic inventions of time and place have been compared with those of American novelist James Branch Cabell, his gothic landscapes with those of Dublin-born Joseph Sheridan Le Fanu. Like Cabell, Dunsany created not just characters but entire nations, even worlds. Like Le Fanu, he imbued the familiar and commonplace with a mysterious presence. Characteristics that distinguish Dunsany are intricately contrived plots (the mark of the chessmaster turned author) and descriptive passages of extraordinary beauty. In his mystery writing Dunsany employs conventions familiar to readers of the genre: contest between intelligence and craftiness, conflict between good and evil, and contrast between the beautiful and the grotesque.

Born in London at 15 Park Square near Regent's Park, Dunsany was a member of the Irish peerage whose family, according to tradition, was Danish in origin, having settled in Ireland before Brian Boru defeated the Danes at Clontarf in 1014. Dunsany Castle in County Meath–still today the family seat–was built in 1190 approximately twenty miles northwest of modern Dublin; that is, within the Pale, the area controlled by the Normans loyal to Henry II, to whom Dunsany's Danish ancestors were linked by marriage. Sir Christopher Plunkett, deputy governor of Ireland in the early fifteenth century, received his baronetcy from Henry VI in 1439. A Dunsany sat in the English Parliament under Henry VII; another was rewarded for his service to Elizabeth I. Dunsany, the eighteenth Baron, was a member of both the Anglo-Irish Ascendancy and the English aristocracy. On his mother's side he was related to the nineteenth-century explorer Richard Burton, whose own writings may have provided ideas for Dunsany's *The Travel Tales of Mr. Joseph Jorkens* (1931). Material for these and other stories also was suggested, according to Dunsany's memoirs, by the assortment of strange objects from other parts of the world, especially the East, that cluttered his father's study.

During the first ten years of Dunsany's life his grandfather, the sixteenth baron, still occupied Dunsany Castle; Dunsany's boyhood home therefore was Dunstall Priory, near Shoreham, in Kent, where his early education was provided first by a governess, then at a local boarding school. At the age of twelve he was sent to Cheam, an English preparatory school whose headmaster had taught Dunsany's father. Earlier he had learned to love the stories of Jacob and Wilhelm Grimm and Hans Christian Andersen; at Cheam he read the Bible, studied Greek, became fascinated with the people of the classical world and biblical lands, and discovered an aptitude for chess that soon led to the tournaments he continued to win throughout his life. (As an adult he became all-Ireland champion; in an exhibition match in London he once fought the world champion José Raoul Capablanca y Grauperra to a draw.) From Cheam he went first to Eton, then to a series of tutors who prepared him for admission to Sandhurst. Meanwhile, his grandfather having died, his father moved to Dunsany Castle, while his mother remained at Dunstall Priory. When Dunsany's father died in 1899 Horace Plunkett, Dunsany's uncle–a member of the Dublin circle that gathered around W. B. Yeats and Lady Gregory–took over the management of family affairs, strengthening a relationship already important to uncle and nephew, for out of all the family, these two shared an interest in lit-

A scene from the first production of A Night at an Inn, *Dunsany's most successful one-act play, in which robbers are pursued because they have stolen the eye of an idol belonging to Indian priests (courtesy of Neighborhood Playhouse)*

erature and writing. Dunsany served with the Coldstream Guards in Gibraltar and South Africa and returned to civilian life in 1901. He was wounded during the Easter Rebellion of 1916 and saw action on the Continent during World War I.

In 1904 Dunsany married Beatrice Villiers, youngest daughter of the Earl and Countess of Jersey, and brought her to live in Dunsany Castle. His first book, *The Gods of Pegāna*, was published in 1905. His second book, *Time and the Gods*, was published in 1906–the year in which his only child, a son, was born and the year in which he stood for Parliament and lost.

Dunsany's early fiction is concerned almost exclusively with the fantastic and the supernatural. His principal contributions to mystery fiction, *The Curse of the Wise Woman* and *The Little Tales of Smethers*, were not published until 1933 and 1952 respectively. However, characters, incidents, and sketches that anticipate these fully developed examples of the genre may be found in many of his tales and novels, including *The Chronicles of Rodriguez* (1922) and *The Charwoman's Shadow* (1926), gothic tales of murder, theft, and narrow escapes from criminal types with supernat-

ural powers. "Mrs. Jorkens" (from *The Travel Tales of Mr. Joseph Jorkens*), which plots the theft of a major tourist attraction, a mermaid; "Ozymandias" and "How Ryan Got Out of Russia" (from *Mr. Jorkens Remembers Africa*, 1934), about the application of deductive reasoning to the problem of recovering a lost treasure and the escape of a spy through a fortuitously misfired rocket are also significant. "Mgamu" and "The Strange Drug of Dr. Caber" (both from *The Fourth Book of Jorkens*, 1948), about bizarre murders; and "Jorkens Leaves Prison" and "The Welcome" (also from *The Fourth Book of Jorkens*), are spy-adventure stories.

The Curse of the Wise Woman is a murder mystery. The narrator–an old man far from his native Ireland, telling a tale of his youth–is not sure whether that remembered land was beautiful and happy or sad and oppressed. Memory takes him back for long periods of recollection: what he does know, as he becomes himself at sixteen, is that he is unhappy, for he is home from Eton for the holidays, and it is nearly time for his return. He has not completed preparation for the new term, and therefore his father will not permit him to go out hunting geese at night on the bog.

Like most boys his age, to him life seems good if he is able to do as he wants, bad if he is thwarted. So when his father disappears mysteriously moments before three armed men break into their house, he is but temporarily shaken. From a cryptic message given him by his father, by a subsequent letter received from him, and by hints from others he deduces that his father's would-be attackers were political enemies bent on assassination, and that he is now alive and well in France. The boy feels free to shoot birds on the bog, join the fox hunt, and even delay his return to Eton.

In the weeks and months that follow, the boy learns for the first time something of the real texture of life in his little part of Ireland, of its grudges, loyalties, and intrigues and of the complex political, social, and economic structures that sustain it and its people. Such knowledge gradually increases as, back at Eton, he is informed that his father has been murdered in Paris, not by his would-be attackers–local men with whom the boy has established a cautious but mutual trust–but by others from a different part of Ireland. He returns home to find that his friend Marlin, son of the Wise Woman who lives at the edge of the bog, has died. He also learns that the Peat Development Syndicate has begun bringing in machinery to remove compressed turf from the bog by the acre, as if it were a coal mine, threatening to change forever not only a source of recreation, sustenance and fuel for local hearths and cookstoves but a link between past, present, and future for those who have lived there for generations. The Peat Development Syndicate is a new cause for terrorism. The poor put their faith in the curse of the Wise Woman, who helps destroy the project to excavate turf.

Dramatic and suspenseful, the novel is enhanced by Dunsany's skillful manipulation of stirring passages of description and detailed knowledge of local customs and manners. At the same time an appropriate vagueness of reference to specific historical events in favor of generalizations provides a universality that keeps it current–a factor, no doubt, in its reissue in England in 1972.

The Little Tales of Smethers and Other Stories belongs more obviously to England of the 1930s and 1940s. It is a cycle of nine stories in which Smethers (the narrator), Linley (the crime-solver), and Inspector Ulton of Scotland Yard are the principal characters. Although not formatted as a novel, the stories are additionally linked by se-

quential episodes in which earlier events often are referred to. The linear narrative that thus emerges establishes that Smethers and Linley were strangers to each other when, shortly before World War II, they happened to be looking for lodgings in the same building at the same time–given their different social, educational, and economic status they would not have met under many other circumstances. They agree to share an attractive if expensive flat, remaining together until called into service, Linley as an officer and Smethers as an enlisted man. During the war and after they continue on good terms, meeting on a few occasions.

In the first story Linley is just down from Oxford and is looking for an attractive but modestly priced flat for a few months. Smethers is a smaller man in every respect–physical, financial, and otherwise–a traveler for Numnumo, a relish for meats and savories, who is barely able to afford his half of the rent but thinks it worth the expense if some of Linley's Oxford manner might rub off on him, for it would help boost sales. "You can make a quarter of an education go twice as far again, if you're careful with it," Smethers assures himself, in a characteristic misidentification. "I mean you don't have to quote the whole of the Inferno to show you've read Milton; half a line may do it."

Shortly after they set up housekeeping together, Smethers tells Linley about a ghastly murder at Unge which he has been following because the chief suspect was a man who had bought two bottles of Numnumo. By then he already has been impressed by Linley's "mind like an acrobat's body"; he is sure Linley will easily interpret facts that have stumped Scotland Yard. Smethers is not disappointed; Linley telephones Scotland Yard to report his deductions based on the clues reported in the Unge case. Inspector Ulton responds to his call. From then on, whenever Scotland Yard is baffled, Ulton brings his clues to Linley.

Linley is indeed ingenious, solving most murders–his specialty–without having to examine the corpse or the scene of the crime but by merely reflecting on what he is told, as if a felonious crime were no more than a chess game. (Like Dunsany, Linley is fond of chess, and very good at it as well.) Why was neither bullet nor exit wound found in one victim? Because the bullet the murderer had fired from an eight-bore shotgun had been crafted from ice. How was a threatened footballer slain on the field despite the tightest security Scotland Yard could provide? The murderer had not even approached the field but had obtained access to the victim's football boots. Under the innersole of one of the boots he had inserted the poisoned fang of a deadly viper which was pushed through to the skin while the victim was running. How did a spy get information to the enemy at a concert broadcast to the Continent? He sat under the microphone and delivered his message in Morse code–coughing for a dot, blowing his nose for a dash–during intermission. How can one identify a murderer who has left but one clue, a nearly completed crossword puzzle? Linley draws a profile of his educational background and hobbies from a study of the words he filled in first and fastest (evidence provided by pressure of pen and pencil) and those he left blank.

Parallels to Sir Arthur Conan Doyle's Sherlock Holmes and Dr. Watson are obvious. Yet Linley, Smethers, and Ulton also have their own individualizing characteristics. Clever, courteous Linley is a reflective man who takes his clues one by one, asking questions about each, thus enabling the reader to keep up with him and perhaps even beat him to the solution. Although self-effacing Smethers reveals through grammar, diction, and literary misidentification that his educational background has been much more limited than Linley's, because he is curious and willing to try, he occasionally comes up with a practical, commonsense observation missed by the others. Ulton is not so stolid, unimaginative, and tied to regulations as Scotland Yard inspectors usually are depicted; he is not above playing little harmless tricks of his own from time to time. Nor, unlike most career policemen in literature, does he resent the outside help on which he has to rely. In fact, although duty and position require him to maintain a professional distance from Smethers and Linley, he never fails to show his appreciation to them both by including them among the privileged admitted to various events.

Those who have examined Dunsany's canon have pointed to a topicality of subject and referents that diminish the relevance of some of his writings and have noted a nineteenth-century tone in his critical statements. Although modernist critics tended to disparage Dunsany's work in the postwar period, reviewers continued to treat Dunsany's new work favorably and loyal readers continued to buy his books, so astute editors continued to publish them. Since his death in 1957, most of Dunsany's titles have gone out of print. One exception is *Gods, Men and Ghosts: The Best Supernatural Fiction of Lord Dunsany*, a collection culled from eight Dunsany books by E. F. Bleiler and first published in 1972. Increased contemporary interest in the supernatural is reflected in its continuing sale.

Biographies:

Hazel Littlefield Smith, *Lord Dunsany: King of Dreams* (New York: Exposition Press, 1959);

Mark Amory, *Biography of Lord Dunsany* (London: Collins, 1972).

References:

Edward H. Bierstadt, *Dunsany the Dramatist* (Boston: Little, Brown, 1917; revised, 1919);

E. F. Bleiler, Introduction to *Gods, Men and Ghosts: The Best Supernatural Fiction of Lord Dunsany* (New York: Dover, 1972);

W. B. Yeats, Introduction to *Selections from the Writings of Lord Dunsany* (Shannon: Irish University Press, 1971).

Papers:

A selection of letters from Lord Dunsany to Mary Lavin is in the manuscript collection of the library of the State University of New York at Binghamton.

Gerard Fairlie

(1 November 1899-12 April 1983)

Joan DelFattore
University of Delaware

BOOKS: *Scissors Cut Paper* (London: Hodder & Stoughton, 1927; Boston: Little, Brown, 1928);

The Man Who Laughed (London: Hodder & Stoughton, 1928; Boston: Little, Brown, 1928);

Stone Blunts Scissors (London: Hodder & Stoughton, 1928; Boston: Little, Brown, 1929);

The Exquisite Lady (London: Hodder & Stoughton, 1929); republished as *Yellow Munro* (Boston: Little, Brown, 1929);

The Reaper (Boston: Little, Brown, 1929);

The Muster of Vultures (London: Hodder & Stoughton, 1929; Boston: Little, Brown, 1930);

Suspect (London: Hodder & Stoughton, 1930; Garden City, N.Y.: Doubleday, Doran, 1930);

Unfair Lady (London: Hodder & Stoughton, 1931);

The Man with Talent (London: Hodder & Stoughton, 1931);

Shot in the Dark (London: Hodder & Stoughton, 1932; Garden City, N.Y.: Doubleday, Doran, 1932);

The Rope Which Hangs (London: Hodder & Stoughton, 1932);

Mr. Malcolm Presents (London: Hodder & Stoughton, 1932);

Birds of Prey (London: Hodder & Stoughton, 1932);

Men for Counters (London: Hodder & Stoughton, 1933);

The Treasure Nets (London: Hodder & Stoughton, 1933);

That Man Returns (London: Hodder & Stoughton, 1934);

Copper at Sea (London: Hodder & Stoughton, 1934);

Moral Holiday (London: Hutchinson, 1936);

Bulldog Drummond on Dartmoor (London: Hodder & Stoughton, 1938; New York: Curl, 1939);

The Pianist Shoots First (London: Hodder & Stoughton, 1938);

Approach to Happiness (London: Hutchinson, 1939);

Bulldog Drummond Attacks (London: Hodder & Stoughton, 1939; New York: Gateway, 1940);

The Mill of Circumstance: A Novelized History of the Life and Times of General Wolfe (London: Hutchinson, 1941);

Captain Bulldog Drummond (London: Hodder & Stoughton, 1945);

They Found Each Other (London: Hodder & Stoughton, 1946);

Bulldog Drummond Stands Fast (London: Hodder & Stoughton, 1947);

Hands Off Bulldog Drummond (London: Hodder & Stoughton, 1949);

Calling Bulldog Drummond (London: Hodder & Stoughton, 1951);

With Prejudice: Almost an Autobiography (London: Hodder & Stoughton, 1952);

Winner Take All (London: Hodder & Stoughton, 1953; New York: Dodd, Mead, 1953);

The Return of the Black Gang (London: Hodder & Stoughton, 1954);

No Sleep for Macall (London: Hodder & Stoughton, 1955);

Deadline for Macall (London: Hodder & Stoughton, 1956; New York: Mill, 1956);

Double the Bluff (London: Hodder & Stoughton, 1957);

Flight without Wings: The Biography of Hannes Schneider (London: Hodder & Stoughton, 1957; New York: Barnes, 1957);

The Reluctant Cop: The Story, and the Cases, of Superintendent Albert Webb (London: Hodder & Stoughton, 1958);

Macall Gets Curious (London: Hodder & Stoughton, 1959);

The Fred Emney Story (London: Hutchinson, 1960);

Please Kill My Cousin (London: Hodder & Stoughton, 1961);

The Life of a Genius, with Elizabeth Cayley (London: Hodder & Stoughton, 1965).

Dust jacket for the first American edition of Fairlie's 1929 novel about an international gang calling themselves the Vultures (courtesy of Otto Penzler)

PLAY PRODUCTIONS: *Bulldog Drummond Hits Out,* by Fairlie and Sapper (H. C. McNeile), London, 1937;

Number Six, with Guy Bolton, London, Aldwych Theatre, 1938.

MOTION PICTURES: *Jack Ahoy!,* screenplay by Fairlie and others, Gaumont-British, 1934;

Open All Night, screenplay by Fairlie, 1934;

Lazybones, screenplay by Fairlie, Universal, 1935;

The Lad, screenplay by Fairlie, Universal, 1935;

The Ace of Spades, screenplay by Fairlie, 1935;

Bulldog Jack (Alias Bulldog Drummond), screenplay by Fairlie, H. C. McNeile, J. O. C. Orton, and others, Gaumont-British, 1935;

Brown on Resolution (Born for Glory), screenplay by Fairlie and Michael Hogan, 1935;

Troubled Waters, screenplay by Fairlie, Universal, 1936;

The Big Noise, screenplay by Fairlie, Universal, 1936;

The Lonely Road (Scotland Yard Commands), screenplay by Fairlie, James Flood, and Anthony Kimmins, 1936;

Chick, screenplay by Fairlie and others, 1936;

Conspirator, screenplay by Fairlie and Sally Benson, Gaumont-British, 1949;

Calling Bulldog Drummond, screenplay by Fairlie and others, M-G-M, 1951.

Gerard Fairlie, a close friend of Herman Cyril McNeile and one of the sources for the character of Bulldog Drummond, carried on the Drummond series after McNeile's death in 1937.

Fairlie was born in London, but his early education took place in Brussels. At the age of thirteen he returned to England to attend Downside School, where he joined the Officers Training Corps in 1914. Fairlie was by no means a brilliant student, but he was determined to pass the entrance examination for the Royal Military College at Sandhurst, and he amazed his parents and schoolmasters by placing sixty-second out of over a thousand candidates. He entered Sandhurst in 1917.

From 1918 to 1924 Fairlie served in the Scots Guards. One of his favorite anecdotes from this period concerns Queen Mary, whom he met under very embarrassing circumstances when he was stationed at Victoria Barracks, Windsor. Having completed his duties as officer of the guard at Windsor Castle, Fairlie retired to his room for a nap. The weather was very hot, so he reclined on his bed stark naked; he was not then aware that it was Queen Mary's practice to make periodic tours of the entire castle when she was in residence there. He awakened to find his door open and Queen Mary and her lady-in-waiting staring at him in stunned silence. The ladies retired in haste, slamming the door. A few weeks later, when several young officers were presented to the queen, she interrupted the introduction of Fairlie by observing that they had already met.

During his years in the Scots Guards Fairlie distinguished himself as an athlete, captaining the army in rugby, golf, and boxing and winning the army heavyweight boxing championship in 1919. He was also a member of the British Olympic Bobsled Team in Chamonix, France, in 1924 and a founding member of the Anglo-French Golfing Society. Fairlie's great physical strength and his proficiency at various sports were among the characteristics with which McNeile endowed his fictional creation Bulldog Drummond.

On 18 July 1923 Fairlie married Joan Roskell, whom he had met several years earlier at a dance for children. For six years he supported his family by working as golf correspondent for various periodicals; during this time he also created his first thriller series hero, Victor Caryll, and established himself as a prolific writer of thrillers. In 1931 Fairlie turned from journalism to screenwriting and spent some time in Hollywood. In 1932 he created his second thriller series hero, Mr. Malcolm.

Fairlie had been a close friend of McNeile since 1919, when they met on the golf course at Nairn (Scotland). McNeile had advised and encouraged Fairlie during his early years as a writer, and in 1935 they collaborated with J. O. C. Orton on a screenplay entitled *Bulldog Jack (Alias Bulldog Drummond)*. Fairlie and McNeile then wrote a stage play, *Bulldog Drummond Hits*

Out, which was produced in London in 1937; it was a critical, although not a commercial, success. After McNeile's death, and in accordance with his wishes, Fairlie added to the series of Drummond novels. He also continued to write other books, primarily thrillers and biographies; but although the Drummond books represent only about one-sixth of his total output, it is chiefly for these that he is remembered.

Bulldog Drummond on Dartmoor (1938) is based on a plot which McNeile and Fairlie had discussed during the last months of McNeile's life. It concerns a middle-aged Drummond who, having retired to the country to raise pigs, goes back into action in order to defend England from troublemaking foreign villains. Fairlie, like McNeile, was politically and socially conservative; and, like McNeile, he incorporated his attitudes into his fiction. However, Fairlie's Drummond is more moderate, on the whole, than McNeile's. The villains are still warmongering foreigners jealous of England's strength and stability, but they are described in much less scathing terms. Further, Fairlie's Drummond usually hands the defeated villains over to the police instead of inflicting a suitable punishment himself, as McNeile's Drummond does.

Fairlie's background as an experienced writer of thrillers is evident in his first original Drummond story. *Bulldog Drummond Attacks* (1939) includes such settings as an underground prison chamber and a madhouse honeycombed with secret passages, and it features an assortment of scarred, lisping, and leering henchmen as well as the recurrent character of Irma Peterson, an exotically beautiful villainess seeking revenge on Drummond for having killed her husband in McNeile's *The Final Count* (1926). Drummond defeats yet another set of foreign malefactors, although his own patriotism is put to the ultimate test when his wife, Phyllis, is taken hostage.

In 1939 Fairlie rejoined the army as a lieutenant colonel in the Royal Sussex Regiment. During World War II he served as head of a commando training school, broadcast over French radio in support of the Resistance, and parachuted into occupied France in order to work with the Maquis, guerilla soldiers in the French underground. He was awarded the Croix de Guerre and a Bronze Star. Fairlie's wartime experiences, or an imaginative version of them, formed the basis of several of his later novels, notably

Dust jacket for the first British edition of Fairlie's 1954 novel, the last of the Bulldog Drummond stories continued after H. C. McNeile's death in 1937 (courtesy of Otto Penzler)

Captain Bulldog Drummond (1945) and *They Found Each Other* (1946).

Like many wartime adventure stories, *Captain Bulldog Drummond* replaces some of the more colorful and melodramatic qualities of the 1930s thrillers with grim reflections of reality. Drummond, reluctantly admitting that he is no longer capable of serving as an officer in the field, has been relegated to Home Guard duties. However, he is eventually called upon to enter occupied France in order to assess the strength and determination of the members of the French Resistance and to report upon their potential value as allies. The book is pervaded by allusions to the real war; for example, chapter 16, which should have told of Drummond's infiltration into France, contains instead a note by Fairlie stating that for reasons of national security he will make no reference to the manner in which agents are, or may be, placed behind enemy lines. On the

other hand, the story includes a number of elements which tie it to the earlier and more traditional Drummond books: Drummond's sense of humor and his characteristic style, the assistance of Algy Longworth and Inspector MacIver, and the villainy of Irma Peterson.

After the war Fairlie returned to his earlier style of writing. Drummond repeatedly rescues beautiful women and their hapless male companions; foils the plots of Irma Peterson and her foreign masters; assists and manipulates the police; and glories in the loyalty, obedience, and companionship of his old friends. Drummond also mellows, gaining in humanity and plausibility but losing some of his stature as a thriller hero: in becoming closer to life, he ceases to be larger than life. Similarly, the plots in which this mellower Drummond appears become, if not actually realistic, less improbable than McNeile's plots. Like the figure of Drummond himself, they gain credibility at the expense of some of the fun which was generated by McNeile's vigorous, if sometimes undisciplined, imagination.

All of Fairlie's Drummond stories are characterized to some extent by a sense of nostalgia for Drummond's own youth and for what Fairlie sees as the simpler and purer world of the 1920s and early 1930s. However, as its title suggests, Fairlie's last Drummond book is the strongest statement of his belief in the superiority of older ways and older values. In *The Return of the Black Gang* (1954) Drummond and his friends again don the black masks, hoods, and robes in which they had terrorized the criminal world in McNeile's novels. Crusading against juvenile delinquency, they rehabilitate potential criminals by means of good old-fashioned lectures and whippings. Carl Peterson, Drummond's old archenemy, is resurrected for one final confrontation with the Black Gang as he attempts to undermine the British way of life by selling weapons to the members of youth gangs. (Drummond had poisoned Peterson in McNeile's story *The Final Count*, but now Peterson reveals that he had used an antidote and therefore was not killed. Fairlie does not offer any convincing explanation for Irma's hysterical vengefulness in the intervening novels.) Despite its improbabilities and its embarrassingly didactic rhetoric, both more characteristic of McNeile's

style than of Fairlie's, *The Return of the Black Gang* does contain some highly entertaining scenes. Nevertheless, after Carl and Irma Peterson have been foiled once again, the Black Gang is finally and formally dissolved, never to reappear. The life-style, values, and attitudes which Drummond and the Black Gang represent no longer had a wide enough appeal to form the basis of a thriller series.

Shortly before he stopped writing the Drummond stories, Fairlie created his last series hero, Johnny Macall. However, even after six books Macall had not aroused much interest, and after the publication of *Please Kill My Cousin* (1961) Fairlie abandoned fiction writing. His last book, a biography of Sir George Cayley which he coauthored with Elizabeth Cayley, was published in 1965. Fairlie spent some time in Malta and then returned to England, where he lived in retirement until his death in 1983.

References:

Otto Penzler, ed., *Private Lives of Private Eyes, Spies, Crime Fighters and Other Good Guys* (New York: Grossett & Dunlap, 1977);

Colin Watson, *Snobbery with Violence: Crime Stories and Their Audience* (London: Eyre & Spottiswoode, 1971).

Anthony Gilbert
(Lucy Beatrice Malleson)

(15 February 1899-9 December 1973)

Mary Helen Becker
Madison Area Technical College

BOOKS: *The Man Who Was London*, as J. Kilmeny Keith (London: Collins, 1925);

The Sword of Harlequin, as Keith (London: Collins, 1927);

Nettle Harvest, as Sylvia Denys Hooke (London: Chapman & Hall, 1927; Garden City, N.Y.: Doubleday, Doran, 1928);

The Tragedy at Freyne, as Anthony Gilbert (London: Collins, 1927; New York: Dial, 1927);

The Murder of Mrs. Davenport, as Gilbert (London: Collins, 1928; New York: Dial/Toronto: Longmans, Green, 1928);

Old Stars for Sale, as Hooke (London: Chapman & Hall, 1928);

The Mystery of the Open Window, as Gilbert (London: Gollancz, 1929; New York: Dodd, Mead, 1930);

Death at Four Corners, as Gilbert (London: Collins, 1929; New York: Dial/Toronto: Longmans, Green, 1929);

Aubrey Dene, as Hooke (London & New York: Longmans, Green, 1930);

The Night of the Fog, as Gilbert (London: Gollancz, 1930; New York: Dodd, Mead, 1930);

The Case Against Andrew Fane, as Gilbert (London: Collins, 1931; New York: Dodd, Mead, 1931);

The Body on the Beam, as Gilbert (London: Collins, 1932; New York: Dodd, Mead, 1932);

The Long Shadow, as Gilbert (London: Collins, 1932);

Strange Guest, as Hooke (London: Murray, 1932);

Death in Fancy Dress, as Gilbert (London: Collins, 1933);

The Musical Comedy Crime, as Gilbert (London: Collins, 1933);

Portrait of a Murderer, as Anne Meredith (London: Gollancz, 1933; New York: Reynal & Hitchcock, 1934);

The Coward, as Meredith (London: Gollancz, 1934);

The Man in Button Boots, as Gilbert (London: Collins, 1934; New York: Holt, 1935);

An Old Lady Dies, as Gilbert (London: Collins, 1934);

The Man Who Was Too Clever, as Gilbert (London: Collins, 1935);

Lady at Large, as Lucy Egerton (London: Cassell, 1936);

Courtier to Death, as Gilbert (London: Collins, 1936); republished as *The Dover Train Mystery* (New York: Dial, 1936);

Murder by Experts, as Gilbert (London: Collins, 1936; New York: Dial, 1937);

The Gambler, as Meredith (London: Gollancz, 1937);

The Man Who Wasn't There, as Gilbert (London: Collins, 1937);

Murder Has No Tongue, as Gilbert (London: Collins, 1937);

Courage in Gold, as Egerton (London: Cassell, 1938);

The Showman, as Meredith (London: Faber & Faber, 1938);

Treason in My Breast, as Gilbert (London: Collins, 1938);

The Bell of Death, as Gilbert (London: Collins, 1939);

The Clock in the Hat Box, as Gilbert (London: Collins, 1939; New York: Mystery House, 1943);

The Stranger, as Meredith (London: Faber & Faber, 1939);

The Adventurer, as Meredith (London: Faber & Faber, 1940);

Dear Dead Woman, as Gilbert (London: Collins, 1940; New York: Mystery House, 1942);

Three-a-Penny, as Meredith (London: Faber & Faber, 1940);

Mrs. Boot's Legacy: A Sketch for Three Female Characters, as Meredith (London: French, 1941);

There's Always Tomorrow, as Meredith (London: Faber & Faber, 1941); republished as *Home*

Dust jacket for the first British edition of Malleson's 1943 novel which focuses on the changes and dangers affecting the old maid Dorothea Capper after she inherits a large fortune (courtesy of Otto Penzler)

Is the Heart (New York: Howell, Soskin, 1942);

The Vanishing Corpse, as Gilbert (London: Collins, 1941); republished as *She Vanished in the Dawn* (New York: Mystery House, 1941);

The Woman in Red, as Gilbert (London: Collins, 1941; New York: Smith & Durrell, 1943); republished as *The Mystery of the Woman in Red* (New York: Quinn, 1944);

The Case of the Tea-Cosy's Aunt, as Gilbert (London: Collins, 1942); republished as *Death in the Blackout* (New York: Smith & Durrell, 1943);

The Family Man, as Meredith (London: Faber & Faber, 1942; New York: Howell, Soskin, 1942);

Something Nasty in the Woodshed, as Gilbert (London: Collins, 1942); republished as *Mystery in the Woodshed* (New York: Smith & Durrell, 1942);

Curtain, Mr. Greatheart, as Meredith (London: Faber & Faber, 1943);

The Mouse Who Wouldn't Play Ball, as Gilbert (London: Collins, 1943); republished as *Thirty Days to Live* (New York: Smith & Durrell, 1944);

He Came by Night, as Gilbert (London: Collins, 1944); republished as *Death at the Door* (New York: Smith & Durrell, 1945);

The Scarlet Button, as Gilbert (London: Collins, 1944; New York: Barnes, 1945); republished as *Murder is Cheap* (New York: Bantam, 1949);

A Spy for Mr. Crook, as Gilbert (New York: Barnes, 1944);

The Beautiful Miss Burroughes, as Meredith (London: Faber & Faber, 1945);

The Black Stage, as Gilbert (London: Collins, 1945; New York: Barnes, 1946); republished as *Murder Cheats the Bride* (New York: Bantam, 1948);

Don't Open the Door!, as Gilbert (London: Collins, 1945); republished as *Death Lifts the Latch* (New York: Smith & Durrell, 1946);

The Spinster's Secret, as Gilbert (London: Collins, 1946); republished as *By Hook or by Crook* (New York: Barnes, 1947);

Death in the Wrong Room, as Gilbert (London: Collins/New York: Barnes, 1947);

Die in the Dark, as Gilbert (London: Collins, 1947); republished as *The Missing Widow* (New York: Barnes, 1948);

The Rich Woman, as Meredith (London: Faber & Faber, 1947; New York: Random House, 1947);

Lift up the Lid, as Gilbert (London: Collins, 1948); republished as *The Innocent Bottle* (New York: Barnes, 1948);

The Sisters, as Meredith (London: Faber & Faber, 1948; New York: Random House, 1949);

Death Knocks Three Times, as Gilbert (London: Collins, 1949; New York: Random House, 1950);

The Draper of Edgecumbe, as Meredith (London: Faber & Faber, 1950); republished as *The Unknown Path* (New York: Random House, 1950);

Murder Comes Home, as Gilbert (London: Collins, 1950; New York: Random House, 1951);

A Nice Cup of Tea, as Gilbert (London: Collins, 1950); republished as *The Wrong Body* (New York: Random House, 1951);

A Fig for Virtue, as Meredith (London: Faber & Faber, 1951);

Lady-Killer, as Gilbert (London: Collins, 1951);

Call Back Yesterday, as Meredith (London: Faber & Faber, 1952);

Miss Pinnegar Disappears, as Gilbert (London: Collins, 1952); republished as *A Case for Mr. Crook* (New York: Random House, 1952);

Footsteps behind Me, as Gilbert (London: Collins, 1953); republished as *Black Death* (New York: Random House, 1953);

The Innocent Bride, as Meredith (London: Hodder & Stoughton, 1954);

Snake in the Grass, as Gilbert (London: Collins, 1954); republished as *Death Won't Wait* (New York: Random House, 1954);

The Day of the Miracle, as Meredith (London: Hodder & Stoughton, 1955);

Is She Dead Too?, as Gilbert (London: Collins, 1955); republished as *A Question of Murder* (New York: Random House, 1955);

And Death Came Too, as Gilbert (London: Collins, 1956; New York: Random House, 1956);

Impetuous Heart, as Meredith (London: Hodder & Stoughton, 1956);

Riddle of a Lady, as Gilbert (London: Collins, 1956; New York: Random House, 1957);

Christine, as Meredith (London: Hodder & Stoughton, 1957);

Give Death a Name, as Gilbert (London: Collins, 1957);

Death against the Clock, as Gilbert (London: Collins, 1958; New York: Random House, 1958);

Death Takes a Wife, as Gilbert (London: Collins, 1959); republished as *Death Casts a Long Shadow* (New York: Random House, 1959);

A Man in the Family, as Meredith (London: Hodder & Stoughton, 1959);

Third Crime Lucky, as Gilbert (London: Collins, 1959); republished as *Prelude to Murder* (New York: Random House, 1959);

Out for the Kill, as Gilbert (London: Collins, 1960; New York: Random House, 1960);

The Wise Child, as Meredith (London: Hodder & Stoughton, 1960);

Uncertain Death, as Gilbert (London: Collins, 1961; New York: Random House, 1962);

She Shall Die, as Gilbert (London: Collins, 1961); republished as *After the Verdict* (New York: Random House, 1961);

No Dust in the Attic, as Gilbert (London: Collins, 1962; New York: Random House, 1963);

Up Goes the Donkey, as Meredith (London: Hodder & Stoughton, 1962);

Ring for a Noose, as Gilbert (London: Collins, 1963; New York: Random House, 1964);

Knock, Knock, Who's There?, as Gilbert (London: Collins, 1964); republished as *The Voice* (New York: Random House, 1965);

The Fingerprint, as Gilbert (London: Collins, 1964; New York: Random House, 1965);

Passenger to Nowhere, as Gilbert (London: Collins, 1965; New York: Random House, 1966);

The Looking Glass Murder, as Gilbert (London: Collins, 1966; New York: Random House, 1967);

The Visitor, as Gilbert (London: Collins, 1967; New York: Random House, 1967);

Night Encounter, as Gilbert (London: Collins, 1968); republished as *Murder Anonymous* (New York: Random House, 1968);

Missing From Her Home, as Gilbert (London: Collins, 1969; New York: Random House, 1969);

Death Wears a Mask, as Gilbert (London: Collins, 1970); republished as *Mr. Crook Lifts the Mask* (New York: Random House, 1970);

Tenant for the Tomb, as Gilbert (London: Collins, 1971; New York: Random House, 1971);

Murder's a Waiting Game, as Gilbert (London: Collins, 1972; New York: Random House, 1972);

A Nice Little Killing, as Gilbert (London: Collins, 1974; New York: Random House, 1974).

OTHER: "The Cockroach and the Tortoise" and "Horseshoes for Luck," in *Detection Medley*, edited by John Rhode (Cecil John Charles Street) (London: Hutchinson, 1939); republished as *Line Up* (New York: Dodd, Mead, 1940);

"You Can't Hang Twice," in *To the Queen's Taste*, edited by Ellery Queen (Frederic Dannay and Manfred Lee) (Boston: Little, Brown, 1946; London: Faber & Faber, 1949);

"Black for Innocence," in *The Evening Standard Detective Book* (London: Gollancz, 1950);

"What Would You Have Done?," in *The Evening Standard Detective Book*, second series (London: Gollancz, 1951);

"The British or the American Story," in *The Mystery Writer's Handbook*, edited by Herbert Brean (New York: Harper, 1956), pp. 235-238.

Anthony Gilbert is the best-known pseudonym of Lucy Beatrice Malleson, who wrote twenty-four books as Anne Meredith, two books

Dust jacket for the first British edition of Malleson's posthumously published novel, the last to feature lawyer/detective
Arthur Crook

as J. Kilmeny Keith, four as Sylvia Denys Hooke, and two as Lucy Egerton. As Anthony Gilbert she wrote more than sixty crime novels, most of them featuring Arthur Crook, a coarse but lovable lawyer with a particular concern for the weak and helpless, who spends more time detecting than practicing law.

Malleson was born 15 February 1899 in Upper Norwood, a suburb south of London. She attended St. Paul's Girls' School in Hammersmith, London, which she left at age fifteen when she did not receive a scholarship and her family could not afford the tuition. In her autobiography, *Three-a-Penny* (1940), she complains of the irrelevance of her education: a chauvinistic concentration on English literature and English history, and mathematics which included logarithms but left students unable to do accounts.

The year was 1914, and she observed: "But within about a fortnight even my ruined life seemed comparatively unimportant, for on the 4th of August Britain went to war." After a childhood she describes as old-fashioned, she learned firsthand about poverty, economic injustice, and woman's rights. She took a course in typing and shorthand, bought a fountain pen, and went to work. At seventeen, with no experience, she began doing clerical work for the Red Cross. Subsequently, she worked for the government in the Ministry of Food and then for the Coal Association. While still in her teens she began to sell verse.

After attending a performance of John Willard's 1922 mystery, *The Cat and the Canary*, she decided to write a thriller. Her first published book was not a success, nor was her second or third. Beginning in 1927, however, she brought out her first mystery under the name Anthony Gilbert, and from then on her mysteries appeared regularly, sometimes two in a year, until 1974. Two reasons are put forward for her use of pseudonyms: that she did not want to trade on the fame of her uncle, the actor Miles Malleson; and that she used a man's name for her crime fiction, fearing that there was prejudice against women writers. When the publishing company Collins accepted the first Anthony Gilbert novel, a publicity photo of Malleson in a wig and with a moustache was made; but the photograph was not used, and her identity was kept secret for many years. She was a founding member of the Detection Club and served as its general secretary. In a tribute in the *London Times* (12 December 1973) mystery writer Michael Gilbert remembered his own entrance into that "august institution . . . hand in hand with Michael Innes, to be introduced to its formidable president, Dorothy L. Sayers," and Malleson's kindness to him on that occasion. He concluded: "Despite the sharing of a writing name, this friendship continued, I am happy to say, down to the day of her death." She died on 9 December 1973 at the age of seventy-four.

The Man Who Was London, Malleson's first book, was published by Collins in 1925 under the name J. Kilmeny Keith. It is a cliché-ridden thriller which features an ancient house, a secret dungeon complete with skeleton, an Oriental dagger, a deaf-mute servant, a locked room, and a villain disguised as a clergyman. The 330-page narrative proceeds slowly and is characterized by stilted and disjointed prose. That it failed is perhaps less surprising than that it found a publisher. Nonetheless, Collins was sufficiently impressed with Malleson's writing talent to publish another Keith novel two years later, in 1927. That year three of Malleson's novels were published, including the first book written as Anthony Gilbert.

The earliest Anthony Gilbert novels often feature a character named Scott Egerton, who is introduced in *The Tragedy at Freyne* (1927) as a member of the House of Commons. In most cases Egerton does not detect but rather takes charge, hiring detectives and lawyers as needed. His role in *The Musical Comedy Crime* (1933) is typical. He hires a detective to help him defend a fellow member of Parliament who is accused of killing an expert bridge player.

Arthur Crook makes his initial appearance in *Murder by Experts* (1936). The tale, long, complicated, and slow moving, resembles the author's early works far more than the fifty-two lively and delightful Arthur Crook mysteries which follow. Crook himself is much less endearing than the irrepressible figure of the later cases.

By 1940 Arthur G. Crook was a fully developed character. A brash and plainspoken Cockney with a passion for pubs and drinking beer in large quantities, as befitting his size, Crook wears off-the-rack brown suits and distributes enormous business cards freely. Often Crook's appearance and attitude lead his opponents to take him for a fool, but these factors reassure his clients (usually elderly women or young people who desperately need help). His disorderly office is on the fifth floor of a building in an unfashionable part of London. His first appearance in *Don't Open the Door!* (1945) is typical. Crook, arriving late at his office, where the elevator has broken down as usual, comes up the 180 steps and enters like "the last of rocket bombs." Although appearing reluctant to take the case of Sammy Parker, whose beloved Nora Deane is missing, when Sammy leaves he consults a file he has begun on her. It is readily apparent that, no matter his appearance and occasional Cockney slang, Crook succeeds through diligence and attention to detail.

Crook thinks well of himself and of his assistant, ex-jewel thief Bill Parsons, and indeed he usually solves his cases very quickly. In *Don't Open the Door!* he is able to get a good lead on the kidnap car in just a few hours. He then moves into a pub to get more information, and a beer, because "pubs are the common denominator." It only takes him a day to find Nora, barely alive after a failed attempt by her kidnapper to murder her. In *Death against the Clock* (1958) he tells the girlfriend of a man condemned to die for murder in less than three weeks, "Just remember you've put this into the hands of the experts, and get yourself a bit of beauty sleep. You'll want to look your best when the boyfriend comes out, won't you? . . . we're going places right away, and if I don't nominate some other chap for the high jump [gallows], I'll–I'll take my pension." Crook discovers the criminal in only a few days in *Don't Open the Door!,* a case in which the criminal is afraid of Crook by reputation. While plotting to murder the recovering Nora Deane, the criminal in disguise is horrified to discover that Crook is also in the hospital: " 'Crook?' Now terror had him fairly by the throat."

Malleson (as Gilbert) was popular in part because Crook is such an individual, but much of her popularity was due to the fact that her mysteries also can stand as good novels. In *Don't Open the Door!*, as in many of the Gilbert mysteries, Crook is not the main protagonist. In fact, he is not even called in by Sammy until well over halfway through the book. And even then the main concern remains the developing relationship between Sammy and Nora. Crook's main function seems to be to provide readers with the assurance that the couple will be joined successfully. *The Mouse Who Wouldn't Play Ball* (1943) is the story of what happens to Dorothea Capper, a prim old maid who is a frequent churchgoer, when she becomes heir to a large fortune. Crook is called in when her hitherto unknown relatives attempt to kill her, but the main focus of interest in the book is on how the money changes her life. *Night Encounter* (1968) is more about how appearances can be deceiving than it is Crook's investigation into who has killed both an elderly woman with little money and an unattractive young girl. The accused is Terry Hunter, an escaped convict who had been in jail for a robbery he had attempted to help his sick child. His wife believes in him and hires Crook, who eventually proves that the murderer is someone who is supposedly above suspicion.

Malleson's Anthony Gilbert books changed markedly from the 1920s and 1930s, when she wrote thrillers that seem contrived today, to the 1940s and beyond, when she wrote well-crafted, satisfying stories. For a period of thirty years, beginning in 1940, she was a sort of quintessential English mystery writer, the creator of successful series character Arthur Crook, whose speech is colorful and common, filled with aphorisms, homespun philosophy, and slang; he protects the weak and the helpless and outwits the establishment. Even her minor characters are individuals with personality, wit, and strength. She is particularly good at portraying single women, the elderly, and persons usually ignored by society. Her settings are homely and familiar, and her plots are ingenious. While Malleson was never ranked among the most distinguished of her Detection Club colleagues, she was a solid, professional writer of enjoyable mysteries.

References:

Jane S. Bakerman, "Bowlers, Beer, Bravado, and Brains: Anthony Gilbert's Arthur Crook," *Mystery Fancier*, 2 (July 1978): 5-13;

Bill Pronzini and Marcia Muller, *One Thousand & One Midnights* (New York: Arbor House, 1986).

Winston Graham
(30 June 1910-   )

Gina Macdonald
Loyola University in New Orleans

BOOKS: *The House with the Stained-Glass Windows* (London & Melbourne: Ward, Lock, 1934);

Into the Fog (London & Melbourne: Ward, Lock, 1935);

The Riddle of John Rowe (London & Melbourne: Ward, Lock, 1935);

Without Motive (London & Melbourne: Ward, Lock, 1936);

The Dangerous Pawn (London & Melbourne: Ward, Lock, 1937);

The Giant's Chair (London & Melbourne: Ward, Lock, 1938);

Strangers Meeting (London & Melbourne: Ward, Lock, 1939);

Keys of Chance (London & Melbourne: Ward, Lock, 1939);

No Exit: An Adventure (London & Melbourne: Ward, Lock, 1940);

Night Journey: An Adventure (London & Melbourne: Ward, Lock, 1941; Garden City, N.Y.: Doubleday, 1968);

My Turn Next (London & Melbourne: Ward, Lock, 1942);

The Merciless Ladies (London & Melbourne: Ward, Lock, 1944; revised edition, London: Bodley Head, 1979; Garden City, N.Y.: Doubleday, 1980);

The Forgotten Story: A Cameo (London & Melbourne: Ward, Lock, 1945); republished as *The Wreck of the Grey Cat* (Garden City, N.Y.: Doubleday, 1958);

Ross Poldark: A Novel of Cornwall, 1783-1787 (London & Melbourne: Ward, Lock, 1945); republished as *The Renegade* (Garden City, N.Y.: Doubleday, 1951); republished as *Ross Poldark* (New York: Ballantine, 1977);

Demelza: A Novel of Cornwall, 1788-1790 (London: Ward, Lock, 1946; Garden City, N.Y.: Doubleday, 1953);

Take My Life (London & Melbourne: Ward, Lock, 1947; Garden City, N.Y.: Doubleday, 1967);

Cordelia (London & Melbourne: Ward, Lock, 1949; Garden City, N.Y.: Doubleday, 1950);

Winston Graham

Jeremy Poldark: A Novel of Cornwall, 1790-1791 (London & Melbourne: Ward, Lock, 1950); republished as *Venture Once More* (Garden City, N.Y.: Doubleday, 1954); republished as *Jeremy Poldark* (New York: Ballantine, 1977);

Night without Stars (London: Hodder & Stoughton, 1950; Garden City, N.Y.: Doubleday, 1950);

Fortune Is a Woman (London: Hodder & Stoughton, 1953; Garden City, N.Y.: Doubleday, 1953);

Warleggan: A Novel of Cornwall, 1792-1793 (London & Melbourne: Ward, Lock, 1953); republished as *The Last Gamble* (Garden City, N.Y.: Doubleday, 1955); republished as *Warleggan* (New York: Ballantine, 1977);

The Little Walls (London: Hodder & Stoughton, 1955; Garden City, N.Y.: Doubleday, 1955);

The Sleeping Partner (London: Hodder & Stoughton, 1956; Garden City, N.Y.: Doubleday, 1956);

Greek Fire (London: Hodder & Stoughton, 1958; Garden City, N.Y.: Doubleday, 1958);

The Tumbled House (London: Hodder & Stoughton, 1959; Garden City, N.Y.: Doubleday, 1960);

Marnie (London: Hodder & Stoughton, 1961; Garden City, N.Y.: Doubleday, 1961);

The Grove of Eagles (London: Hodder & Stoughton, 1963; Garden City, N.Y.: Doubleday, 1964);

After the Act (London: Hodder & Stoughton, 1965; Garden City, N.Y.: Doubleday, 1966);

The Walking Stick (London: Collins, 1967; Garden City, N.Y.: Doubleday, 1967);

Angell, Pearl and Little God (London: Collins, 1970; Garden City, N.Y.: Doubleday, 1970);

The Japanese Girl (London: Collins, 1971; Garden City, N.Y.: Doubleday, 1972);

The Spanish Armadas (London: Collins, 1972; New York: Doubleday, 1972);

The Black Moon: A Novel of Cornwall, 1794-5 (London: Collins, 1973; Garden City, N.Y.: Doubleday, 1974);

Woman in the Mirror (London: Bodley Head, 1975; Garden City, N.Y.: Doubleday, 1975);

The Four Swans: A Novel of Cornwall, 1795-7 (London: Collins, 1976; Garden City, N.Y.: Doubleday, 1977);

The Angry Tide: A Novel of Cornwall, 1798-9 (London: Collins, 1977; Garden City, N.Y.: Doubleday, 1978);

The Stranger from the Sea: A Novel of Cornwall, 1810-1811 (London: Collins, 1981; Garden City, N.Y.: Doubleday, 1982);

The Miller's Dance (London: Collins, 1982; Garden City, N.Y.: Doubleday, 1983);

Poldark's Cornwall (London: Bodley Head/Exeter, England: Webb & Bower, 1983);

The Loving Cup (London: Collins, 1984; Garden City, N.Y.: Doubleday, 1985);

A Green Flash (London: Collins, 1986; New York: Random House, 1987).

MOTION PICTURES: *Take My Life*, screenplay by Graham and Valerie Taylor, Eagle Lion, 1948;

Night without Stars, screenplay by Graham, RKO, 1953.

OTHER: "The Circus," in *Winter's Crimes*, edited by George Hardinge (London: Macmillan, 1974).

PERIODICAL PUBLICATION: "Viewpoint in the Novel," *Writer's Digest*, 52 (October 1972): 25-26, 52.

Although he is perhaps best known for his historical novels, particularly the popular BBC television Poldark series, Winston Graham has brought to the mystery and the spy story a versatility and variety that breaks the formulaic modes and mixes history, romance, adventure, and intrigue. To blackmail, murder, fraud, and theft, Graham has added the mystery of the mind, the exploration of motives and deeds that lie rooted in the past and produce the conflicts, doubts, hesitations, and eccentricities of the present. His power lies in his ability to provide a sense of ordinary people menaced by the sort of trauma and violence that could well occur in the daily lives of his readers. His heroes are not blameless supermen, but guilt-ridden humans touched by the lives of others and forced to make personal decisions about loyalties and values. His mysteries have been translated into fifteen languages, and several have been made into films: *Take My Life* (1947) by Eagle Lion Films in 1948, *Night without Stars* (1950) by Rank in 1951, *Fortune Is a Woman* (1953)–as *She Played with Fire*–by Columbia in 1958, *The Sleeping Partner* (1956) for television in 1958, *Marnie* (1961) (produced by Alfred Hitchcock and starring Tippi Hedren and Sean Connery) by Universal in 1964, and *The Walking Stick* (1967) by M-G-M in 1969.

Born in Victoria Park, Manchester, England, on 30 June 1910 to Albert Henry, a chemist, and Anne Mawdsley Graham, Winston Mawdsley Graham left school at sixteen because of delicate health and at age seventeen moved to the coastal countryside of Cornwall, the setting of many of his novels. He continued his studies with a tutor and by age twenty-one, with the encouragement and support of his widowed mother, began his literary career. His first novel was *The House with the Stained-Glass Windows* (1934). He married Jean Mary Williamson on 18 September 1939. They have a son and a daughter. He served in the coastguard service during World War II and returned to a literary career thereafter. In 1956 he received the Crime Writers' Association prize for one of his finest mysteries, *The Little Walls* (1955). He served as chairman of the London Soci-

Dust jacket for the first British edition of one of Graham's two 1935 novels (courtesy of Otto Penzler)

ety of Authors from 1967 to 1969, and became a fellow of the Royal Society of Literature in 1968.

Graham's detective, when there is one, is an amateur, innocently caught up in an unsuspected crime, brought into it by accident, by circumstance, or by concern for another person. He is sometimes, again by misadventure or because of his deep personal involvement with another, the suspect, or accomplice, or intended victim. Even when the investigator does what he feels is morally and humanly right, he often finds himself on the wrong side of the law, protecting black marketeers, thieves, arsonists, embezzlers, and maybe even murderers. What are most important to Graham are human relationships. In *The Forgotten Story: A Cameo* (1945) a young boy, taken in by distant relatives after his father has abandoned him, joins forces with his cousin's estranged husband and unwittingly uncovers mur-

der, adultery, madness, and betrayal, while his cousin-in-law must act with caution and responsibility to prove his suspicions, save the boy, and demonstrate to his headstrong young wife that he loves her enough to respect her independence and to start a new life that will challenge both of them. In *Fortune Is a Woman* an alienated working-class drifter finds satisfaction and self-worth as an insurance claims adjuster, only to learn that the love of his life may have been part of a conspiracy to cheat the insurance company, perhaps murdering her husband in the process. In *Take My Life* the amateur detective is an opera singer, Philippa Shelley, who, after a successful debut at Covent Garden, learns that her husband, Nicholas Talbot, has previously had an affair with a violinist in the orchestra, a woman bent on renewing the relationship. After a violent quarrel, at the close of which Talbot rushes angrily into the night, Philippa learns that her husband has been accused of murdering his former mistress and that the police seem to have an airtight case against him. She gives up her Covent Garden tour and sets out to prove Talbot innocent, arguing that he might be capable of a flirtation but never a murder, and postulating a murderer who is taking advantage of circumstances and lying low.

Inevitably, because they are amateurs, Graham's characters, male and female alike, do not always do the logical or the rational and as a result often find themselves in complicated and incriminating circumstances that try their courage and their love. Philippa Shelley from *Take My Life* endangers her own life in her dogged pursuit of the murderer. Oliver Brandwell, hero of *Fortune Is a Woman*, finds himself accused of insurance fraud, conspiracy, and arson and suspected of murder because of his failure to consult the authorities about his suspicions and his knowledge of crime or possible crime.

Graham's heroes are normally cautious, pensive characters who take life seriously, who rush into love, but who tend to hesitate and ruminate about all else. They accept the need to test their own assumptions and are willing to experiment, if necessary, to find a workable compromise. *Marnie* follows these same patterns but is unique in his canon in that the man diligently seeking answers and willing to ignore the letter of the law for the sake of love—Marnie's employer and later husband—is not the narrator of the story. Instead it is Marnie, the attractive, competent liar, forger, and calculated thief, who tells her tale. She thereby reveals the psychoneurotic condition formed from a childhood trauma and a puritanical upbringing that makes her incapable of leading a normal life. Graham helps the reader fully understand the changes that psychoanalysis, love, and learning the truth about the past can produce.

In the prologue to *The Forgotten Story* Graham describes those who would reconstruct real events from newspaper accounts as "like paleontologists trying to reconstruct an extinct animal," never certain because of the deceptive nature of appearances, the multiplicity of details that add up to truth but that can also suggest a number of other possibilities. Thus, throughout Graham's canon, men must deal with the disparity of facts and interpretations, and must wade through seeming truths that are at odds with their instinctive feelings. Invariably they must examine a number of contradictory hypotheses before finding a combination that rings true, and even then they have doubts until the final proof is in. A common refrain in his work is "the rest may be fraud but she's genuine–somehow" (*Night without Stars*). To all appearances Marnie, for example, is a scheming, devious criminal, a pathological liar who preys on society and is insensitive to the loss and pain her acts might cause, but with time the reader learns that in reality she is a sensitive, damaged individual, capable of love and kindness, but pushed by forces beyond her understanding to avoid physical or emotional intimacy, to keep others at a careful distance, and to time and again try to win her mother's approval–without success. When at the end, her life in shreds, her self-knowledge only recently and painfully attained, she must confront her accusers and pay for past crimes, readers can appreciate the fury of her assailants but also the courage that allows her to understand that "the way to love is through suffering" and to face the future with hope.

In most Graham novels the past impinges on the present. The present conflicts in *Greek Fire* (1958) grow out of the events and prejudices of wartime Greece, and the hero, of use to the Greek Resistance in the past, employs old alliances to further his present investigation. The evidence that will undo a modern politician consists of wartime letters that identify the politician's secret communist allegiance. In *The Tumbled House* (1959) the besmirching of the late Sir John Marlowe, a reputable barrister turned philosopher, leads most hearers to reconsider their past perceptions in the light of seemingly damning evidence and cry, "sham," but it motivates Sir John's son, Don Marlowe, a successful young conductor, to bring suit, vindicate his father, and restore honor to the family. *The Walking Stick* skillfully interweaves the vulnerable young polio victim's past experiences with life and love with present ones to make credible her acceptance of Hartley's advances and her transformation from wallflower to dancer, skater, and robber. *Woman in the Mirror* (1975) explores the idea that the past can be repeated. The domineering and wealthy Althea Syme employs as secretary a young woman of striking likeness to her dead niece. In fact, the new secretary, Norah, is so much a mirror image of the past owner of Morb House that she resurrects old fears and hatreds that lead to violence and drama. In *Fortune Is a Woman* the suffering of childhood and the betrayal of his father's early death have embittered the hero and made normal human relationships–friendship and love–nearly impossible, but by dealing with the present he learns to come to terms with the past. In *Marnie* the core of the mystery is Marnie's secret past, a past she is reluctant to explore but which she must face if she is ever to be able to deal with life and love normally. Flashbacks to the sordid slum life of her youth provide clues to her present abnormality. However, neither love nor fear, nor psychoanalysis, can help her until she finds out the truth about her past, and that knowledge alone is enough to break down her hidden barriers and allow her to see herself and her world in a new way.

Clearly, a part of Graham's interest in the past is an interest in human psychology, the way experience molds and makes or breaks a person and the way individuals act as catalysts in human relationships, transforming themselves and others when confronted with a difficult situation. His characters inexorably grapple with questions of moral conduct and codes of honor, and must ultimately face issues that challenge who they are and that determine what they will be in the future. *The Walking Stick* raises the question of what really constitutes a crime, with the painter-thief rationalizing that, while crimes against humanity are wrong, crimes against property, especially when insurance will cover the loss, are not. Other characters present evidence to the contrary. In *The Sleeping Partner* two scientists in love with the same woman debate the value of life, the hazards of having children given the impending risk of nuclear holocaust, and the dangers of the scientist blindly seeing only the narrow technical view and ignoring the overall human focus, a debate intensified by the idealist slowly dying of leukemia brought on by his own experimental research. The idealist argues that "science can't emancipate man from his own nature; it can only help him–if he has a certain amount of intellectual modesty–to understand it better," and then he provides a summation of what quite often goes wrong with Graham's heroes: "In times of crisis, if a man has no reference outside himself, even his best moral judgments straggle off into enervation and experience. If you lose your sense of wonder you lose your sense of balance."

After the Act (1965) investigates another area of debate: whether the act of murder changes one profoundly. Its first-person narrator is a successful young playwright who disposes of his older wife by pushing her over a balcony in order to free himself for love with a much younger girl. The question Graham pursues is whether this murderer cannot merely suspend morality for the moment of the act itself, but forever after can convince himself the death was accidental, or necessary, and can carry on as if nothing had happened. In other words, as Anthony Boucher points out in the *New York Times Book Review* (15 May 1966), this novel ambitiously examines a successful murderer by scrapping "all accepted cliches about remorse and retribution" and trying to analyze reactions "completely anew." The first half of the book prepares for the murder, the murderer's motives, justifications, and rationalizations, and ends with the act:

> I pushed her. The muscular movement of deltoid, triceps, biceps and the rest was galvanized into action by some nervous but meditated impulse originating I know not where. I pushed her and she fell. Slowly at first, for the centre of balance was only just tipped. I saw her head half turn as if to look at me; she cried out but not loudly: it was a muffled protest; and she fell. Somewhere between earth and hell my soul was suspended while she dropped. Then there was a tremendous crash and splintering of glass and metal as she went through the glass roof protecting the covered way to the reception desk of the hotel. It was like a bomb exploding in the quiet night. It exploded not only in the night but in my head.
> And thereafter there was silence.

The second half of the book explores the aftermath: the pretense, the police investigation, the necessary lies, the nightmares, the self-delusion, the reevaluations:

> But did I really push her? I went out on the balcony and she was quarrelsome and dogmatic. I could do nothing with her, arguing, persuading. At length I put my hand on her arm, trying to pull her gently in. She shook it off angrily and this sharp movement set her off balance. She cried out and tried to recover and I clutched her frock, trying to hold her. The satin slipped under my fingers. I grabbed at her shoulder but already the weight was too much. In a moment she was whirling down to her death. It was all my fault. If I had not tried to pull her to come in she would never have jerked away from me and over-balanced. It was all my fault that she was accidentally dead.

The narrator becomes increasingly mentally ill. He is haunted: "When they saw me they all stopped whispering, and there was a profound silence. Then I saw Harriet, in the middle of them all. Her face was streaked with blood from broken glass, but she smiled at me as if she had no teeth at all. She was the only one in grave clothes." Finally, there is the desperate urge to confess that leads to the denouement. Thus, in *After the Act* the debate and the psychological study are interwoven as part of the same fabric.

Graham's two spy novels partake of the same qualities as his mysteries. For modern readers they embody an old-fashioned sense of war and men, in which young naval officers, pilots, and spies alike quote Horace and make puns and quips in Latin or Greek, read the classics, and debate questions of values and morality. *Night Journey: An Adventure* (1941) sold seven hundred copies before the stock was destroyed in an air raid. It was revived in the late 1960s with Graham's preface calling attention to its limitations and virtues: a novel "written in the darkest days of the war," but at a time when "the sub-world of espionage" was less savage, less sophisticated, and less ambivalent. It is a straightforward adventure story with the usual Graham twist. The hero who thwarts the Germans is an Austrian scientist, Dr. Mencken, uneasily settled in Britain, fearful of imprisonment as an alien, but a most reluctant spy. Conscripted by British intelligence to secure information about a new kind of poison gas developed by an Italian scientist, he must go to Italy and act as scientific adviser to an Italian naval representative in British pay. But when the Italian scientist is killed in an air raid and the formula for the gas stolen by a Nazi official, he is caught up in an assassination plot and a romance, and despite his amateur meddling is amused to find himself described in a Zurich paper as a "famous British spy and saboteur." The high-tension concluding scene, which takes place on a train speeding through northern Italy and the St. Gotthard Tunnel into neutral Switzerland, was praised by Boucher (*New York Times Book Review*, 28 January 1968), who said it evoked the early Alfred Hitchcock films.

Despite Graham's success in historical novels, his mysteries remain his most enduring achievement for, though building on the traditional techniques for promoting suspense and excitement, they have a freshness of approach and a psychological interest that separates them from other works in this genre. Long after reading a Graham mystery, it is not the mystery itself, the question of who did it and how they did it, that remains; nor is it a sense of place or atmosphere; instead it is the recollection of the moral dilemma—the images of men and women caught up in circumstances beyond their control, not knowing how to act nor to whom to turn, acting impetuously according to the moment and finding themselves thereby trapped in a pattern that plunges them deeper into chaos, discovering that they must look within and face their deepest fears about themselves and their relationships before they can turn outward and deal with the ever more pressing problems around them. Innocence is found culpable, not of the most heinous crimes, but of a failure of humanity, an indifference to others, a betrayal of trust or of need that was not even meant as a betrayal but which simply occurred because of obsessions with one's own concerns.

References:
"Viewpoint in the Novel," *Writer's Digest*, 52 (October 1972): 25-26;

"Winston Graham," *Contemporary Literary Criticism*, 23 (1983): 191-194.

Graham Greene

(2 October 1904-   )

Andrew and Gina Macdonald
Loyola University in New Orleans

See also the Greene entries in *DLB 13: British Dramatists Since World War II; DLB 15: British Novelists, 1930-1959;* and *DLB Yearbook 1985.*

BOOKS: *Babbling April* (Oxford: Blackwell, 1925);

The Man Within (London: Heinemann, 1929; Garden City, N.Y.: Doubleday, Doran, 1929);

The Name of Action (London: Heinemann, 1930; Garden City, N.Y.: Doubleday, Doran, 1931);

Rumour at Nightfall (London: Heinemann, 1931; Garden City, N.Y.: Doubleday, Doran, 1932);

Stamboul Train (London: Heinemann, 1932; revised, 1932); republished as *Orient Express* (Garden City, N.Y.: Doubleday, Doran, 1933);

It's a Battlefield (London: Heinemann, 1934; Garden City, N.Y.: Doubleday, Doran, 1934; revised edition, New York: Viking, 1962);

England Made Me (London & Toronto: Heinemann, 1935; Garden City, N.Y.: Doubleday, Doran, 1935); republished as *The Shipwrecked* (New York: Viking, 1953);

The Basement Room, and Other Stories (London: Cresset, 1935);

A Gun for Sale: An Entertainment (London & Toronto: Heinemann, 1936); republished as *This Gun for Hire* (Garden City, N.Y.: Doubleday, Doran, 1936);

Journey without Maps (London & Toronto: Heinemann, 1936; Garden City, N.Y.: Doubleday, Doran, 1936);

Brighton Rock (London & Toronto: Heinemann, 1938; New York: Viking, 1938; revised, London: Heinemann, 1947; revised, London: Heinemann/Bodley Head, 1969);

The Confidential Agent (London & Toronto: Heinemann, 1939; revised edition, New York: Viking, 1939);

The Lawless Roads (London, New York & Toronto: Longmans, Green, 1939); republished as *Another Mexico* (New York: Viking, 1939);

Twenty-Four Short Stories, by Greene, James Laver, and Sylvia Townsend Warner (London: Cresset, 1939);

The Power and the Glory (London & Toronto: Heinemann, 1940; New York: Viking, 1946); republished as *The Labyrinthine Ways* (New York: Viking, 1940);

British Dramatists (London: Collins, 1942);

The Ministry of Fear: An Entertainment (London & Toronto: Heinemann, 1943; New York: Viking, 1943);

The Little Train, anonymous (London: Eyre & Spottiswoode, 1946); as Greene (New York: Lothrop, Lee & Shepard, 1958);

Nineteen Stories (London & Toronto: Heinemann, 1947; New York: Viking, 1949); expanded as *Twenty-One Stories* (London, Melbourne & Toronto: Heinemann, 1954; New York: Viking, 1962);

The Heart of the Matter (Melbourne, London & Toronto: Heinemann, 1948; New York: Viking, 1948);

Why Do I Write?, by Greene, Elizabeth Bowen, and V. S. Pritchett (London: Marshall, 1948);

The Little Fire Engine (London: Parrish, 1950); republished as *The Little Red Fire Engine* (New York: Lothrop, Lee & Shepard, 1952);

The Third Man and The Fallen Idol (Melbourne, London & Toronto: Heinemann, 1950); abridged as *The Third Man: An Entertainment* (New York: Viking, 1950);

The End of the Affair (Melbourne, London & Toronto: Heinemann, 1951; New York: Viking, 1951);

The Lost Childhood, and Other Essays (London: Eyre & Spottiswoode, 1951; New York: Viking, 1952);

The Little Horse Bus (London: Parrish, 1952; New York: Lothrop, Lee & Shepard, 1954);

Essais Catholiques, translated by Marcelle Sibon (Paris: Editions du Seuil, 1953);

Graham Greene at his apartment in Antibes (Graham Wood/Daily Mail)

The Little Steamroller: A Story of Adventure, Mystery and Detection (London: Parrish, 1953; New York: Lothrop, Lee & Shepard, 1955);

The Living Room (Melbourne, London & Toronto: Heinemann, 1953; New York: Viking, 1954);

Loser Takes All (Melbourne, London & Toronto: Heinemann, 1955; New York: Viking, 1957);

The Quiet American (Melbourne, London & Toronto: Heinemann, 1955; New York: Viking, 1956);

The Potting Shed (New York: Viking, 1957; London, Melbourne & Toronto: Heinemann, 1958);

Our Man in Havana: An Entertainment (London, Melbourne & Toronto: Heinemann, 1958; New York: Viking, 1958);

The Complaisant Lover: A Comedy (London, Melbourne & Toronto: Heinemann, 1959; New York: Viking, 1961);

A Burnt-Out Case (London, Melbourne & Toronto: Heinemann, 1961; New York: Viking, 1961);

In Search of a Character: Two African Journals (London: Bodley Head, 1961; New York: Viking, 1962);

A Sense of Reality (London: Bodley Head, 1963; New York: Viking, 1963);

The Comedians (London: Bodley Head, 1966; New York: Viking, 1966);

Victorian Detective Fiction: A Catalogue of the Collection Made by Dorothy Glover & Graham Greene Bibliographically Arranged by Eric Osborne, by Greene and Dorothy Glover, edited by Eric Osborne (London, Sydney & Toronto: Bodley Head, 1966);

May We Borrow Your Husband? and Other Comedies of the Sexual Life (London, Sydney & Toronto: Bodley Head, 1967; New York: Viking, 1967);

Modern Film Scripts: The Third Man, by Greene and Carol Reed (London: Lorrimer, 1968; New York: Simon & Schuster, 1969);

Travels with My Aunt: A Novel (London: Bodley Head, 1969; New York: Viking, 1970);

A Sort of Life (London, Sydney & Toronto: Bodley Head, 1971; New York: Simon & Schuster, 1971);

The Honorary Consul (London, Sydney & Toronto: Bodley Head, 1973; New York: Simon & Schuster, 1973);

Lord Rochester's Monkey: Being the Life of John Wilmot, Second Earl of Rochester (London, Sydney & Toronto: Bodley Head, 1974; New York: Viking, 1974);

The Return of A. J. Raffles: An Edwardian Comedy in Three Acts Based Somewhat Loosely on E. W. Hornung's Characters in "The Amateur Cracksman" (London, Sydney & Toronto: Bodley Head, 1975; New York: Simon & Schuster, 1976);

The Bear Fell Free (Folcroft, Pa.: Folcroft, 1977);

The Human Factor (London, Sydney & Toronto: Bodley Head, 1978; New York: Simon & Schuster, 1978);

Doctor Fischer of Geneva, or the Bomb Party (London: Bodley Head, 1980; New York: Simon & Schuster, 1980);

Ways of Escape (London: Bodley Head, 1980; New York: Simon & Schuster, 1981);

Monsignor Quixote (London: Bodley Head, 1982; New York: Simon & Schuster, 1982);

Getting to Know the General: The Story of an Involvement (London: Bodley Head, 1984; New York: Simon & Schuster, 1984);

The Tenth Man (New York: Simon & Schuster, 1985; London: Bodley Head, 1985).

Editions and Collections: *Three Plays* (London: Mercur, 1961);

Collected Essays (London, Sydney & Toronto: Bodley Head, 1969; New York: Viking, 1969);

Graham Greene: The Collected Edition, introductions by Greene (London: Bodley Head/Heinemann, 1970);

The Power and the Glory, edited by R. W. B. Lewis and Peter J. Conn (New York: Viking, 1970);

The Pleasure-Dome: The Collected Film Criticism, 1935-40, edited by John Russell Taylor (London: Secker & Warburg, 1972); republished as *Graham Greene on Film: Collected Film Criticism, 1935-1940* (New York: Simon & Schuster, 1972);

The Collected Stories of Graham Greene (London: Bodley Head/Heinemann, 1972; New York: Viking, 1973);

The Portable Graham Greene, edited by Philip Stratford (New York: Viking, 1973; Harmondsworth: Penguin, 1977);

Shades of Greene: The Televised Stories of Graham Greene (London: Bodley Head/Heinemann, 1975).

PLAY PRODUCTIONS: *The Living Room*, London, Wyndham's Theatre, 16 April 1953;

The Potting Shed, New York, Bijou Theatre, 29 January 1957; London, Globe Theatre, 5 February 1958;

The Complaisant Lover, London, Globe Theatre, 18 June 1959; New York, Ethel Barrymore Theatre, 1 November 1961;

Carving a Statue, London, Haymarket Theatre, 17 September 1964; New York, Gramercy Arts Theatre, 30 April 1968;

The Return of A. J. Raffles, London, Aldwych Theatre, 4 December 1975;

Yes and No and *For Whom the Bell Chimes*, Leicester, Haymarket Studio, 20 March 1980.

MOTION PICTURES: *Twenty-one Days*, screenplay by Greene and Basil Dean, Columbia, 1937; rereleased as *21 Days Together*, Columbia, 1940;

The Future's in the Air, commentary by Greene, Strand Film Unit, 1937;

The New Britain, commentary by Greene, Strand Film Unit, 1940;

Brighton Rock, screenplay by Greene and Terence Rattigan, Pathé, 1946; rereleased as *Young Scarface*, Mayer-Kingsley, 1952;

The Fallen Idol, screenplay by Greene, British Lion, 1948; rereleased, David O. Selznik, 1949;

The Third Man, screenplay by Greene, British Lion, 1949; rereleased, David O. Selznik, 1950;

The Stranger's Hand, produced by Greene and John Stafford, British Lion, 1954; rereleased, Distributors Corporation of America, 1955;

Loser Takes All, screenplay by Greene, British Lion, 1956; rereleased, Distributors Corporation of America, 1957;

Saint Joan, screenplay by Greene, United Artists, 1957;

Our Man in Havana, screenplay by Greene, Columbia, 1960;

The Comedians, screenplay by Greene, M-G-M, 1967.

TELEVISION: "Alas, Poor Maling," adapted by Greene, in *Shades of Greene*, Thames Television, 1979.

OTHER: *The Old School: Essays by Diverse Hands*, edited by Greene (London: Cape, 1934);

H. H. Munro, *The Best of Saki*, introduction by Greene (London: Lane, 1950; New York: Viking, 1961);

The Spy's Bedside Book: An Anthology, edited by Greene and Hugh Greene (London: Hart-Davis, 1957; New York: Carroll & Graf, 1985);

Ford Madox Ford, *The Bodley Head Ford Madox Ford*, volumes 1-4 edited by Greene (London: Bodley Head, 1962-1963);

An Impossible Woman: The Memories of Dottoressa Moor of Capri, edited by Greene (London, Sydney & Toronto: Bodley Head, 1975; New York: Viking, 1976);

Victorian Villainies, edited by Greene and Hugh Greene (New York: Viking, 1984; Harmondsworth: Penguin, 1985).

Novelist, short-story writer, dramatist, screenwriter, film critic, news correspondent, editor, essayist, biographer, and writer of children's books, Graham Greene is a recognized master of his craft, a prolific entertainer (self-proclaimed in many of his subtitles) who tells a good tale while challenging values, perceptions, and worldviews. He has been called "the first major English-writing novelist who is also a Catholic" (Harry Sylvester); "one of the really significant novelists now writing in any language" (Sean O'Faolain); and "a searching, irresistible talent and a true magician . . . in the descent of the modern masters" (Morton D. Zabel). In his work Greene has encompassed both the theological and the secular and has combined comedy and tragedy in mixtures labeled "heretical," "Catholic," "sordid" and "wry." Zabel argues that he raised the thriller "to a skill and artistry few other writers of the period, and none in English, had arrived at." Arthur Calder-Marshall finds Greene constructing "an atmosphere of horror, disgust, evil, terror, and loneliness" out of what O'Faolain calls "the broken lives of the betrayed ones of the earth." What sets Greene's mystery fiction apart is his ambition (stated in his introduction to the collected edition of *The Confidential Agent*, 1939) "to create something legendary out of a contemporary thriller." The result has been thrillers that investigate the human condition, the psychology and the heart of man, amid conditions in which the seemingly familiar and benign prove strange and dangerous, and the exotic and uncivilized prove familiar extensions of the ordinary. His urban setting, labeled "Greeneland" by critics, is the seedy underworld of the thief, the spy, and the murderer, a land of universal menace. Greene's most common themes include betrayal and guilt; the complexity of living; the impossibility of finding clear-

Dust jacket for the first American edition of Greene's 1936 novel, published in England as A Gun for Sale: An Entertainment. *Beginning with this book, Greene made a distinction between his novels and "entertainments," which were long fictional melodramas (courtesy of Otto Penzler).*

cut answers; man's psychology when on the run; and man's alienation from himself, his environment, and his fellowman. The movement of his work has been from initial melodramatic excess to more classic directness, with character dominating plot more and more, sinners proving saintly, and idealists dangerous.

Graham Henry Greene was born in Berkhampsted, Herefordshire, England, on 2 October 1904, the fourth of six children of Marion Raymond Greene (a distant cousin of Robert Louis Stevenson) and Charles Henry Greene, the headmaster of Berkhampsted School, where the young Greene was educated. Of his school days, his short stories and essays (such as those in *The Lost Childhood, and Other Essays*, 1951) record games of Russian roulette, conflicts between family and school, attempted escapes of various sorts, and the love-hate relationship with school that has long been the mainstay of the memoirs of upper-middle-class Englishmen. He used his few months of parentally enforced psychoanalysis as the imaginative basis for his negative portraits of mental asylums (as in *The Ministry of Fear: An Entertainment*, 1943). Nonetheless, in general, his childhood was sheltered, and his heritage was a Victorian world order whose values he has questioned ever since. His formative reading included Anthony Hope, H. Rider Haggard, and Marjorie Bowen (Gabrielle Campbell), with the latter providing patterns and concepts for exercise-book imitations. Later it was Ford Madox Ford, Joseph Conrad, and Henry James who provided his models and inspiration. Greene studied modern history at Balliol College, Oxford, and while there edited the *Oxford Outlook*, published a book of verse (*Babbling April*, 1925), and in a spirit of rebellion joined the Communist party for six weeks. In 1926 he became a member of the Roman Catholic Church, an act which has led to his being called a Catholic writer and which has produced a critical search for affirmations of Catholic theology in all his works. After graduation he had a brief unpaid apprenticeship with the *Nottingham Journal*. Greene worked as a subeditor in the *London Times* letters department until 1929, when, inspired by Heinemann and Doubleday's guarantee of six hundred pounds a year on the strength of *The Man Within* (1929), which he had written while recovering from appendicitis, he turned to a full-time writing career.

While with the *London Times* Greene had married Vivien Dayrell Browning, by whom he had two children, but the failure of his second and third novels left his family impoverished and Greene himself frustrated and depressed and ready to give up writing. Nonetheless, he persisted, testing out his method through trial and error, until he developed a style and a form that successfully merged his double interests: serious concerns and melodrama. The success of *Stamboul Train* (1932) gave him the impetus to continue his career as a writer. Greene wrote film reviews for *Night and Day* for two years; in 1935 he became film critic for the *Spectator* and in 1940 its literary editor. His film criticism from this period has been described as brilliant. Then he worked for the British Foreign Office on a confidential mission to Sierra Leone from 1941 to 1943. After the war Greene served as editor and director of the publishing houses Eyre and Spottiswoode (1944-1948) and Bodley Head

(1958-1968). Early in 1952 Greene applied through the American consul in Saigon for a visa to enter the United States but was denied on the basis of the McCarran Act. He was only able to visit for brief periods until the restraint against him was lifted during the presidency of John F. Kennedy.

Greene's autobiography begins in *Journey without Maps* (1936–his early African years) and *In Search of a Character: Two African Journals* (1961–his later African years) and continues in *A Sort of Life* (1971–his life to his twenties) and *Ways of Escape* (1980–his life from 1929 to 1978. In his African autobiographies Greene describes journeys to that continent as metaphors for his own spiritual search, and he explains why he came to reject utopian visions. In *A Sort of Life* and *Ways of Escape* he traces his Georgian childhood among the British intellectual middle class, his attraction to drugs, sex, and danger, his fear of boredom, his deep depressions, and his lifetime of travel, evasion, and escape. He discusses libeling Shirley Temple (he called her "dimpled depravity"); experiencing anticolonial uprisings in Malaysia, Kenya, and Vietnam; being deported from Puerto Rico as a onetime Communist; reveling in Havana; seeking beer and opium to give him "the energy to meet Ho Chi Minh at tea"; and contending with "the Other"–an imposter Graham Greene who creates trouble everywhere for him. He also provides instruction on his craft, but the style of these books overall does not say much about Greene. His personality is much more evident in his work, in what critics call "Greeneland," a landscape of the mind and of the heart–a place of injustice, suffering, guilt and fear. His is a world under seige, in which the safe and familiar are transformed so that the innocent or idealized become the corrupt, the flawed, the annihilated.

William Soskin, in the *Weekly Book Review* (30 May 1943), describes Greene as "an expert in the art" of whetting the "jaded appetites of readers of mystery thrillers" and argues, in effect, that Greene enlivens the genre:

> He has the ability to glamorize the thriller intellectually, give it an upswept hair-do of psychological interest, arch its eyebrows so that its ordinary features seem to involve social questionings, and rouge its lips into a semblance of earnest passion that lifts it out of the boy-meets-girl category.

In other words, Greene's thrillers partake of the same themes, concerns, and approaches as his other work. Both forms are dominated by a search for identity among events that are both devastatingly real, yet somehow of a quality with the unreal. In both there are searches and pursuits and violence.

Greene's protagonists are incapable of remaining detached, despite their initial wish to do so, and once involved are carried along by forces beyond their control—sometimes to the solutions of their puzzles, sometimes to their greater mystification or embarrassment, but always to a revelation of personal character that ultimately outweighs any final denouement. For Greene evil lies not in an individual or an act but in circumstances and mind-sets and is a blurred gray area where the right deed for the wrong motive or the worst of deeds with good cause blend together, and one must reassess one's own absolutes and learn that labels are too easy a game— even in politics. The truly evil man has a childlike egotism—unable to experience empathy, he is self-convinced. "Human nature is not black and white but black and grey," Greene argues, and hence one must be able to write "from the point of view of the black square as well as of the white" if one is to have the "extra dimension of understanding" requisite for meaningful writing. D. in *The Confidential Agent* works faithfully for what he knows is a hopeless cause; Pyle in *The Quiet American* (1955) is blindly committed to a cause which will ultimately destroy those he seeks to help; and the police lieutenant in *The Power and the Glory* (1940) relentlessly tracks down the priest in obedience to the law of his land and his own egalitarian principles. In *The Ministry of Fear: An Entertainment* Arthur Rowe, a man who cannot forgive himself for the mercy killing of his wife and who cannot accept the court's judgment of mercy, eventually races to prevent secret documents from leaving the country, even as he admires the courage of his opponent. In *Our Man in Havana* (1958) Wormold's wish to provide for his daughter Milly leads him to accept funds to spy on Cuba, his adopted land. Then guilt at receiving money without providing some return makes him produce a fictitious network of spies and plots, one that the real spies take all too seriously. Soon innocent lives are lost, others are threatened, and the fabric of Wormold's peaceful life is rent apart.

Greene's central characters are always flawed, but it is this flaw that makes them human and likable and more capable of self-understanding and sacrifice. Having been

Dust jacket for the first British edition of the 1938 entertainment, later reclassified by Greene as a novel, that firmly established Greene as a leading British novelist (courtesy of Otto Penzler)

stripped of illusions, having contemplated self-destruction and lost their most important human connections, they have nothing left to lose and can more realistically confront the world which closes in on them. They are able to smile ironically at themselves and to see through the pretensions and hypocrisies of those around them to recognize their common humanity. Greene's protagonists include a remittance man (Minty in *England Made Me*, 1935), a hired killer (Raven in *A Gun for Sale*, 1936), an adolescent gang leader (Pinkie in *Brighton Rock*, 1938), an alcoholic priest (in *The Power and the Glory*), a mercy killer and amnesiac (Rowe in *The Ministry of Fear*), a fallen Catholic (Scobie in *The Heart of the Matter*, 1948), a failed writer and adulterer (Bendrix in *The End of the Affair*, 1951), an incompetent idealist (Pyle in *The Quiet American*), a jaded journalist gone native (Fowler in *The Quiet American*), an unsuccessful vacuum-cleaner salesman whose wife has left him (Wormold in *Our Man in Havana*), a drunken diplomat (Brown in *The Comedians*, 1966), and an odd priest and his Communist friend (Quixote and Sancho in *Monsignor Quixote*, 1982). In other words, Greene is interested in social outcasts who potentially share his own romantic and anarchistic spirit; he is sympathetic to the poor and oppressed while distrustful of authority. His heroes, despite superficial affiliation with one side or another, doubt, and it is their doubt that makes them seem humane and decent. Humanistic values beneath opposing philosophies dominate his work, and add a depth of perception beyond the norms of the genre.

For all its excesses, Greene's first novel, *The Man Within* (with its title from Sir Thomas Browne's epigraph, "There's another man within me that's angry with me"), includes flashes of brilliance: poetic but tightly controlled imagery, memorable scenes and physical settings, and sharp, if overdone, insights into the psychology of character. It is a paradigm for his work and has all the elements of Greene's later thrillers. Francis Andrews, an orphan taken from school by a smuggler and brought up as a sort of mascot to his crew, is not sure where his allegiance lies. Ultimately, he rejects the romantic but depraved life of the smugglers for the love of his Elizabeth, but only after she has killed herself. What is important to him is that he satisfies the "stern unrelenting critic" within himself; as he discovers, "I am that critic."

Stamboul Train, a cosmopolitan "entertainment" and his fourth novel, published in America as *Orient Express* (1933), reestablished Greene's career after two weak efforts, *The Name of Action* (1930) and *Rumour at Nightfall* (1931), which Greene has chosen to exclude from the collected edition of his works. *Stamboul Train* proved his first really popular success. It is a story of international intrigue involving a motley group of characters: Czinner, a mysterious doctor who is a disguised Communist revolutionary; Carleton Myatt, a rich Jewish merchant obsessed with the current market and racial slurs; Coral Musker, a shy, good-hearted English chorus girl; Mable Warren, a lesbian journalist, with Janet Pardoe, her pretty but stupid companion; Josef Grünlich, a murderous burglar; and so on. The novel takes as its setting a train, the Orient Express, hurtling across Europe from Ostend, Belgium, to Istanbul, Turkey, an image Greene transforms into a metaphor for the thin shell of civilization, a shell as vulnerable as the walls and windows of the

train. The distorted view of the cities through which the train passes heightens the sense of drama and of dislocation ("the great blast furnaces of Liege . . . like ancient castles burning in a border raid," Belgrade a maze like Czinner's battle plan for a coup). The action, segmented into five parts according to the major stops along the route, grows organically from character, as Greene plausibly and realistically provides glimpses into the lives and motives of his creations. As Peter Wolfe has noted, there is "a business merger, an engagement, the deflowering of a virgin, an insurgence, a court martial, two murders, and three arrests" over a three-day period during the Easter season. Czinner is a doomed idealist, a revolutionary who arrives too late for a failed revolution. Lonely chorus girl Coral Musker rightly suspects the motives of men who are good to her. Currant merchant Myatt comes to care for her, and she for him. The other major characters are generally greedy and self-concerned, obsessed with possessions, success, and personal gratification at others' expense. At the heart of the novel is Czinner's court-martial: a debate involving Petkovitch, the army major concerned that proper procedures be followed; the doomed but idealistic Czinner, the "weary and hunted," who seeks a more just world; and the strong-arm Fascist, Colonel Hartep, for whom justice is subservient to state security. Published the year before Hitler took absolute power, Greene's portraits of the conscientious officer, the bureaucrat Hartep, and the self-serving murderer Grünlich ("a man of destiny"–a true menace to society who is ignored in the effort to silence Czinner) sum up what was proving to be the Nazi mentality with its sense of destiny, its approval of violence, and its Teutonic emotionalism. But the central concern of the novel is what happens to the flawed protagonists Czinner, Musker, and Myatt as they learn–or fail to learn–bitter truths about themselves and life. Stylistically, Greene's incorporation, with each train stop, of new sets of characters who are worked into the progressing action makes *Stamboul Train* more modern and more artistic than his preceding works and paves the way for patterns that characterize his canon thereafter.

It's a Battlefield (1934), inspired by Joseph Conrad's *The Secret Agent* (1907), is a grim suspense story that transforms London into a battlefield of ideologies as it depicts how the death sentence of a London bus driver, Jim Drover, an avowed Communist accused of murdering a policeman, affects the lives of various individuals. The murder occurs at a political rally in Hyde Park when Drover strikes out defensively, fearful that the policeman is going to injure his wife; it is a typical Greene incident in which an injurious act is perpetrated by the innocent at heart. A reprieve would signal government weakness to striking laborers, but an execution would arouse their ire and produce a retaliation that could unseat the Minister in the next election. The Minister puts his dilemma into the hands of the Assistant Commissioner, a policeman who does not understand the realities of state policy. The hatreds and guilt unleashed by this controversy lead, among other things, to a supposed assassination attempt on the Assistant Commissioner by Drover's brother Conrad. In the end the Minister arranges the reprieve independently of the Assistant Commissioner, whom he does not bother to inform. Drover, who was content to die and who now fears he will lose his beloved wife, tries suicide without success. Meanwhile, Conrad Drover dies as a result of being struck by a car while shooting at the Assistant Commissioner with a rusty gun loaded with blanks.

As Greene notes in the introduction to the collected edition, *England Made Me* was praised by Ezra Pound and V. S. Pritchett, but little read. His next novel, *A Gun for Sale*, which was eventually filmed by Frank Tuttle, builds on the cinematic techniques Greene absorbed as film critic for the *Spectator* in the late 1930s. It also builds on the thrillers of John Buchan. Certainly its plot is as fantastic as anything Buchan ever wrote. Raven, a man with a harelip and a mutual hatred for everyone and everything but a kitten, is hired to kill a certain old man on the Continent by the obese and supercilious Mr. Cholmondeley. Raven kills the man and his secretary, but when he returns to London, Cholmondeley pays him in marked stolen money. Because the police are soon after Raven (for murder he thinks, but they only want to question him about the money), he has to abandon the only security he has: the kitten, his terrible apartment, and his abused and abusive mistress. He decides that he will track down Cholmondeley and kill him. Meanwhile, chorus girl Anne Crowder, the fiancée of the Scotland Yard man (Jimmy Mather) in charge of tracking Raven, by chance travels on the same train to Nottwich with Cholmondeley and the pursuing Raven. Raven takes her hostage, and she eventually begins to take his side. Escaping from Raven, she investigates Cholmondeley (who is known as

Dust jacket for the first American edition of Greene's 1958 entertainment that he called "really a grey comedy, not a black comedy.... Perhaps in some ways it is a black comedy after all."

Davis in Nottwich, where he is a backer of the show she is in), who almost kills her. Raven rescues her. A little later she helps Raven escape from the police stakeout–an act which alienates Mather from her. Ultimately, Raven kills Cholmondeley-Davis and the mastermind of the plot, a steel magnate who had hoped to start a world war with the murder of the old man; Mather's assistant Sanders kills Raven; and Mather and Anne Crowder are reconciled.

Brighton Rock, the 1938 novel which established Greene's reputation as a leading British novelist, is his first detective novel in that there is an investigator, and the exact cause of the first murder in the book only gradually comes out. *Brighton Rock* was ahead of its time in portraying grim urban realities and in delineating the fallen world of the despairing poor, gangsters, and juvenile delinquents. As such it has evoked much critical commentary and both theological and anti-theological interpretations. Greene's Brighton, though a superficially beautiful seaside resort, is beneath its gleaming facade as grimy and ugly as any decaying urban environment. Its slums are run-down, battered refuse heaps of humanity with broken windows and broken spirits–a sterile wasteland. Its residents, rough social outcasts (bookmakers, carnival people, lower-class workers, the unemployed, Jews, foreigners, Catholics), engage in gang competition, corruption, violence, and even murder. Theirs is a "man's world," wherein razor blade, vitriol, and knife become extensions of that manhood.

The story plunges immediately into the action: "Hale knew, before he had been in Brighton three hours, that they meant to murder him." What follows are two murders, an attempted suicide, and slashings. Hale, a newspaperman, had betrayed Kite, the former leader of a protection racket, to his rival Colleoni and fears the consequences from Kite's gang–as well he should. But the focus of the novel is on the seventeen-year-old leader, the Boy (Pinkie), who replaces Kite and who goes after Hale, a youth embittered by brutality and an impoverished childhood and desperate to lash out cruelly and sadistically before being squashed himself. Pinkie is a typical product of this British netherworld: a young man compelled to prove his manhood by violence, desperate to win loyalty but to avoid personal involvement, an amoral being willing to do whatever it takes to survive–"murder a world" if necessary. His marriage to Rose, a naive tea shop waitress, to stop her testifying against him for Hale's murder, helps lead a headstrong, determined, big-busted, motherly figure, Ida Arnold, to step in, make up for the ineptitude or indifference of the police, and hound Pinkie to his death. Ida, though certainly an unconventional detective, shares characteristics common to most fictional male detectives: curiosity, close observation of details, specialized knowledge appropriate to her case, and standard techniques of checking witnesses and cryptic clues to ferret out the truth. But she is also street-tough and street-wise, with a sense of fair play and loyalty, and compelled by simple notions of right and wrong. Her common refrain is "I want Justice." Her values are old-fashioned and conservative: "an eye for an eye, law and order, capital punishment, a bit of fun now and then, nothing nasty, nothing shady, nothing mysterious." Her investigation forces Pinkie to cover his tracks by killing one of his gang members, and by planning Rose's suicide, and contem-

plating murdering all who get in his way. What could have been a simple tale of detection and vindication is fraught with ambiguity and conflict. Pinkie's youth and inexperience, his devastated childhood, and his conflict with older males–and even his hatred of music and joy–make him pitiable. Ida's stereotypical working-class ways, her savoring of sensual pleasures, her bouts of sentimentality, and her unquestioning self-assurance make it difficult for readers to identify with her cause as they might in a traditional mystery. On the other hand, Pinkie is truly a menace to life, and ultimately readers can be satisfied in his destruction.

The Confidential Agent, written in six weeks in 1938, has been called a paradigm for the espionage novel. In *Ways of Escape* Greene says the Spanish civil war furnished the background and the Munich Agreement "provided the urgency." John Mair of the *New Statesman* (23 September 1939) called *The Confidential Agent* "the best highbrow thriller" he had read in a long time, while Katherine Woods of the *New York Times* (1 October 1939) praised Greene's ingenuity and the fact that the mystery ranges "from the macabre to the apparently trivial." England on the eve of World War II is the setting; it is a place nominally peaceful, polite, and somewhat decadent but in fact the arena for a bitter struggle between competing confidential agents of an unidentified European country in the throes of a civil war. D. (readers are given only his initial) is a former professor of Romance languages who has been sent by his leftist government to buy coal in England in order to continue the war effort against the right-wing forces. He is opposed by L., an aristocrat who is trying to make his own deal for coal while wrecking D.'s chances of success. In Dover D. meets Rose Cullen, the spoiled young daughter of one of the coal magnates with whom he hopes to do business, befriends her, and forms an uneasy alliance with her. D.'s mission is soon subverted: his contacts in London try to withdraw his authority; he is suspected of the murder of a chambermaid in his hotel; he is shot at; and finally his identification papers, on which the coal deal depended, are stolen just before his meeting with the coal magnates. D., on the run from the police, L.'s agents, and even his own people, decides that he will be the "hunter." He comes to realize that he has no heart to be a killer, and, with Rose's help, he travels to her father's company's coal town in a futile attempt to dissuade the miners from supplying L. with coal; but he is captured by the police. He ultimately escapes legal charges and his enemies, with Rose at his side, but their future is uncertain.

The characters of D. and Rose are very well realized and have larger implications. Ever since his wife was shot by the enemy years earlier, D. has lived an emotionless life, cut off from love and hope. He gradually develops feelings for Rose, and she for him, in spite of their differences in age and background. Greene's psychological portraits of them are deft and convincing. Their story allows Greene to comment forcefully on fascism, social injustice, British upper-class frivolity, public blindness about the holocaust forming in Europe, the Spanish civil war, and a multiplicity of other issues of concern in 1939, and to imply that, even if there are no easy answers, questions must be asked.

The Ministry of Fear, which captures the nightmare quality of a bomb-torn London during the early part of World War II, has been called Greene's best thriller and a first-class psychological novel. Arthur Rowe, a middle-aged man, a mercy killer haunted by guilt, stumbles accidentally into the machinations of a group of fifth columnists, who pursue him to his home, attempt to murder him, bomb him, and then confine him in a mental institute after he has become an amnesiac. Amid the madness of not realizing what motivates the malevolence against him he finds love and, for a brief while, escapes from both the horrors of the war and the horrors of his own conscience. By seeing himself objectively, as an outside observer, and only gradually regaining a knowledge of his true identity, he learns to come to terms with his past, accept love and the sacrifices it imposes, and publicly redeem his honor by recovering secrets the police and secret service think lost forever.

Greene agrees with his critics that his 1940 novel, *The Power and the Glory*, is his masterpiece. Set in Mexico during the religious persecutions of 1937 and 1938, it is the story of the pursuit and capture of a priest who buries his fear of his pursuers in alcoholism and the comforts of a sexual relationship but who cannot escape his calling, his beliefs, nor his shame and guilt. The book pits Church against State and soldier against priest and explores the nature of man, the psychology of religion, and the ironies of commitment. It captures the squalor and heat of Mexico, and the venality, sloth, violence, and piteousness of mankind in vivid portraits: a gringo dentist gone to seed, a brutal police lieutenant, a

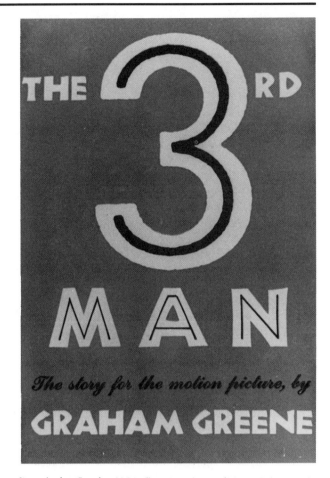

Dust jacket for the 1950 first American edition of the novelette that was published the year after Greene's screenplay of the same title was produced (courtesy of Otto Penzler)

dark and stinking prison hole, and a yellow-faced informer. The action moves from the priest celebrating mass for grateful villagers in an out-of-the-way place, to his confinement for drunkenness, and finally to his Christ-like response to a request which he knows will lead to his capture: to hear the confession of a dying man.

Published in 1948, *The Heart of the Matter* challenges the traditional Roman Catholic attitude toward suicide by implying the potential for salvation in the time that death takes hold. Roman Catholic Major Scobie, for fifteen years a British colonial officer of unquestionable integrity on the coast of Sierra Leone, West Africa, is corrupted by pity for his unattractive wife, Louise, and borrows from a malevolent, disreputable Syrian, Yusef, to send her home to England. Scobie falls in love with Helen, a childlike widow of nineteen, and finds that his love for her turns to pity also. He then indiscreetly exposes his affair with the widow to Yusef. As a result, Yusef blackmails Scobie into smuggling diamonds, an act that leads to dishonor and deceit, the murder of Scobie's houseboy, and finally Scobie's suicide. Greene's use of an omniscient point of view that gives readers the introspections of the other characters, despite the clear focus on Scobie, has the effect of drama, an opposition of perspectives that allows for irony, balance, and ambiguity.

The End of the Affair depicts a heroine, Sarah Miles, who opts for divine love over the purely human although no one believes her. She utters a prayer for life for her lover Maurice Bendrix, whom she thinks is dead, as he is trapped by a V-2 explosion outside their house. When he recovers she takes seriously the commitment she made. Her frigid husband, Henry Miles, and Bendrix are both jealous of her mysterious new lover, not realizing it is God. The novel is another of Greene's odd genre mixes, combining a detective story (false clues leading to false conclusions and detectives emptying wastepaper baskets) with the appearance of a moral tale as Bendrix comes reluctantly to belief in God.

A Burnt-Out Case (1961), set in a leprosarium in the Congo run by priests, nuns, and an atheist doctor, has been called by Charles J. Rolo "strange and haunting . . . , artfully charged with psychological suspense" and "certainly one of Greene's most memorable works," though the critic in the *Catholic World* (April 1961) was put off by the "various types of belief, half-belief and non-belief " within the book. Querry, fleeing his reputation, his past sins, and to some extent himself (he is "the famous Catholic architect"), buries himself alive in a hopeless, depressing labor of self-abnegation. *A Burnt-Out Case* suggests that traditional Christianity is as powerless to aid the spiritual leper as the dedicated doctor is powerless to help end the physical destruction of leprosy until the disease has run its course. Querry learns to care again but ironically dies meaninglessly, the victim of misunderstanding.

Travels with My Aunt (1969) is a Greene self-parody, a metaphor for his work, which details the hilarious adventures of an eccentric aunt (in her late seventies) introducing her highly conventional nephew to a wilder, more carefree side of life. From London to Paris to Istanbul to Asuncion, Paraguay, stodgy Henry Pulling, a retired bank manager, must face the unthinkable at the hands of his Aunt Augusta. He must deal with her disreputable black lover, Wordsworth, with the police who confiscate his mother's ashes believing they are marijuana, with his aunt's illegal ex-

portation of pound notes, with her reminiscences of past lovers, and even with her belly dancing. Forced to hobnob with hippie girls, detective sergeants, and members of the CIA, Pulling begins to awaken to a new life and changed attitudes, to try out marijuana, and to enjoy the con games and the "wickedness."

Our Man in Havana is a comic espionage novel which is also serious because, like all of Greene's books, it questions the nature of belief and its power. Wormold, an English vacuum-cleaner salesman in Havana, is trying to raise his daughter Milly in the Catholic faith in keeping with a promise made to his wife, who deserted both long before; but the daughter uses his devotion to her to manipulate him into fulfilling her every whim. To earn some extra money for her future (and her horse, her stables, and her expensive clothing), he lets himself be talked into working for the British Secret Service and then embarks on an elaborate charade, inventing imaginary agents, concocting intelligence reports, and sending off sketches of vacuum-cleaner parts drawn out of scale as evidence of mysterious military installations in the mountains. When provided extra funds to hire an aviator to photograph the installations and support in the form of Beatrice, a secretary, and Rudy, a radio operator, his charade begins to have unpredictable consequences. The imaginary agents have their counterparts in real life, and innocents die or are pursued as enemy targets. Finally, Wormold feels he must avenge the death of his friend, Dr. Hasselbacher. Yet hilarious scenes occur throughout the book: Wormold engages in a series of comic evasions and inventions to disguise the nonexistence of his spy network; Wormold sticks with a boorish fellow tradesman and goes to comic extremes to avoid being poisoned; and Wormold plays chess with Captain Segura, the chief of police, using miniature liquor bottles for pieces and consuming each piece taken until one or the other is drunk. Wormold is ultimately recalled at the request of Captain Segura, but because the head office simply cannot face the embarrassment of their mistake, he is given an O.B.E. and made staff lecturer on how to run a station abroad. It also looks very much like he will marry Beatrice. Greene mocks the genuine agents' failure to consult experts and to check sources and their mindless competition with an equally mindless opposite. Walter Allen in the *New Statesman* (11 October 1958) feels that the "scenes at the secret service headquarters in London" are "too farcical to be convincing," but that "nothing could be more convincing, in the concreteness of its detail as well as in the beautifully rendered atmosphere of corrupt and seedy luxury, than Mr. Greene's Cuba."

An expert in Victorian and Edwardian crime fiction, Greene, in his play *The Return of A. J. Raffles* (published and produced in 1975), revives the famous Victorian amateur cracksman (safecracker) and cricketer, the creation of E. W. Hornung, in a tongue-in-cheek parody that sets the Victorian against the modern and allows readers to laugh at both. The frothy plot, which follows the conventions of melodrama and mystery, takes second place to character. Supposedly dead, Raffles agrees to aid his associate Bunny's new friend, Lord Alfred Douglas, the notorious lover of Oscar Wilde. He does so by stealing money from Lord Alfred's father to avenge the father's narrow-mindedness and tightfistedness. The Prince of Wales and his mistress as well as an ambitious German cousin intent on blackmail also enter the plot, adding to the potential for disaster. The play contains homosexuality, adultery, and nudity and was originally produced as a Christmas play–a fact that provoked much outrage.

The novelette *The Third Man* (1950) represents an unfinished term of the story effectively rendered in the 1949 Carol Reed movie version. It is a mystery thriller set in postwar occupied Vienna. The action moves against the background of a "smashed" and "dreary" city "of undignified ruins," a city characterized by hunger, black-marketeering, and fear. Like Greene's other thrillers it offers, as Peter Wolfe points out, "a vivid social and political background, a limber journalistic style, adroit cinematic cutting between scenes, and that staple of the thriller, the chase." The story is told by Colonel Calloway, a reasonable and experienced Scotland Yard officer in charge of British military police in Vienna. He uses official files, notes, letters, interviews, and conversations to narrate events and to provide perspectives on the other characters. His story focuses on a hack writer of westerns, Rollo Martins (also known as Buck Dexter). Martins, offered a job by Harry Lime, arrives in town in time for Lime's funeral amid February snows in weather so cold electric drills must be used to dig the grave. When Lime's associates provide different versions of his death, Martins grows suspicious; later, upon hearing Calloway call his friend Lime "about the worst racketeer who ever made a dirty living in this city," he vows to find out the truth. Rollo, like Greene's other amateur detectives, is unconventional. He joins forces with Lime's former mistress, Anna Schmidt, and together they explore the ruins and rubble of Vienna, searching for evidence of the death of their much-admired mutual friend. After the murder of Koch, whose story of Lime's death differs from the official version, they suspect Lime might still be alive, a suspicion that endangers Martins but also leads to his hilarious, impromptu lecture to the British Cultural Relations Society (he at first thinks he has been kidnapped). Thus, Martins and Anna get caught up in a search that leads to painful conclusions: in exchange for asylum Lime betrayed to the Russians the fact that Anna's passport was faked; he distributed diluted penicillin that causes the retardation and death of children; and he has expediently murdered those who would expose him. Convinced that betraying Lime is just, Martins cooperates with British police to set up Lime in a café. Lime flees through Vienna sewers but is ultimately shot by Martins, and Martins exits with the girl.

Lime is another of Greene's amoral villains who has "never grown up." From atop the Great Wheel in Vienna's amusement park he looks down on the dots below and asks Rollo:

> Would you really feel any pity if one of those dots stopped moving–for ever? If I said you can have twenty thousand pounds for every dot that stops, would you really, old man, tell me to keep my money–without hesitation? Or would you calculate how many dots you could afford to spare? Free of income tax, old man. Free of income tax.

Lime is an overreacher, flashy and clever but unable to ever follow through, a qualified physician who has never practiced. He has denied friendship and love and human obligation, but goes to his death because he cannot give them up totally. It is ironic that the final scene plunges him from the heights at which he imagines himself to the depths that are his reality: the sewers of Vienna. Appropriately, his second burial is accomplished with ease.

The Quiet American, set in Saigon and its vicinity, is generally considered one of Greene's finest works. Alden Pyle, the quiet American of the title, an ideological innocent, is set off against Thomas Fowler, a cynical, sophisticated, and jaded English journalist, who has submerged himself in French and Vietnamese culture. The news of Pyle's death begins the novel. Pyle was puritani-

Greene with Jean Seberg (St. Joan) on the set of Saint Joan, *which was adapted by Greene in 1957 from the play by George Bernard Shaw (National Film Archive)*

cal; Fowler is a self-proclaimed hedonist whose attractive Vietnamese mistress, Phuong, went to Pyle on his promise to marry her. Pyle saw people as types and groups; Fowler perceives them as individuals. Pyle was Harvard-educated, enthusiastic, and dangerous in his innocence, his arrogance, and his self-righteousness. He assumed that his perceptions of reality were the same as everyone else's and acted accordingly, while Fowler knows that the Oriental mind does not function like the Western one and that it is almost impossible for a Westerner to understand the political machinations, philosophies, and motivations of the different Asian parties, much less predict their responses. Pyle was a self-convinced believer, headed toward his own destruction and bringing down others with him; Fowler is the atheist, treading carefully, preserving his own life and protecting others. As Greene builds an image of local intrigue, of beleaguered outposts and perilous ventures behind Communist lines, and finally of murder, he incorporates methods and conventions from both the spy and the detective story, but exposes a concern of more far-reaching significance than who killed or will kill whom: rash, unthinking political involvement in a complex culture, whatever the motives.

The Comedians begins on a ship bound for Haiti, with three passengers, Smith (an American do-gooder and vegetarian); Brown (a resident of Port-au-Prince and possibly a hotel-owner); and Jones (a mysterious major whose background as a war hero is dubious), who in time experience the poverty, exploitation, and terror of François (Papa Doc) Duvalier's regime. Brown, the protagonist, is in love with Martha Pineda, wife of the South American ambassador. In the spirit of the Greene crime story the novel contains revolutionary activity, suicide, pursuit, assassination, murder, and even miraculous rescue, all of which change Brown's self-image. A major theme of the novel is the difficulty of distinguishing between illusion and reality when people are disguised and project roles on those around them. Martha Pineda accurately accuses Brown of inventing his friends and acquaintances: "Darling, don't you see you are inventing us?. . . You won't listen if what we say is out of character—the character you've given us. . . . You've turned poor Jones into a seducer and me into a wanton mistress. . . . Perhaps it would not matter so much if your thoughts were not so dark. . . ." Brown views God as "an authoritative practical joker," life as "a comedy" instead of the tragedy he anticipated, and the evil around him as no concern of his. Smith does not even recognize the evil at first, while Jones is ready to make a deal with its representatives. Brown finds in the swimming pool of his hotel the body of a suicide, a member of the Duvalier cabinet, and then watches as one by one his companions are killed or executed or merely disappear mysteriously. The novel seems to say that contemporary life is a degradation. A measure of the novel's success is the fact that it was condemned in a pamphlet that the Haitian government sent to its embassies for distribution.

The Honorary Consul (1973), a hostage drama, builds on an epigraph from Thomas Hardy: "all things merge in one another–good into evil, generosity into justice, religion into politics." The novel is set in a nameless provincial town on the Parana River in Argentina, a backwater significant only because of its proximity to the military dictatorship of Paraguay. Eduardo Plarr is a medical doctor who has settled there, partly because his English émigré father disappeared in a Paraguayan political purge years earlier. Plarr's mother is Paraguayan, and his divided cultural loyalties lead him to be both a member of the three-man British community in the town and a casual sympathizer and helper of Paraguayan guerrilla groups operating across the border. One of the guerrillas is Rivas, a former schoolmate of Plarr's who is a former priest; Rivas's group bungles an attempt to kidnap the American ambassador to Argentina, instead capturing Charley Fortnum, the honorary (British) consul of the title. Fortnum is a sexagenarian alcoholic married to a young girl, a former prostitute and presently Plarr's mistress. When Plarr is brought in to check on Fortnum's physical condition after the kidnapping, the stage is set for a series of agonizing decisions of major moral significance: should harmless innocents like Fortnum (his position is merely honorary) be used as pawns to achieve worthy ends? What role should the Church, in the person of the former priest Rivas, play when confronted by the most appalling injustice? What obligations does Dr. Plarr have to Fortnum, to his mistress, to his profession, and to his mixed cultural heritage?

As usual with Greene, the setting is almost flawlessly rendered, with a strong sense of place, appropriate and accurate local allusions, and an elegant and economical summation of political and social milieus. According to Grahame Smith, several kidnappings actually took place while Greene was finishing the novel, one involving a mistaken identity somewhat similar to Greene's

plot. Dr. Plarr and Rivas are classic Greene figures. Plarr is a man once hurt badly and now determined to remain an uninvolved observer but forced by circumstances to make the moral choice of commitment. Rivas is ethically several steps beyond Plarr, the institutional man turned man of action. Their clash and ultimate resolution in sacrifice show Greene adapting figures from much earlier works–Rose and D. in *The Confidential Agent* parallel Plarr and Rivas in commitment, for example–but making them current and timely. As a result of this book, Greene was approached in 1980 by the South African foreign service to aid in the release of the South African ambassador to El Salvador who had been kidnapped by guerrillas, but his efforts were unsuccessful, and the victim died in captivity.

Doctor Fischer of Geneva, or the Bomb Party (1980) focuses on Fischer, a wealthy, avaricious Swiss dogmatist, who has made millions by inventing a toothpaste but who despises people and takes pleasure in experimenting with toadying guests, exposing their greed, undermining their pretensions and self-respect. The story is an odd mixture of allegorical morality play (with the seven deadly sins marching across the pages), comic hokum, and tragic romance with an aging Romeo and a Juliet who remains little more than a daydream. Lurid party scenes are set off by clever repartee as Fischer defends his behavior to a middle-aged failure named Alfred Jones (the narrator of the novel), who falls in love with and marries Fischer's only daughter, Anna-Luise. There is a poignant scene with Jones waiting impatiently in a hotel restaurant for Anna-Luise's return from the ski slopes (where her father's bomb party occurs) before learning of her tragic death.

The Tenth Man (1985), written as a screenplay in 1944 but shelved and forgotten until rediscovered in 1983, examines the conscience of a man stricken with guilt after a single act of cowardice. In it Jean-Louis Chavel, a wealthy Parisian lawyer held along with thirty other prisoners in a Gestapo prison in occupied France, is one of three to be executed (his fate is decided in a drawing of lots). Whereas the working-class and shopkeeper prisoners accept their fate with resignation and bravado, Chavel panics and in desperation offers his fortune to anyone who will take his place. Janvier Mangeot, in exchange for a firm contract turning over Chavel's family estate and savings to his impoverished family, accepts the deal. After the war a poor, unemployed, and

Greene on the Orient Express (BBC-Television)

exposes his identity and outwits the murderer—at deadly cost. *The Tenth Man* is hallmark Greene, with its failed protagonist, its psychological study, its cinematic images, its economy, and its genre mix. It is not quite a novel, not exactly a thriller, not really a romance, nor a wartime tale of collaborators, but a little of each of these.

The Human Factor (1978) traces the end of the career of Castle, an aging intelligence officer, an old Africa hand returned to England who has made the mechanics of spying into a way of life. He has internalized the rules of security so perfectly that they have become a theology of self-protection, an insulation against fear, hate, and pain. Castle has broken his rules only once, to marry Sarah, a black African woman pregnant with another man's baby. He brings her and the child, Sam, back to England, where in gratitude to the Communist lawyer who helped Sarah escape, he begins to pass secret information about Africa to the Russians. Castle is only a minor official, but his leak triggers a wide investigation which mistakenly settles on Davis, his coworker, as the culprit. Davis is careless about details and reckless by the tight standards of the intelligence service, and one of the authorities, Dr. Percival, quickly "eliminates" him with a synthetic attack of cirrhosis of the liver.

Percival's hasty execution of Davis leads to a number of consequences: with Davis dead, Castle must end his leaks or he will be found out; Colonel Daintry, the security officer supposedly in charge, is racked with guilt because only circumstantial evidence can be found against Davis; and Muller, a South African security man assigned to work with Castle, learns of the leaks in the African section as he develops an intuitive suspicion of Castle, who is an old adversary from South Africa. As guilt and tension mount, the different characters find themselves isolated from their fellows, both physically and spiritually, clinging to whatever shreds of belief motivated them in the first place but without confidence in or assurance of their validity. Belief in any individual is too easily frustrated by realpolitik and even bureaucracy. Only Percival and Castle's mother retain their beliefs whole, and they can only because of cynicism and obsolescent simplicity, respectively. The ending is hardly satisfying in any emotional sense, but it follows inexorably from the premises of the secretive and isolated intelligence world and those of Greene himself in his earlier work.

The Human Factor makes explicit in its main metaphors a theme that Greene has long exam-

conscience-stricken Chavel returns to his family estate, now occupied by Mangeot's mother and sister, introduces himself under a false name, and accepts a job as handyman and special guard on the lookout for the despised Chavel. With time he falls in love with Mangeot's sister, but he is still deeply ashamed of his betrayal of his birthright and his acceptance of another man's sacrifice, and he must constantly be on guard not to betray his true identity. Then, one night, a man calling himself Jean-Louis Chavel appears at the estate. He is an unscrupulous actor, now pursued as a collaborator and in need of aid. He has already murdered once to protect himself, and now he invents a series of lies that undermine the real Chavel's position and prepares himself to take over the property under a decree rescinding all changes of property made during the German occupation. But Chavel, in an act of self-sacrifice,

ined, that of the alienating effect of modern institutional and secular life. The more generalized metaphor may be termed the intelligence world itself; like John le Carré and so many other modern writers, Greene finds in espionage an elegant way of rendering multiple suspicions and betrayals, relativistic truths which refuse to remain stable, isolation, and the polar opposite of a sense of community, shallowness, despair, and corruption. Greene's spies in *The Human Factor* are very ordinary people living in a post-World War II England gone secular (Castle goes into a church on an impulse and listens to the "well-dressed, the middle-aged and the old" sing with "a kind of defiance" until interrupted by a sonic boom). Castle has no faith in any creed or belief, only in his patterned and controlled life with his wife Sarah and her child, in whiskey, in the sleep of oblivion: "This is my fun," he says, "A sense of security." He believes not in "the City of God or Marx, but [in] the city called Peace of Mind."

Greene's more specific metaphors exemplify life under these conditions of consuming despair. Percival introduces the main metaphor, that of boxes:

> "You haven't been a long time with us, have you, or you'd know how we all live in boxes–you know–boxes."
>
> "I still don't understand."
>
> "Yes, you said that before, didn't you? Understanding isn't all that necessary in our business . . . Take a look at that [Ben] Nicholson [lithograph]. Such a clever balance. Squares of different color. And yet living so happily together. No clash. . . . "
>
> Percival pointed at a yellow square.
>
> "There's your Section 6. That's your square from now on. You don't need to worry about the blue and the red. All you have to do is to pinpoint our man and then tell me. You've no responsibility for what happens in the blue or red squares. In fact not even in the yellow. You just report. No bad conscience. No guilt."
>
> "An action has nothing to do with its consequences. Is that what you're telling me?"

The boxes metaphor is repeated by Percival (with approval) and Castle (with anguish) throughout and aptly describes the dilemma of all the characters: how to make human contact in a profession in which no one can talk about his work. As the consequences of Davis's mistaken execution begin to reverberate, the metaphorical becomes literal: one by one the characters become trapped in rooms isolated from the ones they love. Castle is boxed in his house and then in a grim Moscow apartment, Sarah in his mother's house, and Daintry (readers assume) in retirement in his flat. Castle even remarks, referring to a funeral urn, that "Davis is in a box." The metaphor is evoked with particular irony in the confessional box scene of chapter 1 of part 5, where the priest tells Castle to see a doctor.

Few can thrive in a world of isolated boxes. Only Percival ends as cheerily as he began, and that because he is "not the Crusader type. Capitalism or Communism? Perhaps God is a Capitalist. I want to be on the side most likely to win during my lifetime." Percival has no commitment to ideas or ideology and counsels Hargreaves to "beware of people who believe. They aren't reliable players." It is the game that counts, and as the fly-fishing metaphors that Greene puts in Percival's mouth stress, the challenge of a worthy opponent means far more than the results. Percival is unperturbed by Davis's death. His only regret is that "one couldn't throw a man back into the river of life as one could throw a fish."

There are few new themes in *The Human Factor*, but the novel is vigorous and taut, in no way a reworking of Greene's earlier books. The emphasis on Africa and race is as timely and perhaps as prophetic as the focus on American involvement in Vietnam of *The Quiet American*. Castle is an arresting character as a spy manqué, unmistakably a Greene creation from beginning to end. Percival, Sarah, Davis, and the whole panoply of minor characters are sharply and unforgettably drawn. Perhaps the best feature of *The Human Factor* is the relevance of the general metaphor to modern institutional life: Percival's amoral boxes can be found in the flowcharts of government offices, corporations, universities, and all other complex modern social structures that often deny by their very complexity man's obligation to his fellowman.

Of Greene's juvenile works, only one partakes of the thriller format: *The Little Steamroller: A Story of Adventure, Mystery and Detection* (1953). It is a farfetched tale of a London steamroller that foils the plot of a band of smugglers by crashing into the Black Hander's taxi, and it has little to do with the qualities that so intrigue in his adult works.

It is perhaps not surprising that Greene should have had such a successful literary career, for his sensibility is perfectly attuned to that of his time. If the twentieth century is a period of conflicting demands and uneasy alliances, Greene too is a master of contradiction and paradox. He is claimed by both leftists and conservative Catholics; he is an establishment figure (the friend of Omar Torrijos of Panama), who could converse with Ho Chi Minh. He is a very private man who has written two main autobiographies which yet reveal very little. Many would call him a moralist, yet he has a self-confessed taste for drugs and sex. He is a figure from the 1930s, yet as modern as radical priests in Central America; he is solidly British, even disliking America, yet his outlook and sympathies are international and eclectic.

Greene's work is as paradoxical as the man. He is repeatedly ranked among the great serious novelists of the twentieth century, yet his books have had enormous success in the mass culture as well. He is one of the most successfully filmed twentieth-century novelists. Yet, in spite of its modern cinematic nature, his prose owes virtually nothing to the modern and the experimental, and in fact has more in common with the best nineteenth-century models. Greene more than any modern writer has mixed genres, so that his "entertainments" often seem relatively serious and his religious and political books sometimes look like spy or mystery stories.

Whatever his ultimate ranking as an artist, Greene will surely be remembered as the most articulate spokesman for his time. Any American in the distant future curious about attitudes that led to the Vietnam War should read *The Quiet American*. A Latin American living in the twenty-first century might find in *The Power and the Glory* and *The Honorary Consul* representations of emotion and motive lacking in history books. The romantic figure of our times is the international journalist, recording history as it happens. Greene has called his method journalistic, but he has been a journalist of political motive and religious doubt, of alienation and commitment, recording the lives of the underground agent and the teenage tough. His work, a history of our paradoxical and turbulent times, fathers the principle of moral uncertainty which underlies so much of modern spy and political fiction: the individual in conflict with himself.

Interviews:

Martin Shuttleworth and Simon Raven, "The Art of Fiction III: Graham Greene," *Paris Review*, 1 (Autumn 1953): 24-41;

"New Honor and a New Novel: Interview," *Life*, 60 (4 February 1966): 43-44;

G. D. Phillips, "Graham Greene: On the Screen: Interview," *Catholic World*, 209 (August 1969): 218-221;

Michael Mewshaw, "Greene in Antibes," *London Magazine*, 17 (June-July 1977): 35-45;

"Graham Greene at Eighty; Musings on Writing, Religion, and Politics," *World Press Review* (December 1981): 31-32;

Marie-Francoise Allain, *The Other Man: Conversations with Graham Greene*, translated by Guido Waldman (London: Bodley Head, 1983);

Juan Gonzalez Yuste, "Graham Greene Reflects," *World Press Review* (April 1983): 62.

Bibliographies:

William Birmingham, "Graham Greene Criticism: A Bibliographical Study," *Thought*, 27 (Spring 1952): 72-100;

Francis Wyndham, *Graham Greene, Bibliographical Series of Supplements to British Book News on Writers and Their Work, No. 67* (London: Longmans, Green, 1955);

Maurice Beebe, "Criticism of Graham Greene: A Selected Checklist with an Index to Studies of Separate Works," *Modern Fiction Studies*, 3 (Autumn 1957): 281-288;

Phyllis Hargreaves, "Graham Greene: A Selected Bibliography," *Modern Fiction Studies*, 3 (Autumn 1957): 269-280;

Jerry Don Vann, *Graham Greene: A Checklist of Criticism* (Lexington: University of Kentucky Press, 1970);

Robert H. Miller, *Graham Greene: A Descriptive Catalog* (Lexington: University of Kentucky Press, 1979);

R. A. Wobbe, *Graham Greene: A Bibliography and Guide to Research* (New York & London: Garland, 1979);

A. F. Cassis, *Graham Greene: An Annotated Bibliography of Criticism* (Metuchen, N.J. & London: Scarecrow, 1981).

References:

Walter Allen, "The Novels of Graham Greene," in *Penguin New Writing 18* (Harmondsworth: Penguin, 1943), pp. 148-160;

Kenneth Allott and Miriam Farris Allott, *The Art of Graham Greene* (New York: Russell, 1951);

John Atkins, *Graham Greene: A Biographical and Literary Study* (New York: Roy, 1958);

W. H. Auden, "A Note on Graham Greene," *The Wind and the Rain*, 6 (Summer 1949): 53-54;

Gwenn R. Boardman, *Graham Greene: The Aesthetics of Exploration* (Gainesville: University of Florida Press, 1971);

Neville Braybrooke, "Graham Greene, a Pioneer Novelist," *College English*, 12 (October 1950): 1-9;

Arthur Calder-Marshall, "Graham Greene," in *Living Writer: Being Critical Studies Broadcast in the B.B.C. Third Programme*, edited by Gilbert Phelps (London: Sylvan, 1947), pp. 39-47;

Calder-Marshall, "The Works of Graham Greene," *Horizon*, 1 (May 1940): 367-375;

Francis X. Connolly, "Inside Modern Man: The Spiritual Adventure of Graham Greene," *Renascence*, 1 (Spring 1949): 16-24;

Donald P. Costello, "Graham Greene and the Catholic Press," *Renascence*, 12 (Autumn 1959): 3-28;

Beekman W. Cottrell, "Second Time Charm: The Theatre of Graham Greene," *Modern Fiction Studies*, special Greene issue, 3 (Autumn 1957): 249-255;

Fred D. Crawford, "Graham Greene: Heaps of Broken Images," in his *Mixing Memory and Desire: The Waste Land and British Novels* (University Park: Pennsylvania State University Press, 1982), pp. 103-123;

Victor De Pange, *Graham Greene* (Paris: Editions Universitaire, 1953);

A. A. De Vitis, *Graham Greene* (New York: Twayne, 1964);

William D. Ellis, Jr., "The Grand Themes of Graham Greene," *Southwest Review*, 41 (Summer 1956): 239-250;

Robert Evans, ed., *Graham Greene: Some Critical Considerations* (Lexington: University of Kentucky Press, 1963);

Quentin Falk, *Travels in Greeneland: The Cinema of Graham Greene* (London, Melbourne & New York: Quartet, 1984);

Francis Fytton, "Graham Greene: Catholicism and Controversy," *Catholic World*, 180 (December 1954): 172-175;

Harold C. Gardiner, "Graham Greene, Catholic Shocker," *Renascence*, 1 (Spring 1949): 12-15;

Ian Gregor, "The End of the Affair," in Gregor and Brian Nichols's *The Moral and the Story* (London: Faber & Faber, 1962), pp. 190-206;

Henry A. Grubbs, "Albert Camus and Graham Greene," *Modern Language Quarterly*, 10 (March 1949): 33-42;

Ruth Mulvey Harmel, "Greene World of Mexico: The Birth of a Novelist," *Renascence*, 15 (Summer 1963): 171-182, 194;

Haber R. Herbert, "The Two Worlds of Graham Greene," *Modern Fiction Studies*, 3 (Autumn 1957): 256-268;

Gustav Herling, "Two Sanctions: Greene and Camus," *Adam*, 201 (1950): 10-19;

Richard Hoggart, "The Force of Caricature: Aspects of the Art of Graham Greene, with Particular Reference to *The Power and the Glory*," *Essays in Criticism*, 3 (October 1953): 447-462;

Samuel Hynes, ed., *Graham Greene: A Collection of Critical Essays* (Englewood Cliffs, N.J.: Prentice-Hall, 1973);

Douglas Jerrold, "Graham Greene, Pleasure-Hater," *Harper's*, 205 (August 1952): 50-52;

Francis Kunkel, *The Labyrinthine Ways of Graham Greene* (New York: Sheed & Ward, 1959);

F. N. Lees, "Graham Greene: A Comment," *Scrutiny*, 19 (October 1952): 31-42;

David J. Leigh, "Greene, Golding and the Politics of Literature," *America*, 119 (26 November 1983): 331-332;

Laurence Lerner, "Graham Greene," *Critical Quarterly*, 5 (1963): 217-231;

R. W. B. Lewis, "The Trilogy," in his *The Picaresque Saint: Representative Figures in Contemporary Fiction* (Philadelphia: Lippincott, 1959), pp. 239-264;

David Lodge, *Graham Greene* (New York & London: Columbia University Press, 1966);

Jacques Madaule, *Graham Greene* (Paris: Editions de Temps Present, 1949);

François Mauriac, "Graham Greene," in his *Men I Hold Great* (New York: Philosophical Library, 1951), pp. 124-128;

Mary McCarthy, "Graham Greene and the Intelligentsia," *Partisan Review*, 11 (Spring 1944): 228-230;

Frank D. McConnell, "Perspectives: Graham Greene," *Wilson Quarterly*, 5 (Winter 1981): 168-186;

James L. McDonald, "Graham Greene: A Reconsideration," *Arizona Quarterly*, 27 (Winter 1971): 197-210;

Marie-Beatrice Mesnet, *Graham Greene and the Heart of the Matter* (London: Cresset, 1954; Westport, Conn.: Greenwood, 1972);

Modern Fiction Studies, special Greene issue, 3 (Autumn 1957);

Sean O'Faolain, "Graham Greene: I Suffer; Therefore, I Am," in his *The Vanishing Hero: Stud-*

ies in Novelists of the Twenties (London: Eyre & Spottiswoode, 1956), pp. 73-97;

George Orwell, "The Sanctified Sinner," in *The Collected Essays, Journalism and Letters of George Orwell*, edited by Sonia Orwell and Ian Angus (New York: Harcourt, Brace & World, 1968);

W. Peters, "The Concern of Graham Greene," *Month*, 10 (November 1953): 281-290;

Karl Pettern, "The Structure of *The Power and the Glory*," *Modern Fiction Studies*, 3 (Autumn 1957): 225-234;

Gene D. Phillips, S.J., *Graham Greene: The Films of His Fiction* (New York: Teachers College Press, Columbia University, 1974);

Orville Prescott, "Comrade of the Coterie," in his *In My Opinion* (Indianapolis: Bobbs-Merrill, 1952), pp. 92-109;

V. S. Pritchett, "The World of Graham Greene," *New Statesman* (4 January 1958);

David Pryce-Jones, *Graham Greene* (New York: Barnes & Noble, 1967);

Peter Quennell, *The Sign of the Fish* (London: Collins, 1960);

Charles J. Rolo, "Graham Greene: The Man and the Message," *Atlantic Monthly*, 207 (May 1961): 60-65;

P. Rostenne, *Graham Greene Temoin des Temps Tragiques* (Paris, 1949);

Edward Sackville-West, "The Electric Hare: Some Aspects of Graham Greene," *Month*, 6 (September 1951): 141-147;

Barbara Seward, "Graham Greene: A Hint of an Explanation," *Western Review*, 22 (Winter 1958): 83-95;

Elizabeth Sewell, "Graham Greene," *Dublin Review*, 108 (1954): 12-21;

A. J. M. Smith, "Graham Greene's Theological Thrillers," *Queen's Quarterly*, 68 (Spring 1961): 15-33;

Grahame Smith, *The Achievement of Graham Greene* (Sussex: Harvester/Totowa, N.J.: Barnes & Noble, 1986);

John Spurling, *Graham Greene* (London: Methuen, 1983);

Philip Stratford, *Faith and Fiction: Creative Process in Greene and Mauriac* (Notre Dame: University of Notre Dame Press, 1964);

Stratford, Introduction to *The Portable Graham Greene* (New York: Viking, 1973);

Harry Sylvester, "Graham Greene," *Commonweal*, 33 (1940): 11-13;

Derek Traversi, "Graham Greene," *Twentieth Century*, 149 (1951): 231-240, 319-328;

Martin Turnell, *Graham Greene: A Critical Essay* (Grand Rapids, Mich.: Eerdmans, 1967);

John Vinocur, "The Soul Searching Continues for Graham Greene," *New York Times Magazine*, 3 March 1985, p. 38;

Richard J. Voorhees, "The World of Graham Greene," *South Atlantic Quarterly*, 50 (July 1951): 389-398;

Ronald Walker, *The Infernal Paradise: Mexico and the Modern English Novel* (Berkeley & Los Angeles: University of California Press, 1978);

Anthony West, "Graham Greene," in his *Principles and Persuasions* (New York: Harcourt, Brace, 1957), pp. 195-200;

A. D. Wilshire, "Conflict and Conciliation in Graham Greene," *Essays and Studies, 1966* (New York: Humanities Press, 1966), pp. 122-137;

Peter Wolfe, *Graham Greene: The Entertainer* (Carbondale: Southern Illinois University Press, 1972);

George Woodcock, "Mexico and the English Novelist," *Western Review*, 21 (Autumn 1956): 21-32;

Francis Wyndham, *Graham Greene* (London: Longmans, Green, 1955);

Morton D. Zabel, "Graham Greene: The Best and the Worst," in his *Craft and Character in Modern Fiction* (New York: Viking, 1957), pp. 76-96.

Papers:

The Humanities Research Center, University of Texas at Austin, has manuscripts and typescripts of most of Greene's books, plus working drafts and final manuscripts of various short stories and articles, as well as much of the correspondence. There are Greene holdings at the Lilly Library, Indiana University; the Pennsylvania State University Library; the Library of Congress; and the British Museum Library.

Cyril Hare
(Alfred Alexander Gordon Clark)
(4 September 1900-25 August 1958)

T. R. Steiner
University of California, Santa Barbara

BOOKS: *Tenant for Death* (London: Faber & Faber, 1937; New York: Dodd, Mead, 1937);

Death Is No Sportsman (London: Faber & Faber, 1938);

Suicide Excepted (London: Faber & Faber, 1939; New York: Macmillan, 1954);

Tragedy at Law (London: Faber & Faber, 1942; New York: Harcourt Brace, 1943);

With a Bare Bodkin (London: Faber & Faber, 1946;

The Magic Bottle (London: Faber & Faber, 1946);

When the Wind Blows (London: Faber & Faber, 1949); republished as *The Wind Blows Death* (Boston: Little, Brown, 1950);

An English Murder (London: Faber & Faber, 1951; Boston: Little, Brown, 1951); republished as *The Christmas Murder* (New York: Spivak, 1953);

That Yew Tree's Shade (London: Faber & Faber, 1954); republished as *Death Walks the Woods* (Boston: Little, Brown, 1954);

He Should Have Died Hereafter (London: Faber & Faber, 1958); republished as *Untimely Death* (New York: Macmillan, 1958);

Best Detective Stories of Cyril Hare, edited by Michael Gilbert (London: Faber & Faber, 1959; New York: Walker, 1961).

PERIODICAL PUBLICATIONS: "The Boldest Course," *Ellery Queen's Mystery Magazine*, 36 (November 1960);

"The Homing Wasp," *Ellery Queen's Mystery Magazine*, 37 (March 1961);

"Blenkinsop's Biggest Boner," *Ellery Queen's Mystery Magazine*, 38 (September 1961).

Dust jacket for the first British edition of Hare's 1954 novel, in which a creditor's recovery becomes the motive for murder (courtesy of Otto Penzler)

Alfred Alexander Gordon Clark, who wrote under the pseudonym Cyril Hare, was the third son of Henry Herbert Gordon Clark, longtime director and eventually president of the London Life Association. Matthew Clark and Sons of Lon-don, the family firm, were prominent wine and spirit importers; the Gordon Clarks were associated closely with Surrey, of which Henry Herbert was once high sheriff. Alfred Gordon Clark was educated at Rugby and New College, Oxford, where he received a First in history. He was called to the bar of the Inner Temple in 1924 and joined the chambers of the noted criminal lawyer Ronald Oliver. As Gordon Clark pursued the career of a junior barrister, he also began to write light material for *Punch* and other popular papers. He invented a pseudonym that combined the addresses of his residence, Cyril Mansions, Battersea, and of his Temple chambers, Hare Court. He married in 1933 and had one son and two daughters.

With the coming of World War II Gordon Clark entered public service, first as judge's marshal on the Southern Circuit, then in 1940 as an officer in the Ministry of Economic Warfare. From 1940 to 1945 he served as legal assistant in the Public Prosecutions Department. He was appointed judge of the County Court, Surrey, in 1950.

A memoir of Hare (1961) by his friend Michael Gilbert, also a lawyer and detective novelist, presents a man whose experience derived largely from his legal career and public life. "He was a fine speaker," Gilbert notes, whose "beautifully modulated tones" obviously served well on the occasions of his frequent public addresses to academic and literary audiences. When Gilbert first met Gordon Clark at the Detection Club, immediately he was struck by Clark's resemblance to Sherlock Holmes in the Sidney Paget illustrations: "the thin, inquisitive nose, the intellectual forehead, the piercing eye, the Oxford common-room voice."

With the publication of *Tenant for Death* in 1937, Cyril Hare became another in the line of amateur detective-fiction writers who were professionals in another field. His first two books are conventional late Golden Age novels, with complicated detection by a Scotland Yard inspector named Mallett who resembles Freeman Wills Crofts's Inspector French. The deep-fishing lore of his second book, *Death Is No Sportsman* (1938), and the detailed time scheme of its events suggest as one model Dorothy L. Sayers's fishing mystery, *The Five Red Herrings* (1931). However, the sex in Hare's novels is steamier than that in the typical Golden Age mystery. In *Death Is No Sportsman* the rapidly aging outdoorsman Robert Matheson is married to a sensual woman half his age. Euphemia Matheson has a well-hidden affair with the lord of the manor, the overbearing and universally loathed Sir Peter Packer. At the same time she is vigorously courted by a self-important country doctor. Packer is murdered, and eventually Inspector Mallett has many local herrings to pursue, red and otherwise. To promote narrative surprise and a strong ending, Hare uses an effective device from Agatha Christie, in works such

as *Death in the Clouds* (1935); credible revelation in the penultimate chapter of Robert Matheson's guilt is superseded by the true solution in the last. The killer, Dr. Latymer, is the typical hubristic scientist-doctor of classic detective stories.

Suicide Excepted (1939) is an "advance" over the first two novels in its characterization, as critics claim, but its dogged pursuit of the large cast of suspects becomes tedious. When the coroner rules that Leonard Dickinson's death at a small country hotel is suicide, his family loses payment on his insurance policy. To investigate the circumstances of their father's death and prove murder, Dickinson's son and daughter form a team of amateur detectives. (This device, popular in Golden Age novels–for example, Christie's *Murder in Three Acts* [1934] and *The ABC Murders* [1936]– serves to expand the complexity and the narrative of detection.) The amateur investigation turns out to be an ironic red herring. Stephen Dickinson murdered his father and contrived to make it look like suicide; learning of the insurance exception, he had to reverse the signs, prove that the cause of death was murder, and provide a plausible culprit. The ending, in which the unlikely murderer is killed while attempting his next murder, is forced, though certainly unexpected.

The next two books called specifically on Hare's new experiences at the start of World War II. *Tragedy at Law* (1942) is drawn from his service as judge's marshal. Hare's favorite among his books, original in its firsthand material and usually cited as his masterpiece, it has an engaging mix of dotty judges, witty, cynical lawyers, and the realism of a court circuit. As Justice Barber proceeds on circuit, a series of mishaps leads his wife to suspect that someone is trying to murder him, and she organizes from his staff a group of round-the-clock guards. However, as in *Suicide Excepted*, this apparent protector of good turns out to be the murderer. With the murder coming late in the book, systematic investigation plays a relatively small role. The book introduces as investigative partner to Mallett the lawyer Francis Pettigrew, who more and more takes over the protagonist's role in Hare's subsequent novels.

With a Bare Bodkin (1946) is set in the north of England, where a minor government agency removed from London, Pin Control (doubtless resembling Hare's wartime employer, the Ministry of Economic Warfare), is quartered in a converted great house. This book contains some predictable wit about the follies of bureaucracy. Its

Dust jacket for the first American edition of Hare's 1951 novel, involving murders by cyanide poisoning at a Christmas party held in a country mansion

principal contribution to the Hare canon is not detection but romance, the unrecognized growth and final revelation of the middle-aged Pettigrew's love for his agreeable young secretary, Eleanor Brown, who becomes Mrs. Francis Pettigrew.

By contrast with Hare's first detective, the unremarkable Inspector Mallett, Pettigrew is a fascinating English eccentric. Although he appears to be, as he describes himself, "old, unattractive, unsuccessful, crotchety and quirky and set in my ways," Pettigrew is, in fact, a man of intelligence, wit, and true legal acumen. He could be a model for that contemporary favorite of fiction and television, John Mortimer's curmudgeonly Rumpole of the Bailey.

The last three novels, which feature Pettigrew progressing into contented old age, have distinctive features that have attracted readers. *When the Wind Blows* (1949; published in the United States as *The Wind Blows Death*, 1950) presents murder and sensuality in the milieu of a pro-

vincial British symphony orchestra. For its fullness of observation and character and its "unflagging" suspense, Jacques Barzun and Wendell Hertig Taylor judge *When the Wind Blows* "a masterpiece by any standards." In *That Yew Tree's Shade* (1954; published in the United States as *Death Walks the Woods*, 1954) there is a half-attractive scoundrel, the amoral, quick-witted Humphrey Rose. In the last Hare novel, *He Should Have Died Hereafter* (1958; published in the United States as *Untimely Death*, 1958), Pettigrew, on holiday with his wife, returns to Exmoor, an important scene of his childhood. He stumbles across a body in nearly exactly the spot where he had first encountered violent death fifty years earlier. With this event Hare begins, but does not far pursue, an interesting play between the buried memory of a childhood place and present experience in it.

Hare's later novels depend more than the earlier ones on allusion to other detective and nondetective fiction. In *When the Wind Blows* reference to *David Copperfield* and Dickens becomes a thematic clue to reveal the motive for murder. The detection of crime in *He Should Have Died Hereafter* is signaled by veiled reference to Sir Arthur Conan Doyle's "Silver Blaze," which has a comparable horsey milieu and the same surprising instrument of death.

Each detection of the late books featuring Francis Pettigrew turns on a straightforward point of law. For example, marriage to the sister of one's former wife is invalid; therefore, the new Lord Simonsbath of *When the Wind Blows* had to murder his first wife to protect the legitimacy of his newborn son by his second wife, her half sister. Although the property of a bankrupt is sequestered when he cedes it to his wife, a creditor can recover when the bankrupt inherits the property at the wife's death: this recovery motivates murder in both *That Yew Tree's Shade* and the short story "Murderer's Luck." Several points of law operate in *He Should Have Died Hereafter*; one, the "barring of entail," is so exotic that the judge and lawyers in Chancery can hardly contain their excitement as they learn of it.

Pettigrew is absent, however, from what some critics, like Charles Shibuk, estimate to be the most successful of Hare's novels, *An English Murder* (1951). It is also the most blatantly conventional, a clear invocation of the mysteries set in an isolated country house over the holidays, like Christie's *Hercule Poirot's Christmas* (1938). When Robert, son and heir of Lord Warbeck, is killed, all in the closed circle of family, friends, and servants become suspects. Both the characters and incidental details of this novel are more striking than usual for its kind. Robert, the jingoist leader of the League of Liberty and Justice, contrasts with his uncle, Sir Julius, chancellor of the exchequer in a Labor government. Lady Camilla Prendergast, Robert's childhood playmate, has continued to love him; but he is secretly married to Susan Briggs, the butler's daughter, who has borne him a son. Others in the cast include Mrs. Carstairs, the doting wife of a rising assistant to Sir Julius; the butler; and most striking of all, Dr. Wenceslaus Bottwink, a European refugee professor of history, who has been at Warbeck Hall studying the family papers. When the death of Lord Warbeck quickly follows that of Robert, it is revealed that he will be succeeded by his grandson, not by Sir Julius, as all have anticipated. This succession frustrates the murderer—Mrs. Carstairs—who has killed only to advance her husband's political career: if Sir Julius became a peer and therefore no longer could serve as a minister, Carstairs would become chancellor. The murder is distinctively "English" since it has meaning only within the "social and political framework" of England. Dr. Bottwink solves the mystery, helped to his solution by a parallel from the political history of the Pitt family.

Hare's short stories are brief and typically end with a sudden turn, ideals of the detective story for purists like Barzun and G. K. Chesterton, who held that "the whole story exists for the moment of surprise, and it should be a moment." Many seem to be explicit imitations. "A Life for a Life" is dark fantasy like some tales of Poe. "The Tragedy of Young Macintyre" has Chesterton's kind of blatant playfulness. "It Takes Two . . . ," "The Old Flame," and "As the Inspector Said . . . " have the shock and irony of Ellery Queen's or O. Henry's stories.

Using the time that he could spare from a busy public career as barrister, civil servant, and judge, Hare was a detective writer worthy of at least passing notice. He added to detective fiction the milieus of the court circuit and government bureaucracy, scenes of the crime to which few writers have intimate access. He exploited his legal expertise, but lightly; indeed, a reader could wish that there were more knots of the law, more legal complexities to provide surprising and daring twists to the detection. Pettigrew is a splendid Dickensian character, and *He Should Have Died Hereafter* implies that had Hare lived longer, he would have used Pettigrew to explore detection and married love in old age.

References:

Jacques Barzun and Wendell Hertig Taylor, *A Catalogue of Crime* (New York: Harper & Row, 1971), p. 227;

Michael Gilbert, "Introduction," *Best Detective Stories of Cyril Hare*, edited by Gilbert (New York: Walker, 1961), pp. 7-15.

Georgette Heyer

(16 August 1902-5 July 1974)

Earl F. Bargainnier
Wesleyan College

BOOKS: *The Black Moth* (London: Constable, 1921; Boston & New York: Houghton Mifflin, 1921);

The Great Roxhythe (London: Hutchinson, 1922; Boston: Small, Maynard, 1923);

The Transformation of Philip Jettan, as Stella Martin (London: Mills & Boon, 1923); republished as *Powder and Patch*, as Heyer (London: Heinemann, 1930; New York: Dutton, 1968);

Instead of the Thorn (London: Hutchinson, 1923; Boston: Small, Maynard, 1924);

Simon the Coldheart (London: Heinemann, 1925; Boston: Small, Maynard, 1925);

These Old Shades (London: Heinemann, 1926; Boston: Small, Maynard, 1926);

Helen (London & New York: Longmans, Green, 1928);

The Masqueraders (London: Heinemann, 1928; New York: Longmans, Green, 1929);

Beauvallet (London: Heinemann, 1929; New York & Toronto: Longmans, Green, 1930);

Pastel (London & New York: Longmans, Green, 1929);

Barren Corn (London & New York: Longmans, Green, 1930);

The Conqueror (London: Heinemann, 1931; New York: Dutton, 1966);

Devil's Cub (London: Heinemann, 1932; New York: Dutton, 1966);

Footsteps in the Dark (London & New York, Longmans, Green, 1932; New York: Buccaneer, 1976);

Why Shoot a Butler? (London & New York: Longmans, Green, 1933; Garden City, N.Y.: Doubleday, Doran, 1936):

The Unfinished Clue (London & New York: Longmans, Green, 1934; Garden City, N.Y.: Doubleday, Doran, 1937);

The Convenient Marriage (London: Heinemann, 1934; New York: Dutton, 1966);

Death in the Stocks (London & New York: Longmans, Green, 1935); republished as

Dust jacket for the first British edition of Heyer's final mystery (courtesy of Otto Penzler)

Merely Murder (Garden City, N.Y.: Doubleday, Doran, 1935);

Regency Buck (London & Toronto: Heinemann, 1935; New York: Dutton, 1966);

The Talisman Ring (London & Toronto: Heinemann, 1936; Garden City, N.Y.: Doubleday, Doran, 1937);

Behold, Here's Poison! (London: Hodder & Stoughton, 1936; Garden City, N.Y.: Doubleday, Doran, 1936);

They Found Him Dead (London: Hodder & Stoughton, 1937; Garden City, N.Y.: Doubleday, Doran, 1937);

An Infamous Army (London & Toronto: Heinemann, 1937; Garden City, N.Y.: Doubleday, Doran, 1938);

A Blunt Instrument (London: Hodder & Stoughton, 1938; New York: Doubleday, Doran, 1938);

Royal Escape (London: Heinemann, 1938; New York: Doubleday, Doran, 1939);

No Wind of Blame (London: Hodder & Stoughton, 1939; New York: Doubleday, Doran, 1939);

The Spanish Bride (London: Heinemann, 1940; New York: Doubleday, Doran, 1940);

The Corinthian (London & Toronto: Heinemann, 1940; New York: Dutton, 1966);

Beau Wyndham (New York: Doubleday, Doran, 1941);

Faro's Daughter (London: Heinemann, 1941; Garden City, N.Y.: Doubleday, Doran, 1942);

Envious Casca (London: Hodder & Stoughton, 1941; Garden City, N.Y.: Doubleday, Doran, 1941);

Penhallow (London: Heinemann, 1942; Garden City, N.Y.: Doubleday, Doran, 1943);

Friday's Child (London & Toronto: Heinemann, 1944; New York: Ace, 1944);

The Reluctant Widow (London & Toronto: Heinemann, 1946; New York: Putnam's, 1946);

The Foundling (London: Heinemann, 1948; New York: Putnam's , 1948);

Arabella (London: Heinemann, 1949; New York: Putnam's, 1949);

The Grand Sophy (London: Heinemann, 1950; New York: Putnam's, 1950);

The Quiet Gentleman (London: Heinemann, 1951; New York: Putnam's, 1952);

Duplicate Death (London: Heinemann, 1951; New York: Dutton, 1969);

Detection Unlimited (London: Heinemann, 1953; New York: Dutton, 1969);

Cotillion (London: Heinemann, 1953; New York: Putnam's, 1953);

The Toll-Gate (London: Heinemann, 1954; New York: Putnam's, 1954);

Bath Tangle (London: Heinemann, 1955; New York: Putnam's, 1955);

Sprig Muslin (London: Heinemann, 1956; New York: Putnam's, 1956);

April Lady (London: Heinemann, 1957; New York: Putnam's, 1957);

Sylvester; or, The Wicked Uncle (London: Heinemann, 1957; New York: Putnam's, 1957);

Venetia (London: Heinemann, 1958; New York: Putnam's, 1959);

The Unknown Ajax (London: Heinemann, 1959; New York: Putnam's, 1960);

Pistols for Two and Other Stories (London: Heinemann, 1960; New York: Dutton, 1964);

A Civil Contract (London: Heinemann, 1961; New York: Putnam's, 1962);

The Nonesuch (London: Heinemann, 1962; New York: Dutton, 1963);

False Colours (London: Bodley Head, 1963; New York: Dutton, 1964);

Frederica (London: Bodley Head, 1965; New York: Dutton, 1965);

Black Sheep (London: Bodley Head, 1966; New York: Dutton, 1967);

Cousin Kate (London: Bodley Head, 1968; New York: Dutton, 1969);

Charity Girl (London: Bodley Head, 1970; New York: Dutton, 1970);

Lady of Quality (London: Bodley Head, 1972; New York: Dutton, 1972);

The Georgette Heyer Omnibus (New York: Dutton, 1973);

My Lord John (London: Bodley Head, 1975; New York: Dutton, 1975).

Georgette Heyer is more widely known for her forty-five Regency romances than for her dozen novels of mystery. However, the twelve mysteries remain in print; and though they vary greatly in quality, they are, with one exception, a blend of comedy and romance with the conventions of Golden Age detective fiction as employed in the 1930s and 1940s. Heyer's favorite author was Jane Austen, and her Regency romances are evidence of her admiration. When she wrote her mysteries, she did not abandon the romantic formulas she had developed from Austen. These and her comedy are her only distinctive additions to the British detective novel; otherwise, her work is conventional in structure, setting, characters, style, and mysteries to be solved.

One of the most reclusive of writers, Heyer maintained that her books provided all her readers needed to know about her, and so biographical information is scant. Her entry in *Who's Who* is essentially a list of her fiction; not even her address is given. She was educated at various schools, including Westminster College in London, and wrote her first novel at seventeen to en-

Dust jacket for the first British edition of Heyer's only collection of short stories (courtesy of Otto Penzler)

tertain a convalescing brother. In 1925 she married George Ronald Rougier, a mining engineer at the time and later a successful barrister and businessman: he was named Queen's Counsel in 1959. They lived in East Africa until 1928 and in Yugoslavia the following year. Their only son was born in 1932. (Both husband and son are also listed in *Who's Who*.) For many years Heyer lived at The Albany, one of London's most exclusive apartment buildings, where her neighbors included Dame Edith Evans, J. B. Priestley, and Terence Rattigan. There she lived the comfortable, gracious life of an English gentlewoman but also wrote her more than fifty novels—according to her publishers, quickly and with few corrections.

With the exception of *Penhallow* (1942; published in the United States in 1943) Heyer's mysteries fall into the "What Fun!" school of detection. The attitude of many of the characters is that a murder case is something to be enjoyed. Mrs. Haswell and Miss Potterdale, characters in

Heyer's *Detection Unlimited* (1953; published in the United States in 1969) express what is almost a general view: they agree that "although it was disagreeable to persons of their generation to have a murder committed in their midst, it was very nice for the children to have something to occupy them." The young people in that novel and most of the others do seem to enjoy the excitement, the chance to play amateur sleuth, and the opportunity to trade quips about everyone involved, often including the victim. Most of the suspects and witnesses are in some way comic, whether a ludicrous vamp, cowardly constable, absurd Russian prince, or an empty-headed debutante. Most can be described by one word, which sums up the basis of their presentation: irresponsible, domineering, self-dramatizing, or globetrotting. The dialogue is also comic. The characters say exactly what they think, no matter how outrageous. They do not hesitate to discuss who among them may have committed the crime and how, even in the presence of the person being discussed. Though *Death in the Stocks* (1935; published in the United States as *Merely Murder*) contains more such comic dialogue than any of the other mysteries, it is found in all of them, even *Penhallow*.

Greatly contributing to the comedy is Stanley Hemingway, who is progressively Sergeant, Inspector, and Chief Inspector, and Heyer's principal detective. He is not a great detective, though he often says, "I'm never wrong." He solves only four of the eight cases in which he is involved; his early superior Inspector Hannasyde, who is much like Agatha Christie's Superintendent Battle or Freeman Wills Crofts's Inspector French, solves two, and the other two are solved by the romantic hero. Rather than an efficient detective, Hemingway is a genial master of ceremonies for the fun. Cheerful, brisk, birdlike, infinitely talkative and incorrigibly flippant, he disarms hostility with "a certain engaging breeziness of manner," which is the despair of his superiors. This breeziness is a part of what he calls his *flair*, about which he holds no doubts. His droll humor is seen in his treatment of and quarrels with his assistants, usually a mixture of patronization and facetiousness. Particularly good examples of this aspect of his personality are his encounters with the Bible-quoting Constable Glass in *A Blunt Instrument* (1938) and the Scots Inspector Grant in *Duplicate Death* (1951; published in the United States in 1969). Another instance of his drollery is his coining of alliterative epithets for persons in an investigation: "Henna'ed Hannah," "Pretty Paul," "Dismal Desmond," "Granite-faced Gertrude," and many others. Whatever Hemingway's deficiencies as a detective, he is a success as a likable, comic policeman.

In nine of her mysteries Heyer incorporates what might be called the "Pride and Prejudice" formula: apparently overt dislike or indifference between a young man and woman, with waspish or scornful repartee, gradually transformed into affection. Both the young men and the young women are distinct types, repeated over and over, and they are never the culprit. The young women are independent, witty, sensible, and especially "spunky." Yet they are deliberately surly or offensive to the young men or strangely oblivious to the men's interest in them. The young men are developed from Heyer's Regency rakes, but beneath their rakish facade they are all decent and ultrachivalrous. Whether described as "poisonous-tongued," "an amiable snake," or "the rudest man in London," each has a reason for his supposed unpleasantness, and when it is revealed, he is transformed into the hero of romance. These couples enliven Heyer's novels; they are much less insipid than most of the lovers in mystery fiction of the period, because they are characters of the comedy of manners.

Neither Hemingway nor Hannasyde appears in the first three novels. *Footsteps in the Dark* (1932; published in the United States in 1976) involves four young people in a pseudo-Gothic setting, which is a "supernatural" cover for crime organized by a master criminal called The Monk. There are secret panels, underground cells, tunnels entered through a hinged tomb, and a skeleton inside a priest's hole. Occasionally amusing, it reads much like a book for juveniles. More typical is *Why Shoot a Butler?* (1933; published in the United States in 1936); it has the romance and comedy of later novels, as well as the first of Heyer's rakish heroes. However, it is more melodramatic than most of the later ones, particularly in the hero's nick-of-time rescue of the heroine when the villain attempts to drown her. *The Unfinished Clue* (1934, published in the United States in 1937) is a simple variation on Mrs. Henry Wood's *East Lynne* (1861). That teary story of Lady Isabel's leaving her family to run away with another man, only to return unrecognized to watch over her child, is paralleled in Heyer's novel by a runaway wife's returning, again unrecognized, and murdering her former husband to prevent his disinheriting their son.

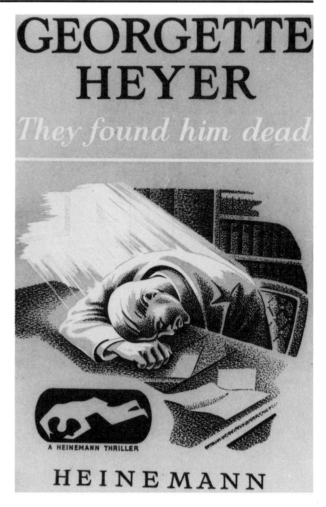

Dust jacket for a later edition of Heyer's 1937 novel in which an elderly victim is murdered at his birthday party

The next seven mysteries, six of which feature Hemingway as detective, were published between 1935 and 1942. In these novels Heyer specializes in upper-class family murders and is often repetitive. Her victims are domestic tyrants, blackmailers, or weaklings. Her murderers are often of the least likely type. Since she is fond of the device of the hidden heir, the murderer is rarely of the immediate family. Among many repeated structural devices are the birthday party of the elderly victim (as in *They Found Him Dead*, 1937, and *Penhallow*); the rigged gun or false shot to provide an alibi (*They Found Him Dead, No Wind of Blame*, 1939, and the final *Detection Unlimited*); and the opening introduction of major characters through a servant or companion (*Behold, Here's Poison!*, 1936, *They Found Him Dead*, and *Penhallow*). As these examples show, *They Found Him Dead* is a compendium of devices found in other mysteries. The best of the seven mysteries in this 1935-1942 group are *Behold, Here's Poison!*, *A Blunt Instrument*, and *Envious Casca* (1941). In *Behold, Here's Poison!*, Heyer's usual elements are handled well, particularly the "Pride and Prejudice" romance, the large family, and the unusual method of murder: nicotine in a tube of toothpaste. *A Blunt Instrument*, which opens with a constable standing beside a corpse, offers a surprising murderer, Hemingway as his most jovial and bewildered self, and a lady detective novelist and a flippant adventurer as the romantic couple. *Envious Casca* presents another surprising murderer, a locked-room murder, a disastrous Christmas reunion, and some of Heyer's cleverest tricks of comic characterization; it is probably her single best work in the mystery genre.

Hemingway is omitted from the most controversial of Heyer's mysteries, *Penhallow*. Some critics consider it her masterpiece because no one in the novel discovers the murderer; only the reader knows. This highly unconventional ploy is managed effectively, but much of its power is vitiated by the unpleasantness of all of the characters and even more by Heyer's lack of control over setting and atmosphere. The Penhallow family in their Cornish manor seem to belong to the middle of the nineteenth century. When after some forty pages there is mention of cars and telephones, the reader becomes disoriented, for until then there has been no indication that the story is taking place in the twentieth century. This is especially true because such a great amount of detail is devoted to physical objects. In spite of the plot twist, *Penhallow* is essentially unsatisfactory. After *Penhallow*, Heyer did not write another mystery for nine years; then came the final two. Hemingway returns in *Duplicate Death* to solve two murders in London society, one occurring at a bridge party. It contains one of Heyer's best romances, and Hemingway is in top form. In *Detection Unlimited*, the last mystery, the comedy becomes so obtrusive as to make the murder and its solution seem minor. The village eccentrics who make up the novel are too extreme, though often amusing in themselves, and even Hemingway becomes pompously ludicrous.

Although Heyer's mysteries have not attracted attention from critics, except for the high praise given them by Jacques Barzun and Wendell Hertig Taylor in *A Catalogue of Crime* (1971), their lasting popularity is evidenced by the continuing appearance of all but the first as Bantam paperbacks, some in their tenth printing. Nevertheless, Heyer cannot be considered among the major writers of detective fiction, for her innovations are idiosyncratic and her mixture of conventions is often uneven, producing either overly melodramatic or simply foolish results. Her achievement as a writer of detective fiction lies in her occasional ability to combine the comic and her special type of romance with the conventions of the Golden Age mystery to create a kind of detective comedy of manners.

James Hilton

(9 September 1900-20 December 1954)

Marvin S. Lachman

See also the Hilton entry in *DLB 34: British Novelists, 1890-1929: Traditionalists.*

BOOKS: *Catherine Herself* (London: Unwin, 1920; New York: Avon, 1946);

Storm Passage (London: Unwin, 1922);

The Passionate Year (London: Butterworth, 1923; Boston: Little, Brown, 1924);

The Dawn of Reckoning (London: Butterworth, 1925);

The Meadows of the Moon (London: Butterworth, 1926; Boston: Small, Maynard, 1927);

Terry (London: Butterworth, 1927);

The Silver Flame (London: Butterworth, 1928);

And Now Good-bye: A Novel (London: Benn, 1931; New York: Morrow, 1932);

Murder at School: A Detective Fantasia, as Glen Trevor (London: Benn, 1931); as Hilton (London: Macmillan, 1935); republished as *Was It Murder?*, as Trevor (New York: Harper, 1933); as Hilton (New York & London: Harper, 1935);

Rage in Heaven (New York: King, 1932);

Contango: A Novel (London: Benn, 1932); republished as *Ill Wind* (New York: Morrow, 1932);

Knight without Armour (London: Benn, 1933); republished as *Without Armor* (New York: Morrow, 1934);

Lost Horizon (London: Macmillan, 1933; New York: Morrow, 1933);

Good-bye Mr. Chips (London: Hodder & Stoughton, 1934; Boston: Little, Brown, 1934);

We Are Not Alone (London: Macmillan, 1937; Boston: Little, Brown, 1937);

Good-bye Mr. Chips: A Play in Three Acts, by Hilton and Barbara Burnham (London: Hodder & Stoughton, 1938);

To You, Mr. Chips (London: Hodder & Stoughton, 1938);

Random Harvest (London: Macmillan, 1941; Boston: Little, Brown, 1941);

Addresses by James Hilton on the Present War and Our Hopes for the Future (New York, 1943);

James Hilton

The Story of Dr. Wassell (Boston: Little, Brown, 1943; London: Macmillan, 1944);

So Well Remembered (Boston: Little, Brown, 1945; London: Macmillan, 1947);

Nothing So Strange (Boston: Little, Brown, 1947; London: Macmillan, 1948);

Three Loves Had Margaret (New York: Avon, 1949);

Twilight of the Wise (London: St. Hugh's, 1949);

Morning Journey (London: Macmillan, 1951; Boston: Little, Brown, 1951);

Time and Time Again (London: Macmillan, 1953; Boston: Little, Brown, 1953);

H. R. H.: The Story of Philip, Duke of Edinburgh (London: Muller, 1956; Boston: Little, Brown, 1956).

MOTION PICTURES: *Camille*, screenplay by Hilton, Zoe Akins, and Frances Marion, M-G-M, 1936;

We Are Not Alone, screenplay by Hilton and Milton Krims, Warner Bros., 1939;

The Tuttles of Tahiti, adapted by Hilton, RKO, 1942;

Mrs. Miniver, screenplay by Hilton, Arthur Wimperis, George Froeschel, and Claudine West, M-G-M, 1942;

Forever and a Day, screenplay by Hilton, Charles Bennett, C. S. Forrester, and others, RKO, 1944.

PERIODICAL PUBLICATIONS: "What Mr. Chips Taught Me," *Atlantic Monthly*, 162 (July 1938): 28-40;

"The Mallet," *Ellery Queen's Mystery Magazine*, 3 (September 1942): 3-19;

"The Perfect Plan," *Ellery Queen's Mystery Magazine*, 7 (March 1946): 43-56;

"Literature and Hollywood," *Atlantic Monthly*, 178 (December 1946): 130ff;

"The King of the Bats," *Ellery Queen's Mystery Magazine*, 21 (March 1953): 16-25.

Though his fiction often dealt with crime and murder, James Hilton's place in the mystery genre rests on a single book, *Murder at School: A Detective Fantasia*, which was published in 1931, before he achieved his enormous success as a popular novelist. Hilton is one of the first British novelists to use his own teaching experience and set a mystery in a school.

Born 9 September 1900 in Leigh, Lancashire, Hilton was the son of John and Elizabeth Burch Hilton. His father was a master, and his mother had been a teacher before her marriage. Hilton grew up in London and attended the Leys School and Christ's College, Cambridge University. He published his first novel, *Catherine Herself* (1920), when he was still at Cambridge, but he had limited success as a writer for more than a decade. As a result, he supported himself during part of that time as a teacher, acquiring knowledge that he would put to use in his mystery as well as in his later fiction, especially *Good-bye Mr. Chips* (1934), his best-seller about a beloved British schoolmaster. In 1934 he was given England's prestigious Hawthornden Prize for *Lost Horizon*

(1933). Six Hilton novels were successfully filmed. In the 1930s Hilton settled in Hollywood, where he continued to achieve renown, although primarily as a writer of screenplays. *Mrs. Miniver*, for which he wrote the screenplay, won an Academy Award in 1942. He divorced his first wife, Alice Brown, in 1937, the same year he married American actress Galina Kopineck. They were divorced in 1945.

Murder at School was reprinted in 1935 under Hilton's own name to capitalize on his growing fame. Hilton's detective protagonist, in his sole appearance, is Colin Revell, a young intellectual who had a "brilliant" career at Oxford. Now, only marginally successful in writing novels and poems, he is glad to accept expenses and return to his former public school, Oakington, at the request of the headmaster, to investigate the bizarre death of student Robert Marshall, who died when a gas fixture fell on him while he was asleep. Revell, like many intellectuals after World War I, reads detective stories, and he fancies the opportunity for some amateur sleuthing.

The unusual setting and Hilton's use of a witty amateur detective nicely balance the morbid events. The school atmosphere is well rendered, especially the social caste system so prevalent in British public schools in the 1920s. Hilton also gives an excellent word picture of the Spartan surroundings at Oakington as, recalling his own days as a schoolboy, Revell notes "the same spluttering hot water pipes in the corridors . . . there was the same curious smell of dust and ink in the deserted classrooms." Hilton makes Revell credible as an intellectual, even providing some examples of witty poetry written by him. He has Revell say bright things: "England expects," replied Revell, lightly purloining someone else's epigram, "that every young man some day will write a novel." There is an especially amusing description of a traditional interschool cricket match. Revell, bored, drifts into sleep, occasionally opening one eye to say, "Well played, sir!" or "Oh, jolly well hit, sir!" Hilton does not make Revell a successful detective at first, and a third death occurs at Oakington. Although Guthrie, a Scotland Yard detective, apparently abandons his efforts, Revell is not convinced. The book's denouement, in which the true killer is revealed, is a small masterpiece.

Murder at School has been a commercial success with frequent reprints in Great Britain and several paperback editions in the United States, including one as recently as 1980. It has been well received critically, though Hilton, like Sir Arthur Conan Doyle before him, deprecated his own efforts as a mystery writer. Jacques Barzun and Wendell Hertig Taylor included *Murder at School* in *Fifty Classics of Crime Fiction 1900-1950*. In their preface they express satisfaction with the book's resolution, feeling that "the identity of the murderer comes as a lively surprise . . . and motives stand up to scrutiny."

Although Hilton would never write another formal detective novel, several other works of fiction by him have elements of the genre. *Rage in Heaven* (1932) is about Philip Monsell, whose paranoiac jealousy leads him to believe that his best friend, Ward Andrews, is trying to take his wife away from him. Monsell commits suicide, arranging evidence so it will lead to Andrews's arrest for his murder. *We Are Not Alone* (1937) also involves an accusation of murder arising from an alleged romantic triangle. (Both books contain well-done courtroom scenes.) In *We Are Not Alone* a doctor in a small British village incurs the jealousy of his neurotic wife when he becomes involved, albeit innocently, with a young Austrian girl who has no job or friends in England. When the wife dies of poison the doctor and the girl are accused. Unfortunately, Hilton removes much of whatever suspense might have been generated by revealing the ending on the very first page. Hilton cowrote the 1939 film version, with Paul Muni giving one of his best performances as the doctor, and wisely left the resolution in doubt until the end. *Contango* (1932), which tells how one chance event affects nine different lives, begins with a murder in the Far East.

Hilton occasionally wrote short stories, three of which had enough mystery elements to be printed in *Ellery Queen's Mystery Magazine*. "The King of the Bats" (March 1953) is set in New Mexico's Carlsbad Caverns and is based on an idea which occurred to Hilton when he first visited the United States. Though never using supernatural elements, Hilton generates a great deal of fear and terror in telling of a man who claims power over the millions of bats who inhabit the caves. The two other stories were more traditional. In "The Mallet" (September 1942) a conversation in the pub of a small British village leads to the solution of an old murder. "The Perfect Plan" (March 1946) is a well-crafted story about a secretary who murders his wealthy employer, using the timing of a BBC radio broadcast for what he hopes will be the perfect alibi. The motivation for the crime is relatively weak, but the ending is very effective.

Hilton's reputation as a novelist has diminished in the decades since his death from cancer of the liver in 1954, and most of his novels, once so popular, are hardly ever reprinted. Ironically, his one detective novel remains available and of considerable interest to mystery readers. Given the book's quality, it is perhaps likely that even if the true identity of the author had not been disclosed, *Murder at School* by Glen Trevor still would be reprinted.

Reference:

Jacques Barzun and Wendell Hertig Taylor, preface to *Was It Murder?*, in their *A Book of Prefaces to Fifty Classics of Crime Fiction 1900-1950* (New York: Garland, 1976), pp. 65-66.

Richard Hull
(Richard Henry Sampson)
(6 September 1896-1973)

Barrie Hayne
University of Toronto

BOOKS: *The Murder of My Aunt* (London: Faber & Faber, 1934; New York: Minton, Balch, 1934);

Keep It Quiet (London: Faber & Faber, 1935; New York: Putnam's, 1935);

Murder Isn't Easy (London: Faber & Faber, 1936; New York: Putnam's, 1936);

The Ghost It Was (London: Faber & Faber, 1936; New York: Putnam's, 1937);

The Murderers of Monty (London: Faber & Faber, 1937; New York: Putnam's, 1937);

Excellent Intentions (London: Faber & Faber, 1938); republished as *Beyond Reasonable Doubt* (New York: Messner, 1941);

And Death Came Too (London: Collins, 1939; New York: Messner, 1942);

My Own Murderer (London: Collins, 1940; New York: Messner, 1940);

The Unfortunate Murderer (London: Collins, 1941); New York: Messner, 1942);

Left-Handed Death (London: Collins, 1946);

Last First (London: Collins, 1947);

Until She Was Dead (London: Collins, 1949);

A Matter of Nerves (London: Collins, 1950);

Invitation to an Inquest (London: Collins, 1950);

The Martineau Murders (London: Collins, 1953).

OTHER: "Mrs. Brierly Supplies the Evidence," in *The Evening Standard Detective Book*, second series (London: Gollancz, 1951).

Writing in 1939, at what is as good a terminus as any other for the "Golden Age," the year of S. S. Van Dine's last and Raymond Chandler's first novel of detection, a reviewer for the *Times Literary Supplement* remarked, "A week in which new novels by Mr. Hull and Mrs. Christie appear should be a red-letter week for connoisseurs of detective fiction." For the reviewer, neither novel (*And Death Came Too* or *Murder is Easy*) was up to standard; but the point is clear that Hull's reputation at this time was very high indeed, at least in

Dust jacket for the first British edition of Hull's first novel, 1934 (courtesy of Otto Penzler)

Britain–perhaps so high that Christie's title even invokes an earlier one of his (*Murder Isn't Easy*, 1936).

That reputation, however (and almost all reviews of Hull's subsequent novels call attention to this fact), is founded very heavily upon his first novel, *The Murder of My Aunt* (1934). Like Raoul Whitefield, Helen Eustis, and one or two other writers, Hull achieved in his first mystery novel a classic of the genre, from which the rest of his career could only be a falling-off. And, like all such writers, he has been the victim of generalization based on reading of that single novel. *The Murder of My Aunt* places Hull in the school of Francis Iles, though Hull's sense of humor is more impishly perverse; and Hull has acknowledged his debt, and even his decision to write mysteries, to Iles's novel *Malice Aforethought* (1931). But it is misleading to classify all of Hull's fifteen novels as crime novels of the "inverted" kind, in which the reader is privy to the criminal's thoughts; and it seems to have been the critic Howard Haycraft who first stated that "all" Hull's novels are written in the first person, a statement duly carried over, in the manner of critical writing in this voluminous genre, into acceptance by repetition. On the contrary, Hull wrote a number of conventional third-person mysteries with the mystery solved by a police detective (*The Ghost It Was*, 1936; *And Death Came Too*, 1939); he wrote a mystery (*Murder Isn't Easy*) in which the murder is seen from the several points of view of those implicated, a device at least as old as Wilkie Collins's *The Woman In White* (1860); he wrote a mystery, three years after Agatha Christie's *Murder in the Calais Coach*, in which, though without the implausibility of Christie's denouement, many people plot to kill the same person (*The Murderers of Monty*, 1937); and he wrote a first-rate courtroom mystery in which the main consciousness is that of the police inspector piecing together the elements of the case, both in and out of court (*Excellent Intentions*, 1938, published in the United States as *Beyond Reasonable Doubt*, 1941), which links him not only with that supreme classic of this subgenre, *The Bellamy Trial* (1927), by Frances Noyes Hart, but also with the school of Cyril Hare, Edward Grierson, and Michael Gilbert.

. It is true that his most esteemed work, including especially *The Murder of My Aunt* but also *My Own Murderer* (1940) and *A Matter of Nerves* (1950), does admit us to the criminal's mind, but all these novels withhold information from the reader, the latter even the identity of the narrator. This mystification, in fact, links Hull more directly to the conventional rather than the inverted crime story. Despite Haycraft's generalization, and though Hull's obvious adeptness at this twist makes him a frequent indulger in *oratio obliqua*, only four of Hull's fifteen novels are written in the first person.

Hull's innovations in the genre are thus ultimately few and tend to link him, with his acidulous sense of humor, to the school Julian Symons called "the Farceurs." Thus, *Last First* (1947), dedicated to those mystery readers who habitually read their endings first, sardonically places the ending at the beginning of the novel. Even *The Murder of My Aunt* is not an innovative work, owing much, as Hull acknowledged, to *Malice Aforethought*. It is perhaps final testimony to Hull's farceur qualities that the narrator of *My Own Murderer*, and one of the most unpleasant of his large gallery of villains of unredeemed viciousness, is called Richard Henry Sampson, the pseudonymous Hull's real name.

The term "inverted" was first used in connection with the mystery genre by R. Austin Freeman, who defined it in this way: "Here the usual conditions are reversed; the reader knows everything, the detective knows nothing, and the interest focuses on the mystery." *Excellent Intentions*, which is often called "inverted," is set mostly during the trial of the accused, whose identity is only gradually revealed, and is told with some aid from flashbacks. It is, in fact, a fairly classic piece of detection. The titles of its seven parts call attention to its construction, beginning with "Prosecution," backtracking to "Investigation," and then proceeding through "Analysis," "Defense," and "Summing-Up" to "Verdict" and "Conclusion." Given the structure, the detective knows everything long before the reader does. The novel thus begins in the mind of the ambitious prosecutor; shifts at once to that of the somewhat cantankerous judge, who knows this is his last case; then shifts to the detective, as well as certain other characters, but never the accused. The detective, Inspector Fenby, who had appeared earlier in *The Ghost It Was*, both during the trial and in retrospect is seen plodding his way to his conclusion in a manner fully in accord with the conventions of the genre, even drawing up a detailed schedule of the whereabouts, throughout the day of the crime, of a crucial snuffbox and preparing sheets which detail the activities of each of the suspects (either list would have won the wholehearted approval of the school of S. S. Van Dine). Such inversions as there are in this relatively conventional novel center our interest in the mind of the judge, who is quite convinced of the guilt of the accused, and who, now at the end of his career, deliberately makes certain errors in his summing-up which he knows will cause the reversal of the jury's decision on appeal. That he is able to do this with the acquiescence of the reader derives from another salient feature of Hull's fiction: the absolute worthlessness of the villain.

This element is present in Hull's work from the beginning, if we recognize the victim in the first novel as the nephew rather than the aunt. In the second novel the victim is the chronic complainer and malicious club nuisance; the rich old uncle of *The Ghost It Was* is a sadistic rider of his hobbyhorse of spiritualism; the manipulative schoolmaster-squire of *And Death Came Too* dies with our strong approbation; and the bureaucrats and officials who are more than once the victims of Hull's postwar fiction would be wished away by any frustrated citizen. This tendency to see the murder as almost the excusable elimination of evil from what W. H. Auden called "The Great Good Place" comes to its peak in *Excellent Intentions,* where the titular motives are those of the murderer, and where the villain has made himself thoroughly unpleasant to the railway officials as he waits for his train and is, after his death, shown to be a cheat and a sadist: "In fact, he had probably done more harm to other people than almost any private individual in the world."

Hull's one important detective, Inspector Fenby, is clearly the descendant of Cuff and even Bucket, rather than a name to be placed among the great detectives: he is Lestrade rather than Holmes, but with more acumen. His unobtrusive insignificance is his main feature and, through the criminal's underestimation, his greatest strength: "it was impossible to do anything else than just accept the fact that he was there and, if possible, avoid tripping over him. Indeed, he really did rather resemble a footstool." Between him and the local Inspector Perceval there is the same kind of interplay as there had been between Superintendent Seegrave and Sergeant Cuff.

But it is *The Murder of My Aunt* that will keep Hull's name in the histories of the genre; and it is one of its essential features that, dealing with a private matter within the family, it does not involve the police at all. The narrator's malice aforethought, about which the reader knows everything from the start, is gradually detected by his aunt, with the aid of various village auxiliaries, especially the doctor, and the tables are turned at the end. The story is told in four parts and a postscript, the latter taking up about one fifth of the whole. The first four parts are the ramblings of a Wildean young man reluctantly but as

Dust jacket for the first British edition of Hull's 1936 mystery featuring Inspector Fenby (courtesy of Otto Penzler)

a matter of financial necessity living in a "small (and entirely frightful) town" in Wales on the beneficence of his aunt. The two are entirely incompatible: she smokes Gold Flakes out of a packet, striking her matches on the sole of her shoe; he smokes scented cigarettes out of an elegant case, ignited by a lighter. He deplores her vulgarity, which we can see as solid English commonsense. He reads French novels, shudders at the manners of the local proletariat, derides all that is not continental ("that tawdry man Gilbert and Sullivan"), and coddles a toy dog called So-So. After attempting to end his aunt's life by automobile accident, fire, and poisoning, he falls victim, as described in the postscript, to her precautionary measures. And the novel, which has well preserved the distinctive voices of nephew and aunt, ends with the aunt's witty observation that the title of the work may stand, since "of " can be possessive as well as attributive. The title is also, no doubt, another kind of double entendre, invoking C. H. B. Kitchin's 1934 *Death of My Aunt,* in which the narrator is present at the murder of his aunt, for which he is not responsible, and it falls to him to discover the real murderer.

The Murder of My Aunt is an exercise in obtuse narration of a kind familiar to readers of Henry James or Ford Madox Ford's *The Good Soldier* but found less often at the less sophisticated reaches of mystery fiction. As his aunt quickly catches on to the young wastrel's plans for her, she makes several of the other characters privy to his design, so that an elaborate dinner-table charade is played out to catch the nephew's conscience and confirm his guilt. When this expendable young man is disposed of at the end, it is clearly in the interests of the aunt, the family, and the village–even the country, given his subversive anti-Englishness. The frightful Welsh town with the unpronounceable name, Llwll, is, could he but know it, "The Great Good Place" from which he must be expelled.

Born in London, Hull was primarily a student of mathematics at school; his career was that of an accountant. His life's work was with the government department, the army, and, eventually, as an official investigator of cost accounts. While this experience could certainly sharpen, or even originate, a sardonic vision, it would also account for the precision of Hull's attention to detail; he plays fair with his reader, defeating him only by the sheer amount of detail provided. While the six novels he wrote after World War II

are markedly inferior to those he wrote before, one of them, *Left-Handed Death* (1946), is worth mention for the ironic eye it turns on the working of the postwar bureaucracy. The murder victim in this story is a thoroughly corrupt official who has denied government contracts to the murderer's engineering company and grown fat on war profits. The frustrations of dealing with paperwork and mindless officialdom are very much in the foreground in these last few novels, written during the period of Hull's most extended government service.

Despite these glances at a changing Britain, the world of Hull's novels moves between the country house and the city club. The village of Llwll and the Whitehall Club are both classic closed circles, and in the manner of the genre the authorial values are on the side of stasis, against change, though rarely in an uncomplicated way. *Keep It Quiet* (1935), generally espousing the values of clubland, at the same time derides the principles of exclusivity and secrecy which inform such a novel as Dorothy L. Sayers's *The Unpleasantness at the Bellona Club* (1928); the club secretary following the principle embodied in Hull's title gets deeper into hot water. Part of the excusability of the accused's crime in *Excellent Intentions* is her humanitarian, if radical, politics set against the victim's truly radical inhumanities. And certainly it is the complexities of *The Murder of My Aunt,* in which young Mr. Edward and his aunt embrace opposite sets of values, both broadly aristocratic, that make it the lasting piece of work it is.

Elspeth Josceline Huxley

(23 July 1907-   )

Gina Macdonald

Loyola University in New Orleans

BOOKS: *White Man's Country: Lord Delamere and the Making of Kenya*, 2 volumes (London: Macmillan, 1935; New York: Praeger, 1968);

Murder at Government House (London: Methuen, 1937; New York: Harper, 1937);

Murder on Safari (London: Methuen, 1938; New York: Harper, 1938);

Death of an Aryan (London: Methuen, 1939); republished as *The African Poison Murders* (New York: Harper, 1940);

Red Strangers (London: Chatto & Windus, 1939; New York: Harper, 1939);

Atlantic Ordeal: The Story of Mary Cornish (London: Chatto & Windus, 1941; New York: Harper, 1942);

East Africa (London: Collins, 1941);

The Story of Five English Farmers (London: Sheldon Press, 1941);

English Women (London: Sheldon Press, 1942);

Brave Deeds of the War (London: Sheldon Press, 1943);

Race and Politics in Kenya: A Correspondence Between Elspeth Huxley and Margery Perham (London: Faber & Faber, 1944; revised edition, London: Faber & Faber, 1956; Westport, Conn.: Greenwood Press, 1975);

Colonies: A Reader's Guide (London: Cambridge University Press, 1947);

Settlers of Kenya (Nairobi: Highway Press, 1948; London: Longmans, Green, 1948; Westport, Conn.: Greenwood Press, 1975);

The Sorcerer's Apprentice: A Journey Through East Africa (London: Chatto & Windus, 1948; Westport, Conn.: Greenwood Press, 1975);

African Dilemmas (London: Longmans, Green, 1948);

The Walled City (London: Chatto & Windus, 1948; Philadelphia: Lippincott, 1949);

I Don't Mind If I Do (London: Chatto & Windus, 1950);

A Thing to Love (London: Chatto & Windus, 1954);

Four Guineas: A Journey Through West Africa (Lon-

Elspeth Josceline Huxley (photograph by Tara Heinemann)

don: Chatto & Windus, 1954; Westport, Conn.: Greenwood Press, 1974);

Kenya Today (London: Lutterworth Press, 1954);

What Are Trustee Nations? (London: Batchworth Press, 1955);

No Easy Way: A History of the Kenya Farmers' Association and Unga Limited (Nairobi: East African Standard, 1957);

The Red Rock Wilderness (London: Chatto & Windus, 1957; New York: Morrow, 1957);

The Flame Trees of Thika: Memories of an African Childhood (London: Chatto & Windus, 1959; New York: Morrow, 1959);

A New Earth: An Experiment in Colonialism (London: Chatto & Windus, 1960; New York: Morrow, 1960);

The Mottled Lizard (London: Chatto & Windus, 1962); republished as *On the Edge of the Rift: Memories of Kenya* (New York: Morrow, 1962);

The Merry Hippo (London: Chatto & Windus, 1963); republished as *The Incident at the Merry Hippo* (New York: Morrow, 1964);

A Man from Nowhere (London: Chatto & Windus, 1964; New York: Morrow, 1965);

Forks and Hope: An African Notebook (London: Chatto & Windus, 1964); republished as *With Forks and Hope* (New York: Morrow, 1964);

Back Street New Worlds: A Look at Immigrants in Britain (London: Chatto & Windus, 1964; New York: Morrow, 1965);

Suki: A Little Tiger (London: Chatto & Windus, 1964; New York: Morrow, 1964);

Brave New Victuals: An Inquiry into Modern Food Production (London: Chatto & Windus, 1965);

Their Shining Eldorado: A Journey Through Australia (London: Chatto & Windus, 1967; New York: Morrow, 1967);

Love Among the Daughters: Memories of the Twenties in England and America (London: Chatto & Windus, 1968; New York: Morrow, 1968);

The Challenge of Africa (London: Aldus, 1971);

Livingston and His African Journeys (London: Weidenfeld & Nicolson, 1974; New York: Saturday Review Press, 1974);

Florence Nightingale (London: Weidenfeld & Nicolson, 1975);

Gallipot Eyes: A Wiltshire Diary (London: Weidenfeld & Nicolson, 1976);

Scott of the Antarctic (London: Weidenfeld & Nicolson, 1977; New York: Atheneum, 1978);

Nellie: Letters from Africa (London: Weidenfeld & Nicolson, 1980);

The Prince Buys the Manor (London: Chatto & Windus, 1982);

Last Days in Eden, by Huxley and Hugo van Lawick (London: Harvill Press, 1984);

Out in the Midday Sun: My Kenya (London: Chatto & Windus, 1985; New York: Viking, 1987).

OTHER: *The Kingsleys: A Biographical Anthology*, edited by Huxley (London: Allen & Unwin, 1973);

Mary Kingsley, Travels in West Africa, edited by Huxley (London: Folio Society, 1976);

Pioneers' Scrapbook, edited by Huxley and Arnold Curtis (London: Evans, 1980).

Elspeth Huxley draws on her knowledge of Africa–the cultural, racial, and social milieus, the unique physical setting, the wildlife, and the tribal and political complexities–to weave Anglo-African detective stories. They are characterized by many of the traditional detective conventions: a murder timetable (who was doing what, when, where), clues (fingerprints, cigarette butts, missing letters, a shot that wasn't heard, bullets, film, mileage), telephone dialing tricks, double shots, multiple suspects, a good many red herrings, and a careful detective who makes intuitive leaps but is at times tied down by interfering political superiors seeking to cover up scandal. However, these mysteries are unique in the scope of the investigation, for Huxley continually points out the potential diversity and richness of crime in Africa, where every plant can be poison, witchcraft has its own secrets and power, and intertribal and interracial conflicts provide a culture from which murder can grow. To the universal motives of jealousy, ambition, blackmail, and greed, Huxley adds the immensely diverse range of African motives, which include fear of sorcery, fear of exposure of one's secret organization, and internecine relationships dependent on tribal ties. Her descriptions of Africa, insights into colonial relationships, and sensitivity to both the virtues and limitations of native cultures intrigue as much as do her plots.

Born in London to Maj. Josceline Grant and Eleanor Lillian Grant, Huxley moved at the age of five with her family to Kenya, where her father had started a coffee plantation. She spent most of her formative years in Africa and clearly cannot escape her African roots. *The Flame Trees of Thika* (1959) and *The Mottled Lizard* (1962; published in the United States as *On the Edge of the Rift*), both best-sellers, dramatize her childhood in Kenya at a time when that country was first opened for white settlement.

Huxley returned to England during World War I to attend school, receiving her degree in agriculture from Reading University in 1927, after which she went to the United States to attend Cornell University for a year. She described those student days in *Love Among the Daughters* (1968). Between 1929 and 1932 she served as an assistant press officer for the Empire Marketing Board in

London. In 1931 she married Gervas Huxley, a tea commissioner who was a distant cousin of Aldous Huxley, and her travels with him, combined with her childhood experiences in Africa, provided material for many of her books. According to Huxley, she began writing the crime books during shipboard journeys in the 1930s in order to pass the time and to avoid playing bridge; three of her detective novels were published between 1937 and 1940. After the war she turned away from mystery writing until her service on the Monckton Advisory Commission in Central Africa inspired a brief return to the detective story, providing background for *The Merry Hippo* (1963; published in the United States as *The Incident at the Merry Hippo*, 1964). Her last crime novel was published in 1964. From 1946 to 1977 Huxley was justice of the peace for Wiltshire, where she and her husband and son settled on a farm, and she served as a member of the general advisory council of the BBC from 1952 until 1959.

Huxley's imagery is drawn from nature. In *A Man from Nowhere* (1964) the protagonist's faltering purpose is compared to "a rock-borne spring that slows to a trickle among reeds and papyrus and may peter out in thirsty shale and sand." In *The Merry Hippo* the chairman stands aggressively, like an angry swan; an African chieftain wishes the chairman's wife the fertility of "the queen of the white ants"; and a young man, startled by love, finds his thoughts "scattering like a flock of startled birds" while in the distance native Shiwans dance and roar triumphantly, their lusty voices as "resonant and full of menace as the grunt of hunting lions." In *Murder On Safari* (1938) poachers "move swiftly as the cheetah" and "travel in the night like bats," and the malevolent faces of malefactors gleam "in the lamplight like an animal's." The commissioner in *Death of an Aryan* (1940) snorts "like a hippopotamus," and a nasty character in *Murder at Government House* (1937) withdraws his face from a safe "like a lizard pulling back its scaly head after darting at a fly."

Much of Huxley's description in her mysteries emphasizes the menace of Africa and the insignificance of man against that ancient land. Thus she writes of Hapana in *The Merry Hippo*:

> Stars, grasshoppers, frogs—too much of everything, crowding you in, menacing you with their profusion and indifference. A man was no more than a mote of dust, a bead of dew on a morning cobweb. The glory, jest and riddle of the world: between Pope's London and Hapana's

bush stretched not only the centuries and miles, but the great gulf between two concepts of life and man's place in it. Here, what was strange or terrible about a murder?

Huxley's first three mysteries have a common detective, Superintendent Vachell, head of the Chania Criminal Investigation Department, and an American with a varied career. He worked for a shipping company in Texas, bought furs from Cajuns in Louisiana, and studied detection with the Federal Bureau of Investigation in Washington, D.C. He has spent time in Canada's Arctic regions with the Mounties, in Delhi with the Indian C.I.D., and finally in Chania as C.I.D. head. His methods are carefully deductive but at the same time unorthodox. He checks and rechecks each link in his chain of reasoning and goes over testimonies bit by bit, "trying to find a flaw," knowing that "sooner or later all murderers were forced to lie about their movements" and believing that "with perseverance some little discrepancy of fact or statement could always be found." However, he is quite willing to mislead witnesses to pry the truth from them, to leave the innocent in jail if it will protect them or make the real villain lower his guard, or even to kidnap a possible murderer from territory where he has immunity in order to confront him with his crime. Given his past experience, he is not a man to be pushed around by those in authority; such pressure simply makes him more suspicious and more determined to pursue his line of investigation, so he is often on the verge of being fired. He understands human nature and toys with how far he can push a man; he knows that African psychology and even African facial expressions differ from European ones, and he judges accordingly. His style changes with his audience. His anthropologist friend Olivia Brandeis, with whom he informally consults on cases, likens his job to that of a witch doctor, hunting down "the enemies of society" and preventing them "from doing further harm," efficiently "eliminating the disruptive elements in society." He has to agree, especially since, in his first case, in *Murder at Government House*, it is really a clever witch doctor whose riddle solves the murder and precipitates the closing of the case.

The murder in this first mystery is politically touchy, the strangulation of a government head in his own study with his guards at his door, possibly by his successor, his jealous rival, an ancient enemy, or even a member of a sinis-

Huxley with her mother, Nellie Grant, London, 1908 (by permission of Elspeth Huxley)

ter African secret society–the League of the Plaindwellers. Vachell confronts suspect after suspect with accusations based on circumstantial evidence and each admits to some crime or potential crime but not to the murder itself. Through Vachell's investigation Huxley introduces readers to colonial types to suggest the infighting and scandals that grow out of being white power figures in a black state and to explore native reactions and native values. She delineates the chain reaction that begins in Africa with drought, which produces hardship, then discontent, and finally a witch-hunt for sorcerers. And she describes the traditional solutions for trouble: the ritual of the warthog tusk, which could result in sudden death; and the poison ordeal, which is generally followed by a slow, painful execution, its victims pinned to the ground with spears and left to be eaten alive by ants and vultures. At one point an execution of a ten-year-old child, designated the evil source of drought, takes place within three hundred yards of the anthropologist's tent. Huxley captures the conflicts of native officials, who are paid by the government to maintain order,

but are also hereditary chiefs, obliged by tribal law to conduct witch-hunts.

Murder at Government House ends with a suicidal plane crash, the near death of Vachell and his anthropologist friend, whom the real murderer sends plunging over a cliff, and a humbled detective. ("I had the whole case in the bag two days after the murder and never knew it. I'm a hell of a detective.")

Murder on Safari, Huxley's second mystery, motivated critic Will Cuppy of *Books* (29 May 1938) to call her "a dangerous rival to Agatha Christie, Mignon G. Eberhart and other ornaments of the international crime choir." E. R. Punshom, writing for the *Manchester Guardian* (25 March 1938) found it "an exciting, well-worked-out problem in detection in an equally exciting framework of hunting and adventure in the African wilds"; and a review for the *Times Literary Supplement* describes it as "a complicated web of clue and counter-clue, clever enough to entrance and entangle even the most experienced detective fan." Huxley was also praised for her wit, her control of dialogue, her effective use of setting, and her touch of the macabre. In *Murder on Safari* a jewel theft along the rural western frontier provides Vachell with an excuse for joining a white hunter on safari. While savoring for a first time the fears and surprises of the hunt, he finds at work the age-old ingredients of civilized crime, greed, and jealousy. When rich Lady Baradale is found shot in the head, her body ravaged by vultures, Vachell, without the usual accoutrements of his profession, must stalk a killer as he has stalked wild beasts and prove or disprove alibis by the testimony of buffalo, hippos, and elephants. In the process he too is stalked, but another member of the safari dies in his stead, gored by a buffalo. When Vachell's plane is sabotaged, he finally stakes himself out as bait: "Leopards, wariest of beasts of prey, were sometimes captured in a trap baited with a living goat. This was to be the model. The murderer was the wary, prowling leopard, and Vachell was to be the living goat." As in Huxley's other novels the detective must eliminate red herrings (theft, poaching, and bribery) to find a killer, but this time the leopard is too wary, the trap sprung too soon.

Death of an Aryan, Huxley's third mystery, is not merely a baffling crime puzzle but a convincing portrait of African farm life. The *New Yorker* reviewer (6 January 1940) called this book "beautifully written," its "mysterious atmosphere . . . thick enough to cut with a knife." An unexpected invitation to a dairy farm involves Vachell in an investigation of cruel, insane violence ranging from the decapitation of prize delphiniums to the brutal mutilation of animals (pigeons and ducks beheaded, dogs and calves slashed and delegged, a fawn butchered). Then a contrary farmer, the former head of the local German bund and the bane of his neighbors, dies suddenly and seemingly of natural causes until Vachell discovers the possibility of a native arrow-poison. In typical fashion Huxley provides many clues (a peculiar will, a broken pipe, an anonymous note, a pinprick hole in a shoe, incubating eggs unturned) and too many suspects, including a young woman Vachell falls irretrievably in love with. Typical too for Huxley's mysteries are the twists of plot in which different types of nefarious activity confuse the issue, in this case secret love affairs, jealousy, blackmail, and espionage. A second death ensues, then multiple poisonings; and Vachell, caught in a leopard trap, finds himself dodging a poison-tipped spear thrust at him in the dark by an insane killer, his earlier predictions confirmed: "Things that had long been hidden, festering in the dark, were bursting out, like pus from a rotten sore too long bandaged up. Once the boil had burst there was no retreat. The evil had to come out, but who would be corrupted by its poison none could say." Once the festering boil is lanced, however, health is restored to the community, and Vachell is free to pursue a beloved as adventurous and as unorthodox as himself.

The Merry Hippo is mildly satiric, a light-hearted but cynical look at a British commission giving advice on the constitutional arrangements for the independence of Hapana, a former African protectorate beset by conflicting factions vying for attention and power. Critic Anna Massa calls it a cross between the works of P. G. Wodehouse and Evelyn Waugh. The character sketches in *The Merry Hippo* are witty but devastating. Hapana's chief minister, for example, holding the coveted distinction of P.G. (Prison Graduate), has invested his family in different ideological banks to make sure that they will always be on the winning side: his eldest son in Moscow, a daughter in Chicago, another in Allahabad, a son in Peking, and the next baby designated for Dundee, Hannover, or Split. Sir Christopher, a Progressive, enlightened on everything from nuclear tests to the color bar to foxhunting, condemns "*apartheid*, hereditary peerages and the Iberian dictatorships" and spends his evenings at plays by Pinter, Wesker, and Ionesco. Tapioca growth and copper production, associated with colonialism and demasculation, become political rallying points that set tribe against tribe. Spies abound, leaking news of the internal working of the commission in politically charged diction to Russians and to local potentates. Anglo-African linguistic misunderstandings, alien tribal rituals, bizarre customs, bungled appointments, and cultural gaffes are depicted with a clear appreciation of the absurd. Facts prove meaningless, only "a dance of politics." Newspapermen totally distort events and misrepresent facts to transform a peaceful affair into what reads like a hotbed of violence and sadism. The sound methods, careful ratiocination, and polite but skilled interrogations of a British colonial detective, John Jacey, are played off against the mercurial, intuitive methods of his pending replacement, Chisango, a man who leaps to swift conclusions and is not averse to backing theory with force and torture. When an expert on pigs dies from a native poison and his wife is strangled soon thereafter, old scandals come to light and mix with recent political machi-

Huxley (right, fifteen years old) with her parents outside their house, Kitimuru, in 1922 (by permission of Elspeth Huxley)

nations to provide enough red herrings to keep readers diverted until the facts are reinterpreted in a new light and the mystery solved. Nonetheless, it is the satiric portrait of cultural clashes and political motives that is Huxley's central concern.

A Man From Nowhere turns *The Merry Hippo* on end and looks at the horrors produced by British arrangements for African independence. It satirizes the English while recounting the story of Dick Heron's personal search for justice after the savage chainsaw murder of his crippled brother; the eruption of a peaceful African state into a wartorn, newly independent nation; the loss of a farm Heron had spent his lifetime developing for his children's inheritance; and the resultant suicide of his wife, a childhood sweetheart whom he loved for her vulnerability. He decides that Peter Buckle, the British cabinet minister most responsible for the violent and destructive independence movement and the man who exonerated and gave power to the leader of the massacre that killed Heron's brother, must be the one to pay. Consequently, Heron leaves his three children with relatives and journeys to the English

country village where Buckle has his estate. There he patiently insinuates himself into the man's home, first as Buckle's milkman, then as his daughter's lover, the native hunter stalking his quarry. But when his first assassination attempt fails and he decides to bide his time, savoring the kill, he begins to find revenge less sweet and more complex. He learns his enemy's weakness, his blindness not only in politics but in his own home; he grows to love the daughter for the same vulnerability that attracted him to his first wife; and he comes to understand the hell that Buckle will suffer when forced to face the truth about his spoiled, amoral, homosexual son and to read in his wife's face the contempt she has long held for him. Ultimately, Heron finds resolution in a murder that will have positive consequences for those most closely involved. The contrast between men with opposite political views–both men of virtue, both warped, both unable to protect their families–prevents any black-and-white interpretation. This novel is highly critical of British games in African politics. It is also critical of much that is at the heart of being English. Heron, as an outsider despite his British ancestry, is appalled by English attitudes and behavior: "It was the past that really brought these people to life. . . . To the future they seemed indifferent, to the present apathetic"; "Here everything had been attenuated, even emasculated: fangs drawn, stings removed, savagery domesticated. People buried life deep under civility, its crassness and cruelty . . . hidden." Here the truly deserving poor are denied any humanitarian aid while the loudmouthed Labour Party bully who is willing to use his family and politics for leverage can renege on all debts without consequence. Huxley's portrait of Buckle's crooked son, Martin, labeled "a picture forger, a blackmailer, a bugger" by his own father, sums up the England of this book: a beautiful facade hiding a cruel, perverted reality.

Huxley's works contain not only a nostalgia for lost African ways, a respect for bush communications and tribal survival skills, and a built-in disdain for European pretensions at African expense but also an awareness of the superstition, ignorance, and disease that limit native Africans. Her descriptions of Africa capture both its beauty and its terror. A character in *The Red Rock Wilderness* (1957) describes "the vast, the utter indifference of time and place like an iron fist squeezing your heart. . . . You could fall and die, the vultures and the ants would strip your bones and everything that was you, a human personality, would vanish off the face of the uncaring earth." African dust is "a universe within a universe, world without end"; and African villages

project "an emanation of age, of knowledge, of lushness, of ancient fears and wrongs, almost of disillusion." In *Murder on Safari* Vachell muses that "there was something very frightening about Africa's utter indifference to the hopes and fears and little dignities of mankind. Only in Africa could a couple of gin cases covered with cheap Japanese calico, resting unattended in a tent, do duty as the coffin of a titled millionairess." Though Huxley is a skilled raconteur, adept at handling clues and juggling red herrings, producing multiple motives, and unveiling the jungle beneath the civilized trappings, it is her picture of Africa–multifarious and splendid–that creates the ultimate mystery made up of beauty and anguish, wisdom and savagery, blended in its land and in its people, challenging European minds and forever evading them. Like her hero in *A Thing to Love* (1954), Huxley cannot look at uncivilized Africa as simpler, more decent, purer than decadent, stale Europe; instead, having seen the evils of hatred and fear and superstition and ignorance and yet having fallen in love with Africa, she finds the dividing line between people "not according to their race or faith or class" but according to their learning to temper hatred with understanding and fear with courage, and to fight senseless waste and destruction by striving for communication despite differences.

Reference:

A. H. Horowitz, "Elspeth Huxley: a Biography," *Wilson Library Biography*, 35 (January 1961): 390.

F. Tennyson Jesse

(1 March 1888-6 August 1958)

Virginia B. Morris
John Jay College, City University of New York

BOOKS: *The Milky Way* (London: Heinemann, 1913; New York: Doran, 1914);

Beggars on Horseback (London: Heinemann, 1915; New York: Doran, 1915);

The Man Who Stayed at Home, as Beamish Tinker (London: Mills & Boon, 1915);

Secret Bread (London: Heinemann, 1917; New York: Doran, 1917);

The Sword of Deborah: First-Hand Impressions of the British Women's Army in France (London: Heinemann, 1919; New York: Doran, 1919);

The Happy Bride (London: Heinemann, 1920; New York: Doran, 1920);

Billeted, with H. M. Harwood (London: French, 1920; New York: French, 1920);

The White Riband: or, A Young Female's Folly (London: Heinemann, 1921; New York: Doran, 1922);

Murder and Its Motives (London: Heinemann, 1924; New York: Knopf, 1924; revised edition, London: Pan, 1958);

Anyhouse (London: Heinemann, 1925);

The Pelican, with Harwood (London: Benn, 1926);

Tom Fool (London: Heinemann, 1926; New York: Knopf, 1926);

Three One-Act Plays (including *The Mask*), with Harwood (London: Benn, 1926);

Moonraker: or, The Female Pirate and Her Friends (London: Heinemann, 1927; New York: Knopf, 1927);

Many Latitudes (London: Heinemann, 1928; New York: Knopf, 1928);

The Lacquer Lady (London: Heinemann, 1929; New York: Macmillan, 1930);

How To Be Healthy Though Married, with Harwood (London: Heinemann, 1930);

The Solange Stories (London: Heinemann, 1931; New York: Macmillan, 1931);

A Pin to See the Peepshow (London & Toronto: Heinemann, 1934; Garden City, N.Y.: Doubleday, Doran, 1934);

F. Tennyson Jesse

Sabi Pas: or, I Don't Know (London: Heinemann, 1935);

Act of God (London & Toronto: Heinemann, 1937; New York: Greystone Press, 1937);

Double Death, by Jesse, Dorothy L. Sayers, Freeman Wills Crofts, and others (London: Gollancz, 1939);

London Front: Letters Written to America, (August 1939-July 1940), with Harwood (London: Constable, 1940; New York: Doubleday, Doran, 1941);

The Saga of San Demetrio (London: HMSO, 1942; New York: Knopf, 1942);

While London Burns: Letters Written to America, (July 1940-June 1941), with Harwood (London: Constable, 1942);
The Story of Burma (London: Macmillan, 1946);
Comments on Cain (London: Heinemann, 1948);
The Alabaster Cup (London: Evans, 1950);
The Compass, and Other Poems (London: Hodge, 1951);
The Dragon in the Heart (London: Constable, 1956).

PLAY PRODUCTIONS: *The Black Mask*, with H. M. Harwood, London, Royalty Theatre, December 1912; New York, Princess Theatre, 1913; as *The Mask*, London, 9 August 1915;
Billeted, with Harwood, London, Royalty Theatre, 21 August 1917; as *Lonely Soldiers*, Pittsburgh, Nixon, 17 September 1917;
The Hotel Mouse, with Harwood, adapted from a play by Paul Armont and Marcel Gerbidon, London, Queens Theatre, 6 October 1921;
Quarantine, London, Comedy Theatre, 6 June 1922; New York, Henry Miller Theater, 16 December 1924;
The Pelican, with Harwood, London, Ambassadors' Theatre, 20 October 1924; New York, 1925;
Anyhouse, London, Ambassadors' Theatre, 12 March 1925;
How to be Healthy Though Married, with Harwood, London, Strand Theatre, 25 May 1930;
Birdcage, with Harold Dearden, London, People's Palace, 15 May 1950;
A Pin to See the Peepshow, with Harwood, London, 1951; New York, 48th Street Playhouse, 17 September 1953.

OTHER: Jean de Bosschere, *The City Curious*, translated by Jesse (London: Heinemann, 1920; New York: Dodd, Mead, 1920);
The Trial of Madeleine Smith, edited, with an introduction, by Jesse (Edinburgh & London: Hodge, 1927; revised 1950);
The Trial of Samuel Herbert Dougal, edited, with an introduction, by Jesse (Edinburgh & London: Hodge, 1928);
Lassiter Wren and Randle MacKay, *The Baffle Book*, edited by Jesse (London: Heinemann, 1930);
The Trial of Sidney Harry Fox, edited, with an introduction, by Jesse (Edinburgh & London: Hodge, 1934);

The Trial of Alma Victoria Rattenbury and George Percy Stoner, edited, with an introduction, by Jesse (London & Edinburgh: Hodge, 1935);
The Trial of Thomas John Ley and Lawrence John Smith, edited, with an introduction, by Jesse (London: Hodge, 1947);
The Trial of Timothy John Evans and John Reginald Halliday Christie, edited, with an introduction, by Jesse (London: Hodge, 1957).

"Miss Tennyson Jesse, who writes when she has a mind to, when she has something to say and no oftener, never says the same thing twice," the *Times Literary Supplement* observed in 1926. What she has to say about crime and punishment in her best-known novel, *A Pin to See the Peepshow* (1934), offers a meticulous analysis of the genesis of catastrophe and a resounding indictment of self-righteousness in the execution of justice. Widely respected as a journalist, novelist, playwright, and criminologist, Fryniwyd Tennyson Jesse chose as the subject for this novel one of England's most controversial murder cases, the trial of Edith Thompson and Frederick Bywaters for the murder of Mrs. Thompson's husband. Her thesis, equally applicable to the fiction and its source, is that women are judged by different standards than men and pay a greater penalty for their follies.

Jesse was also writing a social history of twentieth-century England, and while her own life story is far different from her protagonist's, the novel's verisimilitude depends on many details of her own experience and that of her unhappily married parents. Though a child of social privilege, a grandniece of the poet Alfred Tennyson, she grew up a poor relation, subjected by her father's financial failure and her mother's unpleasant disposition to a childhood of constant quarreling and thinly disguised sexual tensions. Determined to escape, she initially studied painting at the Stanhope school in Cornwall but moved to London in 1909 to become a journalist, the first step in her literary career.

Her first published short story, "The Mask," is a taut tale of marital discord and social disintegration set in the depressed Cornish mine country. Vashti Glasson, frustrated with her tedious husband and repressive marriage, hates the disfigured James Glasson and yearns for sexual excitement with her lover Willie Stark, but their assignation accidentally culminates in murder. Thinking her husband dead, Vashti schemes to escape to America undetected. Her plan ironically back-

Dust jacket for the first British edition of Jesse's 1931 novel featuring Solange Fontaine (courtesy of Otto Penzler)

Jesse makes her thriller terrifyingly real by evoking the hatred that emotional isolation creates in the human spirit. For beyond its shocking denouement, it also forces the reader to assess the consequences of unhappy marriages where divorce does not seem to be an option. In Jesse's own words, quoted by her biographer, Joanna Colenbrander, "It is impossible for the outsider to judge how grindingly the mere presence of one human being in a house may crush down another."

As a direct result of the story's popularity, Jesse collaborated with the popular playwright H. M. Harwood in a dramatization of it which was staged successfully in both England and America. She also signed a long-term contract with the publisher William Heinemann to write fiction. The venture with Harwood had both professional and personal consequences; after their marriage, in 1918, they continued to write together.

During World War I Jesse experimented with form and subject in her writing, working at both fiction and nonfiction and developing the characteristic eclecticism that defines her career. Her attention to women's issues, including divorce, education, and employment outside the home, emerges as a recurrent theme. Unlike many contemporary women writers, especially those writing to a popular audience, she discussed sexual matters, including the dilemmas that abortion and adultery posed in the postwar era. Her forthright approach sometimes outraged the critics, prompting one of them to object to "an abnormal strain of female eroticism" in *Beggars on Horseback*, a volume of short stories published in 1915, and another to reprove "a frankness of expression that seems more masculine than feminine."

The issue of repressed or frustrated sexuality, so clearly tied to Vashti Glasson's temptation to commit adultery in "The Mask," reappears, often in a lighter vein, in Jesse's detective tales featuring the young Frenchwoman Solange Fontaine as an amateur but very clever sleuth. In "The Canary," for instance, a young woman named Marjorie Brownlie is suspected of having murdered her much older and extremely unpleasant husband. Incriminated by an adulterous affair with a mild-mannered bank clerk and openly accused by a venomous sister-in-law, Marjorie is in an extremely vulnerable position. But with the aid of her highly developed, though ironically wrong, intuition, Solange uncovers the real culprit—the malicious husband himself, who has

fires, transforming the lovers into James Glasson's victims. The abandoned mine shaft, site of the accident which had mutilated James Glasson's face and destroyed his soul, becomes both the physical tomb of the murdered Willie Stark and the symbolic pit of the Glassons' marriage. And the black mask which covers Glasson's face is the executioner's mask of death.

Vashti is the strongest character in the story and the most perplexing, as Jesse's women characters always are. Though she cowers before her husband's assertive personality, she tramples on her weak-willed lover. Her frustration with the unresponsive and bitter Glasson is brilliantly and sympathetically sketched. Yet her fury is relentless, and the coldheartedness with which she helps to dispose of the body she thinks is her husband's is chilling. Deliberately Jesse leaves unresolved the question of whether Vashti deserves the horrible punishment her furious husband plans.

committed suicide in order to guarantee that his unfaithful wife will hang for his murder.

In the most revealing conversation in the story, a determined Solange persuades a reluctant mystic, Miss Leman, to stage a séance critical to the investigation. Jesse's detective argues that without their help Marjorie will hang because "a jury is made up largely of husbands and a judge is generally a married man. . . ." To a reader familiar with Jesse's other work, the comment clearly illustrates the novelist's underlying sense of the danger in which an unconventional woman could find herself enmeshed. But in the story itself the social commentary is less significant than either Solange's cleverness or the inexplicable death of the mystic's canary, an event the detective attributes to the evil generated by calling up the spirit of the vicious Brownlie.

Obviously familiar with the theories of writing detective fiction, and comfortable enough with her own skill as a writer to deviate from convention by making her sleuth an intuitive young woman, Jesse discussed the distinction between detective fiction and crime stories in the prefatory essay to *The Solange Stories* (1931). Detective fiction, she wrote, needs an element of surprise which piques curiosity and provides an intellectual puzzle. But the crime story, at which she excelled, must be designed "to give one the shivers."

During the 1920s while Jesse was writing fiction and plays, she was developing a reputation as a self-trained criminologist, producing the sometimes idiosyncratic but influential study *Murder and Its Motives* (1924) and editing several volumes in the Notable British Trials series. That work, coupled with her horrified reaction to the trial and execution of Edith Thompson in 1922-1923, helped her to focus her attention on crime and punishment as a subject for realistic fiction and to take a broader view of the genesis of crime. *A Pin to See the Peepshow* gives readers more than the shivers; it creates a cold knot of dread in the pit of the stomach.

The novel tells Julia Almond's story, a tale of her unhappy marriage to Herbert Starling, her adultery with Leonard Carr, and mindless murder that culminates in an equally mindless execution, a tragedy based overtly on the Thompson case. Its power evolves from the skillful characterization of the doomed Julia, who could bear to live in the world where she belonged only by filtering reality through the romantic haze of her fantasies. Though she is selfish, myopic, and unwit-

tingly destructive, she is profoundly sympathetic, a woman whose punishment so far exceeds her crimes that she becomes a symbol, for Jesse, of the class and gender discrimination endemic in Britain in the 1920s and 1930s.

Julia's world is the London of World War I and the years immediately following, when radical changes in society demanded that women be self-sufficient for the war's duration and then revert to dependence when the men returned. It was a world Fryn Jesse knew very well, for she had lived through it and written about it. Her book on the Women's Army in France, *The Sword of Deborah* (1919), was widely praised for its combination of accurate reportage and sensitive insight into the women's experiences, and her biographer, Joanna Colenbrander, points to the war years as the genesis of Jesse's "lifelong practice of speaking up for women wherever she thought they were being unfairly used."

Tracing Julia's life from late adolescence, Jesse describes a young woman obsessed with self, aspiring to fulfill vague ambitions for happiness and success, by which she means financial security and romantic love. Because she is energetic, she works hard at achieving them, but because she is limited by an indifferent education, rigid social expectations, and a small income, she is repeatedly frustrated and ultimately defeated.

In a novel filled with ironies, Jesse gives Julia's attempts at conventional behavior the most devastating consequences. To escape from the family's encroachment on her privacy at home, Julia turns to marriage without considering the loss of privacy implicit in being a wife. She marries a family friend, an officer in a dashing uniform, forgetting until too late that he is a very ordinary men's shop manager and a widower eager to be cosseted by a devoted and faithful young wife. More like Julia's father than her husband, he is as incapable of understanding her needs as of satisfying them. Yet she is terrified of risking the poverty and disgrace implicit in divorce to gain the independence she craves. The bitterest irony Jesse hammers out, by contrasting her heroine with other characters in the novel, is that Julia would have been an overwhelming success had she been a member of the upper class, among whom divorces were affordable and socially acceptable, or had she been a man, allowed the indulgence of adultery.

The novel brilliantly plays out the counterpoint between Julia's aspirations and her fate.

Jesse, circa 1890, christened Wynifried Margaret

Never understanding what it means to love or be loved, she craves adoration and sexual excitement. Imagining that secret meetings and passionate letters are the essence of romance, she creates a fantasy world of assignations and promises that lead ultimately to Herbert Starling's murder and her own execution. That she never really meant the promises she made in those letters or used any of the poisons she described to get rid of Herbert was clear enough to her. She was more surprised than anyone when Leonard Carr killed him; murder had nothing to do with romance. But neither judge nor jury believed her, as they had not believed Edith Thompson.

At the arrest, throughout the trial, and into the grueling final hours when her appeal is denied, Julia struggles to grasp the reality that has caught her and destroyed her dreams. Meaning no real harm to anyone, frustrated still by never having "had a chance at anything she really wanted," she collapses into screams, heavily sedated and scarcely human. The novelist's message is horrifyingly and didactically clear: nothing Julia Almond has ever done deserves such a punishment.

By making Julia technically innocent yet unwittingly guilty, Jesse took an artistic risk critical to the novel's success. Had her protagonist been either as blameless as she thought herself or repentant for the self-absorption that precipitated the murder, the story would be maudlin. Instead the novel becomes an indictment of the society in which Julia lived and died, because she is punished for refusing to conform to the standards demanded of women of her class. In writing Julia Almond's story, Jesse is advocating equality for women in every social and political sphere. Ironically, of course, Julia is not interested in equality, but in love. That too is part of Jesse's point: her character is tragic because she is so inescapably the product of her time and place.

The novel's structure also contributes to its power. The omniscient but unobtrusive narrator weaves premonitions of doom into Julia's story from the start. The cotton-wool world, "at once amazingly real and utterly unearthly," that Julia

H. M. Harwood, the screenwriter, Jesse's husband

glimpses in a peep show in the prologue is a metaphor for her life: "It was a mad world, compact of insane proportions, but lit by a strange glamour." It is that illusory glamour which Julia pursues as she moves inexorably toward the destruction so painfully described in the epilogue.

For some readers the final chapters, which describe Julia's trial and execution, disrupt the artistic integrity of the novel. Elaine Morgan, who dramatized the story for BBC Television, argues in the afterword to a 1979 Virago edition that Jesse "is no longer writing fiction" because the details are so closely linked to the Edith Thompson case and because the thesis is so clearly an assault on "the pretence of administering justice." Jesse never denied the link to Thompson or her intellectual debt to the histories of women like Edith Carew and Florence Maybrick, who were convicted in the late nineteenth century of similar crimes but reprieved from hanging. In describing her work on the novel, she said that she wrote the beginning and ending first, "and in that frame I placed the life of an over-emotional, under-educated, suburban London girl, who had

no more idea of murder than the unfortunate Mrs. Thompson had." For Jesse as novelist and criminologist, the link to reality did not diminish the story's power any more than the details borrowed from her own experience or that of her family made it autobiographical. Part of Jesse's genius in her best fiction was her ability to work creatively with reality.

The novel's reception was enthusiastic, demanding a second printing in the year of publication. The novelist Ethel Manning compared it to Theodore Dreiser's *An American Tragedy* (1925) for its intense emotional power and stinging social documentation. "It is a book," she wrote, "to move one to tears and anger." Other critics pointed out Julia Almond's relationship to Gustave Flaubert's Emma Bovary, calling the theme of a woman's self-destruction one "that can never grow old."

Because *A Pin to See the Peepshow* is not in the mainstream of popular crime fiction, it is difficult to assess its impact on the genre. Guilty women appear frequently in classic detective fiction, but rarely is a woman's agonizing punishment so deliberately described. Similarly, social criticism is unusual in the fiction Jesse's contemporaries were writing in the 1930s, particularly when it involved such subjects as divorce, abortion, or capital punishment. Nor did the novelist repeat her success by writing other crime novels, although she edited the record of Alma Rattenbury's trial, where a murder in 1935 was a startling replay of many details of the Thompson affair. In any case, *A Pin to See the Peepshow* continues to be read and to make a strong impression on its readers. In 1948 Jesse and Harwood collaborated in its dramatization for the stage, and it was adapted for British television in 1972. While more intense and sophisticated than Jesse's other crime fiction, it shares with those stories a perspective on women at odds with convention, especially with the mores governing sexuality and self-determination. Jesse's women, though they are punished for defying society's expectations, are not actually guilty of murder. She shows little sympathy for killers in either her fiction or her nonfiction, but ambivalent compassion for women desperate to escape from the trap of deadening lives.

Biography:
Joanna Colenbrander, *Portrait of Fryn: A Biography of F. Tennyson Jesse* (London: Deutsch, 1984).

C. H. B. Kitchin
(17 October 1895-2 April 1967)

William Reynolds
Hope College

BOOKS: *Curtains* (Oxford: Blackwell, 1919);
Winged Victory (Oxford: Blackwell, 1921);
Streamers Waving (London: Hogarth Press, 1925);
Mr. Balcony (London: Hogarth Press, 1927);
Death of My Aunt (London: Hogarth Press, 1929;
New York: Harcourt, Brace, 1930);
The Sensitive One (London: Hogarth Press, 1931);
Crime at Christmas (London: Hogarth Press, 1934;
New York: Harcourt, Brace, 1935);
Olive E. (London: Constable, 1937);
Birthday Party (London: Constable, 1938);
Death of His Uncle (London: Constable, 1939;
New York: Harper & Row, 1984);
The Auction Sale (London: Secker & Warburg,
1949);
The Cornish Fox (London: Secker & Warburg,
1949);
Jumping Joan and Other Stories (London: Secker &
Warburg, 1954);
The Secret River (London: Secker & Warburg,
1956);
Ten Politt Place (London: Secker & Warburg,
1957);
The Book of Life (London: Davies, 1960; New
York: Appleton-Century-Crofts, 1961);
A Short Walk in Williams Park (London: Chatto &
Windus, 1971).

OTHER: *Oxford Poetry, 1920*, edited by Kitchin,
Vera M. Brittain, and Alan Porter (Oxford:
Blackwell, 1920).

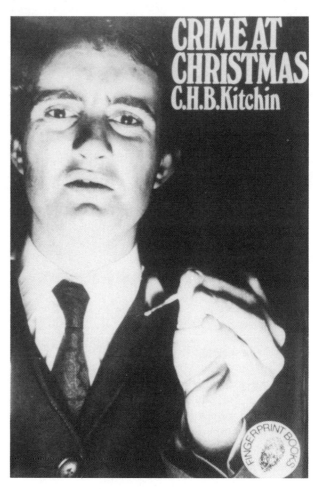

*Dust jacket for a later British edition of Kitchin's 1934
novel, featuring detective Malcolm Warren*

A serious literary artist, C. H. B. Kitchin longed for but never received popular acclaim—perhaps because of his novels' biting wit or, as his friend L. P. Hartley suggested, because Kitchin's four detective novels diverted most readers' attention from his more ambitious and more literary endeavors. Kitchin's early novels have an element of the fantastic which has led critics to compare them to Aldous Huxley's *Crome Yellow* (1921) and L. H. Myers's *The Clio* (1925). His later books became more and more conventional; some critics maintain that in the process Kitchin became a better novelist, while others believe that he lost his individuality and became simply one good novelist among many. Less controversial is the view that Kitchin gradually evolved an attitude toward life which Francis King has likened to that "of an explorer in a diving bell. Insulated by both his wealth and his shyness, he seems to perceive the uneducated and the poor not without sympathy and even affection but at one remove." Kitchin peopled his novels with an impressive range of characters and moved them through well-constructed plots which subtly yet incisively satirize the materialism and self-deception of the British middle class. He is at his best in his elegiac and not unsympathetic re-creations of the past—whether the Edwardian era of *The Book of Life* (1960) or the interwar period of *The Auction Sale* (1949) and *The Secret River* (1956). His detective fiction is less impressive. Compared to the work of other Golden Age novelists, his detective novels lack subtlety and ingenuity, while in their characterization and thematic development they are inferior to his mainstream novels.

Born at Harrogate in 1895, Clifford Henry Benn Kitchin was educated at Clifton College, Bristol, and at Exeter College, Oxford. He served with the British army in France from 1916 to 1918. Following World War I Kitchin published two volumes of his own poetry—*Curtains* (1919) and *Winged Victory* (1921)—and coedited the 1920 volume in Blackwell's *Oxford Poetry* series. He began a career on the stock exchange, and in 1924 he was called to the bar. But because of an inheritance and shrewd investments, Kitchin had no need to earn a living; encouraged by the critical success of his early novels, he decided to retire to Brighton and dedicate himself to writing. He died in April 1967.

Kitchin's first two novels, *Streamers Waving* (1925) and *Mr. Balcony* (1927), combine brilliant wit with serious underlying intentions. *Streamers Waving* centers on the love of Lydia Clame, a shabbily genteel spinster, for Geoffrey Remington. Intending only a joke, Remington allows a report of his death to be circulated; Clame, shattered yet exalted, takes a surrealistic swim in the Thames, contracts pneumonia, and dies. *Mr. Balcony* conceals terror beneath a meticulously described surface. Setting out to make himself the opposite of what nature intended, Mr. Balcony invites several people to travel on his yacht with him to Africa. He murders one of his guests, marries another, sends his wife home to bear his child, and finally joins a group of natives who have castrated him.

While Kitchin may have looked upon *Death of My Aunt* (1929) as an experiment in the realistic mode which dominates all his novels after *Mr. Balcony*, it succeeded beyond all expectation and began his career as a detective novelist on an extremely high note. The book has seldom been out of print and, though he ultimately came to refer to it as "that wretched book," has gained Kitchin more recognition than anything else he wrote. Described by Jacques Barzun and Wendell

Hertig Taylor as "the classic model of the first-person story in which the narrator must do the detecting in order to remove suspicion from himself," *Death of My Aunt* is a closely observed portrait of family life in a provincial town. Its narrator, Malcolm Warren, is a young stockbroker accused of poisoning his rich aunt, Catherine Cartwright. When Kitchin reveals all the clues, the novel's puzzle is not difficult to solve, and Warren is barely adequate as an investigator. Those who praise the novel do so because its characters are clearly drawn and believable, particularly in the way Cartwright's wealth influences her relatives' dealings with her and with one another. Those who find fault with it do so because the inordinate amount of time Warren spends indulging the introspective side of his personality can sap the reader's interest both in Warren and in the outcome of his search for the murderer.

Warren continues his detective career in *Crime at Christmas* (1934), *Death of His Uncle* (1939), and *The Cornish Fox* (1949). As a detective novel, *Crime at Christmas* is less successful than its predecessor. Kitchin achieves suspense only through the most oblique and long-winded storytelling; and, once everything is made clear, what stands revealed are enough coincidences and improbabilities for several thrillers. But, as he makes clear in the amusing "Short Catechism" between the reader and Warren which concludes the book, Kitchin had only a secondary interest in the detective genre. Warren tells the reader, "A detective story is always something of an *étude de moeurs*—a study in the behaviour of normal people in abnormal circumstances. . . . You want the revolver shot, the blood-stained knife, the mutilated corpse—but largely because they bring out the prettiness of the chintz in the drawing-room and the softness of the grass on the Vicarage lawn." The detective story, Warren continues, provides one with "a narrow but intensive view of ordinary life, the steady flow of which is felt more keenly through the very violence of its interruption." Judged by these standards, *Crime at Christmas* is still not a complete success. Kitchin attempts to probe more deeply into Warren's character, but whatever success he achieves is vitiated by the sort of person Warren is. Warren is even more introspective than before and spends still larger amounts of time weeping, not for those who die in the course of the novel but for the effect their deaths have upon his psyche. Moreover, the characters are too stereotyped and atypi-

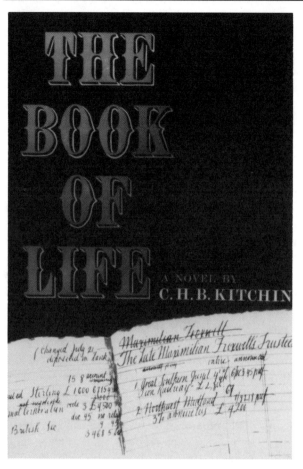

Dust jacket for the first American edition of Kitchin's 1961 novel, in which the baronet, Sir Francis Froxwell, becomes involved in a scandal

cal to allow for an examination of anything resembling ordinary life.

Perhaps because he does not regard himself as a possible suspect, Warren is a much more appealing character in *Death of His Uncle* than in either of the earlier novels. Presented with the task of solving the mystery which surrounds the disappearance of the uncle of his friend Dick Findlay, Warren leisurely works his way to the correct solution. Kitchin's narrative style, far more direct than in his other detective novels, conveys the impression that he is trying to communicate information, not conceal it. So while most readers will hit upon the answer long before Warren, they will feel less impatient with him in the process. As an added bonus, Warren has become a more fully developed character, one through whom Kitchin delivers some marvelously cynical comments on middle-class suburban respectability and resort life.

As in *Crime at Christmas*, in *Death of His Uncle* Kitchin sets forth his ideas about detective

stories, making even stronger claims than in the earlier novel. A good detective story, he writes, "is often a clearer mirror of ordinary life than many a novel written specially to portray it. . . . A historian of the future will probably turn, not to blue books or statistics, but to detective stories if he wishes to study the manners of our age." And *Death of His Uncle* does give a better picture of ordinary life than do Kitchin's other detective novels, bringing to life scenes as diverse as dinner at Aux Trois Pommes, a search of hotels near Paddington Station, a walk along the Cornish coast, and Warren's memorable nude swim in the pond of the Cantervale Nursery. Except for Warren, the characters lack depth, but all come across as reasonably human. One of them, Olive Crowne, is borrowed from Kitchin's novel *Olive E.* (1937), which examines much the same stratum of society as does *Death of His Uncle*.

The last of Kitchin's detective novels, *The Cornish Fox*, is also the least. The most interesting parts involve flashbacks to events in the life of a minor character, Berthe Langeard, who, even though she is the murderer Warren is trying to identify, plays only the most insignificant role in the action of the novel. Warren has become obsessed with algebra, so Kitchin force-feeds his readers passage after passage of ninth-grade mathematics–which, though incredibly boring, has the virtue of diverting attention from a cast of characters so dull that even Kitchin's skillful and detailed chronicle of their day-to-day existence fails to generate any interest after the first few pages. The novel has a few excellent scenes, the most memorable being one near the end when Warren impersonates the Archangel Gabriel to bring peace of mind to Ezekiel Tregwelsoe, the troublemaking Cornish fox of the novel's title, a lonely old man unable to forgive himself for mistakes he made many years earlier. But the overall impression is that Kitchin had grown tired of the detective genre.

Though Kitchin regarded his detective novels too seriously to deserve the "amiable Farceur" label given him by Julian Symons, he never used them to probe deeply. At times Warren seems to be on the point of commenting on someone or something he encounters or even of making a connection between the disorder brought into his world by murder and the apparent randomness of so much of human existence, but he never does so. In addition to pairing *The Cornish Fox* and *The Auction Sale*, published only nine months apart, Kitchin balanced *Death of My Aunt* with *The*

Sensitive One (1931), *Crime at Christmas* with *Olive E.*, and *Death of His Uncle* with *Birthday Party* (1938), using the mainstream novels to reflect a bleaker worldview than he displayed in the detective novels.

Within the detective fiction genre Kitchin's four novels are part of the renewal movement of the 1930s, with affinities to Francis Iles's attempts to secure psychological realism and Dorothy L. Sayers's endeavors to reunite detective fiction with the comedy of manners tradition. But because of his unwillingness to commit himself either to constructing complex puzzles or to writing serious novels into which detective elements are integrated, Kitchin's detective novels never reach the level they could have attained.

Though Kitchin published no detective fiction after 1949, he did write four more novels; and it is on these and *The Auction Sale* that his reputation will rest. *The Auction Sale* has been highly praised by critics as perceptive as Hartley and David Cecil, but others regard *The Book of Life*, the last of Kitchin's works to be published in his lifetime and the only one of his mainstream novels to be published in the United States, as his masterpiece. Despite the popularity of *Death of My Aunt*, Kitchin will probably never be much more than a footnote in the history of detective fiction. His reputation as a talented but minor mainstream novelist working in a well-established subgenre seems more secure, at least among academic critics.

References:

Jacques Barzun and Wendell Hertig Taylor, *A Catalogue of Crime* (New York: Harper & Row, 1971), pp. 266-267;

L. P. Hartley, "The Novels of C. H. B. Kitchin," in his *The Novelist's Responsibility* (London: Hamish Hamilton, 1967), pp. 149-155;

Francis King, "C. H. B. Kitchin," *Times Literary Supplement*, 27 February 1969, p. 206;

Julian Symons, *Bloody Murder* (New York: Viking, 1985), p. 116.

Ronald Arbuthnott Knox
(17 February 1888-24 August 1957)

Brian Murray
Youngstown State University

SELECTED BOOKS: *A Still More Sporting Adventure!*, with Charles R. L. Fletcher (Oxford: Blackwell, 1911);

Naboth's Vineyard in Pawn (London: Society of SS. Peter and Paul, 1913);

Some Loose Stones, Being a Consideration of Certain Tendencies in Modern Theology (London & New York: Longmans, Green, 1913);

The Church in Bondage (London: Society of SS. Peter and Paul, 1914);

An Hour at the Front (London: Society of SS. Peter and Paul, 1914);

Reunion All Around; or, Jaels Hammer Laid Aside (London: Society of SS. Peter and Paul, 1914);

Absolute and Abitofhel (London: Society of SS. Peter and Paul, 1915);

Bread or Stone: Four Conferences on Imperative Prayer (London: Society of SS. Peter and Paul, 1915);

The Essentials of Spiritual Unity (London: Catholic Truth Society, 1918);

A Spiritual Aeneid (London & New York: Longmans, Green, 1918);

Q. Horati Carminium Liber Quintus, with others (Oxford: Blackwell, 1920);

Memories of the Future, Being Memories of the Years 1915-72, Written in 1988 by Opal, Lady Porstock (London: Methuen, 1923; New York: Doran, 1923);

Thesauropolemopompus, with Albert B. Purdie (Ware, Hertfordshire: Edmundium, 1925);

The Viaduct Murder (London: Methuen, 1925; New York: Simon & Schuster, 1926);

The Belief of Catholics (London: Benn/New York: Harper, 1927);

The Three Taps: A Detective Story Without a Moral (London: Methuen, 1927; New York: Simon & Schuster, 1927);

Essays in Satire (London: Sheed & Ward, 1928; New York: Dutton, 1930);

The Footsteps at the Lock (London: Methuen, 1928);

The Mystery of Kingdom and Other Sermons (London: Sheed & Ward, 1928);

Monsignor Ronald Arbuthnott Knox (Elliot and Fry)

The Rich Young Man: A Fantasy (London: Sheed & Ward, 1928);

The Church on Earth (London: Burns & Oates, 1929; New York: Macmillan, 1929);

Caliban in Grub Street (London: Sheed & Ward, 1930; New York: Dutton, 1930);

The Floating Admiral, with others (London: Hodder & Stoughton, 1931; New York: Doubleday, 1932);

Broadcast Minds (London: Sheed & Ward, 1932; New York: Sheed & Ward, 1933);

Difficulties, Being a Correspondence about the Catholic Religion Between Ronald Knox and Arnold Lunn (London: Eyre & Spottiswoode, 1932; revised, 1952);

The Body in the Silo (London: Hodder & Stoughton, 1934); republished as *Settled Out of Court* (New York: Dutton, 1934);

Still Dead (London: Hodder & Stoughton, 1934; New York: Dutton, 1934);

Barchester Pilgrimage (London: Sheed & Ward, 1935; New York: Sheed & Ward, 1936);

Six Against the Yard, with others (London: Selwyn & Blount, 1936); republished as *Six Against Scotland Yard* (New York: Doubleday, 1936);

Double Cross Purposes (London: Hodder & Stoughton, 1937);

Let Dons Delight, Being Variations on a Theme in an Oxford Common-Room (London & New York: Sheed & Ward, 1939);

Captive Flames: A Collection of Panegyrics (London: Burns & Oates, 1940; New York: Spiritual Book Associates, 1941);

In Soft Garments: A Collection of Oxford Conferences (London: Burns & Oates, 1942; New York: Sheed & Ward, 1942);

I Believe: The Religion of the Apostles Creed (Reading: Tablet, 1944);

God and the Atom (London & New York: Sheed & Ward, 1945);

The Mass in Slow Motion (London & New York: Sheed & Ward, 1948);

The Creed in Slow Motion (London & New York: Sheed & Ward, 1949);

A Selection from the Occasional Sermons, edited by Evelyn Waugh (London: Dropmore Press, 1949);

The Trials of Translator (New York: Sheed & Ward, 1949; London: Burns & Oates, 1949);

Enthusiasm: A Chapter in the History of Religion, with Special Reference to the XVII and XVIII Centuries (Oxford: Clarendon Press, 1950; New York: Oxford University Press, 1950);

The Gospel in Slow Motion (London & New York: Sheed & Ward, 1950);

St. Paul's Gospel (London: Catholic Truth Society/ New York: Sheed & Ward, 1951);

The Hidden Stream: A Further Collection of Oxford Conferences (London: Burns & Oates, 1952; New York: Sheed & Ward, 1953);

A New Testament Commentary for English Readers, 3 volumes (New York: Sheed & Ward, 1952-1956; London: Burns & Oates, 1953-1956);

Off the Record (London: Sheed & Ward, 1953; New York: Sheed & Ward, 1953; New York: Sheed & Ward, 1954);

A Retreat for Lay People (London & New York: Sheed & Ward, 1955);

The Window in the Wall and Other Sermons on the Holy Eucharist (London: Burns & Oates, 1956; New York: Sheed & Ward, 1956);

Bridegroom and Bride (London & New York: Sheed & Ward, 1957);

Literary Distractions (London & New York: Sheed & Ward, 1958);

The Priestly Life: A Retreat (New York: Sheed & Ward, 1958; London: Sheed & Ward, 1959);

Lightning Meditations (New York & London: Sheed & Ward, 1959);

Retreat for Beginners (New York: Sheed & Ward, 1960); republished as *Retreat in Slow Motion* (London: Sheed & Ward, 1961);

Occasional Sermons, The Pastoral Sermons, University and Anglican Sermons, 3 volumes, edited by Philip Caraman (London: Burns & Oates, 1960-1963; New York: Sheed & Ward, 1960-1964);

The Layman and His Conscience: A Retreat (New York: Sheed & Ward, 1961; London: Sheed & Ward, 1962).

OTHER: *The Best Detective Stories of the Year 1928*, abridged by Knox and H. Harrington (London: Faber & Faber, 1929);

The Holy Bible, translated by Knox (London: Burns & Oates, 1955).

Ronald Arbuthnott Knox occupies a significant position in the history of British mystery writing. He was the first writer to subject Sir Arthur Conan Doyle's Sherlock Holmes stories to careful–albeit playful–scrutiny; he was one of the first to attempt to codify–somewhat playfully–the principal attributes of quality detective fiction. The enormously prolific Knox also wrote several of his own detective novels. Although they are not particularly distinguished in the areas of characterization and plot, all are gracefully written and intelligently conceived.

Knox was born into a family of clerics on 17 February 1888. His mother's father, the scholarly and multilingual Reverend Thomas French, had served for many years as an Anglican missionary in India, and eventually assumed the bishopric of a vast diocese that included Karachi, Delhi, and Lehore. The Reverend George Knox–Knox's paternal grandfather–was a more theologically and socially conservative man whose rather mediocre ministerial career ended in Rutland, England, where he edited *The Church Missionary Intelligence*. Knox's father, Edmund–who shared George Knox's strong Low Church orientation–was ordained in 1870; in 1878 he wed Ellen Penelope French, whose brief life (she died in 1891) was devoted to the care of her eight children, of whom Ronald was the youngest.

Despite his mother's untimely death, Knox enjoyed a fairly serene childhood. Knox's father—who remarried in 1895—was generally cheerful and kind; Knox's very bright brothers and sisters allowed him to take part in their games and activities, which included the publication of a family newspaper and the frequent discussion of the Sherlock Holmes stories of Conan Doyle. Indeed, all four of Knox's brothers achieved distinction in their chosen fields. Edmund "Evoe" Knox was a well-known wit who in the 1930s and 1940s served as editor of *Punch*. Dilwyn, a close friend of John Maynard Keynes, made notable contributions to the field of cryptology, and—while working for British Intelligence during World War II—played a crucial role in breaking down German codes produced by the infamous Enigma machine. Wilfred, an Anglican priest and a biblical scholar, authored numerous books, including *Sources of the Synoptic Gospels* and *St. Paul and the Church of the Gentiles*.

Knox attended Eton, where he was widely liked for his high intelligence and his sense of humor. He continued his studies in Balliol College, Oxford, where he participated frequently in discussion groups and debating societies and won prizes for his scholarship and Latin verse. In 1910, while a fellow of Trinity College, Knox began preparing himself for ordination as an Anglican priest. Despite his family's evangelical tradition, Knox's own theological biases were by 1910 thoroughly High Church.

In 1911, at a meeting of Trinity College's Gryphon Club, Knox presented what would prove to be a very popular and influential paper entitled "Essays in the Literature of Sherlock Holmes." In this essay—published in *The Blue Book 1912* and later in his own *Essays in Satire* (1928)—Knox parodies the aloof and allusive style of much nineteenth-century textural scholarship as he explains why one finds so many "grave inconsistencies" in Dr. Watson's account of "the Holmes cycle." Knox concludes that while such early adventures as "A Study in Scarlet" and "The Red-Headed League" are "genuine," the "Return Stories"—those that began to appear after the 1891 publication of "The Final Problem"—are in fact "spurious," the "lucubrations" of an impecunious and frequently inebriated Watson who found himself "forced to earn a livelihood by patching together clumsy travesties of the wonderful incidents of which he was once the faithful recorder." Knox's essay gradually achieved a degree of cult status among devotees

of the Holmes stories and is generally regarded as the inspiration for scores of similarly semiserious and—as Julian Symons and others would suggest—extremely tiresome critical studies and "biographies" that pretend that Watson and Holmes were real men whose lives and attitudes can be documented and analyzed. Conan Doyle—writing to Knox in 1912—expressed his "amazement" that "anyone should spend such pains on such material" and admitted that Knox's knowledge of the Holmes stories was clearly far greater than his own. "I am pleased," wrote Conan Doyle, "that you have not found more discrepancies." Thirty years later Knox was himself amazed—and disturbed—by his essay's continuing popularity. "I can't bear books about Sherlock Holmes," he admitted in a letter. "It is so depressing that my one permanent achievement is to have started a bad joke."

Knox entered the Anglican priesthood in 1912 and assumed the chaplaincy at Trinity. But in 1917 he concluded reluctantly that the Church of England "hadn't a leg to stand on" and—much to the bitter disappointment of his father—shifted his allegiance to the Church of Rome. In 1919 Knox was ordained a Catholic priest, "taking"—as Penelope Fitzgerald records—"the antimodernist oath 'against all Liberal interpretations whether of scripture or history.'" In 1919 he accepted a teaching position at St. Edmund's seminary in Hertfordshire; in 1926 he became the Catholic chaplain at Oxford, a position that continued to accord him sufficient time to study and to write. In fact, by 1919 Knox was already well known for *Some Loose Stones* (1913), *Absolute and Abitofhel* (1915), and *A Spiritual Aeneid* (1918): works in which Knox tends—like his friend G. K. Chesterton—to employ humor and nostalgia in his dismissal of most things socially and intellectually "modern."

Knox freely admitted that he began publishing detective fiction in order to supplement his income as a chaplain and don. In Knox's first mystery novel, *The Viaduct Murder* (1925), a quartet of bantering and rather bumbling fellows sets out to discover why a man's body should end up in an osier bed near a golf course and railway arch. *The Viaduct Murder* sold briskly and was favorably received. The *Saturday Review of Literature*, for example, praised its "reasonableness, charm, and gay humor"; the *New York Times* suggested that "in *The Viaduct Murder* Ronald Knox has worked out a detective plot that is seldom excelled except, perhaps, in its ending." For while Knox

Dust jacket for the first American edition of Knox's first mystery (courtesy of Otto Penzler)

does conceal the identity of the murderer until the final chapter, he "violates the unwritten law of detective writing," said the *Times*, when near the novel's end "he allows the police to incriminate the right man."

During the 1920s many critics and writers of detective fiction–including Knox, Chesterton, Dorothy Sayers, and other members of the Detection Club–attempted to codify detective writing's unwritten "laws." In his introduction to *The Best Detective Stories of the Year 1928*, Knox laid down ten rules which he thought necessary for "the full enjoyment of a detective story." He contended that, among other things, "the criminal must be someone mentioned in the early part of the story, but must not be someone whose thoughts the reader has been allowed to follow"; that "all supernatural agencies are ruled out as a matter of course"; that "the detective must not himself commit the crime"; and that "the stupid

friend of the detective, the Watson, must not conceal any thoughts which pass through his mind." Knox also urged that secret passages be used with extreme discretion; that "twin brothers, and doubles generally, must not appear unless we have been duly prepared for them"; and–more facetiously–that "no chinamen must figure in the story." "It is a fact of observation," wrote Knox, "that if you are turning over the pages of a book and come across some mention of 'the slit-like eyes of Chin Loo,' you had best put it down at once; it is bad."

Not surprisingly, Knox's second detective novel, *The Three Taps* (1927), excludes both secret passages and the sort of "chinamen" who were then turning up regularly in the hackneyed and racist pulps. Its victim is a wealthy industrialist found gassed in a rural inn called the "Load of Mischief"; its principal character, Miles Bredon, is described as a "big, good-natured, slightly le-

Dust jacket for the first British edition of the 1934 novel featuring the sleuth Miles Bredon (courtesy of Otto Penzler)

thargic creature still in the early thirties" who successfully investigates the industrialist's death for the Indescribable, an enormous London insurance firm that, like Lloyd's, is famous for taking big risks–and charging big premiums. As in *The Viaduct Murder*–and in his other detective novels– Knox combines an elegant and detailed prose style with a narrative voice which is chatty and sometimes rather patronizingly priestly, and which he sometimes uses to interrupt the story's action and to comment playfully upon his authorial decisions. Thus, early in *The Three Taps* the narrator notes that the major influence in Bredon's life "was that of–how shall I say it?–his wife. I know–I know it is quite wrong to have your detective married until the last chapter. But it is not my fault." While working as an intelligence officer in London during the World War I, Bredon, the narrator informs us, was promptly won over by the young Angela's many charms and made "a hasty but singularly fortunate marriage." For,

"wiser than her generation," Angela–schooled by nuns– "cheerfully accepted the fact that marriages were not 'for the duration'; that she would have to spend the rest of her life with a large, untidy man who would frequently forget that she was in the room."

Bredon continues to appear as the principal sleuth in Knox's other mystery novels. In the meandering and rather predictable *Footsteps at the Lock* (1928), he travels to Oxford to look into the suspicious disappearance of a young Londoner who, it appears, fell from a canoe into the Thames; in *The Body in the Silo* (1934), published in the United States as *Settled Out of Court*, he attempts to discover why a celebrated dilettante should end up dead on the rural estate of an eccentric socialite who keeps a pet ape. As the *Saturday Review* noted, *The Body in the Silo*–quite possibly Knox's best novel–provides "mystery, action, extra-good conversation and surprising denouement."

In *Still Dead* (1934) Bredon investigates the death in Scotland of a young man whose reckless driving in a new sports car had earlier killed the only child of a gardener, "a grim, morose widower, peerless at his craft and a pillar of his local kirk, but with little human contact save for the paternal love now wrenched from him." In his review of *Still Dead* for the *Chicago Tribune*, Mortimer Quick observed that though "the witty and soft-hearted Father Knox wouldn't know how to write about a real crook," he "certainly knows how to write, and this story . . . is entertaining, smooth, and mysterious beyond the power of less intelligent authors of more ordinary murder stories." But in the *Spectator* Sylvia Norman admitted that only Knox's "witty asides" kept her conscious during the thickly plotted *Still Dead*. She thus urged Knox to "multiply the asides" in his next novel, and then "subtract the puzzle."

In Knox's next novel, *Double Cross Purposes* (1937), Bredon–back on the Scottish Highlands– finds himself entangled in a complicated treasure hunt. The book does in fact contain several rather amusing "asides," including, early on, a passage in which the narrator wonders why it is that running water "makes us all want to stop and waste time." "Small boys," he observes, "with all the opportunities of life opening before them, fritter them away the moment they come to a stream; a kind of ritual sense bids them halt, sail paper boats, throw stones at a bottle, or paddle. Bathing itself, the adult's compensation for not being allowed to paddle, would lose half its seductive charm if it were not so evidently a pure waste of time." *Double Cross Purposes* is pleasant enough, but its somewhat labored quality demonstrates that Knox was beginning to grow weary of writing in the detective genre–much to the relief of his bishop, who apparently had long considered it unseemly that a clergyman should write with such verve about crime.

Knox left Oxford in 1939, and during World War II he served as chaplain at a convent school that had relocated in rural Shropshire as a means of escaping German bombs. When in 1947 the school returned to London, Knox–never a parish priest–spent his later years living in quarters provided by wealthy English Catholics, among whom Knox had many friends and spiritual advisees. These included Evelyn Waugh, who published the first biography of Knox in 1959, and Lady Acton (Daphne Strutt), whose friendship and financial support Knox frequently found to be of particular value. Knox devoted much of his literary talent during the final years of his life to producing a Catholic translation of the Bible (1955) which he hoped would read more clearly and felicitously than the Douay version that had long been regarded as the standard Catholic text. When it appeared in 1948, Knox's translation of the New Testament was warmly praised by Catholic reviewers and remained popular until the 1960s, when the more scholarly and textually accurate Jerusalem Bible became officially sanctioned for church use.

Knox died of liver cancer on 24 August 1957. His 1912 essay on Sherlock Holmes is still regarded by Sherlockians as a classic; his 1928 rules for detective story writing are not infre-

quently reprinted and discussed. But Knox's Miles Bredon novels have long been ignored, perhaps largely because in the wake of World War II their facetiousness and priestly asides struck too many readers as irritatingly quaint. Bredon, moreover, has never acquired a legion of fans. Penelope Fitzgerald, for one, has dubbed him "a stick."

Certainly the pipe-puffing Bredon is no Nero Wolfe or Hercule Poirot. But he is probably no less intriguing or memorable than most fictional detectives, and his breezy exchanges with Angela often exhibit plenty of wit. At his worst Knox can be both tiresome and trite; at his best–in *The Body in the Silo*, say, or *The Viaduct Murder*–he cleverly, divertingly combines elegant prose with clever plot. In his recent "defense" of Knox, James Kingman suggested that Knox's novels have often been too harshly dismissed because–as a well-known critic of detective fiction–Knox has been held to an unfairly high standard. Knox, Kingman rightly asserts, "wrote good, but not great detective novels."

Biographies:

Evelyn Waugh, *Monsignor Ronald Knox* (Boston: Little, Brown, 1959);

Penelope Fitzgerald, *The Knox Brothers* (New York: Coward, McCann & Geoghegan, 1977).

References:

James Kingman, "In Defense of Ronald Knox," *Armchair Detective*, 11 (1978): 299;

Robert Speaight, *Ronald Knox the Writer* (London: Sheed & Ward, 1966).

Philip MacDonald
(Anthony Lawless, Martin Porlock)

(5 November 1899?-10 December 1980)

Thomas M. Leitch
University of Delaware

BOOKS: *Ambrotox and Limping Dick*, by MacDonald and Ronald MacDonald, as Oliver Fleming (London: Ward, Lock, 1920);

The Spandau Quid, by MacDonald and Ronald MacDonald, as Oliver Fleming (London: Palmer, 1923);

Gentleman Bill: A Boxing Story (London: Jenkins, 1923);

The Rasp (London: Collins, 1924; New York: Dial, 1925);

Queen's Mate (London: Collins, 1926; New York: Dial, 1927);

Patrol (London: Collins, 1927; New York: Harper, 1927);

The White Crow (London: Collins, 1928; New York: Dial, 1928);

Likeness of Exe (London: Collins, 1929);

The Link (London: Collins, 1930; New York: Dial, 1930);

The Noose (London: Collins, 1930; New York: Dial, 1930);

Rynox (London: Collins, 1930); republished as *The Rynox Murder Mystery* (Garden City, N.Y.: Doubleday, Doran, 1930);

The Choice (London: Collins, 1931); republished as *The Polferry Riddle* (Garden City, N.Y.: Doubleday, 1931);

The Crime Conductor (Garden City, N.Y.: Doubleday, Doran, 1931; London: Collins, 1932);

Harbour (London: Collins, 1931); as Anthony Lawless (Garden City, N.Y.: Doubleday, Doran, 1931);

Murder Gone Mad (London: Collins, 1931; Garden City, N.Y.: Doubleday, Doran, 1931);

Mystery at Friar's Pardon, as Martin Porlock (London: Collins, 1931); as MacDonald (Garden City, N.Y.: Doubleday, Doran, 1932);

Persons Unknown (Garden City, N.Y.: Doubleday, Doran, 1931); republished as *The Maze* (London: Collins, 1932);

The Wraith (London: Collins, 1931; Garden City, N.Y.: Doubleday, Doran, 1931);

Philip MacDonald (courtesy of Otto Penzler)

Mystery in Kensington Gore, as Porlock (London: Collins, 1932); republished as *Escape*, as MacDonald (Garden City, N.Y.: Doubleday, Doran, 1932);

Rope to Spare (London: Collins, 1932; Garden City, N.Y.: Doubleday, Doran, 1932);

Death on My Left (London: Collins, 1933; Garden City, N.Y.: Doubleday, Doran, 1933);

R.I.P. (London: Collins, 1933); republished as *Menace* (Garden City, N.Y.: Doubleday, Doran, 1933);

X. v. Rex, as Porlock (London: Collins, 1933); republished as *Mystery of the Dead Police*, as MacDonald (Garden City, N.Y.: Doubleday, Doran, 1933);

The Nursemaid Who Disappeared (London: Collins, 1938); republished as *Warrant for X* (Garden City, N.Y.: Doubleday, Doran, 1938);

The Dark Wheel, by MacDonald and A. Boyd Correll (London: Collins, 1948; New York: Morrow, 1948); republished as *Sweet and Deadly* (Rockville Centre, N.Y.: Zenith, 1959);

Something to Hide (Garden City, N.Y.: Doubleday, 1952); republished as *Fingers of Fear* (London: Collins, 1953);

Guest in the House (Garden City, N.Y.: Doubleday, 1955; London: Jenkins, 1956); republished as *No Time for Terror* (New York: Spivale, 1956);

The Man out of the Rain and Other Stories (Garden City, N.Y.: Doubleday, 1955; London: Jenkins, 1957);

The List of Adrian Messenger (Garden City, N.Y.: Doubleday, 1959; London: Jenkins, 1960);

Death and Chicanery (Garden City, N.Y.: Doubleday, 1962; London: Jenkins, 1963).

MOTION PICTURES: *The Star Reporter*, screenplay by MacDonald and Ralph Smart, 1931;

C.O.D., screenplay by MacDonald and Smart, 1932;

Hotel Splendide, screenplay by MacDonald and Smart, 1932;

Charlie Chan in London, screenplay by MacDonald, Fox, 1934;

The Last Outpost, screenplay by MacDonald, Paramount, 1935;

The Mystery Woman, screenplay by MacDonald, Fox, 1935;

Ourselves (River of Unrest), screenplay by MacDonald and others, 1936;

The Princess Comes Across, screenplay by MacDonald and others, 1936;

Yours for the Asking, screenplay by MacDonald and others, Paramount, 1936;

The Mysterious Mr. Moto, screenplay by MacDonald and Norman Foster, Twentieth Century-Fox, 1938;

Mr. Moto's Last Warning, screenplay by MacDonald and Foster, Twentieth Century-Fox, 1938;

Mr. Moto Takes a Vacation, screenplay by MacDonald and Foster, Twentieth Century-Fox, 1938;

Blind Alley, screenplay by MacDonald, Michael Blankfort, and Albert Duffy, Columbia, 1939;

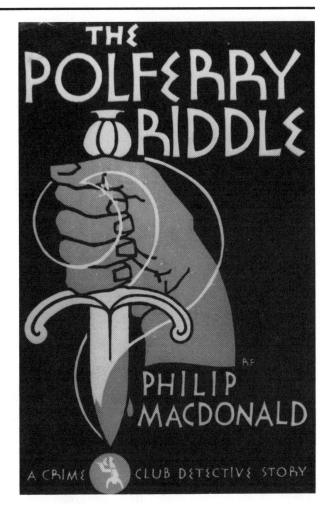

Dust jacket for the first American edition of the 1931 novel published previously as The Choice *(courtesy of Otto Penzler)*

Rebecca, screenplay by MacDonald and others, Selznick/United Artists, 1940;

Street of Chance, screenplay by MacDonald and Garrett Fort, 1942;

Whispering Ghosts, screenplay by MacDonald and Lon Breslow, Twentieth Century-Fox, 1942;

Sahara, screenplay by MacDonald and others, Columbia, 1943;

Action in Arabia, screenplay by MacDonald and Herbert Biberman, RKO, 1944;

The Body Snatcher, screenplay by MacDonald and Carlos Keith, RKO, 1945;

Dangerous Intruder, screenplay by MacDonald, Martin Goldsmith, and F. Ruth Howard, Producers Releasing, 1945;

Strangers in the Night, screenplay by MacDonald, Bryant Ford, and Paul Gangelin, Republic, 1945;

Love from a Stranger, screenplay by MacDonald, Eagle-Lion, 1947;

The Dark Past, screenplay by MacDonald and others, Columbia, 1949;

Circle of Danger, screenplay by MacDonald, Coronado/United Artists, 1951;

The Man Who Cheated Himself, screenplay by MacDonald and Seton I. Miller, Twentieth Century-Fox, 1951;

Mask of the Avenger, screenplay by MacDonald and others, Columbia, 1951;

Ring of Fear, screenplay by MacDonald, Paul Fix, and James Edward Grant, Warner Bros., 1954;

Tobor the Great, screenplay by MacDonald, Richard Goldstone, and Carl Dudley, Republic, 1954.

TELEVISION: "The Fatal Impulse," *Thriller*, NBC, 29 November 1960.

OTHER: "The Star of Starz," in *Ellery Queen's Murdercade*, edited by Ellery Queen (Frederic Dannay and Manfred B. Lee) (New York: Random House, 1975), pp. 222-237.

Philip MacDonald, one of the leading British writers of formal or Golden Age detective stories, remained until his death on 10 December 1980 one of the most mysterious figures in the world of detective fiction. Born in London on Guy Fawkes Day in a year variously given as 1896, 1899, and 1900, and which he described as "quite a long while ago," MacDonald was the son of the novelist Ronald MacDonald and the grandson of George MacDonald, author of such children's classics as *At the Back of the North Wind* (1871) and *The Princess and the Goblin* (1872). Little is known of MacDonald's own life. He served in a cavalry regiment in Mesopotamia in World War I, trained horses for the British Army, and, after being invalided out, turned to show riding and jumping. In 1920 he began to write. His first two novels were written in collaboration with his father; in 1924 he published *The Rasp*, the first of a group of detective novels featuring Colonel (later General) Anthony Gethryn. In 1931 MacDonald and his wife, novelist F. Ruth Howard, moved to Hollywood where MacDonald worked as a screenwriter and breeder of Great Danes and lived until his death. MacDonald, Howard, and Martin Goldsmith collaborated on the screenplay for one of MacDonald's many film projects, *Dangerous Intruder* (1945).

Dust jacket for the first American edition of MacDonald's 1933 novel, originally published as X. v. Rex, *using the pseudonym Martin Porlock (courtesy of Otto Penzler)*

MacDonald's first detective novel, *The Rasp*, is closely modeled on E. C. Bentley's 1912 novel *Trent's Last Case*. In both novels the detective, a journalist of independent means, finds his investigation of the death of a prominent public man in his country house hampered by a romantic attachment to one of the suspects, whom he is finally able to vindicate and marry after writing out a long, circumstantially detailed account of the crime and its perpetrator. Anthony Gethryn, MacDonald's detective in *The Rasp* and many later books, is, like Bentley's Philip Trent, a scholar, a painter, and a wit, by turns ironic and sentimental. *The Rasp* is itself less ironic than Bentley's novel: Gethryn's solution of the crime he investigates, unlike Trent's, is correct in every detail; and Gethryn, though his own tone is often whimsically facetious, is presented without a trace of irony. But the two books share an emphasis on physical evidence and a civilized approach to detection and interrogation characteristic of MacDonald's work.

Throughout *The Rasp* the tone of light comedy is set against suggestions of hatred and lust. In MacDonald's next detective story, *The White Crow* (1928), these suggestions take center stage, giving this novel something of the flavor of a boy's fantasy of romantic adventure. MacDonald's later stories tend to alternate in tone between the drawing-room comedy of *The Rasp* and the melodramatic fantasy of *The White Crow*. Often these two poles are represented respectively as English and American, as in *The Link* (1930), with its American gangster-turned-nobleman victim; *The Nursemaid Who Disappeared* (1938), whose hero is an American playwright in London; and *Guest in the House* (1955), in which the crude American villain is outwitted by the courtly British Colonel St. George. In his final novel, *The List of Adrian Messenger* (1959), MacDonald, now long resident in America, returned to England for his setting but staged the final confrontation between Gethryn and the murderer in California.

Even in the context of other Golden Age detective stories, MacDonald's early books are unusually formulaic. The victim is always the most important character in his world; the police, usually including Assistant Commissioner Sir Egbert Lucas and Superintendent Arnold Pike, are always baffled until Gethryn fortuitously appears; Gethryn is frequently assisted in his investigations by the journalists Dyson and Flood, who do his legwork; and, despite offering a logical explanation of the mystery, Gethryn is never able to produce hard evidence against the criminal and must therefore trick him or her into self-betrayal. In *Rope to Spare* (1932) Lucas observes that Gethryn has "never yet had a case which you were able to bring to a conclusion without yourself either extorting a confession from the guilty person or leading the guilty person to commit himself," and adds, "That, of course, is because those are the sort of cases you've been mixed up in." Lucas gloomily predicts that Gethryn will be unable to conclude the present case because the person he suspects of murder is already dead. But Gethryn's tactics remain unchanged: he bluffs Rosemary Conway into producing a letter in which the murderer incriminates himself. In the few MacDonald detective stories which do not end with an extorted confession, the criminal is either killed or allowed to escape punishment.

The distinction between logical and legal proof so consistent in MacDonald's detective sto-

Dust jacket for MacDonald's final novel

ries elucidates his conception of the detective story as "a sort of competition between the author and the reader," a conception he shares with John Dickson Carr and other Golden Age writers. Because the interest of MacDonald's stories is so forthrightly cerebral–he took pride in the fullness and fairness of his clueing–and because his books are similar in so many ways, his work affords an unexcelled example of the characteristic elements of Golden Age detective fiction.

The principal appeal of MacDonald's work is in its literate and amusing tone and in MacDonald's inventive and logical use of clues. Although these qualities go together in other Golden Age writers, such as Nicholas Blake and Georgette Heyer, MacDonald's detective stories are distinguished by such unusual and effective clues as the boot brushes locked in Kim Kinnaird's trunk in *Death on My Left* (1933) and the notations on the shopping list in *The Nursemaid Who Disappeared*. Anthony Gethryn is often able to construct an elaborate series of suppositions about a crime from only a scant supply of evidence because MacDonald is so ingenious at planting clues which imply a precise, extended chain of conclusions. As he argues in the foreword to

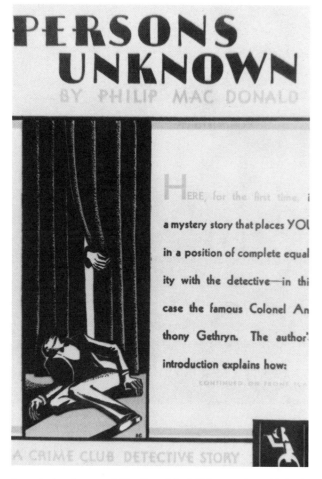

Dust jacket for one of MacDonald's 1931 mysteries, which follows other Gethryn stories by presenting the reader with all of the clues (courtesy of Otto Penzler)

Persons Unknown (1931), MacDonald's first responsibility is to bewilder the reader: his formal detective stories therefore tend to be among the strictest and fairest puzzles ever devised in the genre.

Though the puzzles in the Gethryn stories are highly successful, the character of Gethryn himself is less successful. The man who "from his birth . . . proved a refutation of the adage that a jack-of-all-trades can be master of none," as MacDonald remarks in *The Rasp*, is among the most relentlessly competent of Golden Age detectives; only in *The List of Adrian Messenger* does MacDonald even hint at Gethryn's fallibility. Given his creator's obvious and uncritical affection for him, Gethryn is constructed out of surprisingly few details: he is tall, dark, and lean, with penetrating green eyes. Even his manner of speech depends largely on a few reappearing tags: ("God knows, and he won't split," perhaps Gethryn's favorite, is even mimicked by Alf Widgery in *Guest in the House*, in which Gethryn does not appear.) Mac-

Donald's method of characterization by incantatory repetition of a few details extends to his other characters as well, so that although figures like Selma Bronson (in *The Noose*, 1930) and Lars Kristania (in *The Crime Conductor*, 1931) make a strong initial impression, they have no capacity for further development. MacDonald's principal characters, particularly his women, tend to be striking without being either believable or especially distinctive.

The incantatory nature of MacDonald's characterizations stems from his tendency to emphasize mystery and suspense by focusing on a pregnant detail, but the method frequently lapses into a factitious excitement. Gethryn's most characteristic utterance–"My *God!*"–is frequently used to end chapters on a portentous note. MacDonald's comedy is generally more effective than his melodrama, except in nondetective stories like *Patrol* (1927), the story of a group of British soldiers on a mysterious mission in Africa who one by one are attacked and killed by Arab snipers. In the detective stories the dominant tone is one of civilized inquiry; MacDonald's boys'-adventure sensibility seems misplaced.

The reason MacDonald's detective stories have not enjoyed the popularity of those of his contemporaries Agatha Christie and John Dickson Carr, however, is because of the way his clues are presented. Like the characters, the clues are striking without allowing much development. MacDonald does not have Carr's and Christie's gift of emphasizing his clues and lingering over them in order to sharpen the audience's sense of bewilderment. Because MacDonald cannot draw attention to a clue without elucidating it, his novels are structurally weaker than those of other Golden Age writers. *Death on My Left*, for example, is structurally similar to Christie's *Murder of Roger Ackroyd* (1926): several characters' innocent secrets cause them to behave suspiciously, providing protective camouflage for the real murderer. But unlike Christie, who allows her detective every occasion to speculate about the mysteries of his suspects' behavior, MacDonald presents his red herrings without emphasis and elucidates them mechanically and formulaically. MacDonald's clues, however imaginative they are in conception, have such a short gestation period between presentation and interpretation that MacDonald must either elucidate them immediately (in which case his story becomes episodic, as in *The Choice*, 1931) or present them without any emphasis (so making his stories competent but not memorable, as in *The Link*).

MacDonald seems to have been well aware of these problems, for as early as 1930 he began to experiment with solutions. His first experiments take the form of variations in the presentation of clues corresponding to variations in narrative structure. Unlike Dorothy Sayers and Cyril Hare, who take their detectives from one fictional world to another to investigate mysteries having very much the same form from the audience's point of view, MacDonald emphasizes the variety of the fictional form itself. In *The Noose* Gethryn is required to solve a six-month-old crime in the five days before an innocent man is to be executed. *The Link* is narrated by Michael Lawless, who observes Gethryn attentively without following all his inferences. Gethryn's detective work in *The Crime Conductor* is presented through his letters to his wife in Switzerland. In *Persons Unknown* and *Death on My Left* the evidence is presented through detailed accounts of inquests. In a non-Gethryn book, *Rynox* (1930), MacDonald's experimentation is even bolder; he begins with an epilogue describing the delivery of some three hundred thousand pounds to the Naval, Military, and Cosmopolitan Insurance Company, then proceeds to a story of murder and blackmail, and concludes with a prologue showing how the murder had been planned and explaining the mystery of the epilogue.

Excluding Gethryn from *Rynox, Murder Gone Mad* (1931), *Mystery in Kensington Gore* (1932), and *X. v. Rex* (1933) enabled MacDonald to develop the mystery and detective elements of these stories more freely than in his Gethryn books. The emphasis is not so much on the resolution of a mystery through the elucidation of clues—a formula which had become virtually invariable in Golden Age detective fiction—as on the way in which innocent suspects manage to elude the police and clear their names (in *Mystery in Kensington Gore*) or the way in which the authorities are able to catch a murderer who has apparently left no clues. This transformation from Whodunit to Howcatchem (MacDonald's own term), which constitutes MacDonald's principal contribution to the form of the mystery-detective story, produced his three most distinguished books: *Murder Gone Mad, X. v. Rex,* and *The Nursemaid Who Disappeared.* In these books, and particularly in his masterpiece *The Nursemaid Who Disappeared,* MacDonald makes his limitations—his inventive but foreshortened clues, his habitually episodic struc-

Philip MacDonald, circa 1958

ture, his tendency to melodrama—into virtues, by focusing on clues that give information about the criminal, or suggest ways he or she may be identified but do not reveal the criminal's identity; and by sacrificing interest in the suspicion generated by the readers' intimacy with innocent suspects in favor of interest in the means, whereby the detective is able to identify a criminal whose identity is itself inconsequential. The clues in *The Nursemaid Who Disappeared* do not help Gethryn to identify the criminals but to prevent their crime, thus helping Lucas and the C.I.D. to "exercise your real function—or what should be your real function." The importance of this development in MacDonald's own work, and its formal influence on such different writers as Hillary Waugh and Ed McBain, can hardly be overestimated. Although MacDonald does not have a reputation as an innovator, his later work, like that of Francis Iles, clearly prepares the evolution from the formal detective story characteristic of the Golden Age to the freer forms of the 1940s and after.

The final development in MacDonald's career was his return to the mystery-detective short story, a form ideally suited to his vivid prose and immediately striking clues. His one collected Gethryn story, "The Wood-for-the-Trees," is overwrought and derivative, but his stories about Doctor Alcazar (included in *Something to Hide*, 1952) cleverly mask formal detection in plots involving confidence games, and several of his non-detective stories ("Love Lies Bleeding," "Malice Domestic," "Ten O'Clock") have become classics of the mystery form. MacDonald is best remembered today as an able practitioner of the strict detective novel, but he deserves to be remembered as a writer who triumphed over the limitations of his chosen form by changing it to accommodate his own considerable virtues.

References:

Melvyn Barnes, *Best Detective Fiction: A Guide from Godwin to the Present* (London: Bingley, 1975), pp. 57-59;

Howard Haycraft, *Murder for Pleasure: The Life and Times of the Detective Story* (New York: Appleton, 1941), pp. 149-150;

A. E. Murch, *The Development of the Detective Novel* (New York: Philosophical Library, 1958), p. 224;

H. Douglas Thomson, *Masters of Mystery* (London: Collins, 1931; Folcroft, Pa.: Folcroft Library, 1973), pp. 160-164.

Ngaio Marsh

(23 April 1899-18 February 1982)

Marvin S. Lachman

BOOKS: *A Man Lay Dead* (London: Bles, 1934; New York: Sheridan, 1942);

Enter a Murderer (London: Bles, 1935; New York: Pocket Books, 1941);

The Nursing Home Murder, with Dr. Henry Jellett (London: Bles, 1935; New York: Sheridan, 1941);

Death in Ecstasy (London: Bles, 1936; New York: Sheridan, 1941);

Vintage Murder (London: Bles, 1937; New York: Sheridan, 1940);

Artists in Crime (London: Bles, 1938; New York: Furman, 1938);

Death in a White Tie (London: Bles, 1938; New York: Furman, 1938);

Overture to Death (London: Collins, 1939; New York: Furman, 1939);

Death at the Bar (London: Collins, 1940; Boston: Little, Brown, 1940);

Death of a Peer (Boston: Little, Brown, 1940); republished as *Surfeit of Lampreys* (London: Collins, 1941);

Death and the Dancing Footman (Boston: Little, Brown, 1941; London: Collins, 1942);

New Zealand, with Randal Matthew Burdon (London: Collins, 1942);

Colour Scheme (London: Collins, 1943; Boston: Little, Brown, 1943);

Died in the Wool (London: Collins, 1945; Boston: Little, Brown, 1945);

A Play Toward: A Note on Play Production (Christchurch, N.Z.: Caxton Press, 1946);

Final Curtain (London: Collins, 1947; Boston: Little, Brown, 1947);

Swing, Brother, Swing (London: Collins, 1949); republished as *A Wreath for Rivera* (Boston: Little, Brown, 1949);

Opening Night (London: Collins, 1951); republished as *Night at the Vulcan* (Boston: Little, Brown, 1951);

Spinsters in Jeopardy (Boston: Little, Brown, 1953); republished as *The Bride of Death* (New York: Spivak, 1955);

Scales of Justice (London: Collins, 1955; Boston: Little, Brown, 1955);

Death of a Fool (Boston: Little, Brown, 1956); republished as *Off with His Head* (London: Collins, 1957);

Singing in the Shrouds (Boston: Little, Brown, 1958; London: Collins, 1959);

False Scent (Boston: Little, Brown, 1959; London: Collins, 1960);

Ngaio Marsh (photograph by Mannering and Associates, Ltd.)

Perspectives: The New Zealander and the Visual Arts (Auckland, N.Z.: Auckland Gallery Associates, 1960);

Hand in Glove (Boston: Little, Brown, 1962; London: Collins, 1962);

Dead Water (Boston: Little, Brown, 1963; London: Collins, 1964);

New Zealand (juvenile) (New York: Macmillan, 1964; London: Collier, Macmillan, 1965);

Black Beech and Honeydew (Boston: Little, Brown, 1965; London: Collins, 1966);

Killer Dolphin (Boston: Little, Brown, 1966); republished as *Death at the Dolphin* (London: Collins, 1967);

Clutch of Constables (London: Collins, 1968; Boston: Little, Brown, 1969);

When in Rome (London: Collins, 1970; Boston: Little, Brown, 1971);

Tied Up in Tinsel (London: Collins, 1972; Boston: Little, Brown, 1972);

Black as He's Painted (London: Collins, 1974; Boston: Little, Brown, 1974);

Last Ditch (Boston: Little, Brown, 1977; London: Collins, 1977);

Grave Mistake (Boston: Little, Brown, 1978; London: Collins, 1978);

Photo-Finish (London: Collins, 1980; Boston: Little, Brown, 1980);

Light Thickens (London: Collins, 1982; Boston: Little, Brown, 1982).

PERIODICAL PUBLICATIONS: "I Can Find My Way Out," *Ellery Queen's Mystery Magazine*, 8 (August 1946): 5-24;

"Death on the Air," *Ellery Queen's Mystery Magazine*, 11 (January 1948): 107-128;

"Chapter and Verse," *Ellery Queen's Mystery Magazine*, 61 (March 1973): 6-25;

"A Fool About Money," *Ellery Queen's Mystery Magazine*, 64 (December 1974): 114-118.

PLAY PRODUCTIONS: *The Nursing Home Murder*, by Marsh and Dr. Henry Jellett, Christchurch, N.Z., 1936;

Surfeit of Lampreys, London, 1950;

False Scent, by Marsh and Eileen MacKay, Worthing, Sussex, U.K., 1961;

A Unicorn for Christmas, book by Marsh, music by David Farquhar, Sydney, Aust., 1965;

Murder Sails at Midnight, adapted from *Singing in the Shrouds*, Bournemouth, Hampshire, U.K., 1972.

OTHER: Ngaio Marsh, "Starting with People," in *The Mystery and Detection Annual 1973*, edited by Donald Adams (Beverly Hills, Cal.: Donald Adams, 1974), pp. 208-210;

Marsh, "Roderick Alleyn," in *The Great Detectives*, edited by Otto Penzler (Boston: Little, Brown, 1978), pp. 2-8.

During what is usually referred to as the Golden Age of the detective story, Ngaio Marsh was one of a small group of British mystery writers who set standards of characterization, sophisticated dialogue, and imaginative puzzles which broadened the audience for the genre from people who read them as thrillers to those who read them for many of the same reasons they read mainstream fiction. In a career that spanned almost half a century, her popularity grew steadily, and she became as popular in the United States as she was in England and her native New Zealand.

Born in Christchurch on 23 April 1899, Marsh first studied painting, entering art school when she was fifteen, but her great love was always the theater. Her parents, Henry Edmund and Rose Elizabeth Seager Marsh, had been amateur actors, and she called the appearances of Allan Wilkie's Shakespearean troupe in Christchurch "one of the great events of my student days." She had already begun to write and submitted a Regency play, *The Medallion,* to Wilkie. Though he rejected the play, he returned it in person and invited her to join his company. Her first appearance was as Anna, a German spy, in *The Luck of the Navy.* She toured with Wilkie for two years, meanwhile writing verse, articles, and nondetective short stories for the *Christchurch Sun.*

Upon her return to Christchurch, Marsh resumed painting for a brief period before leaving once again to tour with a local acting company formed by Rosemary Rees. When that company failed, she returned home and was active as actress, producer, and director in a group staging charity shows. Here, she became friendly with a British family of the peerage and accepted an invitation to visit them when they returned to England. She turned them into fictional characters in several of her books, calling them the "Lampreys." Marsh lived in England from 1928 to 1933, doing interior decorating and operating a gift shop. She frequented the London theater at every opportunity.

Mysteries had always been read in the Marsh household in New Zealand, and in her autobiography, *Black Beech and Honeydew* (1965), Marsh mentioned reading such authors as Baroness Orczy, Guy Boothby, and William J. Locke. She also recalled the rainy day she found a treasure trove of *Strand* magazines and discovered Sherlock Holmes. In 1931, on another rainy occasion, a weekend, she began writing her first mystery novel. She created, as her series detective, Roderick Alleyn, named after Edward Alleyn, the great Elizabethan tragedian and founder of Dulwich College, the school her father had attended before immigrating to New Zealand.

Marsh's first book, *A Man Lay Dead,* was not published until 1934, by which time she had returned to New Zealand because her mother was ill. Following her mother's death after what Marsh described as "an illness as cruelly and as excruciatingly protracted as if it had been designed by Torquemada," she remained in New Zealand to care for her father. She also wrote and painted, but she became very ill herself, though, with characteristic understatement, she dismissed this in less than a paragraph of her autobiography, saying, "a long-standing disability that hith-

erto I had contrived to live with, suddenly blew up in a rather nightmarish fashion and I spent three months in hospital undergoing a series of minor operations and a final snorter of a major one." Just as she used painting and the theater in her books, she made use of this experience and collaborated with her physician, Dr. Henry Jellett, on *The Nursing Home Murder* (1935). She returned to England in 1937 and also toured Europe.

Marsh returned to New Zealand in 1938 and stayed during World War II, driving a Red Cross ambulance. She also became increasingly serious about her theater work, producing and directing productions at Canterbury College where she reintroduced Shakespearean productions to New Zealand after a twenty-year absence. After World War II she returned to England to work with the British Commonwealth Theatre Company, a group which she eventually brought on tour to Australia and New Zealand. In 1966 she was appointed a Dame of the British Empire, largely as a result of her work in the theater.

For the rest of her life she divided her time between the theater and mystery writing. She also split her time between England and New Zealand, spending the last years before her death on 18 February 1982 in her native city. In *Black Beech and Honeydew* Marsh has stated that in New Zealand she was seldom interviewed by the media regarding her mystery writing, but more often about her work in the theater. (She always preferred to discuss the latter.) Therefore, she was astonished to find a great deal of interest in her mysteries among serious readers in Great Britain, writing, "it was pleasant to find detective fiction being discussed as a tolerable form of reading by people whose opinion one valued."

Marsh's knowledge of the theater, London's society and art worlds, and the rugged terrain of New Zealand informed her thirty-two novels and a handful of short stories. She classified herself with the mystery writers who create believable characters and use novelistic values, rather than those whose main interest is the puzzle. She once wrote, "I suppose the one thing that can always be said in favour of the genre is that inside the convention the author may write with as good a style as he or she can command. . . . The mechanics in a detective novel may be shamelessly contrived but the writing need not be so nor, with one exception, need the characterization. About the guilty person, of course, endless duplicity is practiced." Indeed, in her books most of the murders occur

Marsh with her mother, Rose Elizabeth Seager Marsh, and father, Henry Edmund Marsh (courtesy of the Estate of Ngaio Marsh)

relatively late so that the reader has the opportunity to know and, occasionally, even care about the victim.

Marsh was always a writer for the mystery reader who wanted detection plus the elements that also make for good nonmystery fiction. She was to break with many traditions in the mystery, including the one that "required" the book to start with the discovery of the corpse. Purists like S. S. Van Dine had warned against the introduction of romance into the mystery novel, but Marsh was undeterred. At first only minor characters fell in love and married. For example, it is Alleyn's friend, Nigel Bathgate, who, having met Angela North at the beginning of *A Man Lay Dead*, woos and wins her. Later, following the lead of Dorothy L. Sayers, one of the most influential writers of the period, Marsh has Roderick Alleyn fall in love with a very talented and liberated woman, the painter Agatha Troy. LeRoy Panek has called Troy "Harriet Vane in a painter's smock." The Alleyn-Troy romance, like that of Sayers's Lord Peter Wimsey and Harriet Vane, does not run smoothly at first, which makes it all the more interesting and believable. Troy is

afraid of losing her independence. She also is slow to overcome her repulsion that Alleyn, as a policeman, must sometimes send people to their death. Theirs was never a static relationship, but rather one that developed throughout the course of Marsh's career.

Alleyn, Marsh's only continuing detective, was drawn in greater depth than most of his contemporary sleuths. Coming along after detectives of the "silly ass" school (Lord Peter Wimsey, Reggie Fortune, and the early Albert Campion), and seeing the light of literary day in the same year as Nero Wolfe, Alleyn is notable for his comparative lack of offensive idiosyncrasies, though his early speech is probably more affected than his adherents might admit. For example, when asked in *The Nursing Home Murder* whether he knows the prime minister, he replies, "I know the old creature, yes." Alleyn was an Oxford graduate, of noble birth and well connected in British society. He was originally in the British diplomatic service but gave it up for "private reasons" never discussed beyond his statement that they would make "a remarkable story." He became a policeman, rising through the ranks from constable to chief superintendent. Though bookish and extremely knowledgeable in many areas, Alleyn wears his erudition more gracefully than Philo Vance. He also shows considerable physical prowess since Marsh decided to make him well rounded, not just an intellect. Until the very end he is capable of demonstrating his stamina and his resources, giving him an extra dimension not possessed by many other detectives. A gentleman in character, as well as by birth, he must still do things as a policeman which repel him, such as invading the privacy of others and using his personal charm to get female suspects to disclose information.

Marsh's successful gentleman detective does not completely dominate her books. She often kept Alleyn "off stage" until fairly late in the proceedings and sometimes used other characters to stand in for her own viewpoint. There are many scenes in Marsh books, beginning with *Artists in Crime* (1938), in which painting is important, and many descriptions in which color is used vividly. Later, Marsh would use a succession of surrogates, intelligent and personable young people, usually of the theater, to give the reader an interesting perspective on the other characters and/or the geographical settings.

Marsh will always be associated with theatrical mysteries, and, indeed, about half of her mysteries can be said to have some form of theatrical background. In her second book, *Enter a Murderer* (1935), and in her last book, *Light Thickens* (1982), murders take place on London stages during actual performances. Many of her mysteries involve murders in theaters or during other presentations before audiences, such as a folk dance ritual in *Death of a Fool* (1956), a private opera performance in *Photo-Finish* (1980), and even a hospital operating theater in *The Nursing Home Murder*. Because Marsh knew so many aspects of stage production, she was able to make the theater a major character in many of her works. An example was her ability to convey the trials and tribulations of mounting and rehearsing a new production and the childish behavior and superstitions of actors.

Writing of actors and actresses enabled Marsh to create some of her most interesting character portrayals and memorable lines. For example, of Francis Liversidge in *Vintage Murder* (1937), Marsh says, "All his actions were a little larger than life. Alleyn found himself thinking of him in terms of stage-craft: '. . . taps cigarette. Takes lighter from pocket. Lights cigarette with deliberation.'" Regarding Valerie Gaynes in the

same book, Marsh says, "She had made use of every conceivable piece of theatrical jargon that she could haul into the conversation in order to show them how professional she was." Of Mary Bellamy, the aging actress in *False Scent* (1959), one reads, "She had 'made an entrance,' comic-provocative, skillfully French-farcical. She had no notion at all of the disservice she had done herself."

Four of Marsh's novels and a short story are set in New Zealand, an unusual twist to the standard British mystery story. Though she came from a family with English roots, Marsh never forgot her homeland and its two distinct cultures, British and Maori. Maori people and their customs play a major role in most of the Marsh mysteries set in the Antipodes and even, through one of the actors, in her last book despite its London theater setting. Ngaio is a Maori word.

Though she felt her career as a writer was a struggle against the limitations the mystery format imposed on someone who wished to present a larger slice of life and deeper characterization, Marsh's respect for the traditions of the detective novel and its audience was apparent. Many writers consider the requirement of "fair play"—that is, presenting all the clues to the reader who then has an equal opportunity to compete with the author's detective—outmoded. Some of that belief may be sincere since novelistic values often suffer when faced with the constraints of inserting clues. However, there is also a self-serving element to this position because it is simply more difficult to write the "fair play" mystery than one in which necessary information may be withheld from the reader. It is especially difficult if the writer, as Marsh did, also wants to create fully developed characters. Never content to be merely a mainstream novelist manqué, Marsh not only played fair, but she advanced the classic mystery puzzle by inventing some of the most original and bizarre murder methods ever devised.

As Panek has pointed out, most Marsh books, especially her early work, invariably follow a structure consisting of an introduction, the murder, police interviews, a recapitulation, additional action, including possibly a second murder, reenactment of the crime, and summary explanation. While there was the established pattern, it and its creator were sufficiently flexible so that readers never perceived the writing as formulaic. Her introductions were invariably longer than those of most mystery writers, providing sufficient time to create atmosphere and introduce

Marsh's school photo, St. Margaret's College (courtesy of Standish and Preece, Ltd.)

the characters, even the impending victim. The murders not only were distinctly original (yet plausible), but Marsh also went further than most mystery writers to make the reader realize that murder is the ultimate violation of another person. Her descriptions of victims tended to be gruesome, though there never was any feeling that she was using literary shock tactics for sensationalism. In rereading her works one comes to appreciate how cleverly she depicted these grisly death scenes so that it was really the reader's imagination which supplied most of the horror and sensation.

Marsh's early works have been justifiably criticized for the number and length of the interviews conducted by the police. At times they were necessary to provide a minute-by-minute account of the movements of a large group of suspects. Even then, the interrogations were overlong. They could not always be justified by what they added in the way of characterization or cru-

cial clues. Incidentally, they demonstrated that most police work is boring routine. With the passing years Marsh shortened the question and answer sessions, at times settling largely for a recapitulation by Alleyn. Later, she even eschewed that device as she found means to add more action to the middle portions of her books.

In her early works the traditional reenactment of the crime came to be expected as Alleyn used it to discover the murderer. Later, she had Alleyn use more conventional, though never pedestrian, means of detection to either trap or uncover the guilty party. As a playwright Marsh was aware of the dangers of anticlimax, and her summaries of Alleyn's reasoning tended to be shorter than the explanations of other mystery writers. Motive usually would prove not to be critical to Marsh's solution since most of her suspects had equally good reasons; often they were being blackmailed. She, despite her stated interest in character portrayal, was also interested in opportunity, the "how" and "when" of the murder, rather than the "why." Physical clues, rather than verbal, are more likely to be the key to the solution in her books.

Another long-standing tradition with which Marsh gradually broke was that of the amateur detective. Even when the policeman, like Alleyn, was a professional, he often relied on a friend who had no official standing. With Marsh it was the flighty journalist Nigel Bathgate, who appeared in eight of the early books, providing comic relief and occasionally requiring Alleyn to rescue him. As Marsh grew more serious, Bathgate was replaced by Inspector Edward Fox, the member of Alleyn's team who played the largest role. Alleyn was never "a lone wolf" and cannot be considered without the Scotland Yarders who appear in most Marsh books, those he refers to as "the usual people," when he encounters a murder and calls for assistance. Fox (variously dubbed "Br'er Fox" or "Foxkins" by Alleyn) is the down-to-earth detective, the perfect foil for his aristocratic, albeit nonsnobbish, superior officer. Fox is especially good at interviewing servants and establishing a rapport with them. He also provides some humor to the series, with the recurring joke of his attempts to learn French through recordings. Though they play far smaller roles, Dr. (later Sir) James Curtis and Sergeants Bailey and Thompson all grace the series with their reassuring presences. Curtis is the Home Office pathologist whom Alleyn has affectionately dubbed "The Great Man." Bailey and Thompson are the photographer and fingerprint expert (the "flash" and "dabs" men), respectively. Indeed, when Alleyn is away from England on a case, Marsh conveys to the reader just how much he misses their support. Through Alleyn and his compatriots, Marsh provided an important transition to the works of Maurice Procter, John Creasey, Ed McBain, Elizabeth Linington, and others who would make the police procedural the most important new subgenre of the mystery in the 1950s.

A Man Lay Dead contains many of the elements of the thriller, whose popularity had not entirely waned with the death of its leading exponent, Edgar Wallace, in 1932. A weekend party at Frantock, the country estate of Sir Hubert Handesley, ends in death when, while everyone is playing "A Murder Game," then very popular in England, the "corpse" is found actually to have been killed. There is then some hugger-mugger in London involving a secret society, one which formerly practiced "various indecent and horrible rites" but now appears to have adopted the tenets of Lenin. (This was the first of many occasions in the Marsh canon in which the far left would be the object of her scorn.) Bathgate has been held prisoner by the group, and Roderick Alleyn detects in the classic manner, reassembling all the guests at Frantock for a reenactment of the crime.

However, beginning with her second book, *Enter a Murderer*, Marsh established her trademark, the "theater mystery." The Unicorn Theatre is presenting *The Rat and the Beaver*, "a melodrama of the opium trade," and Alleyn is in the audience, as Bathgate's guest, when real bullets replace fakes, turning, as in Marsh's first book, a staged murder into a real one. Not only is the solution satisfying and the clues presented fairly in *Enter a Murderer*, but Marsh delivered the first of her many subtle satires of the theatrical profession. She makes Alleyn knowledgeable about the theater and even gives him the opportunity to speak in theatrical metaphor when he takes charge, telling the company, "a drama is being produced which you do not control and in which you play a part that may or may not be significant . . . the flat-footed old Law is stage manager, producer, and critic . . . I embody the Law."

The Nursing Home Murder, Marsh's only collaborative mystery, concerns the murder of the British home secretary, Sir Derek O'Callaghan, on the operating table. The novel strains credulity because the medical staff in attendance all have motives to commit the murder. O'Callaghan

Dust jacket for the first American edition of the 1938 novel about Superintendent Alleyn's courtship of his future wife in London high society (courtesy of Otto Penzler)

argued just prior to the operation with his surgeon who has jealously accused him of being a womanizer. One of the nurses hates the secretary because he has just introduced a drastic bill in the house to deal with radicals. She is called a "Bolshie," and she speaks in stock phrases like "enemy of the proletariat" and "blood-sucking bourgeoisie."

However, the reader learns much about the character of Alleyn in this novel, such as the fact that he is a friend of the prime minister, with whom he modestly admits to having "had an Oppenheimian conversation about anarchists" two weeks previously, and that he reads crime fiction for escape. Alleyn's distaste for some aspects of his job is evident as he replies, with apt analogy, to a physician who sarcastically asks him if he enjoys reading through a suspect's mail. Alleyn replies, "About as much as you enjoy glaring into a septic abdomen, I should think." This book also contains Alleyn's frequently quoted description of the British system of justice when he tells the victim's widow, "You very properly decided to place this tragic case in the hands of the police. In doing so you switched on a piece of complicated and automatic machinery which, once started, you cannot switch off. As the police officer in charge of this case I am simply a wheel in the machinery. I must complete my revolutions." This book is also notable in that, without using a theatrical stage setting, Marsh exercises her flare for the dramatic by having the murder committed in an operating room which is shaped like an amphitheater. Marsh is very authentic regarding the technical medical elements of the plot, providing the reader with a brief course in anesthesia, surgery, and the injection of hyoscine.

Religious cults, those staples of Southern California mystery fiction, also figure prominently in Marsh's mysteries, beginning with her fourth book, *Death in Ecstasy* (1936). The reader knows less of the victim here than usual since she is murdered in the second chapter. Cara Quayne is a novice in the House of the Sacred Flame, a "frenzied" cult which has bilked many wealthy Londoners. She is poisoned when called to their altar to drink the sacral wine, another example of Marsh depicting murder in a quasi-theatrical setting. Alleyn's relationship with Bathgate, who was present in the "church" on a whim, has now evolved into a true Holmes-Watson one, with Bathgate even saying, ironically, "Chief Detective Inspector . . . I am your Watson and your worm. You may both sit and trample on me. I shall continue to offer you the fruits of my inexperience." Alleyn, speaking in Holmesian aphorisms, says of his method of detection, "I receive facts as a spider does flies."

By the time Marsh wrote *Vintage Murder* she had returned to New Zealand. It was dedicated to Allan Wilkie and his wife "in memory of a tour in New Zealand" and is about a theatrical company. Marsh, using her own experiences, masterfully describes the conflicts of such a company, as well as "the homely, knit-together feeling of back stage, the feeling that the troupe was a little world of its own, moving compactly about a larger world." Alleyn is in New Zealand on a rest cure, having recently recovered, like Marsh, from a major operation. He is recognized by one of the company and invited to one of their performances in the fictitious New Zealand city of Middleton and to a backstage party afterward. Here, murder is committed with a jereboam of champagne which has been rigged to drop from the flies and strike the victim. This was the first of

many unusual murder methods which Marsh would invent, and these became another of her trademarks, as was her penchant for long formal interrogations of suspects, which in *Vintage Murder* consume about two-thirds of the book. This is, nevertheless, one of Marsh's strongest mysteries, one in which the humor flows naturally from the characters, and the crime and its solution is a tour de force of plotting.

As Marsh's next book, *Artists in Crime*, begins, Alleyn is sailing back from New Zealand. Aboard ship he meets and falls in love with the British painter Agatha Troy, whose work he knows from a "one man" show the previous year in London. Once back in England he is coincidentally called to investigate the murder of a blackmailing model at the studio for aspiring artists that Troy (Marsh always has Alleyn call her by her last name) operates at her home in Buckinghamshire. Sonia Gluck was stabbed to death, while being placed in the posing position, by a knife unobtrusively protruding through a background drape. Because Marsh had studied painting, the entire book rings true with details about artists' work, including their daily routines and critiques.

Alleyn's love life is well integrated into the plot, and Marsh adds the complication of his being forced to consider Troy, who is uncertain of her feelings about him, as a suspect during his investigation. Both Alleyn and Troy are credible people, with their human strengths and weaknesses well limned. *Artists in Crime* has an intricate puzzle worthy of them.

By *Death in a White Tie* (1938) Marsh was reaching the top of her form. The background, London's social season, is not especially promising; Alleyn and his family are involved because his niece is "coming out." Yet, Marsh causes readers to get more involved than is usual in the classic detective story by creating a compelling victim. The book is perhaps most interesting in its presentation of the conflict between Troy and Alleyn, which at this point is still keeping them apart. In *Death in a White Tie* Troy emerges as a more fully developed character. She admits to a fear of the physical side of love. She also has "an absolute horror of capital punishment," a viewpoint seemingly incompatible with marriage to a policeman whose job it is to send murderers to the gallows.

Though frequently referred to as Marsh's best book, *Overture to Death* (1939) did not escape the critical wrath of Edmund Wilson in his famous essay, "Who Cares Who Killed Roger Ackroyd?" Wilson read the book because critic Bernard DeVoto had referred to Marsh's "excellent prose." Wilson's judgment: "It would be impossible I should think, for anyone with the faintest feeling for words, to describe the unappetizing sawdust which Miss Marsh has poured into her pages as 'excellent prose' or as prose at all except in the sense that distinguishes prose from verse."

Wilson's judgment is decidedly a minority opinion. Jacques Barzun and Wendell Hertig Taylor, agreeing it was Marsh's best work, praised its superb treatment of jealousy, as well as the excellent detection and depiction of life in a small village. Robert E. Briney called it "a superior example of the literate whodunit." Howard Haycraft and Ellery Queen included it on their definitive list of best mysteries.

Overture to Death is set in the Vale of Pen Cuckoo in the Dorset countryside, and the first quarter of the book has to do with village rivalries and jealousies which have arisen during preparations for an amateur theatrical performance to raise funds for the local parish house. Because the murder occurs late in the narrative, the reader has the feeling of knowing the village and its inhabitants. The problems an actress with some professional experience has in directing amateurs is well presented, again reflecting the author's own theatrical background.

The murder method is ingenious. A pistol has been placed in a piano in such a way that with the first use of the soft pedal in the Rachmaninoff "Prelude in C Sharp Minor" it will fire. Marsh even cleverly arranges things so it is not clear who was the intended victim. Seldom has Marsh presented Roderick Alleyn with better opportunities for his superior brand of detection, while still playing eminently fair with the reader in presenting all necessary clues. His character also continues to develop as his marriage to Troy becomes imminent and as clues to his private life are disclosed. The reader learns, for example, that he is a serious devotee of Sherlock Holmes, "of whom nobody shall make mock in my presence."

Death at the Bar (1940) continued Marsh's use of Sherlockian metaphor as Alleyn temporarily acquires a new "assistant," Colonel Brammington, chief constable of South Devon, who says to him, "I shall follow the example of all Watsons and offer blunder after blunder, inviting your compassionate scorn and remembering

the observation that logic is only the art of going wrong with confidence." That speech is a good example of the type of sophisticated language employed by Marsh. It also succinctly establishes the relationship that will exist between the Scotland Yard expert and the local squire who happens to be chief constable. Inspector Fox is also on hand, and this book emphasizes his relationship with Alleyn in ways that are both surprising and poignant.

Alleyn and Fox have been called to investigate a murder that occurred during a dart game at a seaside pub. There is prussic acid on the dart, but in a typical bit of Marshian misdirection, there is a question whether the dart was the murder weapon. Also, Marsh rings another of her clever variations on the theme of suspect likelihood. It is seldom possible to tell in one of her mysteries whether the murderer will be the most obvious suspect or the least likely–or someone in between. Only too many coincidences keep *Death at the Bar* from being Marsh at her best.

Prior to *Death of a Peer* (1940; republished as *Surfeit of Lampreys*, 1947), Marsh had used Roderick and Agatha Troy Alleyn to represent her views, especially with regard to the theater and art. Roberta Grey in this book is the first of many young heroines who, as important characters in her mysteries, would prove to be even more autobiographical. In this book she is Marsh's surrogate regarding her visit with the eccentric "Lamprey" family. "Her heart thumped violently for this was her first sight of England." Roberta finds it hard to believe she is really in London, the city of her dreams, until she sees the statue of Eros in Piccadilly Circus. The sheer noise of the city overwhelms the young girl from down under. There is also a fine sense of the city in the crisis before Munich, with the use of the phrase that was popular at the time, "It can't happen here." These words, also the title of a Sinclair Lewis novel, are used in connection with the world situation, as well as the grisly murder in this book. One of the Lampreys, Lord Wutherwood, is stabbed to death by a skewer which penetrates his eye and brain; he is found alone in the "lift" (elevator) at the family mansion when it has descended to the first floor.

Death and the Dancing Footman (1941) is Marsh's second "weekend houseparty murder" mystery, set in a country manor in Dorset. Jonathan Royal, fancying himself a student of human relationships, stage-manages his own version of a parlor game by deliberately inviting people who

Dust jacket for the first American edition of Marsh's 1939 novel, involving the murder of a pianist in an English country house (courtesy of Otto Penzler)

are enemies in business or rivals in love. Murder inevitably occurs, with a body discovered next to the radio set. Alleyn and Troy happen to be staying nearby, and he is the only Scotland Yard detective who can reach the scene of the crime, which has been isolated by a heavy snowstorm. There is an unusually large number of suspects, and Alleyn must sort through complex relationships and motives to identify a particulary clever killer. This mystery also involves a locked-room murder, unusual for Marsh.

Marsh returned to New Zealand before World War II and spent much of that time driving a Red Cross ambulance. She also wrote two wartime mysteries set there. In *Colour Scheme* (1943) Alleyn appears on the scene late in the book to investigate "leakage of information to the enemy." Although espionage and murder by a German spy are involved, Marsh manages to make an eccentric New Zealand family and a tem-

peramental actor, writing his memoirs, equally important to the plot. Marsh's picture of the actor, Geoffrey Gaunt, is illuminated with flashes of wit. Gaunt admits, "I adore being adored" and says his memoirs will be "the life story of a damn good actor who isn't going to spoil it with gestures of false modesty." At times the murder seems to take a back seat to Marsh's characterizations. Still, Alleyn solves the murder cleverly, through his detailed knowledge of Shakespeare's plays.

There is much more about New Zealand in this book than there was in *Vintage Murder*. The setting is Wai-ata-tapu, a health resort. Many Maoris are important characters; there is even a small glossary of Maori words in the text. *Colour Scheme* and Marsh's next book would stand out as two loving descriptions of a fresh and colorful setting. The background of World War II and the possibility of a Japanese invasion help to convey a sense of New Zealand at a specific time in history.

Alleyn is still engaged in counterespionage in New Zealand in *Died in the Wool* (1945), attempting to keep a secret formula for antiaircraft shells safe. He is forty-seven years old (he would never grow older in Marsh's chronology of his career), still marvelously self-disciplined. "Having left instructions with himself to wake at five, Alleyn did so." Once more, Marsh comes up with an unusual murder method, this time having her victim discovered compacted into a bale of wool. Alleyn solves the murder within twenty-four hours, though the culprit's identity is well hidden by Marsh among the limited group of suspects at a high-country sheep station. The pace is slower than usual, Marsh having eschewed much of her usual wittiness and sophistication in favor of creating an isolated location.

Marsh's first published short story, "I Can Find My Way Out," appeared in *Ellery Queen's Mystery Magazine* in August 1946. She had entered the story in the magazine's first short-story contest, which attracted a prestigious list of entrants. Her entry led to correspondence with its editor, Frederic Dannay, during the course of which she wrote, "I know of no Australasian writer of crime shorts of any distinction." In announcing she had won third prize in the contest, and introducing her story with a brief history of mystery fiction in Australia and New Zealand, Dannay pointed out that this was no longer true. "I Can Find My Way Out" concerns the opening night of a play with the same title at London's Jupiter Theatre. Telling it largely from the viewpoint of its play-

*Marsh with Allan Wilkie, actor-manager of the English Shake-
speare Company, the company she toured with for two years
(courtesy of the Estate of Ngaio Marsh)*

wright, Anthony Gill, Marsh conveys first night
nerves, sketches an entire theatrical company,
and presents a satisfying mystery for Roderick
Alleyn to solve–all in the space of twenty magazine pages.

Final Curtain (1947) is another mystery concerning a large and eccentric family, but it is also
noteworthy for the reunion of Alleyn and Troy
after a separation of over three years. While
Alleyn was a counterspy (and solving murders)
for the Special Branch in New Zealand, Troy did
pictorial surveys for the army. Now they have to
become acquainted again, and Marsh paints their
reunion and its consummation with what Barzun
and Taylor called "a discreet subtlety soon to be
forgotten in the rush to explicit sexuality by inferior writers."

Alleyn has joined Troy at Ancreton, a mansion whose rooms are named for famous actors
and actresses, such as Sarah Bernhardt, Sarah Sid-
dons, Ellen Terry, David Garrick, and Henry Irving. It is the home of Sir Henry Ancred, "the
Grand Old Man of the British Stage," and Troy
has been commissioned to paint him in Macbeth
costume for his seventy-fifth birthday. Gathered
around are the patriarch's actress daughters,
theater-manager son, and stage-designer grandson, as well as his young chorus-girl fiancée.
With the prospect of his leaving the estate to the
last named, there is ample motive for murder,
and Alleyn is fortuitously on the scene when it occurs. The plotting is skillful, and the British
scene is presented with freshness and vigor.

Though it was first published in *Ellery
Queen's Mystery Magazine* for January 1948,
"Death on the Air" was actually written in the
late 1930s and was sent to Frederic Dannay to set
the record straight after Marsh read that "I Can
Find My Way Out" was the first Roderick Alleyn
short story. Tightly plotted, this story involves
the Christmas Day murder of a man (like the victim in *Death and the Dancing Footman*) while he is listening to the radio.

Like many other series detectives, Alleyn is
destined to encounter murder wherever he goes,
even when off duty. In *Swing, Brother, Swing*
(1949; republished as *A Wreath for Rivera*) he and
Troy (now pregnant) are attending the Metro-
nome, a London nightclub. Rivera, a pianist-
accordionist, is murdered while performing his
act. He is shot with what was supposed to have
been a harmless trick revolver. One of Marsh's
lesser works, *Swing, Brother, Swing* is weakened by
the irritating nature of some of the characters,
who include jazz musicians, whining Communists, and an insufferable peer, Lord Bagott, member of still another large, eccentric family. Virtually the only bearable characters are the Alleyns
and Carlisle Wayne, a young woman newly arrived in England but already "the family's favorite confidante."

When she wrote *Opening Night* (1951; republished as *Night at the Vulcan*), Marsh was busy directing stage performances by young theater groups,
and, indeed, she dedicated this book "to the Management and Company of the New Zealand Student Players of 1949 in love and gratitude." Fittingly, the book is a stage mystery with the
archetypal Marsh stand-in, Martyn Trane, a
young actress from New Zealand who is in grave
danger of starving in London until she secures a
part in a show called *Thus to Revisit*. Marsh is excellent in her rehearsal scenes and even better in portraying the company's opening night anxiety, espe-

cially that of Martyn whose own jitters parallel those Marsh described in her autobiography regarding her own acting career. Soon a murder occurs, and once again Alleyn is trodding the boards to solve it. To do so he must memorize the play so that he knows exactly where each member of the cast and crew was during the critical time.

As with *Overture to Death,* there was a wide difference of opinion regarding *Opening Night.* Anthony Boucher, writing in the *New York Times Book Review* (2 December 1951), found it to be a "wonderfully warm and vivid novel of the theater, probably Marsh's best to date." A most interesting review came from Julian Symons who, dissatisfied over the balance Marsh had reached between novels of character and detective puzzles, said in his *Bloody Murder* (1985): "The first half gives a brilliant picture of the intrigues taking place before the opening of a new play. All this is, as it should be, preparation for the murder that is to take place, and after the murder we hope that the book will remain in the same key and that the problems will be resolved as they began, in terms of character. To our disappointment, however, Marsh takes refuge from real emotional problems in the official investigation and interrogation of suspects. The temperature is lowered; the mood has been lost."

Spinsters in Jeopardy (1953) is an atypical Marsh book because it is primarily a thriller. The three Alleyns (though Troy was pregnant only four years ago, Marsh has used literary license and produced as the Alleyn offspring a precocious six-year-old named Ricky) are in the South of France. Roderick is combining an assignment with a family holiday on the Riviera. When Ricky is kidnapped, Alleyn is plunged into a cloak-and-dagger adventure which makes use of subjects Marsh had previously dealt with and was to use again: the international drug trade and a religious cult. Here, it is one whose ceremonies are based on the "Book of Ra" and are described by Marsh as "unbridled Phallicism."

In *Scales of Justice* (1955) Marsh returned to rural England and to the classic puzzle. The setting is a British village named Swevenings which contains houses called Nunspardon Manor, Jacob's Cottage, and Hammer Farm. Trout fishing, a popular English sport, is well integrated into the mystery, with a peer found murdered near a stream. Even the title refers to the theory that "the scales of no two trout are alike . . . in the sense that no two sets of finger prints corre-

spond." Social relationships are well explored and provide an unusual basis for murder. There are many suspects, and Alleyn and Fox must spend several weeks sorting them out before coming up with a well-reasoned, if not totally believable, solution.

"It was glorious to be eighteen, a student at the West London School of Drama and possibly in love, not only with the whole world, but with one young man as well," says Camilla Campion in *Death of a Fool.* Set in rural England, it is about the annual Sword Wednesday of the Mardian family, a December ritual combining folklore, Morris dancing, and mumming plays. A horrible murder, by decapitation, occurs during the staging of a sword dance. Though the pace slackens after the exciting fatal dance, *Death of a Fool* has much to recommend it, including one of Marsh's more interesting supporting characters, a folklorist, Mrs. Anna Bünz.

The serial killer has been a staple of many mystery writers, but *Singing in the Shrouds* (1958) was Marsh's first and only attempt at this subgenre, and she brought it off successfully. Alleyn has been tracking a murderer who leaves flowers strewn on the faces and breasts of his victims and broken necklaces beside their bodies. He follows the suspected killer aboard the ship *Cape Farewell,* bound for South Africa. Typically, Marsh thinks in theatrical terms, remembering a play she had directed with considerable success, when she has Alleyn say to himself, "What is reality? With a psychiatrist, a priest, and a policeman [on the ship] . . . we've got the ingredients for a Pirandello play."

Alleyn identifies the murderer fairly early in his sea voyage, and the book reaches an unnatural plateau as he decides he must keep the identity a secret from his fellow passengers, just as Marsh withholds it from the reader. Still, the characterizations are perceptive and believable and the humor and atmosphere attractive so that one can accept some plot imperfections in this book.

Mary Bellamy in *False Scent* is the female equivalent of Henry Ancred of *Final Curtain.* She is a possessively jealous, fading actress who has gathered family and friends to celebrate a birthday (her fiftieth). Among those present are her husband who is not of the theater and says he has spent the greatest part of his life "among aliens," her playwright son, and Anelida Lee, an aspiring young actress. The depiction of the characters, decidedly three-dimensional, is stronger than the puzzle, though the murder method, poisoning by a perfume atomizer filled with a deadly pesticide, is properly unusual.

Hand in Glove (1962) could be taken as an attempt by Marsh at parody. After all, murder takes place in a village called Little Codling, and the suspects, all members of local society, have names such as Percival Pyke Period, Lord and Lady Bantling, Bimbo Dodds, Alfred Belt, and Mary Ralston, nicknamed "Moppett." One of the more engaging characters is Nicola Maitland Mayne, who, though not directly involved in the theater, is connected to people who are. She is a friend of the Alleyns and was painted on her twenty-first birthday by Troy. *Hand in Glove* never becomes mere satire, not even when the local police call in Scotland Yard, giving clichés about their being understaffed and busy. The book has too much gentle wit to go with a narrative and a solution which are both smooth and satisfying.

An unjustifiably neglected book in the Marsh oeuvre is *Dead Water* (1963) which was dismissed by Barzun and Taylor as "disappointing," stating that they had found the murderer "fairly obvious." The setting, well realized, is Portcarrow's Island in Cornwall, site of a healing spring where a miracle allegedly occurred and now is the scene of a festival. (Boucher, writing in the January 1964 issue of *Ellery Queen's Mystery Magazine,* called the setting "a cut-rate Lourdes.") There are several murders, and then the island is cut off by flood and storm, adding more suspense and action than usual in Marsh. She has gathered an interesting, albeit familiar, group of characters, including Miss Emily Pride, suzeraine of the island, the Reverend and Mrs. Adrian Carstairs, and Maj. Keith Barrimore. There is also the usual Marsh stand-in, Jenny Williams, a young New Zealander in England to do postgraduate research who has taken a job as schoolmistress on the island to augment her scholarship grant.

Not having published a true theater mystery in fifteen years, Marsh returned to her specialty in superlative form in *Killer Dolphin* (1966; republished as *Death at the Dolphin*). For the book's protagonist, Marsh created a male character from New Zealand, Peregrine Jay. He is in London, planning to restore a bombed-out theater, the Dolphin, to produce his own play, *The Glove,* about Shakespeare and his family. In a surprising opening Jay visits the long-closed theater and promptly falls through the stage into five feet of water. That fails to deter him, and, rescued, he

Marsh at home in Montpelier Walk, London (courtesy of the London Daily Express)

goes on with his project, saying, "If you belong to the theater, you belong utterly." The acting company is vividly presented, and there are some biting character portrayals, such as the obnoxious child actor, Trevor Vere, and his stage mother. Due to his knowledge of the theater, Alleyn is regarded by Scotland Yard as "something of an expert on the species." Because the murder occurs relatively late in the book, Alleyn is not as prominent a character as usual, but he is as engaging and sympathetic a sleuth as ever when called in.

While *Clutch of Constables* (1968) is not Marsh's best book, it certainly is her most cleverly titled, with its double reference to police officers and the British painter John Constable. Through what Alleyn concedes is "an outlandish coincidence," he and Troy work on the same case independently. He is in the United States to set up a joint plan of action to combat a successful international art forger and drug distributor, known as "The Jampot." Troy, taking a boat trip on the canals of England, paints and keeps her husband informed by letter of the oddly assorted group who are her companions. When one of them is murdered, she undertakes amateur detection for the first time in their marriage.

It becomes apparent to Alleyn when he returns to England that they have been investigating along parallel lines. There is an affectingly written section in which the seemingly cold Roderick shows his humanity when he says, on seeing Troy again, "I wonder how rare it is for a man's heart to behave as mine does at the unexpected sight of his wife."

Marsh did not write of political rebellion but used drugs and sex in the 1960s and 1970s to bring her books (and Roderick Alleyn) up to date. *When in Rome* (1970) again has Alleyn involved in international crime; he is in Rome to try to catch a mastermind in the drug rackets in what Newgate Callendar called a "blackmail-cum-sex case" (*New York Times Book Review*, 7 March 1971). Alleyn is traveling incognito on a tour in Rome, and drugs are freely used by his fellow tourists. Sex is inserted into the plot during the group's visit to a nightclub and then to a private show, described by the Italian guide as "Keenky Keeks." Alleyn's typically understated reaction to the evening is summed up in one word, "Infamous." An apparent beacon of normality in the tour group is Sophy Jason, the witty character who is a writer of children's books. (Marsh, who has the identical number of letters in her name as Jason, had written a play for juveniles during the 1960s.)

Murders take place in an ancient Roman basilica, apparently patterned after San Clemente's Church, and Alleyn solves the case in a finish with plausible deduction but also more physical action than usual. Though Callendar, who had just become the mystery critic for the *New York Times Book Review*, found the work "too predictable," he later wrote that Marsh "writes better than Christie," a comment that has been advertised by her publishers ever since.

In *Tied Up in Tinsel* (1972) Alleyn returns from an extradition case in Australia to join Troy at a country house, Halberds Manor, where she is painting the portrait of Hilary Bill-Talsman. Alleyn is in time for a very theatrical Christmas party, with traditional Druid elements, which ends in murder. Bill-Talsman is an especially repellent host who employs a houseful of paroled murderers as his servants and makes Alleyn jealous through his unwanted attentions to Troy.

The solution to *Tied Up in Tinsel* is marred by the very unlikely motivation of the murderer. Many other things rescue it, however, especially the stunning, albeit unsympathetic, character portrayals. It is a book best viewed from Troy's perspective as a painter since she sees the characters as people to be placed on a canvas. Though the case is a traditional weekend party mystery, interesting elements of the procedural creep in, including use of police slang, such as "keeping obbo," the expression for an observation or stakeout. Marsh also shows a fine ear for modern argot: trendy words like "scene"; the frequent use of "you know"; and "liase" used as a verb.

In its March 1973 issue *Ellery Queen's Mystery Magazine* published a third, and last, Roderick Alleyn short story, "Chapter and Verse," one which was unearthed as a result of further correspondence between Marsh and Fredric Dannay. It has an intriguing opening as Timothy Bates, a bookseller who met Alleyn in New Zealand, calls on the Alleyns in London, bearing an old rare Bible inscribed with the name of the village in Kent, Little Copplestone, in which they have a second residence. Also inscribed in the Bible are the names of an eighteenth-century family, but investigation shows they never lived in the village. Alleyn cleverly solves what comes as close to being a historical mystery as anything Marsh ever wrote.

Marsh's only non-Alleyn mystery, a short story, was published in *Ellery Queen's Mystery Magazine* for December 1974. "A Fool About Money" is a relatively minor tale; yet, it is a nicely told, nonviolent mystery about Hersey Hancock and her unsettling New Zealand train trip from Christchurch to Dunedin and the stranger who is her companion. The journey, one which Marsh took many times, is well described, especially the frantic queuing up for refreshments during the brief stops at stations on the way.

Marsh continued her efforts to keep up to date in *Black as He's Painted* (1974) with its insights into emerging African states. Bartholomew Opala, the despotic president of fictional "Ng'ombwana," is on a goodwill visit to London and under threat of assassination. Opala (nicknamed "the Boomer") was with Alleyn at Oxford, and the latter is assigned to his security. A modern version of the traditional house party occurs when the guests at a diplomatic reception at Ng'ombwana's London embassy include many with motives to kill Opala. Predictably, a murder does occur, with an unusual weapon, a feathered tribal spear.

While applauding Marsh's use of characters not often found in the mystery, one wishes that

Marsh had presented them in a tighter detective story. Still, the ironic ending is very satisfactory, and the book offers further insights into relations between Alleyn and Troy, who is asked to paint Opala's portrait while he is in London. Alleyn, placing Troy's career above his own, says, "If ever my job looks like so much as coming between one dab of her brush and the surface of her canvas, I'll chuck it and set up a prep school for detectives."

A grown-up Ricky Alleyn, last heard from more than two decades before, returns in *Last Ditch* (1977). He is now a novelist living on one of the British Channel islands, off the coast of France, while working on a book. He becomes involved with the eccentric Pharamond family, one which would have fit perfectly into Marsh's earlier novels; he also falls in love. Roderick Alleyn eventually appears, albeit late in the book, when Ricky becomes immersed in a plot that features murder and the omnipresent international drug trade.

Almost as if the title were prophetic, *Grave Mistake* (1978) stands as probably Marsh's poorest book, one containing relatively little action, either physical or cerebral. Even the setting, Upper Quintern in Kent, is not as well realized as similar British villages in past novels. At times, it is difficult to know whether to take Marsh seriously in this book. She has a gardener named Gardener and a couple named Jobbins who work at odd jobs. Police jargon is again used, but it appears to have been inserted for comic effect, as when one detective, inquiring about fingerprints, talks about "the dibs on the dabs." The best thing about *Grave Mistake* is the murder scene, Greengages Hotel, "a sumptuous sanctuary for super-rich hypochondriacs." Incidentally, there is a Marsh surrogate, Verity Preston, a playwright with a hit currently at the Dolphin Theatre.

For Marsh *Photo-Finish* marked a return both to New Zealand and to better form. It showed her classic puzzle roots in the Golden Age, yet the Mafia, drugs, a Maria Callas-type soprano, and a group of sensational journalists make this novel contemporary, too. Again, one of Troy's painting commissions is used as the excuse for Roderick to be on the scene when a murder takes place. Troy has been commissioned to paint Isabella Sommita, who is giving an operatic performance in the private theater at her luxurious island lodge in the middle of a lake on New Zealand's South Island. When, after a murder, the island is isolated by a severe storm (a throw-back to *Dead Water*), Alleyn takes charge, though he has no official authority. Searching for clues, he says, "When all likely places have been fruitlessly explored, begin on the unlikely and carry on into the preposterous." Marsh spent her last years in New Zealand, and *Photo-Finish* captures much of the country, including areas that retain their primeval wilderness.

Many mystery writers, including Agatha Christie, Erle Stanley Gardner, and Ellery Queen, suffered a decline in their later writings. Marsh's last work, the posthumously published *Light Thickens*, was one of her strongest. Only a slightly obvious murderer and motivation that is a bit farfetched prevents it from being her best book. Never did she do a better job of integrating a theatrical performance into one of her mysteries.

Peregrine Jay is back, staging a new performance of *Macbeth* at the Dolphin. The book traces it from casting, through rehearsals, opening night, a series of macabre practical jokes, and, finally, to murder on stage. Actors' superstitions are essential to the plot (*Macbeth* is a play which especially breeds superstitious feelings among actors, with its possibilities for accident, and the actors in Jay's company follow a long-standing theatrical tradition in not calling it by name, referring to it merely as "the Scot's play"). As one who knows firsthand, Marsh acutely explains this seemingly irrational behavior: "In that most hazardous profession where so many mischances can occur, when so much hangs in the precarious balance on opening night, when five weeks' preparation may turn to ashes or blaze for years, there is a fertile soil indeed for superstition to take root and flourish." Using an apposite analogy to a sea voyage, she describes the company coming together to start, with the goal of a successful production in sight. The company is especially interesting, including a trouble-making leftist who is the union representative and also a member of the Red Fellowship, which Inspector Fox calls "some potty little way-out group." Marsh has the actor profess to see *Macbeth* as "an antiheroic exposure of the bourgeois way of life." The company also includes Rangi, a New Zealand male, who plays one of the three witches and wears a tiki around his neck because he is "Maori through and through."

Though his appearance in *Light Thickens* is delayed, Alleyn quickly makes up for lost time. (Actually, he had been in the audience on opening night, but he was unable to appreciate the performance because his responsibility was security for royalty in attendance.) When he returns two weeks later to see the show, murder takes place. Because knowledge of *Macbeth* is essential to solving the murder and since it is a play Alleyn knows by heart, the mystery is one which few others at Scotland Yard could solve.

While working within the conventions of the classic detective puzzle, Marsh adapted them to her own interests and style. Though her work inevitably bore some resemblances to Sayers and Margery Allingham, who had preceded her, it was sufficiently original that discerning readers found the typical Marsh milieu to be unique. Though she shall always be thought of in terms of murders taking place in theatrical settings, she also brought her standards of well-crafted dialogue, credible characterization, original methods of murder, and fair solutions to other settings, including the seldom-used New Zealand locale. Her series character was one of the most well known, but his creator was not satisfied to allow him to remain merely as another gentleman-detective. As a result, Marsh's Roderick Alleyn was a subtle step in the direction of more authentic policemen, using the procedures that are found in actual criminal investigation. Beginning with *Killer Dolphin* in 1966, she was one of the few mystery writers to regularly appear on the best-seller lists, and her relatively infrequent (because of her theatrical activities) mysteries were eagerly awaited. Even after her death, virtually all of her novels remain available in the English-speaking world through paperback reprints.

Interview:

John Ball, "A Visit with Dame Ngaio Marsh," *Mystery*, 3 (July 1981): 23-25.

References:

Earl F. Bargainnier, "Ngaio Marsh," in *10 Women of Mystery*, edited by Bargainnier (Bowling Green, Ohio: Bowling Green University Popular Press, 1981), pp. 78-105;

Bargainnier, "Ngaio Marsh's 'Theatrical' Murders," *Armchair Detective*, 10 (April 1977): 175-181;

Bargainnier, "Roderick Alleyn: Ngaio Marsh's Oxonian Superintendent," *Armchair Detective*, 11 (January 1978): 63-71;

Jacques Barzun and Wendell Hertig Taylor, Preface to *A Wreath for Rivera* in *A Book of Prefaces to Fifty Classics of Crime Fiction 1900-1950* (New York: Garland, 1976), pp. 83-84;

Anthony Boucher, Introduction to *The Bride of Death* (New York: Mercury, 1955);

Allan J. Dooley and Linda J. Dooley, "Rereading Ngaio Marsh," in *Art in Crime Writing: Essays on Detective Fiction*, edited by Bernard Benstock (New York: St. Martin's Press, 1983), pp. 33-48;

LeRoy Panek, "Ngaio Marsh," in his *Watteau's Shepherds: The Detective Novel in Britain 1914-1940* (Bowling Green, Ohio: Bowling Green University Popular Press, 1979), pp. 185-197;

Julian Symons, *Bloody Murder* (New York: Viking, 1985).

Papers:

Major collections of Marsh's papers are located at the Mugar Memorial Library, Boston University, and the Alexander Turnbull Library, Wellington, New Zealand.

W. Somerset Maugham

(25 January 1874-16 December 1965)

Frank Occhiogrosso
Drew University

See also the Maugham entries in *DLB 10: Modern British Dramatists, 1900-1945* and *DLB 36: British Novelists, 1890-1929: Modernists.*

BOOKS: *Liza of Lambeth* (London: Unwin, 1897; revised, 1904; New York: Doran, 1921);

The Making of a Saint (Boston: Page, 1898; London: Unwin, 1898);

Orientations (London: Unwin, 1899);

The Hero (London: Hutchinson, 1901);

Mrs. Craddock (London: Heinemann, 1902; New York: Doran, 1920);

A Man of Honour: A Play in Four Acts (London: Chapman & Hall, 1903; Chicago: Dramatic Publishing, 1912);

The Merry-Go-Round (London: Heinemann, 1904);

The Land of the Blessed Virgin: Sketches and Impressions in Andalusia (London: Heinemann, 1905; New York: Knopf, 1920);

The Bishop's Apron (London: Chapman & Hall, 1906);

The Explorer (London: Heinemann, 1907; New York: Baker & Taylor, 1909);

The Magician (London: Heinemann, 1908; New York: Duffield, 1909);

Lady Frederick: A Comedy in Three Acts (London: Heinemann, 1911; Chicago: Dramatic Publishing, 1912);

Jack Straw: A Farce in Three Acts (London: Heinemann, 1911; Chicago: Dramatic Publishing, 1912);

Mrs. Dot: A Farce in Three Acts (London: Heinemann, 1912; Chicago: Dramatic Publishing, 1912);

Penelope: A Comedy in Three Acts (London: Heinemann, 1912; Chicago: Dramatic Publishing, 1912);

The Explorer: A Melodrama in Four Acts (London: Heinemann, 1912; Chicago: Dramatic Publishing, 1912);

The Tenth Man: A Tragic Comedy in Three Acts (London: Heinemann, 1913; Chicago: Dramatic Publishing, 1913);

W. Somerset Maugham (photograph by Mark Gerson)

Landed Gentry: A Comedy in Four Acts (London: Heinemann, 1913; Chicago: Dramatic Publishing, 1913);

Smith: A Comedy in Four Acts (London: Heinemann, 1913; Chicago: Dramatic Publishing, 1913);

Of Human Bondage (New York: Doran, 1915; London: Heinemann, 1915);

The Moon and Sixpence (London: Heinemann, 1919; New York: Doran, 1919);

The Unknown: A Play in Three Acts (London: Heinemann, 1920; New York: Doran, 1920);

The Circle: A Comedy in Three Acts (London: Heinemann, 1921; New York: Doran, 1921);

The Trembling of a Leaf: Little Stories of the South Sea Islands (New York: Doran, 1921; London: Heinemann, 1921); republished as *Sadie Thompson: and Other Stories of the South Sea Islands* (London: Readers Library, 1928);

Caesar's Wife: A Comedy in Three Acts (London: Heinemann, 1922; New York: Doran, 1923);

East of Suez: A Play in Seven Scenes (London: Heinemann, 1922; New York: Doran, 1922);

The Land of Promise (London: Heinemann, 1922; New York: Doran, 1923);

On a Chinese Screen (New York: Doran, 1922; London: Heinemann, 1922);

Our Betters: A Comedy in Three Acts (London: Heinemann, 1923; New York: Doran, 1924);

Home and Beauty: A Farce in Three Acts (London: Heinemann, 1923);

The Unattainable: A Farce in Three Acts (London: Heinemann, 1923);

Loaves and Fishes: A Comedy in Four Acts (London: Heinemann, 1924);

The Painted Veil (New York: Doran, 1925; London: Heinemann, 1925);

The Casuarina Tree: Six Stories (London: Heinemann, 1926; New York: Doran, 1926); republished as *The Letter: Stories of Crime* (London: Detective Story Club/Collins, 1930);

The Constant Wife: A Comedy in Three Acts (New York: Doran, 1927; London: Heinemann, 1927);

The Letter: A Play in Three Acts (London: Heinemann, 1927; New York: Doran, 1927);

Ashenden; or The British Agent (London: Heinemann, 1928; Garden City, N.Y.: Doubleday, Doran, 1928);

The Sacred Flame: A Play in Three Acts (Garden City, N.Y.: Doubleday, Doran, 1928; London: Heinemann, 1929);

The Gentleman in the Parlour: A Record of a Journey from Rangoon to Haiphong (London: Heinemann, 1930; Garden City, N.Y.: Doubleday, Doran, 1930);

Cakes and Ale: Or the Skeleton in the Cupboard (London: Heinemann, 1930; Garden City, N.Y.: Doubleday, Doran, 1930);

The Bread-Winner: A Comedy in One Act (London: Heinemann, 1930; Garden City, N.Y.: Doubleday, Doran, 1931);

Dust jacket for the first British edition of Maugham's 1928 collection of short stories based on his experiences as a British espionage agent (courtesy of Otto Penzler)

Six Stories Written in the First Person Singular (Garden City, N.Y.: Doubleday, Doran, 1931; London: Heinemann, 1931);

The Book-Bag (Florence: Orioli, 1932);

The Narrow Corner (London: Heinemann, 1932; Garden City, N.Y.: Doubleday, Doran, 1932);

For Services Rendered: A Play in Three Acts (London: Heinemann, 1932; Garden City, N.Y.: Doubleday, Doran, 1933);

Ah King: Six Stories (London: Heinemann, 1933; Garden City, N.Y.: Doubleday, Doran, 1933);

Sheppey: A Play in Three Acts (London: Heinemann, 1933; Boston: Baker, 1949);

Don Fernando; or, Variations on Some Spanish Themes (London & Toronto: Heinemann, 1935; Garden City, N.Y.: Doubleday, Doran, 1935; revised edition, Melbourne, London & Toronto: Heinemann, 1950);

Cosmopolitans: Very Short Stories (Garden City, N.Y.: Doubleday, Doran, 1936; London & Toronto: Heinemann, 1936);

Six Comedies (New York: Garden City Publishing, 1937);

Theatre. A Novel (Garden City, N.Y.: Doubleday, Doran, 1937; London & Toronto: Heinemann, 1937);

The Summing Up (London & Toronto: Heinemann, 1938; Garden City, N.Y.: Doubleday, Doran, 1938);

Christmas Holiday (London & Toronto: Heinemann, 1939; Garden City, N.Y.: Doubleday, Doran, 1939);

France at War (London: Heinemann, 1940; New York: Doubleday, Doran, 1940);

Books and You (London & Toronto: Heinemann, 1940; New York: Doubleday, Doran, 1940);

The Mixture as Before (London & Toronto: Heinemann, 1940; New York: Doubleday, Doran, 1940);

Up at the Villa (New York: Doubleday, Doran, 1941; London & Toronto: Heinemann, 1941);

Strictly Personal (Garden City, N.Y.: Doubleday, Doran, 1941; London & Toronto: Heinemann, 1942);

The Hour Before the Dawn: A Novel (Garden City, N.Y.: Doubleday, Doran, 1942; Sydney & London: Angus & Robertson, 1945);

The Unconquered (New York: House of Books, 1944);

The Razor's Edge: A Novel (Garden City, N.Y.: Doubleday, Doran, 1944; London & Toronto: Heinemann, 1944);

Then and Now: A Novel (London & Toronto: Heinemann, 1946; Garden City, N.Y.: Doubleday, 1946);

Creatures of Circumstance (London & Toronto: Heinemann, 1947; Garden City, N.Y.: Doubleday, 1947);

Catalina: A Romance (Melbourne, London & Toronto: Heinemann, 1948; Garden City, N.Y.: Doubleday, 1948);

Great Novelists and Their Novels: Essays on the Ten Greatest Novels of the World, and the Men and Women Who Wrote Them (Philadelphia & Toronto: Winston, 1948); revised and enlarged as *Ten Novels and Their Authors* (Melbourne, London & Toronto: Heinemann, 1954); republished as *The Art of Fiction: An Introduc-*

tion to Ten Novels and Their Authors (Garden City, N.Y.: Doubleday, 1955);

A Writer's Notebook (Melbourne, London & Toronto: Heinemann, 1949; Garden City, N.Y.: Doubleday, 1949);

The Vagrant Mood: Six Essays (Melbourne, London & Toronto: Heinemann, 1952; Garden City, N.Y.: Doubleday, 1953);

The Noble Spaniard: A Comedy in Three Acts, adapted from Ernest Grenet-Dancourt's *Les Gaîtés du veuvage* (London: Evans Brothers, 1953);

Points of View (London, Melbourne & Toronto: Heinemann, 1958; Garden City, N.Y.: Doubleday, 1959);

Purely for My Pleasure (London, Melbourne & Toronto: Heinemann, 1962; Garden City, N.Y.: Doubleday, 1962).

Collection: Collected Edition, 35 volumes (London: Heinemann, 1931-1969).

Novelist, playwright, short-story writer, travel writer, autobiographer, and essayist, W. Somerset Maugham wrote only one collection of short stories that justifies his inclusion in any discussion of spy fiction: *Ashenden; or The British Agent* (1928). Statements by Eric Ambler, Graham Greene, and John le Carré (David Cornwell), among others, about that book's influence upon their writing of spy fiction testify to Maugham's importance to the development of that genre.

William Somerset Maugham was born in Paris in 1874 and lived the first ten years of his life there. His mother died in 1882. His father, a lawyer, died in 1884. At age ten he went to live with his clergyman uncle in Kent. His unhappy attendance at an English public school (the King's School in Canterbury), his liberating year of study abroad in Heidelberg (with his concomitant loss of religious faith), and his return to England to take up medical studies in London are all recounted in fictional form in his semi-autobiographical novel *Of Human Bondage* (1915). These events served in part to shape the character of a man who was sensitive and perceptive yet also timorous and withdrawn, an outside observer of life's experiences rather than one totally and passionately immersed in them. In this respect Maugham was like many of his fictional narrators and protagonists, among them his British agent Ashenden.

Financially Maugham was one of the most successful professional writers of all time, and that success enabled him eventually to buy the

John Gielgud (in background) and Peter Lorre (with hat) in a scene from the 1936 Hitchcock film The Secret Agent, *based in part on* Ashenden; or The British Agent.

Villa Mauresque, his fortresslike retreat on the French Riviera, where he entertained writers, statesmen, and members of fashionable society, but where he was also able to withdraw from the world (when he was not traveling). He died there in 1965 at the age of ninety-one.

During World War I Maugham was recruited by British intelligence and spent much of 1916 in Geneva as a British espionage agent. He also worked briefly the following year in Russia (his assignment was to try to prevent the Russian Revolution from happening). It was out of these experiences that the stories in *Ashenden; or The British Agent* came. No doubt the book's influence is due to the fact that it is based on firsthand experience (unlike much of the melodramatic fiction that preceded it). Maugham characterizes his espionage experience, in his preface to the book, as largely humdrum, thereby justifying imparting to the stories a low-key and resolutely antisensational, antiheroic quality. He says, "The work of an agent in the Intelligence Department is on the whole extremely monotonous. A lot of it is uncom-

monly useless. The material it offers for stories is scrappy and pointless; the author has himself to make it coherent, dramatic and probable." The drama that Maugham introduces, and which makes the work rank with his best fiction, is the drama of human beings realistically and compassionately observed as, for the most part, creatures of circumstance rather than as extraordinarily efficacious heroes or fantastically depraved villains.

Ashenden; or The British Agent consistently rejects the conventions and clichés of the spy genre of the time. There are no shoot-outs, no chase scenes, no cloak-and-dagger intrigue in which the clever spy plays cat and mouse with the fiendishly clever counterspy. There are no double agents in these stories. Instead there are situations like that in which the killer hired by British intelligence, a fantastic character called the Hairless Mexican (who would not be out of place in the pages of John Buchan, Sapper [H. C. McNeile], or E. Phillips Oppenheim), boasts of his extraordinary prowess but is ultimately discov-

Maugham with his wife, Gwendolen (Syndication International)

ered, to Ashenden's horror, to have killed the wrong man. In "Giulia Lazzari" a woman is coerced by British intelligence to betray into their hands her lover, an anti-British Indian agitator, only to amaze Ashenden when at the story's end, learning of her lover's suicide, she asks if she can have back the watch she gave him—it cost her twelve pounds and she needs the money. Or in "The Traitor" Ashenden is instrumental in bringing about the capture of a British subject who has turned German spy; but much of the story is devoted to Ashenden's ambivalent feelings about destroying a human being with interesting and appealing qualities, and also with depicting the agonies suffered by the doomed traitor's wife as she slowly realizes he has been delivered over to execution. Repeatedly in these stories the human dimen-

sion receives the major stress, the actual espionage (if there is any) being only the frame upon which that human story is woven.

"Miss King" probably illustrates better than any of the other stories Maugham's resolute refusal to let the melodramatic and sensational dominate in these stories. It is about the very failure of melodramatic intrigue to materialize. Ashenden wonders what conspiratorial meaning can attach to the simultaneous presence at his hotel of the Baroness de Higgins and the Count von Holzminden, both suspected German agents, and the mysterious Egyptian Prince Ali, into whose room Ashenden is lured ostensibly to make a fourth at bridge. These fantastic characters quickly fade, however, as readers realize that the real center of the story is Miss King, the old

Maugham sitting for a portrait by Gerald Kelly, his longtime friend, whom he met in Meudon, 1903 (courtesy of Kentish Gazette)

British governess of the prince's daughters. But when Ashenden is summoned in the middle of the night to the dying old woman's bedside, he still believes intrigue is at the heart of it: the old woman, he thinks, knowing he is a spy, wishes to impart some significant piece of secret intelligence to him. What occurs instead is something both less sensational and more movingly human: with her dying breath the wizened Miss King, who has not seen her native land for many years, whispers in Ashenden's ear the word *England*. The story, ultimately, is not about espionage or intrigue at all but, rather, about a lonely old woman's sad longing in exile.

The character of Ashenden is recognizably human, too, looking, not surprisingly, a lot like Maugham himself (Maugham would use the name Ashenden again, years later, for the semi-autobiographical narrator-protagonist of *Cakes and Ale: Or the Skeleton in the Cupboard*, 1930). Like Maugham he is a successful novelist and playwright; like Maugham also he is a shy and somewhat withdrawn man, who prefers to stand a little to one side of life and watch rather than plunge into its rushing mainstream. But

Ashenden also perceptively observes, as his creator no doubt also did, some of the dehumanizing aspects, and also some of the supreme moral folly, of the spying game and those who control it. He recognizes the ruthlessness of "R.," his control (a character of whom both Ian Fleming and John le Carré would later make much use). He likewise recognizes the basic decency of some of the villains he pursues, men whose only difference from Ashenden and R. is that they are on the other side. About Chandra Lal, the dangerous Indian agitator, Ashenden says to R.:

> "I don't suppose he'd use bombs if he could command a few batteries and half a dozen battalions. He uses what weapons he can. You can hardly blame him for that. After all, he's aiming at nothing for himself, is he? He's aiming at freedom for his country. On the face of it it looks as though he were justified in his actions. . . . I shall carry out your instructions, that's what I'm here for, but I see no harm in realizing that there's something to be admired and respected in him."

And later, Ashenden becomes involved in a plot to blow up a munitions factory in Austria, the positive result of which will be an undermining of the German war effort, but the drawback will be the death and mutilation of many innocent civilians in that factory. Ashenden says:

> It was not of course a thing that the big-wigs cared to have anything to do with. Though ready enough to profit by the activities of obscure agents of whom they had never heard, they shut their eyes to dirty work so that they could put their clean hands on their hearts and congratulate themselves that they had never done anything that was unbecoming to men of honour. . . . They were all like that. They desired the end, but hesitated at the means. They were willing to take advantage of an accomplished fact, but wanted to shift on to someone else the responsibility of bringing it about.

The element of moral ambiguity, which Ashenden's consciousness brings into the stories, is one of Maugham's greatest contributions to the genre of spy fiction. As Julian Symons observed, "Once the convention of the agent as hero had been questioned by Maugham, it collapsed, and from the mid-thirties onward the spy story and thriller became for British writers a vehicle through which to ask the questions about society which still could not easily be expressed in the detective story." Maugham's place as innovator in and shaper of the genre of spy fiction would therefore seem to be established.

Bibliographies:

Charles Saunders, *W. Somerset Maugham: An Annotated Bibliography of Writings about Him* (De Kalb: Northern Illinois University Press, 1970);

Raymond Toole Stott, *A Bibliography of the Works of W. Somerset Maugham,* revised and enlarged edition (London: Kay & Ward, 1973).

Biographies:

Karl G. Pfeiffer, *W. Somerset Maugham: A Candid Portrait* (New York: Norton, 1959);

Garson Kanin, *Remembering Mr. Maugham* (New York: Atheneum, 1966);

Robin Maugham, *Somerset and All the Maughams* (London: Longmans/Heinemann, 1966);

Beverly Nichols, *A Case of Human Bondage* (London: Secker & Warburg, 1966);

Frederick Raphael, *W. Somerset Maugham and His World* (London: Thames & Hudson, 1976);

Anthony Curtis, *Somerset Maugham* (London: Weidenfeld & Nicolson, 1977);

Robin Maugham, *Conversations with Willie: Recollections of W. Somerset Maugham* (London: W. H. Allen, 1978);

Ted Morgan, *Maugham* (New York: Simon & Schuster, 1980).

References:

Laurence Brander, *Somerset Maugham: A Guide* (Edinburgh: Oliver & Boyd, 1963);

Ivor Brown, *W. Somerset Maugham* (London: International Textbook, 1970);

Robert Lorin Calder, *W. Somerset Maugham and the Quest for Freedom* (London: Heinemann, 1972);

Richard A. Cordell, *Somerset Maugham, A Writer for All Seasons: A Biographical and Critical Study,* revised edition (Bloomington: Indiana University Press, 1969);

Anthony Curtis, *The Pattern of Maugham: A Critical Portrait* (New York: Taplinger, 1974);

Klaus W. Jonas, *The World of Somerset Maugham* (New York: British Book Centre, 1959);

Wilmon Menard, *The Two Worlds of Somerset Maugham* (Los Angeles: Sherbourne Press, 1965);

M. K. Naik, *W. Somerset Maugham* (Norman: University of Oklahoma Press, 1966);

F. W. Shropshire, "W. Somerset Maugham as a Mystery Writer," *Armchair Detective,* 14 (1981): 190-191;

Julian Symons, *Mortal Consequences* (New York: Schocken, 1973);

John Whitehead, " 'Whodunit' and Somerset Maugham," *Notes & Queries,* new series 21 (October 1974): 370.

Papers:

Maugham's papers are at the Humanities Research Center, University of Texas at Austin; the Berg Collection, New York Public Library; the Lilly Library, Indiana University; Stanford University; the Houghton Library, Harvard University; the Fales Collection, New York University; the Butler Library, Columbia University; the Olin Library, Cornell University; Beaverbrook Papers, House of Lords Records Office, London; and the University of Arkansas Library.

Herman Cyril McNeile
(Sapper)

(28 September 1888-14 August 1937)

Joan DelFattore
University of Delaware

BOOKS: *The Lieutenant and Others*, as Sapper (London & New York: Hodder & Stoughton, 1915);

Sergeant Michael Cassidy, R.E., as Sapper (London & New York: Hodder & Stoughton, 1915); republished as *Michael Cassidy, Sergeant* (New York: Doran, 1916);

Men, Women, and Guns, as Sapper (London: Hodder & Stoughton, 1916; New York: Doran, 1916);

No Man's Land, as Sapper (London & New York: Hodder & Stoughton, 1917; New York: Doran, 1917);

The Human Torch, as Sapper (London: Hodder & Stoughton, 1918; New York: Doran, 1918);

Mufti, as McNeile (London: Hodder & Stoughton, 1919; New York: Doran, 1919);

Bull-Dog Drummond: The Adventures of a Demobilized Officer Who Found Peace Dull, as McNeile (London: Hodder & Stoughton, 1920; New York: Doran, 1920);

The Man in Ratcatcher and Other Stories, as McNeile (London: Hodder & Stoughton, 1921; New York: Doran, 1921);

The Black Gang, as McNeile (London: Hodder & Stoughton, 1922; New York: Doran, 1922); as Sapper (London: Hodder & Stoughton, 1933);

The Dinner Club, as McNeile (London: Hodder & Stoughton, 1923; New York: Doran, 1923); as Sapper (Bath: Lythway, 1973);

Jim Maitland, as McNeile (London: Hodder & Stoughton, 1923; New York: Doran, 1924);

The Third Round, as McNeile (London: Hodder & Stoughton, 1924); republished as *Bulldog Drummond's Third Round* (New York: Doran, 1924);

Bulldog Drummond: A Play in Four Acts, by McNeile (as Sapper) and Gerald du Maurier (London & New York: French, 1925);

Out of the Blue, as Sapper (London: Hodder & Stoughton, 1925); as McNeile (New York: Doran, 1925);

The Final Count, as Sapper (London: Hodder & Stoughton, 1926); as McNeile (New York: Doran, 1926);

Jim Brent, as Sapper (London: Hodder & Stoughton, 1926);

Word of Honour, as Sapper (London: Hodder & Stoughton, 1926); as McNeile (New York: Doran, 1926);

The Saving Clause, as Sapper (London: Hodder & Stoughton, 1927); as McNeile (New York: Doran, 1926);

When Carruthers Laughed, as McNeile (New York: Doran, 1927); as Sapper (London: Hodder & Stoughton, 1934);

The Female of the Species, as Sapper (London: Hodder & Stoughton, 1928); as McNeile (Garden City, N.Y.: Doubleday, Doran, 1928); republished as *Bulldog Drummond—And the Female of the Species*, as McNeile (New York: Sun Dial, 1943);

Temple Tower, as Sapper (London: Hodder & Stoughton, 1929); as McNeile (Garden City, N.Y.: Doubleday, Doran, 1929);

Tiny Carteret, as Sapper (London: Hodder & Stoughton, 1930); as McNeile (Garden City, N.Y.: Doubleday, Doran, 1930);

Sapper's War Stories, as Sapper (London: Hodder & Stoughton, 1930);

The Finger of Fate, as Sapper (London: Hodder & Stoughton, 1930); as McNeile (Garden City, N.Y.: Doubleday, Doran, 1931);

The Island of Terror, as Sapper (London: Hodder & Stoughton, 1931); republished as *Guardians of the Treasure*, as McNeile (Garden City, N.Y.: Doubleday, Doran, 1931);

The Return of Bull-Dog Drummond, as Sapper (London: Hodder & Stoughton, 1932); republished as *Bulldog Drummond Returns*, as McNeile (Garden City, N.Y.: Doubleday, Doran, 1932);

Knock-Out, as Sapper (London: Hodder & Stoughton, 1933); republished as *Bulldog*

H. C. McNeile (courtesy of Otto Penzler)

Drummond Strikes Back, as McNeile (Garden City, N.Y.: Doubleday, Doran, 1933);

Ronald Standish, as Sapper (London: Hodder & Stoughton, 1933);

51 Stories, as Sapper (London: Hodder & Stoughton, 1934);

Bulldog Drummond at Bay, as Sapper (London: Hodder & Stoughton, 1935); as McNeile (Garden City, N.Y.: Doubleday, Doran, 1935);

Ask for Ronald Standish, as Sapper (London: Hodder & Stoughton, 1936);

Challenge, as Sapper (London: Hodder & Stoughton, 1937); as McNeile (Garden City, N.Y.: Doubleday, Doran, 1937).

PLAY PRODUCTIONS: *Bulldog Drummond*, by McNeile (as Sapper) and Gerald du Maurier, London, Wyndham's Theatre, 29 March 1921;

The Way Out, by McNeile (as Sapper), London, Comedy Theatre, 23 January 1930;

Bulldog Drummond Hits Out, by McNeile (as Sapper) and Gerard Fairlie, London, 1937.

MOTION PICTURE: *Bulldog Jack* (*Alias Bulldog Drummond*), screenplay by McNeile, Gerard Fairlie, J. O. C. Orton, and others, Gaumont-British, 1935.

OTHER: William S. Porter, *The Best of O. Henry*, edited by McNeile (London: Hodder & Stoughton, 1929).

Herman Cyril McNeile was born 28 September 1888 in Bodmin, Cornwall, England, the son of Malcolm McNeile and Christiana Mary Sloggett. His father was a captain in the Royal Navy and, later, governor of the Royal Naval Prison at Lewes. McNeile was educated at Cheltenham College in Gloucestershire and at the Royal Military Academy at Woolwich. At the age of nineteen he joined the Royal Engineers, from whose nickname (the sappers) he later derived his pseudonym. McNeile was promoted to the rank of captain in 1914, served with distinction in World War I, and was awarded the Military Cross. In 1914 he married Violet Baird Douglas, the daughter of a lieutenant colonel in the Cameron Highlanders. They had two sons. McNeile retired from the Army in 1919 with the rank of lieutenant colonel. He and his family moved to Sussex in 1922, where McNeile spent most of the rest of his life, and the Sussex countryside served as the background for many of his stories.

During World War I McNeile wrote several volumes of short stories, most of them concerning the war. Shortly afterward he published his first novel, *Mufti* (1919), which is chiefly notable for its description of a type of Englishman which McNeile called the Breed. Members of the Breed are patriotic and loyal above all else; they are physically and morally intrepid, and usually endowed with great strength; they are interested in sports rather than in the arts; and although they are capable of conceiving plans of action to outwit England's enemies, they are in no way intellectual. Their private incomes make it possible for them to spend their time in the pursuit of adventure, particularly adventure of the type which involves the righting of wrongs and the defense of England.

The attitudes expressed in McNeile's stories are intensely conservative by modern standards. He advocates the use of extreme physical force against those who endanger the morality, prosperity, and stability which he defines as the British way of life; any McNeile character who threatens any aspect of the established order is either a traitorous Englishman for whom no punishment is too severe, or, more often, a warmongering foreigner from whom nothing better is to be expected. Although McNeile's ethnic prejudices would provoke howls of ridicule or of outrage if he were writing today, they were an accepted characteristic of his age and class and an accepted convention of the thriller literature of that period. In McNeile's stories, as in thrillers written by other authors, these prejudices are expressed by means of double adjectives: "homicidal, alien Jews"; "filthy, murdering Boche"; and "stinking, cowardly Bolshevik." In addition to the Jews, Germans, and Russians who seek to subvert world order by inciting wars for monetary gain or by preaching socialism to the working classes, the population of McNeile's world includes "niggers," "wogs," and "dagoes"; but these are minor villains who seldom rate more than one adjective. McNeile's most common generic terms for those who violate his Public School sense of morality, patriotism, and order are "swine," "scum," and "vermin"; or, in extreme cases, "the dregs of the universe." Over and over in McNeile's stories, members of the Breed strike down these "swine" without mercy and without compunction but always with absolute justification.

By far the best-known member of the Breed, as it is represented in McNeile's books, is Hugh Bull-Dog (later *Bulldog*) Drummond. Drummond first appeared in short-story form in the *Strand Magazine* as a detective rather than as the two-fisted knight-errant he later became, but that characterization was not successful, and those stories were not published in book form. The hero, introduced in McNeile's second novel, *Bull-Dog Drummond: The Adventures of a Demobilized Officer Who Found Peace Dull* (1920), is a composite of a friend of McNeile's, Gerard Fairlie; McNeile himself; and McNeile's idealized conception of an English gentleman. Although Drummond is the hero of only about one-third of McNeile's books, McNeile is remembered chiefly as Drummond's creator.

The Bulldog Drummond books make no claim to literary excellence; neither the characters nor the plots in which they appear can by any standard be considered original, plausible, or well rounded. They are, however, good, solid thrillers. In *Bull-Dog Drummond*, for example, most of the action takes place in the villains' country house, which boasts a gorilla in the garden, a hooded cobra on the ground floor, an acid bath in the spare bedroom, and a neck-breaking device implanted in the fifth step of the front staircase. Drummond, of course, strangles the gorilla, foils the cobra, tosses one of the villains into the acid bath, and never forgets to duck on his way upstairs. He also rescues one old man from torture and another from blackmail, marries the heroine, and interferes with the conspiracy hatched by the archvillains Carl and Irma Peterson, who survive to conceive fresh schemes for Drummond to defeat in later books.

McNeile adapted his novel *Bull-Dog Drummond* into a stage play, and he persuaded Gerald (later Sir Gerald) du Maurier, a noted British actor, to read the script. Du Maurier suggested a number of changes; in fact, McNeile later remarked on a radio broadcast that the only dialogue in the original script of which du Maurier approved was the butler's line, "Dinner

Dust jacket for the first edition of McNeile's 1933 novel about Bull-Dog Drummond (courtesy of Otto Penzler)

is served." (Remarks like these, which McNeile made frequently, should be taken with a grain of salt. One of the similarities between Drummond and his creator was their desire to avoid the appearance of being suspiciously intellectual. They succeeded admirably.) The play, entitled *Bulldog Drummond*, was produced at Wyndham's Theatre in London during the 1921-1922 season, with du Maurier in the title role; and, during the same season, in New York City. Both productions enjoyed considerable success. In 1922 the same story appeared on film as *Bulldog Drummond* (Hodkinson Pictures), starring Carlyle Blackwell. However, Drummond did not become a popular film character until Ronald Colman began playing the role seven years later.

McNeile's second Drummond novel, *The Black Gang* (1922), introduces the element of fascism. Drummond and his friends, all strongly built and in excellent physical condition, dress in black masks, hoods, and robes and take it upon themselves to inflict punishment upon those whom they regard as evildoers. Most of the minor villains are unwashed and cowardly, cringing and whining as the Black Gang kicks them downstairs or flogs them with a rhinoceros-hide whip. More dangerous villains are sent to an island off the coast of Mull, where they are kept in a quasi-socialistic concentration camp under the command of a beefy British former sergeant major. Everyone in the story, including the police but probably excepting the villains, considers this a very good joke. Drummond takes even sterner measures against a Bolshevik revolutionary who boasts of having helped to murder the Russian royal family and who has threatened the life of Drummond's wife, Phyllis. He ends up skewered to the wall with his own bayonet. Carl and Irma Peterson, who, as usual, are behind the trouble, escape, although Drummond spends some time throttling Carl before Phyllis intercedes. (Typically, McNeile does not trouble to explain why Drummond, whose wartime exploits included snapping the necks of several German sentries in one second each, should have taken several minutes to strangle Peterson.)

Although the Drummond series included many scenes of violence, Drummond himself is by no means a hard or unattractive character. His bullying is portrayed as a form of patriotism: as a member of the Breed he represents all right-thinking Englishmen when he takes direct and effective measures against warmongers, socialists, and other subverters of peace and prosperity. His friends worship him, and he is capable of both hearty humor and manly tenderness.

Even the archvillains, Carl and Irma Peterson, have their attractive side. They are intelligent, brave, and genuinely loyal to one another. As Richard Usborne observes, "Authors, unless they are careful, fall in love with their big villains. Sapper was always careless. Sapper came to love Carl Peterson dearly, and so did Drummond." Drummond never treats Peterson with the kind of summary justice that he and the Black Gang inflict on lesser villains. Their ongoing struggle is a duel, an affair of honor. For example, at the end of *The Third Round* (1924), Drummond loses an opportunity to kill Peterson outright or to turn him over to the law because he is determined to stage a hand-to-hand fight to the death on the glaciers outside the Petersons' hotel room in Montreux. The fight never takes place because the Petersons, who are less chivalrous but more practical than Drummond, escape the Swiss police by taking a motorboat across the lake to the French town of Evian-les-Bains. Drummond, ignorant of continental geography, has not anticipated this move, and the story ends with the triumphant Peterson sending Drummond a copy of *Our Little Tots' Primer of Geography*.

Despite the good humor and the grudging admiration which sometimes characterize Drummond's relationship with the Petersons, Drummond finally puts an end to Carl Peterson's villainy in *The Final Count* (1926). This story, which Colin Watson describes as "perhaps the most splendidly ridiculous of the entire canon" because of its wild improbabilities, ends with Drummond sprinkling Peterson with a poison with which Peterson himself has murdered several people and intended to murder several more. Irma Peterson, who claims to have been en rapport with Carl at the moment of his death, appears clothed in black to swear vengeance on Drummond. Beginning with *The Female of the Species* (1928) and *Temple Tower* (1929), she does her best to carry out her threat, usually by selling her services to international businessmen whose financial schemes require some highly organized criminal activity. Irma then sees to it that this activity is brought to Drummond's attention, hoping to wreak some terrible punishment on him as he becomes involved in her plots. Irma often attempts to catch Drummond by kidnapping Phyllis, whose incurable propensity for walking into traps became so notorious that it suggested the title for a lecture on thriller stories delivered by William Vivian Butler in 1979: "Good God! The Swine Have Got Phyllis!"

At about the time that he killed off Carl Peterson, McNeile put into book form his second series hero, Ronald Standish. Standish appeared in one story in *The Saving Clause* (1927) and in *Tiny Carteret* (1930); in two volumes of short stories, *Ronald Standish* (1933) and *Ask for Ronald Standish* (1936); and in the last three Drummond novels, *Knock-Out* (1933), *Bulldog Drummond at Bay* (1935), and *Challenge* (1937). In his short stories Standish is a detective of the Philo Vance type, taking cases which interest him but scorning the very mention of a salary. Standish resembles Sherlock Holmes in his approach to apparently insignificant clues and in his philosophy and diction, but the Standish stories are much less complex and much easier to solve than the Holmes stories. In the Drummond books Standish is a British Secret Service agent who is useful primarily because of his access to sources of information and because of his ability to decipher codes and puzzles. Although Standish sometimes takes the initiative in planning strategies because of his admittedly superior intellect, he is always captured or put out of action halfway through the story, leaving the spotlight on Drummond. In addition to Drummond and Standish, McNeile created several less important heroes, notably Jim Maitland, an athletic type who spends most of his time fighting for the British way of life in far-off and exotic places.

Dust jacket for the first British edition of McNeile's second volume of short stories featuring his series hero Ronald Standish (courtesy of Otto Penzler)

In 1930 McNeile returned to writing stage plays with *The Way Out*, and in 1935 he collaborated with J. O. C. Orton and Gerard Fairlie on a screenplay, *Bulldog Jack (Alias Bulldog Drummond)*. This film, which is in a sense a spoof of the more traditional Drummond films, features a Drummond sidekick, Jack, as a bungling playboy who tries to foil a jewel robbery from the British Museum. Two years later McNeile again collaborated with Fairlie, this time on a stage play, *Bulldog Drummond Hits Out*. The play was produced in London and Brighton in 1937.

Although he gave the impression of being a loud and hearty man, McNeile suffered from chronic poor health as a result of a war-related ill-ness which led to his death at the age of forty-eight. During the last months of his life he worked with Fairlie on the plot for a new Drummond novel, which Fairlie published as *Bulldog Drummond on Dartmoor* (1938). After McNeile's death at his home near Pulborough, Sussex, Fairlie continued to write Drummond stories until 1954, when changing values and interests on the part of the public caused him to abandon them. The last traditional Drummond film, *Calling Bulldog Drummond*, was made in 1951. Drummond has appeared since then only in significantly altered form. In the motion pictures *Deadlier Than the Male* (1967) and *Some Girls Do* (1971), Drummond is a James Bond-type agent surrounded by gadgets and girls. His last appearance was in 1974, when he was parodied in *Bullshot Crummond*, produced on Broadway by an English group called the Low Moan Spectacular.

References:

William Vivian Butler, *The Durable Desperadoes* (London: Macmillan, 1973);

Edward Connor, "The Twelve Bulldog Drummonds," *Films in Review*, 7 (October 1956);

Donald McCormick, *Who's Who in Spy Fiction* (New York: Taplinger, 1977);

Otto Penzler, ed., *The Private Lives of Private Eyes, Spies, Crime Fighters and Other Good Guys* (New York: Grosset & Dunlap, 1977);

Richard Usborne, *Clubland Heroes* (London: Constable, 1953);

Colin Watson, *Snobbery with Violence: Crime Stories and Their Audience* (London: Eyre & Spottiswoode, 1971).

A. A. Milne
(18 January 1882-31 January 1956)

LeRoy Panek
Western Maryland College

See also the Milne entry in *DLB 10: Modern British Dramatists, 1900-1945.*

BOOKS: *Lovers in London* (London: Rivers, 1905);

The Day's Play (London: Methuen, 1910; New York: Dutton, 1925);

The Holiday Round (London: Methuen, 1912; New York: Dutton, 1925);

Once a Week (London: Methuen, 1914; New York: Dutton, 1925);

Happy Days (New York: Doran, 1915);

Once on a Time (London: Hodder & Stoughton, 1917; New York & London: Putnam's, 1922);

First Plays (London: Chatto & Windus, 1919; New York: Knopf, 1919)–comprises *Wurzel-Flummery*, *The Lucky One*, *The Boy Comes Home*, *Belinda: An April Folly*, and *The Red Feathers*;

Not That It Matters (London: Methuen, 1919; New York: Dutton, 1920);

If I May (London: Methuen, 1920; New York: Dutton, 1921);

Mr. Pim (London: Hodder & Stoughton, 1921; New York: Doran, 1922);

Second Plays (London: Chatto & Windus, 1921; New York: Knopf, 1922)–comprises *Make-Believe*, *Mr. Pim Passes By*, *The Romantic Age*, and *The Stepmother;*

A. A. Milne

The Sunny Side (London: Methuen, 1921; New York: Dutton, 1922);

The Red House Mystery (London: Methuen, 1922; New York: Dutton, 1922);

Three Plays (New York: Putnam's, 1922; London: Chatto & Windus, 1923)–comprises *The Dover Road, The Truth about Blayds,* and *The Great Broxopp;*

The Artist: A Duologue (London & New York: French, 1923);

The Man in the Bowler Hat (London & New York: French, 1923);

Success (London: Chatto & Windus, 1923; New York: French, 1924);

When We Were Very Young (London: Methuen, 1924; New York: Dutton, 1924);

Ariadne, or Business First (London & New York: French, 1925);

For the Luncheon Interval: Cricket and Other Verses (London: Methuen, 1925; New York: Dutton, 1925);

To Have the Honour (London & New York: French, 1925);

Portrait of a Gentleman in Slippers (London & New York: French, 1926);

Winnie-the-Pooh (London: Methuen, 1926; New York: Dutton, 1926);

Now We Are Six (London: Methuen, 1927; New York: Dutton, 1927);

The House at Pooh Corner (London: Methuen, 1928; New York: Dutton, 1928);

The Ivory Door (London & New York: Putnam's, 1928; London: Chatto & Windus, 1929);

By Way of Introduction (London: Methuen, 1929; New York: Dutton, 1929);

The Fourth Wall (London & New York: French, 1929);

Michael and Mary (London: Chatto & Windus, 1930; London & New York: French, 1932);

Two People (London: Methuen, 1931; New York: Dutton, 1931);

Four Days' Wonder (London: Methuen, 1933; New York: Dutton, 1933);

Peace with Honour (London: Methuen, 1934; New York: Dutton, 1934; revised, 1935);

More Plays (London: Chatto & Windus, 1935)–comprises *The Ivory Door, The Fourth Wall,* and *Other People's Lives;*

Other People's Lives (London & New York: French, 1935);

Miss Marlow at Play (London & New York: French, 1936);

It's Too Late Now (London: Methuen, 1939); republished as *Autobiography* (New York: Dutton, 1939);

Behind the Lines (London: Methuen, 1940; New York: Dutton, 1940);

Sarah Simple (London & New York: French, 1940);

The Ugly Duckling (London: French, 1941);

Chloe Marr (London: Methuen, 1946; New York: Dutton, 1946);

Birthday Party and Other Stories (New York: Dutton, 1948; London: Methuen, 1949);

The Norman Church (London: Methuen, 1948);

A Table Near the Band (London: Methuen, 1950; New York: Dutton, 1950);

Before the Flood (London & New York: French, 1951);

Year In, Year Out (London: Methuen, 1952; New York: Dutton, 1952);

Prince Rabbit and the Princess Who Could Not Laugh (London: Ward, 1966; New York: Dutton, 1966).

Editions and Collections: *Four Plays* (London: Chatto & Windus, 1926)–comprises *To Have the Honour; Ariadne, or Business First; Portrait of a Gentleman in Slippers;* and *Success;*

The Christopher Robin Story Book (London: Methuen, 1929; New York: Dutton, 1929);

Those Were the Days (London: Methuen, 1929; New York: Dutton, 1929)–comprises *The Day's Play, The Holiday Round, Once a Week,* and *The Sunny Side;*

Very Young Verses, preface by Milne (London: Methuen, 1929)–includes selections from *When We Were Very Young* and *Now We Are Six;*

Four Plays (New York: Putnam's, 1932)–comprises *Michael and Mary, To Have the Honour* as *Meet the Prince, The Fourth Wall* as *The Perfect Alibi,* and *Portrait of a Gentleman in Slippers;*

A. A. Milne, edited by E. V. Knox (London: Methuen, 1933);

The Pocket Milne (New York: Dutton, 1941; London: Methuen, 1942);

Winnie-the-Pooh, facsimile edition (London: Methuen, 1971; New York: Dutton, 1971).

PLAY PRODUCTIONS: *Wurzel-Flummery,* London, New Theatre, 7 April 1917;

Belinda: An April Folly, London, New Theatre, 8 April 1917; New York, Empire Theatre, 6 May 1918;

The Boy Comes Home, London, Victoria Palace, 9 September 1918;

Make-Believe, London, Lyric Theatre, 24 December 1918;

The Camberley Triangle, London, Coliseum, 8 September 1919;

Dust jacket for Milne's 1922 detective novel, which influenced British mystery writers of the 1920s (courtesy of Otto Penzler)

The Romantic Age, London, Comedy Theatre, 18 October 1920; New York, Comedy Theatre, 15 November 1922;

The Stepmother, London, Alhambra, 16 November 1920;

The Great Broxopp, New York, Punch and Judy Theatre, 15 November 1921; London, St. Martin's Theatre, 6 March 1923;

The Truth about Blayds, London, Globe Theatre, 20 December 1921; New York, Booth Theatre, 14 March 1922;

The Dover Road, New York, New Bijou, 23 December 1921; London, Theatre Royal, 7 June 1922;

The Lucky One, New York, Garrick Theatre, 20 November 1922; revived as *Let's All Talk about Gerald*, London, Arts Theatre, 11 May 1928;

Success, London, Haymarket Theatre, 21 June 1923; revised as *Give Me Yesterday*, New York, Charles Hopkins Theatre, 4 March 1931;

To Have the Honour, London, Wyndham's Theatre, 22 April 1924; New York, Lyceum Theatre, 25 February 1929;

The Man in the Bowler Hat, New York, Belasco Theatre, 5 May 1924; London, Prince of Wales's Theatre, 27 September 1925;

Ariadne, or Business First, New York, Garrick Theatre, 23 February 1925; London, Haymarket Theatre, 22 April 1925;

Portrait of a Gentleman in Slippers, Liverpool, Liverpool Repertory Theatre, 4 September 1926; London, Royal Academy of Dramatic Art, 19 June 1927;

King Hilary and the Beggarman, London, Polytechnic Theatre, 22 December 1926;

Miss Marlow at Play, London, Coliseum, 11 April 1927;

The Ivory Door, New York, Charles Hopkins Theatre, 18 October 1927; London, Haymarket Theatre, 17 April 1929;

The Fourth Wall, London, Haymarket Theatre, 29 February 1928; revived as *The Perfect Alibi*, New York, Charles Hopkins Theatre, 27 November 1928;

Michael and Mary, New York, Charles Hopkins Theatre, 10 December 1929; London, St. James's Theatre, 1 February 1930;

Toad of Toad Hall, Liverpool, Playhouse, 21 December 1929; London, Lyric Theatre, 17 December 1930;

They Don't Mean Any Harm, New York, Charles Hopkins Theatre, 23 February 1932; revived as *Other People's Lives*, London, Arts Theatre, 6 November 1932;

Sarah Simple, New York, Garrick Theatre, 4 May 1937;

Miss Elizabeth Bennett, London, People's Palace, 3 February 1938;

Gentleman Unknown, London, St. James's Theatre, 16 November 1938.

PERIODICAL PUBLICATIONS: "The Rape of the Sherlock: Being the Only True Version of Holmes's Adventures," *Vanity Fair* (London), 70 (15 October 1903): 499;

"New Explorations in Baker Street," *New York Times Magazine*, 9 March 1952, pp. 10ff.

In his autobiography, *It's Too Late Now* (1939), A. A. Milne complains that his children's books have eclipsed his other kinds of writing. Best known before *Winnie-the-Pooh* (1926) as a playwright, Milne was an important mystery writer, and the popularity of his detective novel, *The Red House Mystery* (1922), helped establish the conventions of British detective fiction between World War I and World War II.

Born in London, 18 January 1882, Alan Alexander Milne was the son of Sarah Maria Heginbotham Milne and John Vire Milne, a head-master. Milne and his two elder brothers grew up at their father's preparatory school, Henley House, where they learned to love the schoolboy life of games, cordial intimacy, routine, and study. At Westminster School Milne settled into mathematics as his favorite subject (in which he later earned his B.A. with honors from Trinity College , Cambridge). While at Westminster and during his early years at Cambridge, Milne and his brother Ken invented a species of comic verse which they called "Milnicks." After having edited the school magazine, *Granta*, at Cambridge, Milne decided upon a career as a writer.

Milne's first piece to appear in the commercial press was a Sherlock Holmes burlesque printed in *Vanity Fair* in 1903. In 1906 Milne became assistant editor of *Punch*, for which he wrote a weekly article and edited correspondence from people who thought that they had invented something humorous. In 1913 he married Dorothy Daphne De Selincourt. Their only child, Christopher Robin Milne, was born in 1920. During World War I Milne found time out from his job as a signal officer to write his first play, *Wurzel-Flummery* (1917).

In *The Red House Mystery* Antony Gillingham arrives at the country estate Red House on an August afternoon to visit his friend Bill Beverley, a houseguest, seconds after Robert Ablett has been murdered. Antony and Matthew Cayley, friend and companion of the murdered man's brother, Mark Ablett, discover the body. Mark Ablett, the head of the household, is missing and a suspect in the murder of his brother, whom he had not seen for fifteen years because of Robert Ablett's dissolute habits. Antony Gillingham literally plays Sherlock Holmes to Bill Beverley's Dr. Watson, drawing a number of false conclusions before he solves the crime.

The Red House Mystery is important both because in it Milne attempted something new to meet the needs of sophisticated mystery fans who wanted witty books and wanted to take part in the detection, and because his popularity as a writer insured the book a wide audience. In an introduction he wrote for the 1926 New York reprinting Milne says he set four goals for himself: the dialogue must be natural, love interest must be minimized, the detective must be an amateur, and there must be a Watson. He argues that stilted language and romantic interludes add nothing to the story. Professional detectives distance the reader, and the absence of a Dr. Watson means that the reader cannot "know from chap-

Milne with son, Christopher Milne, who was depicted in the Winnie-the-Pooh stories, circa 1927 (courtesy of Mrs. Olive Brockwell)

ter to chapter what the detective is thinking." Writing about detective novels in general and this story in particular in *It's Too Late Now*, Milne says, "I had read most of those which had been written, admired their ingenuity, but didn't like their English. . . . I wondered if I could write a detective story about real people in real English. I thought it would be 'fun to try,' my only reason for writing anything." The *London Times Literary Supplement* (20 April 1922) praised the book greatly, as did the *Boston Transcript* (8 April 1922) and the *New York Times* (16 April 1922). Writing in 1936 (16 February), Isaac Anderson said in the *New York Times* that the book had not been forgotten like so many others of its era.

Milne wrote another mystery novel, *Four Days' Wonder* (1933), and a detective play, *The Fourth Wall* (1929; produced, 1928). Although *Four Days' Wonder* was not popular with the reading public (critics found it overrefined), it was made into a 1936 film by Universal. *The Fourth Wall* had a run of 225 performances in New York. Milne suffered a stroke in 1952 which left him partially paralyzed. He died at his home in Sussex on 31 January 1956.

References:

Raymond Chandler, "The Simple Art of Murder," *Atlantic Monthly*, 174 (December 1944): 53-59;

J. Randolph Cox, "Some Notes Toward a Checklist of A. A. Milne's Short Tales of Crime and Detection," *Armchair Detective*, 9 (1975/1976): 270;

Tori Haring-Smith, *A. A. Milne: A Critical Bibliography* (New York & London: Garland, 1982);

Christopher Milne, *Enchanted Places* (London: Eyre Methuen, 1974);

Milne, *The Path through the Trees* (London: Eyre Methuen, 1979);

LeRoy Lad Panek, *Watteau's Shepherds: The Detective Novel in Britain, 1914-1940* (Bowling Green, Ohio: Popular Press, 1979), pp. 64-71;

John M. Reilly, "Classic and Hard-Boiled Detective Fiction," *Armchair Detective* (October 1976): 289ff;

Thomas Burnett Swann, *A. A. Milne* (New York: Twayne, 1971).

Papers:

The manuscripts of Milne's Pooh books are at Trinity College, Cambridge University.

Gladys Mitchell

(19 April 1901-27 July 1983)

Mary Jean DeMarr
Indiana State University

BOOKS: *Speedy Death* (London: Gollancz, 1929; New York: Dial, 1929);

The Mystery of a Butcher's Shop (London: Gollancz, 1929; New York: Dial, 1930);

The Longer Bodies (London: Gollancz, 1930);

The Saltmarsh Murders (London: Gollancz, 1932; Philadelphia: Macrae-Smith, 1933);

Marsh Hay, as Stephen Hockaby (London: Grayson & Grayson, 1933);

Ask a Policeman, by Mitchell, Anthony Berkeley, Mildred Kennedy, John Rhode, Dorothy L. Sayers, and Helen Simpson, as the Detection Club (London: Barker, 1933; New York: Morrow, 1933);

Death at the Opera (London: Grayson, 1934); republished as *Death in the Wet* (Philadelphia: Macrae-Smith, 1934);

Seven Stars and Orion, as Hockaby (London: Grayson & Grayson, 1934);

The Devil at Saxon Wall (London: Grayson & Grayson, 1935);

Gabriel's Hold, as Hockaby (London: Grayson & Grayson, 1935);

Dead Men's Morris (London: Joseph, 1936);

Shallow Brown, as Hockaby (London: Joseph, 1936);

Outlaws of the Border, as Hockaby (London: Pitman, 1936);

Come Away, Death (London: Joseph, 1937);

Gladys Mitchell

St. Peter's Finger (London: Joseph, 1938; New York: St. Martin's, 1987);

Printer's Error (London: Joseph, 1939);

Grand Master, as Hockaby (London: Joseph, 1939);

Brazen Tongue (London: Joseph, 1940);

The Three Fingerprints (London: Heinemann, 1940);

Hangman's Curfew (London: Joseph, 1941);

When Last I Died (London: Joseph, 1941; New York: Knopf, 1942);

Laurels Are Poison (London: Joseph, 1942);

The Worsted Viper (London: Joseph, 1943);

Sunset over Soho (London: Joseph, 1943);

My Father Sleeps (London: Joseph, 1944);

The Rising of the Moon (London: Joseph, 1945; New York: St. Martin's, 1984);

Here Comes a Chopper (London: Joseph, 1946);

Death and the Maiden (London: Joseph, 1947);

The Dancing Druids (London: Joseph, 1948; New York: St. Martin's, 1986);

Holiday River (London: Evans, 1948);

Tom Brown's Body (London: Joseph, 1949);

The Seven Stones Mystery (London: Evans, 1949);

Groaning Spinney (London: Joseph, 1950);

The Malory Secret (London: Evans, 1950);

Pam at Storne Castle (London: Evans, 1951);

The Devil's Elbow (London: Joseph, 1951);

The Echoing Strangers (London: Joseph, 1952);

Merlin's Furlong (London: Joseph, 1953);

Faintley Speaking (London: Joseph, 1954; New York: St. Martin's, 1986);

Caravan Creek (London: Blackie, 1954);

On Your Marks (London: Heinemann, 1954; revised edition, London: Parrish, 1964);

Watson's Choice (London: Joseph, 1955; New York: McKay, 1976);

Twelve Horses and the Hangman's Noose (London: Joseph, 1956; New York: British Book Centre, 1958);

The Twenty-Third Man (London: Joseph, 1957);

Spotted Hemlock (London: Joseph, 1958; New York: British Book Centre, 1958);

The Man Who Grew Tomatoes (London: Joseph, 1959; New York: London House, 1959);

The Light Blue Hills (London: Bodley Head, 1959);

Say It with Flowers (London: Joseph, 1960; New York: London House, 1960);

The Nodding Canaries (London: Joseph, 1961);

My Bones Will Keep (London: Joseph, 1962; New York: British Book Centre, 1962);

Adders on the Heath (London: Joseph, 1963; New York: British Book Centre, 1963);

Death of a Delft Blue (London: Joseph, 1964; New York: British Book Centre, 1965);

Pageant of Murder (London: Joseph, 1965; New York: British Book Centre, 1965);

The Croaking Raven (London: Joseph, 1966);

Heavy as Lead, as Malcolm Torrie (London: Joseph, 1966);

Skeleton Island (London: Joseph, 1967);

Late and Cold, as Torrie (London: Joseph, 1967);

Three Quick and Five Dead (London: Joseph, 1968);

Your Secret Friend, as Torrie (London: Joseph, 1968);

Dance to Your Daddy (London: Joseph, 1969);

Churchyard Salad, as Torrie (London: Joseph, 1969);

Gory Dew (London: Joseph, 1970);

Shades of Darkness, as Torrie (London: Joseph, 1970);

Lament for Leto (London: Joseph, 1971);

Bismarck Herrings, as Torrie (London: Joseph, 1971);

A Hearse on May-Day (London: Joseph, 1972);

The Murder of Busy Lizzie (London: Joseph, 1973);

A Javelin for Jonah (London: Joseph, 1974);

Winking at the Brim (London: Joseph, 1974; New York: McKay, 1977);

Convent on Styx (London: Joseph, 1975);

Late, Late in the Evening (London: Joseph, 1976);

Noonday and Night (London: Joseph, 1977);

Fault in the Structure (London: Joseph, 1977);

Wraiths and Changelings (London: Joseph, 1978);

Mingled with Venom (London: Joseph, 1978);

Nest of Vipers (London: Joseph, 1979);

The Mudflats of the Dead (London: Joseph, 1979);

Uncoffin'd Clay (London: Joseph, 1980; New York: St. Martin's, 1982);

The Whispering Knights (London: Joseph, 1980);

The Death-Cap Dancers (London: Joseph, 1981; New York: St. Martin's, 1981);

Lovers, Make Moan (London: Joseph, 1982);

Here Lies Gloria Mundy (London: Joseph, 1982; New York: St. Martin's, 1983);

Death of a Burrowing Mole (London: Joseph, 1982);

The Greenstone Griffins (London: Joseph, 1983);

Cold, Lone and Still (London: Joseph, 1983);

No Winding Sheet (London: Joseph, 1984);

The Crozier Pharaohs (London: Joseph, 1984).

Gladys Maude Winifred Mitchell was born on 19 April 1901 in Cowley, near Oxford, England, to James and Annie Julia Maude (Simmonds) Mitchell; her father was of Scottish background. She was educated at the Rothschild School in Brentford and the Green School in

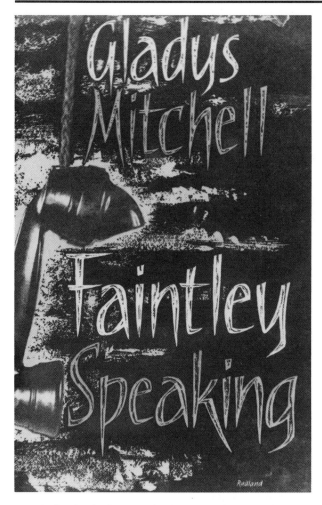

Dust jacket for the first British edition of the 1954 mystery featuring Mrs. Beatrice Bradley and Laura Menzies, her assistant (courtesy of Otto Penzler)

Isleworth; in Middlesex, where she had moved with her family in 1909; and at Goldsmith's College (1919-1921) and University College, London, where she qualified as a teacher and took a diploma in European history (1926).

During her long career Mitchell was not only a prolific writer but also a teacher of history and athletics and an athletic coach. After graduating from University College she taught at a small Anglican school, St. Paul's in Brentford, for over four years and then took a position at St. Ann's Senior Girls' School, Hanwell, where she remained until 1939. After a period of illness she became a teacher of Spanish as well as of history and athletics at Brentford Senior Girls' School. In 1950 she retired from this latter position; in 1953, however, she joined the staff of the Matthew Arnold Secondary School for Girls, where she taught history and English and wrote plays on classical and traditional subjects for perform-

ance by the girls. She finally retired from teaching in 1961. Her experiences in schools contributed greatly to the success of her crime fiction, both in her plots and settings, and in her witty and realistic characterizations of young people. She also put her knowledge of adolescents to use in creating a number of books, mostly mysteries, for young people.

A distinguished crime writer of the Golden Age, Mitchell was an early member of the Detection Club and a member of the Crime Writers' Club. She also belonged to the Society of Authors and was a fellow of the Ancient Monuments Society. In addition, her interest in historical preservation is reflected in the crime novels written under the pseudonym Malcolm Torrie.

Mitchell began writing early, but her first four novels were rejected. Her first novel, *Speedy Death* (1929), introduced the character Mrs. Beatrice Adela Lestrange Bradley, for whom Mitchell is primarily known; Mrs. Bradley (later Dame Beatrice) appears in all of the adult mystery novels written under Mitchell's name. Her most obvious characteristics are her physical eccentricities; she is always described as being exceptionally ugly. Her skin is yellow, her hands are like claws, and her laugh is a cackle. She is often compared to a pterodactyl and sometimes goes by the nickname "Mrs. Croc." Allusions are frequently made to her "basilisk eye." These characteristics remain constant as she ages, but they are less regularly emphasized in later novels. Along with the unpleasant externals, Mrs. Bradley possesses a disconcertingly lovely voice and often reveals an empathetic understanding of others and the ability to elicit warm, almost fanatic support. She is by profession a psychiatrist and frequently introduces herself to persons whom she wishes to question about a crime as a "psychiatric consultant to the Home Office."

As an early member of the Detection Club and a friend of leading practitioners of the genre in its Golden Age, Mitchell followed the established rules, always with wit and originality. The almost comic expertise of her central character helps set her work apart from that of any of her contemporaries but also places her squarely in the mainstream. Mrs. Bradley often informs intimates early on that she knows who is guilty and how the deed was done, the only remaining problem being lack of proof. The comic and artificial tone of the Mrs. Bradley novels places Mitchell clearly in the tradition of the Golden Age. But she both used and parodied some of its conven-

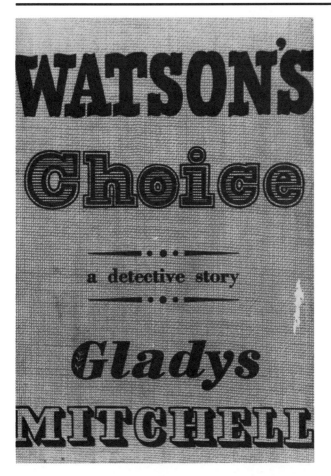

Dust jacket for the first British edition of Mitchell's 1955 mystery, in which a scavenger hunt ends in murder (courtesy of Otto Penzler)

tions; thus, her novels are never predictable.

The Saltmarsh Murders (1932) provides an early example of Mitchell's literary skill. Narrated in the third person (a technique she was to continue to use from time to time) by Noel Wells, a shallow, naive, yet likable young curate, the novel makes use of such staples of the genre as the village fete as a showcase for rural class conflict, and the idealization of youthful femininity, in this case the narrator's love for the virtuous and beautiful young niece of his superior. The novel also presents such stereotypical characters as the kindly yet detached vicar and his malicious and overbearing wife. The narrator has become a clergyman for no better reason than having been bequeathed some money on the condition that he enter orders, but he tries to do his best, and his sincere if bumbling efforts are endearing. Noel's dual function as narrative voice and sidekick to Mrs. Bradley soon becomes clear, but it is Mrs. Bradley who specifically defines it in a structurally interesting appendix. Placed after the

novel proper and thus outside Noel's narrative, the appendix consists of notes that Mrs. Bradley made in her roles as practicing psychiatrist and criminal investigator. The appendix explains the solution to the mystery in a more cogent way than Noel could have managed and avoids the conventional artificiality of forcing Mrs. Bradley to spell it all out to him. Mrs. Bradley describes him as her "invaluable Boswell, Captain Hastings, Doctor Watson" and goes on to epitomize him–and the type he represents–quite aptly: "Child has a head like a turnip. I do not think the Bar suffered any great loss when he went into the Church. Nice enough youth, though. Little Daphne [his sweetheart] will do as she pleases with him." This final passage, though a structural oddity, nevertheless accomplishes a crucial traditional task of the conventional mystery in a way that appropriately sums up and draws together various threads of the novel.

Through the course of the Mrs. Bradley novels the character acquires a circle of family and associates and a firm center of operations. She lives in what is always referred to as "the Stone House," in Wandles Parva, where she is attended by her faithful and philosophical chauffeur George and her equally faithful but often impudent secretary Laura. Her son from a first marriage, Ferdinand Lestrange, is a well-known barrister who occasionally is consulted in his professional capacity. A nephew, Carey Lestrange, a pig farmer, is another recurring character. Various young female relatives also appear. Sally Lestrange, Mrs. Bradley's granddaughter, plays a central role in *Winking at the Brim* (1974), Mitchell's playful novel on the Loch Ness monster theme: Sally is one of the few who actually sight the monster, and she fancies that it winks at her. It is less kindly to the murderer in the novel, for in a device typical of several of Mitchell's denouements, the monster is given the privilege of disposing of the culprit.

Similarly, in a late novel, *The Death-Cap Dancers* (1981), Hermione Lestrange, known familiarly as "Hermy One," a grandniece of Mrs. Bradley (now known as Dame Beatrice), stumbles into a murder mystery. Hermione is central to the plot of the novel, though structurally it is idiosyncratic. The opening directs the reader's attention to Hermione and the group of new friends she has chanced to discover; after they find a body, however, the focus shifts to a group of amateur dancers of which the dead young woman had been a member. The narrative moves back and forth between the two groups as the plot is unwound, and the novel's conclusion draws the two threads together in a frightening climactic scene that employs a device similar to that at the end of *Winking at the Brim*–here the culprit is killed by a boar accidentally freed from his pen on Hermione's father's pig farm.

Other members of Mrs. Bradley's family are mentioned from time to time, but Laura Menzies, later Laura Gavin, is of great interest and importance. She is the kind of confidante and collaborator that Noel Wells, for example, had not the intelligence or objectivity to become. In such novels as *Faintley Speaking* (1954), *Watson's Choice* (1955), and *Winking at the Brim* Laura is an exemplary secretary and investigative assistant. Laura is particularly useful to Mrs. Bradley in *Faintley Speaking* because of her ability to befriend young Mark Street, a boy who unwittingly becomes involved in a disappearance which turns into a murder. Her spunky eagerness to explore dangerous places and her willingness to trespass (as a matter of principle, because she opposes the right of a property owner to close off access to what should, in her view, be public beaches) make her very useful. Later, because she happens to have qualified as a teacher, she is able to substitute at the murder victim's school, where she continues to gather evidence.

Unfortunately, Laura's detecting abilities, again employed by Mrs. Bradley in *Watson's Choice*, are rather repeatedly belittled there; Mitchell's development of her characters was not always completely consistent. Laura's "usual shrewdness," however, is specifically stressed. Her fiancé becomes involved in the detecting this time, and Mrs. Bradley's rather ostentatious fondness for him is established: she regularly refers to him as "our dear Robert," while Laura usually calls him simply "Gavin." Laura and Gavin's affair seems to be a rather lukewarm one: Laura wonders why she doesn't fall more passionately in love with Gavin and doubts that she will be a good wife. Mitchell makes the eventual marriage and, later, Laura's motherhood take second place to her life with Mrs. Bradley.

Watson's Choice is additionally interesting in reemphasizing Mitchell's Golden Age roots. As its title suggests, *Watson's Choice* is based on the work of Sir Arthur Conan Doyle. It begins with a party to which characters are directed to come costumed as Holmesian characters and at which they must play a sort of scavenger hunt in which

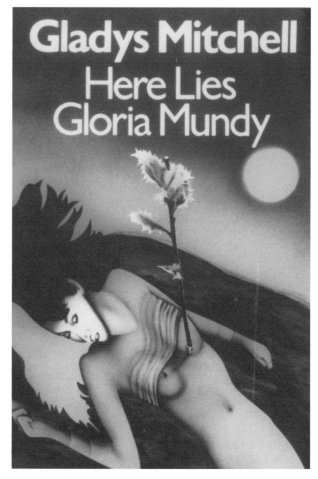

Dust jacket for the first American edition of Mitchell's 1982 Dame Beatrice Bradley mystery, in which the murder victim is seen alive in a London shop after she was found dead

items sought are material allusions to the Doyle stories.

By the time of the publication of *Winking at the Brim* Laura's relationship with Dame Beatrice has matured, and a younger woman, Sally Lestrange, seems more like the Laura of the earlier novels. In *Winking at the Brim*, in fact, the crime is solved by the three women working as a team. In the penultimate chapter they talk through what they know as equals. The chapter effectively uses their conversation both to dramatize their affection for each other and to rewrite the formerly mandatory "revelation scene" in such a way that it gives its readers all necessary information and knits up all the loose ends in a perfectly natural and believable way–an even more functional solution to this problem of the genre than the one Mitchell had employed in *The Saltmarsh Murders*.

Mitchell's plots and settings varied considerably, but she frequently returned to the school or college settings that were most familiar to her. In *Faintley Speaking* and *St. Peter's Finger* (1938) schools are used as settings, while in *Spotted Hemlock* (1958) Mitchell makes use of two adjoining agricultural colleges, one for women and one for men. Her insider's knowledge enabled Mitchell to cast a satiric eye in these novels on students and faculty members alike. Mitchell's treatment of the young people she knew so well, however, was not purely comic. Indeed, a gift for portraying real young folks, warts and all, marks many of her novels. The presentation of young Mark Street in *Faintley Speaking* is both comic and warmly tender. His twelve-year-old's scorn for women, especially women teachers, and his resentment over being cheated out of a much desired bicycle trip in France are as pathetic as they are funny. Mrs. Bradley is humanized by her immediate understanding of his pain, which inspires her to take him off for a quick trip to the caves of Lascaux, in which he had expressed an interest. The fact that an important clue is discovered as a result seems almost parenthetical.

One of Mitchell's favorite novels, however, is an even better example of her wise and sympathetic treatment of young people. In a 1976 interview with B. A. Pike she commented that one of her personal favorites was *The Rising of the Moon* (1945) because it "recalls much of my Brentford childhood (I am Simon in that story and my adorable brother Reginald is Keith)." The narrator, Simon, is portrayed at the age of thirteen, while Keith is two years younger. Their pranks, their dislike of the sister-in-law with whom they live, their longing for adventure, their heedless cruelties, and their inarticulate yearnings for love are all movingly portrayed.

Although many of the same themes inform her other work, Mitchell used two pseudonyms to distinguish her non-Bradley adult novels. For a period in the 1930s she attempted to succeed with "straight" novels published under the name Stephen Hockaby. She later said that she chose a masculine pen name because the first of these books, *Marsh Hay* (1933), had a male narrator, Etin Burntfen, who tells a rather sordid tale of growing up in rural England of the Edwardian period. The novel sets a traditional village society against historical movements of the period—the threat of the coming war is felt, and the woman suffrage movement presages social change. The novel is well written and, like the rest of the Hockaby novels, entirely different from Mitchell's output under her own name.

Dust jacket for the first British edition of Mitchell's last novel, published in 1984, a year after her death

The last of the Hockaby novels to be published, *Grand Master* (1939), is one of Mitchell's finest accomplishments. A richly textured tale of adventure set in the Mediterranean region and depicting the siege of Malta, it follows its English protagonist from boyhood captivity by Moors and Spaniards through a highly dramatic life in which he eventually becomes grand master of the Knights Hospitalers. After *Grand Master* Mitchell wrote one more Hockaby novel, but her publisher rejected it, and she ceased writing under the pseudonym.

Mitchell's other pseudonym, Malcolm Torrie, is attached to six detective novels of the late 1960s and early 1970s. She presumably chose a male pen name for these novels because they center around a male detective, although he eventually is joined by a young wife. Timothy Herring, the protagonist of the Torrie novels, is the secretary (and apparently one of the few working members) of the Society for the Preservation of Historic Buildings, usually called Phisbe. He selects old buildings that are worthy of preservation and works with the restoration projects; these activities regularly lead him to dead bodies and strange situations. In his first appearance, in *Heavy as Lead* (1966), Timothy is a determinedly free bachelor who barely escapes entanglement with an attractive murder suspect; perhaps the suspect's checkered past made her ineligible for such a respectable upholder of tradition as Timothy.

The novel *Your Secret Friend* (1968) introduces Timothy to Alison Marchmont Pallis, a sharp-tongued, embittered, and apparently unlovable teacher who is involved in a most unsuitable and destructive liaison with a married man. Timothy rescues her from the situation and from a group of insensitive young "witches" (pupils at her school who have formed a "coven"), and at the end of the novel she agrees to marry him. From this point on they detect together, as equals, Alison's knowledge of history often turning out to be as useful as Timothy's understanding of old buildings.

The Torrie novels, except for their differing central characters, are much like the works published under Mitchell's given name. The plotting has the same originality, themes show similar variety, and characterizations and settings are familiar. But most recognizable, perhaps, is Mitchell's

clear, witty, penetrating style. Her skill in narration is unexceeded by any of her contemporaries, and her ability to make style characterize her players is exemplary. An early case of such skill in characterization is provided by Noel Wells of *The Saltmarsh Murders*; his mannerism of repeating "of course," as if this incantation could force something to be true or clear, effectively helps underscore his own shallow understanding and his habitually good-humored wishful thinking.

While Mitchell's crime fiction has often been seen as excessively eccentric, with plots that do not always make sense and are not always satisfactorily clarified, her exuberant vitality and variety give her mysteries strong appeal. Her writing is less well known in the United States than in England, and accessibility of her work on this side of the Atlantic has been a problem. In recent years St. Martin's Press has been making some of her best work available in the United States. One may hope she will now find here the readership which she deserves.

Interview:

B. A. Pike, "In Praise of Gladys Mitchell," *Armchair Detective*, 9, no. 4 (1976): 250-260.

Reference:

William A. S. Sarjeant, "The Last of the 'Golden Age' Writers: Gladys Mitchell, 1901-1983," *Armchair Detective*, 18, no. 4 (1985): 351-360.

J. B. Priestley

(13 September 1894-14 August 1984)

Sarah McCarn Elliott

See also the Priestley entry in *DLB 34: British Novelists, 1890-1929: Traditionalists.*

SELECTED BOOKS: *The Chapman of Rhymes* (London: Moring, 1918);

Brief Diversions: Being Tales, Travesties, and Epigrams (Cambridge: Bowes & Bowes, 1922);

Papers from Lilliput (Cambridge: Bowes & Bowes, 1922);

I for One (London: John Lane, 1923);

The English Comic Characters (London: John Lane, 1925; New York: Dodd, Mead, 1925);

George Meredith (London: Macmillan, 1926; New York: Macmillan, 1926);

Talking (London: Jarrolds, 1926; New York & London: Harper, 1926);

Adam in Moonshine (London: Heinemann, 1927; New York: Harper, 1927);

Benighted (London: Heinemann, 1927); republished as *The Old Dark House* (New York: Harper, 1928);

The English Novel (London: Benn, 1927; revised edition, London: Nelson, 1935; Folcroft, Pa.: Folcroft Editions, 1974);

Open House: A Book of Essays (London: Heinemann, 1927; New York & London: Harper, 1927);

Thomas Love Peacock (London: Macmillan, 1927; New York: Macmillan, 1927);

Apes and Angels: A Book of Essays (London: Methuen, 1928);

The Balconinny, and Other Essays (London: Methuen, 1929; New York & London: Harper, 1930);

English Humour (London: Longmans, Green, 1929);

Farthing Hall, by Priestley and Hugh Walpole (London: Macmillan, 1929; Garden City, N.Y.: Doubleday, Doran, 1929);

The Good Companions (London: Heinemann, 1929; New York: Harper, 1929);

Angel Pavement (London: Heinemann, 1930; New York: Harper, 1930);

J. B. Priestley (photograph by Alfred Bernheim)

The Town Major of Miraucourt (London: Heinemann, 1930);

Self-Selected Essays (London: Heinemann, 1932; New York: Harper, 1932);

Faraway (London: Heinemann, 1932; New York: Harper, 1932);

I'll Tell You Everything: A Frolic, by Priestley and Gerald Bullett (New York: Macmillan, 1932; London: Heinemann, 1933);

Albert Goes Through (London: Heinemann, 1933; New York: Harper, 1933);

Wonder Hero (London: Heinemann, 1933; New York: Harper, 1933);

English Journey (London: Heinemann/Gollancz, 1934; New York & London: Harper, 1934);

They Walk in the City: The Lovers in the Stone Forest (London: Heinemann, 1936; New York: Harper, 1936);

Midnight on the Desert (London: Heinemann, 1937; New York & London: Harper, 1937);

The Doomsday Men (London: Heinemann, 1938; New York: Harper, 1938);

Let the People Sing (London: Heinemann, 1939; New York: Harper, 1940);

Rain upon Godshill (London: Heinemann, 1939; New York & London: Harper, 1939);

Britain Speaks (New York & London: Harper, 1940);

Postscripts (London: Heinemann, 1940);

Out of the People (London: Collins/Heinemann, 1941; New York & London: Harper, 1941);

Black-out in Gretley: A Story of and for Wartime (London: Heinemann, 1942; New York & London: Harper, 1942);

Britain at War (New York & London: Harper, 1942);

British Women Go to War (London: Collins, 1943);

Daylight on Saturday: A Novel About an Aircraft Factory (London: Heinemann, 1943; New York: Harper, 1943);

Three Men in New Suits (London: Heinemann, 1945; New York: Harper, 1945);

Bright Day (London: Heinemann, 1946; New York: Harper, 1946);

Jenny Villiers, A Story of the Theatre (London: Heinemann, 1947; New York: Harper, 1947);

Theatre Outlook (London: Nicholson & Watson, 1947);

Delight (London: Heinemann, 1949; New York: Harper, 1949);

Festival at Farbridge (London: Heinemann, 1951); republished as *Festival* (New York: Harper, 1951);

The Other Place, and Other Stories of the Same Sort (London: Heinemann, 1953; New York: Harper, 1953);

Low Notes on a High Level: A Frolic (London: Heinemann, 1954; New York: Harper, 1954);

The Magicians (London: Heinemann, 1954; New York: Harper, 1954);

Journey Down a Rainbow, by Priestley and Jacquetta Hawkes (London: Heinemann-Cresset, 1955; New York: Harper, 1955);

The Writer in a Changing Society (Aldington, Kent: Hand & Flower Press, 1956);

The Art of the Dramatist (Melbourne: Heinemann, 1957);

Thoughts in the Wilderness (London: Heinemann, 1957; New York: Harper, 1957);

Topside; or, The Future of England (London: Heinemann, 1958);

The Story of Theatre (London: Rathbone, 1959); republished as *The Wonderful World of the Theatre* (Garden City, N.Y.: Doubleday, 1959; London: Macdonald, 1969);

Literature and Western Man (London: Heinemann, 1960; New York: Harper, 1960);

William Hazlitt (London: Longmans, Green, 1960);

Charles Dickens (New York: Viking, 1961);

Saturn Over the Water (Garden City, N.Y.: Doubleday, 1961; London: Heinemann, 1961);

The Thirty-First of June; A Tale of True Love, Enterprise, and Progress, in the Arthurian and Ad-atomic Ages (London: Heinemann, 1961; Garden City, N.Y.: Doubleday, 1962);

Margin Released: A Writer's Reminiscences and Reflections (London: Heinemann, 1962; New York: Harper & Row, 1962);

The Shapes of Sleep: A Topical Tale (Garden City, N.Y.: Doubleday, 1962; London: Heinemann, 1962);

Man and Time (Garden City, N.Y.: Doubleday, 1964; London: Aldus, 1964);

Sir Michael and Sir George (London: Heinemann, 1964; Boston: Little, Brown, 1965);

Lost Empires (London: Heinemann, 1965; Boston: Little, Brown, 1965);

The Moments, and Other Pieces (London: Heinemann, 1966);

Salt is Leaving (London: Pan/Heinemann, 1966);

It's an Old Country (London: Heinemann, 1967; Boston: Little, Brown, 1967);

All England Listened: The Wartime Broadcasts of J. B. Priestley (New York: Chilmark, 1967);

The Image Men (2 volumes, London: Heinemann, 1968; 1 volume, Boston: Little, Brown, 1969);

Trumpets Over the Sea (London: Heinemann, 1968);

The Prince of Pleasure and His Regency, 1811-20 (London: Heinemann, 1969; New York: Harper & Row, 1969);

Dust jacket for the first British edition of Priestley's first thriller, 1927, later made into one of Hollywood's earliest talking pictures (courtesy of Otto Penzler)

Anton Chekhov (London: International Textbook, 1970);

The Edwardians (London: Heinemann, 1970; New York: Viking, 1970);

Snoggle (London: Heinemann, 1971);

Victoria's Heyday (London: Heinemann, 1972; New York: Harper & Row, 1972);

Over the Long High Wall (London: Heinemann, 1972);

The English (London: Heinemann, 1973; New York: Viking, 1973);

A Visit to New Zealand (London: Heinemann, 1974);

Outcries and Asides (London: Heinemann, 1974);

The Carfitt Crisis and Two Other Stories (London: Heinemann, 1975);

Particular Pleasures: Being a Personal Record of Some Varied Arts and Many Different Artists (London: Heinemann, 1975);

Found, Lost, Found; or, The English Way of Life (London: Heinemann, 1976; New York: Stein & Day, 1976);

The Happy Dream: An Essay (Andoversford: Whittington Press, 1976);

Instead of the Trees (London: Heinemann, 1977; New York: Stein & Day, 1977).

PLAY PRODUCTIONS: *The Good Companions*, by Priestley and Edward Knoblock, London, His Majesty's Theatre, 14 May 1931;

Dangerous Corner, London, Lyric Theatre, 17 May 1932;

The Roundabout, Liverpool, Playhouse, 14 December 1932; London, 1932;

Laburnum Grove: An Immoral Comedy, London, Duchess Theatre, 28 November 1933;

Eden End, London, Duchess Theatre, 13 September 1934;

Cornelius, London, Duchess Theatre, 20 March 1935;

Time and the Conways, London, Duchess Theatre, 26 August 1937;

I Have Been Here Before, London, Royalty Theatre, 22 September 1937;

When We Are Married: A Yorkshire Farcical Comedy, London, St. Martin's Theatre, 11 October 1938;

Music at Night, Malvern, Malvern Festival, 1938; London, Westminster Theatre, 10 October 1939;

Johnson over Jordan, London, 22 February 1939, New Theatre;

Desert Highway, London, Playhouse, 10 February 1944;

How Are They at Home? A Topical Comedy, London, Apollo Theatre, 4 May 1944;

An Inspector Calls, Moscow, 1945; London, New Theatre, 1 October 1946;

Ever Since Paradise: An Entertainment, Chiefly Referring to Love and Marriage, London, Winter Garden Theatre, 4 June 1947;

The Linden Tree, London, Lyceum Theatre, 23 June 1947;

The High Toby: A Play for the Puppet Theatre, by Priestley and Doris Zinkeisen, London, Toy Theatre, 1954;

Dragon's Mouth: A Dramatic Quartet, by Priestley and Jacquetta Hawkes, London, Winter Garden Theatre, 13 May 1952;

A Severed Head, adapted by Priestley and Iris Murdoch, London, Old Vic Theatre, 1963.

MOTION PICTURES: *Sing As We Go,* screenplay by Priestley and Wellesley Gordon, ATP, 1934;

We Live in Two Worlds, narration by Priestley, Educational Films Corporation of America, 1937;

Jamaica Inn, dialogue by Priestley, Paramount, 1939;

They Came to a City, screenplay by Priestley, Ealing, 1943;

Last Holiday, screenplay by Priestley, ABPC/ Watergate, 1950.

Few English writers have produced as many books as J. B. Priestley, and probably none of the writers who could match him volume for volume have written in so many forms. Priestley wrote more than a hundred books; his works include essays, drama, literary criticism, travel, autobiography, radio talks, radio and television dramas, films, poetry, long novels, short stories, children's stories, and even an opera libretto. Although he is not known as a mystery writer, he did turn his hand to that medium as well.

John Boynton Priestley was born in the wool district of Bradford, Yorkshire. His father, Jonathan Priestley, a Baptist and liberal socialist, was headmaster of the Bradford School. At sixteen Priestley left that school to become a clerk in the wool business and to write essays and articles for local newspapers. In 1914, when he was twenty, his solid provincial life was interrupted by World War I. Priestley was injured several times during the war, but he managed to survive and emerged with a small government grant to study at Trinity Hall, Cambridge. He spent the next three years getting his undergraduate degree, doing graduate studies, and writing articles. In 1919 he married Patricia Tempest, who was also from Yorkshire, and moved to London, where he began working as a free-lance writer, turning out reviews and critical essays for half a dozen magazines during the day and writing fiction at night. His wife, still in her twenties, was dying slowly of inoperable cancer; Priestley drove himself not only to pay the bills but also as a distraction from her dying.

Priestley's second novel and first thriller, *Benighted* (1927), is set on a stormy night in the mountains of Wales, where five motorists take shelter in the somber house of a strange and disordered family. One of the stranded travelers is Roger Pendrel, a war survivor who sits by the fire and suddenly slips into a gray world akin to shell

A New Novel by the author of "The Good Companions," "Midnight on the Desert," etc.

J. B. PRIESTLEY

Black-out in Gretley

Dust jacket for the first American edition of Priestley's 1942 mystery, depicting England under blackout conditions during wartime

shock. He rouses himself, falls in love, sees his world beginning to open out, and ends the night and his life in mortal combat. Each traveler's story is revealed to the others during the course of the evening, as is the mystery of the house. In the United States *Benighted* was published as *The Old Dark House* (1928) and sold twenty thousand copies. Priestley resisted offers to make it a play but allowed Hollywood to turn it into one of the first talking motion pictures, produced in 1932. Patricia Priestley had died in 1925, and Priestley married Mary Wyndham Lewis in 1926.

Hugh Walpole met Priestley in 1929 and suggested they write *Farthing Hall* (1929) together. Walpole's name on the novel meant a large advance and gave Priestley enough uninterrupted time to write *The Good Companions* (1929). In a time of short novels, this book was a quarter of a million words in length and achieved not only immediate but lasting popularity; it has never been out of print. The success of *The Good Companions* released Priestley from financial cares and made him a literary lion. *Angel Pavement* (1930), which followed, also was a best-seller.

Priestley has said he was not a born novelist, but he found writing novels an irresistible challenge. After he had two best-sellers, plays became the challenge, and from 1932 onward he wrote more plays than novels–more than forty during his long life–and became one of England's foremost dramatists. His first attempt at play writing, with the aid of Edward Knoblock, was the 1931 dramatization of *The Good Companions*. His next was influenced by his work as a reviewer. In 1927 he had reviewed W. J. Dunne's *An Experiment With Time*, and Dunne's ideas about time transcendence bolstered Priestley's belief in the individual's ability to delve into past time to help shape the present and future. In 1932 he used this idea in a play called *Dangerous Corner,* in which a group of people play a version of the game "Truth." In this game each person is, in turn, compelled to make damning revelations about himself. The players learn how their friend Martin died, but they also learn, in the words of one of the characters, that "telling the truth is as dangerous as skidding round a corner at sixty"; the results are tragic for all the participants. *Dangerous Corner* eventually became Priestley's most popular play, but it started with a chilly reception and nearly closed after five performances. Priestley took over the company at that point, and the play ran for nearly a year. The company went on to produce more of Priestley's plays, and in time he worked with most of the stars of the English stage. *Dangerous Corner* became a film in 1934.

Priestley joined forces with a Cambridge friend, Gerald Bullett, to write a spoof of early murder mysteries called *I'll Tell You Everything* (1932). The words of the title are said early and often to Simon Heath, whose innocence matches that of Candide and who assists in the appearance and disappearance of mysterious steel caskets. Each character who utters the title sentence to Simon follows it with a story that conflicts with the other characters' stories. Eventually villains, detectives, and an army of superpatriots are sorted out, and Simon's prize is the beautiful Zoe-Ann. In the last chapter the authors enter the novel and speak with the characters, tying up the remaining threads of the plot.

In 1937 Priestley was told by his wife's doctor that she should winter in a warm, dry climate. He took his family to the rocky moonscape of northern Arizona, where he worked on Hollywood scripts for which he received money but he refused to have his name listed in contracts or credits. A year later the Priestleys returned with three friends, and he processed enough movie scripts to support nine people. He put his companions into an adventure story called *The Doomsday Men* (1938), a novel about three mad brothers out to destroy the world from their secret arsenal in the desert. Some of Priestley's plays and novels have had, as he said, a strange trick of catching up with life, and this work is one of them. *The Doomsday Men* begins with religious crazies in California and ends with political crazies in the desert of the American Southwest. Though it was written long before the development of the nuclear bomb, the characters and location seem chillingly contemporary to readers today. Priestley's concerns while writing it were the events in Europe that brought on World War II.

Priestley had fought the First World War with a rifle; he fought the second with a typewriter and his voice. Every Sunday night he gave talks called "Postscripts" over BBC radio to encourage war-weary Britons and overseas listeners. The talks brought in an abundance of fan mail, and Priestley often was stopped on the London streets by people who wanted to talk to him and touch him. He hated the hero-worship but enjoyed the work. One night he was called back to the BBC and so escaped the bomb that made a direct hit on his hotel rooms.

Priestley combined the real-life blackouts he hated with enemy spies in a wartime Midland town in the plot of a light 1942 thriller, *Black-Out in Gretley*. Humphrey Neyland, the novel's main character, is a sour young widower and government agent who sorts out all the clues, catches the spies, and wins the charming but terrified Dr. Margaret Bauernstern.

When the war ended, Priestley decided to enter politics, though he had never been a member of any political party. In 1945 he stood for Parliament as an Independent and was almost elected to represent Cambridge University. He continued to be politically active, primarily through his writing.

Priestley again used time as a plot device in the 1945 play *An Inspector Calls* (1947), in which a self-satisfied family is having a party when an inspector arrives to interview them about a girl's suicide. Questioning reveals they are all morally responsible for her despair. The time warp figures

Priestley visiting with a miner and his family in their home, 1941 (BBC Hulton)

in the play's powerful ending, which gives the characters a chance to rectify their behavior toward the girl by replaying the past; but they meet this opportunity with the selfishness they have already exhibited.

An Inspector Calls had its premiere in Moscow in 1945 because all the London theaters were booked. It opened in London in 1946 at the Old Vic with a cast that included Ralph Richardson and Alec Guinness. History, like time, repeated itself. The play received a chilly, almost hostile reception but, like *Dangerous Corner,* went on to become a phenomenal success. In 1954 it was made into a film. Revived as a play in 1973, it was wildly popular with young people and had sixteen hundred performances in Germany alone. Priestley commented that the play later became more topical than it was when he wrote it: "Greed, selfishness and callousness have come back amongst older people and younger people are rebelling against it; and that's what this play is about."

In 1952 Priestley's second marriage ended in divorce. In 1953 he married Jaquetta Hawkes, an archaeologist from Oxford. Together they wrote two plays and a travel book and worked

for UNESCO and nuclear disarmament. Priestley railed at postwar England during this time, saying that private stupidity had been cemented into public stupidity, stiffened by whole armies of bureaucrats, civil servants, and advisers, all at vast expense. He believed that pollution, stress, and crowding were reducing life to the dreariest mediocrity.

In a 1961 intellectual thriller, *Saturn Over the Water,* Priestley poses a set of powerful men, working under the cover of a science institute, who form an international conspiracy to destroy the world with the intention of then rebuilding it to their tastes and dictates. Also in 1961 Priestley traveled in Germany to get local color for his next thriller, *The Shapes of Sleep,* published in 1962. In this improbable story, free-lance reporter Ben Sterndale is drawn into a mystery surrounding the disappearance of a sheet of figures from an advertising agency. Priestley employed an aspect of the time transcendence concept, the possibility of drawing on the past to make wiser present choices, in both *Saturn Over the Water* and *The Shapes of Sleep.* Both novels also revolve around international conspiracies that threaten the world, as did *The Doomsday Men.*

The international conspiracy is one element of Priestley's last mystery story, *Salt is Leaving* (1966). Lionel Humphrey Salt, Priestley's doctor-detective in the novel, sets out to find a severely ill patient who has disappeared, and he meets a young woman who is looking for her missing father, a bookseller. The two disappearances are related, and the action grows to involve the town's most prominent man.

In his later years Priestley was offered various awards and honors. Prime Minister Harold Wilson tried to make him a knight, but Priestley refused. The one honor he wanted was the Order of Merit, which is strictly limited to twenty-four living recipients. He received it in October 1977. In response he had two things to say: "First, I deserve it. Second, they have been too long about giving me it. There'll be another vacancy soon." But he was wrong. He lived seven more years and died at home in Stratford-upon-Avon, one month short of his ninetieth birthday.

It has been said that Priestley will be remembered for his plays rather than his novels. If so, perhaps the reason is that most of the plays were minutely revised for and with the players, and they were performed before they were published. This was particularly true of the comedies. His suspense stories are among his minor novels. They always have an interesting idea and flashes of mood and scenery, but they are not convincing. The critic John Braine says of the thrillers that they are splendidly ingenious; their pace never slackens and they carry the reader along to a satisfying and wholesome ending. But John Atkins (1981) points out that Priestley fails to transmit to the reader a kind of evil madness, a convincing destructive element. Instead of showing evil at work, he presents clichés. Having survived two world wars, Priestley certainly believed in the power of evil of global proportions, as many of his suspense stories show. Perhaps he believed in evil so much that he had to hold it at arm's length, not just for the reader but for himself.

Priestley's two famous suspense plays will fare better than the novels. David Hughes comments that *Dangerous Corner* and *An Inspector Calls* are of the same type, "the thriller that closes breathlessly on an unexpected twist of time's tail. Unity of time and place hold [them] intensely together, and the action is continuous." But these are plays about social responsibility, not flirtations with the dark power of evil madness.

It has often been said of Priestley that he would have written better if he had written less. In his eighties, Priestley agreed. "I have written far too much," he stated in *Instead of the Trees* (1977), "far too much for my own good." When he was working at his best, a play or novel seemed to arrive without any conscious effort. Too much work with the front of his mind, he feared, had prevented these unconscious gifts from the back of his mind. He felt he was "standing in [his] own light, overshadowing [his] better self." In his sixties, when he was in a more complacent mood, Priestley had summed up his work this way in *Margin Released* (1962): "It could have been better, but it could have been worse." Much of it is very good indeed.

References:
John Braine, *J. B. Priestley* (London: Weidenfeld & Nicolson, 1978);
Ivor Brown, *J. B. Priestley. Writers and Their Work*, No. 84 (London: Longmans, Green in association with the British Council, 1957);
Susan Cooper, *J. B. Priestley: Portrait of an Author* (London: Heinemann, 1970);
A. A. DeVitis and A. E. Kalson, *J. B. Priestley* (Boston: Twayne, for G. K. Hall, 1980);
J. W. Dunne, *An Experiment with Time* (London: A. & C. Black, 1927);
David Hughes, *J. B. Priestley: An Informal Study of His Work* (London: Rupert Hart-Davis, 1958);
P. D. Ouspensky, *A New Model of the Universe* (London: Kegan Paul, 1931);
Colin Wilson, "A Hell of a Talent," *Books and Bookmen*, 21 (January 1975): 26ff.

John Rhode
(Cecil John Charles Street, Miles Burton)
(1884-December? 1964)

Charles Shibuk

BOOKS: *With the Guns,* as F.O.O. (London: Nash, 1916);

The Making of a Gunner, as F.O.O. (London: Nash, 1916);

The Worldly Hope, as F.O.O. (London: Nash, 1917);

The Administration of Ireland, as I.O. (London: Philip Allan, 1921);

Ireland in 1921, as C.J.C. Street (London: Philip Allan, 1922);

Rhineland and Ruhr, as Street (London: Couldrey, 1923);

Hungary and Democracy, as Street (London: Unwin, 1923);

The Treachery of France, as Street (London: Philip Allan, 1924);

East of Prague, as Street (London: Bles, 1924);

A. S. F.: The Story of a Great Conspiracy, as John Rhode (London: Bles, 1924); republished as *The White Menace* (New York: McBride, 1926);

The Double Florin, as Rhode (London: Bles, 1924);

The Alarm, as Rhode (London: Bles, 1925);

The Paddington Mystery, as Rhode (London: Bles, 1925);

Dr. Priestley's Quest, as Rhode (London: Bles, 1926);

The Ellerby Case, as Rhode (London: Bles, 1926; New York: Dodd, Mead, 1927);

Mademoiselle from Armentières, as Rhode (London: Bles, 1927);

Lord Reading, as Street (London: Bles, 1928; New York: Stokes, 1928);

The Murders in Praed Street, as Rhode (London: Bles, 1928; New York: Dodd, Mead, 1928);

Slovakia Past and Present, as Street (London: King, 1928);

Tragedy at the Unicorn, as Rhode (London: Bles, 1928; New York: Dodd, Mead, 1928);

The Case of Constance Kent, as Rhode (London: Bles, 1928; New York: Scribners, 1928);

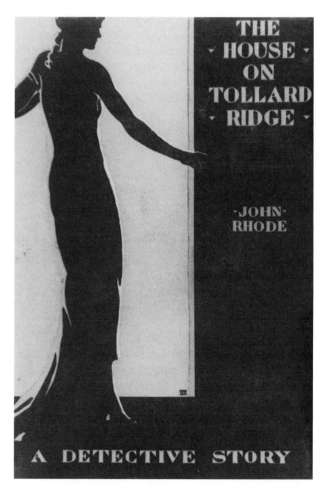

Dust jacket for the first American edition of Street's 1929 novel in which a wealthy recluse is murdered (courtesy of Otto Penzler)

The House on Tollard Ridge, as Rhode (London: Bles, 1929; New York: Dodd, Mead, 1929);

The Davidson Case, as Rhode (London: Bles, 1929); republished as *Murder at Bratton Grange* (New York: Dodd, Mead, 1929);

The Hardway Diamonds Mystery, as Miles Burton (London: Collins, 1930; New York: Mystery League, 1930);

Peril at Cranbury Hall, as Rhode (London: Bles, 1930; New York: Dodd, Mead, 1930);

President Masaryk, as Street (London: Bles, 1930); republished as *Thomas Masaryk of Czechoslovakia* (New York: Dodd, Mead, 1930);

The Secret of High Eldersham, as Burton (London: Collins, 1930; New York: Mystery League, 1931); republished as *The Mystery of High Eldersham* (London: Collins, 1933);

Pinehurst, as Rhode (London: Bles, 1930); republished as *Dr. Priestley Investigates* (New York: Dodd, Mead, 1930);

The Menace on the Downs, as Burton (London: Collins, 1931);

Tragedy on the Line, as Rhode (London: Collins, 1931; New York: Dodd, Mead, 1931);

The Three Crimes, as Burton (London: Collins, 1931);

The Hanging Woman, as Rhode (London: Collins, 1931; New York: Dodd, Mead, 1931);

The Death of Mr. Gantley, as Burton (London: Collins, 1932);

Murder at the Moorings, as Burton (London: Collins, 1932; New York: Sears, 1934);

Mystery at Greycombe Farm, as Rhode (London: Collins, 1932); republished as *The Fire at Greycombe Farm* (New York: Dodd, Mead, 1932);

Dead Men at the Folly, as Rhode (London: Collins, 1932; New York: Dodd, Mead, 1932);

Death at the Crossroads, as Burton (London: Collins, 1933);

Fate at the Fair, as Burton (London: Collins, 1933);

The Motor Rally Mystery, as Rhode (London: Collins, 1933); republished as *Dr. Priestley Lays a Trap* (New York: Dodd, Mead, 1933);

Tragedy at the Thirteenth Hole, as Burton (London: Collins, 1933);

Ask a Policeman, by Rhode and others (London: Barker, 1933; New York: Morrow, 1933);

The Claverton Mystery, as Rhode (London: Collins, 1933); republished as *The Claverton Affair* (New York: Dodd, Mead, 1933);

The Venner Crime, as Rhode (London: Odhams Press, 1933; New York: Dodd, Mead, 1934);

The Charabanc Mystery, as Burton (London: Collins, 1934);

The Robthorne Mystery, as Rhode (London: Collins, 1934; New York: Dodd, Mead, 1934);

To Catch a Thief, as Burton (London: Collins, 1934);

Poison for One, as Rhode (London: Collins, 1934; New York: Dodd, Mead, 1934);

Shot at Dawn, as Rhode (London: Collins, 1934; New York: Dodd, Mead, 1935);

The Corpse in the Car, as Rhode (London: Collins, 1935; New York: Dodd, Mead, 1935);

Hendon's First Case, as Rhode (London: Collins, 1935; New York: Dodd, Mead, 1935);

The Milk Churn Murder, as Burton (London: Collins, 1935); republished as *The Clue of the Silver Brush* (Garden City, N.Y.: Doubleday, Doran for the Crime Club, 1936);

The Devereux Court Mystery, as Burton (London: Collins, 1935);

Mystery at Olympia, as Rhode (London: Collins, 1935); republished as *Murder at the Motor Show* (New York: Dodd, Mead, 1936);

Death at Breakfast, as Rhode (London: Collins, 1936; New York: Dodd, Mead, 1936);

Death in the Tunnel, as Burton (London: Collins, 1936); republished as *Dark Is the Tunnel* (Garden City, N.Y.: Doubleday, Doran for the Crime Club, 1936);

Murder of a Chemist, as Burton (London: Collins, 1936);

In Face of the Verdict, as Rhode (London: Collins, 1936); republished as *In the Face of the Verdict* (New York: Dodd, Mead, 1940);

Where Is Barbara Prentice, as Burton (London: Collins, 1936); republished as *The Clue of the Silver Cellar* (Garden City, N.Y.: Doubleday, Doran for the Crime Club, 1937);

Death in the Hop Fields, as Rhode (London: Collins, 1937); republished as *The Harvest Murder* (New York: Dodd, Mead, 1937);

Death at the Club, as Burton (London: Collins, 1937); republished as *The Clue of the Fourteen Keys* (Garden City, N.Y.: Doubleday, Doran for the Crime Club, 1937);

Death on the Board, as Rhode (London: Collins, 1937); republished as *Death Sits on the Board* (New York: Dodd, Mead, 1937);

Murder in Crown Passage, as Burton (London: Collins, 1937); republished as *The Man with the Tattooed Face* (Garden City, N.Y.: Doubleday, Doran for the Crime Club, 1937);

Proceed With Caution, as Rhode (London: Collins, 1937); republished as *Body Unidentified* (New York: Dodd, Mead, 1938);

Death at Low Tide, as Burton (London: Collins, 1938);

Invisible Weapons, as Rhode (London: Collins, 1938; New York: Dodd, Mead, 1938);

The Platinum Cat, as Burton (London: Collins, 1938; Garden City, N.Y.: Doubleday, Doran, 1938);

The Bloody Tower, as Rhode (London: Collins, 1938); republished as *The Tower of Evil* (New York: Dodd, Mead, 1938);

Death Leaves No Card, as Burton (London: Collins, 1939);

Death Pays a Dividend, as Rhode (London: Collins, 1939; New York: Dodd, Mead, 1939);

Death on Sunday, as Rhode (London: Collins, 1939); republished as *The Elm Tree Murder* (New York: Dodd, Mead, 1939);

Mr. Babbacombe Dies, as Burton (London: Collins, 1939);

Drop to His Death, by Rhode and Carter Dickson (John Dickson Carr) (London: Heinemann, 1939); republished as *Fatal Descent* (New York: Dodd, Mead, 1939);

Murder in the Coalhole, as Burton (London: Collins, 1940); republished as *Written in the Dust* (Garden City, N.Y.: Doubleday, Doran for the Crime Club, 1940);

Death on the Boat Train, as Rhode (London: Collins, 1940; New York: Dodd, Mead, 1940);

Mr. Westerby Missing, as Burton (London: Collins, 1940; Garden City, N.Y.: Doubleday, Doran for the Crime Club, 1940);

Murder at Lilac Cottage, as Rhode (London: Collins, 1940; New York: Dodd, Mead, 1940);

Death Takes a Flat, as Burton (London: Collins, 1940); republished as *Vacancy With Corpse* (Garden City, N.Y.: Doubleday, Doran for the Crime Club, 1941);

Death at the Helm, as Rhode (London: Collins, 1941; New York: Dodd, Mead, 1941);

Death of Two Brothers, as Burton (London: Collins, 1941);

Up the Garden Path, as Burton (London: Collins, 1941); republished as *Death Visits Downspring* (Garden City, N.Y.: Doubleday, Doran for the Crime Club, 1941);

They Watched by Night, as Rhode (London: Collins, 1941); republished as *Signal for Death* (New York: Dodd, Mead, 1941);

The Fourth Bomb, as Rhode (London: Collins, 1942; New York: Dodd, Mead, 1942);

This Undesirable Residence, as Burton (London: Collins, 1942); republished as *Death at Ash House* (Garden City, N.Y.: Doubleday, Doran for the Crime Club, 1942);

Night Exercise, as Rhode (London: Collins, 1942); republished as *Dead of the Night* (New York: Dodd, Mead, 1942);

Dead Stop, as Burton (London: Collins, 1943);

Dead on the Track, as Rhode (London: Collins, 1943; New York: Dodd, Mead, 1943);

Murder, M.D., as Burton (London: Collins, 1943); republished as *Who Killed the Doctor?* (Garden City, N.Y.: Doubleday, Doran for the Crime Club, 1943);

Men Die at Cyprus Lodge, as Rhode (London: Collins, 1943; New York: Dodd, Mead, 1944);

Four-Ply Yarn, as Burton (London: Collins, 1944); republished as *The Shadow on the Cliff* (Garden City, N.Y.: Doubleday, Doran for the Crime Club, 1944);

Death Invades the Meeting, as Rhode (London: Collins, 1944; New York: Dodd, Mead, 1944);

The Three Corpse Trick, as Burton (London: Collins, 1944);

Vegetable Duck, as Rhode (London: Collins, 1944); republished as *Too Many Suspects* (New York: Dodd, Mead, 1945);

Not a Leg to Stand On, as Burton (London: Collins, 1945; Garden City, N.Y.: Doubleday, Doran for the Crime Club, 1945);

Bricklayer's Arms, as Rhode (London: Collins, 1945); republished as *Shadow of a Crime* (New York: Dodd, Mead, 1945);

Early Morning Murder, as Burton (London: Collins, 1945); republished as *Accidents Do Happen* (Garden City, N.Y.: Doubleday for the Crime Club, 1946);

The Lake House, as Rhode (London: Bles, 1946); republished as *The Secret of the Lake House* (New York: Dodd, Mead, 1946);

The Cat Jumps, as Burton (London: Collins, 1946);

Death in Harley Street, as Rhode (London: Bles, 1946; New York: Dodd, Mead, 1946);

Situation Vacant, as Burton (London: Collins, 1946);

Nothing But the Truth, as Rhode (London: Bles, 1947); republished as *Experiment in Crime* (New York: Dodd, Mead, 1947);

Heir to Lucifer, as Burton (London: Collins, 1947);

Death of an Author, as Rhode (London: Bles, 1947; New York: Dodd, Mead, 1948);

A Will in the Way, as Burton (London: Collins, 1947; Garden City, N.Y.: Doubleday for the Crime Club, 1947);

Death in Shallow Water, as Burton (London: Collins, 1948);

The Paper Bag, as Rhode (London: Bles, 1948); republished as *The Links in the Chain* (New York: Dodd, Mead, 1948);

The Telephone Call, as Rhode (London: Bles, 1948); republished as *Shadow of an Alibi* (New York: Dodd, Mead, 1948);

Devil's Reckoning, as Burton (London: Collins, 1948; Garden City, N.Y.: Doubleday for the Crime Club, 1949);

Blackthorne House, as Rhode (London: Bles, 1949; New York: Dodd, Mead, 1949);

Death Takes the Living, as Burton (London: Collins, 1949); republished as *The Disappearing Parson* (Garden City, N.Y.: Doubleday for the Crime Club, 1949);

Up the Garden Path, as Rhode (London: Bles, 1949); republished as *The Fatal Garden* (New York: Dodd, Mead, 1949);

Look Alive, as Burton (London: Collins, 1949; Garden City, N.Y.: Doubleday for the Crime Club, 1950);

Ground for Suspicion, as Burton (London: Collins, 1950);

The Two Graphs, as Rhode (London: Bles, 1950); republished as *Double Identities* (New York: Dodd, Mead, 1950);

A Village Afraid, as Burton (London: Collins, 1950);

Family Affairs, as Rhode (London: Bles, 1950); republished as *The Last Suspect* (New York: Dodd, Mead, 1951);

Beware Your Neighbor, as Burton (London: Collins, 1951);

Dr. Goodwood's Locum, as Rhode (London: Bles, 1951); republished as *The Affair of the Substitute Doctor* (New York: Dodd, Mead, 1951);

Murder Out of School, as Burton (London: Collins, 1951);

The Secret Meeting, as Rhode (London: Bles, 1951; New York: Dodd, Mead, 1951);

Murder on Duty, as Burton (London: Collins, 1952);

Death in Wellington Road, as Rhode (London: Bles, 1952; New York: Dodd, Mead, 1952);

Death at the Dance, as Rhode (London: Bles, 1952; New York: Dodd, Mead, 1952);

Heir to Murder, as Burton (London: Collins, 1953);

Something to Hide, as Burton (London: Collins, 1953);

By Registered Post, as Rhode (London: Bles, 1953); republished as *The Mysterious Suspect* (New York: Dodd, Mead, 1953);

Death at the Inn, as Rhode (London: Bles, 1953); republished as *The Case of the Forty Thieves* (New York: Dodd, Mead, 1954);

Murder in Absence, as Burton (London: Collins, 1954);

The Dovebury Murders, as Rhode (London: Bles, 1954; New York: Dodd, Mead, 1954);

Dust jacket for the first British edition of one of the seven mysteries by Street published in 1933 (courtesy of Otto Penzler)

Death on the Lawn, as Rhode (London: Bles, 1954; New York: Dodd, Mead, 1955);

Unwanted Corpse, as Burton (London: Collins, 1954);

A Crime in Time, as Burton (London: Collins, 1955);

Murder Unrecognized, as Burton (London: Collins, 1955);

The Domestic Agency, as Rhode (London: Bles, 1955); republished as *Grave Matters* (New York: Dodd, Mead, 1955);

Death of a Godmother, as Rhode (London: Bles, 1955); republished as *Delayed Payment* (New York: Dodd, Mead, 1956);

Death in a Duffle Coat, as Burton (London: Collins, 1956);

An Artist Dies, as Rhode (London: Bles, 1956); republished as *Death of an Artist* (New York: Dodd, Mead, 1956);

Found Drowned, as Burton (London: Collins, 1956);

Open Verdict, as Rhode (London: Bles, 1956; New York: Dodd, Mead, 1957);

The Chinese Puzzle, as Burton (London: Collins, 1957);

Robbery With Violence, as Rhode (London: Bles, 1957; New York: Dodd, Mead, 1957);

The Moth-Watch Murder, as Burton (London: Collins, 1957);

Death of a Bridegroom, as Rhode (London: Bles, 1957; New York: Dodd, Mead, 1958);

Bones in the Brickfield, as Burton (London: Collins, 1958);

Murder at Derivale, as Rhode (London: Bles, 1958; New York: Dodd, Mead, 1958);

Death Takes a Detour, as Burton (London: Collins, 1958);

Death Takes a Partner, as Rhode (London: Bles, 1958; New York: Dodd, Mead, 1958);

Licensed for Murder, as Rhode (London: Bles, 1958; New York: Dodd, Mead, 1958);

Return from the Dead, as Burton (London: Collins, 1959);

A Smell of Smoke, as Burton (London: Collins, 1959);

Three Cousins Die, as Rhode (London: Bles, 1959; New York: Dodd, Mead, 1960);

Legacy of Death, as Burton (London: Collins, 1960);

Death Paints a Picture, as Burton (London: Collins, 1960);

Twice Dead, as Rhode (London: Bles, 1960; New York: Dodd, Mead, 1960);

The Fatal Pool, as Rhode (London: Bles, 1960; New York: Dodd, Mead, 1961);

The Vanishing Diary, as Rhode (London: Bles, 1961; New York: Dodd, Mead, 1961).

OTHER: Daniel Halévy, *Vauban, Builder of Fortresses,* translated by Street (London: Bles, 1924);

Jean de Pierrefeu, *French Headquarters, 1915-1918,* translated by Street (London: Bles, 1924);

Maurice Thiéry, *Captain Cook, Navigator and Discoverer,* translated by Street (New York: McBride, 1930);

The Floating Admiral, By Certain Members of the Detection Club, includes contributions by Street, as John Rhode, and others (London: Hodder & Stoughton, 1931; Garden City, N.Y.: Doubleday, Doran for the Crime Club, 1932);

Detection Medly, edited by Street as Rhode (London: Hutchinson, 1939); abridged as *Line Up: A Collection of Crime Stories by Famous Mystery Writers* (New York: Dodd, Mead, 1940).

Best known for the detective novels he wrote under the pseudonym John Rhode, Cecil John Charles Street was a prolific writer of straightforward detective stories in the demanding tradition of Freeman Wills Crofts. Also using the pseudonym Miles Burton, he produced some 140 mystery novels. There have been other equally productive writers, but few have been able to match Street's usual high standards and merit. Many of his novels were extremely popular–especially in England, where they were republished at frequent intervals.

Little is known of Street, who was reclusive and extremely reticent about his private life. A professional soldier, he eventually rose to the rank of major, was awarded the Military Cross, and became an officer in the Order of the British Empire. His interests–history, politics, science, and criminology–are apparent in the nonfiction books, mostly on historical and political subjects, with which he began his writing career. He also produced three French translations and a novel, *The Worldly Hope* (1917), before turning his full energies to crime fiction.

For his first attempt at crime writing, Street, whose work is not noted for its humor, adopted the pseudonym John Rhode–possibly as a pun on his own name. The thriller *A. S. F.: The Story of a Great Conspiracy* (1924), which deals with the menace of cocaine traffic, was followed in the same year by *The Double Florin* (1924), a spy novel about a secret organization that enlists a young English aristocrat with severe financial problems in its struggle against Bolshevism.

Rhode's third thriller, *The Alarm* (1925), which deals with a British citizen's attempt to smuggle arms into Portugal, includes some feeble attempts at detection. Rhode continued in this new direction with *The Paddington Mystery* (1925), an extremely minor work notable only for its introduction of Dr. Lancelot Priestley. The novel involves Harold Merefield (pronounced "Merryfield"), who finds himself falsely accused of murder. He is saved by Priestley, who eventually becomes his employer and father-in-law. This novel is included in the "Haycraft-Queen Definitive Library of Detective-Crime-Mystery Fiction" because of its premier position in the Priestley saga–certainly not for its merit.

Dr. Priestley is a mathematician and scientist who resides in an old house in London's Westbourne Terrace with his daughter, April (who is mentioned but otherwise completely absent from the Priestley series), and—after the first book—his new secretary Harold Merefield. Priestley, who has aristocratic features that have resolved themselves into rather grim lines somewhat reflecting his personality, once held a chair of higher mathematics and a professorship at a prestigious London university, but a long series of intolerable arguments with the university hierarchy has forced him to abandon his chair. Since he is in an extremely comfortable financial position, this step caused no hardship and provided the leisure for Priestley to write a series of books on abstruse mathematical subjects and to spend much time shattering popular but totally erroneous theories through a strict application of logic. Priestley's favorite hobby is solving murder mysteries by treating them as impersonal problems that will yield their secrets to pure logic. Conundrums of this nature are frequently brought to him by Scotland Yard Inspector (later Superintendent) Hanslet and his successor, Inspector (later Superintendent) Jimmy Waghorn. Priestley calls these mysteries the very breath of life to him, but he usually has no particular empathy for the people involved or for any abstract idea of justice. Once the problem is solved, Priestley promptly loses all interest and devotes his attention to something else. A dry, academic person, he hazards a humorous remark only once in his long series of investigations. He is well known as a lavish and genial host—especially if one of his guests is going to present him with a crime problem after dinner.

At the start of his crime-solving career Priestley is a fully ambulatory sleuth, but as he grows older, he becomes more sedentary (somewhat resembling Rex Stout's detective, Nero Wolfe). To the detriment of the series, his appearances in the later novels are limited and all the detective work is left to Waghorn. Priestley's consistent refusal to use the telephone further limits contact between the two of them.

Rhode was not noted for his characterization, but one of his major achievements was the creation of Dr. Priestley, who would become one of the best-known and most impressive detectives in British crime fiction. Priestley's second investigation, *Dr. Priestley's Quest* (1926), demonstrates improvements in characterization and especially in detection. It is narrated by Merefield, who would

continue in this function for the next several novels, including *The Ellerby Case* (1926), about the murder of Sir Noel Ellerby (caused by an illicit drug), and is just about equal in merit to its predecessor.

Two other books of this period are sometimes listed, incorrectly, as crime fiction. *Mademoiselle from Armentières* (1927) is a novelization of a well-known British silent war film of 1926 and stands among Rhode's poorest works. *The Case of Constance Kent* (1928), the account of a true crime, received highly favorable reviews.

Rhode's novel *The Murders in Praed Street* (1928), one of his most popular works, also appears on the Haycraft-Queen list. In the course of investigating a series of bizarre and unrelated murders, Priestley discovers that he is due to be the next victim. The plot and puzzle are well conceived, but, as in many earlier works, Rhode uses too many words for too little effect. Subsequent novels display greater economy (and effectiveness) with a tighter prose style. *The Murders in Praed Street*, the only Rhode novel to be adapted for the screen, was considerably reworked for *Twelve Good Men* (1936), whose scriptwriters entirely dispensed with Priestley.

The next Priestley novel, *Tragedy at the Unicorn* (1928), is not one of the best in the series, but *The House on Tollard Ridge* (1929) is one of Rhode's finest efforts. The novel starts with the murder of the house's reclusive owner and continues with suspicion being directed toward his ne'er-do-well son. While its subject matter is less sensational than that of *The Murders in Praed Street*, Rhode's prose style is equal to the demands of this narrative.

By 1930 Street's production of crime fiction was so extensive that he decided to publish some of it under a new pseudonym, Miles Burton. Street was able to convince everyone that "Miles Burton" was the pen name of another author born in 1903, and managed to keep his identity as Burton secret throughout his lifetime. He even had the temerity to give two separate novels—one published as by Burton (1941) and the other as by Rhode (1949)—the same title, *Up the Garden Path*. Four years after Street's death Lenore S. Gribben's *Who's Whodunit* (1968) cited John Dickson Carr (Carter Dickson), "Rhode's" collaborator on *Drop to His Death* (1939), as the source for the information that Street was Miles Burton as well as John Rhode. Later "Burton's" editor at the London publishing house Collins admitted to Jacques Barzun that Burton was Street.

Dust jacket for the 1958 American edition of Street's novel in which a threatened family fortune leads to murder

The first Burton novel, *The Hardway Diamonds Mystery* (1930), a minor thriller about a supercriminal with a maniacal laugh, was followed by Burton's second, *The Secret of High Eldersham* (1930)—an improvement over its predecessor. This novel was recently selected for an American reprint edition by Barzun and Wendell Hertig Taylor, who think few stories of its era have stood up so well. Desmond Merrion, Burton's most popular detective, makes his debut in this novel, meets the woman he will later marry, and is able to render considerable assistance to the intelligent Inspector Young.

Never as popular as Dr. Priestley, Merrion is a former member of the British Admiralty, whose wartime experiences as an intelligence agent have given him a taste for detective work. He instantly responds any time Scotland Yard requests his help with the investigation of a difficult crime. Merrion's status as an unofficial adviser to Scotland Yard is later interrupted by World War II, when he returns to his duties as a

captain in the Admiralty. At the end of the war he resumes his activities for Scotland Yard. A lighthearted and whimsical person with a vivid imagination—the complete antithesis of Dr. Priestley—he enjoys driving his car—especially outside London—and is often to be observed smoking a cigarette.

Burton's *The Menace on the Downs* (1931) is a rural tale about the death of an errand boy, who is found with his throat cut. Was it accident, suicide, or murder? Warmer than most of the Burton stories, it introduces Inspector Henry Arnold, who works (and bickers) with Merrion through most of the series.

The Burton novels tend to be colder and less vivid than the Rhode novels—whose effectiveness is enhanced by the commanding presence of Dr. Priestley. Yet Barzun and Taylor have noted that Burton's tend to be wittier and less dependent on mechanical devices, as well as more concerned with scenery and character. They are often less solid, too, the outcome being sometimes pulled out of a hat rather than demonstrated.

Rhode's novels of the 1930s include *The Hanging Woman* (1931), one of the best Dr. Priestley stories of this decade. One of Rhode's best of any period, *Mystery at Greycombe Farm* (1932) is about arson in a cider barn and the subsequent discovery of a charred corpse. The plot and characters are more involving than in most of the Priestley series.

In Rhode's *The Motor Rally Mystery* (1933) death at night during the annual motor race at Torquay demands Priestley's investigation, which Barzun and Taylor call a classic performance. They describe the plot and motivation as "first-class" and rate the novel with *The Claverton Mystery* (1933), *Hendon's First Case* (1935), and *Death in Harley Street* (1946), as among Rhode's best. *The Claverton Mystery*, which concerns spiritualism and murder, has been cited by Barzun and Taylor for its sound puzzle, menacing atmosphere, and unusual method of murder. *Hendon's First Case* introduces Cambridge graduate Jimmy Waghorn, who has studied at Hendon's Metropolitan Police College and plays an increasingly more important role in the series.

Another Rhode novel of the 1930s, *Invisible Weapons* (1938), is a locked-door mystery worthy of the early Ellery Queen or John Dickson Carr, with whom Rhode successfully collaborated on a variation on the same subgenre. Their *Drop to His Death* is an atmospheric tale of murder committed by unknown means in an elevator located on the premises of a pulp-magazine publisher.

Some notable Burton novels also appeared during this period. Barzun and Taylor rank *Death in the Tunnel* (1936) high on their list of the best railway detective novels. A cleaning woman finds a body on the premises of the local elementary school in *Murder in the Coalhole* (1940), notable for its humor, its approach to sex, and the bickering of Merrion and Arnold. *Death Takes a Flat* (1940) is a straightforward tale about a retired Indian army officer and his wife, who view a potential new home that contains an unexpected and very dead occupant. *Murder, M.D.* (1943) contains some of Burton's best plotting.

Rhode's *Night Exercise* (1942) is a rare break from the Priestley series. The novel details civilian-defense preparations on the eve of World War II and presents the problem of a missing (and disagreeable) officer. Barzun and Taylor praise its action and characterization.

Yet, by the mid 1940s the effects of Street's prodigious output began to show. Many of his novels began to seem mechanical and routine. He also produced some excellent fiction, however. In Rhode's *Death in Harley Street* Priestley is at the height of his powers on page one, and the novel's ingenious method of revenge involves Street's scientific expertise. Barzun and Taylor consider this novel the best of the Priestley saga. Rhode's

The Telephone Call (1948), a masterly reconstruction of the well-known Julia Wallace case, presents a highly plausible (fictional) solution. *The Two Graphs* (1950), which deals with the confusion of identity between brothers, is possibly the last first-rate Rhode novel, although *Dr. Goodwood's Locum* (1951), another tale of impersonation, disappearance, and murder, has much to recommend it. Of the later Burton novels, *The Cat Jumps* (1946), *A Will in the Way* (1947), *Murder in Absence* (1954), and perhaps *The Chinese Puzzle* (1957) are of value.

Street's last novel, *The Vanishing Diary*, was published under the pseudonym John Rhode in 1961. He died in late 1964 at an Eastbourne hospital near his home in Seaford, England.

Street has frequently been praised for his ingenious and meticulously crafted plots. Many of his later works have been characterized as dull, with some justice. Street, unlike such authors as Queen and Carr, was usually unable to apply atmosphere to his puzzles, and his people—with the notable exception of Priestley—have been characterized as "cardboard." Few critics, however, have noticed Street's ability to depict rural areas and their inhabitants with a great deal of verisimilitude. Yet, the John Rhode novels, especially, are notable for their inventive plots, and Dr. Lancelot Priestley remains an impressive character.

Dorothy L. Sayers

(13 June 1893-17 December 1957)

Bernard Benstock
University of Miami

See also the Sayers entries in *DLB 10: Modern British Dramatists, 1900-1945,* and *DLB 36: British Novelists, 1890-1929: Modernists.*

BOOKS: *Op. I* (Oxford: Blackwell, 1916);
Catholic Tales and Christian Songs (Oxford: Blackwell, 1918);
Whose Body? (New York: Boni & Liveright, 1923; London: Unwin, 1923);
Clouds of Witness (London: Unwin, 1926); republished as *Clouds of Witnesses* (New York: Dial, 1927);
Unnatural Death (London: Benn, 1927); republished as *The Dawson Pedigree* (New York: Dial, 1928);
The Unpleasantness at the Bellona Club (London: Benn, 1928; New York: Payson & Clarke, 1928);
Lord Peter Views the Body (London: Gollancz, 1928; New York: Payson & Clarke, 1929);
The Documents in the Case, by Sayers and Robert Eustace (Dr. Eustace Robert Barton) (London: Benn, 1930; New York: Brewer & Warren, 1930);
Strong Poison (London: Gollancz, 1930; New York: Brewer & Warren, 1930);
The Five Red Herrings (London: Gollancz, 1931); republished as *Suspicious Characters* (New York: Brewer, Warren & Putnam, 1931);
The Floating Admiral, by Sayers and others (London: Hodder & Stoughton, 1931; New York: Doubleday, Doran, 1932);
Have His Carcase (London: Gollancz, 1932; New York: Brewer, Warren & Putnam, 1932);
Murder Must Advertise: A Detective Story (London: Gollancz, 1933; New York: Harcourt, Brace, 1933);
Ask a Policeman, by Sayers and others (London: Barker, 1933; New York: Morrow, 1933);
Hangman's Holiday (London: Gollancz, 1933; New York: Harcourt, Brace, 1933);
The Nine Tailors: Changes Rung on an Old Theme in Two Short Touches and Two Full Peals (Lon-

Dorothy L. Sayers (portrait by Walter Edward Blythe/ courtesy of Otto Penzler)

don: Gollancz, 1934; New York: Harcourt, Brace, 1934);
Gaudy Night (London: Gollancz, 1935; New York: Harcourt, Brace, 1936);
Papers Relating to the Family of Wimsey, by Sayers and others, as Matthew Wimsey (London: Privately printed, 1936);
Busman's Honeymoon: A Detective Comedy in Three Acts, by Sayers and Muriel St. Clare Byrne (London: Gollancz, 1937; New York: Dramatists' Play Service, 1939);

Busman's Honeymoon: A Love Story with Detective Interruptions (New York: Harcourt, Brace, 1937; London: Gollancz, 1937);

The Zeal of Thy House (London: Gollancz, 1937; New York: Harcourt, Brace, 1937);

An Account of Lord Mortimer Wimsey, Hermit of the Marsh (Oxford: Privately printed, 1937);

The Greatest Drama Ever Staged (London: Hodder & Stoughton, 1938);

Double Death: A Murder Story, by Sayers and others (London: Gollancz, 1939);

Strong Meat (London: Hodder & Stoughton, 1939);

The Devil to Pay: Being the Famous History of John Faustus, the Conjurer of Wittenberg in Germany; How He Sold His Immortal Soul to the Enemy of Mankind, and Was Served XXIV Years by Mephistopheles, and Obtained Helen of Troy to His Paramour, with Many Other Marvels; and How God Dealt with Him at the Last: A Stage-Play (London: Gollancz, 1939; New York: Harcourt, Brace, 1939);

In the Teeth of the Evidence and Other Stories (London: Gollancz, 1939; New York: Harcourt, Brace, 1940);

He That Should Come: A Nativity Play in One Act (London: Gollancz, 1939);

Begin Here: A War-Time Essay (London: Gollancz, 1940; New York: Harcourt, Brace, 1941);

Creed or Chaos?: Address Delivered at the Biennial Festival of the Church Tutorial Classes Association in Derby, May 4th, 1940 (London: Hodder & Stoughton, 1940);

The Mysterious English (London: Macmillan, 1941);

The Mind of the Maker (London: Methuen, 1941; New York: Harcourt, Brace, 1941);

Why Work?: An Address Delivered at Eastbourne, April 23rd, 1942 (London: Methuen, 1942);

The Other Six Deadly Sins: An Address Given to the Public Morality Council at Caxton Hall, Westminster, on October 23rd, 1941 (London: Methuen, 1943);

The Man Born to Be King: A Play-Cycle on the Life of Our Lord and Saviour Jesus Christ, Written for Broadcasting (London: Gollancz, 1943; New York: Harper, 1949);

Even the Parrot: Exemplary Conversations for Enlightened Children (London: Methuen, 1944);

The Just Vengeance: The Lichfield Festival Play for 1946 (London: Gollancz, 1946);

Unpopular Opinions (London: Gollancz, 1946; New York: Harcourt, Brace, 1947);

Making Sense of the Universe: An Address Given at the Kingsway Hall on Ash Wednesday, March 6th, 1946 (London: St. Anne's Church House, 1946);

Creed or Chaos? and Other Essays in Popular Theology (London: Methuen, 1947; New York: Harcourt, Brace, 1949);

The Lost Tools of Learning: Paper Read at a Vacation Course in Education, Oxford 1947 (London: Methuen, 1948);

The Emperor Constantine: A Chronicle (London: Gollancz, 1951; New York: Harper, 1951);

Introductory Papers on Dante (London: Methuen, 1954; New York: Harper, 1955);

Further Papers on Dante (London: Methuen, 1957; New York: Harper, 1957);

The Poetry of Search and the Poetry of Statement and Other Posthumous Essays on Literature, Religion and Language (London: Gollancz, 1963);

Christian Letters to a Post-Christian World: A Selection of Essays, edited by Roderick Jellema (Grand Rapids, Mich.: Eerdmans, 1969); republished as *The Whimsical Christian: 18 Essays* (New York: Macmillan, 1978);

Talboys (New York, Evanston, San Francisco & London: Harper, 1972);

Striding Folly, Including Three Final Lord Peter Wimsey Stories (London: New English Library, 1973);

Wilkie Collins: A Critical and Biographical Study, edited by E. R. Gregory (Toledo, Ohio: Friends of the University of Toledo Libraries, 1977).

OTHER: *Great Short Stories of Detection, Mystery and Horror*, edited by Sayers (London: Gollancz, 1928); republished as *The Omnibus of Crime* (New York: Payson & Clarke, 1929);

Tristan in Brittany: Being Fragments of the Romance of Tristan, Written in the XII Century, by Thomas the Anglo-Norman, translated by Sayers (London: Benn, 1929; New York: Payson & Clarke, 1929);

Great Short Stories of Detection, Mystery and Horror, Second Series, edited by Sayers (London: Gollancz, 1931); republished as *The Second Omnibus of Crime* (New York: Coward-McCann, 1932);

Great Short Stories of Detection, Mystery and Horror, Third Series, edited by Sayers (London: Gollancz, 1934); republished as *The Third Omnibus of Crime* (New York: Coward-McCann, 1935);

"Blood Sacrifice," in *Six against the Yard*, by Sayers and others (London: Selwyn & Blount, 1936), pp. 197-233; republished as *Six against Scotland Yard* (New York: Doubleday, Doran, 1936), pp. 197-233;

Tales of Detection, edited by Sayers (London: Dent, 1936);

"The Murder of Julia Wallace," in *Great Unsolved Crimes* (London: Hutchinson, 1935), pp. 111-122; revised in *The Anatomy of Murder: Famous Crimes Critically Considered by Members of the Detection Club* (London: Lane, 1936; New York: Macmillan, 1937), pp. 157-211;

Wilkie Collins, *The Moonstone*, introduction by Sayers (London: Dent/New York: Dutton, 1944);

Garet Garrett, *A Time Is Born*, introduction by Sayers (Oxford: Blackwell, 1945);

The Comedy of Dante Alighieri the Florentine, Cantica I: Hell, translated by Sayers (Harmondsworth, U.K.: Penguin, 1949);

The Comedy of Dante Alighieri the Florentine, Cantica II: Purgatory, translated by Sayers (Harmondsworth, U.K.: Penguin, 1955);

The Song of Roland, translated by Sayers (Harmondsworth, U.K.: Penguin, 1957);

The Comedy of Dante Alighieri the Florentine, Cantica III: Paradise, translated by Sayers, completed by Barbara Reynolds (Harmondsworth, U.K.: Penguin, 1962).

Her dozen detective novels and two dozen short stories in the genre established the reputation of Dorothy Leigh Sayers in the 1920s and 1930s as a major writer of mysteries; they also established Lord Peter Wimsey as an equally famous fictional detective. Since the success of Sir Arthur Conan Doyle's Sherlock Holmes stories in the last decade of the nineteenth century, the fame of the serial detectives had threatened to eclipse that of their authors, yet it had become essential that a forceful personality be created for a writer in the genre to succeed in capturing an audience. Sayers conceived of Lord Peter as a fascinating if somewhat eccentric charmer, following the Conan Doyle tradition that the character of the detective took precedence over all other facets of the detective fiction. Like Conan Doyle she found herself eventually wanting to rid herself of Wimsey and what she termed "literature of escape," and unlike Conan Doyle she succeeded. Even with the high literary achievement of her Wimsey stories, Dorothy Sayers was uncomfortable with the necessity of writing them in order to achieve financial security and independence, and once she was relieved of economic necessity, she dedicated her writing career to "literature of expression," which she interpreted for herself as religious essays and dramas and translating Dante's *Divina Commedia*.

The tandem writing careers of Dorothy L. Sayers (as she insisted on being referred to), the detective fictions that spanned the years 1923 to 1937, and the "serious" literature that occupied her until her death in 1957, reflect important aspects of her existence as a woman attempting to lead an independent life in twentieth-century English society. Educated and erudite as she was as a young woman, Sayers nonetheless found herself alone and unemployed, despite a genteel and privileged background, and possibly unemployable in the wake of returning veterans from the Great War and reduced industrial needs. Her first important job was in an advertising agency in London, from which she derived the setting and ambience for her highly successful *Murder Must Advertise* (1933). The success of the Wimsey novels enabled her to quit her advertising job and devote herself exclusively to writing. *Murder Must Advertise*, although an excellent example of Sayers's "literature of escape," nonetheless captures the fear of unemployment among the British white-collar employees and professionals. And all of Sayers's detective novels are skillfully fictionalized representations of English social and economic life in the period between the two world wars.

Dorothy Leigh Sayers's life began in Oxford, which she left as a child, only to return later as a student at the University. Her father was an Anglican clergyman and schoolmaster at the Choir School of Christ Church College, who undertook the initial education of his only child with seriousness, tutoring her in Latin, and passing on her subsequent education to tutors. In Oxford her mother, whose family name of Leigh was retained by Dorothy L. Sayers, lived an active social life, which changed drastically when the family moved to the bleak Fen countryside during Dorothy's childhood. The Reverend Henry Sayers gladly gave up the onerous job as a schoolmaster for the Cambridgeshire living that provided his family with a much larger house that could include their extended family, a grandmother and an aunt, and Helen Sayers devoted herself thereafter to the basic needs of her husband's parishioners. The grim and watery countryside of the Fen provided the novelist daughter

Sayers impersonating Dr. Hugh Allen, in the Going-Down Play, *Oxford, 1915*

with the atmospheric potency of *The Nine Tailors* (1934), rivaled only by Conan Doyle in his *The Hound of the Baskervilles,* and the personality of Reverend Sayers added elements to the characterization of the vicar in *The Nine Tailors.*

The life of Dorothy L. Sayers could be casually summarized as relatively uneventful, and yet it provides its mysteries and puzzles to keep several biographers active, one of them "official" and the others of varying degrees of intensity and high-spiritedness. Her life could be summarized in stages: a vicarage childhood (which could have been written under the heading of "My Edwardian Childhood," as Sayers once attempted but abandoned after thirty-three pages); a solid education which qualified her as a teacher of languages and a potential medievalist; a strong sexual drive that broke the bounds of bourgeois propriety and resulted in an illegitimate child fostered out; the early adult years of sexual frustration and financial worries; the advertising job; the subsequent writing career; success and fame; a belated marriage to a feckless husband; and a tendency throughout to eccentricity. Some of these biographical details were understandably late in being disclosed and resulted in a trio of biogra-

phies. Sayers herself was an indifferent and highly ambivalent autobiographer, as witness the furtive pages on her childhood and an equally furtive fictionalization that she never finished and never herself allowed to have published. She had set a fifty-year moratorium on any biography of her after her death; but within twenty years the gossipy unofficial entry in the field appeared, and it was only a matter of time before the official version was forced into print. It was the exciting and rather blameless life of Lord Peter Wimsey that obviously excited interest in the relatively unexciting but peculiar life of Dorothy Leigh Sayers.

It is interesting to consider whether Dorothy Sayers's education trained her to write the Lord Peter series of detective narratives, or whether instead her training and inclinations were literary and esoteric, and the mystery writing career was an aberration brought on by her confrontation with economic necessity. Until the age of fifteen she was tutored at home, by her father in Latin and by private tutors in French and German. She then attended Godolophin School in Salisbury, where she felt ill at ease and none too popular with her schoolmates, a private and somewhat brooding persona already. At Godolophin she became aware of an interest in and talent for writing, and she submitted poetry and nonfiction to the school magazine, her first publications. In her own words, she adopted a "corsage of defiance" to cover her feelings of insecurity in the first experiences outside the vicarage. She distinguished herself at Oxford, attended Somerville College, one of the two women's colleges at the University, a setting that she more than immortalized and dissected in her major novel, the one that comes closest to transcending the confines of the criminal novel, *Gaudy Night* (1935), as Shrewsbury College. Her depiction of an exclusively feminine intellectual community has raised more than one eyebrow among her critics and not a few hackles. Sayers took a first-class honors degree at Oxford in 1915 in modern languages and received both a B.A. and M.A. degree in the same ceremony in 1920, when Oxford relented and awarded degrees to its women students. Sayers was among the first women to be granted Oxford degrees.

After leaving Oxford, Sayers attempted various odd jobs in order to earn a living, primarily teaching but also working as a reader for the Oxford publishing firm of Basil Blackwell, where she published some of her own verse, the religious literary bent that would return to claim her full attention after the Wimsey series made her fortune. The longest tenure at a job was at the advertising agency in London, Benson's, on Southampton Row, from which Wimsey eventually rescued her. She began at Benson's in 1922, the year in which she also began work on her first Wimsey venture, published as *Whose Body?* (1923). As she confided obliquely to her friend Muriel Jeager at the time, she was working on what she called "Lord Peter," and although there were occasional non-Wimsey stories that she published, particularly with Montague Egg as her detective, it was Lord Peter who took central stage in her important detective narratives. The creation of a wealthy aristocrat as her functioning persona has attracted a good deal of commentary, especially when one considers her total lack of experience with the upper classes, her basically prim middle-class origins, much less her plebeian employment, as well as her rarely satisfied sexual interest in men. As is often the case with women writers of serial detective fiction, the mere existence of a male detective gives rise to speculation on the adopting of a masculine alter ego, the reliance on a strong male alternative. With Sayers the eventual introduction of Harriet Vane halfway through the series, first as a victim requiring Wimsey's protection, then as a woman detective fiction writer turned amateur detective, and eventually as Wimsey's bride, has intensified the psychosexual investigation of the woman author.

The major role played by women writers in the detective fiction genre began in the early 1920s with Agatha Christie and Dorothy L. Sayers, ushering in what has been designated as the Golden Age of crime fiction, the period between the wars. From the earliest Sherlock Holmes story in 1887 the genre enjoyed a healthy popularity in Britain, and although it continued on unabated through the first two decades of the twentieth century, it needed the revivification that came with Christie and Sayers, primarily because the Sherlockian version of the format limped along without much change; it was locked in a time frame of fog-enveloped, gaslit London and the grim moors of the rural backwaters, a world of trains and hackneys, telegrams and messages delivered by commissionaires, the late-Victorian world. Christie and (to an even greater degree) Sayers brought the detective novel into the twentieth century, a world of fast motorcars and cocktail parties, bobbed hair and shortened skirts, the politics and life-styles of the postwar age. And both of them saw the possibilities of the comic in the detective novel. Detective fiction has always required a subsidiary technique to augment the puzzle aspect, either a heavy dose of atmosphere or, more recently, an element of the comic. Sayers's comic substyle is more artificially literary and urbane than Christie's, and more than that of her many imitators along those lines. In commenting on Sayers's "refreshing humour," P. D. James notes that it "was born of a keen eye and a frank relish for the vagaries, inconsistencies and absurdities of life. No changes of fashion can diminish the humour of Mr. Hankin's irruption into the office sweepstakes in *Murder Must Advertise*, the Bohemian party in *Clouds of Witness*, the Village Inquest in *The Nine Tailors*, or the literary cocktail chat about the Book of the Moment in *Gaudy Night*."

Sayers's literary style in the Wimsey series allowed for very few compromises with the popular genre in which she was working, although various practitioners have taken their cue from her and attempted to write a highly literary type of crime narrative. She used as much of her education and training as she dared in her writing style: fully developed paragraphs and compound-complex sentence structures that bear no resemblance to the journalistic prose that usually serves the purposes of the crime novel; a sense of language and deployment of phrases in foreign languages, as well as literary and cultural allusions, many of them quite esoteric, which indicate a parallel with the High Modernism in vogue in the 1920s; captions and epigraphs that betray her intellectual underpinnings and probably evade the uninformed reader. The incorporation of such literary embellishments has earned her a mixed reaction, from the accusation of snobbish pretentiousness to praise for raising the genre to belletristic heights. In "Who Cares Who Killed Roger Ackroyd?" (1950) Edmund Wilson reports that when he leveled his heavy critical artillery against crime fiction in an earlier article, he was instructed to read Dorothy L. Sayers, so that he could appreciate a rare writer who was a stylist. Wilson found her style stilted and said so, probably missing the significance that her style contained the preciosities that befit the social level of her characters, both reflecting and parodying their life-styles, and that like many another fine practitioner of the crime fiction art, Sayers developed a narrative style that was particular to her artistic format.

Magazine cover showing Sayers at a meeting of the London Detection Club

Sayers's career as a writer of detective mysteries divides between the novels of the 1920s and those of the 1930s, and even within the short span of her involvement in the field the elements of significant change are apparent. Although one might assume that in her first works she was still the neophyte learning her craft, there is almost no hesitancy at all or amateurishness even in her initial ventures: the writing is always elegant, the command of her materials assured, and (despite some implausibilities in methods of murder and the carrying out of the murder, an area where she has never been given consistently good marks) an ingenuity and originality of design characterizes and individualizes each work. Of the first series of novels Mary Brian Durkin comments that they essentially deal with "Murder and Mirth," an apt description of crime novels that seem to follow the rules of fair play, supply the reader with the clues necessary for accurate detection, minimize the use of coincidence, and shy away from romantic entanglements. *Whose Body?*, *Clouds of Witness* (1926), *Unnatural Death* (1927), *The Unpleasantness at the Bellona Club* (1928), and *The Documents in the Case* (1930)–the last an un-

usual collaborative effort in an epistolary style that does not include Lord Peter at all–illustrate Sayers's initial concerns with the telling of the tale as well as the success of the denouement, featuring a fresh development in the often formulaic genre of detective fiction. Also, they are all highly characteristic of the mood and mores of the 1920s, which, despite Dorothy Sayers's personal awareness of the disadvantages to many of unemployment and unpleasant jobs, retained the features of a mindlessly carefree age.

Whose Body? introduced Lord Peter to the world of crime fiction readers in the process of unraveling a brace of puzzling dilemmas surrounding bodies–one dead and unidentified and one missing and presumed dead–undoubtedly Sayers's most comic situation. The novel is her most relaxed and pleasantly mischievous, indicating that she may well have intended a more frivolous variant of the art form than later developed and perhaps accounting for what she later called the "silly ass" aspects of her detective hero, which her detractors stress in characterizing Lord Peter. (The whimsey pun is therefore diagnostic.) To an extent *Whose Body?* is a gentle spoof of the detective genre and the English aristocracy, elements of which surface at various instances throughout the Wimsey canon, although to a lesser extent during the second phase of her productivity. Although it at times veers toward the facetious, the characterization of Lord Peter is indeed established from the outset as a wit, a connoisseur, an aristocrat with a malicious boyishness, a debunker and teaser, an accomplished pianist casually playing Scarlatti while Inspector Parker waits to resume discussion of the two cases, and a collector of incunabula–he is deflected from attending an auction by the discovery of the dead body and sends his valet Bunter in his place. One assumes early on that the silliness is a facade to disarm those he comes in contact with, a disguise which allows him the advantage over everyone around him, his perceptions remaining sharp and incisive throughout. Yet, one also assumes that Wimsey is enjoying his silliness to an extraordinary degree.

Only later on does the balancing half of Wimsey's personality define itself; he is a war hero with horrible nightmares of the trenches, having been buried alive until he was rescued by his batman Bunter, now his valet and invaluable assistant in detection, an accomplished photographer who can capture telltale fingerprints and a suave servant who can inconspicuously interrogate other servants. The later characteristics of Lord Peter Wimsey accumulate in slow sequence as the series develops: his distinguished good looks (an afterthought, apparently, since at first only the comic aspects of his features are emphasized); his athletic prowess, especially as a skilled cricketer, despite early indications that he is somewhat undersized; his charms as a deceiver of women, although he eventually matures into the avid and romantic wooer and winner of Harriet Vane. The process that builds up in the first four novels delineates the puckishness and potential of the aristocrat-sleuth, with a concomitant factor of vulnerability, while the last seven novels achieve his domestication of the vulnerable male.

Domestication reveals itself in *Whose Body?* in the introduction of the Dowager Duchess of Denver, Lord Peter's mother and the instigator of the investigation of the materialized naked corpse, whose run-on monologues are as much a mask of her shrewdness as is Wimsey's put-on silliness, marking her from the beginning as his natural collaborator: they are the two members of the family who are most alike and of mutual support. The presence of Inspector Charles Parker at the outset of the series sets up the investigative team of professional and amateur, a counterpart to the Wimsey-Bunter team of "upstairs/downstairs" access. The romance that will bring Parker into the family as Lord Peter's brother-in-law is still only in the wings as yet.

The second Lord Peter tale, *Clouds of Witness*, is the one that displays the full range of the Wimsey clan, and Sayers's dissection of the aristocracy (which balances her idolization of the class through the pro-Peter faction of the family) takes on a more serious note. Murder here is "brought home" to Wimsey when his older brother, the Duke of Denver, is accused of the crime and refuses to exonerate himself by openly explaining his whereabouts at the time of the killing. The pig-headed and stuffy Duke and the priggish and dull Duchess are in sharp contrast to the younger brother and the indomitable mother. The variable factor in the family is Lord Peter's sister Mary, who is also the one responsible for the disruptions that have led to the death of her fiancé, himself something of a cad who has already been denounced as a cardsharp. Nor is this the only unfortunate alliance that Lady Mary Wimsey has undertaken: her previous "suitor," a Bolshevik and of course anathema to the family, resurfaces in the investigation as a suspect who shoots and wounds Lord Peter. Mary's "liberation" had

Dust jacket for the first American edition of Sayers's 1930 novel, Strong Poison, *which introduced Lord Peter Wimsey's consort, Harriet Vane (courtesy of Otto Penzler)*

taken place during the war, when she was released temporarily from family confines to participate in war-related work in London, and she now is determined to make the most of that newfound freedom. Her position as a "tainted" woman anticipates that of Harriet Vane, and, despite the censure of the Duke and Duchess, she commands the sympathy of Lord Peter and the Dowager Duchess. Even more important, Lady Mary attracts the interest of Inspector Parker, so that the possibility of an alliance between the titled Mary and the middle-class policeman presents itself as *Clouds of Witness* is resolved, the author about to bring together the "best elements" of the two classes. The Duke of course is cleared by his frivolous younger brother despite his refusal to sanction or cooperate with Lord Peter's investigations, and in effect the aristocratic family perseveres.

There is something of a change of tone between the first two books, between the more remote case of the two "bodies" and the more pressing instance in which a peer of the realm and the head of the Wimsey family faces a trial in the House of Lords which cannot but go against him unless Lord Peter breaks the airtight case against the Duke. What could pass as a casual dalliance with amateur sleuthing becomes a serious concern and a test of Wimsey's professionalism despite his amateur standing. The "Murder and Mirth" aspects are still there in the background, in the satiric presentation of the Soviet Club and such, but the new seriousness takes front stage. "Murder and Mores" characterizes *Clouds of Witness* and will remain as a substratum for many another Sayers mystery novel.

Nor is Sayers's awareness of 1920s England as still suffering from the aftermath of World War I always to remain below surface; in *The Unpleasantness at the Bellona Club* the war is the dominant subtext throughout. The timing of the murder, during the two-minute reverential silence on the commemoration of the Armistice, provides the solemnity of the situation, while the setting of the murder, the stuffy Bellona Club, where ninety-two-year-old generals snooze away the day, provides the comic relief. Wimsey's own shell-shocked condition, from which he still suffers with nightmares but which he is progressively overcoming, primarily with the help of Mervyn Bunter, is replicated in the grandson of the dead general, a veteran whose shattered nerves have prevented him from earning a living and are poisoning his domestic situation. Less concerned with mores than with deeper human values, *The Unpleasantness at the Bellona Club* mystery displays concerns that seem to be at the heart of Dorothy Sayers's religious instincts, while Wimsey's ability to restore his psychic strength where others succumb suggests her view that only the fittest are likely to survive.

The other two novels of the early period, *Unnatural Death* and *The Documents in the Case*, are not as important in the creation of the Wimsey mystique or in establishing the essentials of the Sayers terrain. To an extent they take murder out of the genteel world, and, although they hardly place it in the "mean streets" of Raymond Chandler's arena, they emphasize an aspect of brutishness and nastiness that will eventually affect Lord Peter to a marked degree in the last Sayers novel. *Unnatural Death* depicts serial murders perpetrated so that the murderer would emerge as the sole beneficiary of an oral last will and testament and culminates in a bizarre twist with the murderer's desperate final move to avoid punishment. The epistolary novel *The Documents in the Case*, a non-Wimsey mystery, was written in collaboration with Robert Eustace, a pseudonym for Dr. Eustace Robert Barton. Sayers was in the process of becoming more involved in the technicalities of murder methods, conceiving of unique and unusual methods, and a medical collaborator and available adviser became advantageous for her. The demands of the age of murder mysteries turned away from the hypothetical and suspect secret poisons unknown to medical science but had not yet fixed on the exactness of scientific research for the means of causing death. P. D. James, who has acquired that degree of knowledgeability, faults Dorothy Sayers for methods that she finds "over ingenious and at least two are doubtfully practicable" as well as "unnecessarily complicated." "But if she was sometimes wrong," James adds in lauding Sayers, "she was never wilfully careless and her papers bear witness to the scholarly trouble she took to get her details right."

The 1920s witnessed the rise of Lord Peter Wimsey into prominence and the career of Dorothy L. Sayers into granting her financial security, and after seven years at the S. H. Benson advertising agency she quit in 1929. The decade began with several love affairs, most of them little more than desperate flirtations, but all of them ending unhappily, with one of them resulting in the birth of a son whom the mother sent to be raised by a cousin who had been her closest childhood friend. The need to be gainfully employed was intensified by Sayers's determination to provide for her child. She visited the boy during his childhood and later legally adopted him when she married, giving him her husband's name. The marriage in 1926 was to Oswald Atherton Fleming, a handsome newspaperman who proved to be irresponsible and soon unemployed as he became increasingly alcoholic. Sayers had never been a particularly attractive woman (although the 1915 photograph from Somerset College displays at least a temporary beauty), her thinning hair the result of a childhood illness, and the marriage paired the unattractive breadwinner and the handsome ne'er-do-well, whom she supported until his death in 1950. Fleming did have one talent that he practiced as an excellent cook, and even published a cookbook—which many suspect the diligent Dorothy Fleming ghostwrote for him.

When she left Benson's, Sayers moved with her husband from London to their own house in Witham, Essex. Although she did some translating from the French at the time, the 1930s found her primarily involved with the detective narratives, writing Wimsey novels and assorted short stories, editing mystery anthologies, and participating in the founding of the Detection Club, with herself as *prima inter pares*. The Detection Club sought to establish the rules by which the profession functioned and thrived, and raising the basic levels of the art form by insisting that the fictional detective solve the complex crime through cerebration and deductive reasoning, rather than depend upon some sort of deus ex machina. The membership consisted of such writers as Agatha Christie, Freeman Wills Croft, Anthony Berkeley, G. K. Chesterton, and Ronald A. Knox, and among their activities was the writing of communal novels of detection, for which each member would contribute a particular chapter.

The Wimsey novels of the second phase have been characterized as those of "Murder and Manners," and Sayers had indeed come to utilize aspects of the comedy of manners in her embellished technique. The shift tended to move her approach away from the fixed rules of the genre, the tightly constructed puzzles that highlighted the English novel of detection. Her locales became more diversified and somewhat exotic (a Fen country village, a Scottish fishing area, a coastal resort), unusual settings that set the tone for the particular crime situation, and she employed further facets of her acquired specialized knowledge. These changes did not always meet with critical approval, although by this time she had won a permanent audience for her fictions, and she defended them against the charge that they diluted the necessary elements of the format, contending that modifications were needed to add sophistication and significance, factors most often lacking in conventional crime books. In particular she offended by breaking the cardinal rule that disallowed romance to mix with detection, especially when it "compromised" the objectivity of the detective. With *Strong Poison* (1930) Harriet Vane appeared to complicate Wimsey's life and Sayers's fictional scheme of things.

Four of the last seven Wimsey books feature Harriet Vane in her shifting capacities and with varying intensity: *Strong Poison*, *Have His Carcase* (1932), *Gaudy Night*, and *Busman's Honeymoon*

Sayers with the Detection Club skull

(1937), and each in its own way marks a particular departure. (The subtitle for the last one discloses the significance of the departure: *A Love Story with Detective Interruptions*–critics who have concluded that Lord Peter Wimsey had been invented for the primary purpose of providing a husband for Dorothy L. Sayers's surrogate self point directly at that subtitle.) If Lord Peter had seemed an almost perverse alter ego for the plainfaced vicar's daughter, Harriet Vane seems uncomfortably close to an autobiographic self, not just as a writer of detective fiction (with a male detective of her own creating), but as a woman who had had an illicit affair with a scoundrel unworthy of her affection. It only remained for the scorned woman to become a potential murderer of her ex-lover to satisfy a deep-seated wish-fulfillment, as well as for her attractive detective hero (he has become decidedly better-looking and possibly a few inches taller since *Whose Body?*) to rescue her from certain execution for a murder she did not commit. Harriet Vane's gratitude, however, prevents her from accepting Wimsey's courtly attentions, which evolve through several novels from admiration to obsession, span some five years and escape-travel on his part, and display themselves in multiple proposals of marriage. She herself becomes involved in attempting to solve a murder in *Have his Carcase* and a criminal outrage in *Gaudy Night*, although he is eventually called in to provide his expertise. And in the second case he is finally rewarded: in

Oxford he plies his troth in Latin and is accepted in Latin. Their honeymoon is the immediate occasion of another murder mystery to be solved (*Busman's Honeymoon*), a literary afterthought that has done very little to enhance Sayers's literary reputation.

Harriet Vane's entrance was apparently intended as Lord Peter Wimsey's exit, and *Strong Poison* scheduled to be the last in the canon, but Wimsey's popularity persuaded Sayers (as Conan Doyle had been persuaded by public insistence) to delay her detective's retirement. Readers might have suspected that the author's total commitment was no longer in her next work, *The Five Red Herrings* (1931), and it is usually placed fairly low on the list of her best books. Nonetheless, in some ways it is vintage Sayers: an exquisite puzzle with a half dozen equally qualified suspects, a mood throughout that sets the scene, dependence on the intricacies of timetables, and the complex solution provided by a ratiocinative detective to a complex murder plot. Before revealing his findings and eliminating the five red herrings that have obfuscated the track of the guilty suspect, Wimsey claims for himself that ultimate mantle: "At last I feel like Sherlock Holmes." (Years earlier he had embarked on the case of the naked corpse by announcing, "Enter Sherlock Holmes, disguised as a walking gentleman.") No mention of Harriet Vane appears in this successor to *Strong Poison*, and Lord Peter might just as well been the misogynist Sherlock; but in *Have His Carcase* Lord Peter is very much in the thoughts of neophyte detective Harriet Vane as she, having discovered a dead man on the beach with his throat slashed, tries to put her "fictional" detective abilities to work for her–in effect negating the necessity of having Lord Peter Wimsey on hand. Complications arise when the tide claims the body, but she attempts to read the evidence left behind. It is Lord Peter who is eventually called in and succeeds in solving the murder, but Harriet refuses to accept his offer of marriage. The added importance of locale in the Sayers pattern can be noted in her introductory comment: "In *Five Red Herrings*, the plot was invented to fit the locality; in this book, the locality has been invented to fit the plot."

The next two novels, *Murder Must Advertise* and *The Nine Tailors*, are usually ranked among Sayers's best, and it is difficult to imagine what the Wimsey series would have been like without them, had Sayers given up as a writer of detective fiction in 1930. Of equal importance, they draw so perfectly from her years at Benson's and her earlier years in Bluntisham-cum-Earith in the Fens, evocative of the sights and smells of atmospherically familiar areas for her. The first captures not only the professional workplace in London, the tensions, jealousies, suspicions, friendships, camaraderie, and pulsations of an advertising concern in a metropolis but also the wild and frantic lives of the young rich, and in each Lord Peter Wimsey moves with facility and in disguise: he takes his two middle names, Death Bredon, as his operational name as he poses as an ad writer at the agency where a murder has occurred (disguised, as so often in Sayers's work, as an accident), and as the masked Harlequin among the fast set where drugs are being bought and used. If *Murder Must Advertise* is Sayers at her most "modern" *The Nine Tailors* is Sayers at her most old-fashioned, perhaps at her most traditional. The book was actually begun before *Murder Must Advertise* and had to be abandoned temporarily while she met contractual obligations and quickly produced the book she claimed to dislike; on the other hand, she called *The Nine Tailors* "a labour of love." In the novel she returned to a village like the one in which she spent her childhood and immortalized an aspect of her vicar father; also she took the opportunity to write a paean of praise and even exaltation for the Church in which she had deep roots and to express admiration for a facet of old England to which she felt politically committed, making the book an examination of the tradition of bell-ringing as much as a murder mystery. And as a murder mystery it is one of her starkest and most terrifying.

Busman's Honeymoon, which ostensibly and belatedly closed the Wimsey series, first took life as a play co-authored in 1937 by Sayers and Muriel St. Clare Byrne and is distinguished not only by the dominant elements of romantic marital love upstaging detection, but by the excessive reaction that Lord Peter experiences to the execution of the thoroughly unpleasant murderer whom he brought to justice. The agonies of conscience that he suffers over the hanging of the unrepentant villain breaks the bounds of the fictional assumptions, the willing suspension of disbelief necessitated by the escapist nature of detective fiction, although it fulfills the logic established in the opening novel of a sensitive war hero, the shell-shocked and tormented Major Wimsey. True to form, Sayers's concluding novel contains one of her more outlandish murder methods, so that

Dust jacket for the first American edition of Sayers's 1933 novel based in part on her experiences at an advertising agency (courtesy of Otto Penzler)

the fictionality of that aspect contrasts sharply with the reality of Wimsey's anguish. After 1937 the dashing detective was withdrawn by his creator from public view; his career as an amateur sleuth and hers as a writer of detective narratives ended, and yet during the first year of World War II he does make a new appearance (the story is set in 1939, and was written in 1942, though it was not published until 1972), perhaps analogous to Holmes's World War I reappearance in "His Last Bow," in a short story titled "Talboys." The domestication of Lord Peter Wimsey is completed by his role as the father of three sons.

The Wimsey canon stands as the mainstay of Dorothy L. Sayers's literature of detection, consisting of the eleven novels and two dozen short stories, supplemented by the epistolary novel and assorted stories, a half dozen of which concern her supplementary detective, the wine salesman Montague Egg, a prosaic bourgeois who is so obviously an antihero to the heroic Lord Peter. Even

the minor pieces indicate an author of consistently high literary quality, perhaps overly so for the demands of the genre, displaying a penchant for witty repartee and elegant epigrams. The personal involvement of the author with both Lord Peter and Harriet is apparent, as are her personal views and prejudices. There is no objective, indifferent narrator masking Sayers the author in her major novels: a high moral stance, which nonetheless makes allowances for women in love having illicit affairs, or for Wimsey manipulating unscrupulous women for his own higher purposes; a staunch patriotism in defense of the traditional values of England and its ruling classes; a contempt, mirrored in her caustic depictions, of such "undesirables" as cads and communists, drug dealers and dizzy debutantes, as well as scientific atheists. Sayers was often rather unsubtle in the various intrusions of anti-Semitic sentiments in her detective writings, although the primary case against her—in *Whose Body?*—may actually be a matter of misinterpreting the comic intentions that somehow went awry. That Sir Reuben Levy is a self-made Jewish financier is at the core of the conflict, since he succeeds in winning the love of the woman that the Englishman with the "proper credentials" desires. Both men become successful and are knighted for their accomplishments, but Sir Julian Freke waits some two decades to exact his revenge, his "perfect murder" plot depending on his finding a dying derelict who looks Semitic enough to pass for Sir Reuben. Lord Peter's astuteness in recognizing that the naked corpse was not that of the Jewish financier originally rested on the absence of any sign of his having been circumcised, but that salient observation was wisely excised by the publisher. In effect the decent Sir Reuben is a far more sympathetic victim than the cold-bloodedly atheistic doctor who kills him.

One need not rely on the later career Dorothy Sayers embraced to read the strong implications of her particular code in the detective fictions: in many ways her major Wimsey works define her values in very definite patterns. Her authorized biographer, James Brabazon, reminds readers of "the deep sense of tradition and continuity" deriving from her rural background, describing "Dorothy's England, traditional, ordered, conventional, untouched by—indeed resentful of—the social disturbances of the Industrial Revolution and the intellectual excitements of the age." In response to the "excitement" of the Russian Revolution Sayers can be categorical: as early as the first novel she gratuitously introduces a Russian mother and daughter who escaped from the revolution-torn country and elicit Lord Peter's sympathy for the nerves-shattered daughter. The conversation takes place mostly in French, her lingua franca with the English aristocrat. More frequently, it is the satiric mode that Sayers employs in her virulent anti-Communism, especially in the second novel, where the obnoxious Bolshevik actually shoots Wimsey. "A Socialist Conchy with neither bowels nor breedings" is how Wimsey dismisses him, but he nonetheless has to endure a wretched and sloppily served meal at the Soviet Club. Most often Sayers broadens the scope of her satiric thrusts and somewhat vitiates her own prejudices by putting the more lurid examples of chauvinism, class bias, and racism in the mouths of satirized characters. The Dowager Duchess, on the other hand, has a license to say almost anything; her sentiments can be smiled at but not despised, and she herself is meant to be greatly admired. "The lower orders are so prejudiced," she announces; "what unfinished-looking faces they have—so characteristic, I think, of the lower middle-class." The tongue-in-cheek sense of play through most of the "Murder and Mirth" novels are a dominant characteristic of Sayers's literary tone.

There is an important modulation in the Wimsey canon between the early snobbism and the later patriotism, although the consistent vein of class-consciousness persists throughout. The Dowager Duchess in *Whose Body?* blithely maintains that "Dad always hated self-made people and wouldn't have 'em at Denver," and that as the present Duke, "old Gerald keeps up the tradition." Lord Peter has already echoed the same sentiment, but without indicating actual approval. A bias against financiers may be at the heart of the sentiment, as Lord Peter indicates when he refers to those "whose breath devastated whole districts with famine or swept financial potentates from their seats," yet he allows that Sir Reuben was in his private life a decent and prudent man. In *Unnatural Death* Wimsey remembers the look on the face of "a great financier as he took up his pen to sign a contract. Wimsey had been called to witness the signature, and refused. Incidentally, the financier had been murdered soon after, and Wimsey had declined to investigate the matter." This incident is certainly gratuitous and therefore all the more diagnostic of a genuine attitude on the part of the author. An occasional humanitarian concern in *Strong Poison* becomes a harbinger of others in the later works; in this case

Sayers in the winter of 1949-1950 (photograph by Atherton Fleming)

Wimsey contrasts the English care for animals with unconcern for the plight of the underprivileged: "It's all of a piece with people who write to the papers about keepin' dogs in draughty kennels and don't give a hoot—or a penny—to stop landlords allowin' a family of thirteen to sleep in an undrained cellar with no glass in the windows." He has come a long way in a short time from his role as "silly ass" to that of a committed ideologue of rather complex hues.

Direct statements such as these by Lord Peter are quite another matter from his more casual conversations, where he tends to at least politely pretend to agree with whomever he is talking to. He might begin with an innocuous complaint against advertising, for example, but the conversation escalates: "Wetheridge said that in his time, by gad, a respectable Club would have scorned advertisements, and that he could remember the time when newspapers were run by gentlemen for gentlemen. Wimsey said that nothing was what it had been; he thought it must be due to the War." A nostalgia for the past and a reaction against the present progressively invade the Wimsey books, culminating in Lord Peter's assertion in *Gaudy Night*: "One may either hulloo on the inevitable, and be called a bloodthirsty progressive; or one may try to gain time and be called a bloodthirsty reactionary" (it is apparent in which direction he tips the balance). Statements replace innuendo and ambivalent small talk during the 1930s volumes, where the names (and ideas) of Mussolini and Hitler appear more than just occasionally. Harriet Vane in particular is disturbed by the realization that her books would be burned by Fascists, and her role as an independent wage-earning woman would not be allowed. Also in *Gaudy Night*, however, there is the conversation between the college porter and a foreman in which the two agree that "Wot this country wants . . . is a 'Itler." Such ideas expressed by the "lower" classes are apparently not intended to be taken as having the author's imprimatur, yet bits and pieces of just such dialogues pepper all of Sayers's books.

Against the backdrop of English class stratification Sayers sets her murder drama, and in the two novels in which class differences are particularly pertinent (*Clouds of Witness* and *Gaudy Night*) it may be significant that no murder takes place, in the first because the death was actually suicide and in the second because scare tactics are the full extent of the criminal intention. Sayers is quite categorical in *Clouds of Witness* when she informs the reader that "in the kind of society to which the persons involved belonged, such a misdemeanour as cheating at cards was regarded as far more shameful than such sins as murder and adultery," and consequently the cardsharp does away with himself, obviating murder, and the Duke's adultery is excused and even justified. In *Gaudy Night* the scholars at Shrewsbury College halfheartedly search among themselves for the perpetrators of the scurrilous offenses, preferring to assume that that person was outside their class: "Surely . . . it is far more likely to be one of the scouts than one of ourselves. I can scarcely imagine that a member of this Common Room would be capable of anything so disgusting. Whereas that class of persons–" (and even among themselves complete homogeneity no longer exists, so that a prejudice is voiced against a "lively young woman" whose "antecedents are not particularly refined"). The frequently expressed wish in many genteel murder mysteries is that the murderer is in reality an outsider (the wish in *Busman's Honeymoon* reads: "unless the crime could be traced to a passing tramp or somebody"), but never is that the real case in the self-contained puzzle. In *Gaudy Night*, however, the Oxford community of women scholars remains intact, and it is indeed the lowly menial who is unmasked as the terrorizer.

There is no doubt that in Dorothy Sayers's cosmogony England is in danger, externally from dangerous ideologies and internally from foreign elements and a lowering of standards and values. Vilified throughout the fictions either by those in whom we are expected to endow our trust or by those who are admittedly questionable themselves, are such people as socialists, pacifists, conscientious objectors, proletarians, lesbians, cardsharps, financiers, the nouveau riche, Jews, Scots (and to compound the vices of avarice, some are even Scottish Jews!), Irish, Italians, atheists, and attorneys. Social deterioration is observed by Lord Peter even at Oxford ("The Cherwell's not what it was, especially on Sunday. More like Bank Holiday at Margate, with gramophones and bathing-dresses and everybody barging into everybody else.")–in her Author's Note Sayers expresses her own gripe ("The Corporation Dump . . . is, or was, a fact, and no apology for it is due from me"). To counter the encroachment on the civilized values of England, Sayers conceives of a perfect blend of the elements of the bourgeoisie and aristocracy, not just in the marriage of Harriet and Peter, but in the alliance of Peter Wimsey and Charles Parker: "Wimsey was the Roland of the combination–quick, impulsive, careless, and an artistic jack-of-all-trades. Parker was the Oliver–cautious, solid, painstaking, his mind a blank to art and literature and exercising itself, in spare moments, with Evangelical theology." The actual marriage takes place between Parker and Lady Mary Wimsey, and the effected balance is demonstrated in a bit of reverse snobbism: "It pleased Mary to have the management of their moderate combined income, and incidentally did her a great deal of good. She now patronized her wealthy brother with all the superiority which the worker feels over the man who merely possesses money."

Wimsey himself, it turns out, is a balance of originating forces, having a French antecedent in his family tree. His uncle, a Delagardie, is called upon to write a biographical introduction to *Unnatural Death* in which he mentions that he perceives in his nephew "that underlying sense of social responsibility which prevents the English landed gentry from being a total loss, spiritually speaking." If Lord Peter's spirituality is ever in question, it can be verified as early as in *Whose Body?* when he is in Salisbury tracking down a lead, but avails himself of the opportunity in the

Dust jacket for the first American edition of Sayers's 1934 novel set in the Fen country, where she grew up (courtesy of Otto Penzler)

cathedral town to attend Evensong. In a later novel Harriet finds to her surprise that the urban aristocrat she married fits in well in the small village, and she recognizes in attending a village concert that there is an underlying facet to the husband, as he corroborates her own rural background: "In London, anybody, at any moment, might do or become anything. But in a village—no matter what village—they were all immutably themselves; parson, organist, sweep, duke's son and doctor's daughter, moving like chessmen upon their allotted squares." Her conclusion is an astounding one: "I have married England."

And it is England that is ultimately extolled through the person of Lord Peter, and his peregrinations over the English landscape are calculated to expose what is best in England. First, it is the countryside itself and country people, especially that brand of English "pluck" immortalized in the closing chapter of *The Nine Tailors*: the vicar

and his parishioners braving the floods and persevering to ensure a kind of normal life for those in refuge: "The Rector's organization worked brilliantly." *The Nine Tailors* was Sayers's special project since it embodied her salute to her country childhood; her reverence for the Anglican church, its spiritual essence, its ritual, and its architecture; and her depiction of even the bleakest of English landscapes as intrinsically beautiful. What to many seemed an aberration in the detective story, the emphasis on bell-ringing in the church steeple, was to Sayers the essence of the narrative, at once a magnificent experience and a uniquely English one, as she understates it by saying, "The art of change-ringing is peculiar to the English, and, like most English peculiarities, unintelligible to the rest of the world."

Have His Carcase and *Five Red Herrings* are the texts that allowed Dorothy Sayers the finest opportunities to describe with pleasure the rural landscape. The invented coastal landscape in the first is idyllic, despite the corpse on the beach, and as initially described returns the England of the 1930s to a serene rural past: "Except for an occasional tradesman's van, or a dilapidated Morris, and the intermittent appearance of white smoke from a distant railway-engine, the landscape was as rural and solitary as it might have been two hundred years before." In the second instance, the locale is specifically Galloway in Scotland, and Wimsey's arrival there evokes a long paragraph of exaltation of the gleaming coast, the farms and inns, the scent hanging in the air, the jetty and the cottages, the flowers and the church spire and the hillside—a rural paradise. And *Gaudy Night* is redolent of many of the same essences set in Oxford: long paragraphs celebrate an April morning in the town, a city of "withdrawn and secret beauty" during vacation time. But more important is the university itself, which the Warden of Shrewsbury extols as: "the home of lost causes: if the love of learning for its own sake is a lost cause everywhere else in the world, let us see to it that here at least, it finds its abiding home."

As a celebration of the rituals and traditions, the pomp and circumstance, of "Dorothy's England," the Wimsey tales are a series of patriotic statements, although as mirthful pieces of fiction they range somewhere between the novels of P. G. Wodehouse and Evelyn Waugh. Primary among that celebration is the aura emitted by the House of Lords in *Clouds of Witness*, an institution already in question in democratic England of the

Dust jacket for the first American edition of the novel in which newlyweds Lord Peter Wimsey and Harriet Vane find a corpse in their honeymoon cottage (courtesy of Otto Penzler)

1920s, but one which Sayers endows with regal importance and seriousness as it prepares to try Gerald, Duke of Denver, on murder charges. The fate of the Duke is never in question for the reader since Lord Peter is winging his way to America to obtain the last piece of evidence that will exonerate him: it is the institution itself that is awesome in its majesty and apparently fully justified in its time-honored rights to sit in judgment of a peer. Only as she approached the winding down of the series, and the special attention that she devoted to *The Nine Tailors* and *Gaudy Night* in their celebrations of the time-hallowed Anglo-Catholic Church and Oxford University, did Sayers deal with an aspect of her society somewhat repugnant to her: the urban London scene of *Murder Must Advertise*, a novel that she had to write quickly. Nonetheless, *Murder Must Advertise* is not without its own celebration of an English in-

stitution, as Lord Peter distinguishes himself as a crack cricketer toward the end of the novel, and the sentiment of Mr. Brotherhood echoes sonorously: "I don't care who wins or who loses, sir, provided they play the game." Nor does the despised practice of commercial advertising fail to redeem itself somewhat: having satisfactorily solved the mystery, Wimsey insists on finishing his advertising campaign, and brings it to a successful conclusion, very much proud of his efforts and a job well done.

It is important to note that the panorama of Sayers's England also includes Sayers herself—and not only in her obverse/reverse images of herself in Lord Peter and mirror image of herself in Harriet Vane, but in minor character of Miss Climpson, introduced in *Unnatural Death* and of occasional service thereafter. "A Use for Spinsters" is the chapter in which Wimsey sets up an investigative agency under Miss Climpson's competent guidance, utilizing the untapped talents of spinsters who have nothing to do, but as devoted gossips and ferreters of information can prove invaluable. Miss Climpson's diligently Catholic approach to the Anglican Church reflects the author's specific concerns, and religion becomes a subject mentioned often through Miss Climpson's prodding. And in *Murder Must Advertise* a Sayers surrogate is presented as well in the ad agency, modeled on the one for which she worked for seven years, a Miss Meteyard, whose name contains an anagram for Sayers (MiSS metEYARd).

The detective writing career finally abandoned and the 1930s drawing to a close, Dorothy Leigh Sayers involved herself enthusiastically in her religious plays, essays, and talks, and in her translations, primarily of Dante's *Commedia*. By then she was certainly a celebrity as the creator of Lord Peter Wimsey, as well known as an eccentric, famous for her domesticated pet pig, Francis Bacon, who shared her living quarters until he finally wound up in her frying pan during the austere years of World War II. An honorary doctorate of letters was awarded her by the University of Durham the year that her husband died, and she later became a churchwarden at St. Thomas's in London, where she had one of her religious dramas produced. On 16 December 1957 Sayers returned alone to her cottage in Witham after a Christmas shopping trip to London; and the next day was found dead at the foot of the stairs, apparently the victim of a sudden stroke.

As one of the most accomplished practitioners of the mystery writer's art, and with Agatha

Sayers's home at Witham, 1980 (photograph by James Brabazon)

Christie vying for the dust-jacket-blurb designation as the Queen of the Golden Age of mystery fiction, Sayers was distinguished for her new and unusual methods of murder, tapping the knowledge of toxicologists and the medical profession so that her plots evolved frequently around highly original–and as often widely improbable–modi operandi. After the first handful of novels and stories, and with a captured readership assured, she sharpened her talents within the format: the later volumes disclose exceptionally fine characteristics only hinted at in the earlier ones, although the Wimsey family had their immediate inception as wonderfully developed characters and carried the weight of the first narratives. *Murder Must Advertise* rises to the level of a comedy of manners and mores in the manner of Evelyn Waugh, while *The Nine Tailors* is unique in its grim and austerely atmospheric capturing of hardened people in a remote and somber countryside. Either of these two qualifies as her most accomplished piece of detective fiction, although for a handful of aficionados of the Wimsey books *Gaudy Night* vies with them for honors and has its own special place in the canon, especially since it moves beyond the assumed constraints of the format. It is an overly long narrative of carefully limned characterizations, a particularly large cast of characters when one considers the bounds of allowable

"suspects," and without the expected murder that is at the center of every crime novel (a few writers, Nicolas Freeling for one, have since attempted the full-length nonmurder mystery). In place of the obligatory murder or murders *Gaudy Night* depends upon a series of disturbing hate messages and ugly acts of vandalism.

Gaudy Night has its detractors who maintain that it violates the carefully built-up structures of the generic form, but its advocates view it as an expansion of as well as a liberation from the constraints of that form. It retains all the chilling effects of the legitimate crime novel and balances well the celebration of the feminine academy with a scrutiny of the limited lives of women cut off from normal contacts and concerns, and it strongly anticipates Sayers's interests outside the scope of detective fiction. Sayers's ambivalence toward the kind of writing that made her financially free of a time-consuming office job never conflicts with the dedication that went into the writing of the Wimsey books in particular, and *Strong Poison*, as it introduces crime writer Harriet Vane, even presents an apologia for the profession along her own particular lines. "Damn it," exclaims Lord Peter in Harriet's defense, "she writes detective stories and in detective stories virtue is always triumphant. They're the purest literature we have." Such a justification would only

269

Portrait of Sayers by Sir William Oliphant Hutchinson, 1950 (National Portrait Gallery)

have mollified Dorothy Sayers temporarily. The same Wimsey in *Gaudy Night* seeks to transform Harriet from the writer of detective fiction to perhaps the kind of writer Sayers herself sought to become when he says, "You haven't yet . . . written the book you could write if you tried," having in mind the required specifics of such a literature when he noted, "You would have to abandon the jigsaw kind of story and write a book about human beings for a change." For the millions of readers of the Lord Peter Wimsey books, Sayers had constantly demonstrated her mastery of those puzzles and created some delightful and meaningful human beings as well.

Bibliographies:
Robert B. Harmon and Margaret A. Burger, *An*

Annotated Guide to the Works of Dorothy L. Sayers (New York: Garland, 1977);

Colleen B. Gilbert, *A Bibliography of the Works of Dorothy L. Sayers* (London: Macmillan, 1977; Hamden, Conn.: Anchor, 1978);

Ruth T. Youngblood, *Dorothy L. Sayers: A Reference Guide* (Boston: G. K. Hall, 1982).

Biographies:
Janet Hitchman, *Such a Strange Lady: An Introduction to Dorothy L. Sayers, 1893-1957* (New York: Harper & Row, 1975);

Ralph E. Hone, *Dorothy L. Sayers: A Literary Biography* (Kent, Ohio: Kent State University Press, 1979);

James Brabazon, *Dorothy L. Sayers: A Biography* (New York: Scribners, 1981).

References:

Elaine Bander, "The Case for Sir Charles Grandison," *Sayers Review*, 1 (1977): 8-9;

Bander, "Dorothy L. Sayers and the Apotheosis of Detective Fiction," *Armchair Detective*, 10 (1977): 362-365;

Lionel Basney, "God and Peter Wimsey," *Christianity Today*, 17 (14 September 1973): 27-28;

Miriam Brody, "The Haunting of *Gaudy Night*: Misreadings in a Work of Detective Fiction," *Style*, 19 (Spring 1985): 94-116;

Carol Ann Brown, "Notes for a Lost Eulogy," *Bulletin of the New York C. S. Lewis Society*, 9 (1978): 106;

SueEllen Campbell, "The Detective Heroine and the Death of Her Hero: Dorothy Sayers to P. D. James," *Modern Fiction Studies*, 29 (Autumn 1983): 497-510;

John G. Cawelti, *Adventure, Mystery, and Romance* (Chicago: University of Chicago Press, 1976), pp. 120-125;

Joe R. Christopher, "Dorothy L. Sayers and Inklings," *Mythlore*, 4 (1976): 8-9;

Christopher, "Dorothy L. Sayers, Duchess of Redonda," *Armchair Detective*, 17 (Fall 1984): 418-419;

Christopher, "Lord Peter Views the Telly," *Armchair Detective*, 12 (1979): 20-27;

Christopher, "The Mystery of Robert Eustace," *Armchair Detective*, 13 (1980): 365;

S. L. Clark, "The Female Felon in Dorothy L. Sayers's *Gaudy Night*," *Publication of the Arkansas Philological Association*, 3 (1977): 59-67;

Alzina Stone Dale, *Maker and Craftsman: The Story of Dorothy L. Sayers* (Grand Rapids, Mich.: Eerdmans, 1978);

Mary Brian Durkin, *Dorothy L. Sayers* (Boston: Hall, 1980);

Lee Edwards, "Love and Work: Fantasies of Resolution," *Frontiers*, 2 (1977): 31-38;

William R. Epperson, "The Repose of Very Delicate Balance: Postulants and Celebrants of the Sacrament of Marriage in the Detective Fiction of Dorothy L. Sayers," *Mythlore*, 6 (Fall 1979): 33-36;

Dawson Gaillard, *Dorothy L. Sayers* (New York: Ungar, 1981);

Martin Green, "The Detection of a Snob," *Listener*, 49 (14 March 1963): 461-464;

E. R. Gregory, "From Detective Stories to Dante: The Transitional Phase of Dorothy L. Sayers," *Christianity and Literature*, 26 (Winter 1977): 9-17;

George Grella, "Dorothy Sayers and Peter Wimsey," *University of Rochester Library Bulletin*, 28 (Summer 1974): 33-42;

Trevor H. Hall, *Dorothy L. Sayers: Nine Literary Studies* (Hamden, Conn.: Shoe String Press, 1980);

Margaret P. Hannay, "Head versus Heart in Dorothy L. Sayers' *Gaudy Night*," *Mythlore*, 6 (Summer 1979): 33-37;

Hannay, ed., *As Her Whimsey Took Her: Critical Essays on the Work of Dorothy L. Sayers* (Kent, Ohio: Kent State University Press, 1979);

Barbara G. Harrison, "Dorothy L. Sayers and the Tidy Art of Detective Fiction," *Ms.*, 3 (November 1974): 66-69;

Howard Haycraft, *Murder for Pleasure* (New York: Appleton-Century, 1941), pp. 135-142;

Caroline Heilbrun, "Dorothy L. Sayers: Biography Between the Lines," *American Scholar*, 51 (Autumn 1982): 552-561;

Heilbrun, "Sayers, Lord Peter and God," *American Scholar*, 37 (Spring 1968): 324-330;

Lillian M. Heldreth, "Breaking the Rules of the Game: Shattered Patterns in Dorothy L. Sayers's *Gaudy Night*," *Clues*, 3 (Spring-Summer 1982): 120-127;

Nancy Y. Hoffman, "Mistresses of Malfeasance," in *Dimensions of Detective Fiction*, edited by Carry N. Landrum, Pat Browne, and Ray B. Browne (Bowling Green, Ohio: Popular Press, 1976), pp. 97-101;

Kathleen Gregory Klein, "Dorothy Sayers," in *10 Women of Mystery*, edited by Earl F. Bargainnier (Bowling Green, Ohio: Popular Press, 1981), pp. 8-39;

Thomas D. Lane, "Dignity in the Detective Novel," *Clues*, 1 (Spring 1980): 119-122;

Q. D. Leavis, "The Case of Miss Dorothy Sayers," *Scrutiny*, 6 (December 1937): 334-340;

G. A. Lee, *The Wimsey Saga: A Chronology* (Witham, U.K.: Dorothy L. Sayers Historical and Literary Society, 1980);

Donald G. Marshall, "*Gaudy Night*: An Investigation of Truth," *Seven*, 4 (1983): 98-114;

John F McDiarmid, "Reality and Romance: Dorothy Sayers' Intention and Accomplishment," *Clues*, 6 (Fall-Winter 1985): 123-134;

Bruce Merry, "Dorothy L. Sayers: Mystery and Demystification," in *Essays in Detective Fiction*, edited by Bernard Benstock (London: Macmillan, 1983), pp. 18-32; republished as *Art in Crime Writing* (New York: St. Martin's Press, 1984), pp. 18-32;

Virginia B. Morris, "Arsenic and Blue Lace: Sayers' Criminal Women," *Modern Fiction Studies*, 29 (Autumn 1983): 485-495;

Doris T. Myers, "Lord Peter Wimsey's Answer to Pilate," *Cimarron Review*, 33 (1975): 26-34;

Seta Ohanian, "Dinner with Dorothy L. Sayers or 'As My Whimsey Feeds Me,' " *Journal of Popular Culture*, 13 (1980): 434-446;

Nancy-Lou Patterson, "Beneath the Ancient Roof: The House as Symbol in Dorothy L. Sayers' *Busman's Honeymoon*," *Mythlore*, 10 (Winter 1984): 39-46;

Patterson, "Images of Judaism and Anti-Semitism in the Novels of Dorothy L. Sayers," *Sayers Review*, 2 (June 1978): 17-24;

Laura K. Ray, "The Mysteries of *Gaudy Night*: Feminism, Faith, and the Depths of Character," *The Mystery and Detection Annual 1973* (Beverly Hills, Cal.: Donald Adams, 1974), pp. 272-285;

Barbara Reynolds, "The Origin of Lord Peter Wimsey," *Times Literary Supplement*, 22 April 1977, p. 492;

William Reynolds, "Dorothy L. Sayers' Detective Short Fiction," *Armchair Detective*, 14 (Spring 1981): 176-181;

Reynolds, "Literature, Latin, and Love: Dorothy L. Sayers' *Gaudy Night*," *Clues*, 6 (Spring-Summer 1985): 67-78;

H. P. Rickman, "From Detection to Theology: The Work of Dorothy Sayers," *Hibbert Journal*, 60 (July 1962): 290-296;

Karen Rockow, "Blowing the Whistle on Dorothy Sayers and Lord Peter," *Unicorn*, 3 (1974): 37-38, 41;

Elizabeth Bond Ryan and William J. Eakins, *The Lord Peter Wimsey Cookbook* (New Haven, Conn.: Ticknor & Fields, 1981);

William M. Scott, "Lord Peter Wimsey of Piccadilly: His Lordship's Life and Times," *Armchair Detective*, 13 (1980): 212-218;

C. W. Scott-Giles, *The Wimsey Family* (New York: Harper & Row, 1977);

P. L. Scowcroft, "The Detective Fiction of Dorothy L. Sayers: A Source for the Social Historian?," *Seven*, 5 (1984): 70-83;

Julian Symons, *The Detective Story in Britain* (London: Longman's, 1962), pp. 26-28;

Richard Tillinghast, "Dorothy L. Sayers: Murder and Whimsy," *New Republic*, 175 (31 July 1976): 30-31;

Nancy M. Tischler, *Dorothy L. Sayers: A Pilgrim Soul* (Atlanta: John Knox Press, 1979);

Colin Watson, *Snobbery with Violence: Crime Stories and Their Audience* (London: Eyre & Spottiswoode, 1971), pp. 146-148, 153-156, 160-162;

Joyce Lannom Watts, "The Androgynous Aspects of Harriet and Peter," *Sayers Review*, 4 (January 1981): 1-11;

Edmund Wilson, "Who Cares Who Killed Roger Ackroyd?," in his *Classics and Commercials: A Literary Chronicle of the Forties* (New York: Farrar, Straus, 1950), pp. 257-265;

Fritz Wölken, "Dorothy Sayers," in *Englische Dichter Der Moderne*, edited by Rudolf Sühnel and Dieter Riesner (Berlin: Schmidt, 1971), pp. 30-31.

Papers:
Dorothy L. Sayers's papers are at Wheaton College in Wheaton, Illinois.

Helen Simpson

(1 December 1897-14 October 1940)

Barrie Hayne
University of Toronto

SELECTED BOOKS: *Truth, The Real Helena, The Witch, Masks: Lightning Sketches* (Oxford: Blackwell, 1918);

Philosophies In Little (Sydney: Angus & Robertson, 1921);

A Man of His Time (Sydney: Angus & Robertson, 1923);

Acquittal (London: Heinemann, 1925; New York: Knopf, 1925);

The Baseless Fabric (London: Heinemann, 1925; New York: Knopf, 1925);

The Women's Comedy (London: Pelican Press, 1926);

Cups, Wands, and Swords (London: Heinemann, 1927; New York: Knopf, 1928);

Enter Sir John, by Simpson and Clemence Dane (London: Hodder & Stoughton, 1928; New York: Cosmopolitan, 1928);

Mumbudget (London: Heinemann, 1928; Garden City, N.Y.: Doubleday, Doran, 1929);

The Desolate House (London: Heinemann, 1929); republished as *Desires and Devices* (Garden City, N.Y.: Doubleday, Doran, 1930);

Printer's Devil, by Simpson and Dane (London: Hodder & Stoughton, 1930); republished as *Author Unknown* (New York: Cosmopolitan, 1930);

'Vantage Striker (London: Heinemann, 1931); republished as *The Prime Minister Is Dead* (Garden City, N.Y.: Doubleday, Doran, 1931);

Boomerang (London: Heinemann, 1932; Garden City, N.Y.: Doubleday, Doran, 1932);

Re-Enter Sir John, by Simpson and Dane (London: Hodder & Stoughton, 1932; New York: Farrar & Rinehart, 1932);

Ask a Policeman, by Simpson and others (London: Barker, 1933; New York: Morrow, 1933);

The Spanish Marriage (London: Davies, 1933; New York: Putnam's, 1933);

The Woman on the Beast, Viewed from Three Angles (London: Heinemann, 1933; Garden City, N.Y.: Doubleday, Doran, 1933);

Helen Simpson

The Happy Housewife: A Book for the House That Is or Is to Be (London: Hodder & Stoughton, 1934);

Henry VIII (London: Davies, 1934; New York: Appleton-Century, 1934);

The Female Felon (London: Dickson & Thompson, 1935);

Saraband for Dead Lovers (London: Heinemann, 1935; New York: Doubleday, 1935);

Imaginary Biographies, with others (London: Allen & Unwin, 1936);

Under Capricorn (London: Heinemann, 1937; New York: Macmillan, 1938);

A Woman Among Wild Men: Mary Kingsley (London: Nelson, 1938);

Maid No More (London: Heinemann, 1940; New York: Reynal, 1940);

A Woman Looks Out (London: Religious Tract Society-Lutterworth Press, 1940).

PLAY PRODUCTIONS: *Masks*, Sydney, 1921;
A Man of His Time, Sydney, 1923;
The Cautious Lovers, London, Lyceum Club,
1 June 1924;
The School For Wives, adapted from Molière, London, 1925;
Gooseberry Fool, with Clemence Dane, London, Players' Theatre, 1 November 1929.

MOTION PICTURE: *Sabotage*, dialogue by Simpson and others, Gaumont-British, 1937; rereleased as *The Woman Alone*, 1937.

OTHER: *Pan in Pimlico*, in *Four One-Act Plays* (Oxford: Blackwell, 1923); republished as *Double Demon and Other One-Act Plays* (New York: Appleton, 1924);
L. -S. Mercier, *The Waiting City: Paris, 1782-88*, an abridgement, translated and edited by Simpson (London: Harrap, 1933);
Heartsease and Honesty, being the Pastimes of the Sieur de Grammont, Steward to the Duc de Richelieu in Touraine, translated by Simpson (London: Golden Cockerel Press, 1935);
The Cold Table: A Book of Recipes for the Preparation of Food and Drink, compiled and edited by Simpson, with the assistance of Petrie Townshend (London: Cape, 1935; New York: Macmillan, 1936).

Helen Simpson was born in Sydney, Australia, on 1 December 1897 of French aristocratic stock (she made use of this background in her novel *Boomerang*, 1932). She left Australia before she was twenty years old and lived out her life in England, dying in the Blitz in 1940. Simpson was one of the earliest women undergraduates at Oxford, and her acquaintance with Dorothy Sayers and others led her to become a charter member of the Detection Club; she contributed to the group's *Ask a Policeman* in 1933. The range of work produced during her forty-two years is wide: plays, translations from the French, histories and biographies, even recipe books. Her claim on present interest, out of the dozen novels she wrote, are the five mystery or detective novels, three of which were written in collaboration with Clemence Dane.

Of the five novels within the mystery genre, the three written with Dane have attracted the most attention, in large part because of their superior plotting and the presence of a detective who deserves to be better known. But 'Vantage Striker* (1931), a much more psychological and darkly in-

trospective work, shows what she might have written without Dane's theatrical hand and background. Her first novel, *Acquittal* (1925), is also more of a psychological study than a crime novel. It begins with the heroine's acquittal on a charge of murdering her husband and ends with the necessity of her choosing between two suitors, one of whom unquestioningly accepts her innocence, while the other, less convinced, does not care. Although there is no concentration on the trial or the actual crime, it seems likely that her friend Dorothy Sayers may have taken this apprentice work as a model for her own later work.

Howard Haycraft, in *Murder For Pleasure* (1968), regards the three novels Simpson wrote with Dane, *Enter Sir John* (1928), *Printer's Devil* (1930), and *Re-Enter Sir John* (1932), as foreshadowing the marriage of the novel of detection and the novel of character, a marriage Dorothy Sayers may be said to have consummated in the late 1930s. Although Simpson and Dane's novels are historically significant and Sir John is an interesting amateur detective, Simpson is quite often ignored in the critical literature. Her work deserves more prominence.

The nature of the collaboration between Dane and Simpson is quite easy to understand. Dane was primarily a dramatist, several of whose novels deal with the stage, and whose most famous one, *Broome Stages* (1931), is a roman-fleuve of the English theater. It was clearly Dane who sketched the background for the actor-detective and no less clearly Simpson who provided the mystery and detective elements.

The three novels of Simpson and Dane sketch a fully realized world of the theater, in which characters recur and Sir John is developed. In *Enter Sir John* he is the great personage of the stage, who might have been modeled on one of the great actor-managers, Irving, Tree, or (later) Olivier. But behind the mask of the great actor–the duality is a characteristic trait in Simpson's work–is "plain Johnny Simmonds," though not so plain that "Johnny" stands for "John," but rather for "Jonathan." What drives Sir John to detection is professional pride; he is offended by a reviewer who has charged him with living in art rather than life–"if Sir John Saumerez would occasionally go out into the highways and hedges of real life for a model, instead of depending entirely on his shaving-glass, he would cease to be the extremist example of Narcissism since Louis XIV."

Dust jacket for the first American edition of the 1933 novel in which Simpson repudiated fascism, a political philosophy with which she had shown sympathy in her 1931 mystery 'Vantage Striker

Though Haycraft preferred the third of the Simpson-Dane trio, *Re-Enter Sir John*, the first book is surely the more interesting, primarily because it provided the donnée for the greater artist, Alfred Hitchcock, and his film *Murder*. The main literary interest of *Enter Sir John* lies in the development of the relationship between Sir John and Martella, and in the entrance of Sir John himself. Martella is a young actress in her twenties in whose acting career Sir John has taken an interest and who is accused of murder. He attends her trial and sees her convicted. He then pursues his own inquiry, uncovers the criminal, and persuades the girl to enter into a permanent "engagement" (the pun is his) with him at the end.

Sir John, who has detected the criminal but not his rather tortured motive, traps him—

mousetraps him—using the device Hamlet used to catch the conscience of the king: he has him read for a part which is a reconstruction of his crime. The reader is already aware that he is the guilty party, so that the novel contains at least four climaxes: the conviction of the heroine, our recognition of the murderer, the revelation of his motive, and Sir John's coup de theatre in unmasking him. The plot is poorly constructed, with the murderer known to the reader two-thirds of the way through, and thirty pages remaining even after he makes his escape. It is, indeed, at that point that the elements of the novel of character usurp those of the novel of detection.

If Sir John's dualities give this first appearance much of its interest, Martella is at least as interesting a character, and darker psychologically.

"A dark, defiant girl" who once whipped a native driver in India for ill-treating a horse, Martella is subject to irrational rages and may even, it is suspected, have committed the murder in one of the fugue states to which she is subject.

It is regrettable that Martella figures less in the two Sir John novels which follow. In the second, *Printer's Devil*, even Sir John's role is peripheral, one of four knights who contributed to the fame of an egomaniacal playwright who is writing his sensational memoirs, and whose publisher is murdered to suppress them. Sir John's contribution to the solution is small. He is present at the obligatory Golden Age gathering in the library where all is revealed, in this novel transferred to a balcony Japanese Garden, so that the murderer may step gracefully off the parapet when he is unmasked. In the third of the series, *Re-Enter Sir John*, the actor returns to center stage, still more of a personage than a personality. This last novel is the most skillfully plotted: a young man is accused of cheating at cards, and a murder follows which resurrects his twice-married mother's tangled past. Sir John makes a crucial deduction based on the left-handedness of the suspect, and he closes his case, here, with a coup de cinema, using a projected film to mousetrap his murderer. Martella, who is his largely offstage business associate in *Printer's Devil*, is his active helper in *Re-Enter Sir John*. Though lending him more assistance than she did when she herself was the accused, she urges him at the end of the novel to leave detecting in the future to the police. And so he does.

In these three collaborative novels there is a dark view of human personality, highlighting the possibilities of mental dissociation, something approaching split personality. Harmlessly channeled, it is the basis of Sir John's art as both actor and detective. Both he and Martella are actors first and people second: when he proposes to her, she mistakes him to mean that he wants her as his stage leading lady. "We artists have a double function," he says. "We use life to create art, and we use art to—how shall I put it?—criticize life." His detectival method is to "apply the technique of his art to a problem of real life." In Sir John, and to a lesser extent Martella, this divided nature is beneficial. In *Printer's Devil*, however, where the center of attention is the murderer, a psychopathic artist who is intent on sweeping aside all that stands in the way of his artistic success, the novel Simpson wrote in between the second and third collaborations with Dane is foreshadowed.

'Vantage Striker makes it clear that Simpson contributed the dark tones in the collaborations with Dane. The title refers to the two major characters, both of whom are in a position of power with right of first service–the actual tennis champion who is suffering from blind rages of violence as a result of his war service, and the great statesman, who has insane delusions of omnipotence. The same psychiatrist who testified in *Enter Sir John* as to Martella's fugue states returns here in a principal role. Both the tennis player, who knocks a man down on the first page, and the statesman, who justifies murder for the general good, are suspects when the prime minister is murdered, and the word of the one is set against the other's as to who was last with him. When the tennis player's dual personality is cured by a counterirritant, a blow on the head during a match, the psychiatrist tries the same remedy on the cabinet minister by injecting him with malarial germs, and unmasks his guilt (these bizarre medical procedures were presumably discussed with Dennis J. Browne, Simpson's physician husband, and must have had some basis in contemporary medical knowledge). But the criminal is unmasked in a peculiarly British way: the prime minister's death is attributed to heart disease, and the statesman's only punishment is his enforced retirement from public life.

'Vantage Striker appeared in 1931, a resonant year for its political undertones. With the National Government just taking power in the disarray of the Depression, and with Churchill and the other future leaders of 1940 carefully excluded, the mediocre figures of James Ramsey MacDonald and Stanley Baldwin were in power. As did much of the world, Great Britain clearly yearned for a strong hand at the helm, and even Oswald Moseley's brownshirts seemed the answer to some. Simpson's answer is not fascism, a solution she strongly repudiates in her apocalyptic *The Woman on the Beast* (1933) two years later, but her presentation of Brazier, the cabinet minister, and her virtual absolution of him at the end of the novel, suggests ambivalence, if not sympathy, to what he represents. The novel also presents the battered generation of young men of 1914-1918 as they reach the midpoints of their lives, some even feeling guilty at being alive; the parallel treatment of the tennis player and the statesman manages to fuse the plight of the postwar youth with the malaise of the nation itself.

What Simpson seems to favor politically in the novel is a strong central authority, one which, for the public good, does not keep the governed fully informed. That political tenet, though presented in a rather more comic vein, is the basis of the relationship between Sir John Saumerez and his Martella in the Dane-Simpson novels.

While 'Vantage Striker is a more sophisticated, less frivolous work than the three collaborative novels, it is by its nature dated, both politically and psychologically. If Simpson is to retain an important place in detectival history, it will be as a collaborator with Dane, as the creator of Sir John, the actor-detective. Although Sir John is no intellectual, and therefore little of a ratiocinator, and even in his profession more of a showman than a technician, he still holds our interest. It is his outer self which charms the reader, his ease with people, his self-assurance, and his persistence in pursuing what he wants, a solution to a crime. Clemence Dane may well have first brought Sir John Saumerez on stage, but it was surely Helen Simpson who gave him his symbolic divided quality.

Bibliography:
E. Morris Miller and Frederick Macartney, *Australian Literature: A Bibliography to 1938, Extended to 1950* (Sydney: Angus & Robertson, 1956).

Reference:
Howard Haycraft, *Murder for Pleasure: The Life and Times of the Detective Story*, enlarged edition (New York: Biblio & Tarmen, 1968).

C. P. Snow

(15 October 1905-1 July 1980)

Brian Murray
Youngstown State University

See also the Snow entry in *DLB 15: British Novelists, 1930-1959*.

SELECTED BOOKS: *Death Under Sail* (London: Heinemann, 1932);

New Lives for Old, anonymous (London: Gollancz, 1933);

The Search (London: Gollancz, 1934; Indianapolis & New York: Bobbs-Merrill, 1935; revised edition, London: Macmillan, 1958; New York: Scribners, 1958);

Strangers and Brothers (London: Faber & Faber, 1940; New York: Scribners, 1960); republished as *George Passant* (New York: Scribners, 1970);

The Light and the Dark (London: Faber & Faber, 1947; New York: Macmillan, 1948);

Time of Hope (London: Faber & Faber, 1949; New York: Macmillan, 1950);

The Masters (London: Macmillan, 1951; New York: Macmillan, 1951);

The New Men (London: Macmillan, 1954; New York: Scribners, 1954);

Homecomings (London: Macmillan, 1956); republished as *Homecoming* (New York: Scribners, 1956);

The Conscience of the Rich (London: Macmillan, 1958; New York: Scribners, 1958);

The Two Cultures and the Scientific Revolution (London & New York: Cambridge University Press, 1959); enlarged as *The Two Cultures and A Second Look* (London & New York: Cambridge University Press, 1964);

The Affair (London: Macmillan, 1960; New York: Scribners, 1960);

Science and Government (London: Oxford University Press, 1961; Cambridge, Mass.: Harvard University Press, 1961);

Corridors of Power (London: Macmillan, 1964; New York: Scribners, 1964);

Variety of Men (London: Macmillan, 1967; New York: Scribners, 1967);

Charles Percy Snow (photograph by Jane Brown/courtesy of the Observer)

The Sleep of Reason (London: Macmillan, 1968; New York: Scribners, 1968);

The State of Siege (London: Macmillan, 1969; New York: Scribners, 1969);

Last Things (London: Macmillan, 1970; New York: Scribners, 1970);

Public Affairs (London: Macmillan, 1971; New York: Scribners, 1971);

The Malcontents (London: Macmillan, 1972; New York: Scribners, 1972);

In Their Wisdom (London: Macmillan, 1974; New York: Scribners, 1974);

Trollope: His Life and Art (London: Macmillan, 1975; New York: Scribners, 1975);

The Realists (London: Macmillan, 1978; New York: Scribners, 1978);

A Coat of Varnish (London: Macmillan, 1979; New York: Scribners, 1979).

Though extensively trained as a scientist, Charles Percy Snow became one of the most productive and accomplished fiction writers of his generation. He is best known, certainly, for the eleven highly autobiographical novels that make up the "Strangers and Brothers" sequence. But Snow also produced two very effective detective novels, *Death Under Sail* (1932) and *A Coat of Varnish* (1979). These well-constructed and widely praised works strongly suggest that Snow's literary career would have been equally successful had he more frequently channeled his narrative skills into the mystery genre.

Snow, the second of four children, was born on 15 October 1905 in what he once labeled a "petty-bourgeois-cum-proletarian" suburb of Leicester, an industrial city located in the British Midlands. Snow's mother, Ada, was the daughter of servants; his father, William, worked at a local shoe factory and played the organ at area church services, despite the fact that–unlike his wife–he refused to accept the basic tenets of orthodox Christianity. Often describing himself as "tone-deaf," Snow did not inherit his father's musical abilities. But he was clearly influenced by the fact that both his father and his paternal grandfather were themselves intellectually curious and the readers of serious books. Snow described his grandfather as "a very striking example of the superior Victorian working man"–one who, for example, "made me read Renan's *Life of Jesus* at the age of eight."

As a child Snow was enrolled in a small, private school kept–he much later remembered–by "some rather clever spinsters"; between the ages of eleven and sixteen he attended a local secondary school, Alderman Newton's, where he distinguished himself in the areas of science and math. In 1925 Snow won a scholarship to University College, Leicester, where he earned a bachelor's degree in chemistry and a master's in physics. In 1928 Snow entered Christ's College, Cambridge, where–in 1930–he earned his doctorate in physics after completing a dissertation on "The Infra-Red Spectra of Simple Diatomic Molecules." Throughout the 1930s Snow remained in Cambridge as a fellow at Christ's Church and was thus able to work with an unusually gifted group of colleagues, including the physicist Ernest Rutherford, who was then directing the Cavendish Laboratory and at the peak of his power and influence. As Snow later observed, this "was perhaps the most brilliant period in Cambridge intellectual history. The place was stiff with Nobel Prize winners."

At Cambridge Snow continued to conduct significant research in the fields of spectroscopy and crystallography. But at eighteen Snow had already decided that he was much more interested in writing fiction than in carving out a career in science and academia. As an undergraduate Snow completed his first novel, "a rather typical story of young people," he recalled, "trying to find love and purpose and so on." Soon realizing that there was little in this unfocused, unoriginal, and unpublishable manuscript that was worth saving, Snow destroyed it.

In *Death Under Sail*, Snow's first published novel, Roger Mills–a young Harley Street cancer specialist–is shot to death while sailing with six friends on the Norfolk Broads, a group of small, linked lakes in northeastern England. Initially all of Mills's guests–four men and two women–are considered suspects in his murder. One of them, Ian Capel, narrates the story. He is a witty and frank bachelor of fifty-three who–in a local newspaper's sensationalized summary of the case–is not inappropriately identified as a "well known clubman." As the reader soon realizes, Capel is also the least likely of the guests to commit first-degree murder and then coolly, consistently contend that he was elsewhere on the yacht during the early-morning moments when it occurred.

Assigned to investigate the crime is Detective-Sergeant Aloysius Birrell, an excitable young Irishman who combines, Capel suggests, "the susceptibilities of a Victorian heroine" with "a flaming enthusiasm for anything that was connected with crime." Birrell has virtually memorized Gross's *Handbook of Criminology;* he has read a great many detective novels, which he particularly, vigorously praises for their consistent portrayal of policemen routing the forces of evil. The excitable Birrell requires considerable help, however, from a man identified only as Finbow, a friend of Capel's whose suave manner and highly logical mind have long been admired by his colleagues in the British Civil Service. These contrasting figures are effectively drawn; their differing approaches to the investigation of the Mills murder provide *Death Under Sail* with much of its conflict and humor. In fact, compared to the dispassionate Finbow, Birrell is something of a buffoon–a representative, Finbow suggests, "of all the virtues and vices of an age of words." For "an age of words," Finbow notes, means not only that everyone has easier access to useful information,

Dust jacket for Snow's 1968 novel, in which two women are accused of torturing and murdering a young boy

but also, unfortunately, that "everyone imbibes an immense amount of nonsense."

Writing in 1980, the British journalist and critic Anthony Lejune dismissed *Death Under Sail* as "a quite straightforward, if rather ponderous" example of the modern detective story. But upon publication the book was largely praised by reviewers, who agreed that the "six pleasant people" who sail with Mills at the start of *Death Under Sail* remain effectively individualized–and suspicious–throughout its duration. Forty-four years after its first publication, Jacques Barzun and Wendell H. Taylor included *Death Under Sail* in their reprint series of *Fifty Classics of Crime Fiction 1900-1950*, pointing out in a prefatory note that the work remains "a neat little tale of classic mould: the murder among friends in a setting automatically restricted." Barzun and Taylor praise Snow's use of Capel, Birrell, and Finbow as a means of providing "incessantly various interpretations of what is said and done, while the five other people act out their lies and concealments before our eyes." Snow, they suggest, moves deftly to the crime's solution "through many wayward conversations, numerous ironic maxims about life and character, and a sound detective philosophy about the interplay of material and psychological clues."

Years later Snow recalled that, after *Death Under Sail*, both "Heinemann and I think someone at Doubleday offered to guarantee me what was then a little fortune to just go and write detective stories." But by 1935 Snow had decided to focus entirely on the completion of a series of novels that would cover several decades and be linked by common characters, situations, and themes. The first of these, *Strangers and Brothers* (later retitled *George Passant*), was published in 1940, shortly after Snow had joined a Royal Society subcommittee designed to help direct the research centers of Britain's universities toward projects that would benefit a nation rearming itself for war. In 1942 Snow was named the Ministry of Labour's director of technical personnel and for the duration of World War II played a crucial part in ensuring that the talents of British scientists were being effectively channeled toward the defeat of Germany and its allies. Snow's wartime services not only made him a C.B.E. (Commander of the British Empire) but enabled him to observe at close range the maneuvers and power plays of high-level politicians and governmental officials. Snow's insider's knowledge of British politics is perhaps best displayed in *The Light and the Dark* (1947), *Homecomings* (1956), and *Corridors of Power* (1964), which, along with *George Passant, Time of Hope* (1949), *The Masters* (1951), *The New Men* (1954), *The Conscience of the Rich* (1958), *The Affair* (1960), *The Sleep of Reason* (1968), and *Last Things* (1970), make up the "Strangers and Brothers" series. These eleven novels chronicle the life of the series narrator, Lewis Eliot, whose good mind and intense "craving not to be unknown" enable him to leave a small city in the Midlands for a career that would make him a barrister and a government minister, and that would involve him in many intriguing episodes. In *The New Men*, for example, Eliot is close to a group of British scientists working to develop an atomic bomb; later, in *Corridors of Power*, he finds himself involved in the long and heated debate over whether or not Britain should simply divest itself of all nuclear arms. In *The Sleep of Reason*, one of the most gripping volumes in the series, Eliot witnesses the trial of two young women

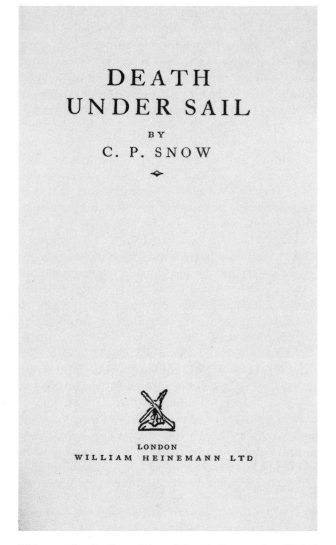

DEATH
UNDER SAIL
BY
C. P. SNOW

LONDON
WILLIAM HEINEMANN LTD

Title page for the first edition of Snow's first novel, published in 1932

accused of the torture and murder of an eight-year-old boy. In a 1978 interview with John Halperin, Snow admits that many of the more fascinating men and women who appear and reappear in the "Strangers and Brothers" series owe much to real-life models; that Eliot, moreover, owes a great deal to C. P. Snow. Both, for example, have mildly eccentric fathers who live with a fierce independence well into old age; both are fond of cricket and prefer the visual arts to music. Both are involved in academics as well as politics; both have eye problems and—late in life—suffer cardiac arrest.

Undoubtedly, Snow's reputation as a writer of fiction rests principally on the novels in the "Strangers and Brothers" sequence, most of which sold well in both Britain and North America throughout the 1950s and 1960s. Many reviewers and critics have praised these works not only for their thorough characterizations but also for their intelligence, compassion, and frank willingness to deal with controversial issues in the public debate. Others, however, have argued that most of Snow's characters are mechanical and flat; that his plots tend to drag; that his prose is frequently stilted and bland. They suggest also that throughout his literary career Snow remained a living fossil, reactionarily employing a plodding, documentary, message-laden style of novel writing more appropriate to the nineteenth century. Indeed, Snow bluntly insisted on several occasions that he found the works of Anthony Trollope and Charles Dickens far more satisfying and important than those produced by such influential modernists as James Joyce and Virginia Woolf. To the great annoyance of many of his contemporaries, Snow argued–too sweepingly–that much highly praised modernist fiction was simply too self-absorbed and trivial; that it was characterized by "bad thinking," by a preoccupation with technique and content, by the immaturely romantic notion that intellectuals and artists must oppose "the scientific-industrial revolution" and stand alienated from the rest of society.

Snow's most controversial publication was surely *The Two Cultures and the Scientific Revolution* (1959), a brief, argumentative essay informed by Snow's belief that Western civilization–having entered the atomic age and, with it, a period of unprecedented and potentially cataclysmic social change–was more than ever in need of unified guidance from its brightest minds. Unfortunately, argues Snow, intellectuals in the West tend to align themselves into two opposing camps or "cultures"–one of them "scientific," the other literary, or "traditional." As a result they tend to regard each other with hostility and contempt. Snow does urge scientists to become more aware of the humanities, to study the works of Dickens and Rainer Maria Rilke, among others.

But much more energetically, Snow condemns "literary intellectuals" for their "Luddite" hostility to science, calling it "bizarre how very little of twentieth-century science has been assimilated into twentieth-century art," and scoring the fact that, for example, "the great edifice of modern physics goes up, and the majority of the cleverest people in the Western world have about as much insight into it as their neolithic ancestors would have had." And–to the particular irritation of such Lawrentians as F. R. Leavis–Snow, like

Dust jacket for Snow's 1970 novel, part of the "Strangers and Brothers" series

H. G. Wells, argues that science and, more particularly, "industrialisation" represent "the only hope for the poor." "With singular unanimity," he notes, "in any country where they have had the chance, the poor have walked off the land into the factories as fast as the factories could take them."

Much of Snow's later writing–particularly his fiction–reveals his growing sense that men and women in the West have, in fact, lost control of their environment; that the codes and customs that once kept irrationality and barbarism in check have simply fallen apart; that, as a result, the center cannot hold. Such pessimism is much in evidence in Snow's last novel, *A Coat of Varnish*, which–like his first book–is a mystery, its center of attention the gruesome murder, in 1976, of Madge Ashbrook, a cranky and rather wealthy but "parsimonious" old woman who is herself convinced that England is being ruined by Marxists and assorted political "crooks."

Whatever the cause, the England that Snow portrays in *A Coat of Varnish* is in deep trouble, with its unemployment rate soaring and its pound declining daily on the stock exchange. The novel is set in a largely upper-middle-class quarter of London, where–Snow strongly implies–dangerous forces are festering just beneath a surface that appears settled and safe. Early in the book Humphrey Leigh–a semiretired intelligence officer and the book's principal character–is harassed by a "mob" of youths while drinking with a friend, Alec Luria, in a normally quiet pub. Soon afterward Leigh learns that Lady Ashbrook, his neighbor and friend, has been savagely beaten to death in her own home with the hammer which, "for do-it-yourself purposes," she "kept in the tool-box about the room."

Leigh is able to follow closely the official investigation of what the press dubs "The Belgravia Murder" because of his friendship with Frank Briers, an efficient Scotland Yard detective assigned to head up the case. Briers gradually narrows down the field of suspects to several of Lady Ashbrook's acquaintances and supposed friends. But as the taut final chapters reveal, Briers finds it difficult to secure the arrest of the greedy, calculating figure he knows committed the crime. *A Coat of Varnish* does not then offer the sort of neat, climactic ending that one generally finds in murder mysteries. It is, however, a tightly structured work that features believable characters, solid subplots, and particularly vivid descriptions of Belgravia and environs during the historic heat wave of 1976. "I know the streets, the churches, the clubs," wrote Anthony Lejune in his review of *A Coat of Varnish*. "I remember those broiling summer nights and the rain-soaked autumn which followed: and I can testify that everything is exactly as Lord Snow describes."

Certainly, the book's central themes are bluntly stated. "None of Humphrey's friends," we learn, "had been bubbling with optimism about the state of the nation, or its economy, or, deeper down, of the state of the Western world." One of those friends is Luria, an American academic based on Snow's friend Philip Rieff, who in several books has discussed what he generally considers to be the rather bleak consequences of living in an era of "endless transitionality"; who has noted, for example, that "released from authoritative pasts, we progress towards barbarism, not away from it." After witnessing the ugly violence in the pub, Luria reminds Leigh that "peo-ple who live in a nice pretty cushioned world" are prone to forget the fact that "civilisation is hideously fragile." "There's not much," he notes, "between us and the horrors underneath. Just a coat of varnish, wouldn't you say?" "And," he continues, "the same applies to you and me. And the rest of us. There's not much between us and our beastly selves. Human beings aren't nice, are they?"

Briers, too, broods about the barbarism he must witness daily while on the job. Once, he admits, "I was a starry-eyed young policeman," believing that "some sort of good feeling or good instinct" led most "ordinary men" to heed "ordinary human rules." Now, however, echoing somewhat the later Snow, Briers fears that "the crude answer" to the problem of barbarism and chaos is, quite simply, "sanctions." And most of these–including the "fear of judgment and the after life," and the "fear of what other people think"–have largely disappeared. Today, "it's mostly fear of the law" that barely maintains order; "without the law, there wouldn't be much left in the way of moral rules. I wish I believed something else, but nowadays I can't."

Lejune, reviewing *A Coat of Varnish* for *National Review*, suggested that the book's "respectable but featureless prose" resembled "a moderately good rice pudding" but added approvingly that its plainly conservative slant revealed that Snow's "left-wing views, if they exist at all, have become quite unobtrusive." In the *New York Times Book Review* Julian Moynahan pointed out that Snow had always revealed "an informed interest, rare in a novelist, in how a bureaucracy–in this case the London police–sets about organizing its work." He found "the detectives' planning sessions in what is called the Murder Room and the long sessions of interrogation of the chief suspect" to be "the best things in the book." "Much less good," wrote Moynahan, "are the several conversations–between Humphrey and Briers, and between Humphrey and Alec–in which it is insisted that there is a close connection between Lady Ashbrook's violent demise and the general collapse of civilization."

Snow–married since 1950 to the novelist Pamela Hansford Johnson–died on 1 July 1980. Though he remained active in public affairs throughout the final decades of his life (serving as Harold Wilson's technology minister in the 1960s, for example), Snow continued to devote most of his energy to writing essays and novels, including *In Their Wisdom* (1974), which also warns

Bert Howard, Pamela Hansford Johnson, and Snow at the 1950 wedding reception for Johnson and Snow (courtesy of the Estate of C. P. Snow)

of the dangers of assuming a "false optimism about human beings," and which many of Snow's admirers consider one of his finest efforts. One of those admirers, Suguna Ramanathan, is admirably balanced and astute, admitting, for example, that when Snow's writing is bad, "it is horrid. It can sound uninspired and monotonous and it can fall into bathos." But as she also points out, Snow at his best utilizes a lean, "deliberately plain" prose style "which has its own austere appeal"; he reveals not only "an excellent ear for contemporary idiom," but the ability to address important questions regarding human nature even as he constructs a convincing, suspenseful story. Snow is at his best in both *Death Under Sail* and *A Coat of Varnish*.

Interview:

John Halperin, *C. P. Snow: An Oral Biography* (Brighton, Sussex: Harvester Press, 1983).

References:

Bernard Bergonzi, *The Situation of the Novel* (London: Pelican, 1972);

Rubin Rabinovitz, *The Reaction Against Experiment in the English Novel: 1950-1960* (New York: Columbia University Press, 1967);

Suguna Ramanathan, *The Novels of C. P. Snow: A Critical Introduction* (London: Macmillan, 1978);

David Schusterman, *C. P. Snow* (New York: Twayne, 1975).

Josephine Tey
(Elizabeth Mackintosh, Gordon Daviot)
(1896?-13 February 1952)

Virginia B. Morris
John Jay College, City University of New York

See also the Gordon Daviot entry in *DLB 10: Modern British Dramatists, 1900-1945.*

BOOKS: *The Man in the Queue*, as Gordon Daviot (London: Methuen, 1929; New York: Dutton, 1929); as Josephine Tey (London: Davies, 1953; New York: Macmillan, 1953); republished as *Killer in the Crowd* (New York: Mercury, 1954);

Kif: An Unvarnished History, as Daviot (London: Benn, 1929; New York: Appleton, 1929);

The Expensive Halo, as Daviot (London: Benn, 1931; New York: Appleton, 1931);

Richard of Bordeaux, as Daviot (London: Gollancz, 1933; Boston: Little, Brown, 1933);

The Laughing Woman, as Daviot (London: Gollancz, 1934);

Queen of Scots, as Daviot (London: Gollancz, 1934);

A Shilling for Candles, as Tey (London: Methuen, 1936; New York: Macmillan, 1954);

Claverhouse, as Daviot (London: Collins, 1937);

The Stars Bow Down, as Daviot (London: Duckworth, 1939);

Leith Sands and Other Short Plays, as Daviot (London: Duckworth, 1946);

Miss Pym Disposes, as Tey (London: Davies, 1946; New York: Macmillan, 1948);

The Franchise Affair, as Tey (London: Davies, 1948; New York: Macmillan, 1949);

Brat Farrar, as Tey (London: Davies, 1949; New York: Macmillan, 1950); republished as *Come and Kill Me* (New York: Pocket Books, 1951);

To Love and Be Wise, as Tey (London: Davies, 1950; New York: Macmillan, 1951);

The Daughter of Time, as Tey (London: Davies, 1951; New York: Macmillan, 1952);

The Privateer, as Daviot (London: Davies, 1952; New York: Macmillan, 1952);

The Singing Sands, as Tey (London: Davies, 1952; New York: Macmillan, 1953);

Josephine Tey (photograph by Angus McBean)

Plays, by Gordon Daviot, 3 volumes (London: Davies, 1953-1954).

PLAY PRODUCTIONS: *Richard of Bordeaux*, as Daviot, London, Arts Theatre Club, June 1932; revised version, London, New Theatre, 2 February 1933;

The Laughing Woman, as Daviot, London, New Theatre, 7 April 1934;

Queen of Scots, as Daviot, London, New Theatre, 8 June 1934;

The Little Dry Thorn, as Daviot, Hammersmith, London, Lyric Theatre, 11 November 1947;

Valerius, as Daviot, London, Saville Theatre, 3 October 1948;

The Stars Bow Down, as Daviot, Malvern, Malvern Festival Theatre, 10 August 1949;

Dickon, as Daviot, Salisbury, Salisbury Arts Theatre, 9 May 1955.

Josephine Tey's reputation as a detective novelist rests on eight mysteries. Like her contemporaries in the genre, Tey portrayed a world in which crimes are solved; but she rejected the tidy conclusions characteristic of classic detective fiction, preferring to leave her readers vaguely uneasy, often disconcerted, at the novel's end. Those responsible for inflicting pain and suffering, even death, sometimes emerge completely unscathed. Others, wrongfully accused, find their lives unalterably changed by the unprovoked evil that has overtaken them.

Tey structures her novels like the conventional mysteries they seem to be: there are motives to discover, clues to follow, alibis to check, and conclusions to draw. In the end, logic (sometimes assisted by Providence) unravels the mystery; but questions linger: How can an adolescent from a good family murder his twin in cold blood and feel no remorse (*Brat Farrar*, 1949)? What defense does an unconventional woman have against accusations of abuse by an unscrupulous and self-serving girl (*The Franchise Affair*, 1948)? Tey's criminals are not thugs. Typically they are evil because their egotism destroys their compassion and their capacity for restraint.

Over and over in Tey's novels innocence is destroyed by exposure to evil. Sometimes loss of innocence means simply being forced to admit that a friend or relative is corrupt. As Marion Sharpe observes in *The Franchise Affair*: "What *can* be more shattering than to find the person you have lived with and loved all those years not only doesn't exist but has never existed? That the person you have so much loved not only doesn't love you but doesn't care two hoots about you and never did? What is there *left* for someone like that? She can never again take a step on to green grass without wondering if it is bog." Often the innocent suffer more directly. In half of Tey's novels completely blameless people are murdered because of their killers' unrestrained ambition, and the discovery of such evil creates a sense of implication. As Tad Cullen says in *The Singing Sands* (1952) when he discovers why his friend died, "I feel dirty all over."

Tey's detectives are implicated in the same way. Though they are honest and act with the highest motives, none is infallible. Through their errors in judgment, they also inflict pain on the innocent, and so contribute to Tey's thesis that there is no protection against the insidious influence of crime, which poisons everything it touches.

Tey's private life is cloaked in mystery. The most reliable information comes from two sources: the material she supplied to the 1948 edition of *Who's Who* and the brief foreword John Gielgud wrote for *Plays, by Gordon Daviot* (1953-1954).

The writer known as Josephine Tey and Gordon Daviot was born Elizabeth Mackintosh in Inverness, Scotland, the daughter of Colin and Josephine Horne Mackintosh. The exact date of her birth is unknown. She studied at the Royal Academy in Inverness and then attended Anstey Physical Training College in Birmingham for three years, from about 1915 to 1918. In 1926 she resigned from a position as physical-education instructor and returned home to care for her widowed and ailing father. Apparently resolved to make a career as a writer, she published a mystery novel, *The Man in the Queue*, in 1929, under the pen name Gordon Daviot. Although she continued to use her own name privately, she asked to be listed as Gordon Daviot in *Who's Who*. She published two more novels before Gordon Daviot became well known as the author of *Richard of Bordeaux* (1933), a successful history play whose 1933 London production starred John Gielgud as Richard II. Her second mystery, *A Shilling for Candles*, was published in 1936 under the pseudonym Josephine Tey, her great-great-grandmother's name, presumably because she wanted to establish separate identities as playwright and as mystery novelist.

Because so little is known about her life, reading biographical details into her fiction has become a frequent practice. There is little question that her own attitudes are revealed in the fondness and occasional, gentle mockery with which she portrays Scotland, in her characters' passion for horses and fishing, and in their fervor for all things English. The tendency to identify Tey with any or all of the sympathetic unmarried women in her novels or even with her detective Alan Grant is more problematic, as it is likely to be for most writers. Like Tey, many of her characters are independent and connected with the theater. Tey does appear to be poking fun at herself when Madeleine March, a much-sought-after playwright in *The Daughter of Time* (1951), reneges on a promise to write a historical play so that she can finish "one of her awful little detective stories . . . while it is still fresh," but in general Tey's novels should not be read as disguised autobiography.

Her first two novels, *The Man in the Queue* and *A Shilling for Candles*, share many characteristics of the classic Golden Age detective novels of the period in which they were written. Each focuses on the hunt for a murderer whose initially unidentified victim is discovered in the opening chapter.

In *The Man in the Queue* Detective Inspector Alan Grant investigates the murder of a man whose body is found wedged in the line waiting to attend a popular musical. Initially he seeks out a suspect who fits his own preconception of the kind of man who might have committed the crime. He follows the hapless Lamont on a wild chase through London and the Highlands, nearly precipitates his death by drowning, and arrests him for murder despite an intuitive feeling that the physical evidence is somehow wrong. Only when Mrs. Wallis unexpectedly confesses that she has killed Albert Sorrell to prevent him from murdering her daughter is Lamont absolved.

In *A Shilling for Candles* Robert Tisdall seems the logical suspect in actress Christine Clay's murder because Grant discovers that he had much to gain from her death. Terrified by the prospect of arrest and aware that proving his innocence would be virtually impossible, Tisdall disappears. This time police pursuit arouses more than Grant's uneasy conscience. The press seizes on Tisdall's flight as an example of police inhumanity, and Grant must struggle with bad publicity as well as self-doubt.

Once again the suspect is absolved unexpectedly, this time by the determined investigative work of the local chief constable's daughter, Erica Burgoyne, who finds Tisdall's missing overcoat and proves that the button entangled in the victim's hair did not belong to him. Erica, like Lamont's defender Miss Dinmont, is one of Tey's most appealing creations: a young woman with an uncanny knack for judging character and an unspoiled self-confidence. A fascinating contrast to the novel's more jaded adults, she is so firmly convinced that Tisdall is not guilty that she is willing to risk her own position by helping Tisdall elude capture.

In many ways *A Shilling for Candles* is a more mature work than *The Man in the Queue*. No timely confession solves this crime. Instead, Grant stumbles on the solution while he is waiting impatiently in a barbershop: an old movie magazine describes the intuitive genius of Lydia Keats—a woman who has predicted that a famous actress will drown—and concludes, rather snidely, that whoever the star is, she should be careful not to go swimming with Keats. Intuiting the way the crime must have been committed, Grant uncovers the incriminating evidence and arrests Keats, who—hoping to enhance her reputation as a clairvoyant—had apparently chosen her victim at random.

Like the other fictional detectives of the era, Grant, a detective inspector at Scotland Yard, is intelligent, persistent, intuitive, and successful; but he does not fit the contemporary stereotypes. Neither iconoclastic amateur nor methodical professional, he is considerably more convincing than Dorothy Sayers's Wimsey or Agatha Christie's Poirot, and clearly less plodding than Crofts's Inspector French. Grant's interest in crime combines both passion and profession. Tey emphasizes his individuality from the first: he does not look like a policeman, and his methods sometimes evoke the disapproval of his superiors. Despite his skill and his ultimate success, he is distinguished in these early novels as much by the mistakes he makes as by his achievements. More than once he is brutally critical of himself, and in *A Shilling for Candles* he comments that he would like to be "one of these marvelous creatures of super-instinct and infallible judgment who adorned the pages of detective stories." Yet his errors make him sympathetic. The motivation in *A Shilling for Candles* points the way to Tey's later fiction. In her first novel Mrs. Wallis is a likable, even admirable woman, driven to crime by blind maternal love, and when she confesses, it is to prevent anyone else from being punished for her crime. Grant is convinced—and gratified by the thought—that no English jury will convict her. Lydia Keats, on the other hand, kills because vanity has driven her beyond reason. Her crime is clearly the result of madness generated by blind ambition, a theme that recurs in later novels. It is typical of Tey that neither novel contains descriptions of violence. Tey is more interested in exploring the aftermath of crime than she is in chronicling the confrontation between killer and victim.

Distancing the reader from the victim's physical suffering is typical of the kind of classic detec-

Dust jacket for the first American edition of Tey's murder mystery without a murder

tive fiction Tey was writing in these novels. It is crucial if the emphasis of the novel is to remain centered on the detective. If too much sympathy is evoked for the victim, the novel takes on a different perspective. Sorrell is a typically appropriate victim: an undefined character murdered as he was about to commit a violent crime.

The treatment of Christine Clay's death, however, reveals Tey's emerging, more complex approach to the unmourned victim. On the surface her death creates an unrestrained outpouring of grief, but underneath the public tears there is little real feeling. None of her colleagues misses her very much; no one's life is altered by her death.

Since Tey had been deeply involved in the theater for several years when she wrote *A Shilling for Candles*, her choice of an actress as her victim is particularly interesting. The self-absorption and opportunism of the other theater people in the novel suggest that Tey's attitude toward the glamorous world of the theater was at best ambivalent.

Christine Clay is portrayed more sympathetically than the ambitious actress Ray Marcable in *The Man in the Queue*. Grant sees Marcable as the chief villain because she is totally self-centered; but it is in Marta Hallard, the actress who takes over Clay's starring role, that Tey provides her most revealing insight into the character of a theatrical star. Hallard, who appears regularly in the

Alan Grant novels, is a curious combination of charm and self-absorption. Though her character fluctuates not only from novel to novel but within individual ones as well, she is portrayed in a complimentary manner as a successful, independent woman.

Since Tey is reputed to have written *The Man in the Queue* in two weeks in order to enter it in a competition sponsored by the publisher Methuen, it is not surprising that the novel has some stylistic and structural flaws. Its weakest quality is its florid style, full of laborious descriptions and stilted conversations. The stylistic evolution in Tey's work demonstrates most persuasively her growing sophistication as a novelist. In *A Shilling for Candles* the writing is tighter and the dialogue more natural. The xenophobia characteristic of so much Golden Age fiction has been moderated into a gentler ethnocentrism. The awkward first-person narrator has disappeared, and the multiple narrators speak in distinctly different voices.

Neither *The Man in the Queue* nor *A Shilling for Candles* received much critical notice when it was published. The second novel, however, served as the basis for Alfred Hitchcock's 1937 movie *Young and Innocent*, reportedly his favorite among his English films. When these early novels were republished in 1954, after Tey had gained a reputation as a first-class mystery writer, they were generally praised. Anthony Boucher commented, with the wisdom of hindsight, that *The Man in the Queue* was far ahead of its time (*New York Times*, 16 September 1953)–probably because of Tey's conception of Alan Grant, whose place in the development of the fallible, self-doubting detective hero is clearly established in these early novels.

In the ten years between *A Shilling for Candles* and *Miss Pym Disposes* (1946), Mackintosh published plays under her Daviot pseudonym but no detective fiction. John Gielgud quotes her as calling her detective fiction her "yearly knitting." Whether that remark, made to a theatrical colleague, justifies Sandra Roy's conclusion that Tey was scornful of the mysteries is debatable. There is no convincing reason to believe that Tey was dismayed by her mysteries' success, especially since they were frequently praised for their intelligence and wit. If anything, her experimentation with the form suggests that she saw the mystery novel not only as a creative challenge but as a legitimate vehicle for exploring human behavior.

Miss Pym Disposes illustrates Tey's innovative approach to the form. It is a locked-room mystery in the best Golden Age tradition. Murder disrupts a women's physical-education college just before graduation. The victim, admired by the headmistress and disliked by everybody else, evokes little sympathy; her killer is a member of the college community; a piece of critical evidence is discovered almost immediately; and the motive is obvious.

Everything else in the novel is unconventional: the killer escapes with neither punishment nor remorse; the innocent suspect faces a lifetime of guilt and self-imposed punishment for her unknowing motivation of the murderer; the detective, Miss Pym, resolves never to get involved in criminal investigation again. Miss Pym's dismay at the havoc she has helped to create and the suffering she imposes is part of the novel's theme.

This evidence of Tey's continuing interest in the psychology, rather than the skill, of the detective links *Miss Pym Disposes* to Tey's earlier novels. Tey's pattern of "revealing . . . at great length the mental processes of the detective," which an anonymous reviewer for the *New York Times* (28 July 1929) faulted in *The Man in the Queue*, became a central element of Tey's work and one of its greatest strengths. She develops conflict through interior dialogue. The author of a best-selling book on psychology for laymen, Miss Pym is particularly adept at conducting such debates within herself to clarify her thoughts and justify her actions. In deciding to "dispose" instead of leaving things to God or the law where they belong, she has good intentions but is responsible for the worst possible outcome. Her suspicions force Mary Innes to acknowledge that her best friend, Beau Nash, has committed murder in order to insure that Innes gets the job she deserves. It is consistent with Innes's character that she condemns herself to return to the little market town she has struggled so hard to escape and work there, rather than take the job that Nash's crime made possible for her.

Miss Pym is aware of the tensions created in the community of women striving to finish their rigorous physical and academic training and find suitable jobs; yet she wants to deny that those tensions can be ultimately destructive. She tries to cling to the illusion that the students are normal, healthy children and is unwilling to confront the corrupting elements of the cloistered life and the dangers of obsessive absorption in one's job. Her friend Henrietta, the headmistress, feels as much passion for her school as a lover feels for the beloved. Her favoritism toward one student and the students' mania for success are at the heart of what is wrong at the college. The murder is only a symptom of this far greater evil, whose innocent victim is Mary Innes.

One of the novel's strengths is Tey's ability to create a realistic setting in which her abstract considerations of good and evil can be played out. By juxtaposing detailed descriptions of people and events with fast-paced, realistic dialogue, she creates an absorbing environment. Even the minor characters come vividly alive. For example, Teresa Desterro, a sophisticated South American who has spent a year at the college, is an astute judge of character and refreshingly disrespectful of the conventions of English life. Like Erica Burgoyne in *A Shilling for Candles*, she can see through the pretensions of authority. She recognizes the destructive power of the stress under which the students operate. Though she cannot predict the catastrophe, she prepares both Pym and the reader for its shock.

Several other elements of the novel demonstrate its relationship to Tey's earlier mysteries: the real criminal is once more discovered by chance; an innocent person is assumed guilty because of the detective's misperceptions and preconceived notions. Yet, despite those similarities, *Miss Pym Disposes* is the first of Tey's great successes and a clear indication of the innovative direction her work was to take.

Like *Miss Pym Disposes*, *The Franchise Affair* explores the suffering of the innocent, in this case a mother and daughter falsely accused of imprisoning and beating a young girl in order to secure her services as a maid. The story comes from eighteenth-century English legal history, but Tey gives her novel a familiar, contemporary setting. Tey combines the story of the infamous Mrs. Brownrigg, who was hanged in 1767 for savagely torturing young girls, with that of Elizabeth Canning, who in 1753 perjured herself by accusing a gypsy named Mary Squires and an old woman called "Mother" Wells of imprisoning and abusing her. The novel gains power from being set in the present time. It makes the ugliness of the mob and the hysteria created by the press seem more immediate and threatening than they might appear in a historical setting. Tey is using historical reality as a vehicle for examining modern behavior.

Tey makes no attempt to rehabilitate either Brownrigg or Canning. Rather, she takes their culpability at face value and uses them as personifications of evil. The opposition between guilt and innocence, grotesque inhumanity and false accusation, provides the underlying tension of the novel. Implicit in Tey's historical source is the possibility that Mary Squires and Mother Wells are guilty, but their fictional counterparts, Marion Sharpe and her mother, are innocent. To be sure, Tey tantalizes the reader with vague suspicions; the Sharpes are, after all, somewhat bizarre, with their ancient car, ramshackle house, and private habits. Marion's swarthy skin not only recalls Mrs. Brownrigg's appearance but is decidedly un-English, usually a confirmation of guilt in a typical Golden Age detective novel.

But despite their appearance and their habits, the Sharpes are witty, delightful women, with enormous resilence; and the novel's focus is their difficulty in defending themselves against overwhelming, deliberately false evidence. Neither their solicitor, Robert Blair, nor their defense counsel believes that they have kidnapped, imprisoned, and beaten Betty Kane, and neither does the reader. The mystery lies in uncovering the evidence that will clear them in the face of enormous public hostility and an amoral, self-confident accuser.

The name of Betty Kane, the girl who claims they have held her prisoner, not only echoes "Elizabeth Canning" but marks her as a true daughter of Cain. She superficially resembles one of Tey's favorite character types, the charming, innocent adolescent with a sharp mind and the strength of her convictions. Just as Beau Nash, in *Miss Pym Disposes*, was able to carry out and cover up a murder because she seemed an absolutely unlikely suspect, so Betty Kane perpetrates her lies by appearing innocent and vulnerable. Tey was enough of a cynic to know that such charm can be manipulated for self-serving ends.

Though she does not commit murder, Kane is more reprehensible than Nash because her motives are entirely selfish. While Nash's lack of remorse for her crime seems inhuman, she has the self-justification of intending to correct an injustice done to someone else. Kane's motivation is to preserve her reputation and attract sympathetic attention. Tey explains her behavior as, in part, the consequence of heredity. She is the selfish child of a long-dead selfish mother, despite the loving environment of her adoptive home.

As in other Tey mysteries Betty is undone by a combination of diligence and good luck. Ironically, the same outrageous press coverage which gained her national recognition and forced the po-

Dust jacket for the first American edition of Tey's best-known mystery, in which Inspector Grant investigates the case against King Richard III

lice to bring charges against the Sharpes is the means for her undoing. Her picture is recognized by a Danish hotelkeeper, who identifies her as the "wife" of a traveling salesman. Robert Blair had long suspected that a sexual escapade must be an element in the case, and, in fact, the fifteen-year-old invented the story of the kidnapping to account for the time she spent with the salesman.

Blair, the novel's primary investigator, is the Sharpes' most passionate defender and their deliverer as well. Like Alan Grant (who appears briefly in the novel representing the police), Blair is a bachelor, comfortable in his ways and good at what he does. Although he has had no experience with criminal cases, he throws himself into the work, hiring a detective and tracking down elu-

sive clues. In a dramatic courtroom scene the case against the Sharpes is discredited by the testimony of witnesses whose existence the police had never even suspected. It would be wrong to conclude, however, that the novel is an attack on police methods or integrity. Rather, it explores a characteristic Tey subject: the devastating and destructive effects of misinterpreting physical evidence.

Unlike Tey's other detectives, Blair makes no incorrect assumptions. His emotions do not mislead him and neither does the apparently overwhelming evidence of his clients' guilt. Like the others, he learns a lot about himself, his prejudices, and his limitations. His interior dialogues illustrate strength not apparent in his habit-ridden bachelor's way of life.

At the end of the novel, unwilling to return to his old routine, he falls in love with Marion Sharpe, proposes marriage, and, when she declines his offer, follows her to Canada. What attracts him to this rather unlikely romantic heroine is her intelligence and her dignity. Tall, lean, dark, and vaguely exotic, she is Tey's most fully developed independent woman, older and wiser than the typical heroine but no less intriguing. She can be compared to several minor characters from *Miss Pym Disposes*, especially Catherine Lux the theory mistress, and anticipates both Aunt Bee in *Brat Farrar* and, in some ways, Marta Hallard in *To Love and Be Wise* (1950), *The Daughter of Time*, and *The Singing Sands*.

She turns down Blair's "generous" offer, arguing that any man who has not married before he is forty is not interested in having a wife, any more than he wants the flu or rheumatism. "I don't want to be just something that has overtaken you," she explains, and she insists that his devoted maiden aunt has accustomed him "to all the creature comforts and the cosseting that I wouldn't know how to give you–and wouldn't give you if I knew how." Their romance is unresolved at novel's end, but the relationship between Marion and Robert Blair is the closest Tey comes in her novels to describing romantic love between adults.

The Franchise Affair has been one of Tey's most popular novels. Tey is explicit in delineating her thesis: "Your true criminal . . . has two unvarying characteristics, and it is these two characteristics which make him a criminal. Monstrous vanity and colossal selfishness. And they are both as integral, as inerradicable, as the texture of the skin." This statement might define any of her villains, but none of them is more vicious or destructive than Betty Kane, in part because her victims matter to the reader so much.

The Tey character who most closely resembles Kane in her pure selfishness is Simon Ashby, the twin who is defrauded of his inheritance in *Brat Farrar* but emerges as the novel's real criminal. At age thirteen Simon murdered his older twin in order to inherit the family fortune. Having covered his crime by making the death appear to be suicide, he seems never to have felt the slightest remorse. The novel begins with a scheme engineered by a ne'er-do-well actor to insinuate Brat Farrar, an orphan with an uncanny resemblance to Simon Ashby, into the family as the missing Patrick, whose body has never been found. Farrar is a quick study and a successful po-

seur. Having explained that rather than killing himself he ran away to sea, the false Patrick is exhilarated when his deception works: " 'You're in!' gloated the voice inside him. 'You're in! You're sitting as of right at the Ashby table, and they're all tickled to death about it.' " The family, with the notable exception of Simon, quickly comes to love and accept him, and he them. The novel poses a dilemma: How can Farrar be so charming if he is so corrupt?

His crime is fraud, not murder, which simplifies the issue somewhat. No one but Simon loses anything, and even before his crime is revealed his surly behavior diminishes any sympathy the reader might feel for him. Yet Brat Farrar does not deserve, on the basis of his charm alone, to inherit Latchetts, the family estate. In *A Shilling for Candles* Tey labeled charm the "most insidious weapon in all the human armoury."

For much of the book Tey makes it difficult for the reader to decide how to judge Brat and Simon. Yet, by introducing allusions to the biblical stories of Jacob, who cheated his brother Esau out of his birthright, and of Joseph, whose jealous brothers threw him into a pit in Dothan to die before they relented and sold him into slavery, she prepares the reader for Simon's confession, which confirms Brat's suspicions about Patrick's fate. Then the imposter assumes the role of proving that the person he pretends to be has, in fact, been murdered, fully aware that if he is successful he will expose his own crime as well as Simon's. It is consistent with Brat's character that he persists and consistent with the novel's theme that he is rewarded for his honesty, not punished for his deception. His interior dialogues demonstrate his decency and true heroism, as he struggles with his conscience and with the anguish his discoveries will bring to the family he has come to love.

Beatrice Ashby, the unmarried aunt who runs the household with enormous competence and affection, resembles both Miss Pym and Marion Sharpe, though for many readers Aunt Bee is more realistic than any of Tey's other adult women because she lives in a more conventional setting. A professional breeder and trainer of horses, she is a complex and appealing character with an enormous capacity for love and for coping with her family's unexpected tragedies. The eldest Ashby daughter, Eleanor, whose love for Brat shocks her into concluding that he cannot be her brother, is very like her.

Tey puts much emphasis on being well brought up. Brat is able to carry off his impersonation not only because–unknown to him–he is the illegitimate child of Aunt Bee's cousin and thus bears a strong family resemblance, but because he has good manners. One sure clue to Simon's true character is that he is ungentlemanly. Yet, Tey does not suggest that environment or heredity alone is responsible for the way people behave. The novel is full of contrasting siblings whose unique personalities cannot be attributed to the influence of one over the other, a more traditional approach than Tey used in explaining Betty Kane's behavior.

The countryside setting is an idyllic world corrupted by greed and ambition. The novel sets in opposition benign appearance and destructive hatred, a contrast that explodes in the dramatic and tense climax, in which Simon and Brat struggle and fall into the same pit where Simon had thrown Patrick's body, an accident in which Simon is killed and Brat is seriously injured. At that moment the narrative perspective changes, and the novel's pace quickens. Events are reported, questions answered, legal issues resolved. Brat slowly recovers and discovers that he is, to his surprise, an Ashby after all.

Part of the solution to Brat's situation is provided by what can be politely described as an official cover-up, atypical in Tey's novels and in classic detective fiction in general. The police play a different role in this novel than in Tey's others. The police at "the highest level" are told everything and engage in "smoothing out the mess to the best of their ability without breaking any of the laws they were engaged to uphold. . . . By a process of not saying too much, the ritual of the Law might be complied with, leaving unwanted truths still buried. . . ." *Brat Farrar* helped cement Tey's reputation as one of the best mystery novelists of the 1940s. Particularly impressed with her originality and skill in creating a believable imposter, most reviewers agreed with James Sandoe that the setting created by her "devotion to English tradition and the English countryside" was one of its outstanding pleasures.

In *To Love and Be Wise* Tey returned to the character of Alan Grant, her Scotland Yard detective, and to the less idyllic world of theatrical stars and other public personalities. She continues to examine the corrosive power of egomania, and she explores the subject of impersonation from a different angle. Leslie Searle is a woman who enjoys role playing and who is thorough in

planning the murder of Walter Whitmore, the current golden boy of broadcasting, a pompous man with no humility and less charm.

As Leslie Searle, artist and photographer, she maintains two identities. The artist is a woman, and the photographer is a man. Her transvestism has professional, rather than sexual, motivation: she has found it easier to move around and work as a man. During the events the novel describes she uses her masculine identity to get close to her intended victim. Things do not work out as planned; she abandons her murder plot and disappears from the trip she has been making with Whitmore to gather material for a book. Suspecting that the missing "man" has drowned, perhaps the victim of foul play, the local police call in Alan Grant of Scotland Yard.

There are sexual implications in Searle's impersonation of a man. She has an all-consuming obsession with her actress-cousin Marguerite Merriam, whose suicide after being jilted by Whitmore has inspired Searle's murder plot. Yet, it is characteristic of Tey's work that the more bizarre overtones of Searle's behavior are ignored or glossed over in solving the mystery. Instead, the novel emphasizes her dual role of victim and perpetrator.

Inspector Grant and most of the other characters sense from the beginning that there is something "unreal" and even "wrong" about Leslie Searle. To Grant "he" is "disconcerting," to Lavinia Fitch "uncanny," and to Toby Tullis "a materialized demon." Serge Ratoff, searching for the worst possible insult, calls him a "middle-west Lucifer." These foreshadowings, logical in context, are even more satisfying in rereading. Once the mystery has been resolved, the reader recognizes how brilliantly the clues are laid down and is able to appreciate the complexity of the characterizations.

Alan Grant intuits the truth before he can find the evidence to support his hunches. The contrast provided by his warm friendship with Marta Hallard and his forceful interrogation of possible suspects adds dimensions to his personality that are only hinted at in the earlier novels. He does not experience the self-doubt that has troubled him in earlier novels. Beneath the structure of the detective plot is a consideration of personal relationships, particularly the nature and consequences of love. Relationships between mother and child, between husband and wife, and those between lovers, friends, and enemies are examined. Very few of the relationships are good, sup-

Dust jacket for the first American edition of one of the mysteries in which Tey drew on her experiences with theater people

porting the allusion to Shakespeare's *Troilus and Cressida* (III, 3) in the novel's title: "to be wise and love exceeds man's might . . . . " Many characters are linked by selfishness, sometimes disguised.

Only independent, self-confident people who are able to function alone can appreciate companionship rather than manipulate it. Ironically, the best relationship in the novel is between Alan Grant and Marta Hallard, the actress who appeared briefly in *A Shilling for Candles*. Grant admires her intelligence and her self-sufficiency, as well as her beauty and fame, and while he never puts the conclusion into words, he implies that successful people do not seek fulfillment through others–including through marriage–but through themselves. That assumption, echoing the theme of Tey's early short story, "Madame Ville D'Au-

bier" (*English Review*, February 1930), may explain Tey's choice not to include romance as an element in the Grant novels. In a slightly different way it also explains Leslie Searle's change in plans, for she abandons her plan to kill Walter Whitmore when she is forced to question her own obsessive devotion to Marguerite.

To Love and Be Wise undercuts any attempt to describe Tey as an essentially conservative writer who supported "law and order" and the maintenance of the status quo. There is no rigidity, no moral judgment, in Grant's response to the criminal elements of Searle's deception, just as there is none in the Ashbys' response to Brat Farrar's impersonation. In his final interview with the unmasked Searle, Grant jokes about the desire to kill and takes a good-natured poke at the softness of the criminal-justice system.

"There are quite a few people I would have willingly killed in my time. Indeed, with prison no more penitential than a not very good public school, and the death sentence on the point of being abolished, I think I'll make a little list à la Gilbert. Then when I grow a little aged I shall make a total sweep . . . and retire comfortably to be well cared-for for the rest of my life." Tey's point is that many people have the urge to kill, though some lack the capacity and others are rational enough to understand that their motives are not sufficient justification for the deed. In this novel without a murder Tey is also examining the psychology of the killer.

Witty repartee, acidic observations, and evocative descriptions, always part of Tey's style, are abundant in the novel, as is the fluent dialogue that is her hallmark. She defines characters by their habits of speech. Grant's repeated references to the conjurer's trick of a "lady sawn in half" emphasizes his astute perception that Searle is not what he seems to be. It also provides an idiom for discussing Searle's dual identity. As in Tey's earlier novels the minor characters are drawn as distinctive individuals who contribute to the energy of the work, rather than simply fill up space.

To Love and Be Wise has fans and detractors. James Sandoe describes it as an "exceptional . . . and notably rewarding piece of work," but several contemporary American reviewers were much less impressed, calling it "slim," even "staggeringly unlikely," and insisting that Tey could write better mysteries than she had done here.

Tey's next novel is a radical departure from her pattern of creating unusual crimes in ordinary settings. Alan Grant is still at Scotland Yard, and Marta Hallard is waiting impatiently to be made Dame Marta; but Grant is in the hospital recovering from a fall through a trapdoor, depressed as well as sore, and the suspect he investigates has been dead for 450 years.

The Daughter of Time is Tey's best-known and most controversial mystery, with most serious critical attention focused on its subject rather than on its structure or style. Like Tey's other novels it involves murder, character assassination, and fraud. The crime is the murder of the Yorkist princes, Edward and Richard, in the Tower of London at the time when King Richard III's brief reign was ended by his death at Bosworth Field. Though Grant, like the other characters in the novel, begins by assuming Richard to be the murderer of the princes and the evil man that

Shakespeare portrays, he concludes that Richard was the victim of character assassination perpetrated by historians loyal to his successor, Henry Tudor, to validate Henry's almost nonexistent claim to be King Henry VII of England.

To support this conclusion—which is also accepted by some historians—Tey combines detective techniques with historical research. Grant, intuitively convinced that the National Gallery portrait of Richard reveals a good, not an evil, man, tries to apply all the police methods he knows to uncover the facts of the case. Since he is immobilized, Marta finds him a young American researcher, Brent Carradine, who is delighted to look up all the things Grant is eager to know. The novel is essentially static, reflecting the process of historical investigation, which, Tey suggests, is apt to move in fits and starts and run into dead ends at least as frequently as police work.

Initially well reviewed by critics such as Sandoe and Boucher, the novel prompted debate in the 1970s—an unusual fate for a detective story. On one side Guy Townsend argued passionately that Tey hated historians, manipulated evidence, and mocked scholarly research. Defending her and the novel, M. J. Smith pointed out that while novelists can do as they like with historical facts, historians such as Townsend compromise their integrity by ignoring research with which they do not agree. Townsend failed to acknowledge Paul Murray Kendall's scholarly and comprehensive biography of Richard III, published in 1956, which also supports the argument for Richard's innocence. Since Richard has provoked both passionate defense and vehement hatred since his death in 1485, the debate about Tey's conclusions is not surprising. Whether it is accurate to describe Tey's treatments of historical subjects in her plays, as well as this novel, as "whitewashing," as Sandra Roy has done, or as reassessments, is a matter of debate, as is the question of whether or not her partisan conclusions weaken *The Daughter of Time* as a detective novel. What is undeniably imaginative about the novel is its employment of a contemporary detective to solve crimes that took place in the distant past. Other novelists, such as Umberto Eco in *The Name of the Rose*, transform their premodern characters into highly skilled detectives, but Tey mixes old and new, and the frequency with which the novel is republished suggests that her approach has great appeal.

Despite its differences from her earlier books, the novel is pure Tey. Grant's intuitive "flair" that something is amiss when he looks at the portrait of the reputed monster recalls her earlier books. Furthermore, the self-aggrandizing destruction of another's reputation in *The Daughter of Time* links it firmly to Tey's earlier novels. Henry VII's court historians anticipate contemporary journalists as the purveyors of character assassination to an audience greedy for "backstairs gossip" and willing to believe what they are told. In the process of clearing Richard's reputation to his own satisfaction, Grant is convinced of their calumny. He insists that they are amoral in their eagerness to write the history their audience and their patron want to read. For Grant, as for Tey, such manipulation of truth is the most reprehensible crime.

The physical injury for which Grant is hospitalized in *The Daughter of Time* is followed in Tey's next novel by his emotional exhaustion. As *The Singing Sands* begins, he takes sick leave to fish in Scotland and to recover his equilibrium–a task that takes concerted effort and is finally achieved through work, not relaxation. That work is the quest to identify the young man whose body he discovers on the train to Scotland and then to find his murderer.

Grant seems older here than in earlier novels and thinks briefly of retirement; but by the time he has solved the riddle of the dead man on the train he has recovered completely. Gone is the irritability that comes with lying in a hospital bed and the embarrassment of having to confess the panic of shattered nerves. Gone, too, is the fear that he has lost his talent for investigation.

A famous archaeologist, the killer, Heron Lloyd, is driven by the same kind of ambition that Grant ascribes to Henry VII in *The Daughter of Time*. Completely scornful of moral and legal restraint, Lloyd will do anything to maintain his preeminent position. He has murdered Bill Kenrick to keep him from announcing his discovery of a fabled desert paradise that Lloyd was on the verge of discovering himself, and, when Grant is about to solve the case, he commits suicide, hoping to preserve his reputation. Grant takes enormous satisfaction in knowing that Lloyd's vanity and his crime will be common knowledge and that Kenrick will get the credit he deserves: "As long as books were written and history read, Bill Kenrick would live; and it was he, Alan Grant, who had done that. They had buried Bill Kenrick six feet deep in oblivion, but he, Alan

Grant, had dug him up again and set him in his rightful place as the discoverer of Wabar."

This novel divides into two parts: Grant's investigation, which is the heart of the novel, and his visit to the Scottish Highlands and the Hebrides. Although Kenrick's body is discovered on the trip north and Grant begins his inquiries there, the two elements are not totally integrated. Scotland holds out the promise of relaxation, and of marriage and family, but they appeal to Grant only in passing. His brief infatuation with Lady Kentallen does not survive when it must compete with his real love: his work.

As might be expected in a novel where the actual mystery is less compelling than the characters and setting, the book had a mixed critical reception. Tey's recent death perhaps softened some reviewers' objections, particularly to the resolution of the case through the criminal's confession and suicide. Yet Boucher commented on her "gracefully skilled writing," and reviewers were unanimous in praising her masterful descriptions of Scotland and in recognizing (without always agreeing on its merits) that she was, in fact, more interested in her detective's psychology than in writing a conventional detective story.

For the most part within the conventions of the classic detective story Josephine Tey examined the nature of crime and the suitability of punishment. Her work is distinguished by its complex characters and skillful dialogue. As Dorothy Salisbury Davis has observed, "if any one characteristic most distinguished Miss Tey's work it was her power to evoke character, atmosphere, mores by conversation" (*New Republic*, 20 September 1954).

She has sometimes been faulted for weak plotting and excessive dependence on chance, confession, and suicide to resolve her stories. In traditional mystery novels a detective's skill is the key element in solving crime. He earns his victory either by dogged work or brilliant insight, by working with the evidence rather than questioning it. Tey takes a different approach. Her detectives are fallible and often misinterpret physical evidence.

If Tey is unconventional in some ways, her work is still in the mainstream of classic detective fiction. There is always a motive for crime, and when it is uncovered the criminal is discovered. Her books contain no random violence, little bloodshed, and no police corruption. Even her experiments are often within the framework of the genre's tradition as she tries her hand at a locked-room mystery in *Miss Pym Disposes*, armchair detection in *The Daughter of Time*, and fair-play discovery of clues in *To Love and Be Wise*.

Yet, to think of her as an exemplar of tradition rather than a framer of it seriously underestimates her place in the history of the detective novel. Later writers, such as Ruth Rendell and P. D. James, have followed her lead in creating their detectives and in treating the character of the independent woman. Hampered by a lack of biographical information, literary biographers face serious handicaps in discussing the woman and her work, but these limitations have not diminished the enthusiasm of her readers.

References:
Sandra Roy, *Josephine Tey* (Boston: Twayne, 1980);
Nancy Ellen Talburt, "Josephine Tey," in *Ten Women of Mystery*, edited by Earl F. Bargainnier (Bowling Green, Ohio: Bowling Green State University Popular Press, 1981).

Roy Vickers
(David Durham, Sefton Kyle)
(1888?-1965)

Paul McCarthy
University of Kansas

BOOKS: *Lord Roberts: The Story of His Life* (London: Pearson, 1914);
The Mystery of the Scented Death (London: Jenkins, 1921);
Hounded Down, as David Durham (London: Hodder & Stoughton, 1923); as Vickers (London: Newnes, 1935);
The Vengeance of Henry Jarroman (London: Jenkins, 1923);
The Woman Accused, as Durham (London: Hodder & Stoughton, 1923); as Vickers (London: Newnes, 1926);
The Exploits of Fidelity Dove, as Durham (London: Hodder & Stoughton, 1924); as Vickers (London: Newnes, 1935);
Ishmael's Wife (London: Jenkins, 1924);
The Man in the Shadow, as Sefton Kyle (London: Jenkins, 1924);
A Murder for a Million (London: Jenkins, 1924);
Dead Man's Dower, as Kyle (London: Jenkins, 1925);
Four Past Four (London: Jenkins, 1925; New York: Jefferson House, 1945);
The Pearl-Headed Pin, as Durham (London: Hodder & Stoughton, 1925); as Vickers (London: Newnes, 1935);

His Other Wife (London: Jenkins, 1926);
The Unforbidden Sin (London: Jenkins, 1926);
Guilty. But–, as Kyle (London: Jenkins, 1927);
The White Raven, (London: Jenkins, 1927);
The Radingham Mystery (London: Jenkins, 1928);
A Girl of These Days (London: Jenkins, 1929);
The Gold Game (London: Jenkins, 1930);
The Hawk, as Kyle (London: Jenkins, 1930); as Vickers (New York: Dial, 1930);
The Rose in the Dark (London: Jenkins, 1930);
The Deputy for Cain (London: Jenkins, 1931);
The Bloomsbury Treasure, as Kyle (London: Jenkins, 1932);
The Marriage for the Defence (London: Jenkins, 1932);
The Vengeance of Mrs. Danvers, as Kyle (London: Jenkins, 1932);
The Whispering Death, as John Spencer (London: Hodder & Stoughton, 1932); as Vickers (London: Newnes, 1935; New York: Jefferson House, 1947);
Bardelow's Heir (London: Jenkins, 1933);
Red Hair, as Kyle (London: Jenkins, 1933);
Swell Garrick, as Spencer (London: Hodder & Stoughton, 1933); as Vickers (London: Newnes, 1935);

The Life He Stole, as Kyle (London: Jenkins, 1934);

Money Buys Everything (London: Jenkins, 1934);

The Forgotten Honeymoon, as Durham (London: Jenkins, 1935);

Hide Those Diamonds! (London: Newnes, 1935);

Kidnap Island (London: Newnes, 1935);

The Man in the Red Mask (London: Newnes, 1935);

The Man without a Name, as Kyle (London: Jenkins, 1935);

Silence, as Kyle (London: Jenkins, 1935);

The Durand Case, as Kyle (London: Jenkins, 1936);

Number Seventy-Three, as Kyle (London: Jenkins, 1936);

The Body in the Safe, as Kyle (London: Jenkins, 1937);

The Girl in the News (London: Jenkins, 1937);

I'll Never Tell (London: Jenkins, 1937);

The Notorious Miss Walters, as Kyle (London: Jenkins, 1937);

Terror of Tongues! (London: Newnes, 1937);

During His Majesty's Pleasure, as Kyle (London: Jenkins, 1938);

The Enemy Within (London: Jenkins, 1938);

The Girl Who Dared, as Durham (London: Jenkins, 1938);

The Life Between (London: Jenkins, 1938);

Missing!, as Kyle (London: Jenkins, 1938);

Against the Law, as Durham (London: Jenkins, 1939);

The Judge's Dilemma, as Kyle (London: Jenkins, 1939);

Miss X, as Kyle (London: Jenkins, 1939);

The Girl Known as D 13, as Kyle (London: Jenkins, 1940);

Playgirl Wanted (London: Jenkins, 1940);

The Shadow Over Fairholme, as Kyle (London: Jenkins, 1940);

She Walked in Fear (London: Jenkins, 1940);

Brenda Gets Married (London: Jenkins, 1941);

A Date With Danger (London: Jenkins, 1942; New York: Vanguard, 1944);

The Price of Silence, as Kyle (London: Jenkins, 1942);

War Bride (London: Jenkins, 1942);

Love Was Married, as Kyle (London: Jenkins, 1943);

The Department of Dead Ends (New York: Spivak, 1947);

Six Came to Dinner (London: Jenkins, 1948);

The Department of Dead Ends (London: Faber & Faber, 1949; Roslyn, N.Y.: Detective Book Club, 1953);

Gold and Wine (London: Jenkins, 1949; New York: Walker, 1961);

Murder of a Snob (London: Jenkins, 1949; New York: British Book Centre, 1958);

Murdering Mr. Velfrage (London: Faber & Faber, 1950); republished as *Maid to Murder* (New York: Mill, 1950);

Murder Will Out (London: Faber & Faber, 1950; Roslyn, N.Y.: Detective Book Club, 1954);

They Can't Hang Caroline (London: Jenkins, 1950);

The Sole Survivor and The Kynsard Affair (Roslyn, N.Y.: Detective Book Club, 1951; London: Gollancz, 1952);

Murder in Two Flats (London: Jenkins, 1952; New York: Mill, 1952);

Eight Murders in the Suburbs (London: Jenkins, 1954); abridged as *Six Murders in the Suburbs* (Roslyn, N.Y.: Detective Book Club, 1955);

Double Image and Other Stories (London: Jenkins, 1955; Roslyn, N.Y.: Detective Book Club, 1955);

Find the Innocent (London: Jenkins, 1959); republished as *The Girl Who Wouldn't Talk* (Roslyn, N.Y.: Detective Book Club, 1959);

Seven Chose Murder (London: Jenkins, 1959; Roslyn, N.Y.: Detective Book Club, 1959);

Best Detective Stories of Roy Vickers (London: Faber & Faber, 1965);

The Department of Dead Ends (New York: Dover, 1978).

OTHER: *Some Like Them Dead,* edited by Vickers (London: Hodder & Stoughton, 1960);

Crime Writers' Choice, edited by Vickers (London: Hodder & Stoughton, 1964);

Best Police Stories, edited by Vickers (London: Faber & Faber, 1966).

Roy Vickers was the author of at least sixty-seven novels published in hardcover or in serial form, and at least eighty-four short stories which have appeared in various magazines and in collections and anthologies. Almost all of his novels and short stories concern crime in some way, and their very number makes Vickers stand out as a writer to whom some attention must be given by those interested in the literature of crime. Taken together, his novels are not of high quality by the standards of today. Most of them were written for the mass market of the 1920s and the 1930s,

Dust jacket for the first British edition of the 1924 collection of short stories, featuring Miss Dove, thief and swindler (courtesy of Otto Penzler)

and while the reader of those times may well have found them entertaining, the reader of today would find many of them dated. The situation is quite the reverse with respect to Vickers's short stories. Although some of the earlier ones are as dated in style and content as many of his novels, the majority of the short stories have a quality which sets him apart as a major contributor to mystery fiction.

Roy C. Vickers was born in 1888, or possibly in 1889, and he died in 1965. He was educated at Charterhouse School in Surrey and at Brasenose College, Oxford, which he left without a degree. He studied law for some time at the Middle Temple in London, but he did not practice.

Vickers was married and had one son. From the beginning of his adult life Vickers resolved to make his living by writing. While accumulating rejection slips he worked as a salesman. He found some success as a ghostwriter, but left that after finding himself in some difficulty for being too original in a ghosted article. He was a crime reporter for a newspaper and a contest editor for a weekly publication. Vickers wrote a large number of nonfiction articles and sold hundreds of them to newspapers and magazines. The time frame for all of this activity is hazy, but most of it must have occurred during the second decade of this century. It was during this period that Vickers's

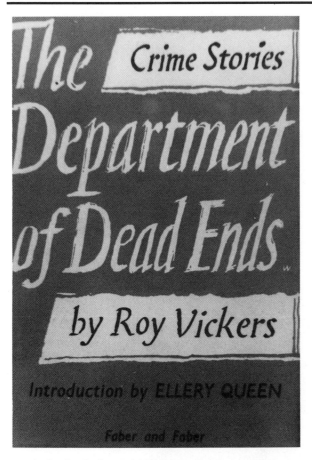

Dust jacket for the first British edition of Vicker's 1949 Department of Dead Ends stories (courtesy of Otto Penzler)

first book, a biography of Frederick, Earl Roberts, was published.

It was also during this period that he began to sell his fiction. From November 1913 through February 1917, twenty short stories by Vickers were published in the *Novel Magazine,* a popular British fiction magazine he edited for some time. Three of the stories were under the name Sefton Kyle, a pseudonym which Vickers used later for a number of his novels. A novel by Vickers, apparently his first, was also published in the *Novel Magazine,* serialized in four issues, March 1916 through June 1916. He called it *The Unforbidden Sin,* a title which he used for a different novel in 1926.

Generally well plotted and well written, Vickers's novels can best be described as sensational thrillers with a romantic element which is, in the case of some of them, the dominant theme. They are filled with master criminals and their gangs, plots of immense proportions, handsome and daring heroes who rescue, and fall in love with, beautiful and innocent maidens—some

of them are not so innocent after all. Some of his plots are extremely involved, and in his better novels, the sensationalism is turned down to an acceptable level.

Only nine of Vickers's novels have been published in the United States. Fortunately, among them is one which can be considered as representative of his better novels, *Murdering Mr. Velfrage* (1950). This novel is an inverted mystery, with the identities of the criminals more or less clear from the beginning, while it is not at all obvious just who has been murdered. Furthermore, it is not until the very end that the true motive for the crime is revealed. The principal character is a handsome young man whose attention is focused, at least partially, on two attractive young women, and at the end of the novel he chooses one of them to marry. The romantic element of the story is skillfully intertwined with the crime element, and it does not distract the reader from the mystery.

The early short stories by Vickers, those published in the *Novel Magazine,* are virtually unknown today. None of them has been collected, or even reprinted. They are as dated as many of the novels, and they are important only insofar as they are the first stories by a writer whose reputation rests largely on the quality of his short stories. One set of four stories features the head of security of one of Britain's railways and a beautiful and brilliant female criminal. With the repartee between these two and with the detailed reporting of the crimes, Vickers created an early model of one of his famous works, *The Exploits of Fidelity Dove,* a collection of sixteen stories published in 1924 under the name David Durham. *The Exploits of Fidelity Dove,* stories about the fascinating swindler and thief Miss Dove and her gang, demonstrates a considerable increase in Vickers's maturity as a writer of short stories from his days with the *Novel Magazine.* The plots are highly imaginative, and the stories show a control of characters and situations which not every writer of the popular fiction of the day could exercise.

Miss Dove's adversary in many of her exploits is Inspector Rason of Scotland Yard. Vickers had many names which he used over and over for his characters. Rason is one of them. At least two, if not three, of his detectives are called Rason, and there is still some debate about the actual number of different characters named Rason in Vickers's short stories and novels.

In September 1934 one of Vickers's finest stories, "The Rubber Trumpet," the first of thirty-

Dust jacket for the first British edition of Vicker's 1950 collection of stories about the fictitious Department of Dead Ends in Scotland Yard (courtesy of Otto Penzler)

seven stories which feature the fictitious department of Scotland Yard called the Department of Dead Ends, appeared in *Pearson's Magazine*. Over the following twenty or so years, forty-eight more of his stories appeared in *Pearson's*. All but five of the stories about the Department of Dead Ends have been included in one or more collections of Vickers's stories. Three collections with the title *The Department of Dead Ends* were published in 1947, 1949, and 1978, each with some stories not in the other. With the publication of these and other collections in the United States and in Britain, Vickers's reputation grew, and he is considered now to have been one of the finest writers of short detective stories in the middle years of this century.

The Department of Dead Ends stories are in-verted mysteries. In each there is a finely detailed description of a situation which leads up to a murder, or murders. The reader knows the circumstances of the crime. The question is how the identity of the murderer will be discovered by the police. The characters of the murderers and the victims are fully developed in each story, and it was Vickers's strong point that he was able to do this so completely in relatively few pages. He made real people of his characters, with feelings and motives the reader can understand, and in some cases with which the reader can sympathize. Vickers's characters come from a wide spectrum of the classes of English society, and the stories record many aspects of life in England, especially in Edwardian times and during the

Roy Vickers (caricature by 'Rich')

1920s and 1930s. In the early stories the detective in the Department of Dead Ends is Superintendent Tarrant, and in the later ones it is Inspector Rason, probably not the same Rason of the *Exploits of Fidelity Dove* stories, and certainly not the Rason who is the detective in some of Vickers's novels.

Each of the stories is about a crime which the regular forces of Scotland Yard fail to solve. The Department of Dead Ends is the final resting place of these and other unsolved cases, the depository of pieces of evidence such as a rubber trumpet and other clues which become forgotten in time. Later, sometimes years later, a detective is reminded of some item deposited with the department. He makes a connection and solves an old case. This formula was applied, with success,

over and over again by Vickers to a bewildering variety of situations. *Murder Will Out* (1950); *Eight Murders in the Suburbs* (1954); *Seven Chose Murder* (1959); and *Best Detective Stories of Roy Vickers* (1965), published shortly after Vickers's death, also contain some stories about the Department of Dead Ends. They are filled out with other stories.

References:

Paul McCarthy, "EUREKA! More Stories by Roy Vickers," *Poisoned Pen*, 5 (October 1983): 31-32;

McCarthy, "The Short Stories of Roy Vickers," *Poisoned Pen*, 5 (July 1982): 3-9;

Barry Pike, "PEN Profiles 24," *Poisoned Pen*, 5 (July 1982): 10-18.

Henry Wade
(Henry Lancelot Aubrey-Fletcher)
(10 September 1887-30 May 1969)

James and Joan Gindin
University of Michigan

BOOKS: *The Verdict of You All* (London: Constable, 1926; New York: Payson & Clarke, 1927);

A History of the Foot Guards to 1856, as H. L. Aubrey-Fletcher (London: Constable, 1927);

The Missing Partners (London: Constable, 1928; New York: Payson & Clarke, 1928);

The Duke of York's Steps (London: Constable, 1929; New York: Payson & Clarke, 1929);

The Dying Alderman (London: Constable, 1930; New York: Brewer & Warren, 1930);

No Friendly Drop (London: Constable, 1931; New York: Brewer, Warren & Putnam, 1932);

The Hanging Captain (London: Constable, 1932; New York: Harcourt, Brace, 1933);

Policeman's Lot (London: Constable, 1933);

Mist on the Saltings (London: Constable, 1933);

Constable, Guard Thyself! (London: Constable, 1934; Boston: Houghton Mifflin, 1935);

Heir Presumptive (London: Constable, 1935; New York: Macmillan, 1953);

Bury Him Darkly (London: Constable, 1936);

The High Sheriff (London: Constable, 1937);

Released for Death (London: Constable, 1938);

Here Comes the Copper (London: Constable, 1938);

Lonely Magdalen (London: Constable, 1940; revised, 1946);

New Graves at Great Norne (London: Constable, 1947);

Diplomat's Folly (London: Constable, 1951; New York: Macmillan, 1952);

Be Kind to the Killer (London: Constable, 1952);

Too Soon to Die (London: Constable, 1953; New York: Macmillan, 1954);

Gold Was Our Grave (London: Constable, 1954; New York: Macmillan, 1954);

A Dying Fall (London: Constable, 1955; New York: Macmillan, 1955);

The Litmore Snatch (London: Constable, 1957; New York: Macmillan, 1957).

Author of twenty detective novels and two volumes of short stories over a career of more than thirty years, Henry Wade (the pseudonym for Henry Lancelot Aubrey-Fletcher) was born in Surrey on 10 September 1887. He was a baronet, educated at Eton College and New College, Oxford. Marriage in 1911 to Mary Augusta Chilton resulted in four sons and a daughter. Wade was also a decorated officer of the Grenadier Guards in both world wars and (from 1925) the high sheriff of Buckinghamshire. He has frequently been acknowledged as one of the pioneers of the classic detective fiction of the Golden Age of the late 1920s and early 1930s. Like John Dickson Carr's, Wade's work is carefully plotted; like Margery Allingham's or Anthony Berkeley's, crime is contingent on something gone wrong with the established English social world through the terrors and upheavals of World War I.

For example, in Wade's third novel, *The Duke of York's Steps* (1929), set in the world of London bankers in the collapsing markets of 1929, most of the established figures of society have great difficulty admitting that anything has gone wrong. A leading banker, Garth Fratten, dies as a result of what is apparently a casual blow by a passerby as he walks down the Duke of York's steps. His friends and family immediately assume that the cause of death is an aneurysm, accidental and unpredictable. When the detective suggests a more deliberate possibility, the doctor who signs the death certificate is outraged and states that since he is a physician to the king his judgment cannot possibly be questioned. Only Fratten's daughter, a young woman of the jazz age, born in the early years of the new century, senses that something is wrong and begins to ask questions. Subsequent questions about the organization of financial networks reveal an economic and social world as tangled and complicated as that of Charles Dickens's Jarndyce and Jarndyce, to which Wade refers. The traditional and respect-

Dust jacket for one of Aubrey-Fletcher's collections of realistic short stories

able old generals and financiers who head the organizations are, in varying degrees, duped by international figures, by those emerging from newer commercial classes, and by those who have responded with sardonic selfishness to the shattering experiences of the war. Double identities mystify the complacent and solid English economic world. Cosmopolitan Jews, in particular, are suspect, seen as one of the forces unleashed to debase the social and economic structure. *The Duke of York's Steps* depends, as does much of classic detective fiction, on inheritance, on who would kill in order to take over the appropriate lineage of social tradition. For a long time Fratten's feckless and illegitimate son is suspected. But the son is cleared, as the machinations of an assortment of

financiers, headed by a Jewish banker who had seemed to flourish under Fratten's broad-minded confidence and who was actually holding Fratten's arm as they walked down the steps in their silk hats, are revealed as the agents destroying the English world. No reconciliation is suggested in a novel that pursues both its problems and its methods relentlessly.

Like six of Wade's other novels (*No Friendly Drop*, 1931; *Constable, Guard Thyself!*, 1934; *Bury Him Darkly*, 1936; *Lonely Magdalen*, 1940; *Too Soon to Die*, 1953; and *Gold Was Our Grave*, 1954), *The Duke of York's Steps* uses a series detective, Inspector Poole. Poole is a committed man who is nonetheless aware of the social embarrassment of asking questions and is deferential to established

Dust jacket for the 1946 revised edition of Aubrey-Fletcher's 1940 mystery, in which the strangled body of a prostitute, Bella Knox, is discovered on Hempstead Heath. A map on the endpapers allows the reader to follow Inspector Poole's pursuit of the murderer.

society, whose protective insularity he must penetrate to discover the truth. He almost considers his inquiries ill-mannered, although, as a reader of Henry James, he is sensitive to the complexity of human motives. As in all his criminal investigations, he follows conventional patterns of detection in *The Duke of York's Steps*, putting clues together carefully, working out all the possible entrances and exits to apparently enclosed spaces, and staging reconstructions of the crime that are never entirely adequate. In the process he is helped by Fratten's liberated daughter, who tracks down the source of a vulgar and distinc-

tive perfume that first seems to implicate and then to clear her brother. Poole himself is responsible for understanding the more intricately contorted financial and legal network that has led to the usurpation of the society.

Another kind of English society decimated by World War I is visible in *Mist on the Saltings* (1933), one of Wade's most moving novels. John Pansel, badly injured in the war "in which a group of young firebrands in Sarajevo threw a bomb which shattered the whole firmament of creation into a million fragments and turned all the thoughts and efforts of men for years to destruc-

Dust jacket for the first American edition of the book regarded by some critics as the first mystery to portray accurately the changes in postwar British society

tion, destruction, destruction," had been nursed back to precarious health by Hilary, an upper-class young woman looking for a social function. They marry and move to the flat North Sea coast, where John paints brilliantly described skies and subtle changes in light. After twelve years the romantic idyll has worn off, John's painting is increasingly unsuccessful, and the world presents a barren combination of depressing economic conditions and rising fears of another war. The village where they live, though called Bryde-by-the-Sea, offers no sense of community, for almost everyone has drifted there as detritus from somewhere else, worn down by poverty. Feeling and passion are still possible among some, like

Christian Madgek, an itinerant boatman and smuggler who abandons his understandably calculated design when he sees the genuine passion of the daughter of the town's prosperous pub owner. A successful novelist and womanizer, Dallas Fiennes, also moves to a hut on the marshy saltings between the village and the sea, looking for the isolation and quiet necessary to write his next novel. He recognizes Hilary's growing unhappiness and plans to exploit her. She, thwarted by years of John's increasingly surly depression, responds. Wade writes the scenes of the complex and emotional relationship, in which each character is made both self-justifying and self-abnegating simultaneously, with compressed and convincing skill.

Dallas Fiennes is found drowned in the mud of the saltings under circumstances that make it seem likely that John has killed him in a jealous rage over what he only partly understood (Hilary's infidelity is displaced emotion never quite consummated). The people of Bryde-by-the-Sea, characteristically slow in speech and movement, are unable to believe that the death was anything other than an unhappy accident. The police, working slowly, hampered by the tendency of Hilary and others to shroud partial truths in misleading accounts, have considerable difficulty establishing the existence of an actual crime. Suspicions switch (in a stunning style in which Wade builds details effectively to manage quick reversals) from one lover to another. The plot ends in a series of confessions, in a way that illustrates the difference between those who can love what is not themselves, and the victim, Fiennes, who can love only his own triumphs. The confessions, which are the authentic acknowledgment of passions within complicated and responsive psyches, have a sacrificial or redemptive quality that leaves justice shrouded in mist. Wade leaves a deeply appealing and ambiguous cover over social and human crime, as if all the apparatus of rational detection can only understand a proportion of human evil, nobility, and sympathy. Justice, as in some of Wade's other work, like *The Missing Partners* (1928), seems, in contrast, a minor issue.

Some of Wade's detective novels have neither the ratiocinative focus of *The Duke of York's Steps* nor the emotional depth of *The Mist on the Saltings*. They are more comic in tone, like *Heir Presumptive* (1935), which is told primarily through the point of view of a callow and stupid young member of a family's inferior branch who imagines he can murder his way to inheritance. Although qualified as a doctor, Eustace Hendel, the central figure of the novel, has been a wastrel, steadily losing enough at cards and nightclubs to need money when he learns of the sudden drowning of both the immediate heirs to the family title and land. Eustace then charts the family tree and assumes that only two distant cousins stand between him and the title. Wade introduces numerous comic legal tangles: discussions of the laws of entail; succession through the female line; and the possibility of inheriting the title with none of the money necessary to sustain it. In the meantime Eustace kills one cousin in a staged hunting accident on an isolated Scottish estate. He also plans to murder the cousin's invalid and dying

son, who must be eliminated before he can block Eustace from succession. Issues crucial to classical detective fiction are satirized: Sir Arthur Conan Doyle's work seems reflected in the fact that the current baron, a splenetic old man of ninety, stigmatizes Eustace as part of the "dark" side of the family he must prevent succeeding on grounds that are neither rational nor moral; Anthony Berkeley's famous novel *The Poisoned Chocolates Case* (1929) is lampooned through the elaborate use of poisoned chocolates as a means of eliminating the invalid cousin. Eustace is both suspected and outfoxed, subtly manipulated into thinking himself capable of succession, no matter how immoral, by a lawyer, a wiser criminal, married to one of the cousins on the female line who will inherit. Eustace had always used women, valued them only for rank and status, although his current mistress, a seedy actress, had reversed issues and pushed him to murder his way to succession. Eustace's superficial pride in his idea of the male is reversed. Even the lawyer's more clever and entangling schemes are reversed, for the final line of the novel suggests that he, too, is apprehended in Wade's comic treatment of how families and the law become intricately involuted, out of all humane control.

Wade's focus on the cultural dislocations emerging from World War I persisted through World War II. In 1947 he published *New Graves at Great Norne*, set in a depressed town on the East Anglian coast that had been losing trade and population ever since the coming of the railroads. In the despair following Chamberlain's bargain with Hitler at Munich in 1938, Great Norne seems a static world until a series of apparently accidental deaths—the vicar drowned, an old colonel shooting himself, an old drunken farmer burned in a farmhouse conflagration—shocks the town. Like the communities in Wade's other novels, the townspeople are hesitant to acknowledge the possibility of crime, of deliberate disruption of the social order. At the inquest on the vicar's death the doctor refuses to notice whiskey on his breath or the broken whiskey bottle in his pocket, for everyone knows that the vicar did not drink; they see "no point in causing unnecessary distress by an exploratory autopsy." The doctor does not want to ask a question he is not forced to ask. The detective, turning the issue around, wants to ask questions to eliminate possibilities, realizing that an autopsy that showed no alcohol in the vicar's stomach would prove that he must have been murdered. When the chain of killings continues,

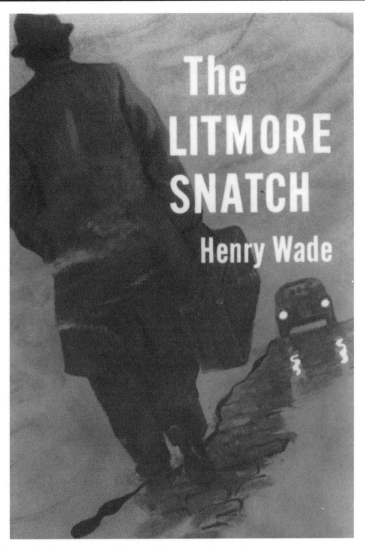

Dust jacket for the first American edition of Aubrey-Fletcher's last mystery, in which Poole pursues the kidnapper of a newspaper publisher's son

the police, including both local and London detectives of varying degrees of knowledge and perception, realize that the murdered were all members of the local church council that, just after World War I, had heavily censured a young wife, who later committed suicide, for infidelity.

At first, suspicion centers on the young wife's husband, a hard, grim, silent builder, the only one of his compatriots not to have served during World War I. He and the town have resented each other ever since. But the judgmental builder never changed his values; the real killer, brought into focus only on the last pages of the novel—a breach of the rules of conventional fictional deduction—is the long-dead woman's avenging lover, a sailor who had lived in the village disguised for ten years as a bent and indigent barrow man in order to discover the habits of his eventual victims. As a murder mystery the novel (as Wade's later ones sometimes do) rings slightly false, as if the enormous emotional impact of the disruptions of World War I could no longer be sustained. The novel, however, has a tamer and more successful parallel theme. The principal early suspect in the old colonel's murder is his son-in-law, a cheerful, aimless, casual sponger who plays golf. His intense, emotional wife is also unsatisfied, likely to be unfaithful. But the generations are different, and no life-denying hostility justifying homicide emerges in the newer social world. Unlike the builder or the old church council, the golfer is capable of understanding both his wife and his own limitations, just as he is about to redeem his genteel, feckless life in the necessary struggle of World War II.

Wade's implicit sense of an England regenerating or redeeming passion apart from issues of class through World War II did not last through the 1950s. He begins one of the best of his last novels, *A Dying Fall* (1955), by outlining the partial recovery of a class in 1952 with the return of Churchill, the gradual ending of austerity, and the renewed interest in horses and steeplechase racing. The world of the 1950s has also changed in that the police, now far more professional and competent, are often thought to force confessions from criminals illegitimately, and slippery, fashionable psychiatrists are likely to persuade juries to ignore the conclusions of honest police work. Wade's central figure is a slightly maimed veteran of the war, Charles Rathlyn, part of the "hunting folk who had a sort of freemasonry that beat the Freemasons themselves" as a less overtly privileged substitute for what once was an upper class. Lacking the money to live, race, and hunt as he would like, Charles still maintains the gentlemanly code of behavior, which attracts a rich widow in the racing set. She proposes marriage because she genuinely loves him, and Charles, not then in love with anyone, accepts. The marriage of unequal passions palls after a few months, and Wade's sympathies follow the woman who feels strong, honest passion, as in *Mist on the Saltings* or *New Graves at Great Norne*, or like Griselda, whose impotent husband might possibly have been murdered by either the county's high sheriff or the local priest, both of whom love her, in *The Hanging Captain* (1932). Charles falls in love with Anne, a younger member of the same horsing freemasonry, but they are both too scrupulous to consummate their love. When Charles's wife, who had walked in her sleep before, falls to her death over the balustrade outside their bedroom, others and the police suspect that the quiet and decorous Charles had pushed her. Investigation reveals dishonesty, blackmail, jealousy, and resentment within the structure of the widow's world, but none of the ancillary crimes can be attributed to Charles. Rather, the criminals are the two secretaries, one male, one female, refugees from more deprived classes whom the widow had rescued and kept on long after she needed their services. The parasites on what were the upper classes fracture the brave remnants of the great house society, doing more damage than do the upper classes themselves. The child of the prisoner, trained as an accountant, and the social secretary who cannot conceal the anger originating in her illegitimate childhood prevent the society from reestablishing any unity. Charles is free, and he and Anne marry and establish their stables in another country, but the reader still does not know whether or not Charles pushed his wife over the balustrade. The novel ends with an ambiguity like that of *Mist on the Saltings*, although in this, a thinner novel, Wade seems to rely too much on doubt concerning a single incident rather than on the doubt that involves redemptions, confessions, sacrifice, and the human spirit in the earlier novel. Like *Heir Presumptive*, although less comic, the simple plot of *A Dying Fall* is handled with skill and grace. But it lacks the human depth and texture of some of Wade's best fiction, at all stages of his career, like *Mist on the Saltings* and *New Graves at Great Norne*.

Reference:

Charles Shibuk, "Henry Wade," *Armchair Detective*, 1 (1967-1968): 111-115; 2 (1968-1969): 45.

Patricia Wentworth
(Dora Amy Elles)
(1878-28 January 1961)

Christopher Smith
University of East Anglia

BOOKS: *A Marriage under the Terror* (London: Melrose, 1910; New York: Putnam's, 1910);

A Child's Rhyme Book (London: Melrose, 1910);

A Little More Than Kin (London: Melrose, 1911); republished as *More Than Kin* (New York: Putnam's, 1911);

The Devil's Wind (London: Melrose, 1912);

The Fire Within (London: Melrose, 1913);

Simon Heriot (London: Melrose, 1914);

Queen Anne Is Dead (London: Melrose, 1915);

Earl or Chieftain? The Romance of Hugh O'Neill (Dublin: Catholic Truth Society of Ireland, 1919);

The Astonishing Adventure of Jane Smith (London: Melrose, 1923; Boston: Small Maynard, 1923);

The Red Lacquer Case (London: Melrose, 1924; Boston: Small Maynard, 1925);

The Annam Jewel (London: Melrose, 1924; Boston: Small Maynard, 1925);

The Black Cabinet (London: Hodder & Stoughton, 1925; Boston: Small Maynard, 1926);

The Dower House Mystery (London: Hodder & Stoughton, 1925; Boston: Small Maynard, 1926);

The Amazing Chance (London: Hodder & Stoughton, 1926; Philadelphia: Lippincott, 1928);

Anne Belinda (London: Hodder & Stoughton, 1927; Philadelphia: Lippincott, 1928);

Hue and Cry (London: Hodder & Stoughton, 1927; Philadelphia: Lippincott, 1927);

Grey Mask (London: Hodder & Stoughton, 1928; Philadelphia: Lippincott, 1929);

Will-o'-the-Wisp (London: Hodder & Stoughton, 1928; Philadelphia: Lippincott, 1928);

Fool Errant (London: Hodder & Stoughton, 1929; Philadelphia: Lippincott, 1929);

Beggar's Choice (London: Hodder & Stoughton, 1930; Philadelphia: Lippincott, 1931);

The Coldstone (London: Hodder & Stoughton, 1930; Philadelphia: Lippincott, 1930);

Kingdom Lost (Philadelphia: Lippincott, 1930; London: Hodder & Stoughton, 1931);

Danger Calling (London: Hodder & Stoughton, 1931; Philadelphia: Lippincott, 1931);

Nothing Venture (London: Cassell, 1932; Philadelphia: Lippincott, 1932);

Red Danger (London: Cassell, 1932); republished as *Red Shadow* (Philadelphia: Lippincott, 1932);

Seven Green Stones (London: Cassell, 1933); republished as *Outrageous Fortune* (Philadelphia: Lippincott, 1933);

Walk with Care (London: Cassell, 1933; Philadelphia: Lippincott, 1933);

Fear by Night (London: Hodder & Stoughton, 1934; Philadelphia: Lippincott, 1934);

Devil-in-the-Dark (London: Hodder & Stoughton, 1934); republished as *Touch and Go* (Philadelphia: Lippincott, 1934);

Blindfold (London: Hodder & Stoughton, 1935; Philadelphia: Lippincott, 1935);

Red Stefan (London: Hodder & Stoughton, 1935; Philadelphia: Lippincott, 1935);

Hole and Corner (London: Hodder & Stoughton, 1936; Philadelphia: Lippincott, 1936);

Dead or Alive (London: Hodder & Stoughton, 1936; Philadelphia: Lippincott, 1936);

The Case Is Closed (London: Hodder & Stoughton, 1937; Philadelphia: Lippincott, 1937);

Down Under (London: Hodder & Stoughton, 1937; Philadelphia: Lippincott, 1937);

Mr. Zero (London: Hodder & Stoughton, 1938; Philadelphia: Lippincott, 1938);

Run! (London: Hodder & Stoughton, 1938; Philadelphia: Lippincott, 1938);

The Blind Side (London: Hodder & Stoughton, 1939; Philadelphia: Lippincott, 1939);

Lonesome Road (London: Hodder & Stoughton, 1939; Philadelphia: Lippincott, 1939);

Who Pays the Piper? (London: Hodder & Stoughton, 1940); republished as *Account Rendered* (Philadelphia: Lippincott, 1940);

Dust jacket for the first American edition of Elles's 1955 novel in which Miss Silver investigates murders that follow an outbreak of poison-pen letters

Rolling Stone (London: Hodder & Stoughton, 1940; Philadelphia: Lippincott, 1940);

Unlawful Occasions (London: Hodder & Stoughton, 1941); republished as *Weekend with Death* (Philadelphia: Lippincott, 1941);

In the Balance (Philadelphia: Lippincott, 1941); republished as *Danger Point* (London: Hodder & Stoughton, 1942);

Pursuit of a Parcel (London: Hodder & Stoughton, 1942; Philadelphia: Lippincott, 1942);

The Chinese Shawl (London: Hodder & Stoughton, 1943; Philadelphia: Lippincott, 1943);

Miss Silver Deals with Death (Philadelphia: Lippincott, 1943); republished as *Miss Silver Intervenes* (London: Hodder & Stoughton, 1944);

The Key (Philadelphia: Lippincott, 1944; London: Hodder & Stoughton, 1946);

The Clock Strikes Twelve (Philadelphia: Lippincott, 1944; London: Hodder & Stoughton, 1945);

She Came Back (Philadelphia: Lippincott, 1945); republished as *The Traveller Returns* (London: Hodder & Stoughton, 1948);

Silence in Court (Philadelphia: Lippincott, 1945; London: Hodder & Stoughton, 1947);

Beneath the Hunter's Moon: Poems (London: Hodder & Stoughton, 1945);

Pilgrim's Rest (Philadelphia: Lippincott, 1946; London: Hodder & Stoughton, 1948); republished as *Dark Threat* (New York: Popular Library, 1951);

Latter End (Philadelphia: Lippincott, 1947; London: Hodder & Stoughton, 1949);

Wicked Uncle (Philadelphia: Lippincott, 1947); republished as *Spotlight* (London: Hodder & Stoughton, 1949);

The Case of William Smith (Philadelphia: Lippincott, 1948; London: Hodder & Stoughton, 1950);

Eternity Ring (Philadelphia: Lippincott, 1948; London: Hodder & Stoughton, 1950);

Miss Silver Comes to Stay (Philadelphia: Lippincott, 1949; London: Hodder & Stoughton, 1951);

The Catherine Wheel (Philadelphia: Lippincott, 1949; London: Hodder & Stoughton, 1951);

The Brading Collection (Philadelphia: Lippincott, 1950; London: Hodder & Stoughton, 1952);

Through the Wall (Philadelphia: Lippincott, 1950; London: Hodder & Stoughton, 1952);

Anna, Where Are You? (Philadelphia: Lippincott, 1951; London: Hodder & Stoughton, 1953); republished as *Death at Deep End* (New York: Pyramid, 1963);

The Ivory Dagger (Philadelphia: Lippincott, 1951; London: Hodder & Stoughton, 1953);

The Watersplash (Philadelphia: Lippincott, 1951; London: Hodder & Stoughton, 1954);

Ladies' Bane (Philadelphia: Lippincott, 1952; London: Hodder & Stoughton, 1954);

Vanishing Point (Philadelphia: Lippincott, 1953; London: Hodder & Stoughton, 1955);

Out of the Past (Philadelphia: Lippincott, 1953; London: Hodder & Stoughton, 1955);

The Pool of Dreams: Poems (London: Hodder & Stoughton, 1953; Philadelphia: Lippincott, 1954);

The Benevent Treasure (Philadelphia: Lippincott, 1954; London: Hodder & Stoughton, 1956);

The Silent Pool (Philadelphia: Lippincott, 1954; London: Hodder & Stoughton, 1956);

Poison in the Pen (Philadelphia: Lippincott, 1955; London: Hodder & Stoughton, 1957);

The Listening Eye (Philadelphia: Lippincott, 1955; London: Hodder & Stoughton, 1957);

The Gazebo (Philadelphia: Lippincott, 1956; London: Hodder & Stoughton, 1958); republished as *The Summerhouse* (New York: Pyramid, 1967);

The Fingerprint (Philadelphia: Lippincott, 1956; London: Hodder & Stoughton, 1959);

The Alington Inheritance (Philadelphia: Lippincott, 1958; London: Hodder & Stoughton, 1960);

The Girl in the Cellar (London: Hodder & Stoughton, 1961).

Patricia Wentworth is the pseudonym of Dora Amy Elles. The daughter of a distinguished soldier, Lt. Gen. Sir Edmund Roche Elles, she was born in 1878 in Mussoorie, one of the favorite summer stations of the Indian army in the foothills of the Himalayas. At first she was educated privately but later attended Blackheath High School for Girls, a well-to-do day school located not far from the military establishments at Woolwich, London. She was first married to Lt. Col. George Dillon, who died in 1906, and then, in 1920, to Lt. Col. George Oliver Turnbull, by whom she had one daughter. Despite her growing reputation as a writer, she never courted fame, preferring a quiet existence devoted to such typical British middle-class pleasures as the theater, gardening, motoring, and the keeping of pet dachshunds. Her second husband assisted her in the preparation of her manuscripts for submission to the publishers.

Wentworth's first published work appeared, like Rudyard Kipling's, in the pages of the *Civil and Military Gazette*, the leading newspaper for the British Raj in the Punjab. Her earliest inclination was to write historical romances, and with *A Marriage under the Terror* (1910), a sentimental tale set during the French Revolution, a period which the British reading public knew well, thanks to Charles Dickens's *A Tale of Two Cities* (1859) and Baroness Orczy's *The Scarlet Pimpernel* (1905), she won a prize for the then considerable sum of 250 guineas (or about four hundred dollars) for a first novel. *A Little More Than Kin* (1911) and a number of other romances are in much the same vein, and she also published some verse, which is testimony to her concern for the precise and disciplined use of language. The first of her thrillers was *The Astonishing Adventure of Jane Smith* (1923). It is, however, with books known loosely under the collective title of the "Miss Silver Mysteries" that Wentworth chiefly made her mark. Part of the secret of her success lies no doubt in the way she maintained a strong sense of continuity of character, circumstance, and tone among these novels without, however, making them into a series which has to be read in order. There is, too, an accurate and even affectionate portrayal of English middle-class life which many of her contemporaries undoubtedly found comforting amid all the changes in British society and which today's readers probably enjoy as a portrayal of what they like to regard as typical English manners and customs.

Miss Maud Silver–the Christian name is rich in late-Victorian resonances, and the policemen with whom she works mock it when they venture to call her "Maudie" behind her back–is a retired governess who in middle age sets up a detective agency. Some comparisons with Agatha Christie's Miss Jane Marple are inevitable, though there are important differences, too. Miss Silver has acquired remarkable powers of observation through long experience of living in middle-class homes where her subordinate but, to a degree, privileged position had permitted her to see much that her employers might have preferred to pass unnoticed. Where Miss Silver differs essentially from Miss Marple is in being a professional. Though she will occasionally chance to be in the vicinity when some crime is committed, it is more usual for clients, who are often following a recommendation from acquaintances or who know of her work by reputation, to write or to call at her flat and ask for help. Before she will take on a case she always insists on frankness from the client, and it is made clear that an appropriate fee will have to be paid in due course, even if actual sums of money are genteelly not mentioned. Though a successful private detective, Miss Silver is not rich. With a modest inheritance she had been able to give up work as a governess, and now she lives in a small but comfortable flat in Montague Mansions, which is a rather grand name for a quite ordinary apartment block in London. She has a maid who does the housework for her, shows in the visitors, and provides countless pots of tea. The furnishing and decoration of the flat are Victorian in style, and the carpets and upholstery are beginning to look shabby and need replacing. Wentworth coyly tells the reader that the walls were decorated with reproductions of such old-fashioned and hackneyed sentimental paintings as Edward Henry Landseer's *Monarch of the Glen*, John Everett Millais's sensationally popular *Bubbles*, and G. F. Watts's *Hope*. On the mantelshelf, the top of the bookcase, and every other available space stand framed photographs. These are not, however, just the souvenirs of a spinsterish existence; they are also the human records of a life of solving crime.

Miss Silver is described as a dowdy spinster with neat features and mouse-colored hair. She cannot afford to buy clothes very often–the ones she wears are often said to be at least two years old–and as she has little dress sense and picks dull colors and long skirts, she generally looks rather out of fashion. She invariably wears at her throat a bog-oak brooch in the form of a rose with a pearl at the center, and her pince-nez is held on a thin gold chain looped from the left side of her bodice. These details add up to an accomplished portrait of an ex-governess who might be expected to be kindly but rather ineffectual. Part of Miss Silver's abiding charm is the constant questioning of the stereotype.

Though Miss Silver makes a living by her work and takes a professional pride in her success as a detective, she does not display any special skills or expertise or have recourse to unusual equipment or apparatus. Her chief aid is something that might well be found in any schoolroom, a red copybook (or exercise book), in which she systematically makes notes, and her method as an investigator is based essentially on painstaking observation and the processes of elimination which lead inevitably to the right conclusion. Hers is a method that might be used by anybody who happened to possess Miss Silver's patience and penetration, and this has undoubtedly helped endear her to readers who feel some kinship with her.

Unlike some private detectives, Miss Silver enjoys good relations with the police. Once the local bobby has been forced to admit that the case is quite beyond him–and that generally does not take long–Chief Inspector Lamb of Scotland Yard, stolid and solid, and his young assistant Frank Abbott, who, as a child, had been one of Miss Silver's charges and now emerges as one of the new breed of police detectives, are called in. There is no animosity between the three, and though Chief Inspector Lamb is sometimes tempted to think that his younger colleague is a little too precocious, discussions between the three are full and frank. What makes Miss Silver especially useful in investigations is her ability to sit in a corner watching suspects as she knits small garments for her niece's children, apparently oblivious to what is going on around her, though, of course, she is, in fact, shrewdly analyzing the situation. Sometimes, too, she is prepared to enter premises and carry out searches without needing, as the police would, to go through the formality of obtaining a warrant in advance.

Dust jacket for the first British edition (1959) of Elles's 1956 mystery in which a fingerprint provides a perplexing clue

Miss Silver investigates the crimes of the English middle classes. They are committed in the home counties, in the prosperous country districts around London, and Miss Silver often has the chance of thinking the matter through and even of making some interesting first contacts while on the relatively short journey from the capital by train, for she naturally cannot afford a car and has not, in any case, lost the habit of thinking that rail travel is the normal way of getting about. The scene of the crime is generally a comfortable country house where more than one generation of the family will live at ease, though without aristocratic splendor, with one or two servants to attend to their creature comforts. Wentworth usually sets her novels in a closed community, where it is relatively easy for Miss Silver (and the reader, of course) to become acquainted with all the members, although occasionally a whole village will fall under suspicion, and in *Miss Silver Deals with Death* (1943) the focus of attention is a London block of flats. The cast of characters often includes recently demobilized army officers returning to an uneasy situation at home, professional people (such as publishers, solicitors, and doctors, as well as clergymen) and their wives who devote their time to the social round and to running the home which may well house a number of other members of the family, such as unmarried sisters, and a variety of guests. Usually some pretext is found to enable Miss Silver to stay at the house, too.

The crime is always murder, and the victim may die in a variety of ways, by poisoning, by drowning, by being pushed from the parapet of a house, or by being shot. But the unpleasantness of the act is not dwelt on, so that there is no horror from the description of violent death. In fact, death is simply the starting point of an intellectually intriguing investigation, not a matter of shock or even of sadness, though there may be a lot of tension and foreboding when it is appreciated that the killer may strike at any moment. The motives include cupidity, as when an attempt is made to withhold a heritage in *The Alington Inheritance* (1958), and long-lasting family squabbles. False accusations fly, and those under suspicion frequently find it hard to clear themselves because of some mistake they had made at an earlier date or because they are guilty of some lesser crime. Blackmail is a common element, which can lead to a second murder and a further scattering of clues. As well as the crime there is a secondary source of interest in love. Wentworth reveals her original taste for romance when young lovers, parted through war or misunderstanding, come together again, or when estranged couples are reconciled and new relationships are forged. There is something undeniably cozy here, for not only is crime the prerogative of the well-heeled, but solutions are always found which favor the young or the deserving.

Wentworth's plotting is dense and complex, but rarely confusing and generally straightforward. Context and situation are set before the reader either in the build-up to the crime or in its immediate aftermath, and when Miss Silver intervenes, her briefing provides a second opportunity for explaining what is going on and for clarifying the personal relationships that are the basis of the story. The plot moves forward in a simple chronological fashion toward important events, confrontations, and a conclusion which is never entirely predictable.

The lasting success of Wentworth's work, especially her Miss Silver mysteries, is probably explained by a multiplicity of factors: a solid, believable character for whom the reader can feel both sympathy and admiration; believable characterizations and well-drawn settings; and a combination of crime and mystery with romance which can puzzle without causing alarm or distress and charm without becoming too sentimental. Her novels, though unassuming on the surface, are complex and tightly structured and seldom failed to satisfy a devoted public.

Dennis Yates Wheatley

(8 January 1897-11 November 1977)

J. Randolph Cox
St. Olaf College

BOOKS: *The Forbidden Territory* (London: Hutchinson, 1933; New York: Dutton, 1933);

Old Rowley: A Private Life of Charles II (London: Hutchinson, 1933); republished as *A Private Life of Charles II* (London: Hutchinson, 1938);

Such Power Is Dangerous (London: Hutchinson, 1933);

Black August (London: Hutchinson, 1934; New York: Dutton, 1934);

The Fabulous Valley (London: Hutchinson, 1934);

The Devil Rides Out (London: Hutchinson, 1934);

The Eunuch of Stamboul (London: Hutchinson, 1935; Boston: Little, Brown, 1935);

Contraband (London: Hutchinson, 1936);

Murder Off Miami, by Wheatley and J. G. Links (London: Hutchinson, 1936); republished as *File on Bolitho Blane* (New York: Morrow, 1936);

They Found Atlantis (London: Hutchinson, 1936; Philadelphia: Lippincott, 1936);

Red Eagle: A Life of Marshal Voroshilov (London: Hutchinson, 1937);

The Secret War (London: Hutchinson, 1937);

Who Killed Robert Prentice?, by Wheatley and Links (London: Hutchinson, 1937); republished as *File on Robert Prentice* (New York: Greenberg, 1937);

The Golden Spaniard (London: Hutchinson, 1938);

The Malinsay Massacre, by Wheatley and Links (London: Hutchinson, 1938; New York: Rutledge, 1981);

Uncharted Seas (London: Hutchinson, 1938);

Herewith the Clues!, by Wheatley and Links (London: Hutchinson, 1939; New York: Mayflower Books, 1982);

Sixty Days to Live (London: Hutchinson, 1939);

The Quest of Julian Day (London: Hutchinson, 1939);

The Scarlet Imposter (London: Hutchinson, 1940; New York: Macmillan, 1942);

Faked Passports (London: Hutchinson, 1940; New York: Macmillan, 1943);

Dennis Wheatley

The Black Baroness (London: Hutchinson, 1940; New York: Macmillan, 1942);

Three Inquisitive People (London: Hutchinson, 1940);

Strange Conflict (London: Hutchinson, 1941);

The Sword of Fate (London: Hutchinson, 1941;
    New York: Macmillan, 1944);
Total War (London: Hutchinson, 1941);
Mediterranean Nights (London: Hutchinson, 1942);
"V" for Vengeance (London: Hutchinson, 1942;
    New York: Macmillan, 1942);
Gunmen, Gallants, and Ghosts (London: Hutchinson, 1943);
The Man Who Missed the War (London: Hutchinson, 1945);
Codeword–Golden Fleece (London: Hutchinson, 1946);
Come Into My Parlour (London: Hutchinson, 1946);
The Launching of Roger Brook (London: Hutchinson, 1947);
The Haunting of Toby Jugg (London: Hutchinson, 1948);
The Shadow of Tyburn Tree (London: Hutchinson, 1948; New York: Ballantine, 1973);
The Rising Storm (London: Hutchinson, 1949);
The Seven Ages of Justerini's (London: Riddle, 1949); revised and republished as *1749-1965: The Eight Ages of Justerini's* (Aylesbury, Buckinghamshire: Dolphin, 1965);
The Second Seal (London: Hutchinson, 1950);
The Man Who Killed the King (London: Hutchinson, 1951; New York: Putnam's, 1965);
Star of Ill-Omen (London: Hutchinson, 1952);
To the Devil–a Daughter (London: Hutchinson, 1953);
Curtain of Fear (London: Hutchinson, 1953);
The Island Where Time Stands Still (London: Hutchinson, 1954);
The Dark Secret of Josephine (London: Hutchinson, 1955);
The Ka of Gifford Hillary (London: Hutchinson, 1956);
The Prisoner in the Mask (London: Hutchinson, 1957);
Traitor's Gate (London: Hutchinson, 1958);
Stranger Than Fiction (London: Hutchinson, 1959);
The Rape of Venice (London: Hutchinson, 1959);
The Satanist (London: Hutchinson, 1960; New York: Ballantine, 1974);
Vendetta in Spain (London: Hutchinson, 1961);
Saturdays with Bricks (and Other Days under Shell-Fire) (London: Hutchinson, 1961);
Mayhem in Greece (London: Hutchinson, 1962);
The Sultan's Daughter (London: Hutchinson, 1963);
Bill for the Use of a Body (London: Hutchinson, 1964);
They Used Dark Forces (London: Hutchinson, 1964);
Dangerous Inheritance (London: Hutchinson, 1965);

The Wanton Princess (London: Hutchinson, 1966);
Unholy Crusade (London: Hutchinson, 1967);
The White Witch of the South Seas (London: Hutchinson, 1968);
Evil in a Mask (London: Hutchinson, 1969);
Gateway to Hell (London: Hutchinson, 1970; New York: Ballantine, 1973);
The Ravishing of Lady Mary Ware (London: Hutchinson, 1971);
The Devil and All His Works (London: Hutchinson, 1971; New York: American Heritage, 1971);
The Strange Story of Linda Lee (London: Hutchinson, 1972);
The Irish Witch (London: Hutchinson, 1973);
Desperate Measures (London: Hutchinson, 1974);
The Time Has Come: The Young Man Said, 1897-1914 (London: Hutchinson, 1977);
The Time Has Come: Officer and Temporary Gentleman, 1914-1919 (London: Hutchinson, 1978);
The Time Has Come: Drink and Ink, 1919-1977, edited by Anthony Lejeune (London: Hutchinson, 1979);
The Deception Planners: My Secret War, edited by Lejeune (London: Hutchinson, 1980);
Collection: *The Lymington Edition* 54 volumes (London: Hutchinson, 1961-1972).

MOTION PICTURE: *An Englishman's Home*, screenplay by Wheatley and others, Aldwych, 1939.

OTHER: *A Century of Horror Stories*, edited by Wheatley (London: Hutchinson, 1935);
A Century of Spy Stories, edited by Wheatley (London: Hutchinson, 1938).

Dennis Wheatley, who also wrote history and political analysis, was called "Prince of Thriller Writers" by a critic in the *Times Literary Supplement* (8 June 1940), and this motto was emblazoned on the spines of the collected edition of his works. In his lifetime he published more than sixty volumes of fiction, principally in the fields of adventure, espionage, and historical romance. They sold over twenty million copies. The majority of them are long, three hundred to four hundred pages, for he believed in giving the reader his money's worth.

Wheatley's works of fiction can be divided into six categories: four sets of books with continuing characters (the Duke de Richleau, Gregory Sallust, Julian Day, and Roger Brook), plus stories

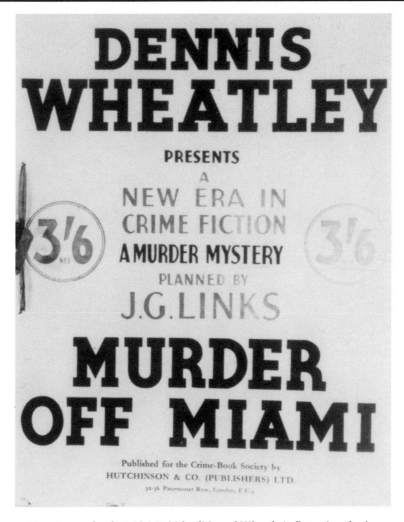

Front cover for the 1936 British edition of Wheatley's first crime dossier

of black magic and straight adventure novels. The hero of each series was developed to exist in his own world, as though the books in that series formed his official biography. For example, novels about the Duke de Richleau were designed to fill in gaps in the character's life, which extends from 1894 to 1960.

Dennis Yates Wheatley was born in London, 8 January 1897, and educated at Dulwich College, on board H.M.S. *Worcester*, and privately in Germany. He served in the Royal Field Artillery, the City of London Brigade from 1914 to 1917, and then with the Thirty-sixth Ulster Division between 1917 and 1919, when he was gassed and invalided out. His father and grandfather before him had been vintners, so it was natural for him to join the family wine firm, Wheatley and Son, in 1919 after his military service. He became the sole owner of the firm on his father's death in 1927. Prior to that, in 1923, he married Nancy

Robinson; they had one son, Anthony, and were divorced in 1931.

Wheatley's career as a writer began in the 1930s. The firm of Dennis Wheatley, Ltd., was affected by the Great Depression in the early 1930s, and the company went into liquidation with Wheatley himself sustaining a loss of several hundred thousand pounds. With his new bride, the former Joan Johnstone, Wheatley practiced every possible economy including limiting themselves to a glass of sherry each in the evenings. Encouraged by his wife, who had read his short stories in manuscript, Wheatley bought some paper and sat down to write a thriller. The result was *Three Inquisitive People* (1940), a detective story which involves formal deduction in which Richard Eaton's mother is murdered in her Mayfair flat. In quick succession Wheatley wrote several short stories, selling one ("The Snake") to *Nash's* in London and *Cosmopolitan* in New York, and

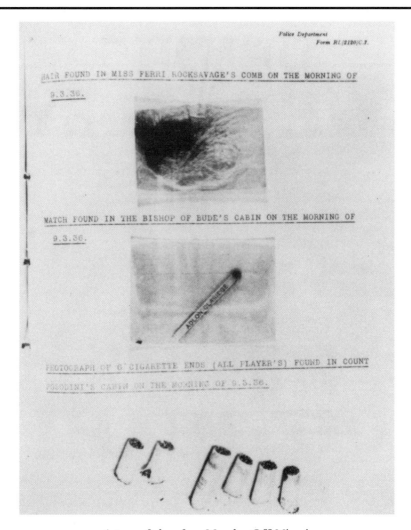

A page of clues from Murder Off Miami

wrote a second novel, *The Forbidden Territory* (1933). Both he and his publisher (Hutchinson and Company) thought this a much better story than *Three Inquisitive People*, which they had accepted, so it was published first. Determined to help market his own work, Wheatley sold some pictures and furniture and used the money to print two thousand postcards advertising the book, which became a worldwide best-seller.

Alexandre Dumas was a great influence on Wheatley, who ascribed his lifelong interest in history to reading his novels. The characters in *The Forbidden Territory* have direct counterparts in Dumas. The Duke de Richleau himself is Athos, the conservative Richard Eaton is d'Artagnan, Simon Aron (the liberal Jew) is Aramis, and the democratic American, Rex van Ryn, is Porthos. Wheatley readily acknowledged that *The Golden Spaniard* (1938) was his version of Dumas's *Twenty Years After* (1845), while *The Prisoner in the*

Mask (1957) was inspired by the Man in the Iron Mask section of Dumas's *The Vicomte de Bragelonne* (1848-1850).

Following Dumas's lead in *The Three Musketeers* (1844), Wheatley saw the potential for writing several stories about a single set of characters, but he did not want to confine himself to endless sequels. Again following the practice of Dumas, he alternated stories featuring the duke with others about Gregory Sallust. Wheatley took nearly a year to write *Black August* (1934), his Wellsian account of a Russian revolution set in the future (roughly 1960). The hero, Sallust, was based in part (his appearance and personality) on a friend of Wheatley's from World War I, Gordon Eric Gordon-Tombe, was to appear in ten additional novels, the majority belonging to a series of spy thrillers set during World War I. *Black August* is greatly informed by Wheatley's knowledge of the Soviet Union, which he displayed in his

Wheatley, age eighteen, as a lieutenant in the Royal Field Artillery

1937 biography of the Russian marshal, Kliment Voroshilov.

After two novels (*Black August* and *Contraband*, 1936) with Sallust as hero, Wheatley conceived the idea of using him in a series set during the early years of World War II. The first novel, *The Scarlet Imposter* (1940), sent Sallust into Germany as a spy and involved him with the conspiracy to assassinate Hitler. Wheatley quickly followed up the success of this with a direct sequel, *Faked Passports* (1940), which continued Sallust's adventures in Germany and during the Finnish-Russian War (1939-1940). Since he had not published two consecutive books about the same

character before, he was uncertain whether to continue with the Sallust saga or to turn to another subject. He left it up to his readers by including a request for suggestions at the end of the second novel. When the votes were tallied, he began the third in the series, *The Black Baroness* (1940), about the 1940 German invasion of Norway.

Anxious to find a way to use his imagination on some project more directly connected with the war, he accepted an offer from the British Intelligence branch, MI5, to write a paper outlining measures for countering a possible invasion of Britain. The reception of this by the Imperial General Staff encouraged the production of further papers on resistance to invasion and the utilization of the Home Guard for village defense. This led to his accepting a position as a member of the Joint Planning Staff of the War Cabinet from 1941 to 1944. In 1945 he was made a wing commander on Sir Winston Churchill's staff. He was awarded the Bronze Star by the United States for his services to the Allied war effort.

After the war the Wheatleys bought a two-story Georgian mansion, Grove Place, in Lymington, a small, ancient town, about halfway between Southampton and Bournemouth. Wheatley and his wife expended much time and money restoring the house and grounds. Wheatley also devoted much time to raising his son by his first wife and the sons of his second wife by an earlier marriage.

While a member of the Joint Planning Staff, Wheatley acquired an intimate knowledge of many matters which could have been used as background for his thrillers. Unfortunately, the Official Secrets Act prevented him from capitalizing on this source. He confided his dilemma to Air Commodore Kenneth Collier, then director of plans, who provided a solution. He suggested Wheatley set his stories in Napoleonic times. From this germ came the inspiration for his postwar stories about Roger Brook.

The Roger Brook series began with *The Launching of Roger Brook* in 1947 and was carefully planned from the start as a finite series with a specific number of volumes. Twelve volumes covering the period of 1783 to 1815: the French Revolution, the rise and fall of Napoleon, and Roger Brook's missions for Prime Minister William Pitt were conceived, written, and published over a twenty-seven-year period. The subplots running throughout the series include Brooks's love affair with Georgina Thursby, his erstwhile mistress, and the antagonism with the school bully, George Gunston, later Brigadier Gunston. Individual novels involve his search for the lost Dauphin, the reconciliation between Napoleon and Josephine, a plot to assassinate the emperor, and the daring rescue of his own daughter at a Black Mass on Walpurgis Night. The series has received much praise for the skillful way in which Wheatley combined his melodramatic plots with accurate historical detail.

Wheatley only describes his fictional heroes in general physical details. For example, de Richleau is a slim, delicate-looking man with an aquiline nose, a claret-colored vicuna smoking jacket, and gray "devil's eyebrows," who enjoys his Hoyo de Monterrey cigars. Gregory Sallust is satanic, sardonic, and cynical, with a lantern-jawed face and a white scar running from his left eyebrow to his dark, smooth hair. His background is filled in with paragraphs of block description, as is that of his chief, Sir Pellinore Gwaine-Cust. A lone wolf, Sallust is the ideal hero who will dare anything, if the stakes are high enough.

Wheatley was one of the most financially successful writers in the field of the occult. A totally serious, self-conscious student of the subject, he used his novels as vehicles for a coherently developed theory of Black Magic. Personally, he claimed to have never attended or assisted at an occult ceremony and that his knowledge came from research, but a reader of *The Devil Rides Out* (1934) or *The Haunting of Toby Jugg* (1948) would come away convinced that the author believed in what he wrote about. Some of his other Black Magic novels are not as convincing as these. The diabolists could just as well have been gangsters. Wheatley's reputation as a writer of occult fiction is out of proportion to the actual number of books he wrote in that genre. The Lymington edition of his collected works labeled only one fifth of the volumes as belonging to that subseries. As far as his actual belief is concerned, the closest Wheatley ever came to subscribing to any organized religion or cult was his belief in reincarnation.

His political views are apparent and undisguised in all of his works. One need not read between the lines to decide that he was a monarchist, chauvinist, racist, and individualist, yet his readers never seem to have complained. Apparently enough of them shared his views or just enjoyed his exotic situations for his books to continue in popularity.

One of Wheatley's contributions to the mystery field, his crime dossiers, underwent a renaissance in the 1980s when they were reissued. Planned and executed in collaboration with J. G. Links, the crime dossiers were murder mysteries in which the physical clues (photographs, broken matches, cablegrams, newspapers) were actually reproduced in the publications. Readers could have the satisfaction of solving the mystery by examining the same clues, in a physical sense, as the detective. The solution was in a sealed envelope. They inspired a number of imitators in both their incarnations. The four titles were *Murder Off Miami* (1936), *Who Killed Robert Prentice?*

Wheatley's memorial to his friend Gorden Eric Gordon-Tombe, a bookplate showing Tombe as a satyr. Tombe was the model for Wheatley's Gregory Sallust (designed by Frank C. Papé).

(1937), *The Malinsay Massacre* (1938), and *Herewith the Clues!* (1939).

Wheatley's life apart from his writing sometimes appears as if it consisted of equal parts of public service, travel, bricklaying, and gracious living. His tremendous output can be attributed to a disciplined work schedule. His secretary would arrive at half past nine in the morning for about an hour of dictating replies to his correspondence. From half past ten to one o'clock he worked on his current book. After lunch he would continue for half an hour, take a nap, be awakened for tea at four o'clock, and continue work until dinner. He often worked after dinner until midnight or two in the morning. This schedule was kept up six days each week.

Each novel was a combination of the back-ground history of its locale and the plot of the story. They were uniformly 160,000 words long, or twice the length of the ordinary thriller. In a day when most writers had become automated to the extent of composing their novels on the typewriter, Wheatley still wrote in longhand, in pencil, with a good eraser. He never corrected his manuscripts until most of the book had been written, but he used four people besides himself to proofread the galleys.

After having decided that *Desperate Measures* (1974), the final Roger Brook novel, was to be his last work of fiction, he began work on his autobiography. In it he claimed that *The Second Seal* (1950), a novel of the Duke de Richleau's life during World War II, was his best work. In failing health Wheatley devoted the last few years of his life to continuing his memoirs. Planned to appear in five volumes, he had only completed two when death came on 11 November 1977. With the overall title of *The Time Has Come* (1978), the first two volumes give quite detailed accounts of his life to the end of World War I. Two more volumes, edited from his notes by Anthony Lejeune, were published posthumously (1979), beginning with 1919 and containing the story of his career as a writer through World War II. Wheatley wrote to entertain and was paid well for his success. That his works do not seem destined to survive him makes him a probable source for studies in popular taste in the second quarter of the twentieth century.

References:

Glen St. John Barclay, *Anatomy of Horror: The Masters of Occult Fiction* (London: Weidenfeld & Nicolson, 1978; New York: St. Martin's, 1979);

Reg Gadney, "The Murder Dossiers of Dennis Wheatley and J. G. Links," *London Magazine*, new series, 8 (March 1969): 41-51;

Iwan Hedman, "Dennis Wheatley: A Biographical Sketch and Bibliography," *Armchair Detective*, 2 (July 1969): 227-236;

David Thomas, "The Black Magic Books of Dennis Wheatley," *Book and Magazine Collector*, no. 54 (September 1988): 4-11.

Ethel Lina White
(1887-1944)

Barrie Hayne
University of Toronto

BOOKS: *The Wish-Bone* (London: Ward, Lock, 1927);

'Twill Soon Be Dark (London: Ward, Lock, 1929);

The Eternal Journey (London: Ward, Lock, 1930);

Put Out the Light (London: Ward, Lock, 1931; New York: Dial, 1933); republished as *Sinister Light* (New York: Paperback Library, 1966);

Fear Stalks the Village (London: Ward, Lock, 1932; New York: Harper, 1942);

Some Must Watch (London: Ward, Lock, 1933; New York: Harper, 1941); republished as *The Spiral Staircase* (Cleveland: World, 1946);

The First Time He Died (London: Collins, 1935);

Wax (London: Collins, 1935; Garden City, N.Y.: Doubleday, Doran for the Crime Club, 1935);

The Wheel Spins (London: Collins, 1936; New York: Harper, 1936); republished as *The Lady Vanishes* (London: Collins, 1962; New York: Paperback Library, 1966);

The Elephant Never Forgets (London: Collins, 1937; New York: Harper, 1938);

The Third Eye (London: Collins, 1937; New York: Harper, 1937);

Step in the Dark (London: Collins, 1938; New York: Harper, 1939);

While She Sleeps (London: Collins, 1940; New York: Harper, 1940);

She Faded Into Air (London: Collins, 1941; New York: Harper, 1941);

Midnight House (London: Collins, 1942); republished as *Her Heart in Her Throat* (New York: Harper, 1942); republished as *The Unseen* (New York: Paperback Library, 1966);

The Man Who Loved Lions (London: Collins, 1943); republished as *The Man Who Was Not There* (New York: Harper, 1943);

They See in Darkness (London: Collins, 1944).

OTHER: "An Unlocked Window," in *My Best Mystery Story* (London: Faber & Faber, 1939);

"The Gilded Pupil," in *Detective Stories of Today*, edited by Raymond Postgate (London: Faber & Faber, 1940).

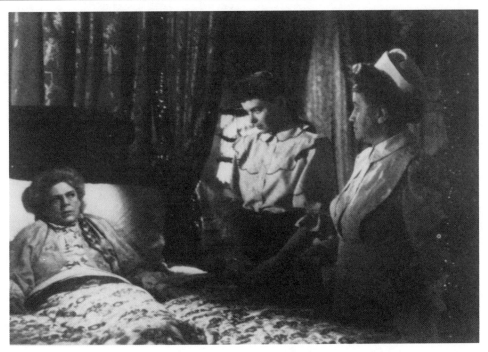

Scene from the 1946 movie The Spiral Staircase, *based on White's 1933 novel,* Some Must Watch. *Dorothy McGuire (center) plays the mute servant of an imperious bedridden woman (Ethel Barrymore) in a New England community where an unknown person is killing people whom he perceives to be imperfect (courtesy of RKO).*

Ethel Lina White belongs ineluctably to what has been called derisively "The Had-I-But-Known School" of mystery fiction, with its endangered heroine, its closed and threatening circle (which in her best novel is not an old dark house but a train), its association of terror with the commonplace, and its resolution in marital pairing. The opening of her best novel, *The Wheel Spins* (1936), suggests most of these elements: "The day before the disaster, Iris Carr had her first premonition of danger. She was used to the protection of a crowd.... Their constant presence tended to create the illusion that she moved in a large circle.... The crowd had swooped down on a beautiful village of picturesque squalor, tucked away in a remote corner of Europe.... On this holiday she heard Pan's pipes, but had no experience of the kick of his hairy hindquarters."

Little information on White's personal life is available. She was born in Abergavenny, Monmouthshire, Wales, and is known to have worked for the Ministry of Pensions in London. It was not until her third novel, *The Eternal Journey* (1930), that she began to work the vein of mystery or adventure, and then not in what would become her characteristic way. It is a tale of atonement, in which a young woman who has been responsible for a death in 1794 is given a chance to live again in 1930 and is then projected into 2331. Like other Gothic writers, White often flirted with the supernatural: only in this novel such elements remain unexplained.

There is little of conventional mystery or detection in White's novels. The secret which lies at the heart of both Gothic and detective fiction, and which is sprung upon the reader in the first case and left to his rational deduction in the second, is almost always sprung in White's books. An interesting exception is White's next novel, *Put Out the Light* (1931), where the author tells the reader in a preface that because the victim is the most dominant character in the novel, she is retained as long as possible. Readers may "decide" who is going to kill her, and no doubt "the reader will reach the goal before the detective, who is built to last, and not for speed." Superintendent Pye, an engagingly commonsensical detective, plods his way to a solution, much aided by his clairvoyant sister. *Put Out the Light* is as close to a detective novel as any White ever wrote, and its originality lies in the fact that the victim, a most unpleasant owner of a chain of lingerie shops, has given her three adopted children and two other characters ample reason for wishing her dead, though her murder does not take place until the twenty-ninth of thirty-five chapters.

Some Must Watch (1933) begins with a note of foreboding that is characteristic in White's novels: "Helen realized that she had walked too far just as daylight was beginning to fade. . . . Over all hung a heavy sense of expectancy, as though the valley awaited some disaster." But "fortunately," the third paragraph begins, "Helen was a realist . . . and not prone of self-pity." More than the heroines of Mary Roberts Rinehart, who tend anyway to be middle-aged, White's typical heroines are courageous, inquisitive, and pertinacious, though sufficiently lacking in these qualities as to make necessary the final interventions of heroes. Hired as a companion in a strange old mansion in Cornwall peopled by a matriarch, her stepson and stepdaughter, and a variety of servants and nurses, Helen, who finds herself in the midst of a series of murders of young women, contradicts her elders. She feels fear but not despair as the men of the household leave or are incapacitated one by one in the course of a terrifying and constantly rainy night, and she is generally quite her own person.

It is suggestive that White's two best novels, *Some Must Watch* and *The Wheel Spins*, are both more widely known through their film versions, which make important changes in the transfer to the screen. Out of *Some Must Watch* Robert Siodmak made *The Spiral Staircase* (1946), a classic film noir in a dark and brooding New England, where the old woman now has two sons, one of whom turns out to be a perfectionist who destroys all imperfection; and the girl of the film, who like her counterpart in the novel becomes the murderer's final quarry, is mute. (The villain's motive is less effective in the novel; he kills women because of his dedicated opposition to world overpopulation.)

The characteristic mixture of horror and the mundane in *Some Who Watch* and *The Wheel Spins* is certainly what drew Alfred Hitchcock to the latter novel, out of which he made *The Lady Vanishes* (1939), one of his most admired films. He adds intimations of coming war, underlining White's relatively playful satire of British chauvinism, and makes the hero a figure of much greater charm and substance. In each case the source of the film is fully in evidence, but the something additional raises the film to a higher level of art. One element Hitchcock toned down is White's typical touch of suspense. The effectiveness of both novel and film is due to Iris's frustration when no one will believe her story of the existence—and disappearance from a speeding train—of Miss Froy. In one way the novel is superior: in the film the audience sees Miss Froy and can testify to her reality; in the novel the reader must consider the possibility that Miss Froy is indeed a figment of Iris's imagination. Once the reader believes that Miss Froy exists, the suspense as to whether she will be saved before she is submitted to murderous surgery is great and typical of White. The fact, often pointed out, that no murder takes place in the novel in no way diminishes the suspense, for murder is but a step away throughout.

Wax (1935), published between White's two greatest successes, is an unusual novel for White inasmuch as it locates commonplace events in bizarre surroundings rather than the reverse. Here the suspense resides in Sonia's valorous night in a waxworks gallery, where each figure seems to threaten to come to life at any moment. It is this attributing sinister human qualities to the seemingly inanimate that is one of the most effective features of *Some Must Watch*, where the last tree in a long avenue suddenly comes to life as the stalking murderer, a major poetic motif of that novel.

White rarely strayed far from the formulas of her success. The works which follow *The Wheel Spins* include *The Elephant Never Forgets* (1937), in which an idealistic student of proletarian life in Soviet Russia has her friends disappear into political prisons one by one, until she herself is threatened; *The Third Eye* (1937), in which a young games mistress, caught up in murder at an exclusive girls' school, is then transferred, somewhat gratuitously, to the care of Miss Bat of Bat House, where the stalking and the endangerment continue; *Step in the Dark* (1938), which places a quaint little English widow with two charming young daughters in the clutches of a Swedish count and his associates, who would kill her for the royalties she receives as a writer of bestselling mysteries; and *While She Sleeps* (1940), in which Miss Loveapple—much like Miss Froy—is randomly selected as a murder victim and escapes her fate largely through good luck, never learning that she was endangered at all.

In *Midnight House* (1942), which deserves a renewed readership, a young governess is introduced to the Romeo-and-Juliet love that separated two families eleven years before. Since then the mansion next door has been barred and empty. Its opening, attended by a good deal of suspense as the heroine, with typical fortitude, enters it through a secret passageway, literally brings to light some skeletons long hidden in its closets. While it does little more than combine the usual elements of White's work, *Midnight House* balances them all perfectly and brings the hero and heroine together at the end, the detection having been accomplished primarily by the girl. This novel also was made into a film, *The Unseen* (1945), but in this case the film version does not illuminate the source.

All White's heroines, even the mousiest, are their own women. Ann Sherbourne in *The Man Who Loved Lions* (1943), one of White's weakest novels, is a young orphan girl who attends a reunion of schoolfriends, arranged seven years before, in a mansion now converted into a zoo. To the usual perils of stabbing, shooting, and strangling are now added the fangs of a hungry lion; the heroine survives all with fortitude, and the last scene of the novel, the villain having been unmasked, is the heroine's recognition of her long-lost love.

White's last novel, published after her death, remains characteristic. In *They See in Dark-ness* (1944) the commonplace town of Oldtown ("by day, a homely huddle of roofs, clustering in a tree-lined valley; but by night . . . a black bowl filled to the brim with shadows") is terrorized by a murderer who is eliminating one by one the legatees of a large estate. On the peripheries of the action is a sinister group of nuns, who supervise an insane asylum and unwittingly harbor the criminal. The heroine, who is the companion of an old lady, is also—no less than her predecessors—the object of both the murderous villain and the romantic hero.

Of all the Gothic writers whose work descends from Charlotte Brontë's *Jane Eyre* (1847), adapting their lady-companions and governesses to the alien world of the first half of the twentieth century, and leading those heroines through avenues, houses, or compartments of terror, Ethel Lina White, after Daphne du Maurier, is the most artistically successful and, without a peer, the most suspenseful.

Emlyn Williams

(26 November 1905-   )

William Nelson
Wichita State University

See also the Williams entry in *DLB 10: Modern British Dramatists, 1900-1945.*

BOOKS: *A Murder Has Been Arranged* (London: Collins, 1930; New York: French, 1931);

The Late Christopher Bean (London: Gollancz, 1933);

Night Must Fall (London: Gollancz, 1935; New York: Random House, 1936);

He Was Born Gay (London: Heinemann, 1937);

The Corn Is Green (London: Heinemann, 1938; New York: Random House, 1941);

The Light of Heart (London: Heinemann, 1940);

The Morning Star (London: Heinemann, 1942);

A Month in the Country (London: Heinemann, 1943; New York: French, 1957);

The Druid's Rest (London: Heinemann, 1944);

The Wind of Heaven (London: Heinemann, 1945);

Spring, 1600, revised edition (London: Heinemann, 1946);

Thinking Aloud: A Dramatic Sketch (London: French, 1946);

Trespass (London: Heinemann, 1947);

Pepper and Sand: A Duologue (London: Deane, 1948);

Accolade (London: Heinemann, 1950);

Someone Waiting (London: Heinemann, 1954; New York: Dramatists Play Service, 1956);

Beth (London: Heinemann, 1959);

The Collected Plays (London: Heinemann, 1961; New York: Random House, 1961)–includes *Night Must Fall, He Was Born Gay, The Corn Is Green, The Light of Heart;*

George: An Early Autobiography (London: Hamilton, 1961; New York: Random House, 1962);

The Master Builder (New York: Theatre Arts Books, 1967);

Beyond Belief: A Chronicle of Murder and Its Detection (London: Hamilton, 1967; New York: Random House, 1968);

Emlyn: An Early Autobiography: 1927-1935 (London: Bodley Head, 1973; New York: Viking, 1974);

Headlong (London: Heinemann, 1980; New York: Viking, 1981);

Cuckoo (London & New York: French, 1986);

Dr. Crippen's Diary: An Invention (London: Macdonald, 1988).

SELECTED PLAY PRODUCTIONS: *Vigil*, Oxford, Playhouse, November 1925;

Full Moon, Oxford, Playhouse, 28 February 1927; London, Arts Theatre, 30 January 1929;

Glamour, London, Embassy Theatre, 10 December 1928;

A Murder Has Been Arranged, London, Strand Theatre, 9 November 1930;

Port Said, London, Wyndham's Theatre, 1 November 1931; revised as *Vessels Departing*, London, Embassy Theatre, 3 July 1933;

Night Must Fall, London, Duchess Theatre, 31 May 1935;

The Corn Is Green, London, Duchess Theatre, 20 September 1938;

Thinking Aloud, London, Stage Door Canteen, July 1945;

Someone Waiting, London Globe Theatre, 25 November 1953.

OTHER: *Vigil*, in *The Second Book of One-Act Plays* (London: Heinemann, 1954);

"Dr. Crippen's Diary," in *Great Cases of Scotland Yard* (Pleasantville, N.Y.: Reader's Digest Association, 1978), pp. 417-514.

Emlyn Williams is known primarily as an actor-playwright, perhaps more particularly in the United States as a reader-impersonator of Charles Dickens since 1951 and of Dylan Thomas since 1955. He has performed in many plays and motion pictures; directed plays; and written plays, novels, and film and television scripts. He was named a Commander of the British Empire in 1962. His contribution to the mystery genre consists of an early one-act play, four full-length plays, and two documentary novels.

Emlyn Williams (courtesy of the Welsh Arts Council, University of Wales Press)

George Emlyn Williams was born on 26 November 1905 near Mostyn, Flintshire (now Clwyd), Wales, to Richard and Mary Williams. His father had been a stoker in a coal mine; at the time of Williams's birth his father was an unsuccessful greengrocer. In 1906 the family moved to Pen-y-maes, Glanrafon, Wales, where Richard Williams became the landlord of a pub. Williams received his earliest education at a convent of French nuns and at a council school.

Williams's interest in the macabre can be traced in part to his experiences with death during his childhood in Wales: the death of a village girl and the suicide of a neighboring farmer impressed him profoundly. Williams earned a scholarship at Holywell County School; he was eleven years old when he met Sarah Grace Cooke, the teacher who both inspired his interest in education and provided moral and financial support for him to continue. She encouraged his interest in language and sent him to St. Julien, France, when he was fifteen to study French with a teacher of her acquaintance. Williams describes the relationship with Miss Cooke in his two autobiographical books, *George* (1961) and *Emlyn* (1973); it also served as a source of inspiration

Scene from the 1937 film version of Williams's play Night Must Fall, 1935. Robert Montgomery (right), the psychopathic murderer, is interviewed by Dame Mae Whitty (left), playing Mrs. Bramson, and Rosalind Russell (center), her spinster niece (MGM).

for his play *The Corn Is Green* (1938).

Williams earned a scholarship to Oxford University and entered the university in 1923. While he did well in school, it soon became clear to him that he was not a scholar. His main interest was in theater, and he became a member of the Oxford University Dramatic Society. It was at Oxford that he decided to drop his first name in favor of his unusual middle name. His "sinister" bent was first manifested in a one-act drama, *Vigil*, which was produced in 1925 by the dramatic society and was successful on the stage; it was published in 1954. The play centers on the hypnotic power of "The Master" to enthrall visitors to his manor on the Welsh border until he is ready to dispose of them. Two intended victims, Richman and Atherton, plot to murder him to free themselves but lack the will to do so; when the master suddenly dies, they find that his servant, Isaiah–played by Williams in the Oxford production–has been slowly poisoning him. The dialogue is melodramatic, and some effects are theatrical in the bad sense of the term. The play does afford an introduction to the direction that Williams would take with the crime story: he would be more concerned with atmosphere and

the psychology of the murderer and his victim than in the ratiocinative solution of the mystery.

Williams's first full-length play, *Full Moon*, was produced at Oxford in 1927. Later that year he received his degree and moved to London to seek a career in the theater, making his professional acting debut as Pelling's 'Prentice in J. B. Fagan's *And So to Bed* in 1927. A series of other roles followed, including that of Jack in his own *Glamour* in 1928.

Williams's next venture in the realm of the mystery was *A Murder Has Been Arranged*, which began its run at London's St. James's Theatre on 26 November 1930 with Williams as director; it was published the same year. The play combines a story of murder with the supernatural: the occultist Sir Charles Jasper celebrates his birthday with a costume ball on the stage of a purportedly haunted theater; the guests are dressed as famous ghosts of history. Sir Charles is to inherit two million pounds if he is still alive at 11:00 that night; otherwise the money will go to his nephew, Maurice Mullins. In a reenactment of the murder that led to the haunting of the theater, Sir Charles is killed by Mullins in an ingenious manner that makes the crime appear to be a suicide; but the dead man's ghost returns and forces Mullins to confess. Richard Findlater remarks, "The interest of the play lies not in the facts of the crime, but in the portrait of the murderer": Mullins says, "I don't take furtive sniffs at the cup of vice. I drink it to the dregs, with a gesture. I am the Complete Criminal." The play received favorable reviews, which emphasized Williams's command of atmosphere and sense of the theater, but it was not a commercial success.

From April 1930 to January 1931 Williams played the role of the Chicago gangster Angelo in Edgar Wallace's *On the Spot*. When the play concluded its run, he went to Germany for four days to research the mass murders of Fritz Haarman, the "Butcher of Hannover." In August 1931 he opened in Wallace's crime drama *The Case of the Frightened Lady* in the role of Lord Lebanon.

Williams's next play, *Port Said* (1931), was, like *A Murder Has Been Arranged*, a failure; its setting is the underworld of the disreputable port city, and it incorporates melodramatic tactics similar to those in the earlier play. Although murder is the mainspring of the plot, the major theme of the play is the divided character of an Anglo-Turkish clerk, Youssef el Tabah, played by Williams; it is a crime story rather than a mystery. It was no more successful when it was revised in 1933 as *Vessels Departing*. Williams went on to appear as a young Frenchman in another crime drama, *The Man I Killed*, by Reginald Berkeley, in 1932.

In 1935 Williams married Molly O'Shann, whom he had known since 1930; they had two children. She died in 1970. In *Emlyn* Williams frankly discusses his relationships with several men prior to his marriage, including the actor Bill Wilson and a younger man named Fess Griffiths. The latter is thought to be the model for the character Dan in *Night Must Fall* (1935), Williams's first successful play using a mystery motif.

Night Must Fall opens with the rejection by the Lord Chief Justice of an appeal from a death sentence; the rest of the play is a flashback. The murderer is Dan, a charming but psychopathic bellhop, who, despite his sinister actions, manages to elicit cooperation from his intended victims by a kind of hypnotic power. Carrying the severed head of his first victim in a hatbox, Dan insinuates himself into the household of the invalid Mrs. Bramson and her niece, Olivia. Although Olivia soon guesses that he murdered a guest at the hotel where he works, she does not give him

Williams performing as Charles Dickens (photograph by Bryan Heseltine)

away and even protects him from discovery by the police. Finally, Dan is compelled by his homicidal tendencies to murder Mrs. Bramson and is arrested. In *Emlyn* Williams describes his discovery that his companion, Griffiths, attempted to defraud him. His reaction is wonderment and horror that he had not really known someone to whom he had been so close. Williams's amazement and fascination are comparable to the reactions of his characters in the play when they encounter the remarkable villainy of Dan, who displays a subhuman indifference to the lives of others.

Night Must Fall established Williams as a playwright, and his portrayal of Dan furthered his reputation as an actor. The play opened at the Duchess Theatre in London on 31 May 1935 and ran for 435 performances, then moved to the Ethel Barrymore Theater in New York. It was filmed in 1937 with Robert Montgomery as Dan and again—less successfully—in 1964, with Albert Finney in the role. Williams toured in the part in 1943 and for the armed forces in the Middle East in 1944. In 1945 he wrote a crime sketch, *Thinking Aloud*, about the thoughts of an actress who has murdered her husband. It was performed at the Stage Door Canteen in London in July 1945, published in 1946, and revived in New York in 1975.

In 1953 Williams completed *Someone Waiting*, his last play to study the psychology of a criminal; it opened at the Globe Theatre in London on 25 November, with Williams in the role of Fenn, and was published in 1954. In the play Nedlow, a rich industrialist, has murdered a woman and permitted a younger man, Paul, to take the blame. Paul already has been executed for the crime when the play begins. Fenn, who comes to tutor Nedlow's adopted son, Martin, for his law exams, is actually Paul's father, bent on avenging the death of his son. Martin hates his adoptive father and joins the plot. Fenn, at first a sympathetic character, becomes forbidding as he uses innocent persons as pawns in his plans; when one intended pawn does not appear, he kills Hilda, the maid, who was not involved in the original crime. His plans fail due to one mishap after another; finally, he places a gun in the hand of a drunken Nedlow and shoots himself in the heart, making it appear that Nedlow is the killer. Meanwhile, Martin, who is a pilot, dumps Hilda's body at sea and then kills himself by crashing the plane. Thus, all of the guilty parties are punished except Nedlow's wife, Vera, who knew about the original crime but let Paul be hanged. She has been drawn into protecting Nedlow by perceiving him as her helpless child rather than as a guilty husband. Characteristically, Williams is more concerned with the psychology of the killer and those associated with him than with presenting the crime as a puzzle to be solved.

Beyond Belief (1967), a "nonfiction novel" similar to Truman Capote's *In Cold Blood* (1966), is an account of the "moors murders" of 1963-1964, a series of torture-killings of children. It is closer than his plays to the mystery tradition; it is a police procedural in which the reader knows who the criminals are, and the methodology of the police in apprehending them is detailed. The book also explores the background and psychology of the criminals, Ian Brady and Myra Hindley.

Dr. Crippen's Diary, published in 1978 in *Great Cases of Scotland Yard* and separately in 1988, is another documentary novel about an actual crime; here Williams permits his imagination freer rein than in *Beyond Belief*. The work purports to be a diary kept by Crippen; there is also a third-person account of the trial and hanging of Crippen and details about the later life of his mistress-secretary, Ethel LeNeve. According to the diary, the doctor was actually innocent of his wife's death: in a dark bathroom she took an overdose of a sedative, mistaking it for her headache pills. Faced with the body, the doctor cut it up, buried all but the head in the basement, and placed the head in a suitcase. He then dropped the suitcase into the English Channel on a hastily arranged trip to Dieppe with his young mistress. At his trial Crippen maintained that the remains found buried in his basement were not those of his wife; he never made the argument that she had died accidentally. Dr. Crippen was executed at Pentonville Prison, London, on 23 November 1910.

Although Williams used a modern form for his documentary novels, the form of his plays is dated and appears artificial to modern audiences; according to Don Dale-Jones, "His acknowledged influences are Maugham, Ibsen, Barrie and Galsworthy, writers of 'well-made' plays." If Williams, faithful to his mentors rather than innovative, is not adventurous in structure, he is a good storyteller, and he is always entertaining. His contribution to the crime story is in his penetrating studies of the personality and psychology of the criminal and those who are caught up in crime. His documentary novels are models of the genre, which maintain their power to hold the reader as enthralled as Williams is with the inexplicable criminal mind.

References:

Don Dale-Jones, *Emlyn Williams* (Cardiff, U.K.: University of Wales Press, 1979);

Richard Findlater, *Emlyn Williams* (London: Rockliff, 1956; New York: Macmillan, 1956).

Valentine Williams

(20 October 1883-20 November 1946)

J. Randolph Cox
St. Olaf College

BOOKS: *With Our Army in Flanders*, as G. Valentine Williams (London: E. Arnold, 1915; New York: Longmans, 1915);

Adventures of an Ensign, as Vedette (Edinburgh: W. Blackwood, 1917);

The Man with the Clubfoot, as Douglas Valentine (London: Herbert Jenkins, 1918); as Valentine Williams (New York: R. M. McBride, 1918);

The Secret Hand: Some Further Adventures by Desmond Okewood of the British Secret Service, as Douglas Valentine (London: Herbert Jenkins, 1918); republished as *Okewood of the Secret Service*, as Valentine Williams (New York: R. M. McBride, 1919);

The Yellow Streak (London: Herbert Jenkins, 1922; Boston: Houghton Mifflin, 1922);

The Return of Clubfoot (London: Herbert Jenkins, 1922); republished as *Island Gold* (Boston: Houghton Mifflin, 1923);

The Orange Divan (London: Herbert Jenkins, 1923; Boston: Houghton Mifflin, 1923);

Clubfoot the Avenger: Being Some Further Adventures of Desmond Okewood, of the Secret Service (London: Herbert Jenkins, 1924; Boston: Houghton Mifflin, 1924);

The Three of Clubs (London: Hodder & Stoughton, 1924; Boston: Houghton Mifflin, 1924);

The Red Mass (London: Hodder & Stoughton, 1925; Boston: Houghton Mifflin, 1925);

Mr. Ramosi (London: Hodder & Stoughton, 1926; Boston: Houghton Mifflin, 1926);

The Pigeon House (London: Hodder & Stoughton, 1926); republished as *The Key Man* (Boston: Houghton Mifflin, 1926);

The Eye in Attendance (London: Hodder & Stoughton, 1927; Boston: Houghton Mifflin, 1927);

The Crouching Beast (London: Hodder & Stoughton, 1928; Boston: Houghton Mifflin, 1928);

The Knife Behind the Curtain: Tales of Secret Service and Crime (London: Hodder & Stoughton, 1930; Boston: Houghton Mifflin, 1930);

Mannequin (London: Hodder & Stoughton, 1930); republished as *The Mysterious Miss Morrisot* (Boston: Houghton Mifflin, 1930);

Death Answers the Bell (London: Hodder & Stoughton, 1931; Boston: Houghton Mifflin, 1932);

The Gold Comfit Box (London: Hodder & Stoughton, 1932); republished as *The Mystery of the Gold Box* (Boston: Houghton Mifflin, 1932);

The Clock Ticks On (London: Hodder & Stoughton, 1933; Boston: Houghton Mifflin, 1933);

Fog, with Dorothy Rice Sims (London: Hodder & Stoughton, 1933; Boston: Houghton Mifflin, 1933);

The Portcullis Room (London: Hodder & Stoughton, 1934; Boston: Houghton Mifflin, 1934);

Masks Off at Midnight (London: Hodder & Stoughton, 1934; Boston: Houghton Mifflin, 1934);

The Clue of the Rising Moon (London: Hodder & Stoughton, 1935; Boston: Houghton Mifflin, 1935);

Dead Man Manor (London: Hodder & Stoughton, 1936; Boston: Houghton Mifflin, 1936);

The Spider's Touch (London: Hodder & Stoughton, 1936; Boston: Houghton Mifflin, 1936);

Mr. Treadgold Cuts In (London: Hodder & Stoughton, 1937); republished as *The Curiosity of Mr. Treadgold* (Boston: Houghton Mifflin, 1937);

The World of Action: The Autobiography of Valentine Williams (London: Hamish Hamilton, 1938; Boston: Houghton Mifflin, 1938);

The Fox Prowls (London: Hodder & Stoughton, 1939; Boston: Houghton Mifflin, 1939);

George Valentine Williams, circa 1924, when he wrote news coverage of the Howard Carter excavation of the tomb of Tutankhamen in Egypt

Courier to Marrakesh (London: Hodder & Stoughton, 1944; Boston: Houghton Mifflin, 1946);

Skeleton Out of the Cupboard (London: Hodder & Stoughton, 1946).

PLAY PRODUCTION: *Berlin*, by Williams and Alice Crawford, New York, George M. Cohan Theatre, 30 December 1931.

SCREENPLAY: *Land of Hope and Glory*, screenplay by Williams and Adrian Brunel, 1927.

OTHER: *Double Death*, Supervised and with a Preface and Prologue by John Chancellor; suggested and edited by James W. Drawbell and William Lees, with contributions by Dorothy L. Sayers, Freeman Wills Crofts, Valentine Williams, F. Tennyson Jesse, An-

thony Armstrong, and David Hume (London: Gollancz, 1939).

PERIODICAL PUBLICATIONS: "The Purple Cabriolet," *Collier's, the National Weekly*, 72 (27 October 1923): 5-6, 22-24. (This story and the five entries from *Collier's* below were collected as *Clubfoot the Avenger*.)

"The Secret of the Silver Icon," *Collier's, the National Weekly*, 72 (10 November 1923): 8-9, 27-29;

"The Top Flat," *Collier's, the National Weekly*, 72 (24 November 1923): 14-15, 24, 26, 28;

"The Constantinople Courier," *Collier's, the National Weekly*, 72 (8 December 1923): 13-14, 35-36;

"Gaboriau, the Father of the Detective Novel," *National Review*, 82 (December 1923): 611-622;

"The Girl at the Hexagon," *Collier's, the National Weekly*, 73 (5 January 1924): 11, 24, 26, 28;

"The Chamois Leather Packet," *Collier's, the National Weekly*, 73 (19 January 1924): 13-14, 30-31;

"Putting the Shocks into 'Shockers'," *Bookman (New York)*, 66 (November 1927): 270-272;

"Detective Fiction," *Bookman (New York)*, 67 (July 1928): 521-524;

"The Detective in Fiction," *Fortnightly Review*, 134 (September 1930): 381-392;

"Crime Fiction According to Hoyle," *Saturday Evening Post*, 204 (11 July 1931): 33, 108-109; revised as "Crime Fiction" in *Writing Detective and Mystery Fiction*, edited by A. S. Burack (Boston: The Writer, 1945), pp. 45-58; revised edition (Boston: The Writer, 1967), pp. 271-280.

Valentine Williams was a gifted writer with a journalist's ability to get the story and hold his readers' attention. While he wrote both detective and spy fiction and held strong opinions on how each should be written, it is for his tales of the British Secret Service and its struggle against the villain Dr. Adolph Grundt, known as Clubfoot, that Williams is remembered. As Williams himself remarked in his autobiography, *The World of Action* (1938), it was the villains of fiction who fascinated him. The hero was most effective in conjunction with a plausible and human villain. Despite the variety of his other published work, Williams is best known for creating Clubfoot, just as Sax Rohmer is remembered for Fu Manchu.

Williams had just two basic tenets of writing fiction, both of which are expounded in every article he wrote on the mechanics of the mystery genre. First, while the standard for the romance-adventure-espionage story was higher than the detective story, the latter was more difficult to write. Plot construction was therefore of paramount importance. Second, authenticity of setting made for plausibility, and plausibility was the essence of the successful adventure story. Plausibility of character was equally significant. Throughout his career the critics commented on the well-conceived characters in his stories.

George Valentine Williams was born on 20 October 1883; his father was George Douglas Williams, chief editor of Reuter's News Agency. A Roman Catholic, Williams was educated at Downside School and privately in Germany. In 1902, at age nineteen, Williams joined Reuter's as a subeditor, following in the family tradition established by his father and grandfather of working for the news agency. Williams later recounted his time at Reuter's was an education in itself; it was there he learned to avoid the split infinitive.

Soon after Williams joined Reuter's his father resigned from the firm due to ill health, continuing, however, a close watch on his son's career. Because of Williams's exceptional fluency in the German language, he was assigned as a correspondent to Berlin in 1904. During the five years he spent there, from 1904 to 1909, he came to learn much of the German character. While he found much to admire, he was not deceived by German pretensions of friendship with his own country. His autobiography contains many anecdotes and shrewd observations of people, famous and little known, from those early years.

In 1910 he was offered the post of Paris correspondent of the *Daily Mail*, the flashy newspaper owned by Alfred Harmsworth, Lord Northcliffe. Against his father's wishes, he accepted. His father, brought up on the more traditional journalism of the *Times* and the *Standard*, distrusted both Northcliffe and his newspaper. Williams held this post for four years and went to Lisbon as a special correspondent during the Portuguese revolution in 1910 and to the Balkans in 1913.

In 1915 he joined the Irish Guards and entered World War I. That same year Williams published an account of his experiences during the first year of the war. The book, *With Our Army in Flanders*, received favorable reviews on both sides of the Atlantic. The following year, as a second lieutenant in the Irish Guards, Williams experienced injuries at the front which indirectly turned him into a writer of fiction. On 25 September 1916, during the Battle of the Somme, a 6-inch shell blew up near Williams and seriously wounded him. While recovering from his injuries in the hospital he had recurring dreams of being in Berlin as a British spy without papers, pursued by the military and the police. After the most serious of his injuries had healed, Williams was sent to Scotland to convalesce. To combat the boredom of his recovery and to give an outlet to his battlefield memories Williams wrote "The Adventures of an Ensign" for *Blackwood's* magazine. This account of life in the Irish Guards was published as a book in 1917.

Adventures of an Ensign might not have been published at all without the intervention of John Buchan, then director of information at the For-

Dust jacket for the first American edition of Williams's first short-story collection, published in 1930 (courtesy of Otto Penzler)

eign Office. It was Buchan who read the book and passed it through the official censor. It was also Buchan who urged Williams to try his hand at a novel, a "shocker," as he himself had done with *The Thirty-Nine Steps* (1915). Williams, in dire need of money, took Buchan's advice and turned his Berlin spy dream into *The Man with the Clubfoot* (1918).

In the novel Desmond Okewood learns that his brother Francis is in Germany in the service of the British government and goes behind the lines to search for him. On finding the body of a Dr. Semlin, Okewood assumes his identity and bluffs his way into a meeting with the Emperor William II and with Dr. Adolph Grundt, the chief of the emperor's personal secret service. The goal of both sides is the recovery of an indis-

creet letter written by the emperor on the eve of World War I. There is much in the novel to suggest Buchan, especially the discussion of the theory of true disguise, of *being* a German instead of just pretending.

Grundt, or Clubfoot, appeared in seven novels in all. Huge, bestial, with a vast temper, he is larger than life rather than just a caricature of the German as seen by the English in 1918. There is a decidedly human and humane aspect to the character which makes him seem credible, despite his grotesque villainy. He was based on an amalgam of people Williams had met: a German with an uncontrollable temper, a clubfooted man seen in church as a child, as well as "Old C.," the mysterious and legendary power behind the British Secret Service. The last possessed a wooden leg, a tremendous drive, a large body, and a certain fondness for gallows humor.

It seems clear that the Okewood brothers, Desmond and Francis, share some of the traits of the Williams brothers, Valentine and Douglas. The choice of espionage as a genre was based on his recollections of having seen William Gillette on the stage in Gillette's melodrama *Secret Service* (1895), a performance which impressed Williams with the romantic possibilities of the spy as a character.

Williams followed the success of *The Man with the Clubfoot* with another story of Desmond Okewood, *The Secret Hand* (1918). In the novel Francis Okewood is unavailable for service, and the chief of the Secret Service asks Desmond to take a hand in investigating the murder of an old-time music hall performer; the assignment also concerns rumors of a newly organized German spy ring operating in England. Narrated by Okewood, the novel ends with its protagonist agreeing to accept a commission in the Secret Service. Dr. Grundt makes no appearance in the novel, supposedly having perished at the end of the first book.

Williams then turned to the classic country house detective story in *The Yellow Streak* (1922); the title refers to the cowardice of the murdered man. It is lighthearted in style and clichéd in construction with appropriately atmospheric comings and goings of the chief suspects. It introduces Detective Inspector George Manderton of Scotland Yard, a big, burly man with a heavy, dark mustache. Manderton is always neatly dressed and has keenly observant eyes which seem to be in perpetual motion. Manderton appears in six of Williams's novels.

By 1921 Williams was foreign editor of the *Daily Mail*, but growing differences with Lord Northcliffe led to his resignation in 1922; he planned to devote himself to fiction. He was, however, recalled to cover the opening of Tutankhamen's tomb in 1923 and 1924 and was never able to abandon completely his original profession.

As Williams had never described Dr. Grundt's demise in detail he was able to resurrect him for a return encounter with Desmond Okewood in *The Return of Clubfoot* (1922). Their confrontation on Cock Island during a search for gold treasure is classic. Grundt, shot by Francis Okewood at the climax of the earlier novel, is revealed to have been only slightly wounded. A

clever cipher imbedded in a scrap of music and a German verse is the key to the treasure.

Manderton returns as the detective in Williams's next novel, *The Orange Divan* (1923). This is more maturely plotted than *The Yellow Streak* and is written in a less pedestrian style. Williams uses humor and shrewd observation of character in contrasting the ungainly Manderton with the sleek, retired French detective, Boulot.

Clubfoot returns again in *Clubfoot the Avenger* (1924), which utilizes a third-person narrative. Desmond Okewood, having retired from the Secret Service, is aided by Inspector Manderton in the confrontation with Grundt which is presented in six related episodes. This experiment in construction is explained by the source of the episodes, six short stories which Williams published in *Collier's* in 1923 and 1924. The addition of bridging material and some other changes converted the six short works into a book-length novel.

The Three of Clubs (1924) had appeared serially in *Collier's* prior to the Clubfoot stories. Melodramatic, overly romantic, and overwritten, the novel is Williams's contribution to the literature of the Orient Express. It presents a game of international intrigue in which the destinies of Godfrey Cairsdale and Virginia Fitzgerald are mixed up with the significance of the emblem of the three clubs. Surprisingly, it received better reviews than the Clubfoot books, the critics feeling he had risen above his material in this case.

Williams never really settled into the pattern of producing uniform works of fiction. He varied his work between detective novels and adventure thrillers and did not return to the character of Clubfoot too often for him to become stale.

In *The Red Mass* (1925) he produced an historical adventure set in 1794, a story firmly in the tradition of the Baroness Orczy's *Scarlet Pimpernel* (1905). For the next three years Williams lived in Cannes and devoted himself to his novels and occasional short fiction. His material came from his own travels and experiences. *Mr. Ramosi* (1926), with its opening chapter reminiscent of the prologue to Sapper's *Bull-Dog Drummond* (1920)–the gathering of men of varied national backgrounds to meet a mysterious Egyptian–was based on material collected on his trips to cover the tomb of Tutankhamen. *The Pigeon House* (1926), with its French foreign legionnaires who are loyal to their fellow Basques, was the result

Dust jacket for the first British edition of Williams's 1937 collection of ten short stories, featuring Mr. Horace B. Treadgold, first seen in his 1936 novel Dead Man Manor *(courtesy of Otto Penzler)*

of a summer in Basque country followed by a tour of French Morocco.

His 1927 novel, *The Eye in Attendance*, is again a vehicle for George Manderton, whose character is more deeply delineated than in previous novels. The conflict of characters (the murder suspect is reluctantly given an alibi by his wife) is especially well presented. A minor character named Ronald Dene is perhaps a forerunner of Williams's later series detective, Trevor Dene.

In 1928 the Williamses (he was married to Alice Crawford, the Australian actress) returned to London when his mother became ill (she died in May). For the next two years he divided his time between his fiction and a weekly political article for the *Sunday Graphic*. *The Crouching Beast*

(1928) is another Clubfoot story, this time lacking the Okewood brothers. The story is set in World War I and is narrated by Olivia Dunbar, who is assigned a mission by an escaped British Secret Service agent. The plot served as the basis for a 1936 film, under its own title, and a stage play, *Berlin*, produced in 1931. The play, written by Williams and his wife, lasted just over two dozen performances.

In 1930 Williams visited the United States, where his brother was serving as Reuter's representative in New York City. The same year he published his first short-story collection, *The Knife Behind the Curtain*, and a novel of love, murder, and mystery in Paris and the Riviera, *Mannequin*. The novel received high praise from Will Cuppy in

Orville Wright, Col. N. G. Thwaites, Frederick W. Wile, and Valentine Williams, Berlin, 1908, where Williams served as a correspondent for the Reuter's News Agency

the *New York Herald Tribune* for being a worthwhile reading experience as well as a good mystery.

The Williamses returned to the United States in December 1930 for an extended stay. He wrote four radio plays for NBC, "Moon Maiden," presented 7 April 1931, "The King's Messenger," "Mata Hari the Spy," and "The Mummy Hand." He and his wife appeared in the first one, Williams himself taking a dual role. This was followed by a series of lectures called "Gallery of Famous Britons" which he wrote for radio and delivered Sunday evenings for eighteen weeks. The American years ended in 1937, but Williams returned to a post with the British Embassy in Washington in 1941 and 1942, then traveled to Hollywood to write screenplays for three years prior to his death.

Williams produced books at a rate of at least one or two each year until 1939. After 1930 he began to employ American settings. *Death Answers the Bell* (1931), about the murder of Barrasford Swete, was another case for Inspector Manderton but also introduced Trevor Dene of the Fingerprint Division. Dene had attended Cambridge and was known as the Boy Sherlock.

The Gold Comfit Box (1932) was the fifth novel about Clubfoot. Set in 1913 and narrated by Philip Clavering of the Secret Service, it concerns the search for the gold box of Charles Forest and the secret hidden within it. The opening is as artistically realistic a description of inclement weather as any mystery reader could wish.

The Clock Ticks On (1933), *Masks Off at Midnight* (1934), and *The Clue of the Rising Moon* (1935) are all vehicles for Trevor Dene, the young man from Scotland Yard on holiday or assignment in America. Williams accomplished something of a feat for a British writer in making his Americans speak like Americans and not as caricatures of Americans.

The action in *Fog* (1933) all takes place on the transatlantic liner *Barbaric* bound for Southampton and Cherbourg. Williams wrote this in collaboration with Dorothy Rice Sims, whose husband was a famous authority on bridge. This collaboration accounts for the authenticity of the bridge-game scenes which are ingeniously worked into the mystery plot.

Another shipboard scene serves as an opener to *The Portcullis Room* (1934), but the action soon shifts to Toray Castle in Scotland. *Dead*

337

Man Manor (1936) introduces Mr. Horace B. Treadgold, an English tailor living in New York, who solves a murder while on vacation in Quebec. Treadgold is a delightful character, a stamp collector whose favorite reading is Laurence Sterne's *Tristram Shandy* (1759-1767). Williams brought him back in *Mr. Treadgold Cuts In* (1937), a collection of ten short stories, and *Skeleton Out of the Cupboard* (1946). And as though to prove he could write about villains other than Dr. Grundt, Williams created an international crook, Baron Alexis De Bahl, alias "The Fox" in *The Fox Prowls* (1939).

But to most readers Williams's name will always be linked to that of his most famous creation, Clubfoot. *The Spider's Touch* (1936) is the first story in the series not firmly rooted in World War I. It is also the first to make use of an American antagonist for Clubfoot. James Fane of the American Embassy in London disappears into Europe with some papers. He is pursued by the Secret Service, the United States government, and his twin sister, Patricia, who enlists the aid of four soldiers of fortune to find him. Each of these pursuers has a score to settle with Dr. Grundt, whose agent had been an intermediary in the attempted sale of the papers to the United States.

A decade later Dr. Grundt made his last

bow in *Courier to Marrakesh* (1944). Set in 1943 the book is narrated by a singer of folk songs, Andrea Hallam. The story involves her search for a friend in Marrakech, her accidental involvement with the British Secret Service, and an encounter with Dr. Grundt. Clubfoot is part of the famous German General-Staff plot to get rid of Hitler and settle for peace. In a memorable scene Clubfoot predicts that there will be no room for politicians in the postwar world. The end of the novel reveals that Hitler himself ordered a wreath for Dr. Grundt's bier, but Clubfoot's death is again not certain. Any planned return, however, was cut short by the author's death.

Valentine Williams died on 20 November 1946 in New York City. As a writer he received such uniformly positive reviews from the critics that it is surprising to find so little critical attention paid to his work. Williams's works are firmly rooted in the times in which he lived and wrote, yet plausible and original. They ought not be overlooked by anyone interested in the evolution of the spy story.

Reference:
H. F. Manchester, "How Philo Vance, Clubfoot and Charlie Chan were Born," *The Writer*, 43 (September 1931): 249-252.

Dornford Yates
(Cecil William Mercer)
(7 August 1885-5 March 1960)

J. Randolph Cox
St. Olaf College

BOOKS: *The Brother of Daphne* (London: Ward, Lock, 1914);

The Courts of Idleness (London: Ward, Lock, 1920);

Berry and Co. (London: Ward, Lock, 1920; New York: Minton, Balch, 1928);

Anthony Lyveden (London: Ward, Lock, 1921); republished with *Valerie French* as *Summer Fruit* (New York: Minton, Balch, 1929);

Jonah and Co. (London: Ward, Lock, 1922; New York: Minton, Balch, 1927);

Valerie French (London: Ward, Lock, 1923); republished with *Anthony Lyveden* as *Summer Fruit* (New York: Minton, Balch, 1929);

And Five Were Foolish (London: Ward, Lock, 1924);

As Other Men Are (London: Ward, Lock, 1925);

The Stolen March (London: Ward, Lock, 1926; New York: Minton, Balch, 1933);

Blind Corner (London: Hodder & Stoughton, 1927; New York: Minton, Balch, 1927);

Perishable Goods (London: Hodder & Stoughton, 1928; New York: Minton, Balch, 1928);

Maiden Stakes (London: Ward, Lock, 1928);

Blood Royal (London: Hodder & Stoughton, 1929; New York: Minton, Balch, 1930);

Fire Below (London: Hodder & Stoughton, 1930); republished as *By Royal Command* (New York: Minton, Balch, 1931);

Adele & Co. (London: Hodder & Stoughton, 1931; New York: Minton, Balch, 1931);

Safe Custody (London: Hodder & Stoughton, 1932; New York: Minton, Balch, 1932);

Storm Music (London: Hodder & Stoughton, 1934; New York: Minton, Balch, 1934);

She Fell Among Thieves (London: Hodder & Stoughton, 1935; New York: Minton, Balch, 1935);

And Berry Came Too (London: Ward, Lock, 1936; New York: Minton, Balch, 1936);

She Painted Her Face (London: Ward, Lock, 1937; New York: Putnam's, 1937);

Cecil William Mercer

This Publican (London: Ward, Lock, 1938); republished as *The Devil in Satin* (Garden City, N.Y.: Doubleday, Doran, 1938);

Gale Warning (London: Ward, Lock, 1939; New York: Putnam's, 1940);

Shoal Water (London: Ward, Lock, 1940; New York: Putnam's, 1941);

Period Stuff (London: Ward, Lock, 1942);

An Eye for a Tooth (London: Ward, Lock, 1943; New York: Putnam's, 1944);

The House That Berry Built (London: Ward, Lock,
1945; New York: Putnam's, 1945);

Red in the Morning (London: Ward, Lock, 1946); republished as *Were Death Denied* (New York:
Putnam's, 1946);

The Berry Scene (London: Ward, Lock, 1947; New
York: Putnam's, 1948);

Cost Price (London: Ward, Lock, 1949); republished as *The Laughing Bacchante* (New York:
Putnam's, 1949);

Lower Than Vermin (London: Ward, Lock, 1950);

As Berry and I Were Saying (London: Ward, Lock,
1952);

Ne'er-Do-Well (London: Ward, Lock, 1954);

Wife Apparent (London: Ward, Lock, 1956);

B-Berry and I Look Back (London: Ward, Lock,
1958).

PLAY PRODUCTION: *Eastward Ho*, by Yates and
Oscar Asche, London, Alhambra, 9 September 1919.

OTHER: Charles William Stamper, *What I Know*,
ghostwritten by Yates (London: Mills &
Boon, 1913); republished as *King Edward as
I Knew Him* (New York: Dodd, Mead, 1913).

PERIODICAL PUBLICATIONS: "Temporary Insanity," anonymous, *Punch*, 138 (25 May
1910): 392;

"The Babes in the Wood," *Pearson's Magazine*, 30
(September 1910): 306-316;

"Rex v. Blogg," *Pearson's Magazine*, 33 (February
1912): 179-184;

"Valerie," *Windsor Magazine*, 50 (October 1919):
353-370;

"Court Cards," *Windsor Magazine*, 65 (December
1926): 16-26;

"The Real Thing," *Windsor Magazine*, 85 (April
1937): 610-620.

The books of Dornford Yates are an acquired taste for some readers. His style has an elegance that resembles no other artisan in the English language; his content is rooted in the work
of Robert Louis Stevenson, Anthony Hope, Stanley Weyman, and Sir Arthur Conan Doyle. His
works fall into three categories: light humor,
light romance, and thrillers. Some of the characters in one category have a habit of showing up
in books in the other two categories. Yates was a
writer who merged his own life with that of his creations, and he created a world into which he and
his readers could escape from mundane reality.

*Dust jacket for the first British edition of the sixth book featur-
ing Mercer's series detectives Jonah Mansel and
Richard Chandos*

It was a world with unending sunshine and the
best vintage wine, when one war was behind and
the next not even on the horizon.

Yates valued the light romance more highly
than the thriller, but the latter made enough
money for him to live the life to which he as-
pired. Of the light humor, it is the Berry books,
about Maj. Bertram Pleydell of White Ladies in
the County of Hampshire, which are ageless, in
the same way that the works of P. G. Wodehouse
are ageless. By contrast, the thrillers are stern, serious stuff. If they all sound a bit like Anthony
Hope (Hawkins's) *The Prisoner of Zenda* (1894) or
its sequel, *Rupert of Hentzau* (1898), that seems to
be what Yates's readers wanted. They also
seemed to want the combination of the strong, silent bachelor, Jonathan (Jonah) Mansel, and the
beefy young man who narrates most of the stories, Richard (William) Chandos. Mansel was the
man with the accessory-laden Rolls Royce and a

way with political intrigue; Chandos was the unsophisticated man who was attractive to girls.

Cecil William Mercer, who began using the pen name Dornford Yates as early as 1911, was born in Upper Walmer, Kent. Descended from Dornfords as well as Mercers, he counted the short-story writer Saki (Hector Hugh Munro) as his cousin. He was educated at St. Clare, Walmer, from 1894 to 1899, attended Harrow from 1899 to 1904, and took a B.A. in jurisprudence from University College, Oxford, in 1907. He was active in the Oxford University Dramatic Society, but his reading was primarily in those writers who influenced his choice of material as well as his style when he turned to writing.

Little is known about Mercer's early years in London, but he appears to have worked as a clerk in or near Crutched Friars in 1908. He served as a clerk and pupil to the solicitors Wontners of Bedford Row as a kind of "back door" to the bar, thus avoiding the time-consuming rigors of law school. Becoming a barrister of the Inner Temple in 1909, he was taken into Treasury Chambers by Travers Humphreys.

In those days one way up the ladder to a higher status was to write articles for *Punch*. Mercer did this with a not very funny article about conversations over crossed telephone lines. It was his only appearance in the magazine. His position in Travers Humphreys's office provided him with a lot of paperwork and the opportunity to observe cases which supplied him with material for later novels. One of the more famous cases involved the trial for murder of Dr. Crippen in which he had no more active part than that of observer. This bothered him at the time and may account for the amount of space he devotes to the case in one of his quasi-autobiographies, *As Berry and I Were Saying* (1952).

He published his first short story, "Busy Bees," in the *Windsor Magazine* in 1911. It was collected with several of its successors in his first book, *The Brother of Daphne*, in 1914. That was the year he began his military service as a second lieutenant in the Third County of London Yeomanry. He spent part of the war in Egypt and the Balkans before being discharged because of serious muscular rheumatism. This affliction caused him to move to Pau in southwestern France in 1922, taking with him his American wife, the actress Bettine Stokes Edwards, whom he had married in 1919. By then he had published four collections of short stories, all in the Berry series, and one novel, *Anthony Lyveden*

(1921). He had also suffered something like a nervous breakdown brought on by family problems, his father's disapproval of his marriage, and his father's death.

Mercer was a slow writer. It took him about six weeks to write a short story; and while his first novel went smoothly, it was not rushed to completion. At the time he was writing *Anthony Lyveden*, he read an article in the *Spectator* which made him examine his style more closely. An admirer of Fowler's *The King's English* (1906), he took to heart a passage about the use of the colon and the formal period and incorporated them into his writing. As a result, his style took on a gravity that has been compared to sixteenth-century English. Richard Usborne, in his *Clubland Heroes* (1953), points out the choriambic rhythm at the end of first sentences of short stories. Usborne also suggests (in the introduction to the 1984 Dent edition of *Perishable Goods*) that Mercer owed much of his inimitable style to a 1913 book by C. W. Stamper, *What I Know*. The dedication to Dornford Yates in the book suggests to Usborne that Yates's formal, stilted prose style was just lying below the surface, that the *Spectator* article only released it.

From 1922 on, Mercer lived most of his life abroad, journeying to London only for meetings with his publishers, staying at the Conservative Club, where he was a member. He also began to evidence the behavior traits about which people whispered: his fits of temper and his almost pathological, though genuine, dislike of publicity. His working methods paralleled his behavior. He spent mornings in his library, where no one, not even his wife, dared disturb him. He wrote each story first in longhand, section by section, then typed, corrected, cut, expanded, and rewrote them. Not one to mix in society, he had no real friends beyond those of his own invention. The closing of the library door shut out the real world as well. It is not surprising that his marriage came to an end a decade later.

In 1925 Mercer was forty years old; he began to wonder if he should vary his pattern of alternating light romance with the humorous escapades of the Berry group. He thought the thriller might prove possible and took a look at the leaders in the field: John Buchan, Sapper (H. C. McNeile), and Edgar Wallace. As he wrote his first thriller, he kept three books in mind: McNeile's *Bull-dog Drummond* (1920), Buchan's *The Thirty-Nine Step* (1915), and Robert Louis Stevenson's *Treasure Island*, (1883).

Dust jacket for the first British edition of the 1939 novel in which an ordinary young man named John Bagot relates how he joined with Mansel and Chandos to take on a mastermind thief and murderer named Barabbas

Blind Corner (1927) uses Jonah Mansel from the Berry books as the adventurer-protagonist. For the narrator, Mercer created Richard (William) Chandos, a heavy, solemn young man who could make the improbable incidents seem perfectly plausible. On a motor tour of France, Chandos witnesses a murder and finds a dog collar with an inscription on it which leads to a buried treasure in Austria. It is Jonah Mansel who deciphers the inscription and joins Chandos in a race to reach the treasure before the infamous "Rose" Noble and his gang find it.

The novel sold well, and Mercer followed it with a sequel, *Perishable Goods* (1928). Even Berry was set aside while he wrote this variation on *The Prisoner of Zenda*. Adele, Boy Pleydell's wife, strays over from the other series for the thriller. Kidnapped by "Rose" Noble, she is held for ransom in Castle Gath in Austria.

Maiden Stakes (1928), a collection of ten short stories, mostly of lighthearted love, followed. One of the stories, "Letters Patent," be-

longs to the Berry series and tells of Boy Pleydell, who writes a novel about Jonah Mansel. Mercer was blending fact and fancy in a way to confuse most readers who wanted one or the other but not necessarily both.

Blood Royal (1929) is yet another variant on Anthony Hope as Chandos and his friend George Hanbury return to Austria to assist the offensive young claimant to the throne of Reichtenburg in regaining his kingdom. Mansel is absent from this story, which also tells how Chandos meets and falls in love with the Duchess Leonie.

If *Blood Royal* leaned heavily on *The Prisoner of Zenda* for its plot, then its sequel, *Fire Below* (1930), had *Rupert of Hentzau* (the sequel to *The Prisoner of Zenda*) for its model. In *Fire Below* Chandos and Leonie return to Austria and become involved in the rescue of Leonie's former lady-in-waiting from Prince Paul of Reichtenburg.

Adele & Co. (1931), a novel in the Berry series, just barely makes the crime novel/thriller category by virtue of the theft of the Pleydell jewels, which serves as the pivot to the plot. *Safe Custody* (1932) does not feature any of the Dornford Yates characters encountered heretofore. It is an adventure novel in which the goal is rightful possession of a castle that hides Pope Alexander VI's jewels. There is a game of king-of-the-hill as the castle exchanges hands and a pitched battle before the dreadful discovery that occurs when the treasure is found. Another visit to Austria, another castle, another murder, and a crook named Pharaoh, once involved in the Bell Hammer murders, are the ingredients in *Storm Music* (1934).

She Fell Among Thieves (1935) brings back Mansel and Chandos, who are disguised as chauffeur and traveler in their investigation of the notorious Vanity Fair, whose reputation for being unscrupulous and ruthless is borne out in the course of the novel. *And Berry Came Too* (1936) is another collection of short stories about the Pleydell group. Some skirt close to the thriller genre, especially "Cock Feathers," in which a police sergeant takes over the Rolls (Boy at the wheel) to chase a stolen car driven by some jewel thieves.

By now Mercer was producing a new book every year, though there had been none in 1933, the year he divorced Bettine. He was also making many journeys from Paris to London now to keep in touch with his son, Richard, and with his publishers. In 1934 he married Elizabeth Lucy

*Dust jacket for the first American edition of the mystery pub-
lished in Britain as* Red in the Morning. *Soon after its appearance Mercer moved to Umtali, Southern Rhodesia.*

Bowie, whom he had met in 1932. She must have
seemed to have stepped out of his own literary
world, for he referred to her as Jill, after one of
the Pleydells.

At the age of fifty Mercer was working
harder than ever. If his plots and characters may
be classed as stock, at least they came from his
own private stock. His faithful readers must have
derived much comfort from the certainty that
there would be no unpleasant surprises in a
Dornford Yates novel.

In *She Painted Her Face* (1937) Richard Exon
rescues a countess from her uncle, who is holding her in an Austrian castle. *This Publican* (1938;
published in the United States as *The Devil in
Satin*) is an exception in the Yates oeuvre. The
strange story of Rowena Bohun, who uses guile
to make her husband David seem the guilty party
in her suit for divorce, has enough improbabilities to make the reader welcome the sanity which
Forsyth, the solicitor, brings to the novel. Unlike
other Yates novels, which repay rereading, once
seems enough here. With *Gale Warning* (1939) Mer-

cer was back on course again in a high adventure
with Mansel and Chandos, this one narrated by
John Bagot, whose benefactor, George St. Omer,
has been murdered by a master villain appropriately named Barabbas.

During this time Mercer was building his
dream house, Cockade, in Eaux Bonnes, France,
some twenty miles from Pau. It was modeled
closely on Gracedieu in *The House That Berry Built*
(1945). The last two decades of Mercer's life saw
a number of changes, but his books came out on
schedule, if not as frequently. The house near
Pau had to be evacuated when France fell to Germany during World War II, and the Mercers fled
by car to Portugal in scenes that could have been
lifted from any of his thrillers. From there they
moved to Rhodesia, where Captain Mercer was
recommissioned as a second lieutenant in the
Royal Rhodesian Regiment. By 1944 he was promoted to field rank and remained Major Mercer
for the rest of his days. The return to Cockade
after the war was disappointing. Life had
changed too much and so had the attitudes of
the people in Pau toward their English colonists.
Rising expenses made a final move necessary,
and a new house, Sacradown, was built in Umtali,
Southern Rhodesia. Mercer died in the Isolation
Hospital there on 5 March 1960.

There were no changes in Mercer's last
books. His ideas had been formed before 1914
and never moderated. This was one of the reasons he revered the nobility and wrote of it in his
books. Many of the later books have been referred to as "labor-saving" since they went back
to earlier days and took up where other books
had left off. The constant reader found reassur-
ance in familiar stories about characters who had
become like old friends.

In *Shoal Water* (1940) Jeremy Solon, a young
Englishman on holiday in France, rescues a
lovely girl from a gang of jewel thieves, with
Mansel's aid. *Period Stuff* (1942) contains detective
stories about Inspector Falcon. *An Eye for a Tooth*
(1943) must be fitted in plot between *Blind Corner*
and *Perishable Goods*. *The House That Berry Built* further merges the worlds of fact and fancy in Mercer's life, containing a murder mystery to be
solved as only Berry can do it. *Red in the Morning*
(1946) brings back Mansel and Chandos to rescue yet another lady in distress while exterminat-
ing some crooks.

The Berry Scene (1947) does not belong to
the category of the thrillers but is interesting as
an overview of the Berry series. It begins in

Berry's youth and concludes with the group's retiring to Portugal. It is the last of the Berry books proper, but the two quasi-autobiographies, *As Berry and I Were Saying* and *B-Berry and I Look Back* (1958), use the characters in conversation and anecdote.

Cost Price (1949), the last of the Chandos-Mansel thrillers, is a story about smuggling the Borgia jewels out of Austria to England between the world wars. The characters return for one last bow in *Ne'er-Do-Well* (1954), a detective novel with Superintendent Falcon, C.I.D., in charge.

In *Lower Than Vermin* (1950) Mercer paid tribute to a way of life which he knew would never return. A family history story related by the governess, Miss Carson, it roughly covers the years from the Diamond Jubilee (1897) until right after World War II. Mercer's final thriller, *Wife Apparent* (1956), concerns a demobilized officer with a head wound that makes him amnesiac. Not one of Mercer's best, it sounds in summary too much like past works, including *Random Harvest* (1941) by James Hilton.

Since Mercer had begun with Berry in 1911, it may have seemed appropriate to conclude with him in 1958 with *B-Berry and I Look Back*. His thrillers represent a world of nostalgia for many readers, as gallant knights battle the dragons for the lady and the gold. They are eminently readable and, since the details are easily forgotten, equally rereadable. If the Dornford Yates books are an acquired taste, enough readers acquired that taste to keep the author solvent. In his final years it was the writing itself that mattered to Mercer rather than the money. He wrote to please himself, not his readers alone, but he succeeded at both.

Biography:

A. J. Smithers, *Dornford Yates: A Biography* (London: Hodder & Stoughton, 1982).

References:

J. Randolph Cox, "Letters," *Armchair Detective*, 14 (Spring 1981): 185-186;

Tom Sharpe, "Introduction," in Yates's *Blind Corner* (London: Dent, 1983), pp. vii-xiv;

Sharpe, "Major Mercer and Mr. Yates," *Radio Times*, 218 (25 February-3 March 1978): 4-5;

Richard Usborne, "Dornford Yates," in his *Clubland Heroes*, revised edition (London: Barrie & Jenkins, 1974), pp. 27-78;

Usborne, "Introduction," in Yates's *Perishable Goods* (London: Dent, 1984), pp. vii-xiii.

Books for Further Reading

Adey, R. C. S. *Locked Room Murders and Other Impossible Crimes.* London: Ferret, 1979.

Aisenberg, Nadja. *A Common Spring: Crime Novel and Classic.* Bowling Green, Ohio: Bowling Green University Popular Press, 1979.

Albert, Walter. *Detective and Mystery Fiction: An International Bibliography of Secondary Sources.* Madison, Ind.: Brownstone Books, 1985.

Altick, Richard D. *Victorian Studies in Scarlet.* New York: Norton, 1970.

Ball, John, ed. *The Mystery Story.* San Diego & Del Mar: University of California, 1976.

Bargainnier, Earl F., and George N. Dove, eds. *Cops and Constraints: Amerian and British Fictional Policemen.* Bowling Green, Ohio: Bowling Green University Popular Press, 1986.

Barnes, Melvyn. *Best Detective Fiction: A Guide from Godwin to the Present.* London: Bingley/Hamden, Conn.: Linnet, 1975.

Barzun, Jacques, and Wendell Hertig Taylor. *A Book of Prefaces to Fifty Classics of Crime Fiction, 1900-1950.* New York: Garland, 1976.

Barzun and Taylor. *A Catalogue of Crime,* second impression, corrected. New York, Evanston, San Francisco & London: Harper & Row, 1974.

Benvenuti, Stephano, and Gianni Rizzoni. *The Whodunit: An Informal History of Detective Fiction.* Translated by Anthony Eyre. New York: Macmillan, 1980.

Borowitz, Albert. *Innocence and Arsenic: Studies in Crime and Literature.* New York: Harper & Row, 1977.

Breen, Jon L. *What About Murder? A Guide to Books about Mystery and Detective Fiction.* Metuchen, N.J. & London: Scarecrow, 1981.

Cassidy, Bruce, ed. *Roots of Detection.* New York: Ungar, 1983.

Cawelti, John G. *Adventure, Mystery, and Romance: Formula Stories as Art and Popular Culture.* Chicago: University of Chicago Press, 1976.

Champigny, Robert. *What Will Happen: A Philosophical and Technical Essay on Mystery Stories.* Bloomington: Indiana University, 1977.

Charney, Hannah. *The Detective Novel of Manners: Hedonism, Morality and the Life of Reason.* Rutherford, N.J.: Fairleigh Dickinson University Press, 1981.

Cook, Michael L. *Mystery, Detective, and Espionage Magazines.* Westport, Conn.: Greenwood Press, 1983.

De Vries, P. H. *Poe and After: The Detective Story Investigated.* Amsterdam: Bakker, 1956.

345

Eco, Umberto, and Thomas A. Sebeok, eds. *Dupin, Holmes, and Pierce: The Sign of Three.* Bloomington: Indiana University Press, 1983.

Edwards, P. D. *Some Mid-Victorian Thrillers: The Sensation Novel, Its Friends and Its Foes.* St. Lucia, Queensland: University of Queensland Press, 1971.

Gribbin, Lenore S. *Who's Whodunit: A List of 3218 Detective Story Writers and Their 1100 Pseudonyms.* University of North Carolina Library Studies, no. 5. Chapel Hill: University of North Carolina, 1968.

Haining, Peter. *Mystery! An Illustrated History of Crime and Detective Fiction.* London: Souvenir Press, 1977.

Harper, Ralph. *The World of the Thriller.* Cleveland: Press of Case Western Reserve University, 1969.

Haycraft, Howard. *Murder for Pleasure: The Life and Times of the Detective Story,* enlarged edition. New York: Biblio & Tannen, 1968.

Haycraft, ed. *The Art of the Mystery Story: A Collection of Critical Essays.* New York: Simon & Schuster, 1946.

Hubin, Allen J. *Crime Fiction, 1749-1980: A Comprehensive Bibliography.* New York & London: Garland, 1984.

Hughes, Winifred. *The Maniac in the Cellar: Sensation Novels of the 1860s.* Princeton: Princeton University Press, 1980.

Johnson, Timothy W., and Julia Johnson, eds.; Robert Mitchell, Glenna Dunning, and Susan J. Mackall, assoc. eds. *Crime Fiction Criticism: An Annotated Bibliography.* New York & London: Garland, 1981.

Kalikoff, Beth. *Murder and Moral Decay in Victorian Popular Literature.* Ann Arbor: UMI Research Press, 1986.

Keating, H. R. F. *Crime and Mystery: The 100 Best Books.* New York: Carroll & Graf, 1987.

Keating. *Murder Must Appetize.* London: Lemon Tree Press, 1975.

Keating. *Whodunit? A Guide to Crime, Suspense & Crime Fiction.* New York: Van Nostrand Reinhold, 1982.

Keating, ed. *Crime Writers.* London: BBC, 1978.

La Cour, Tage, and Harald Morgensen. *The Murder Book: An Illustrated History of the Detective Story.* Translated by Roy Duffell. London: Allen & Unwin, 1971.

Lambert, Gavin. *The Dangerous Edge.* London: Barrie & Jenkins, 1975.

The Lilly Library, Indiana University. *The First Hundred Years of Detective Fiction, 1841-1941, By One Hundred Authors. On the Hundred Thirtieth Anniversary of The First Publication in Book Form of Edgar Allan Poe's "The Murders in the Rue Morgue," Philadelphia, 1843,* introduction by David A. Randall. Bloomington: Lilly Library, 1973.

Mandel, Ernest. *Delightful Murder: A Social History of the Crime Story.* London: Pluto, 1984.

Mann, Jessica. *Deadlier than the Male: Why Are Respectable English Women So Good At Murder?* New York: Macmillan, 1981.

McCleary, G. F. *On Detective Fiction and Other Things*. London: Hollis & Carter, 1960.

McSherry, Frank D., Jr. *Studies in Scarlet: Essays on Murder and Detective Fiction*. San Bernardino, Cal.: Borgo, 1985.

Meet the Detective. London: Allen & Unwin, 1935.

Menendez, Albert J. *The Subject Is Murder; A Selective Subject Guide to Mystery Fiction*. New York: Garland, 1986.

Merry, Bruce. *Anatomy of the Spy Thriller*. Dublin: Gill & Macmillan, 1977.

Modern Fiction Studies, special "Detective & Suspense" issue, 29 (Autumn 1983).

Most, Glen W., and William W. Stowe, eds. *The Poetics of Murder: Detective Fiction & Literary Theory*. New York: Harcourt Brace Jovanovich, 1983.

Murch, A. E. *The Development of the Detective Novel*. London: Owen, 1958.

Nevins, Francis M., Jr., ed. *The Mystery Writer's Art*. Bowling Green, Ohio: Bowling Green University Popular Press, 1970.

Olderr, Steven. *Mystery Index: Subjects, Settings and Sleuths of 10,000 Titles*. Chicago: American Library Association, 1987.

Osborne, Eric. *Victorian Detective Fiction: A Catalogue of the Collection Made by Dorothy Glover & Graham Greene*. London, Sydney & Toronto: Bodley Head, 1966.

Ousby, Ian. *Bloodhounds of Heaven: The Detective in English Fiction from Godwin to Doyle*. Cambridge: Harvard University Press, 1976.

Palmer, Jerry. *Thrillers: Genesis and Structure of a Popular Genre*. London: Arnold, 1978.

Panek, Leroy L. *The Special Branch: The British Spy Novel, 1890-1980*. Bowling Green, Ohio: Bowling Green University Popular Press, 1981.

Panek. *Watteau's Shepherds: The Detective Novel in Britain, 1914-1940*. Bowling Green, Ohio: Bowling Green University Popular Press, 1979.

Pate, Janet. *The Book of Sleuths: From Sherlock Holmes to Kojak*. London: New English Library, 1977.

Pate. *The Book of Spies and Secret Agents*. London: Gallery Press, 1978.

Peterson, Audrey. *Victorian Masters of Mystery*. New York: Ungar, 1983.

Phillips, Walter C. *Dickens, Reade and Collins, Sensation Novelists*. New York: Columbia University Press, 1919.

Prager, Arthur. *Rascals at Large: Or, The Clue in the Old Nostalgia*. Garden City: Doubleday, 1971.

Quayle, Eric. *The Collector's Book of Detective Fiction*. London: Studio Vista, 1972.

Queen, Ellery. *The Detective Short Story: A Bibliography*. Boston: Little, Brown, 1942.

Queen. *Queen's Quorum: A History of the Detective-Crime Short Story as Revealed in the 106 Most Important Books Published in This Field Since 1845*, new edition, with supplements through 1967. New York: Biblio & Tannen, 1969.

Reilly, John M., ed. *Twentieth-Century Crime and Mystery Writers*, revised and enlarged edition. New York: St. Martin's, 1985.

Routley, Erik. *The Puritan Pleasures of the Detective Story: A Personal Monograph*. London: Gollancz, 1972.

Skene Melvin, David, and Ann Skene Melvin. *Crime, Detective, Espionage, Mystery and Thriller: Fiction and Film: A Comprehensive Bibliography of Critical Writing through 1979*. Westport, Conn.: Greenwood Press, 1980.

Smith, Myron J., Jr. *Cloak and Dagger Fiction: An Annotated Guide to Spy Thrillers*, revised and enlarged edition. Santa Barbara & Oxford: ABC-Clio, 1982.

Smyth, Frank, and Myles Ludwig. *The Detectives: Crime and Detection in Fact Fiction*. Philadelphia & New York: Lippincott, 1978.

Steinbrunner, Chris, Charles Shibuk, Otto Penzler, Marvin Lachman, and Francis M. Nevins, Jr. *Detectionary: A Biographical Dictionary of the Leading Characters in Detective and Mystery Fiction*, revised edition. Woodstock, N.Y.: Overlook Press, 1977.

Steinbrunner and Penzler, eds., with Lachman and Shibuk. *Encyclopedia of Mystery and Detection*. New York, St. Louis & San Francisco: McGraw-Hill, 1976.

Stewart, R. F. *. . . and Always a Detective: Chapters on the History of Detective Fiction*. Newton Abbot, U.K. & North Pomfret, Vt.: David & Charles, 1980.

Symons, Julian. *Bloody Murder*, revised edition. New York: Viking, 1984.

Thomson, H. Douglas. *Masters of Mystery: A Study of the Detective Story*. London: Collins, 1931. Republished, with an introduction and notes by E. F. Bleiler. New York: Dover, 1978.

Watson, Colin. *Snobbery with Violence: Crime Stories and Their Audience*. New York: St. Martin's, 1971.

Winks, Robin W. *Modus Operandi: An Excursion into Detective Fiction*. Boston: Godine, 1982.

Winks, ed. *Detective Fiction: A Collection of Critical Essays*. Englewood Cliffs, N.J.: Prentice-Hall, 1980.

Woeller, Waltraud, and Bruce Cassidy. *The Literature of Crime and Detection: An Illustrated History from Antiquity to the Present*. Translated by Ruth Michaelis-Jena and Willy Merson. New York: Ungar, 1988.

Contributors

Earl F. Bargainnier ....*Wesleyan College*
Mary Helen Becker ....*Madison Area Technical College*
Bernard Benstock ....*University of Miami*
J. Randolph Cox ....*St. Olaf College*
Joan DelFattore ....*University of Delaware*
Mary Jean DeMarr ....*Indiana State University*
Janet Egleson Dunleavy ....*University of Wisconsin-Milwaukee*
Sarah McCarn Elliott...*New York, New York*
James Gindin ....*University of Michigan*
Joan Gindin ....*University of Michigan*
Dorothy Goldman ....*University of Kent*
Barrie Hayne ....*University of Toronto*
H. R. F. Keating ....*London, England*
H. M. Klein ....*University of East Anglia*
Marvin S. Lachman ....*Santa Fe, New Mexico*
Thomas M. Leitch ....*University of Delaware*
Andrew Macdonald ....*Loyola University in New Orleans*
Gina Macdonald ....*Loyola University in New Orleans*
Paul McCarthy ....*University of Kansas*
Virginia B. Morris ....*John Jay College, City University of New York*
Brian Murray ....*Youngstown State University*
William Nelson ....*Wichita State University*
Frank Occhiogrosso ....*Drew University*
LeRoy Panek ....*Western Maryland College*
Nancy Pearl ....*Tulsa, Oklahoma*
B. A. Pike ....*London, England*
William Reynolds ....*Hope College*
Charles Shibuk ....*New York, New York*
Christopher Smith ....*University of East Anglia*
T. R. Steiner ....*University of California, Santa Barbara*
Nancy Ellen Talburt ....*University of Arkansas*

Cumulative Index

Dictionary of Literary Biography, Volumes 1-77
Dictionary of Literary Biography Yearbook, 1980-1987
Dictionary of Literary Biography Documentary Series, Volumes 1-4

Cumulative Index

DLB before number: *Dictionary of Literary Biography*, Volumes 1-77
Y before number: *Dictionary of Literary Biography Yearbook*, 1980-1987
DS before number: *Dictionary of Literary Biography Documentary Series*, Volumes 1-4

C

I

J

M

N

Q

R

S

Cumulative Index

W

Y

Dictionary of Literary Biography